Movement education in physical education:

A guide to teaching and planning

Movement education in physical education:

A guide to teaching and planning

Hayes Kruger
James Madison University

Jane Myers Kruger
James Madison University

WM. C. BROWN COMPANY PUBLISHERS

Dubuque, Iowa

Physical Education

Consulting Editor
Aileene Lockhart
Texas Woman's University

Parks and Recreation

Consulting Editor
David Gray
California State University, Long Beach

Health

Consulting Editor
Robert Kaplan
The Ohio State University

Copyright © September 1977 by Wm. C. Brown Company Publishers

Library of Congress Catalog Card Number: 76-42585

ISBN 0-697-07142-1

Printed in the United States of America

Contents

Chapter VI

First steps in teaching   155

Chapter VII

Movement learning lessons   185

Chapter VIII

Units of instruction: themes i to v   223

Chapter IX

Units of instruction: themes vi to xi   281

Chapter X

Units of instruction: themes xii to xvi   325

Chapter XI

Division of the program   343

Chapter XII

**The games
program   359**

Chapter XIII

Gymnastics   405

Preface

■ Movement education can no longer be considered a novelty in the
United States, although there undoubtedly are many physical educators
who have yet to hear of it, much less understand it. Its growth during the
past twenty years appears to have slowed as a combination of factors, some
economic, others based on ignorance, seem to have limited its use to young
children and the handicapped. Few authors of the books most popular in
college preparatory programs include discussion of movement education
beyond third grade. Often confused with movement exploration, movement education is sometimes included as a six-week unit of instruction. Little wonder, then, that many teachers consider they have "done" movement
education when they have hardly scratched the surface of the most important concept to appear on the physical education scene in the past quarter
century.

The present state of affairs—the limited growth of the fundamental
core of physical education and the confusion of terms—is destined to continue until teachers who have developed working models of physical education programs with a movement orientation to publicize the successes
they have had beyond those that may have been achieved by the traditional
emphasis on competitive games and directed activity with no unifying
structure. Unfortunately, many teachers hop from job to job or leave teaching before they have completed the struggle to learn what physical education program planning leads to. Most programs at the elementary school
level never go beyond the beginning stages. Few teachers today really know
how well the children with proper basic movement education are prepared
for upper levels of instruction. Even fewer teachers are able to apply the
basic movement concepts and methods to instruction in skills and related

traditional programs. There is a reluctance to let go the reins of authoritarian methodology when the children reach an age that questions authority. But how will children learn to make decisions if they do not learn how to live with the freedom to make choices? Physical education with a movement orientation requires freedom to experiment, to choose alternatives, to think, and to discipline one's self. Self-disciplined learning is a viable option to authoritarian discipline when teachers work toward its achievement.

This book is the result of many years of work with children, work that has proved the validity of movement education in physical education. Although most of the effort in movement education is still directed toward early childhood and the handicapped preschooler, the authors' experience includes the upper level elementary student and a liberal involvement at the secondary and college level both in skills classes and in coaching such sports as football, gymnastics, swimming, track and field, and synchronized swimming. It appears just as imperative to treat physical education as movement education at these upper levels of instruction, as it does for the young child. Gaps in basic movement education must be identified and treated sensitively and intelligently, for they represent real obstacles to the acquisition of desired levels of skill.

Such is the background and some of the convictions that have gone into the writing of this book. Its contents are directed not only at teaching a specific activity, because there are many books that do that now, but also at the development of understandings that will enable the reader to plan and carry out a sensible program of movement education within the framework of physical education as it is constituted today. Change will come but only one step at a time. Each step will have to prove itself over and over again for every kind of physical educator under a variety of instructional circumstances.

Critics of movement education have often based their criticism on very limited information or misinformation. Their concerns appear to center mainly around the area of competitive games, the traditional sports in particular, and are expressed as doubt that movement education works beyond the primary grades. These doubts or fears may be the main reason for so little progress in the development of movement-oriented curricula in physical education. After twenty years or more of movement education, the upper elementary and secondary school physical education programs still resemble a patchwork of unrelated activities. Skills are often badly taught even by teachers who make the effort to teach rather than merely to supervise activity. There appears to be little understanding of the nature of skill learning and methods of presentation that do not turn the student away from learning. Without an appreciation of the basic structure of skills, their root patterns, and the movement variables that describe them and to which they are bound in their variation from situation to situation, there is little hope for the development of excellence in teaching and its correlate, learning.

The fact that college skill classes are generally at the beginner level is evidence that physical education in the public schools is not fulfilling a major part of its educational role, the development of competence in motor skills. Low levels of competence are seen not only in activity skills but also in such fundamental activities as running, jumping, throwing, and catching. Investigation even of a cursory sort quickly reveals the basic problem, a lack of instruction. Correction involves a retreat to what is fundamental to the so-called basic skills, awareness. Awareness of what the body is doing, where the movement is going, and how it is going must be demonstrated with clarity at the general movement level and at increasingly more complex levels of movement if skillful movement is to be acquired. Of course, it is much easier to teach fundamental grammar at an early age and proceed with instructional sequences that build on, broaden, and deepen the initial experience than it is to begin at the beginning with older children and adults whose movement patterns have become fixed. But that is what physical education is all about, solving movement problems.

This book takes a new look at physical education. Its chapters are arranged to permit flexible development of reader concepts. Much attention is given to the use of themes, stating objectives, and planning the unit or the lesson. Basic movement is viewed as fundamental and is taught separately in relation to different physical environments before being integrated into the other learning track called developmental movement education. The games, dance, and gymnastic programs that usually constitute this track are given close attention in separate chapters. Space does not permit a detailed development of each of the programs, but an appendix contains a sample curriculum prepared by physical education students to help illustrate development of one guide to teaching. From the beginning descriptions of fundamental motor patterns to the final chapter on the goals and objectives of physical education, there are illustrations, pictures, and suggestions to clarify the role of basic movement education in the attainment of competence, in the release of potential, in problem solving, and eventually in the attainment of the ability to operate in a self-actualized manner.

The central theme of movement education in physical education is that the learner is central to product and process objectives. His needs determine the program, but the goals of education must guide the planning and monitor the process. Neither the goals, nor the teaching skills, nor the physical setting will be enough if in the hearts of those who teach there is not the fundamental understanding that, as Pestalozzi observed, "the essential principle of Education is not teaching but love."

Hayes and Jane Kruger

Chapter I

The implications of change for physical education

The school must represent life, life as real and vital to the child as that which he carries on in the home, in the neighborhood, or on the playground.

John Dewey

■ Today's mechanized and computerized society is taking a closer look at what schools are doing *to* children as well as what they are doing *for* children. Population mobility, particularly in the United States, justifies a search for ways to meet the need to develop more meaningful human relationships. The disappearance of opportunities to exercise the body by means of work and play in and about the home justifies, at least in part, development of systematic physical education. Two fundamental needs—the need for exercise to attain and maintain optimum health and fitness for living and the need for social contact to attain meaningful human relationships—can be met through early and repeated involvement in the new physical education developing throughout the United States.

The New Look in Physical Education

Physical education programs in modern elementary schools have updated goals. No longer is a program acceptable simply because it provides children with an opportunity to release tensions built up during tedious classroom sitting or because physical fitness is the major goal of physical education. The new physical education fosters opportunities for children to develop their potential for physical movement in all kinds of ways, not just within the restrictions of a particular game or exercise. It challenges children to think, to operate creatively within the limits of their abilities, to solve problems, and to share thoughtfully and with consideration for others the facility within which the movement experience takes place.

Within the parameters of this new physical education there is a new vision of what physical education can be for every child, the weak, the strong, the able, and the disabled. Central to every issue, to every program, to every activity are the children. Who they are, what they are, how they are, and where they are going matters. It matters because each child is im-

1

Movement education
focuses on the learner

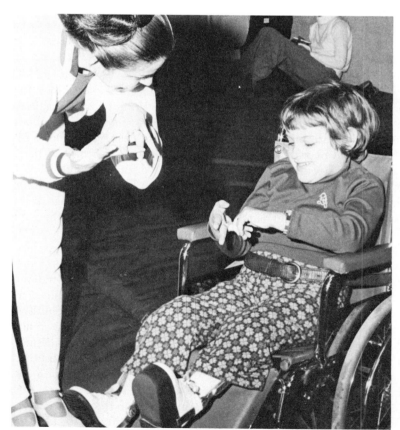

All children can be
successful in movement-
oriented programs

portant. Each child's needs and interests are important. Because they are, the success of the new physical education is not judged by the attainment of certain standards on normed tests, by the successes of competitive teams, nor by any other means that lumps children into namelessness. The success of the program is measured by the individual successes of each and every child in the many progressions needed to achieve fully functioning maturity.

Movement reveals the person

Moving children express a variety of needs through the manner in which they move and relate to various aspects of their environment. If they choose not to move when others are enjoying the movement experience, that says something. So does movement that is cramped, awkward, and hesitant; or the opposite, free, smooth, and confident. Observations of children in motion provide fruitful additions to information one may have received in other ways about the self-image of certain children. Some seem to be saying, "I think well of myself. I am a successful person." Others are quite obviously saying something else like, "I'm no good. Nobody likes me. I'm afraid of making more mistakes."

The next most important feature of the new physical education, after the central importance of the child, is its orientation to movement as an expression of the individual rather than as a part of skills and activities that children participate in by behaving in specified ways. By playing with movement, by experimenting with movement, and by thoughtfully studying movement under the guidance of a sensitive, knowledgeable teacher, it is possible for children to become quite proficient in a variety of movement abilities and grow increasingly happier with themselves at the same time. This occurs because the program is child centered. Decisions about the worthwhileness of activities are based on how well the needs of the children involved are being met. No activity or program area is sacred. Activities are modified, even eliminated, if a conflict with the needs of children arises. Movement competency is important only to the extent that it serves the needs and interests of the mover.

New vs. old goals

In the process of attaining movement learning proficiency and gaining a positive self-image, children are encouraged to develop important supportive behaviors that become self-reinforcing as each new level of attainment opens up additional opportunities for growth and fulfillment. Among these supportive behaviors are those that demonstrate self-discipline, independent thinking, cooperative learning and sharing, self-reliance, and perseverance. These attributes are no longer merely hoped-for outcomes that are somehow supposed to develop as by-products of participation in relays, games, and the other competitions that have played major roles in the physical education of the past. However, it is not the elimination of competition that is being called for; it is its reassignment to a position that reflects more accurately the humanistic values of individual

Implications of change

growth, positive self-image, and acceptance of obligations and responsibilities to build and maintain a society in which each human life has meaning and value regardless of national origin, color, or creed. Competition is viewed as a challenging way of testing skills, abilities, and knowledge; as an outgrowth of having learned; and as a vehicle through which learning may be continued. Competition has value when employed not for its own

Understanding movement principles

Problem solving

sake but for a purpose more directly related to immediate need, perhaps confirmation that one has achieved a desirable degree of mastery. Above all, competition is not the sole reason for participation in physical education.

A movement-oriented physical education program includes all program areas of traditional physical education, such as games, dance, gymnastics, and aquatics, when available. It does not necessarily include all the activities listed for those program areas, and the objectives are not likely to be the same. With a child-centered, rather than an activity-centered, approach, the physical education teacher structures activities around the needs of children instead of structuring the children around the needs of the program. There is quite a difference.

The new physical education is movement education within the framework of the current general concept of physical education. The new physical education uses the traditional content but adds its own subject matter to serve as the underpinning, the foundation, for this content. The new concept emphasizes awareness—awareness of what the body is doing as it moves, awareness of where the movement is going in the surrounding space, awareness of the qualities of force and speed, and awareness of the social and physical environments to which the movement relates. A movement-oriented physical education program acknowledges the primacy of body awareness in the physical education of the individual.

Finding different ways

Implications of change

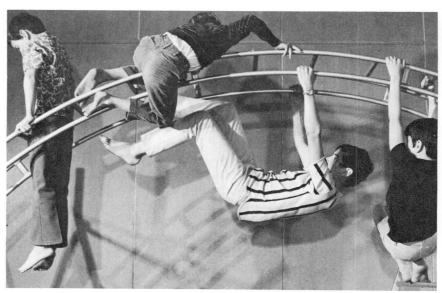

Exploring the
environment

Working together
through movement

School cannot be a happy place for children who fail all the time. Yet physical education has been guilty, sometimes cruelly so, of contributing additional sadness, humiliation, and disappointment to the daily lives of children already overburdened with failure. Many teachers have turned to some form of movement education to provide children with a more adequate ratio of successes to failures. These teachers have discovered the limitations of the traditional program of physical education, the major one being the difficulty of meeting individual needs. How does one structure the lesson for success when the content consists of dodgeball, relays, and other forms of competition?

To deal with the unhappy state of mind created by activity-oriented traditional physical education, children rebel in some fashion. They ask for and receive medical excuses or letters from their parents, requesting or demanding excuse from participation in some areas of the program. If all else fails, children may just refuse to participate, no matter what. Who can blame them?

Something should be done to make physical education a subject that provides worthwhile fun and productive learning for every child. The first step is to make the child central to the program, a process that is easier said than done, for it may require retooling the attitudes of the physical education teacher. Unless this is done, however, there is not much hope either for the unhappy child in physical education or for the future of physical education as a viable force for good in the education of young children.

The "life" represented by the school should be that of hope, promise, and enough fulfillment to motivate attendance, attention, participation, and thinking. It should lead by little steps toward responsible, independent decision making on the part of the learner, an objective not often charac-

Engaging in
experimentation

Implications of change

teristic of a school program, but certainly one that is sorely needed. As the child demonstrates growing mastery over himself, he is rewarded by increased freedom and responsibility. In this area physical education properly taught can make a significant contribution because it is quite evident from observation of movement not only how well the child moves but also how responsibly he behaves. Complete success in movement-oriented physical education can come only when learners are allowed increasing amounts of freedom to structure their own learning, to determine what is worth knowing, and to determine learning priorities. This freedom cannot be granted willy-nilly. It must be earned, and the arenas in which physical education takes place offer excellent conditions under which to operate a program that gradually frees learners from dependence and makes them responsibly independent.

Discovering
something new

The teacher's responsibility

The agent for effecting change in the physical education program is the teacher, of course. Without the full support of the teacher, little will happen to transform the program into one that is germane to the needs of the learners. Dramatic changes can take place, however, if the teacher enthusiastically embraces new ideas, is willing to experiment, and is not afraid to make mistakes and own up to them. Mistakes will surely be made, but patience with one's self and lots of reading, thinking, observing, and restructuring of one's philosophy will eventually shape a physical education program worthy of a place in the modern elementary school.

Activities important
to the learner

Change from an outmoded concern for simple activity to a child-centered program includes the teacher's ability to accept and respect the different, the clumsy, the learning disabled, the slow, and even the disruptive child. Teachers who have participated in labeling children will have to strip away the labels that have prevented their getting to know children. The physically handicapped child will have to be viewed not as a child who *cannot* but rather as a child who *can*. Mental, emotional, and physical disabilities should not exclude children from participation in physical education. Their needs for movement learning experiences may be greater

Implications of change

9

than those of normal children. If one accepts this position, then the need to diversify lessons sufficiently to assure successful learning experiences for all children must be accepted also. A stronger argument for movement education within the physical education program is hardly required.

Now, let us look at the physical education programs currently used in elementary schools.

Current programs

■ Four types of physical education programs are distinguishable in today's elementary schools. None is all bad, at least not for every child, but the degree to which a program is able, even with the best of teachers, to meet the needs of all children varies considerably. Good teachers make a big difference, of course, but if the program is restricted by shortsighted goals, even a good teacher will not be effective.

1. Recess or supervised play physical education

One may argue that this is not physical education. Still, many schools meet their physical education requirement by scheduling twenty or thirty minutes of free play or recess daily. In some situations the classroom teacher is relieved by an aide, or another teacher covers two classes at once. A sensitive, concerned teacher will make the most of this situation by using student leadership, discussing objectives, seeing to it that human values are honored, and handling other important matters while leaving most of the activity decisions to the children. Of course, skill learning is minimal, and there is endless repetition of the same activity. In less controlled situations there is much bullying as the few dominate the activity and the equipment.

Exchanging ideas

2. Organized conventional physical education

Taught either by the classroom teacher, a physical-education specialist, or a combination of both, the organized program is generally composed of a rigidly organized sequence of activities ostensibly progressing from the simple to the complex. Games are usually the mainstay of the program, team games being preferred. Skills are taught, put in the framework of drills, and practiced until the class is ready to employ them in games. Dance, if included, is folk and square dancing. Gymnastics consists of stunts and tumbling, set patterns performed to teacher-established standards. All in all, the program resembles a watered-down version of what the children can expect at junior high school. Younger children play such games as Duck, Duck, Goose; Hill Dill Come Over the Hill; and Giant's Cave—chasing and fleeing activities, for the most part. Dodgeball and modified sportslike activities are added gradually, so that as fifth and sixth graders they can play the games at that level. There is little time for individualized learning. Decisions are usually made to favor the majority; therefore, whatever suits them best becomes the program.

3. Movement exploration physical education

During the past twenty years there has been an upsurge and proliferation of programs that may, in part, be considered a trend away from the rigidity of the conventional games-dominated program toward individualized programs, featuring exploration of movement possibilities. Either a classroom teacher or a physical education specialist may "teach" movement exploration. Scattered formations are used, and each child is expected to explore the possibilities for movement either within his or her space, in the general space without collision, or in relationship to some piece of apparatus or manipulative equipment.

"How many different ways can you find to get from where you are to another place?" "How many ways can you balance yourself?" "How many ways can you find to go under the equipment?" "How many ways can you find to control the ball without using your hands?" These and similar questions are followed by others after suitable remarks to positively reinforce behavior have been made. Resourceful teachers can think of many questions and keep as many as ninety or one hundred children busy for a half hour.

Many different ways of relating to apparatus and manipulative equipment are sought. Junk equipment is often used to supplement commercially made apparatus, and many innovative settings are created to stimulate exploration and to keep it going. It is common for such programs to be reserved for the primary level. Games programs along more conventional lines take over at upper grade levels.

The extent to which movement exploration programs are movement education is debatable. In some cases only the semantics need to be clarified, while in others there is no question that movement education is severely limited by the manner in which tasks are presented.

4. Movement education physical education

The major feature of these programs is emphasis on the study of movement both to provide a foundation for activities and to develop the movement potential of all children. The approach to movement study sometimes takes on an undisguised British flavor complete with British program subdivisions. In the British program each subdivision is taught independently of the other two, although they have a common basis. Educational gymnastics, games, and modern educational dance are the subdivisions of the British program that some American programs emulate, but these may serve more as inspiration than as actual models to other programs.

The approach to movement education in physical education presented in this book differs from the British program. There are no real philosophical differences. However, whereas the British have three distinct programs or subdivisions of physical education, this book suggests the inclusion of a program division that studies and develops the elements of movement common to *all* the subdivisions but with emphasis on specific application. This *basic movement* "track" will be fully developed in later chapters so that the threads that bind even the most advanced sport and dance techniques to fundamental movements are easily recognized. We believe this program offers the best solutions to the dilemma of American physical education as it tries to meet modern standards with yesterday's methods and materials.

British programs are generally taught by classroom teachers supervised by physical education organizers. These teachers do a remarkable job, often superior to the performance of American specialists teaching similar lessons. The clarity of British teachers' objectives and their familiarity with problem-solving methodologies may account in part for this difference.

Americans have a different physical education, more slanted toward team sports than toward body-management skills. Male students majoring in physical education have particularly weak backgrounds; many have chosen physical education simply because they want to be coaches. Both male and female students have often been deprived of an opportunity to develop skills in programs other than team sports. Gymnastics and dance are usually very weak areas for them. It is left to the colleges to change this condition while simultaneously teaching the prospective teacher how to teach and what to teach.

Nothing can be done about a college student's poor physical education background except to try to undo as much of the damage as possible. This requires a willingness on the part of students to undertake the many tasks needed to improve not only their competency in motor behaviors but also their attitudes about physical education for children. The growth of movement education within the current framework of physical education will gradually cause the two terms to become synonymous. Eventually, one of the terms will drop out of general use, but the new orientation to movement study and application will remain.

College preparatory programs in physical education are gradually changing their course offerings and course objectives. It is gratifying to note the adoption of more movement-oriented courses and of specialized programs for those interested in physical education in elementary schools, for preschool children, and for the handicapped. The common foundation of all of these programs is the study of movement. Gymnastics courses are moving away from stunt and Olympic orientation to something more basic. Games courses seek to analyze the components of games and their implications for learning. There seems to be a wider acceptance by undergraduates of dance in physical education that may lead to the increasing inclusion of dance in public school programs. Finally, student teachers are gradually finding more opportunities to teach elementary school physical education in movement-oriented situations. They are not required to "teach" their supervisors the "new" movement approach as often, because many supervising teachers are experienced teachers of movement.

The reader should be able to relate to at least one of the four types of physical education programs. It should be evident by now that the physical education curriculum described in this book is, in all likelihood, quite different from that experienced by most students. It will resemble the fourth type of program, a program that is only slowly developing, but one that we believe is needed desperately to provide an important educational opportunity for all children.

To begin the process of education in movement for the purpose of improving physical education, consider carefully the remaining parts of this chapter. The first step toward the goal is to understand, then to attempt to formulate a concept, and finally a philosophy of physical education. We have provided some help in these tasks with our own definitions of movement exploration, movement education, and physical education.

Definitions

Movement exploration

This term connotes method rather than content of a movement program. It is a process used by a learner that involves experimentation with possibilities for movement within restraints imposed by the teacher's way of stating the task. Obviously, movement exploration is not taught; it is used to promote learning by discovery. Teachers may guide the child's exploration, giving clues or asking questions that draw the child's attention to some previously unnoticed aspect of the task. Movement exploration programs are not extensively concerned with movement study, but they are sometimes the forerunners of movement education with more sophisticated lesson formats and course content.

Movement education

This term embraces the content, methods, and objectives of a creatively oriented learning experience that seeks to develop learner awareness of where and how the body moves to fulfill some expressive or functional purpose. The term, movement education, embodies the concept of efficient and/or expressive movement as the individualized goal of instruction. A basic movement vocabulary expressed both verbally and through move-

Implications of change

ment is developed to guide the learner's movement education in games, gymnastics, dance, and (when possible) aquatics.

Some physical education authorities prefer almost a purely British approach, as described earlier, of a totally separate program for each subdivision. We have had more success with American physical education majors using a separate "track" or program for basic movement that leads the learner into the specific motor competencies of gymnastics, dance, and games.

Basic movement education assumes that learners have the necessary awarenesses of the *what*, the *how*, and the *where* to permit them to modify the interrelationships of motion factors to achieve a desired skill objective. A simple example will be sufficient.

> A learner of any age is taking swimming instruction. If the learner is afraid of the water and demonstrates extreme reluctance to follow directions that would lead into deeper water, change the body position from the vertical to the horizontal, or in any other way disturb the feeling of security given by holding on to the edge of the pool in the shallow area, there is no point in proceeding with standard swimming instruction. The learner is not ready for that. But what *is* the learner ready for? What needs to be done for that person? A complete answer is beyond the scope of this chapter, but the following is a partial answer: The learner needs to "play" to become familiar with buoyancy, stability, water temperature, changes in relationship to the surface, and a host of other factors that will give assurance of the ability to begin taking direct steps toward the desired swimming competency. Once any step is taken wherein the objective is motor performance, the learner must rely on his or her level of basic movement awareness for achievement. If it is sufficient, the objective will be attained; otherwise it will not.

Physical education

This term means the application of understandings, facts, principles, and beliefs to the subject of movement learning experiences in the school setting to modify behavior, broaden perception, develop appropriate concepts and skills, and enrich the quality of life in conjunction with the accepted goals of education.[1] It is a composite of three interrelated program areas. The first area emphasizes understandings of self-movement through basic movement education; the second stresses the development of skilled and associated knowledge in games, dance, gymnastics, and aquatics; and the third serves as the vehicle for organized or formal expression of movement abilities, the extracurricular program area. Physical education seeks, through regular participation in planned physical activity, to develop students' ability to think, to solve problems and to apply knowledge to the process of learning and its desired objectives. Good physical education

---

1 A description of physical education as an applied field, in contrast with human movement as a larger field of inquiry, is presented by Ruth Abernathy and Maryann Waltz in "Toward a Discipline: First Steps First," *Quest*, 2, April 1964, pp. 1-7.

encompasses the previous definition given of good movement education. The concept of movement education gives physical education its "new look."

■ Communication at the learner's level of understanding, something movement education can do, makes education meaningful. Children need confidence in their teacher's ability to help them reach desired goals. The proper kind of communication is needed to inspire this confidence. A strong concept of physical education will help the teacher to put goals and objectives in proper perspective and lead to clarity of thought and communication with the learner. Each teacher should have his or her own definition of physical education and recognize that, in many cases, it will change with experience.

Webster's Third New International Dictionary defines physical education as "education in methods designed to promote the development and care of the body and usu. involving instruction in hygiene and systematic exercises and in various sports and games."[2] Although we do not agree, many people probably consider this to be a reasonably accurate description of their own experience. A stronger relationship to sports is given by the American Heritage definition: "Education in the care and development of the human body stressing athletics and including hygiene."[3]

Irrespective of the value of such definitions for the layman, the physical education teacher should seek more clarity, particularly if the elementary schoolchild is to be the target of instruction. If the teacher investigates the meanings of the terms "physical" and "education" separately, a much richer assortment of concepts is revealed. According to Webster, "physical" is defined in part as "of or belonging to all created existences in nature . . . relating to or in accordance with the laws of nature." Another meaning states, "of or relating to the body. . . ."[4] The projection of these concepts to physical education illuminates a potential that many authorities have insisted is essential to proper understanding of physical education's role. But this is only half the story.

"Education" is defined as: "1 : the act or process of educating : training through study or instruction . . . 2 : knowledge, skill, and development gained from study or training 3 : the study or science of the methods and problems of teaching."[5] Attention is called to the terms "act or process" because something other than an end product of instruction is important also.

The two definitions identify key concepts that should not be allowed to go astray when the terms "physical" and "education" are combined to form "physical education." By grouping key concepts according to the way

2 By permission. From *Webster's Third New International Dictionary,* © 1971 by G. & C. Merriam Co., Publishers of the Merriam-Webster Dictionaries.
3 Reprinted by permission from *The American Heritage Dictionary of the English Language.* © 1969, 1970, 1971, 1973, 1975, 1976, by Houghton Mifflin Company.
4 *Webster's Third New International Dictionary,* p. 1706.
5 By permission. From *Webster's New Elementary Dictionary,* © 1975 by G. & C. Merriam Co., Publishers of the Merriam-Webster Dictionaries.

Building a new concept of physical education

they appear to relate to each other best, one is led to an interesting arrangement, which is, to some persons (the reader, hopefully) perhaps a provocative one (fig. 1.1). Capping the arrangement with the term "physical education," the two words from which the key concepts derive, provides the student of physical education with direction for the formulation of a sound, modern definition of elementary school physical education.

Fig. 1.1 The key concepts underlying physical education, as defined by the words "physical" and "education"

PHYSICAL EDUCATION		
KNOWLEDGE	PROCESS	BODY
LAWS	TEACHING	DEVELOPMENT
PROBLEMS	STUDY	SKILLS
	TRAINING	
	METHOD	

The *body* as the instrument for movement is engaged in a sequence of *study* and *training* in an orderly *development*. *Problems* engaged in through movement are solved through the application of *knowledge* and the *laws* governing and regulating the body. Of great importance is the *process* employed in teaching whereby a variety of *methods* is used to attain the goals of physical education, chief among which is the acquisition of skills.

Now, try to arrange the concepts in another way, or leave them as they are and put them together in a way that defines physical education.

The challenge to the physical education teacher is to make each concept a vital part of a dynamic, movement-oriented physical education program that reaches into the lives of all participating children at all levels of ability. Regarding movement learning as the core to which activity skills relate, offers the opportunity to build a two-way communications bridge between teacher and student. Without this bridge there is little chance that physical education can win the long, uphill battle for recognition and acceptance by all aspects of the educational community.

Subsequent chapters will develop the most meaningful ideas suggested by the key words elicited from the three dictionaries, with the role of movement education, of course, a very important issue.

Before proceeding further, complete the following assignment. A list of selected readings has been included. These will help to provide the kind of foundation necessary to further study of movement education in physical education.

1
Complete the following statement:
Physical education is defined as—

2
Save the statement until you have completed reading this book or completed a course of study. Reread it then, and rewrite any portions with which you are no longer satisfied.

Abernathy, Ruth. "Implications for Physical Education in the Current Re-Examination of American Education." *Journal of Health, Physical Education and Recreation,* January 1961, pp. 19-20.

———. "The Search for Significant Persistent Themes in Physical Education." *Journal of Health, Physical Education and Recreation,* March 1965, pp. 26-28.

Abernathy, Ruth, and Waltz, Maryann. "Toward a Discipline: First Steps First." *Quest* 2 (April 1964): 1-7.

Arnold, Peter. *Education-Physical Education and Personality.* New York: Atherton Press, 1968.

Boyd, Barbara, and others. "Whatever Happened to Basic Movement Skills." *Journal of Health, Physical Education and Recreation,* May 1966, pp. 21-47.

Davis, Elwood Craig, ed. *Philosophies Fashion Physical Education.* Dubuque, Iowa: Wm. C. Brown, 1963.

Diem, Liselott. "Basic Movement Education." *Education Panorama* 9, no. 1:17-20.

Findlay, Elsa. "Rhythm and Creative Expression." *Journal of Health, Physical Education and Recreation,* September 1962, pp. 37-57.

Howard, Shirley. "The Movement Education Approach to Teaching in English Elementary Schools." *Journal of Health, Physical Education and Recreation,* January 1967, pp. 31-33.

Jenkins, Gladys Gardner. "The Child's Self Image." *Education Panorama* 9, no. 1:13-16.

———. "These Are Your Children." *Journal of Health, Physical Education and Recreation,* November-December 1966, pp. 34-37.

Jordan, Daniel C., and Streets, Donald T. "The Anisa Model: A New Basis for Educational Planning." *Young Children,* 28, no. 5 (June 1973):289-307.

Ludwig, Elizabeth A. "Basic Movement Education in England." *Journal of Health, Physical Education and Recreation,* December 1961, pp. 24-28, 77.

———. "Toward an Understanding of Basic Movement Education in the Elementary Schools." *Journal of Health, Physical Education and Recreation,* March 1968, pp. 27-77.

Nixon, John E., and Jewett, Ann E. *Physical Education Curriculum.* New York: Ronald Press, 1964.

Porter, Lorena R. "The Movement Movement." *Today's Education— NEA Journal,* May 1972, pp. 42-44.

Smith, Hope M. "Creative Expression and Physical Education." *Journal of Health, Physical Education and Recreation,* May-June 1962, pp. 33-39.

Stecher, Miriam B. "Concept Learning Through Movement Improvisation: The Teacher's Role as Catalyst." *Young Children,* January 1970, pp. 143-53.

Implications of change

Chapter II

The foundations for curricular design

According to my experience, success
depends upon whether what is taught
to children commends itself to them
as true through being closely connected
with their own personal observations
and experience.

Johann Heinrich Pestalozzi

Introduction to curriculum

■ Physical education programs should aim to help all children, regardless of ability or disability, to grow up successfully. This commitment to all children requires the adoption of appropriate practices and procedures to permit inclusion of children with handicapping conditions in either regular or special classes. Statements of goals and program objectives that accompany a curriculum guide should describe behaviors that will assure the fulfillment of this aim.

These statements support a belief that administration—from the school board to the supervisor and the instructional staff—has an obligation to decide upon curriculum content rather than leaving it to individual teachers to decide. The choices of subject matter and teaching methods must be given explicit direction. Not everything can and should be taught. Priorities can be given substance by appropriate statements of program objectives that will aid achievement of the goals of the school system. Goal-oriented program direction will assure that each child will benefit from participation in a broad curriculum of physical education under the guidance of teachers committed to the achievement of identified instructional and program objectives. Such objectives should include the knowledge, the physical skills and abilities, and the attitudes to be acquired.

Curriculum development in physical education has not emphasized knowledge as much as activity skill development. Skill goals are often described in detail, with elaborate sequences from the simple to the complex; knowledge goals are often so generally described that they become merely a neglected component of the program. Safety rules and game rules are often the only things emphasized. Little effort has been directed to thinking and doing, to analysis of motor behavior, or to understanding movement principles, the laws of motion, and other scientific foundations of human movement that could help the learner be a more effective, more understanding learner. Unless the body of knowledge supporting physical education is made a viable part of the curriculum, the goals of physical education cannot be met. The "why" should be taught along with the "how," to enable children to become increasingly self-reliant and intelligent about their physical well-being, about their growth and development.

Growth and development of personal attitudes are the most important objectives of all. Good attitudes, good feelings about oneself and toward others, are outcomes of participation in activity that has the psychological welfare of the learner uppermost on its list of objectives. If this objective ranks low or is missing, the commitment to help each child grow up successfully cannot be met.

Physical education's concern for developing healthy attitudes, both social and physical, is associated with equal concern for the growth of personality in the total process of what Maslow calls becoming a more fully functioning person.[1] Teachers must attend most carefully to the process, the procedures, and practice of teaching the curriculum of knowledge and skills if they are to help children to become self-actualized human beings. Provision must be made for allowing children to assume an increasingly larger share of the responsibility for directing their own learning, for making decisions, and for assuming the obligations toward others associated with such freedom. Maslow states:

> We can certainly now assert that at least a reasonable, theoretical, and empirical case has been made for the presence within the human being of a tendency toward, or need for growing in a direction that can be summarized in general as self-actualization, i.e., he has with him a pressure toward unity of personality, toward spontaneous expressiveness, toward full individuality and identity, toward seeing the truth rather than being blind, toward being creative, toward being good and a lot else.[2]

The new physical education asserts that freedom to learn is primary to personality growth as a part of the total process of becoming a more fully functioning person. Freedom demands the ability to make choices that will have an effect upon growth. Given a facilitating environment and a broad range of options, children are free, all else being equal, to make purposeful decisions affecting their growth and satisfy this tendency toward self-actualization. The child is becoming a more fully functioning person—is growing up.

Consider the following statement by Gladys Gardner Jenkins and the implications for curriculum for physical education.

> The more we learn about children through research and clinical studies, the more we realize the importance of the picture a child develops of himself. A child gains his self-image from those around him. If he finds himself

1 Abraham H. Maslow. *Toward a Psychology of Being* (New York: D. Van Nostrand, 1962).
2 Maslow, *Psychology of Being*, p. 155.

liked—if parents, teachers and other boys and girls respond to him positively—he can be free of anxiety about himself, free to learn within the framework of his abilities. But when a child has experienced too much failure and discouragement, when the expectations of what he must do have exceeded his capabilities, background, or experience, he begins to doubt his personal worth. When this happens, anxiety crowds out the positive feelings and he may hit out against a world which is depriving him of confidence.[3]

It should be clear by now that we believe a curriculum is more than a list of activities to be taught at each grade level. The variability of individual needs, capacities, and abilities coupled with different environmental circumstances direct attention to the need for flexibility welded to progressive, forward-looking practices. This chapter examines some elements that must be considered in constructing a useful and viable curriculum for elementary school physical education.

■ Three aspects of growth should be given prominence: (1) the sequential stages of motor learning experience (psychomotor development), (2) personality and the development of social competence (affective behaviors), and (3) knowing and understanding (comprehension and thinking behaviors). Each of these aspects of growth makes an important contribution to the development of the individual and none should be neglected. The only way that physical education can ever hope to achieve recognition of its potential as an educative force is through development of a curriculum that considers the learner as the principal reason for being.

General content and definition

The structure of physical education is given clarity and an entirely new dimension when psychomotor objectives are actively supported by cognitive and affective objectives. Overhand throwing is part of a developmental psychomotor sequence supported by a rationale that explains its mechanics, methods of utilization, purpose, and consequences to the learner. It relates to activity that came before and activities that will follow. A look at many physical education lesson plans today suggests that what Jerome S. Bruner described as necessary to improve science is just as appropriate for physical education.

> Grasping the structure of a subject is understanding it in a way that permits many other things to be related to it meaningfully. To learn structure, in short, is to learn how things are related.[4]

Bruner speaks of the role or importance of structure as "learning that serves the future through the transference of principles and attitudes." He speaks of the "mastery of fundamental ideas" as "involving a grasp of general principles" and the development of an attitude toward learning and inquiry, toward guessing and hunches, toward the possibility of solving problems.[5]

3 Gladys Gardner Jenkins. "These Are Your Children," *Journal of Health, Physical Education, and Recreation,* November-December 1966, p. 34.
4 Jerome S. Bruner. *The Process of Education* (New York: Random House, 1960), p. 7.
5 Ibid, p. 20.

Teaching specific topics or skills without making clear their context in the broader fundamental structure of a field of knowledge is uneconomical. The best way to create interest in a subject is to render it worth knowing, which means to make the knowledge gained usable in one's thinking beyond the situation in which the learning has occurred.[6]

Methods and means, the process used by the instructor to teach and by the student to learn, are important in this definition by Cowell and France.

The curriculum is that body of experience by means of which we translate our social and educational philosophy into teaching procedures. This is done by having teachers consciously select and organize experiences for the purpose of developing the personalities of pupils by new insights, senses of value, skills, or other abilities. Its function is to stimulate the students through appropriate experiences so that the objectives set up by the curriculum will be achieved. The curriculum then becomes a series of rich and guided experiences with some order of priority (progression) and directed toward the achievement of certain objectives. It is education viewed from the standpoint of the means.[7]

This is a useful definition, although it might be stronger if the phrase "our social and educational philosophy" were replaced by the expression "societal goals." This expression implies the needed direction and provides a note of authority. Goal statements are made to describe values. The values cherished by the people of a nation, state, or community, whether written or not, support the existing educational programs and give direction for new programs.

Factors that influence curriculum

■ Figure 2.1 presents an overview of the factors that influence curriculum development. These factors are stated in the form of questions that require answers before any serious attempt to construct a curriculum should be made.

1 *Where* is the program to be conducted?
2 *When* will the program be scheduled?
3 *Who* will benefit from the program?
4 *What* is to be taught?
5 *How* will the objectives be achieved?
6 *Why* is it important to have the program?

Any one of these questions might be asked first. Taxpayers and upper-level administrators who are answerable to taxpayers have a right to the answers before monies for the programs are considered. Curriculum writers, too, feel more comfortable about their work when they know that the rationale behind each answer is accepted by responsible authority. The answers, then, serve as guidelines to curriculum writers.

6 Ibid, p. 31.
7 Charles C. Cowell, and Wellman L. France. *Philosophy and Principles of Physical Education* (Englewood Cliffs, N.J.: Prentice-Hall, 1963), p. 146.

Fig. 2.1 An overview of questions that require answers
before writing a new curriculum

CURRICULUM

WHERE?	Environment	Space
		Facilities
		Equipment
WHEN?	Time	Schedule
		Lessons
		Supervised Play
		Extracurricular
WHO?	Children	Boys and Girls
		Ages
		Abilities
		Likenesses
		Differences
		Development
		Needs
		Interests
WHAT?	Content	Experience
		Activities
		Skills
		Concepts
		Knowledge
HOW?	Strategies	Behaviors
		Methods
		Organization
		Administration
		Progressions
		Sequence
WHY?	Rationale	Goals
		Program objectives
		Instructional objectives

Where? (Facilities, Equipment, Space, Environment)

A variety of spaces must be available where children can learn through movement. Space near and above the ground, outdoors and indoors, and in various shapes provides the best stimulation for motion at all ages of a child's development.

Indoor space means a gymnasium large enough and high enough to provide space for indoor games and apparatus work. Playrooms are generally satisfactory only for children up to second grade; they are poor substitutes for wooden-floored gymnasiums.

Field areas, smooth hardtop surfaces, and semi-improved natural areas offer an assortment of spaces for many purposes from creative to structured forms of play. Older children need field space or flat surfaces for seasonal sports. Younger children need the opportunity to enjoy creative and imaginative play among trees, on little hills, and in sand areas. Dr. Minnie Berson of the United States Office of Education, Office of Early Childhood Education, made the following remarks at a perceptual-motor symposium:

Foundations for
curricular design

23

We can strengthen children by having a place where they can climb trees, by hanging ladders around, by having more tunnels, and by having all kinds of wheel toys that a child can use. But there is more to it than that. Think of the sensory development we encourage when we develop an outdoor facility. This is where the child has first contacts with water in a pool, with sand that he can manipulate. He certainly can develop many fine skills from this.[8]

Variety is essential to provide for the diverse needs of young children. Apparatus that lends itself to rearrangement provides new challenges in

8 Excert from *Perceptual-Motor Foundations: A Multidisciplinary Concern,* Proceedings of the Perceptual-Motor Symposium sponsored by the Physical Education Division of the American Association for Health, Physical Education, and Recreation (Washington, D.C.: AAHPER, 1969), pp. 123-24.

Utilizing available
outdoor space

Using available indoor
space effectively

creative movement learning experiences. Things to climb on, jump from, swing on, move along, and go through stimulate imagination and challenge children to find new ways to use them. Shaded spaces where children can escape from the sun are also important.

When? (Time, Schedule, Lessons)

Although some children enjoy daily periods of physical education, many others have fewer than two per week. A physical education lesson may vary from thirty to forty minutes for the primary level with somewhat longer periods for older children. What matters most, however, is not how much time is given but how well it is used.

Creating a game

Things to climb on,
jump from, swing on
stimulate the imagination

Creative and resourceful teachers will find ways of making good use of whatever time and space are available. The practice of having children get busy as soon as they enter the gymnasium is a time-saver. Small group activity with sufficient equipment avoids long waiting for turns, one of the biggest time-wasting practices. Good organizational practices and procedures enable children to spend time in relevant "doing," another time-saver.

Additional time for related programs or extracurricular activities may be found before and after regular school hours and during recess periods. These are valuable periods that provide time for laboratory experiences tied to the instructional periods in which concepts and skills are first introduced.

Who? (Children, Boys and Girls, Needs, Interests)

Physical education should start as early as possible. This means kindergarten or at least first grade. All children should be included.

Many children have handicaps of some kind. Physically handicapped children, usually the easiest to recognize, are movers who need help in coping with their special problems. Emotionally handicapped children are often overlooked or considered annoyances. The hyperkinetic child tries the teacher's patience and disturbs others by constant energy outbursts, by flitting from one thing to another. The hypokinetic child, at the opposite pole, is lethargic, without dynamic energy, passive; therefore, these children are no particular trouble to the teacher. Emotionally handicapped children cry out for understanding. Movement learning experiences help them, and ways should and must be found to include them in physical education.

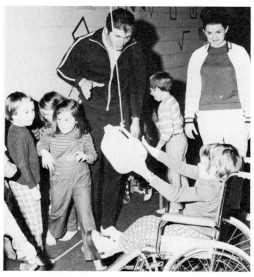

Developing "I can"
attitudes

Mentally retarded children are found in many classes. They learn more slowly than normal children but derive as much enjoyment from successful movement learning experiences as their more fortunate classmates do. Perhaps their enjoyment is even greater than that of a normal child. Experience has shown that these children benefit enormously from movement-oriented educational programs.

Children who appear to be normal but have difficulty learning may have some kind of learning disability. Whatever the cause, movement learning experiences can be structured to assist these children, too.

All children means just that—*all* children.

Developmental track   Basic movement track

What? (Content, Dual-Track Program, Skills, Awareness)

Although the content is somewhat at variance with the traditional view of elementary school physical education, much of the activity is familiar. It is organized along different lines, however, and includes specified cognitive objectives that are often absent from most programs. The influence of basic movement education has provided a substantial foundation to all movement activities, from the simple to the complex, but it has also complicated understanding the relationships of the various parts of the program to each other.

A physical education curriculum that truly reflects the needs of children requires an organizational structure that permits flexibility and progression, concentration and variety, and all manner of individual opportunities for growth, at the same time providing for the needs of groups. A very simple principle is behind the major organizational tool for this curriculum: basic movement education (with its focus on the development of awareness) and the acquisition of goal-oriented motor skills are fundamentally different in purpose, yet their purposes are mutually compatible. Awareness is needed to develop skills; skills are natural outcomes of the development of awareness. That is the purpose of the curriculum itself. To understand this relationship, it is necessary to refer to figure 2.2.

Foundations for curricular design

Fig. 2.2 The dual-track physical education program. Each track supplies needed information that the child assimilates to form a new base for learning. Sometimes one track supplies his need, sometimes the other.

Learning Track for Developmental Movement Education	leading to the acquisition of tool skills
The Child attitude knowledge skills	assimilation of new knowledge and skills
Learning Track for Basic Movement Education	leading to awareness of body, space, effort, relationship

Improving awarenesses

The basic movement track and the developmental movement track make up the instructional core of physical education.

Basic movement education.

The sum of all experiences that make an individual aware of his or her body movements, of the direction of the movement in surrounding space, and of the relation of that movement to space, time, force (weight), and flow is one's basic movement education. It begins early in life through exploration and discovery and, if experiences are adequate, will provide the individual with an adequate kinesthetic awareness of the body and the relationship among its parts and to the external environment.

Although movement patterns with varying degrees of complexity are employed, no specific skills are associated with the objectives of basic movement education. Aside from awareness of movement and nonmovement, the learner's awareness of similarities and differences in movement is most significant. Obviously different movements are performed by beginners, who progress toward more subtly different movements that require higher levels of sensitivity. Teachers ask questions, present new challenges, ask more questions; students learn to think, to problem solve, to find a variety of answers, to analyze, and to ask their own questions.

Skill learning is dependent upon sensitivity (1) to bodily changes of position, (2) to similarities and differences that extend to awareness of shapes made by movement, and (3) to likenesses and differences in the relationship to people and objects that is required by whatever skill or understanding is being acquired. Accidental or concurrent skill learning, particularly large motor skills like new ways of turning, jumping, and rolling, are often by-products of the process of exploration and discovery used in enhancing one's basic movement education.

Informal exploration and discovery, the single source of awareness until entry into formal programs of movement education, is made an important educational force through its "grammar" or "vocabulary." Structured movement lessons, which appear unstructured by virtue of the options given the learner, are teacher efforts to fill in the gaps of informal and deficient movement education caused by limited play space, infrequent opportunity to participate, overprotective or poorly informed parents, and inadequate learner motivation or ability.

The term IQ means intelligence quotient and connotes an ability to function intellectually. There may some day be an MQ, or movement quotient, to indicate ability to apply oneself to the solution of movement problems. This psychomotor potential would be demonstrated as the abilities to perceive possible solutions and to perform actions resulting in a solution that meets the functional or expressive requirements of the problem. Further processing would result in refinement of whatever pattern emerged or its replacement by a new and either more efficient or more expressive pattern. Much research will be needed to determine the feasibility of such a quotient and any hereditary or environmental variables that affect it.

Basic movement lessons are emphasized in preschool programs and in the primary grades up to age seven, when the developmental movement track begins to dominate physical education lessons (fig. 2.3).

Developmental movement education. Skills and activities and the understandings related to them that lead to the development of specific motor competencies and knowledge are the individual learner's developmental movement education. Four areas of competence—games, gymnastics, dance, and aquatics—are included in the developmental track of move-

Fig. 2.3 Beyond the third grade the percentage of instructional time shifts from an emphasis on basic movement to developmental movement.

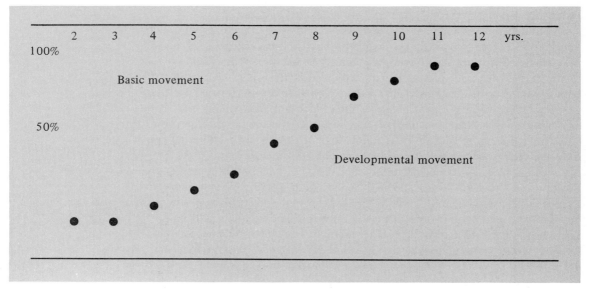

ment learning. Each area offers the learner opportunity to enrich specific competencies through the acquisition of tool skills that, in turn, strengthen self-concepts or open the way toward social competency. Skills enable individuals to cope efficiently with everyday problems and challenges. Skill learning objectives are very important to the purpose of elementary school physical education.

First through exploration and discovery and later through more directed forms of learning the child seeks to acquire skills. Immature skill forms are practiced and refined; in time, an efficient form is achieved. The joy of the first success—the first jump, bicycle ride, or front somersault—is the intrinsic reward for success. It serves to stimulate further effort to acquire skills. There is nothing quite like the feeling of "I can."

Movement education for the young child is physical education, in which emphasis is mainly on *basic* movement education. This does not mean a lack of any specific skill instruction. While developmental skill learning experiences are not as formal or as long and complex as they are for older children, they do play an important role in development. Therefore, they should not be left to chance.

Foundational skills in the preschool experience include fundamental locomotor and nonlocomotor patterns, such as jumping and turning; body management skills, such as hanging, climbing, and swinging on apparatus; and manipulative patterns, such as striking and throwing. The elementary school physical education program is built upon this foundation. Unfortunately, not all children bring an adequate set of motor skills to kindergarten or first grade. Deficiencies must be corrected before useful progress can be made. "I can't" attitudes must be changed to positive, success-oriented behaviors, a sure sign of "I can" feelings.

Time to explore—
basic movement

Working on control—
developmental move-
ment

Fundamental locomotor
pattern—jumping

Preschool experiences

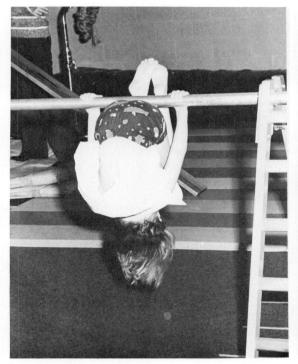

Body management skills   Building self-confidence

Activities that should be included in the elementary school physical education program are illustrated in figure 2.4. It is important to include related cognitive and affective (attitudinal) objectives that should be acquired along with motor skills competency.

Games. Even simple games should stress behavior appropriate to the winner or the loser and understandings about special formations and directions of movement. Questions should be posed that permit students to compare or to contrast one form of behavior or play with another form so that they may draw conclusions. A less effective way of teaching standards of conduct is for the teacher to list the rules and to identify acceptable standards, although this method may be necessary on occasion.

Students should be encouraged to make decisions about class activities. Adults, particularly physical education teachers, who always make the decisions for the learners will considerably diminish opportunities to shape attitudes or to form values. Even simple games offer participant choices: the particular adaptation of a throwing skill; a strategy of play; or, perhaps, the number of people to include in the game.

.Gymnastics. Activities that stress body management rather than object management or offensive and defensive tactics are classified as gymnastics. Movement competencies are sought through a wide range of activities from jumping, turning, rolling, and balancing to climbing, swinging, and vaulting.

Foundations for
curricular design

33

Games	Gymnastics
Games of low organization	Educational gymnastics
Contests	Stunts and pyramids
Sports	Olympic gymnastics
	Rhythmic gymnastics

**Developmental
Movement
Education**

Aquatics	Dance
Drownproofing	Modern educational dance
Swimming	Folk and square
Water stunts	Social
Diving	Gymnastic

Games program

Limited programs can be conducted without the benefits and advantages of apparatus; for example, by the use of ingenious adaptations of partner relationships and sturdy sticks, such as broomsticks, that enable the performer to grip, to hang, and to support himself while his partners hold on tightly to the stick. However, apparatus is essential to a well-rounded gymnastics program. Experience has proved the value of apparatus work for young children, whose confidence is expressed by an "I

Gymnastics program

Aquatics program

can" attitude. This attitude is based on motor competence acquired through countless opportunities to experiment with and to think about movement in obviously challenging situations presented by apparatus that has been thoughtfully arranged by student or teacher.

Mastery of movement is the primary objective of this gymnastics program. Competitive forms of activity, such as track and field meets or gymnastics meets, are potential but not essential outgrowths of this program.

Dance. Dance should be a varied experience for elementary school children. Like other aspects of physical education, it should begin with exploration. Unstructured forms are more easily managed by young children. Their ideas can be given expression through dancelike activity, and this activity will establish a foundation of movement abilities, rhythmic awareness, and knowledge of value that will enable extension of this program

Foundations for
curricular design

Dance program

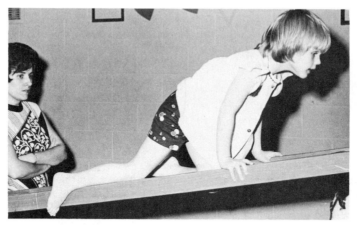

Apparatus work for
young children

to modern dance and to such structured forms as folk, square, and social dance.

The rhythmic experience should not be limited to basic dance forms. Ball, hoop, ribbon, and rope routines can be student- as well as teacher-created. Even gymnastics apparatus can be used to expand the rhythmic experience.

A good dance program provides children with opportunity to express

Dancelike activity—
rhythmic awareness

themselves through movement. This is the major difference between dance and the other programs where the objectives are functional in nature.

Aquatics. Aquatics has been long neglected in elementary school physical education for many reasons: lack of facilities, lack of personnel, lack of interest, and so forth. Even recreational swimming programs are inadequate in many communities. Little if any attention is given to proper swimming instruction in programs for young children. Swimming pools are constructed for use by older children, age eight and up. Shallow-water and portable pools suitable for giving instruction to younger children are only now being constructed. In addition, there are few trained personnel who know much about the art of teaching the very young how to swim. Knowing how to swim and how to lifeguard is not sufficient background; it often does more harm than good.

In swimming programs for young children the exploratory approach should be advocated, a familiarization process so necessary to orientation prior to formal instruction. Water safety for everyone should be a major aim of physical education. Unfortunately, except for rare instances, it has been completely ignored or left to summertime recreation programs. The importance of swimming skills for everyone should be accepted by communities and should be implemented through community-supported instruction either directly or indirectly under physical education. No child should be deficient in skill simply because his or her parent could not pay for lessons or transport the child to a facility. The recreational lure of swim-

Foundations for
curricular design

ming, boating, diving, surfing, snorkeling, and scuba diving make approved swimming programs a must for all children. Swimming is first of all a survival skill and secondly a recreational or competitive activity.

Progressions

■ Developmental progressions in games, dance, gymnastics, and aquatics become increasingly complex and specific to individuals as needs, interests, opportunity, and teacher stimulation interact. About the time a child reaches third grade, peer group pressures become a strong force. Refinement of motor patterns is influenced by the capability and need of the learner. High levels of skill are developed by children who pursue special interests in gymnastics, basketball, swimming, soccer, and other sports, and in dance. Most children try to develop skills that will enable them to participate in team games and activities with their peers. A few prefer to limit their involvement to more individual activities, such as competitive gymnastics and swimming. Interest in specialization should not exclude a child from the development of other skills.

Flotation devices

Useful water toys

Exploratory approach

Fig. 2.5 The stages of skill learning and attainment of mastery start with a generalized pattern. Skills evolve through usage and practice to become automatic under almost all conditions.

Personal style: Mastery of the skill

Specificity of skill attained

Developmental activities for further differentiation and refinement

Acquisition of the fundamental motor pattern

Generalized exploratory or directed learning experience leading to the outlining of a motor pattern

Figure 2.5 illustrates the stages of skill learning experiences at any age. The length of time varies considerably according to the ability of the learner and the complexity of the skill. In time, each skill is personalized by the individual, with some styles being unmistakably the property of only one person (for example, Olga Korbut).

The route to automatic performance of a skill begins with rough efforts to reproduce the refined pattern. The first fumbling efforts to walk on a level surface develop to a point where the individual can adapt his walk to different requirements. Special interests lead to special refinements of walking patterns, such as those required for the balance beam. Uncertain, hesitant, fine motor patterns, such as those required for buttoning buttons, handling a knife and fork, or playing a musical instrument, gradually increase in efficiency, too.

Fundamental movement patterns arise out of individual effort to produce purposeful movement out of generalized, undifferentiated movement. Trial-and-error experimentation with movement eventually succeeds in enabling an infant to turn over, to manipulate an object, to walk, and so on. These immature, beginning forms of fundamental patterns gradually develop into refined forms, even as they undergo such differentiation as modifying the level-surface walking pattern to walk on a slope, on a slippery surface, to the sound of a drum; at the same time, they become smoother and better coordinated with movements of other parts of the body.

The developmental track introduces activities that foster the need for further differentiation of fundamental movements. Each of the four major program areas—dance, games, gymnastics, and aquatics—consists of developmental activities organized in order of complexity and difficulty. The demands thus made upon learners will lead to the refinement of specific skills needed for successful performance.

In summary, then, games, dance, gymnastics, and aquatics are the four

Practicing specific skills

Foundations for
curricular design

major programs of the developmental movement learning track of elementary school physical education. Each of these programs consists of various activities. For example, under the title of "Games," there are such activities as individual games and sports, team sports, hunting and chasing games, and relays. In turn, these activities progress from the simple to the complex, including skills, organization, and strategies or concepts. Structure can vary from informal, loosely organized forms to highly organized, formal activities governed by precise rules.

Instructional methods tend to favor more directed forms rather than indirect teaching strategies, often because the teacher is not knowledgeable enough about the subject matter and how to teach it to use guided discovery and task analysis techniques. However, whenever the objective is to teach a specific skill, the direct method of "show and tell" is quickest for learners who have the necessary background to follow the instructions. Learners who do not have this background must be taught differently so that they can acquire the skills, too.

Each of the four program areas of the developmental movement track is supported by the objectives of the basic movement track. Awareness of and familiarization with basic movement make possible intelligent focus upon specific abilities. Although basic movement and developmental movement are separated as programs, this separation is only a means for leading learners to high levels of movement mastery through the intelligent application of awareness, understanding, and knowledge of how to learn.

Preschool basic
movement

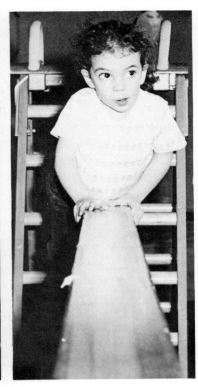

Finding her own way

Emphasis on correct
landings

Relating to new
environments

How? (Methods, Organization, Sequence)

There is an old saying, "There are many ways to skin a cat." Left without direction, teachers may employ any teaching method that works, sometimes at great cost to the self-esteem of the learner. It is not enough merely to list skill objectives for the physical education program. The "how" of learning is often as important or more important than the "what." Instructional methods determine not only what will be learned but how it will be learned. Unless there is an expressed commitment to procedural objectives, there is no way to assure that these objectives will be met or even recognized. As an example, if it is important for children to learn how to apply principles of movement to new situations, children must be given the opportunity to think about what they are doing. They must be able to apply, analyze, and snythesize; to make errors and correct them; to make choices among alternatives. The method used for attaining objectives should be compatible with all aspects of those objectives.

Teaching methods vary from the very directed command style, in which the teacher makes all the decisions relative to a program objective, to the most permissive style, in which the learner decides what to learn and when and how to learn it. In between there are several alternative methods,

Foundations for
curricular design

which use more or less indirect modes of instruction. The knowledgeable teacher knows when to employ direct methods and when to take a more indirect approach.

Why? (Goals, Rationale, Values, Objectives)

The modern American child, often the product of a society that no longer has sufficient safe places for young children to explore, a society that overprotects, overfeeds, and underexercises its children, needs school-provided movement learning experiences. Kindergarten is almost too late for many children to develop essential movement abilities and related self-concepts. There is quite a bit of evidence that the preschool years are tremendously important to a child's growth and development, that about half of the child's knowledge is acquired before the age of five. Each year, as a new group of little ones enters kindergarten, this belief is reinforced. But there are many among them who have not fared so well, who appear to have missed out, who have been deprived somehow of opportunities to develop as fully as their more fortunate peers. Furthermore, there seems to be no actual mental or physical *deficiency*, only an *inability* to perform, to move, to relate meaningfully to a new environment of people and things and the new objects and spaces that differentiate it from the familiar.

To offset the effects of poor environment, parent misunderstandings of child needs, and various kinds of disabling conditions, preschool programs with strong emphasis on movement learning experiences are appearing in many communities. The importance of motor skills to child growth and development is supported by Espenschade and Eckert, who observe that:

> Opportunities for the perfecting of the skills that have been developed during infancy and early childhood remain of considerable importance in later childhood if the child is to maintain a level of performance similar to his age mates.[9]

The reference to peers is an important one; even very young children soon recognize whether or not they are as capable as their playmates. If attention to deficiencies is not given soon enough and effectivly enough, these children will be so badly outstripped that they will resist participation in activities with others. The embarrassment of failure in front of one's peers is a strong deterrent to further participation. For that reason alone, it is important to minimize handicapping conditions as much as possible before it is too late.

Skills and concepts achieved in early childhood through grade two are the foundation for the middle years, from grades three to six, approximately, when the fundamental skills of almost all games, gymnastics, and swimming are acquired. Perhaps that holds true for dance, too, but not enough has been done in this area to be certain. The desire for self-expression is clearly evidenced by the popular dance styles these children use to emulate their older brothers and sisters. Perhaps, if they begin by exploring, by doing their own thing, they can comfortably be guided to more challenging

---

9 Anna S. Espenschade, and Helen M. Eckert. *Motor Development* (Columbus, Ohio: Merrill, 1967), p. 172.

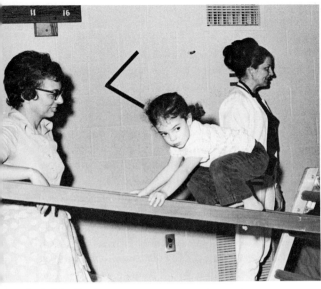

Individualized
instruction

Self-realization

dance forms. Once children discover they are capable of handling higher level challenges, there is no stopping their desire to go on.

Simplified forms of football, such as touch and flag football, stress formation and spatial relationships different from those of the increasingly popular games of soccer and its close kin, basketball. Field hockey for girls and ice hockey for boys explore spatial relationships similar to soccer and basketball. The manipulative instruments **differ** for each of these games, as do the rules, surfaces, and boundaries, but the essential characteristics of offense and defense remain the same—attack space on offense, defend space on defense.

Involvement in the mainstream of living is required to produce a fully functioning human being. The potential for social growth cannot be released if the learner is unable to form meaningful relationships with others. Movement skills—sport skills for many—serve a dual purpose: they provide personal satisfaction as a reward for achievement and the opportunity to interact for extended periods of time with one's peers.

Whereas movement learning experiences for the young child serve to strengthen cognitive development in general, similar experiences at later stages tend to serve more specific purposes. Getting along in society demands special skills that can be acquired only through actual participation in the struggle for identity and for acceptance. Future citizens of an adult society must learn through active participation in childhood society. The ticket to such participation among children, especially boys, is skill.

Because skill is so important as the means through which boys and girls interact with their human and physical environments, children must be assured from the earliest age onward of maximum opportunity to learn proper body management and manipulative skills so that they can pursue

Foundations for
curricular design

43

meaningful objectives within the spectrum of physical education. Skill learning should not be left to chance.

To assure readiness for skill learning, programs should be structured to increase the level of physical fitness as a natural outcome of joyful participation. Because the potential for psychomotor development cannot be realized if minimum levels of strength, endurance, and flexibility are absent, movement learning experiences must challenge each child's capacity to meet higher fitness levels. Individualized progression, understanding the importance of physical fitness, and positive teacher support for all efforts to achieve will gradually build attitudes needed to bond fitness to skill learning. This matter will be expanded upon in future chapters, but several thoughts about physical fitness are important at this stage.

Physical fitness, like social competence, is a by-product of skill learning, not an end product; therefore, physical fitness is one of the means through which the individual's potential for growth and development may be fully realized. Lack of sufficient strength or any other fitness factor can thwart the struggle toward self-realization and the fulfillment of meaningful personal goals.

If physical education "is education viewed from the standpoint of the means" as Cowell and France state, the curriculum cannot be weak or misdirected. It is a means of assuring optimum growth and development of a child, if for no other reason than to assure taxpaying parents that their children are getting a fair return for their money.

Experiences must
challenge each child's
capacity

■ The reader has been introduced to general concepts of curriculum with a two-track arrangement of objectives. One track deals with movement in general, the other with movement as skill. Only a broad overview is required at this time, like the skeleton of a house under construction. Details will follow so that construction may proceed with a clear picture of the final product and knowledge of the workings of all parts.

Two major areas of concern will be investigated. Curricular content will focus on the two learning tracks, the principles of movement in basic movement education and the skills and associated understandings in developmental movement. This area of study concerns content, the *What* that should be considered.

Process, the *How*, is the second major area of study, which looks at the organizational structure of the content from the standpoint of facilitating learning. This area is concerned with how the on-paper structure translates into actual teacher and learner behavior.

Learner characteristics will be considered in discussions of the rationale for the curriculum as it unfolds. The reader should have a knowledge of characteristics of children at the various stages of development to facilitate understanding the rationale. The list of references at the end of this chapter will provide interested students with sources for additional information.

General summary and a look ahead

Assignments

1
Visit the library and locate helpful references in addition to the ones given. Make note of particular chapters that contain references to curriculum development, especially in elementary school physical education.

2
Write an essay with the title, "The Most Important Aspects of a Curriculum in Elementary School Physical Education."

3
Identify the important aspects of the physical education program in the local school system or in another, more familiar or more accessible one.

Readings

■ The following references are but a few of many that may help the reader to appreciate the complexity of the process of making decisions affecting the physical education curriculum.

Allport, Gordon W. *Becoming.* New Haven, Conn.: Yale University Press, 1955.

American Association for Health, Physical Education, and Recreation, Physical Education Division. *Perceptual-Motor Foundations: A Multidisciplinary Concern,* Proceedings of the Perceptual-Motor Symposium. Washington, D.C.: AAHPER, 1969.

Bilbrough, A., and Jones, P. *Physical Education in the Primary School.* London: University of London Press, 1963.

Bruner, Jerome S. *The Process of Education.* New York: Random House, 1960.

Cameron, W. McDonald, and Pleasance, Peggy. *Education in Movement.* England, Basil, Blackwell & Mott, 1963.

Cowell, Charles C., and France, Wellman L. *Philosophy and Principles of Physical Education.* Englewood Cliffs, N.J.: Prentice-Hall, 1963.

Cratty, Bryant J. *Movement Behavior and Motor Learning.* 2d ed. Philadelphia: Lea & Febiger, 1967.

Espenschade, Anna S., and Eckert, Helen M. *Motor Development.* Columbus, Ohio: Merrill, 1967.

Godfrey, Barbara B., and Kephart, Newell C. *Movement Patterns and Motor Education.* New York: Appleton-Century-Crofts, 1969.

Jenkins, Gladys Gardner. "These Are Your Children." *Journal of Health, Physical Education, and Recreation,* November-December 1966, p. 34.

Kirchner, Glenn. *Physical Education for Elementary School Children.* 4th ed. Dubuque, Iowa: Wm. C. Brown, 1977.

Maslow, Abraham H. *Toward A Psychology of Being.* New York: D. Van Nostrand, 1962.

Miller, Arthur C.; Cheffers, John T. F.; and Whitcomb, Virginia. *Physical Education, Teaching Human Movement in the Elementary Schools.* Englewood Cliffs, N.J.: Prentice-Hall, 1974. (rev. ed. of *Physical Education in the Elementary School Curriculum,* 3d ed.).

Nixon, John E., and Jewett, Ann E. *Physical Education Curriculum.* New York: Ronald Press, 1964.

———. *An Introduction to Physical Education,* 8th ed. Philadelphia: Saunders, 1974.

Raths, Louis E.; Wassermann, Selma; Jonas, Arthur; and Rothstein, Arnold M. *Teaching for Thinking.* Columbus, Ohio: Merrill, 1967.

Singer, Robert N. *Motor Learning and Human Performance.* New York: Macmillan, 1968.

———, and Walter, Dick. *Teaching Physical Education (A Systems Approach).* Boston: Houghton Mifflin, 1974.

Willgoose, Carl E. *The Curriculum in Physical Education.* Englewood Cliffs, N.J.: Prentice-Hall, 1969.

Chapter III

The dual-track program

The overall impact of movement education on American physical education could be beneficent. So long as its supporters are not driven to harden their position into a pedagogical "hang-up" we can look forward to a fruitful synthesis that blends the best part of the old with the new.

Lawrence F. Locke

■ The single track of activities worked reasonably well when the program consisted of units of games, dance, and gymnastic stunts. Movement education requires a core course of basic movement in a curricular continuum in which emphasis on and frequency of basic movement lessons vary according to the demonstrated needs of children. The content is introduced through a series of themes and integrated with previous learning that regularly takes place in different kinds of learning environments. A second learning track, with its emphasis on the broad development of readiness abilities, offers a solution to the conflict of objectives between specific skill-oriented activities and the generalized explorations of basic movement lessons.

The particular environment established for basic movement becomes the link between the two tracks. Learner readiness, need, and interests are on-the-spot determinants of instructional objectives. If the time is right, a gymnastic skill is taught in the apparatus environment or a throwing pattern is corrected in the manipulative environment. Too much instruction too soon causes such behavior as learner apprehension and leads to failure. But too long a delay results in the loss of opportunities for teacher intervention and instruction.

Separation of the two programs makes it possible for the instructor to use basic movement as the support system for the sequences of skills and activities that form the multiactivity learning experience of the developmental movement education track. As one example, instead of performing useless calisthenic fitness exercises, the learner works on tasks that continue the development of general body management abilities and prepares for specific activities to come. One of the weaknesses of the multiactivity, block-learning experience in physical education is that the specific fitness performance levels required by a given activity may be inadequate at the beginning of the unit. Consequently much valuable skill-learning time is forfeited to conditioning. In the dual-track program, basic movement and its extension, body management, provide preinstructional preparation of the learner so that valuable skill-learning time is not lost. How all this comes about is probably not clear to the inexperienced reader but will be made so in later chapters. Meanwhile it should be understood that a poor basic movement foundation is a handicap to the learner of skills because it does not provide the learner with sufficient awareness of what is being observed and how to reproduce it. Skill learners have to be good observers of movement.

Two basic movement lessons

■ In the basic movement lesson, the movement experiences develop and enrich awareness. The following lesson description illustrates how this might happen.

The learners are traveling in various ways from place to place within the boundaries of allowable floor space. The teacher asks, "*What* are you doing to travel?" One answers, "Running." Another says, "Jumping." Others name different forms of locomotion on the feet or on the hands and feet. Then the teacher asks, "In terms of direction, *where* is the movement going?" Some children answer, "Forward," while others say, "Backward" or "Sideward." If they are traveling forward only, the teacher asks a question such as, "Can you travel in different directions?" However, these questions as to direction of course assume that the concept of direction is understood. With young children, a different approach is taken so that the concept of direction is tied to awareness of which part of the body is leading. If the front leads, the direction is forward, for example. Finally, the questions "How are you traveling?" might be answered "Lightly," "Fast," or "Crooked," typical replies from beginners.

This description of a lesson, or an episode within a lesson, illustrates the differences between traditional, directed physical education and efforts to help learners become aware of the nature of the learning experience.

To explain further, a typical basic movement lesson will be described in more detail. The theme of the lesson is Traveling in Different Ways with Change in Speed and Level. The movement challenges are designed to evoke appropriate movement responses to each of the conditions of the theme. A series of lesson episodes is usually necessary for fully exploring and developing the many possibilities inherent in such a broadly stated theme.

The floor or a grass area is often the environment for basic movement learning. Boundaries are identified by walls, lines, or markers. The lesson begins with a challenge such as, "Can you show me some different ways in which you can travel?" A flurry of activity follows, interrupted occasionally by the teacher's request to stop and answer questions to determine whether the learners are aware of what they are doing and to stimulate the exploration of other possibilities. The instructor looks for clarity of movement as each step in the lesson unfolds. Time, as evidenced by awareness of speed, is introduced with a similar movement challenge, "Can you change speeds as you travel?" Then later, perhaps in another episode, the instructor adds awareness of level while traveling and while traveling at different speeds. Throughout the lesson episodes, with comments and questions, the instructor supports creative thinking, good listening, and courteous behavior toward classmates. The lesson moves quickly, with time to rest and observe how others are solving the movement problem.

Floor lesson episodes usually last no longer than fifteen minutes, often less. The movement theme may be expanded by shifting the focus from an environmental relationship to the floor surface to an environment in which balls, hoops, and ropes are employed or perhaps to one in which apparatus is used for traveling under, over, and around. Other environments are water, such as a swimming pool, and rhythm, the adaptation to sound, drums, clapping, music. Each environment offers opportunities for enriching the learner's understandings and for improving ability to manage oneself through discovery learning.

Teacher behavior throughout the lessons shows concern for individual growth and development. The whole teaching process is a series of little steps geared to the responses of the students. Progress is controlled by the rate at which students learn to differentiate the elements of movement, to

Demonstrating readiness
for another challenge

Learning to manage
herself

Dual-track program

49

integrate them in new ways, to assimilate them into their enlarging repertoire of movement capability and understandings, and finally to generalize the new findings and thereby demonstrate their readiness for another challenge. Teacher guidance is governed by the theme of the lesson. As the main ideas are explored and discoveries made, the possibility for additional fields of exploration are uncovered.

Two lessons in skill learning

■ Contrast the preceding lesson with two examples of lessons focusing on skill learning. The first lesson follows the traditional format, while the second reflects the problem-solving, exploration orientation of the basic movement track. The first example typifies the directed teaching of subject matter so characteristic of instructors who are training their students to perform according to preconceived standards. The second example might be said to emphasize the education of the student.

Lesson One—traditional format

Opening exercises. The four squad leaders lead the exercise sequence while the instructor counts the cadence.

Skill learning—mimetic throwing. The instructor, with back to the class, explains and demonstrates form for the overhand throw. The class is asked to copy the movements several times. Left-handers are asked to perform the same pattern on the opposite side.

Skill learning—ball handling. The instructor throws a six-inch playground ball back and forth with one of the leaders, while explaining the mechanics of focus and technique. The leaders are each given a ball and now repeat the throw-and-return sequence with each member of their squad. The instructor makes corrections as needed. After several turns during which other members may have a turn as leader, the activity is stopped.

Culminating activity—endball. Each squad occupies one of the four divisions of a rectangular area, 30 × 40 feet. Two squads in alternate areas team up against the other two. The object of the game is to throw the ball over an opposing squad or through the spaces between individuals into the next area where, if the ball is caught, a point is scored. The game continues, with the ball going back and forth over one squad or the other while the instructor reminds the participants to use the overhand throw, enforces the rules, and keeps score.

Lesson Two—basic movement orientation

In this lesson the focus is directed toward the development of the same competencies as in the preceding lesson, but the approach is different, and so is the culminating activity.

Preinstructional activity. As the children arrive, each finds a space and begins a sequence of on-the-spot created movement emphasizing twisting. The instructor reminds the class that the arms, legs, and other body parts can give support while the action of twisting is explored. Handstands, bridgelike positions, rolls, and jumps are among the great variety of actions performed.

Locomotor phase. The children are challenged to travel with emphasis on an approach run and a jump for height. A twist emphasis is added, followed by a safety roll. Starting and stopping times are determined by the student. Unique combinations are repeated and observed, and there is discussion concerning the flow of the action or its uniqueness.

Manipulative phase. Each child receives a ball, finds space, and begins spontaneous play that includes tossing and catching the ball, striking it with various body parts, and balancing it on various parts of the body. Balls that go out of control are retrieved without disturbing other students. The teacher moves about, talking to this one and that one, making comments, offering suggestions, and asking questions. Then the children are challenged to concentrate on performing an overhand throwing action directed toward the walls. It is obvious from the response that the children have had practice differentiating various types of throws from the general category of throwing.

Manipulative phase—analysis. The instructor selects several students to perform their overhand throw, and similarities in the throwing patterns are discovered through a series of questions and observations. The instructor asks questions such as, "Does the right-handed thrower move the left or the right foot forward? During which part of the throwing action is the step taken?" The children observe each other, discuss the problem posed, and participate actively in seeking the answer to the problem.

Culminating activity. The group is divided into pairs, and partners throw and catch one of the balls. The overhand throw is used. Pairs who are ready for an additional challenge are urged to move farther apart to increase the throwing distance. Each pair decides upon its own rules for the activity.

Closing activity. The class evaluates the learning experience. Other activities in which the overhand throw is effective are discussed. The balls are returned to their storage space. A brief run ends the class activity.

The need for a variety of techniques

The two preceding lessons are significantly different from each other. How? Which lesson offers students opportunities to make decisions about what they will do? Which lesson appears to promote the importance of process? Of end product?

Lesson Two is typical of a movement-oriented skills lesson. Some lessons are more specifically movement oriented, others less so, depending upon the objectives. All are dependent on the learners having acquired a basic movement vocabulary so that directions, questions, observations, analysis, and assessment are easily understood—so that it is possible for learners to acquire the ability to teach each other.

It is important to keep in mind that the developmental track is oriented to the pursuit of skill objectives and that it is possible to teach skills by using a variety of techniques or teaching strategies ranging from the very strict, formal, by-the-numbers approach to a free, guided discovery approach. Learning styles differ, too. Some learners learn better when the teacher employs a very direct method. Here the teacher assumes the responsibility for thinking about the specific objective and the way to achieve it, for deciding the amount of time to devote to the task at any one period, and for deciding about the use of learning aids. Until students are able to assume some of the responsibilities themselves, teachers and coaches find it easier and more efficient to make all of the decisions themselves. It is somewhat frustrating, however, for the teacher to have to think of everything for everybody, and in the long run this method is probably the least efficient means of teaching. Students can learn to make many decisions about their own progress, which makes them less dependent and gives the instructor more opportunity to use instructional talents elsewhere. In Lesson Two's culminating activity, for example, the students were given the opportunity to make decisions about space intervals and rules for the activity. This is a small step, to be sure, but one that can be expanded until students are able to make major decisions about their own learning.

More characteristics of the basic movement lesson

Basic factors

Although it is possible, in fact highly desirable, to conduct a skills lesson in which most of the following factors operate, a basic movement lesson requires the fusion of these factors with the content.

1 The basic movement lesson is process-oriented with open-ended outcomes.
2 Basic movement education is a problem-solving experience. The teacher organizes the learning environment to stimulate the involvement of students in problems, or presents tasks within which there are one or more problems requiring solution.
3 The main thrust of the movement lesson must be exploratory. Pursuit of a variety of movement options through divergent thinking is encouraged.
4 The lesson must foster integration of elements differentiated out of the exploratory experience. As new elements are discovered, the student is urged to find ways to combine them with familiar movement sequences or to combine them in a way that creates an entirely new sequence.
5 To effect complete assimilation, opportunities to generalize new understandings must be given optimum expression. New knowledge should be used in new ways.

In Lesson One described previously, the instructor challenges students to think about what they are doing that causes them to travel. Young children learn the names of the locomotor skills as they acquire them or observe others performing. But that is not enough at the primary age, and a dialogue of questions and movement supported by oral responses ensues.

You are running? Which body parts are taking the weight of your body so that you can travel? Your feet. In running, the feet go one after the other. Can you travel in a way that is different from that?

Noting that some children are jumping with feet held together while others are skipping and galloping, the instructor calls for an observation period in which children demonstrate the travel forms they have been using. The similarities and differences, as compared with running, are noted, and everyone is given an opportunity to try all the different methods of traveling and any others that come to mind.

The concepts of *same* and *different*

The concepts of *same* and *different*, usually present in some form, are expanded on in the lesson we have been describing. If the children are ready, their observations will take them from an understanding that a gallop requires one foot to lead and the other to follow to the fact that gallops are not all alike. Some gallops are higher, land harder, travel faster, look smoother, and so forth. Gradually such important, but subordinate, actions as those of the arms and head will be noted for similarity and difference, too.

The importance of individuality

Basic movement lessons should always reinforce the importance of individuality in movement expression. The fact of individual differences should be pointed out and given positive support. The differences between themselves and others that children sense should be allowed oral expression so that the children are guided in perceiving the value of individuality. Inexperienced teachers are not always aware of the repressive nature of many of the environments from which children come to school. Unfortunately, there are teachers who are repressive, too; not consciously, perhaps—they are only trying to make sure that children do things the "right" way. Children develop anxiety in unfamiliar situations, ones in which the risk of being wrong is great. This anxiety causes many children to imitate the few children they think do things the right way. Physical educators must fight to preserve or restore the individuality that is the prerogative of every child by praising enthusiastically and lavishly the child who "dares to be different." If the teacher is sincere, the children will respond by being inventive, and a major barrier to the release of potential will have been overcome.

The teacher continues the lesson.

In what way is your manner of traveling different? ("Before I was running, now I am jumping." Or, "I have my hands and feet on the floor—now.") *Let's see how others have solved the problem of finding different ways of traveling. Who can show us a different way?*

The instructor has set the stage for the observation of and verbalization about difference. After three or four observations, the class investigates further possibilities. Meanwhile, there has been clarification of the concept of *different,* a very important instructional objective of this lesson, and the children have demonstrated their awareness of the concept through their movement behaviors.

Because basic movement lessons are noncompetitive, children can give full expression to their own movement ideas without fear of unfavorable comparison.

The reader may wonder why it is so important to be insistent about clarifying the meaning of basic concepts such as *same* and *different*

Dual-track program

through observation and verbalization. Movement experiences are made more meaningful by a continual clarification of what the movement lesson is all about—the concepts that in their aggregate form the objectives of the lesson or sequence of lessons. Movement analysis is an important aspect of physical education for the learner as well as for the instructor. A continual emphasis on analysis will build the understandings necessary for the complex tasks of analysis, choreography, and design that should be higher level objectives in the developmental track. It all begins with observations of *same* and *different*.

Matching movements

Expansion of basic movement concepts

■ The fundamental concepts pertaining to posture, actions, qualities, and spatial relationships of movement are applied to basic movement education before being applied to the analysis of skills, dances, or offensive and defensive deployment of players. Young children especially enjoy the challenge of being different. For them the exploration of the *what,* the *where,* and the *how* of movement can go on and on, particularly if the instructor knows ways to vary the environment.

The following examination of how simple concepts are expanded uses the theme Traveling in Different Ways with Change in Speed and Level. Exploration of this theme on the floor, grass area, or other flat surface will soon exhaust the limited movement ideas and capacities of the inexperienced learner. Prolonged efforts to "think about still other different ways" lead to boredom, so it is best to shift the scene to a different environment. This is another way in which the basic movement track differs from the developmental track. In skill learning, the instructor shifts from one drill to another and then into a game to maintain interest and continuity of the learning experience. When movement concepts are involved, however, the instructor changes the environment but maintains the integrity of the concepts. The actions may change but the concepts do not.

Environmental changes

Environmental changes may be accomplished in one of two ways.

1 Change the relationship of self to floor to a relationship of self to other things.
2 Change the relationship of self operating alone in the mass of others to a relationship of self in close cooperation with others.

Although a more precise treatment of physical and social environmental change will be given in chapter 5, some understandings that will help clarify the overview of the dual-track physical education program will be discussed here.

Note that the environmental changes that are so important for the expansion and deepening of movement ideas presented in the basic movement curriculum are natural introductions to the major programs of the developmental movement curriculum. The foundation for psychomotor, perceptual, cognitive, and affective behavioral competencies is laid by the systematic environmental changes made throughout the basic movement education track. The child can, without unusual stress, be led into rather than forced into the competitive environment of the developmental track through the manipulation of the social and physical environments by the knowledgeable instructor.

From floor to apparatus. The change from floor to apparatus expands or reinforces such concepts as traveling and balancing while introducing new actions—such as hanging, climbing, and supporting on hands—required for traveling on the apparatus. Space words such as *on, under,* and *around* are given new meaning when related to apparatus.

Floor and apparatus lessons in basic movement lead directly to and are compatible with educational gymnastics and the conventional forms of Olympic gymnastics.

Working with space
words—**on, under,
around**

Dual-track program

55

From floor to water. Motor behavior in water requires many adaptations and adjustments. Swimming pools vary in depth and size. Configurations are different, too. Some are round, others angular, and still others are free form. Textures vary from the smooth, slippery feel of polyvinyl to the roughness of concrete. The walls may have gutters, allowing the learner to obtain a secure handhold while experimenting with movement of other body parts or going deeper into the water. Too low a water temperature will cause the learner to get out early and thus limit the extent of the movement experience.

Traveling in the water can be performed in a number of ways from simple adaptations of walking to swimming on front, back, or sides. Swimming aids such as tubes, boards, swim vests, and egg-shaped bubbles allow nonswimmers to explore locomotor and nonlocomotor possibilities without concern for the immediate need to be proficient in swimming mechanics. Drownproofing is the first major goal of water play, so relationships to above and below the water surface have to be explored and the discoveries of breath control made and practiced at appropriate times. Ways of getting into and out of the water are other avenues for exploration that give the beginner confidence and extend abilities.

Exploring ways to
enter the water

Beginner confidence

From floor to manipulation. Visual contact is a main ingredient of manipulatory experiences. The manipulation of balls, hoops, beanbags, wands, and ropes requires the ability to use the eyes to track the object as it travels on the floor or in the air. Adaptations to size, weight, texture, and shape are made through countless exploratory movements. Traveling while controlling the object adds another dimension to the task. Changing the speed and level of the body or the object is even more challenging.

Possible manipulations of equipment are so various that they are almost numberless. Balls can be manipulated in relation to floors, markings on the floor, walls, other objects on the floor or hanging from the ceiling or walls, and people. Much the same can be said for other manipulative equipment. Cooperative relationships are easily fostered through manipulative play. One child throws, bats, or kicks while the other catches, traps, or retrieves. Then the roles are reversed. These are simple but meaningful ways by which cooperative behavior develops.

Developing cooperative relationships

Traveling while controlling the object

From floor to sound. The fourth category of environments to which a floor lesson can turn is called rhythm. Rhythm involves movement responses to selected sounds that lead to or cause alterations in the quality of motor patterns such as walking, galloping, and skipping or that stimulate a change in existing patterns such as the change from a walk to a skip. The sounds may be live, made by the clapping of hands, the stomping of feet, the swishing together of hands, the beating or scratching of the tambourine's tautly stretched skin, the playing of an instrument, or by the modulations of the human voice. Recorded sounds are quite good today, especially recorded natural sounds, street noises, sounds of machines and animals. Also useful are folk tunes and adaptations of music for modern dance, fitness exercises, and so forth.

Change in the intensity, tempo, and duration of sound is easily translated to movement of the body, the legs, the arms, or the entire self. Rhythms can be variously interpreted with all kinds of movements. Gradually learners make the transitions from simple explorations of the *what, where,* and *how* of movement, as related to sound and rhythm, to dance and to the expression of moods, feelings, and ideas through dancelike activity, and finally to dance compositions. As in the other environments, the shift from basic to developmental movement can be made very subtle.

Additional possibilities. Beyond these main environmental situations, it is possible to explore such combinations of environments as: (1) ball

Dual-track program

Ideas relating to
dance composition

Expression of moods
and feelings

handling to music; (2) ball handling around, on, and under the apparatus; (3) apparatus work to music; (4) ball handling in the water; (5) ball, beanbag, hoop, ribbon, rope, or wand handling related to music and apparatus at the same time. Environmental relationships like these can be used if the instructor feels such involvement is productive.

The overview of basic movement lessons in summary

A fully treated movement theme is one in which the concepts implied by the theme are introduced, developed, clarified, and enriched through free and guided exploratory experiences in as many different environments as the learner can operate in comfortably. It is a fact of life that adequate facilities are not always available, but resourceful, imaginative teachers find ways of minimizing the limitations of poor situations.

The learner in a basic movement program, having had a broad experience in coping with the problems inherent in different environments as well as with the especially designed tasks presented by the instructor, is now ready to deal with the specifics, the set forms and principles, that govern participation in the developmental track of movement learning experiences. The learner also brings to the specific objectives of the developmental program of activities a learning set that has successfully tolerated frustrations, that has solved movement tasks, and that has learned to observe and analyze. A varied basic movement education improves the learner's potential for achievement, and the likelihood of failure of many skills programs can be avoided.

Figure 3.1 illustrates the relationship of the primary learning environments to the basic movement track.

Fig. 3.1 The relationship of the primary learning environments to the basic movement track

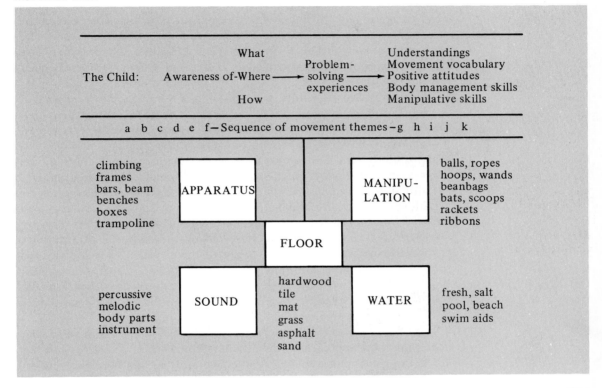

There is much confusion about the place of movement education, exploration, and problem solving in physical education beyond the third grade. Some physical educators do not attempt a movement program in the upper elementary and junior high school grades. A more direct route to skill learning, they feel, is directed, command style teaching, often considered the traditional approach. Their rationale is that movement education is for the young, less inhibited child, a child who, upon reaching the upper level of elementary school experience, will want and need specific skill learning along with the traditional games and sports. Further, it is felt that the exploratory experiences in the primary grades provide the necessary familiarization for success in the so-called conventional activities.

This is a weak position because children are not all alike, and they will not all be able to take the big step from a free, exploratory situation to a

Movement education beyond the third grade

Dual-track program

59

level where learning is dictated by specific forms. The step is too abrupt a change, for one thing, and it eliminates or reduces considerably the opportunity to operate cognitively at levels of thinking above mere recall. Not all of the upper level program requires directed learning to achieve its objectives. Educational goals include the attainment of objectives that cannot be achieved through directed learning. Children need to grow in their ability to think and to operate independently with a growing understanding of the obligations and responsibilities of citizenship. Children need to learn how to live with freedom, an objective that cannot be achieved from directed learning. The aims of physical education should be supportive of all facets of the broad goals of education. One way to assure the compliance of physical educators is to require them to identify their objectives with these goals.

A few physical educators, probably only a very few, have eliminated entirely the traditional emphasis on sport skills and seasonal activities. Games and their skills, and dances, too, have been made subjects for exploration and discovery. Children are solving the problems of skills and creating their own games instead of learning the rules of conventional game forms. All dance is creative, with no traditional steps and patterns.

Although many physical educators, sensing the need for change, have experimented with the elimination of traditional activities and mindless participation in which children perform without knowing what they are doing or why, certain felt needs have not been met. Social expectations, particularly for boys and increasingly for girls, must be acknowledged through instruction in culturally relevant skills. There comes a time when problem solving is not the best approach to learning. It is then that the instructor provides explicit instructions in the mechanics of the particular skill and the steps leading to its acquisition.

Movement education does not mean problem solving. Problem solving is an important approach to the attainment of certain objectives but not all. If the child understands the objective and has the necessary understandings and subskills, he is in a good position to apply himself intelligently to the given task. Problem solving plays an important role after the directed experience has established the basic pattern of the new skill, and the efficiency, accuracy, and speed of the skill must be improved. Now the observational powers acquired through a proper basic movement program are applied to the analysis of a specific movement pattern, a complex, goal-oriented skill. Movement education is not solely basic movement education. It is also specific skill education. But because of the basic movement emphasis, the learning of specific skills can be managed in a freer, more self-disciplined environment than in an environment in which training instead of education occurs.

Our experience has shown the need to blend the desires of both the traditionalist and the creative, nontraditionalist. There are values in both programs. The following statements argue for a movement-oriented physical education program that supports the traditional activities for children who are emotionally, socially, and physically able to manage the challenges they represent. We also present a case for the continuation throughout the curriculum of the principles of movement learned through basic movement education.

Statement One—implications of movement education

Movement education refers to (1) learning about the motion factors that influence movement and what the individual can do to increase movement capabilities and abilities to analyze, to construct, and to assess movement; and (2) increasing the individual's appreciation of movement as a functional and expressive tool of human beings. Physical education has by tradition meant games, sports, dance, and sometimes swimming. In the early days of physical education, the term applied merely to training; now it often means simply physical recreation. Movement education, on the other hand, is an all-encompassing effort to educate for movement in such diverse activities as work, play, drama and other art forms, and the seriously competitive activity of sports. The core of its knowledge base is found in basic movement, but it radiates outward and upward to provide a continuing rationale and support for increasingly complex human activity in increasingly complex social and physical environments.

Statement Two—exploration and analysis in traditional skills

Exploration, and the subsequent discovery of facts, principles, relationships, and qualities, is a method used by movement educators in creative learning situations. This method is the basic means for involving young children safely in a variety of movement activities. It is a method that can also be used with older learners in the creation of offensive plays, dances, or gymnastic patterns and sequences, in the development of exhibition routines, and in the diversification of a specific motor skill. Regarding the latter, the learner in basketball, after learning a specific skill such as the lay-up shot, may spend considerable time trying to exploit the possibilities of that shot, to be its master, so to speak. Different angles of approach to the basket may be tried, different speeds, different combinations with the dribble and the pivot, or use of the other hand. Each challenge entails a number of problems to overcome, a variety of situations to analyze, and many opportunities to assess the skill level attained and to make decisions about further practice. It is a time for setting personal goals and making value judgments. Physical education offers many such opportunities, and all quite naturally, in the play-work of the child. But not all skills lend themselves to such a wide range of exploratory efforts. The pitch of a baseball, however, as narrowly limited as it is by rules and size of target is still subject to some variations of grip, target, speed, and combinations with other movements. In movements that must be executed in technically correct ways, such as in gymnastic and ballet skills, the direction or combination and sometimes the speed are variables. Starting and ending positions are often good possibilities for exploration. All of which says, in effect, that the traditional skills are sound areas for the exercise of

Dual-track program

61

analytical and divergent thinking behaviors that, when taken advantage of, enrich the growth and development of the participants.

Statement Three—the need for flexibility

As pointed out earlier, physical educators should be versatile and flexible in their teaching. There are times when a direct, command style teaching method is better, and there are other times when an indirect, guided discovery or problem-solving approach will achieve the objective. When the movement-oriented approach is discarded, it is usually because the instructor either has a too simplistic understanding of movement education and basic movement or has not learned to analyze skills and their related activities. Either cause for dropping movement education is a signal that there is probably much that is wrong with the primary program, too. Basic movement is not the only program that should be offered at an early age. The developmental track has much to offer and is in fact necessary at an early stage to assure the attainment of certain skills by the third grade. Skills acquired at the lower end of the continuum of learning form the foundation for those that are to be learned later. There needs to be a separate emphasis or learning track to assure the development of skills, the tools of play. When such learning occurs in environments that give strong support to individualized learning, the readiness level of the learner will be the primary determiner of emphasis either in the direction of a movement-oriented experience or a skill-learning experience, either a problem-solving approach or a more direct approach.

The ability to analyze skills and activities, to sort out relevant motion factors, and to compare task requirements with an accurate assessment of learner abilities will help to solve the problems faced by upper elementary and junior high school physical education teachers as they view the high percentage of failures among their students. Blaming previous teachers or the students is not the solution. The flexible use of command style and problem-solving teaching methods in concert with the real needs of the children will help as a starter.

Directed or command style teaching is an effective means of imparting information when its limitations are recognized. Learners must be ready to learn, or this method results in failure for many. When all learners are ready, the direct method may be employed with an entire class simultaneously and successfully. Under other circumstances, as illustrated below, a part of the class or just a single individual may be involved in directed instructional situations.

Illustration One. The entire class is working on approach steps to a jump for height, as in high jumping. Most students use variations of the scissors or hurdle jump. The instructor involves the class in the additional task of turning before landing from the jump and rolling, if off balance. Then those who would like and are ready to learn the straddle roll join the instructor in one section of the area while the remainder of the class either continues independently or changes to a different activity. Under circumstances like this, directed teaching goes very well with the individualized learning commitment of good physical education.

Illustration Two. The gymnastics class is tumbling. The children are working on sequences of previously learned skills when the behavior of one child who is especially skillful and strong comes to the attention of the instructor. The instructor asks whether the child would like help in learning a back handspring. Help is welcomed, and the rest of the class, still under nominal supervision, carries on with tasks not requiring teacher intervention. Many will work in small groups and give each other assistance.

Statement Four—the need for a combination of instructional patterns at upper levels

The need for differentiated instructional patterns is as important in the upper elementary school and secondary levels of instruction as it is during the early learning years. In most instances the objectives are different, as well they should be, but that is not always the case. Children mature at different rates, a situation that cannot be changed. There are circumstances, too, when the skill learning experiences have to be generalized, even for these other children to provide a foundation for more specific learning. "Typically, skill learning consists of reorganizing and repatterning subroutines learned from prior experiences, and using them in the new task," according to Sage,[1] an assumption that there has been previous learning to restructure. In many cases, the learner has missed out. Fathers transferring from job to job, the lack of peers in the neighborhood, overprotective parents, embarrassment during skill learning resulting in withdrawal, and other circumstances deprive many children from adequate motor learning experiences. Well-meaning parents of a pretty girl are afraid that exercise will produce bulging muscles. Fear of injury is a frequent reason for parental restriction. One of the more ridiculous reasons is concern that exercise will make the child perspire.

A physical education program that purports to meet individual needs cannot ignore the children who, because of maturational lags, movement learning deprivation, and other handicapping conditions, are not able to meet the demands of conventional skill objectives in competitive learning environments. If utilized properly, with the welfare of the child foremost, physical education offers every child opportunities to become a more fully functioning individual.

■ Skills have to be learned. Aside from reflexive actions, all other motor behavior is acquired through purposeful interactions with the many and various environments with which the learner comes in contact. Athletes are not born; neither are dancers or pianists. Genetic differences place limitations on potential, but without learning, the potential is never released. The potential for skill in physical activity is freed for growth and development by soundly conceived physical education programs. Motor skill learning is a major instructional goal of physical education.

**Motor
skill
learning**

1 George H. Sage, *Introduction to Motor Behavior* (Reading, Mass.: Addison-Wesley, 1971), p. 299.

Motor skill defined

An acceptable definition of motor skill is not easy to find in the literature. All authors appear to agree in substance that accuracy and precision are major characteristics of the resulting motor performance. Cratty asserts that "the term *skill* denotes that some learning has taken place and that a smoothing or an integration of behavior has resulted. Extraneous movements have been omitted, and the performance is executed with increasing speed and accuracy, a decrease in errors, or perhaps the ability to apply greater force."[2] Sage states, "A skill may refer to a task which requires a series of responses. A skill may also refer to an integrated series of responses which are directed at bringing about a specific result."[3]

Harrow prefers to separate movement skill from movement pattern, stating that, "A movement skill implies the development of a degree of proficiency or mastery."[4] The movement pattern is described as a more fundamental motor behavior like walking and skipping. This distinction between skill and pattern is shared by Godfrey and Kephart,[5] but it is one that is not as easy to make as their proponents indicate. We prefer to consider all voluntary motor behavior as motor patterns, with the term *motor skill* or just *skill* referring to those patterns that have evolved distinguishing characteristics not attainable merely by maturation.

> *A movement skill is a smoothly integrated, precisely and accurately executed movement pattern ranging from the simple to the complex in its organization that is employed to obtain a desired result or to express a desired quality.*

Following this definition, a well-executed jump—such as one performed on a balance beam or a leap in a basketball—is a skill. The jump for its own sake is the pattern that, with refinement, becomes a skill. In dance, a jump may be skillfully employed in a Hungarian folk dance or to express fright in a modern composition.

A movement pattern, as distinguished from random, sometimes involuntary movements, is characterized as having a specific shape. It proceeds from a beginning shape into one or more directions, always forming new shapes, and ends as a shape. Its behavior has a rhythm that to a degree characterizes it but that is capable of certain adjustments to achieve its purpose. The overhand throwing pattern, for example, whether skilled or

2 Bryant J. Cratty, *Movement Behavior and Motor Learning* 2d ed. (Philadelphia: Lea & Febiger, 1967), p. 10.
3 Sage, *Motor Behavior*, p. 295.
4 Anita J. Harrow, *A Taxonomy of the Psychomotor Domain* (New York: McKay, 1972), p. 76.
5 Barbara B. Godfrey and Newell C. Kephart, *Movement Patterns and Motor Education* (New York: Appleton-Century-Crofts, 1969), p. 8.

Jumping, refined,
becomes a skill

not, has a characteristic shape that distinguishes it from other throwing patterns. Its rhythm is *slow-quick*, slow for the preparation and quick for the execution. The intensity or strength of the action depends on such factors as the weight of the object to be overcome, the distance, and the urgency of the situation.

Characteristics of skilled motor behavior. According to Sage,[6] skilled behavior in motor performance has three clearly defined characteristics. His description closely supports the definition supplied previously.

1 It is an organized sequence of movements.
2 It requires spatial and temporal organization.
3 It involves accuracy and uniformity of execution, and it is done to accomplish a purpose.

Categories of skill. In addition, Sage[7] cites three categories of skill derived from scanning the literature.

1 *Infant and child learning.* Harrow[8] calls this category basic-fundamental movements that are built on a foundation of reflex movements. In-

6 Sage, *Motor Behavior*, p. 297.
7 Ibid., p. 297.
8 Harrow, *Psychomotor Domain*, p. 51.

Dual-track program

Organized sequence
of movements

Accuracy and uniformity
of execution

cluded in this category are grasping, manipulating an object, crawling, creeping, and walking. Chapter IV will deal with these patterns and others in detail.

2 *Communication learning.* Handwriting, reading, manipulating puzzles, and sign language for the deaf are major examples of motor skills required to achieve academic educational objectives. Reference to this category of skill will be made only for the purpose of pointing out possible relationships to certain early childhood movement experiences.

3 *Vocational and recreational learning.* Skills for games, sports, gymnastics, dance, and aquatic activities fall into this category.

Changes in skill development. In addition to knowing a vast variety of skills, the physical education instructor should be able to assist the learner in monitoring the development of skill. Sage[9] describes the following changes that occur in skill development.

1 A reduction in errors
2 Improvement in accuracy
3 Improvement in rate
4 Reduction in overall muscular tension
5 Smoothness of performance
6 Greater consistency of performance
7 Greater freedom from the effects of distractions
8 Decreased feeling of effort

Phases in motor skill acquisition

According to Fitts and Posner, as recorded by Sage,[10] there are three phases of motor skill acquisition.

9 Sage, *Motor Behavior,* p. 300.
10 Ibid., p. 300-3.

Cognitive phase. The first phase is cognitive and involves an attempt on the part of the learner to understand what is involved and by what means the goal will be achieved. A mental picture of the pattern is formed. The pattern is given shape, and a rough idea of the rhythm is employed. During this phase there is a great reliance on visual cues.

Associative phase. The second or associative phase is an intermediate stage in which the feedback control shifts from visual to proprioceptive (muscle sense). The learner relies more and more on the feeling of the movement for data concerning the correctness of the action. In the initial stage of learning the breast stroke, for example, many beginners attempt to see what their feet are doing, which is sometimes facilitated by instructors who teach the kick for the elementary backstroke first. Since the learner can sit on the edge of the pool and watch the pattern of the feet, control is an easy matter. The steps that follow are more difficult and often result in the performer attempting to receive visual feedback instead of relying on muscle sense. Practice gradually overcomes this reliance on the eyes, eliminates extraneous movements, and shapes the pattern more and more correctly. Along with improved spatial organization of the pattern is an improved use of energy and time. The rhythm of the effort achieves a harmony that allows it to proceed without interference from distractions. This phase may take a considerable period of time, depending on previous experience, practice of the pattern, teaching and learning strategies, and, of course, the motivation of the learner. In practice, the learner demonstrates an ability to utilize the skill in an increasing number of situations. Speed and accuracy show improvement from poor to consistently good.

Autonomous phase. Finally, there is the third or autonomous phase when the skill is internalized to the point of automaticity. Some say the action becomes "habitized." No thinking is required beyond the initiation of the action. In fact, the action is so much a part of the performer that concentration on other things is possible while the skill is performed with accuracy. The performer can think ahead, plan strategies, make subtle adjustments at will, or, as a dancer, give the action a special expression. The basketball player dribbles through the opposition and either shoots, passes, or pivots without loss of control, adjusting the speed and direction of movements according to the defensive actions of the opponents. The gymnast performs a series of tumbling movements to music and makes a smooth transition into a turn, the facial expression showing pleasure, the bodily attitude expressing confidence. This final step, this final refinement, signifies the mastery of movement.

■ The developmental track contrasts sharply with the basic movement track because its end products are skills ranging in complexity from generalized locomotor, nonlocomotor, and manipulative skills that are often associated with maturation to the most highly complicated motor patterns imaginable. Skills are the primary objectives of the developmental track. They are as fundamental to it as addition and subtraction are to arithmetic and as vocabulary is to language arts.

Developmental track characteristics

Dual-track program

The difficulty factor of a skill is relative to the experience and age of the performer. Young, inexperienced children find the coordination needed for batting a ball off a batting tee as difficult as their older friends find hitting a pitched ball. Learning skills and their related shapes and rhythms is dependent upon the mastery of simpler versions of the same skill with shapes and rhythms that are similar but not so complicated. This is where involvement in basic movement education creates a link with skill learning. Basic movement produces its own by-products of movement patterns acquired through exploration. These patterns are the forerunners of more deliberately refined patterns in developmental movement education.

Subtly and inevitably, the fundamental body management and manipulative skills derived from free and guided explorations lead to the teacher structuring tasks out of which desired skills are developed. This shift in emphasis from the cognitive to the psychomotor is not immediately apparent to the learner, nor does it have to be. The learner is busy learning, one moment absorbed with the feeling of an action, the next giving attention to the specific structure of a pattern demonstrated by the teacher or a partner. The instructor is conscious of awakening certain awarenesses of the learner to the *what*, the *how*, or the *where* for the specific purpose of bridging the gap between what the learner knows and the action, shape, or rhythm not known or in need of correction.

Categories of learner readiness

The instructor should be so knowledgeable in the variables in skills and in activities involving skills that the task structure can be manipulated according to the specific needs of each learner. In general, these needs fall into one of the following categories of learner readiness.

1 The learner is not ready for any part of the specific structure of the skill or activity. More time is needed to experience related movements at the exploratory level that will strengthen the awareness of the elements of motion factors operative in skill structure or activity structure.
2 The learner is ready for involvement in the general pattern of the skill but would be frustrated with too specific a task. The general pattern of the underhand pitch would be a more comfortable skill to learn than the very specific version desired for softball play.
3 The learner is ready for a detailed task assignment that might involve the entire skill or, if very complex, one of the parts in the sequence.
4 The learner is ready for the details of skill refinement. Depending on the age of the learner and knowledge of mechanics or aesthetic principles, instruction is aimed at the highest level of accomplishment of which the learner is capable.

Factors in the acquisition of motor skills

When determining in which of the categories the learner belongs with reference to a particular skill or set of skills, the instructor should be able to state, before putting a learner into the first category, that one or more of the factors from a list such as the following are absent to a degree that would impair learning or, in some instances, would create a danger to the learner, the instructor, or partners in the situation. It is evident, of course, that gymnastic skills often fall in the latter situation.

1. **Psychomotor ability**
   a. Physical fitness level
      The learner has—
      (1) Strength of muscle groups required to execute skill
      (2) Endurance to maintain action for required time
      (3) Flexibility of body parts for required range of motion
   b. Body management ability
      The learner is able to—
      (1) Demonstrate sufficient agility
      (2) Execute alternative safety movements such as a proper fall if required
      (3) Be spatially oriented (knowledge of where one is in space)
      (4) Display required level of movement memory, the ability to recall the positions or sequences of an action or series of actions

2. **Attitude**
   The learner displays—
   a. Tolerance to frustration of "not getting it" or of the repetition of failure to succeed
   b. Lack of distractibility, allowing attention to the task at hand
   c. Perseverance despite task monotony, environmental factors like heat, cold, and humidity, pain, soreness, and fatigue
   d. Courage to execute a hazardous maneuver that is "safe" if attention to the task is maintained
   e. Self-control and self-discipline that allows the practice of the skill or its elements without direct instructor supervision and without which the skill cannot be learned because instructor time per learner is limited

3. **Cognitive ability**
   The learner is able to—
   a. Remember directions accurately, especially the sequence
   b. Apply a given principle if required
   c. Construct or reconstruct a sequence if required
   d. Select alternative courses of action if required
   e. Demonstrate awareness of the elements of movement with reference to body, effort-rhythm, space, and environmental relationship relevant to the task

This completes the discussion of motor learning. The reader is urged to become familiar with one or more of the references listed at the end of this chapter for a more complete treatment of the subject.

■ Progression is upward in the developmental track, from lower echelons of simple skills and activities requiring few rules to complex skills and activities requiring many rules. This is another difference between skill learning and basic movement education. Progression in basic movement education is spiral, that is to say, circularly upward. Each new theme in-

The structural outline of the developmental track

volves all the previous learning plus the added emphasis that requires much restructuring of previously acquired understandings to include the new concepts and awarenesses.

Skill learning proceeds very directly from a given starting point to a given ending. When completed, learners can say with satisfaction that they have learned how to do something, and give that something a name such as forward roll, lay-up shot, or instep kick. Each learner may say something more general to describe the skill such as, "Today I kicked the ball so it went up," or something more specific, "I put in two left-handed lay-up shots coming in off a dribble." The hierarchical structure of progression on the developmental track is linear and specific to an activity or even a portion thereof.

For the sake of clarity, consideration is given to the many progressions in developmental movement education by grouping them in program areas that are then divided according to categories of activity. Games, gymnastics, dance, and aquatics are the four major program areas. As illustrated in figure 3.2, the major headings are broken down into more easily handled substructures. These, in turn, are also subject to division and redivision until the specific skill or activity to be taught is clearly identified.

Fig. 3.2 A structural outline of the developmental movement track in a fully implemented movement education program

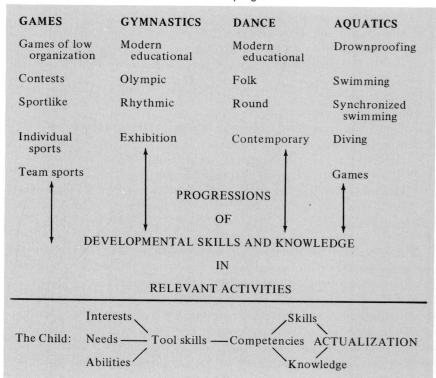

The child as integrator of learning tracks

The child as a learner is the integrator of the two learning tracks. To the learner there is just one program of physical education, consisting of separate activity areas that receive either a continuing emphasis (basic movement education) or an intermittent, seasonal emphasis (developmental movement education). Each child is a blender of information from both tracks, the amount of information depending upon instructional and learning techniques, need, interest, ability, and motivation. The quality of instruction, time allotment, and equipment may strongly influence the outcome.

Human movement

Human movement as a discipline is a rich source of knowledge with important implications for physical education. While some advocates of human movement learning experiences would go so far as to change physical education by doing away with the title and renaming it "kinesiology," as Mackenzie[11] would have it, other leaders appear to be primarily concerned with some form of reorganization of the content.[12] We are particularly interested in a view expressed by Abernathy and Waltz in which physical education is considered an applied field of the discipline of human movement.

> It is important to emphasize the distinction between terms, for physical education and human movement are not synonymous. Physical education is viewed as the school or college program utilizing movement experiences in developing concepts, enriching percepts, and otherwise modifying the organism in keeping with broad educational goals. Physical education is, in this sense, an applied field. It is concerned with facts and beliefs derived from the meaning of movement in human life and with the foundation for and the conditions of significant application of such facts and beliefs in the process of education. Inquiry into the phenomenon of human movement, on the other hand, obviously encompasses a search for knowledge beyond the scope of immediate or even subsequent application in physical education.[13]

When physical education is viewed as the application of relevant knowledge from the larger field of inquiry known as *human movement,* the reference to movement learning experiences is, at least in part, an acknowledgement of this relationship. As scholarly research and inquiry into the art and science of human movement continues to elaborate and to synthesize understanding, clarification of structure, content, and method in physical education and other specific applications in public and private educational and recreational areas will become a major benefit. Physical education programs as reflections of the instructor's activity biases should

11 Marlin M. Mackenzie, *Toward a New Curriculum in Physical Education* (New York: McGraw-Hill, 1969), pp. 8 ff.
12 Daryl Siedentop, *Physical Education—Introductory Analysis* (Dubuque, Iowa: Wm. C. Brown, 1972), pp. 105-47.
13 Ruth Abernathy and Maryann Waltz, "Toward a Discipline: First Steps First," *Quest* 2(1964):1-2.

become a phenomenon of the past. The new physical educator will pursue the universally accepted objectives for the physically educated man and woman.

Summary of basic movement and developmental movement relationships to physical education

■ The dual-track physical education program described in this book is meant to assure the appropriate emphasis upon each of the two main thrusts in a movement-oriented physical education program—movement awareness and skills. To slight either one is to risk the reduction in the potential of physical education as a vital influence on the lives of boys and girls. That basic movement is a distinct experience apart from the goal-oriented activity of skills learning is not a new concept by any means. Included in an often quoted article by Dr. Marion R. Broer, "Movement Education: Wherein the Disagreement?" are three important definitions agreed upon at the National Association for Physical Education of College Women Workshop in 1956.

Body Mechanics—the application of physical laws to the human body at rest or in motion. (The term does not denote any specific set of activities or course content.)

Basic Movement—movement carried on for its own sake, for increased understanding, or for awareness of the movement possibilities available to the human body.

Basic or Fundamental Activities—motor skill patterns that form the foundation for the specialized skills required in daily life, work, sports, dance (standing, walking, running, jumping, pushing, lifting, throwing, etc.)[14]

The motor skills considered *basic* to the acquisition of more highly specialized skills are the foundation of the developmental movement track. They will be described in detail in the following chapter and elaborated upon further in the program areas that constitute this aspect of the physical education curriculum.

Basic movement education is considered separately so that its contribution to physical education can be better understood. The motion factors that constitute the content of this program are described in chapter V and then elaborated on in subsequent chapters concerned with lessons and method. Of interest to many students and teachers of physical education is the question of basic movement lessons beyond the third grade. The special techniques for meeting the basic movement needs of older children and men and women, if necessary, are described separately because the purposes are different. Young children move for the fun and enjoyment of moving. Older children tend to be goal oriented. The specific reasons for their movements do not rule out their need for basic movement education. It just means that the physical education teacher must make the student aware that the basic movement experience leads to skill acquisition. Then basic movement makes sense to the learner, who will cooperate enthusiastically.

Attention will next be given to the fundamental motor patterns out of which complex skills evolve. The reader might ask why the discussion of

14 Marion R. Broer, "Movement Education: Wherein the Disagreement?" *Quest* 2(1964):22.

this subject precedes the discussion of basic movement. There is no satisfactory answer. Experience in teaching has shown us that student physical education majors need to review the fundamental patterns young children should acquire through the natural combination of maturation and exploration of various environments. Once these understandings have been achieved, the student physical education major is better able to understand the concept of body awareness as employed in the basic movement track.

Assignments

1
Visit and observe children at play at a local school. Note the motor skills being demonstrated. What differences in the quality of movement do the children show? Are clumsy behaviors in evidence? Do some children appear fearful, anxious, or overly cautious? Is the entire group active or are many children sitting down or just watching while the main players participate? Comment.

2
To clarify the concept of awareness of what, how, and where in movement, select a familiar specific motor pattern of a fairly high level of complexity, such as the cartwheel, the dribble and lay-up shot, or the tennis serve. Perform the action with the opposite side of the body; for example, if your normal tennis serve is right-handed, do a left-handed serve. Note the attention that must be given to what parts of the body are performing and in what order. Note how the elements of rhythm are suddenly a major source of attention. How fast? When is the force accented? Note the spatial aspect of direction. What is the shape of the action through space?
Would generalized concepts relevant to what, where, and how be helpful in establishing a core of awarenesses before skill instruction is a major part of the curriculum? Comment.

3
Identify with the initials for basic movement or developmental movement the track to which the following elements of a physical education lesson belong.

Throwing a beanbag	( )
Fast and slow contrasted	( )
Sequencing actions	( )
Tension and relaxation	( )
High skipping	( )
Using different balances	( )
Catch and throw overhand	( )
Lay-up shot	( )

Readings

Abernathy, Ruth, and Waltz, Maryann. "Toward a Discipline: First Steps First." *Quest* 2(1964):1-2.

Broer, Marion R. "Movement Education: Wherein the Disagreement?" *Quest* 2(1964):22.

Cratty, Bryant J. *Movement Behavior and Motor Learning.* 2d ed. Philadelphia: Lea & Febiger, 1967.

Espenschade, Anna S., and Eckert, Helen M. *Motor Development.* Columbus, Ohio: Merrill, 1967.

Godfrey, Barbara B., and Kephart, Newell C. *Movement Patterns and Motor Education.* New York: Appleton-Century-Crofts, 1969.

Harrow, Anita J. *A Taxonomy of the Psychomotor Domain.* New York: McKay, 1972.

Inner London Education Authority. *Educational Gymnastics.* London: The County Hall, 1969.

Laban, Rudolf. *The Mastery of Movement.* 2d ed., rev. Lisa Ullmann. London: MacDonald & Evans, 1960.

Mason, Bernard S., and Mitchell, Elmer D. *Active Games and Contests.* New York: A. S. Barnes, 1935.

Mackenzie, Marlin M. *Toward a New Curriculum in Physical Education.* New York: McGraw-Hill, 1969.

North, Marion. *Movement Education.* London: Maurice Temple Smith, 1973.

Russell, Joan. *Modern Dance in Education.* London: MacDonald & Evans, 1958.

Sage, George H. *Introduction to Motor Behavior.* Reading, Mass.: Addison-Wesley, 1971.

Siedentop, Daryl. *Physical Education—Introductory Analysis.* Dubuque, Iowa: Wm. C. Brown, 1972.

Singer, Robert N. *Motor Learning and Human Performance.* London: Collier-Macmillan, 1968.

Sweeney, Robert T., ed. *Selected Readings in Movement Education.* Reading, Mass.: Addison-Wesley, 1970.

Chapter IV

Movement patterns and fundamental skills

It is a curious fact that one may observe many lessons in physical education without finding much intelligent instruction in the fundamental activities in which man engages every day.

Jesse Feiring Williams

What the body can do

■ When young children are asked, "What can your body do?" any number of interesting ways of moving or posturing may result. Young children speak the language of the body more eloquently and more accurately than they speak the language of the intellect. They will show rather than tell. "This!" might be the enthusiastic response, followed by a posture or pose of some kind. Or, they may stand on their hands, jump with a turn, or travel about. More probing, with questions such as, "Can you do it another way?" will usually elicit an even greater variety of behaviors. Many movements will be invented right on the spot, because the joy of moving and of having an appreciative audience is a delightful experience for young children. They like to express themselves through body movement.

The primary school and the preschool offer the greatest opportunity for teachers and parents alike to capitalize on the tremendous interest children have in exploring their environments, in discovering new ways of managing their bodies, and of acquiring the language skills and concepts related to these explorations. Teachers as observers of movement know what children can do and what they cannot do. This is the basis upon which teachers interact with the children in the learning process. They arrange environments that are challenging and ask questions that encourage children to explore, to move, to think, and to discover. These explorations include the fundamental movement patterns that children need if they are to acquire additional skills.

Teachers of movement should commit to memory all of the fundamental motor (movement) patterns described in this chapter. They should have a clear image of each pattern to compare with the motor patterns demonstrated by the children. Teachers should be able to identify with great

The excitement
of a challenge

Language of the
body speaks

The importance of
teacher interaction

Time to explore, move,
think, and discover

accuracy the motor abilities of every child. Is the child's performance of a particular motor activity acceptable? If not, what is the problem and how can it be corrected? The child just might need more time to explore, to mature, to experience. Or the child might need some specific instruction.

In this chapter we will examine some psychomotor activities. We will define some of the terminology important to motor learning, describe the motor patterns on which complex skill learning is based, and identify preschool motor behaviors that the elementary school teacher should know about. The reader is urged to become acquainted with the suggested readings listed at the end of the chapter.

■ Authorities are generally agreed on three major learning domains: the cognitive, having to do with knowing; the affective, having to do with feeling; and the psychomotor, having to do with doing. The word *psychomotor* signifies a mind-body relationship in movement. *Perceptual-motor,* another term that is in vogue, refers to perceiving and interpreting a stimulus and making a motor response to it. Because the mind is involved, Harrow is of the opinion that "psychomotor and perceptual-motor appear to be synonymous."[1] That question will not be debated here. *Psychomotor* will be used to denote the broad field of voluntary movement behaviors. Perceptual-motor will be used to denote development of sensory discriminations and appropriate motor responses. Perceptual-motor programs are aimed at correcting children's identifiable motor deficiencies. Psychomotor programs include all those leading to enhancement of motor behaviors from preschool to old age.

The purpose of classifying behaviors is to identify fundamental teaching objectives. For example, the movement of the vocal cords produces sounds, which are symbols standing for ideas. Therefore, this physical movement has a cognitive purpose—to produce language. A speech therapist might have psychomotor objectives for preparing a child to speak. Exercises to strengthen certain muscles or to produce coordination would fall in the psychomotor class. After these objectives have been met, the child is ready to attack the cognitive or symbolic objectives of speech. While all this has been going on, the therapist has taken great pains to help the child feel good, demonstrate a positive attitude toward therapy, try hard, and be patient. The child's attainment of these affective objectives may bear upon the acquisition of the psychomotor and cognitive objectives.

We teachers in physical education today need a taxonomy for the psychomotor domain. A taxonomy is a classification, and Anita J. Harrow has developed one. It is hierarchical in that it begins at the lowest level of movement behaviors and builds by levels to the most complex motor behaviors. At least, that is Harrow's intention. If there are any imperfections in her taxonomy, we still should not close our eyes to its usefulness in facing

The psychomotor domain

1 Anita J. Harrow, *A Taxonomy of the Psychomotor Domain* (New York: McKay, 1972), p. 183.

Movement patterns and fundamental skills

an otherwise confusing array of objectives in curriculum development for physical education. So, despite some reservations, we have followed Harrow's *Taxonomy of the Psychomotor Domain* in classifying objectives in the motor area.

Skill learning is a primary goal of physical education. Fundamental movements and sport and dance skills are often taught without regard for previous learning or sufficient appreciation of the interrelationships involved. Harrow elaborates on this concept in the following statement.

> The efficiency and degree of skilled movement attained by any learner is based upon the learner's control of his basic or fundamental movements, the degree of efficiency with which he perceives stimuli, and the level of development he has attained in the fourth category of physical abilities. Once the learner has acquired a skilled movement vocabulary he has the necessary tools (an efficient body—an accurate perceptual system—and skilled movement repertoire) for modifying and creating aesthetic movement patterns.[2]

A child's movements at birth are reflexive. Motor activity often involves the entire body, as both sides work simultaneously. During the first two years of life, a remarkable change occurs, particularly in children who are properly nourished and environmentally stimulated.[3] Through a combina-

Attending to the task

2 Ibid., p. 33.
3 Brain damage caused by malnutrition and understimulation during the first two years of life that results in clumsiness and feeblemindedness is reported on by Roger Lewin, "Starved Brains," *Psychology Today* 9, no. 4 (September 1975):29-33.

tion of maturation and learning, various motor patterns and communication skills develop, climaxed by the attainment of upright carriage. Infant children or neonates become toddlers who are able to travel about and to manipulate objects they find in their travels. Movement skills and concepts grow together, fostered by positive feelings of "ableness." Each child's self-image as a successful person supports a growing awareness of self, others, and physical environments. Further differentiation of locomotor and manipulative behaviors follows, based on experimentation. In time, these voluntary fundamental movements will undergo changes induced by more formal learning. The potential for the development of different movements and of different combinations of motor patterns is enormous, if the right circumstances prevail. Our interpretation of Harrow's classification of various behaviors follows.[4]

Level	Behavior	Interpretation
1.00	Reflex movement	Involuntary movement
2.00	Basic fundamental movements	Voluntary fundamental movement patterns
3.00	Perceptual abilities	Interpretation of sensory data leading to appropriate and coordinated movement
4.00	Physical abilities	Physical fitness components on which further learning depends
5.00	Skilled movements	Voluntary skilled motor patterns
6.00	Nondiscursive communication	Forms of movement communication leading to advanced, aesthetic motor expression

Each of these levels is divided into subcategories. Level 1.00, reflexive behavior, is of interest only in that it serves as the springboard for Level 2.00 skills. Level 2.00 behaviors are subdivided into locomotor movements, nonlocomotor movements, and manipulative movements. These patterns will be elaborated on later in this chapter. We will draw on the remaining levels as we develop our own concept of curricular structure. However, we will not violate the integrity of the taxonomy.

■ A clear definition of terms to be used throughout this text is in order. Some terms have been used in the previous section and may require immediate clarification. Others will be defined as the need arises. Many of the following terms will appear in the suggested readings.

Definitions

1 *Basic-fundamental skills*: This is Harrow's term for "those inherent movement patterns which form the basis for specialized complex skilled

4 Harrow, *Taxonomy*, p. 32.

movements."[5] Wickstrom's definition of *fundamental skill*, "a common motor activity with a general goal," is not as clear, but he adds, "It is the basis for more advanced and highly specific motor activities. Running, jumping, throwing, catching, galloping, skipping, kicking, and climbing are typical of the identifiable general motor activities included in the category of fundamental skills."[6] We prefer to use the term *fundamental motor pattern* when the generalized form only is considered and the term *fundamental motor skill* when the attainment of proficiency is clearly marked by the development of accuracy and precision of movement.

2 *Development*: According to the Anisa theory of curriculum and pedagogy as expressed by Jordan and Streets, development is "the process of translating potentiality into actuality."[7] Cowell and France state that development means "progress toward maturity and represents the unfolding of the child's native abilities within the limits of his inherent capacity. It is the expression of heredity in a favorable environment and indicates the degree to which a person approximates the limits of his potential."[8] Note the reference to potential in both definitions, a clear indication of the importance attached to helping children develop to their individual maximums, rather than limiting their development through set forms of progression and through expectations that are too high for some and too low for others.

3 *Developmental motor pattern*: According to Wickstrom, this is ". . . any movement used in the performance of a fundamental skill that does not measure up to the mature pattern for the skill."[9] The sequences of motor behaviors leading up to terminal skills are the developmental motor patterns. A child attempts a jump in the first stage, then gradually learns to push off with both feet simultaneously and to coordinate the arm action with the extension of the legs. Finally, the child puts it all together and performs the total action in its mature form. This process may take several years. Some children may never attain the mature form, while a few may achieve it long before kindergarten. We also use the concept of developmental motor pattern as an immature form in the description of progressions leading to the acquisition of sport skills.

4 *Differentiation*: The principle of differentiation "states that development proceeds from the simple to the complex, from the homogeneous to the heterogeneous, from the general to the specific."[10] In terms of chil-

5 Ibid., p. 52.
6 Ralph L. Wickstrom, *Fundamental Motor Patterns* (Philadelphia: Lea & Febiger, 1970), p. 5.
7 Daniel C. Jordan and Donald T. Streets, "The Anisa Model: A New Basis for Educational Planning," *Young Children* 28, no. 5 (June 1973):297.
8 Charles C. Cowell and Wellman L. France, *Philosophy and Principles of Physical Education* (Englewood Cliffs, N.J.: Prentice-Hall, 1963), p. 109.
9 Wickstrom, *Fundamental Motor Patterns*, pp. 5-6.
10 L. Joseph Stone and Joseph Church, *Childhood and Adolescence*, 3d ed. (New York: Random House, 1973), pp. 156-57.

dren's motor development, it means the ability to single out a specific motor pattern from a generalized motor pattern. Children who can execute a simple high jump and a simple broad jump are demonstrating differentiation of a motor pattern. They show progression from a general ability to elevate the body momentarily to attainment of the more specific patterns of a high jump after an approach run or a long jump after an approach run. Even the character of the approach run will differ for the two jumps.

5 *Form:* According to Singer, "Form refers to economy of effort."[11] Wickstrom expands on this concept.

> Form includes movements, the time-space arrangement of movements, and the total visual effect produced. It refers to the complete manner in which a motor task is done. The term form is best understood if its meaning is not fragmented by too many qualifying terms. One especially useful qualifying term is good. It is used to describe the high standards which apply to the form used in fundamental skills and in advanced sport skills. The specific standards for good form at these two levels are different, but the quality of the form is equally high relative to its level. In both instances, good form implies economy of movement and requires conformance to good body mechanics. At both levels good form is a compound of the similarities in the performance of the highly skilled.[12]

Jump executing **form**

11 Robert N. Singer, *Motor Learning and Human Performance* (London: Collier-Macmillan, Ltd., 1968), p. 6.
12 Wickstrom, *Motor Patterns,* p. 6.

The description of form as movement economy, proper body mechanics, and visually pleasing alignments of body parts adequately defines the term.

6 *Growth*: Espenschade and Eckert refer to growth as "measurable physsical and biological changes in the development of the individual...."[13] The term *growth* should not be used when *maturation* is meant. Another term with which it is often confused is *development,* which applies to activities characterized by a progression in refinement rather than by an increase in size.

7 *Kinesthesis*: Scott uses the term *kinesthesia* and defines it as "Movement sense, a collective function of the muscle spindles, the Golgi tendo organs, and the joint receptors."[14] Sinclair refers to these organs "as the organs of 'muscle sense' or kinesthesis."[15] Singer adds, "Kinesthesis is a consciousness of muscular movement and effort and a keenly developed sense required of beginners and experts alike for proficiency in many motor skills."[16] He goes on to state that the terms *kinesthetic* and *proprioceptive* generally refer to the same sense—the sense that provides information about the body's position in space and the relationship of its parts.

8 *Law of use*: The principle that the human body "develops and grows through use,"[17] is how Sinclair defines the law of use. Muscles that are not used over a period of time atrophy; ". . . the muscle becomes flaccid, probably will decrease in girth, potential strength capacity is reduced, capillary function is decreased, and the muscle cells take on more of the characteristics of the light cell rather than the red muscle cell," opines Scott.[18] It is important to remember this principle when working with motor skills. The fitness component is ever present. As exercise makes demands on the body, new capillaries grow, muscle cells increase in size, and so on.

9 *Learning*: According to Perkins, learning is "a modification of behavior as a result of experience or training."[19] Singer defines it as "the relatively permanent change in performance or behavioral potential resulting from practice or past experience in the situation."[20] Learning may be inferred from measurements taken of performance. The single, accidental performance of a skill such as a back dive does not mean that learning has occurred, although instructors have been known to

13 Anna S. Espenschade and Helen M. Eckert, *Motor Development* (Columbus, Ohio: Merrill, 1967), p. 78.
14 M. Gladys Scott, *An Analysis of Human Motion,* 2d ed. (New York: Appleton-Century-Crofts, 1963), p. 435.
15 Caroline B. Sinclair, *Movement of the Young Child* (Columbus, Ohio: Merrill, 1973), p. 3.
16 Singer, *Motor Learning,* p. 73.
17 Sinclair, *Movement,* p. 3.
18 Scott, *Human Motion,* p. 100.
19 Hugh V. Perkins, *Human Development and Learning* (Belmont, Calif.: Wadsworth, 1969), p. 338.
20 Singer, *Motor Learning,* p. 3.

grade the performance as passing. This is not learning. The test only indicates that a dive was performed. Cratty's definition emphasizes learning as ". . . a long-range change, demonstrable retention measures col-
lected over a period of time."[21] If the instructor has never seen the
student execute the dive before it occurs in the test situation, the instructor should ask the student to repeat the dive to strengthen the in-
inference that learning has in fact occurred.

10 *Maturation*: This is "the term most frequently used to describe
changes which develop in an orderly fashion without direct influence
of known external stimuli but which are almost certainly, in part at
least, a product of the interaction of the organism and its environment."[22] Cratty calls it "an ongoing process which is evidenced during
the formative years by an increasing potential to perform a variety of
tasks."[23] Maturation and learning are linked as conditions determining
"readiness," an expression often used by physical educators as a rationale for instruction, program adjustments, and the introduction of
special circumstances such as competition.

11 *Mature form*: According to Wickstrom, a "major goal in the development of the skill is the achievement of the standards of mature form after the minimal standards of a fundamental skill have been achieved."[24]
It is the desired final shape and rhythm of a series of developmental
motor patterns. A young child may achieve the mature form of basic
skipping prior to entering school, while other children may not achieve
the same standard of form for a year or more. Immature form in some
patterns may persist even into the adult years. Witness the number of
adults who display an immature overhand throwing pattern. Wickstrom
identifies four possible ways in which an individual may progress in
the development of a particular pattern.

One: A child might skip one or several stages that most other children
seem to pass through and achieve a mature pattern at an age as early as 3
or 4 years.
Two: A child might linger at an early stage of skill development and then
quickly pass on through one or more stages without pause.
Three: A child might not fit neatly into any typical stage of development
but might progress according to the developmental trend for a particular
part of the skill pattern.
Four: A child might fail to make significant progress in motor pattern development, and remain at an immature level or stage indefinitely.[25]

Wickstrom, furthermore, identifies mature form as the second of
three major goals in skill development. The first is the minimal form of
a fundamental skill. When the alternating feet in the run make the body
airborne for just a moment between steps, even if the runner is poorly

21 Cratty, *op. cit.*, pp. 245-46.
22 Espenschade and Eckert, *Motor Development,* pp. 78-79.
23 Cratty, p. 107.
24 Wickstrom, *Motor Patterns,* p. 11.
25 Ibid., p. 11.

coordinated, the first goal is achieved. Goal two in running is achieved when the leg action is proper and the arms move in opposition. The third goal is mature form—internalized behavior, readiness for adaptation to the balance beam, the sprint, or the distance run. Each adaptation requires a different form on the mature level of the fundamental skill.[26]

12 *Movement*: The easiest way to define movement of the body is Wickstrom's "change in position by any segment of the body."[27]

13 *Movement behavior*: A more precise term than *movement* is *movement behavior*, defined by Cratty as "observable movement of the body, excluding such functions as visceral changes, the conduction of nerve impulses, and circulation of body fluids. Movement behavior is *observable* and not simply *recordable* movement, for most internal fluctuations are measurable by various devices."[28] Movement behavior and motor behavior are synonymous.

14 *Motor ability*: Singer considers motor ability "the immediate state of the individual to perform in a wide range of motor skills."[29] Whole classes cannot be tested in motor ability. So, instructors often formulate their own tests, usually a group of fundamental skills that the instructor can observe an entire group doing at the same time. The results of these tests are used to select certain children for special help in motor learning. Strictly speaking, these instructor-designed tests do not determine motor ability, but they do help instructors make some decisions until such tests can be designed. Arnheim and Sinclair describe several tests for use with small groups of children.[30] The tests are purported to measure impairment in motor ability. Mentioned are the Oseretsky Test of Motor Proficiency, the Frostig Movement Skills Test Battery, and the Hamm-Marburg Body Coordination Test for Children. All of the tests are time-consuming to administer.

15 *Motor-base*: This is a relatively new expression connoting "the internal organization and representation of motor activity experiences," according to Early in *Perceptual Training in the Curriculum*, as reported by Jordan and Streets in "The Anisa Model" in *Young Children*, a publication of the National Association for the Education of Young Children (NAEYC). Jordan and Streets consider the formation of the motor-base and the achievement of psychomotor competence to "comprise one of the most important developmental requirements of the infant and the pre-schooler."[31] The motor-base is the awareness of the body, how it moves and relates to its environment at a given time and place.

26 Ibid., p. 12.
27 Ibid., p. 4.
28 Cratty, p. 9.
29 Singer, *Motor Learning*, p. 107.
30 Daniel D. Arnheim and William A. Sinclair, *The Clumsy Child* (St. Louis: Mosby, 1975), pp. 34-38.
31 Jordan and Streets, "The Anisa Model," p. 299.

16 *Motor capacity*: Although the terms *ability* and *capacity* are not synonymous, their association with the term *motor* appear to make them so. Singer states, "Motor capacity depicts the maximum potential of an individual to succeed in motor-skill performance. It is a person's innate ability, his motor aptitude."[32] Motor ability seems to refer to basic abilities to coordinate the body, while motor capacity seems to involve many such coordinations.

17 *Motor fitness*: Cratty defines motor fitness as "individual capacity to perform . . . the potential one has to perform a motor skill. . . ." Cratty suggests there are "other performance dimensions: capacity to utilize space effectively in the accurate performance of a task, as well as the application of speed and the effective combination of various factors when performing a skilled act."[33] The instructor may determine that the reason for a lag in a child's motor behavior development is a low level of motor fitness. If this is the case, the instructor may choose to institute remedial measures to correct the deficiency and speed up learning of the desired motor skill.

18 *Motor educability*: "The ease with which one learns new athletic skills" is the way Singer defines motor educability.[34] Cratty calls it "the capacity to learn."[35] The motor educable individual is one who can easily learn new skills. Of course, there are individuals for whom motor learning is difficult. Although they are not uneducable, their poor *motor ability* or low *motor fitness* restrict their *motor capacity* by increasing the time it takes them to learn new skills.

19 *Motor learning*: Cratty defines motor learning as ". . . the rather *permanent change* in motor performance brought about through practice and excludes changes due to maturation, drugs, or nutrients. The concept of learning involves two main inferences: (1) that a rather permanent change in behavior, verifiable by comparing performance trials separated in time, has occurred, and (2) that the change has been caused by practice."[36]

20 *Motor pattern*: There is some confusion in the literature about the meaning of motor pattern. Godfrey and Kephart attempt to differentiate pattern from skill,[37] while Singer uses the term *generalization* instead of *pattern*. He lists the following "generalized motor experiences."
1 Balance and posture
2 Propulsion and receipt
3 Locomotion
4 Contact and manipulation[38]

32 Singer, *Motor Learning*, p. 108.
33 Cratty, p. 11.
34 Singer, *Motor Learning*, p. 108.
35 Cratty, p. 11.
36 Ibid., p. 10.
37 Barbara B. Godfrey and Newell C. Kephart, *Movement Patterns and Motor Education* (New York: Appleton-Century-Crofts, 1969), p. 8.
38 Singer, *Motor Learning*, p. 140.

Movement patterns and fundamental skills

Wickstrom identifies sport skills as precise patterns arising out of less precise movement patterns. "A fundamental motor pattern is the underlying skeleton and the essence of what is accepted as good form for a fundamental skill."[39] We agree with Wickstrom in this because the concept of pattern and the feeling for pattern are important concerns in a movement-oriented approach to physical education. Gerhardt states:

> That which connects builds a relationship. Relationships define patterns. Patterns become tools for understanding because they enable man to predict. They order, define, and structure experience. Similarities are juxtaposed with differences in a whole, a unit for subsequent comparison and prediction.[40]

21 *Motor plan:* This term connotes the ability of the individual to plan a sequence of motor behaviors for the purpose of achieving a specific objective. A prerequisite would appear to be an adequate motor-base, that is, sufficient prior experience and skill from which to draw. Planning may involve a complex sequence of behaviors, such as a segment of a gymnastics routine, or a much more limited activity, such as climbing a tree to retrieve a kite. Arnheim and Sinclair state that once the ability to motor plan has been achieved, the individual will be able to "solve unique movement problems utilizing the backlog of movement skills that have been acquired earlier."[41]

22 *Movement memory:* The ability to recall the sequence and the attributes of a previously performed movement through motor reproduction is our definition of movement memory. When learners repeat an action, they demonstrate the ability to remember what they did before and how they did it. They recall the pattern of the action, its direction, speed, fluency, and so on. Instruction in motor skills is followed by practice that requires learners to recall through movement memory patterns performed earlier. The recall of verbal instructions requires a quite different sort of memory. Again, movement memory is established on the motor-base.

23 *Perceptual-motor:* This term is often used in conjunction with such words as activity, perceptual-motor activity, process, development, and learning. Capon refers to perceptual-motor development as "one's ability to receive, interpret, and respond successfully to sensory information."[42] Perception is the act of interpreting relevant stimuli recorded through one's sensory apparatus. Motor refers to the response produced. Arnheim and Sinclair refer to "the accurate processing of information that comes to the individual through his sense organs."[43]

39 Wickstrom, *Motor Patterns,* p. 12.
40 Lydia A. Gerhardt, *Moving and Knowing* (Englewood Cliffs, N.J.: Prentice-Hall, 1973), p. 6.
41 Arnheim and Sinclair, *Clumsy Child,* p. 51.
42 Jack Capon, *Perceptual-Motor Lesson Plans* (Alameda, Calif.: Front Row Experience, 1975), p. 1.
43 Arnheim and Sinclair, *Clumsy Child,* p. 6.

Other compound expressions are easily defined on the basis of the foregoing information.

24 *Performance*: Wickstrom defines performance as "a motor activity that is to be done or that has been done. The term can be used acceptably to refer to the act (the child threw a ball) or to signify the outcome (a distance of 150 feet)."[44] Performance is merely the act. Whether learning has occurred or not must be inferred from other performances by the learner. A performance may be planned that requires learning and practice to accomplish. The relative merits of a motor performance may be determined by comparing it with a performance standard, such as the expected level of achievement or other performances by either the performer or someone else. "A measured performance is not good, bad, satisfactory, or unsatisfactory in absolute terms. It is relatively good or bad depending upon the extent to which an expected outcome is achieved."[45]

25 *Relaxation*: An increase in muscle contraction, or tonus, is required in all large muscle skills except for relaxation, which Scott calls "a conscious release of muscular tension in a general sense or in a differential sense."[46] The purpose of relaxation is to reduce unnecessary muscular tension, to give in to gravity, and to eliminate unnecessary movements. Relaxation as a skill is practiced separately at first and later used in refining other skills, making their performance more efficient.

26 *Skill*: "Skill is a relative quality, not to be defined in absolute terms," according to Singer.[47] The quality of a motor performance rated by a knowledgeable observer will be compared with minimal standards and, beyond that, with potential high-level performance. An incredible range of skill can sometimes be seen even among young children when they have received excellent instruction early. Skilled performance may be exhibited in either set or variable circumstances. In team games, tennis, and other competitive activities circumstances differ because the actions of opponents show great variability and require participants to make continual adjustments in their motor patterns. Skill in timing and in spatial determinants are called for under these circumstances. Swimmers, track and field contestants, divers, and gymnasts perform under fairly set environmental circumstances, although there may be certain variations in equipment and climatic conditions. Top performers exhibit the highest level of efficiency in keeping with their having achieved optimum standards of physical fitness.

27 *Teaching*: Jordan and Streets define teaching as "arranging environments and guiding the child's interaction with them to achieve the educational goals."[48] Mosston writes about teaching behaviors as "a cumulative chain of decision making—of deciding among known

44 Wickstrom, *Motor Patterns*, p. 7.
45 Ibid.
46 Scott, *Human Motion*, p. 388.
47 Singer, *Motor Learning*, p. 5.
48 Jordan and Streets, "The Anisa Model," p. 297.

choices."[49] These are the decisions about what to teach, how to teach it, and how to involve students as decision-makers in their own learning. Mosston describes teaching styles ranging from highly authoritarian to highly democratic—from telling students what to do to allowing them progressively greater freedom and responsibility for making decisions. Teaching is much more than just "telling." Humphrey describes it as "guidance, direction, and supervision of behavior that results in desirable and worthwhile learning."[50] It would appear that teaching style is determined in part by instructional objectives and educational goals. We will devote a special section in this book to objectives and goals.

Characteristics of fundamental motor patterns

■ Fundamental motor patterns may be divided into three categories.

1 *Locomotion*: Movement patterns involving change in place or traveling. The body does not remain fixed, except on a slippery surface, so that the center of gravity is definitely transported.

2 *Nonlocomotion*: Movement patterns involving no change in place. The body may or may not remain fixed, but it remains over one spot so that there is minimum movement from the center of gravity.

3 *Manipulation*: Movement patterns involving the handling of objects. Toys, tools, and recreational equipment are manipulated in a variety of ways.

Human bodies, like the bodies of other primates and most mammals, can move in a great variety of ways. Diarthrodial (freely movable), joints permit humans to make many motions, technically classified as flexion, extension, abduction, adduction, circumduction, and rotation. These terms may be familiar to the reader, but movement educators find it easier to classify these motions in three categories: stretching, curling, and twisting. It may be argued that all other actions involve these three.

Curling involves joint flexion or bending. It is drawing the body toward its center when the spine is involved, or moving one body segment toward another within the same part when fewer joints are involved. Curling causes a rounding of the body or its parts.

Stretching is the opposite of curling. It is more than straightening body parts when stretching is used fully. Body parts elongate or move away from the body center. Arrowlike or wall-like shapes result from stretching.

Twisting is rotating motion that, because of physical limitations, results in one end of a part turning against the hip, knee, elbow, shoulder, or spinal attachment at the other end. The body can also twist against its supporting parts such as the feet.

Curling, stretching, and twisting are easily observed in all forms of human motor behavior. For example, in walking, the legs curl and stretch with a bit of a twist to maintain a forward direction, while the upper body twists in opposition. Lessons to improve the quality or range of movements are often necessary not only with young children but also with individuals

49 Muska Mosston, *Teaching Physical Education: From Command to Discovery* (Columbus, Ohio: Merrill, 1966), p. 3.

50 James H. Humphrey, *Child Learning Through Elementary School Physical Education,* 2d ed. (Dubuque, Iowa: Wm. C. Brown, 1974), p. 65.

of all ages. Limited movement experiences frequently result in an inadequate motor-base, which may be recognized by lack of completeness in actions requiring a full stretch, curl, or twist.

LOCOMOTOR PATTERNS

1.0 Rolling
- 1.1 Rocking
- 1.2 Turning over, logrolling
- 1.3 Forward rollover
- 1.4 Backward shoulder rollover

2.0 Quadruped locomotion
- 2.1 Hitching
  - 2.11 Rabbit hopping
- 2.2 Crawling
- 2.3 Creeping
  - 2.31 All fours, hands and feet
  - 2.32 Climbing
  - 2.33 Vaulting
  - 2.34 Wheeling

3.0 Biped locomotion
- 3.1 Walk
- 3.2 Run
- 3.3 Jump
  - 3.31 Hop
  - 3.32 Leap
- 3.4 Gallop
- 3.5 Slide
- 3.6 Skip

NONLOCOMOTOR PATTERNS

4.0 Balance
- 4.1 Sitting
- 4.2 Standing
- 4.3 Using different body parts

5.0 Axial movements and gestures
- 5.1 Stretching
- 5.2 Bending or curling
- 5.3 Twisting
- 5.4 Swinging
- 5.5 Swaying
- 5.6 Shaking
- 5.7 Rotating, pivoting, or turning

6.0 Relaxation or tension reduction
- 6.1 Whole body
- 6.2 Selected parts

MANIPULATIVE PATTERNS

7.0 Maintaining contact
- 7.1 Carrying
- 7.2 Shaking
- 7.3 Swinging
- 7.4 Lifting
- 7.5 Pushing
- 7.6 Pulling
- 7.7 Balancing
- 7.8 Wringing
- 7.9 Prehensile dexterity

8.0 Propulsion: release of contact
- 8.1 Striking
  - 8.11 Blocking
  - 8.12 Punching
  - 8.13 Kicking
  - 8.14 Batting
  - 8.15 Butting
- 8.2 Throwing
  - 8.21 Push or thrust
  - 8.22 Underhand
  - 8.23 Overhand
  - 8.24 Heave

9.0 Reception: absorption of force
- 9.1 Trapping
- 9.2 Catching
  - 9.21 Body and arms
  - 9.22 Hands alone

10.0 Suspension
- 10.1 Hanging from hand grip
  - 10.11 Upper arm or armpit
  - 10.12 Straight arm
  - 10.13 Bent arm
- 10.2 Hanging from hand and knee grip
- 10.3 Hanging from knee grip

These motor patterns are fundamental to the complete psychomotor development of the child. Included are all of the basic patterns for classroom activity, work skills involving tools, and play skills involving equipment, dance, games, gymnastics, and aquatics. Each program area will involve additional skills that are fundamental to success in those particular activities. However, the motor patterns listed are fundamental to all program areas. This is not to say that, because the patterns are fundamental, all children will perform them satisfactorily or even acquire all of them without instruction.

Usually by the age of two, children can walk, having successfully learned to travel about in some other fashion first, such as hitching, crawling, or creeping. Through much trial and error, children learn to sit and later to stand. Walking eventually leads to running, and somewhere along the way the jump evolves. Meanwhile, countless manipulative patterns are being learned through the handling of various objects. The behaviors may appear primitive at first, but with growth and continued learning, more mature patterns develop. Actualization of children's potential abilities is enhanced by experience: the richness of the environment that stimulates all of the senses in new and different ways; the opportunity to explore safely but also to dare the new and different; the stimulation of social contact with other children and with adults who reinforce positively.

Locomotor patterns

The development of locomotor patterns is not altogether predictable. Not all children progress from crawl to creep to stand to walk. Some hitch about, stand, and walk. Even the steps vary in learning to stand and walk. The movement patterns described in this section are capable of almost endless variation. Speed, force, and direction are the major variables in continued progress and skill refinement.

1.0 Rolling

Rolling is the transfer of weight to adjacent body parts. Rotation is either sideways around the long axis or forward and backward around the horizontal short axis.

1.1 *Rocking*: Although not strictly locomotion, except with continual change of direction, rocking is the transfer of weight. There is some change in the position of the body weight, and the manner in which the weight is shifted can lead to rolling as the action becomes more forceful. One may rock from side to side or forward and backward while lying curled up on one's back. Rocking is an incomplete roll.

1.2 *Turning over*: Turning over from the back onto the stomach or vice versa is a pattern acquired during the first six months or so of life. The turn from back to belly usually comes first.[51] Children should know the stretched body turnover before receiving instruction in logrolling, that is, continuous sideward rolling. The

51 Stone and Church, *Childhood and Adolescence*, p. 65.

log roll should be performed with arms stretched beyond the head so that the hips and shoulders initiate the shift of weight.

1.3 *Forward rollover*: This is not the common gymnastic forward roll. One simply tucks in the head, lowers the back of the head and neck to the mat between the hands, and rolls forward with a curved back to a sitting position. The spine must be flexible if the body is to roll smoothly along the length of the spine from the neck to the tailbone. If the spine is stiff, a flopover results, as the entire back hits the mat at one time with a characteristic thump.

1.4 *Backward shoulder rollover*: From either vigorous forward and backward rocking or from completion of a forward rollover, those with flexible spines can easily execute the backward shoulder rollover to the knees. Young children will often not bother to use their hands, and some will fail to execute the pattern until they pull their heads to one side. The backward rollover is important precisely because it allows for continuation of movement that dissipates the force of falling backward while protecting the head from injury or the neck muscles from strain.

2.0 Quadruped locomotion

Four-footed locomotion normally precedes biped or two-footed locomotion. However, not all quadruped motor patterns will be acquired without instruction.

2.1 *Hitching*: Parts of the trunk are used for support in hitching, after the fashion of a caterpillar. The pattern is that of a reaching out followed by a drawing toward. Some infants use this pattern as a temporary means of locomotion. Older children may use a scooter in performing this motor pattern when an arm-strengthening activity is desired.

2.11 *Rabbit hopping*: This pattern is performed from the squatting position with the hands reaching forward and taking all the weight while the feet are moved forward. This hands-then-feet pattern may be repeated as desired. When performed to imitate a rabbit, the movement is usually taught as a squat-jump, and the hands are used to form the ears of the rabbit. Note the similarity of this pattern to wheeling.

2.2 *Crawling*: Fundamental crawling is performed on the belly with the hands reaching and pulling while the feet draw up and then push rearward. The arm and leg on one side move forward as the limbs on the opposite side thrust to the rear, propelling the body forward. Variations are used to change direction and to combine with hitching.

2.3 *Creeping*: Creeping is executed on the hands and knees. In coordinated movement, the left knee and right hand travel forward while balance is maintained by the opposite members, that then move forward in an alternation of steps. One variation that can be practiced resembles crawling, in that the limbs on each side alternate with those on the opposite side. Other variations have a distinct character.

2.31 *All fours*: Raising the knees off the floor when creeping puts the bottom of the feet in contact with the floor, raises the hips, and shifts the weight forward onto the hands. With the feet placed wider apart than hip-width and the hands placed wider apart than shoulder-width, this position can be relatively comfortable and used for agile changes in direction or for forward travel. An excellent coordinator of arm and leg movement and a strength-builder, this pattern is fundamental to gymnastics, wrestling, and football. Care should be taken not to raise the hips too high. This makes it difficult for the performer to see forward and causes the head to be cocked to one side. When this happens, almost invariably forward travel will not be evenly accented but will take on a sideward slant as one side leads the other.

2.32 *Climbing*: Creeping behaviors in the infant lead to climbing, first to a standing position, and later to a series of steps. Either the creeping or the crawling pattern may be used in climbing. If the ladder is inclined at a fairly steep angle, the first step may be made with the foot followed by the hand on that side. In effect, the child walks up the ladder using hands to support a little weight but principally to help with balance. Rope climbing resembles hitching if both arms and legs are used, the legs pushing and the arms pulling. For more details read Godfrey and Kephart's *Movement Patterns and Motor Education*.

2.33 *Vaulting*: It may seem strange that vaulting is a fundamental motor pattern. This vault does not resemble the gymnastic vault over the side horse or long horse. It is more closely related to the rabbit hop. The hands are placed on an obstacle such as a bench, and with a quick push and lift the legs are swung over to the other side as the hands support the weight of the body. The feet usually go over one after the other; more highly skilled performers lift them over simultaneously. For this vault the hands are placed sideways on the object and travel is lateral to the point of departure. The pattern should be practiced to both sides.

2.34 *Wheeling*: This pattern is similar to the cartwheel but without the outstretched body and straight, widespread legs. The performer turns sideways from a crouched stance. Weight is taken on the hands either simultaneously or on one after the other, with the feet following one after the other. An effort should be made to place the hands and feet in a straight line. The next turn follows the first without interruption.

3.0 Biped locomotion

All of the motor patterns in this category involve use of the feet. The first three patterns should be considered primary, the remaining motor patterns developing out of them as variations or combinations. Some authors categorize these variations and combinations as fundamental skills; we do not.

3.1 *Walk*: After children balance on two feet, they are ready to start walking. The toddler's walk with feet spread wide and arms held still is gradually replaced by a more mature pattern—heel-to-toe transfer of weight over the foot, movement of the arms in opposition to the feet, and a narrower stance. The turned-out feet of the toddler gradually shift forward to the most efficient walking position.

3.2 *Run*: In running, the feet alternate evenly and rhythmically as they do in walking, except that there is a momentary loss of contact with the ground after each step. The immature run is similar to the immature walk. Gradually, the arms are moved in opposition to the feet, and the runner learns to land on the balls of the feet to absorb shock and to gain additional leverage. As speed increases, the elbow is bent more, but the stance remains fairly erect.

3.3 *Jump*: The desired pattern is a symmetrical push-off with both feet, simultaneous forward/upward movement of the arms, and a landing on both feet at the same time. Researchers have pointed out that the difficulty shown by young children as they perform their first jumps arises from adapting to symmetrical patterns when their experiences in walking and running have stressed asymmetrical movement. Many children enter school still unable to jump as described, frequently because they have not been encouraged to do so or have lacked an opportunity. They push off

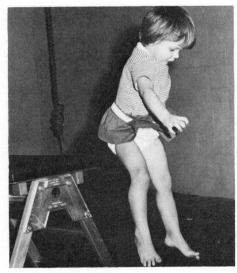

Preschoolers jumping
from different levels

with one foot, even though their stance is parallel, and land first on one foot and then the other. They either fail to move their arms or move them back and up. For further information on the jump read Godfrey and Kephart, Sinclair, or Espenschade and Eckert.

3.31 *Hop*: It takes a lot of strength for young children to push all of their weight up into the air from a standing position. They are usually past the age of four before they can perform a series of hops successfully. Hopping requires pushing off with one foot and landing on the same foot. After children learn to hop on one foot, they must learn to hop on the other if they are to acquire the ability to skip. Rhythmic lifting of the arms to assist in the hop may develop as clapping patterns and rope-turning skills are acquired. Rhythmic jumping in place is a good way to lead into rhythmic hopping.

3.32 *Leap*: The leap is the most difficult locomotor pattern to acquire because, like the hop, it requires a push-off on one foot, but its greater height also increases the force of the landing, which is made on the opposite foot. If the child pushes off on the foot preferred for hopping, then the landing will be on the weaker foot, causing the leaper to either collapse and fall or make certain preventive movements. Leaping should be done first off one foot and then off the other, as if learners were leaping from stone to stone across a brook. The arms assist in the lift, but the leap itself, like other forms of the jump when performed in gymnastics or dance, should involve only the lower part of the body. However, technically this is difficult to achieve. Rhythmic lifting of the arms should be permitted in execution of the leap. Other movements can be added later.

3.4 *Gallop*: In the gallop, one leg leads while the other moves forward to catch up but never to lead. The rhythm for a right-foot lead is RIGHT-left-RIGHT-left. As the left foot moves forward toward the right, the right foot quickly moves ahead and the left foot displaces it. Of course, the gallop should be learned leading with either foot. Most children can gallop by the time they enter school, but many may appear awkward and heavy. Pretending that the knee on the rear leg is hurt will give pattern clarity to the movements of those children whose gallops look too much like a run.

3.5 *Slide*: The slide is similar to the gallop, except that the direction of movement is sideways. In a slide to the right, the right foot steps sideways, pulling the body over it, whereupon the left foot immediately moves to the position vacated by the right foot, which has already started the next sideward step. The rhythm is the same as that for the gallop so it should not be confused with the step-draw motion of folk dancing. Children demonstrate agility by changing the direction of their slides quickly. Like the gallop, the slide is fundamental to sport and dance skills.

3.6 *Skip*: The skip is a combination of walking and hopping, but it has the rhythm of the gallop. That is one reason why the gallop should be taught first. The pattern is step-hop, step-hop, and so on. Emphasizing the lift of the knees and arms helps establish the uneven rhythm characteristic of the skip pattern. Some children in first grade may not yet know how to skip. A little private attention at the end of class, with the instructor and performer moving side by side holding inside hands, may help establish the rhythm. Often the problem lies in the children's inability to hop several times on either foot. Practice this with everyone, and skipping will improve quickly in most cases.

Nonlocomotor Patterns

Nonlocomotor patterns are either *functional* or *expressive*. Functional patterns are those meant to accomplish some objective, like bending to avoid bumping one's head, twisting to avoid contact, or balancing carefully. Expressive actions are those meant to communicate. They are called gestures. Nonlocomotor movement patterns may be used either functionally or expressively. They are described here merely to make you aware of their existence, if that is necessary, and to assure that you will pay attention to their development in young children. As in the case of locomotor patterns, more complex motor skills depend upon the proper development of fundamental nonlocomotor patterns.

Again, speed, force, and spatial variables such as direction influence the quality of nonlocomotor patterns. Correct technique is highly dependent on awareness of body parts, their alignment with each other and with the center of gravity. Movement requires controlled muscular tension if it is to be efficient. Also we agree with Scott that relaxation is a fundamental skill, and we have included it here.

4.0 **Balance**

Awareness of balance means awareness of the center of gravity in relation to the base of support. This awareness is accompanied by the awareness of unbalance when the center of gravity moves outside the base of support. Both awarenesses are necessary to good balance. We are concerned here with static balance, which is balance without motion as opposed to dynamic balance which is balance achieved during energetic activity. "The maintenance of a particular body position with a minimum of sway is referred to as static balance while dynamic balance is considered to be the maintenance of posture during the performance of a motor skill which tends to disturb the body's orientation."[52] Balance is achieved and monitored by the coordinated efforts of the stretch reflex, proprioceptors, the reticular formation of interlaced nerve cells, the vestibular apparatus of the ear, and the

52 Espenschade and Eckert, *Motor Development*, p. 163.

eyes. Singer[53] is a good source for additional information on the mechanisms that affect balance. The physical education teacher who is concerned with the acquisition of fundamental motor patterns should be alert to problems in maintaining balance. Three categories of static balance may be identified.

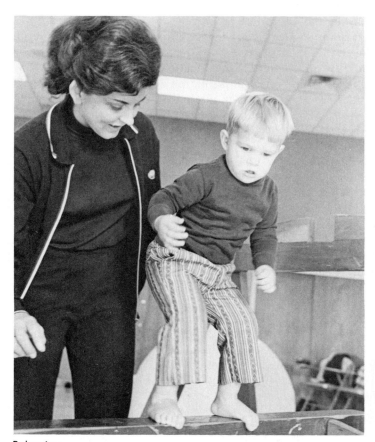

Balancing

4.1 *Sitting*: Sitting is maintaining the upper body in an erect posture on a base of support that includes the pelvic bones, their surrounding muscle tissue, and the feet or legs held in a bent position. Variations are common, and any one position is not held long. Legs may be crossed, feet may be spread wide apart, and, if the person is sitting on the floor instead of on a chair, the legs may be positioned in front of the body, to one side, or, in very young children, bent to the rear. This latter position resembles kneeling, except the seat is on the floor between the feet. Children, as they grow older, usually stop using that position.

53 Singer, *Motor Learning*, pp. 58-61.

4.2 *Standing*: Standing requires more critical alignment of the body in relation to the center of gravity than is necessary for sitting. The higher center of gravity and the smaller base of support make it harder to achieve and maintain equilibrium. Godfrey and Kephart stress "standing tall" and "holding the chest up" as ways to help children experience the feeling of good posture. "Standing tall or erect in good alignment will make the shoulders drop back into proper position, as long as they are not held stiffly or used to force the action."[54]

4.3 *Using different body parts*: Balanced posture using different body parts is subject to wide variation from simple to complex forms. Examples of balancing on two body parts include using the feet to support the body when it is fully bent in a squat, using the hands in a handstand, and combinations using one hand with one foot, knee, or hip. One may balance on a single body part or on more than two body parts. The possibilities are many, and with encouragement young children will explore different ways just for the fun of it. Many of these balance positions are fundamental to sport skills—witness the stance in football, the start in track or in wrestling, the positions in gymnastics used on the floor and on apparatus.

5.0 Axial movements and gestures

Voluntary actions not involving locomotion or movement of specific body parts required for support are called axial movements or gestures. Dance instructors are more apt to use the term gesture, parti-

54 Godfrey and Kephart, *Movement Patterns*, p. 100.

Using different body
parts for balance

cularly if expression is the purpose of the movement. These fundamental actions are limited to those that take place on the spot or occur in addition to the actions that transport the body. Aside from manipulative behaviors which are treated separately, these actions include counterbalancing the body in response to a shifting center of gravity; movement in opposition to the action of the legs as in walking or running; movement adding impetus to the downward thrust of the legs to elevate the body as in jumping; widening, narrowing, or otherwise adjusting the size of the body to make a more functional or a more expressive use of available space; changing the orientation of the body in space so as to face different ways. Seven subcategories of axial movements are identified.

5.1 *Stretching*: This is the extension of body parts and the straightening out of joints that results in movement away from the body center. It is most important for the instructor to gradually increase the student's awareness of a complete stretch in all of the body parts and the stretch of the body as a whole in all directions.

5.2 *Bending or curling*: Folding the body or a body part is called bending or curling, bending having a connotation of being more angular. Curling conveys the sense of moving into a compact, round shape. It is the opposite of stretching, and psychologically it is associated with feelings of inwardness accompanying a drawing in toward the body center. Instructors should make sure that

Extension of body
parts—stretching

Curled shape

learners feel the contrast between the full stretch and the curl and the many positions in between.

5.3 *Twisting*: The twist may incorporate the curled or the stretched body shape, but its action changes the spatial orientation of the body parts involved. The hand may move directly toward the shoulder in a curl, whereas a twist of the lower arm during the action will change the direction that the hand faces as it arrives at the shoulder. The asymmetrical shapes produced by twisting actions enhance the body's functional and expressive abilities. Consider how difficult it would be to move your body without making the slightest twisting motion.

5.4 *Swinging*: Pendular movements, particularly from the shoulder, knee, and hip joints, are called swinging actions. The arm, because of the way it is articulated at the shoulder, is capable of circling in a wider range of movement than the leg, the foot, or the hand. Circling might be considered a subcategory of swinging inasmuch as it is the continuation of a swinging action in one direction until a full circle is made. Swinging or circling is usually characterized as a free rather than a restricted or bound action.

5.5 *Swaying*: Swaying is shifting from one edge of the base of support to the opposite edge. Swaying while standing with the feet close together is more limited in range than swaying with the feet spread apart. The mover must be able to control the sway

Twisting using a hoop

Collapsing:
selective tension
reduction

so as not to take a step or make a change in the size of the base. This may entail counterbalancing the movement of the center of gravity in one direction with the movement of a body part in the opposite direction.

5.6 *Shaking*: Exaggerated trembling is shaking, a visible, vigorous back and forth movement of body parts at a fairly rapid rate. Shaking may include rapid twisting, slight to be sure, but necessary to the character of this action. To shake, the individual's body must be loose enough to allow the action to happen. One cannot shake if there is too much tension in the muscles.

5.7 *Rotating, pivoting, or turning*: Rotating involves twisting one body part in relation to an adjacent body part. It is also the turning of the entire body as in spinning or pivoting on one foot. A twist in one direction is often followed by a turn in the opposite direction, the twist being used to increase the distance over which force for turning can be developed. Discus throwing is probably the most outstanding example of this kind of behavior, but it occurs with less exaggeration in many other activities as well. Pivoting in basketball often begins with a twist, as the player fakes in one direction and pivots in the other.

6.0 Relaxation or tension reduction

"Relaxation is a conscious release of muscular tension in a general sense or in a differential sense. The latter implies localized lowering of tonus in relation to increased muscular activity for a particular movement. Relaxation skill is based on the kinesthetic awareness of feelings of tonus. It is a motor skill which must be learned in much the same way as any other motor skill."[55] Two subcategories are identified.

6.1 *Whole body*: Muscle tonus of the entire body is consciously reduced when a person is lying down and there are minimal distractions. A general awareness of tension reduction is developed by progressively relaxing the body, beginning with the head and working toward the feet. Isometric tension is followed by tension reduction until the entire body is relaxed. Frostig,[56] Scott,[57] and Cratty[58] describe specific techniques for developing this motor skill.

6.2 *Selected parts*: "Any activity that requires maximum flexibility or is attempting to increase flexibility must provide relaxation of the antagonistic muscles first."[59] Selected body parts are chosen to move in a free-swinging manner to demonstrate looseness of

55 Scott, *Human Motion*, pp. 388-89.
56 Marianne Frostig, *Movement Education: Theory and Practice*, (Chicago: Follett, 1970).
57 Scott, *Human Motion*, pp. 388-95.
58 Bryant J. Cratty, *Movement, Perception and Thought*, (Mountain View, Calif.: Peek Publications, 1969), pp. 26-27. Bryant J. Cratty, *Movement Behavior and Motor Learning*, 2nd ed., Philadelphia: Lea & Febiger, 1967, p. 182.
59 Scott, *Human Motion*, p. 394.

Differential relaxation

the opposing muscle groups or relaxation in unrequired parts is stressed such as face and neck musculature or the muscles of extension to permit the follow-through of flexion in throwlike actions. Breathing is related to differential relaxation. Through relaxation of body parts, the force of gravity may be taken into account. For example, with a loss of equilibrium, one may relax and allow the body to collapse rather than risk injury in fighting the fall. Such differentiated ability to relax is directly related both to the awareness of effort and to the acquisition of all motor skills.

Manipulative patterns

Objects lend themselves to various manipulations depending on their properties. Rigidity as a property ranges from the flexibility of a ribbon used in rhythmic gymnastics to the firmness of a baseball bat. Balls vary in elasticity, making them more or less suitable for certain activities. Weight, texture, size, shape, and to some extent even color are variable properties that influence the manner in which objects are manipulated. Consider the effect of using a basketball of regulation size and weight on the throwing patterns of small children. Incorrect patterns that individuals have developed in learning to cope with manipulative objects (during childhood, and adolescence), such as the basketball, may be exhibited by college-age students whose skills never matured to efficient form. For example, many people are unable to apply their body forces correctly in shooting a basketball. Basic skills should evolve out of the intelligent refinement of

Movement patterns and fundamental skills

basic manipulative patterns. The physical education instructor should be able to guide and structure the required learning experiences.

All of the basic manipulative patterns may be grouped in three categories according to the principal behavior of the manipulator. It is assumed that the instructor will carefully select appropriate equipment. Also the instructor should consider varying the size, weight, texture, shape, and color of objects to stimulate development of adaptive abilities. The instructor can guide the learner in selecting and developing appropriate adaptive patterns if the learner needs help. If the child is trying to manipulate a heavy ball with one hand without much success, the teacher should suggest that the child use both hands. Colors of objects are important, too. Some colors contrast better with the background color of a floor, wall or ceiling, making the object easier to track visually. Instructors should observe what children do with objects and how they do it, so that they can guide the children in flexible, adaptive development of manipulative behaviors.

7.0 Maintaining contact

Under this heading are listed all of the patterns required to maintain continuous contact with an object while it is being manipulated. Infant children follow an interesting sequence of development after they are able to focus on and track objects with their eyes. They progress from reaching for and gathering in objects with both hands to grasping objects with one hand. The use of the thumb in opposition to the fingers for grasping replaces the earlier finger-to-palm grasp. By the time most children are seven months old, they can reach for, grasp, and release objects with one hand, and by the age of ten months the pattern is smoothly coordinated.[60, 61] As infants are learning to walk they are perfecting manipulative skills they have already acquired.

7.1 *Carrying*: The manipulative pattern observed earliest in infancy is carrying, when the child first grasps and holds an object. We are concerned here, however, with the ability to employ the pattern properly to objects of different weights, sizes, and shapes. The learner demonstrates efficiency in carrying skill by varying choice and movement of body parts to maintain control of different objects. Carrying movements involve holding objects between body parts ranging all the way from thumb and finger if the object is very small, to thumb and hand, to both hands, to both arms applied in a corralling or encircling manner. The object may be carried by a handle from which it hangs suspended, or it may be grasped from underneath if it is too heavy or too large to be grasped from above.

7.2 *Shaking*: Infants may be observed to shake an object to dislodge it from their own grasp before they have learned to release objects voluntarily. Later, infants may shake objects such as rattles

60 Espenschade and Eckert, *Motor Development*, pp. 993-95.
61 Stone and Church, *Childhood and Adolescence*, pp. 63-81.

to cause something to happen. Much later, children may be seen using a shaking motion to move an object such as a ribbon in an undulating fashion. A cloth or blanket used in play may be shaken in imitation of mother hanging up the washing. Skilled shaking behavior requires the relaxation of the opposing muscle groups so that the movement has sufficient flexibility.

7.3 *Swinging*: This pattern was described previously under nonlocomotor behavior. The rhythmic, pendular movement of the arm is transferred to an object in this variation on the carrying pattern. The object may be swung forward and back, side to side, or up and down. The object may be attached to a string, a stick, or some other device. The object may also be held like a bat or club and used as an extension of the arm. The weight thrown in field events and the cowboy's lasso are examples of objects that are swung. We are not considering the release of the object here.

7.4 *Lifting*: Lifting involves the displacement of objects varying in weight from light to heavy with consequent application of increased force and involvement of additional body members. Heavy lifting requires the performer to use leg and back muscles while keeping the object as close to the line of gravity as possible. Lifting a heavy object requires strong flexion of the arms, as in pulling, and strong extension of the legs and back, as in pushing. In fact, the legs push downward when an object is raised.

7.5 *Pushing*: Continuous contact with an object while pushing it moves it. The action is one of extension in a straight line. Light objects may be pushed by extension of the arm or even just a finger, while heavier objects may require the muscular force of the entire body in extension. Pushing heavy objects requires that the back be kept straight to transmit the force of the extending legs efficiently.

Lifting and pushing

7.6 *Pulling*: Pulling, the opposite of pushing, may involve flexing just the arm or, when greater force is needed, extending the leg, too, as in "digging in." Continuous pulling of an object such as a wagon combines locomotion with the drawing-toward action of pulling. The weight of the body is applied in the direction of intended movement.

7.7 *Balancing*: An object too large to be grasped may be balanced on a body part such as an open hand. Care must be taken to position the object on the center of gravity on the body part. Simple balancing involves a single object such as a large ball, a plate, or a tray held in the open hand. Slightly more complicated movements are required to balance such objects on other body parts or to balance irregular or long objects on the hand. Even greater ability is required to balance objects turned on end, particularly on a small body part such as the tip of a finger.

7.8 *Wringing*: Wringing is a twisting action such as that used to turn a screw or to spin a ball. Screwing caps on and off jars is a wringing action, as is the action for which the pattern is named, that of wringing a cloth as if to squeeze it dry.

7.9 *Prehensile dexterity*: Finger dexterity requires, at least in the initial stages, coordination of visual perceptual abilities and manipulation of the fingers and thumb. This much ability is fundamental, and even preschool children are capable of manipulating small objects such as beads, cups, and string fairly well. When children enter school, they spend much time learning skills such as writing and drawing that require finger dexterity. Even tying shoes, a fundamental activity, gradually becomes so internalized that learners pay less and less attention to the details of the action. Advanced levels of prehensile dexterity are evident in the playing of musical instruments, in typing, in carrying out various office duties, and in doing fine craftwork.

8.0 Propulsion: release of contact

Many of the patterns previously described are employed in some part of the actions covered in this category. The major difference is that objects are released or given impetus through striking behaviors.

8.1 *Striking*: Striking is imparting a blow to an object to propel it. Any body part may be used, although objects are usually struck with the hand, fist, foot, knee, or forehead. An implement such as a bat, club, paddle, or racket may be used as an extension of the body. There are five subcategories of striking. Eye focus on the target area is essential for successful striking performance.

8.11 *Blocking*: Blocking is stopping the movement of an object along the ground or in the air with the whole body or a body part. The entire object is the target area.

8.12 *Punching*: Punching is a combination of two patterns: a thrust or jablike action and a slashing, overhand action. A ball suspended from a rope is easier to strike by punching than a ball that is thrown, and a suspended balloon is easier to punch than a heavy, suspended ball. It is customary to clench the hand to form a striking surface on the palm side, the little finger end, or the knuckles of the fist. The object should be hit in the center.

8.13 *Kicking*: A blow struck with any part of the leg is called a kick, although the action is usually performed with the toe or instep. A ball should be kicked just below its center to raise it off the ground. Kicking a ball held by the kicker requires considerably more coordination than kicking a ball that is lying still or is rolling along the ground. A good kick is initiated by the backward swing of the thigh with the knee well flexed. The lower leg is extended quickly just before the thigh is in line with the ball, which imparts maximum velocity to the foot just before it contacts the ball. The ankle is held firm for either the toe kick or the instep kick. The arms are used to maintain equilibrium.

Striking skills

8.14 *Batting*: Objects may be batted with the hand, the fist, or a held implement. The movement is a swing directed at a stationary or thrown object. Fundamentally, it is the action used in baseball, tennis, and golf. Implements used in batting may be held with one or both hands. The feet are placed wide apart for stability. A poor swing is accompanied by loss of a stable base as the batter pivots on the forward foot, causing the body to turn. In a good swing there is a strong twist of the trunk with no loss of footing.

8.15 *Butting*: The growing popularity of soccer provides many children with the opportunity to learn different ways of butting with the head. In simple butting, performers should focus their eyes on the ball when the head makes contact. This allows them to position the ball high on the forehead.

8.2 *Throwing*: Except for pushing or thrusting, all throwing movements incorporate some form of the swing to develop the force needed to propel the object. Children just learning to throw usually do not stand with their feet in the right position or follow through on the throwing motion. All four throwing patterns require the thrower to focus on the target throughout the action.

8.21 *Push or thrust*: The pattern of pushing or thrusting is similar to that used in the basketball push-pass. The object to be pushed is usually held close to the chest with both hands and then thrust toward the target, the release accompanied by rapid wrist and finger flexion. Light objects may be pushed with one hand.

8.22 *Underhand*: Either one or both hands may be used in the underhand throw. When both hands are used, the feet and knees are spread apart and slightly flexed so that they may be extended on the upward swing of the arms. One-handed throws are swung alongside of the hip.

8.23 *Overhand*: In the overhand throw the object is swung

Movement patterns and fundamental skills

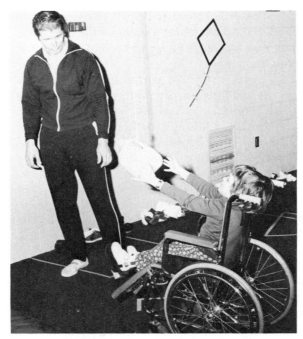
Pushing or thrusting

above the shoulder. The position from which the object is thrown is some point above and behind the ear. The throw is executed by bringing the elbow forward and then snapping the forearm forward into full extension with a final flicklike flexion of the wrist to propel the object to a release. The arm may be swung back, up, and over the shoulder to bring the ball into throwing position. This motion is not appropriate when a quick throw must be made. A more direct way to bring the object into throwing position is to carry it straight up and then back over the shoulder. The overhand throw is extremely versatile and may be used when accuracy, speed, distance, and power are required. Wickstrom describes the mature pattern for the right-handed throwing as follows:

Preparatory movements
1. Pivot, rotating the body to the right and shift the weight to the right foot.
2. Swing the throwing arm backward and upward.
Throwing movements
3. Step forward in the direction of the throw with the left foot.
4. Rotate the hips, the trunk, and the shoulders to the left while retracting the throwing arm to the final position before starting the forward arm action.
5. Swing the right elbow forward horizontally, extend the forearm and snap the wrist just before releasing the ball.

No follow-through

Follow-through
6. Continue the pattern of movement in the follow-through until the momentum generated in the throwing action can be dissipated.[62]

    Although there are many variations on the overhand throw, including differences in preparatory and follow-through movements, the sequence is the same for all.

8.24 *Heave*: Essentially a side or side-underarm throw, the heave is best exemplified by the discus throw, which is the most advanced or complex form of heave. Great power is generated by unwinding the trunk from its preparatory twisted position. The arm remains straight unless the object is so large that the hand and forearm must curve around it to grasp it. Sometimes, to generate additional force, performers spin around rapidly one or more times before releasing the object. Another way to generate additional force is to attach a rope to the object and swing the object around the head before heaving it. There is a German heaving ball that looks like an undersized volleyball, but weighs

62 Wickstrom, *Motor Patterns*, p. 82.

more, and comes with a leather strap handle. (A supplier for German heaving balls is listed in the appendix.)

9.0 Reception: absorption of force

It is more difficult to receive an object than to propel it because of the judgments that must be made just prior to reception, as well as during reception. The object may roll, bounce, or travel through the air to the receiver. The rolling object is easiest of the three to track visually; then comes the bouncing object, and last the airborne object. Variations in each of these pathways to the receiver affect the ease or difficulty of reception. Objects on a direct path to the receiver are easiest to receive. Those traveling to the right or left require the receiver to move laterally to intercept, which is still easier than traveling forward or back, particularly to intercept an aerial object.

9.1 *Trapping*: Children usually learn to trap an object before they learn to catch it, which is not to say that all trapping is easier than catching. Simple trapping is receiving a ball, beanbag, or other object and holding it against the floor or the body. As a means of stopping a moving object, trapping may be the forerunner of catching objects with the hands alone or stopping an object with the foot and body—skills associated with the game of soccer because all players except the goalkeeper are denied use of the hands to receive the ball. The term trapping is often used to mean the act of stopping an object between any part of the body and the ground or other part of the body. Stepping on a moving ball with enough pressure to stop it without shifting all one's weight onto the ball is one means of trapping. Other ways to trap a ball are between the arm or arms and body, between the legs, and between the hands, arms, or body and another surface such as the floor or wall. Trapping with the feet particularly requires the development of additional blocking abilities to absorb the force of the initial contact with the moving object. The bouncing or airborne object is first blocked by a body part that reduces its velocity with a "giving" motion, allowing the object to fall to the ground where the foot takes over.

9.2 *Catching*: The first stage of catching is trapping. Wickstrom describes the child's first catching efforts: "He sits with his legs spread and when a ball is rolled slowly at the central axis of his trunk, he attempts to grasp it or tries to trap it against one of his legs."[63] This form is often used by kindergarten children who have not had many experiences playing with balls. Other catching behaviors leading to successful manipulative activity include chasing a rolling ball and trapping it with the hands or with the arms and body assisting the hands; controlling the bouncing or thrown ball with the body and arms, and catching with the hands alone.

63 Ibid., p. 97.

9.21 *Body and arms*: Catching with the body and arms is an immature form of the behavior. The ball is corralled against the body with a traplike action. Large balls are handled in this way, but some children continue to use this pattern even when they change to the use of smaller balls. Young children often catch a football by trapping it against the body in the mistaken belief that this is the correct technique. The action of catching a football with the hands and immediately bringing it to the body to prevent fumbling may be misinterpreted by children as body-and-arms catching.

9.22 *Hands alone*: The mature form of catching requires that the hands reach for the ball, grasp it, and simultaneously give in the direction of its path so as to dissipate its force. Immature forms of the hands-catch include reaching out and waiting for the ball to fall into the hands; clutching at the ball on reception without "giving" rearward to soften the impact; pushing at the ball, which causes it to rebound off the hands; and holding the hands together like the beak of a bird in pursuit of food, waiting for the ball to enter the pocket. The proper method of catching involves two ball-control principles:

1. Force must be applied to change the velocity of a moving object (to decelerate it).
2. The shock of catching the object is diminished by absorbing the force over a greater distance or over a greater area, or both (the catcher must give with the ball).[64]

The preparatory position of the hands in catching is forward with thumbs and fingers up for balls arriving above the waist and down for balls arriving below the waist. The hands form a cup or funnel shape. The ball, whether rolling, bouncing, or aerial, must be watched until caught. If children have acquired these fundamental behaviors by third or fourth grade, they can learn the variations needed in specific sports.

Patterns of Suspension

The explorations of young children usually include climbing, which results in suspension of the body from one or more members of the body. Unfortunately, the literature on motor development contains little useful information on suspension or hanging activity. In climbing on ropes, trees, or playground equipment, children must suspend themselves at least momentarily by the arms while they secure a better or a different grip with the feet or legs. Children must have enough strength in the grip, in the arms, and in the arm and back muscles that make up the shoulder girdle to control suspension. This prerequisite is different from all other pre-

64 Ibid., p. 106.

Suspension from hands

requisites for motor learning we have previously described. Play on apparatus, of which young children from preschool upward are so fond, develops patterns of suspension. The increasing use of apparatus in preschools and in elementary schools requires the inclusion of suspension patterns in any list of fundamental motor behaviors.

10.0 Suspension

Although there are skills involved in supporting oneself on the apparatus, these may easily be considered variations of movement patterns commonly executed on the floor. Suspension patterns are different. The body hangs from a support in the grip of the body part or parts being used for control. There are three categories of suspension. Within each category there is room for development from static hanging to swinging or traveling.

10.1 *Hanging from hand grip*: There are several different patterns of suspension from the hand grip. Each requires the use of the hands with some assistance from the muscles of the shoulder girdle.

10.11 *Upper arm or armpit*: The body may be suspended from two parallel bars or a single bar by bringing the elbows over the bar or bars and resting the weight on the upper arm or armpit. In climbing out of a hole or pit, or over a ledge, you would use this technique to pull your shoulders up and over the arms and bring the hands into position for support in further lifting. Young children require a low bar for these suspensions.

10.12 *Straight arm*: The straight arm suspension is often the one first attempted by the young child, who must reach high for the rung of a ladder supported parallel to the ground above the head. Grip strength is most important in maintaining straight arm suspension for the performance of other actions that may follow. The child may try to swing or to bring the feet up to the same rung or to a different rung. Without sufficient strength of grip, the child usually will shift to the more secure upper arm grip if the opportunity arises.

10.13 *Bent arm*: Bent arm suspension is the most difficult because it involves the use of all of the muscles of the shoulder girdle. It is fundamental, because without it children cannot be expected to progress in the development of apparatus skills and other climbing behaviors. Any bent arm position is difficult to maintain, but those with the arms bent only slightly (at approximately 120 degrees) require the greatest strength, while those with the arms bent almost double (at approximately 45 degrees) require the least. The easiest way to maintain a bent arm hang is to rest the chin on the bar. Rope climbing requires use of the bent arm hang to give the feet and legs time to secure a new grip. The bent arm hang also is used to help bring the hips and legs up to a higher position than would be possible with straight arm suspension.

10.2 *Hanging from hand and knee grip*: The child must have the strength to curl the trunk and flex the legs upward to hang suspended from a hand and knee grip. Suspension may be from one bar or from two in any number of variations, some being more difficult than others.

10.3 *Hanging from knee grip*: Suspension from the knees alone requires a certain mastery of skills in each of the foregoing categories of suspension. The grip is secured by maintaining a flexed position of the legs. Careful uncurling of the trunk allows the body to hang fully suspended with the head down and the arms hanging free. To reestablish the upright position, the child must either curl the body and regrasp the bar so that the knee grip may be released or place the hands on the floor for support while disengaging the knees and bringing the feet down under control.

We have identified and described motor patterns fundamental to the acquisition of skilled movement behavior. Once children have become skilled in the fundamentals they can proceed safely to the more complex adaptations required in interaction with new environments and under other social and physical conditions.

Movement patterns and fundamental skills

Assignments

● Beginning with this chapter, we suggest assignments that students may undertake on their own or that the instructor may make to increase understanding of the concepts.

1
Observe filmed, videotaped, or live performances of children engaged in free movement or manipulation of objects in a variety of environmental situations such as a playground, neighborhood area, gymnasium, or laboratory setting. Identify orally or in writing all of the fundamental motor patterns exhibited during a given period of time such as ten or twenty seconds. Determine the category to which each of the motor patterns belongs.

2
Observe filmed, videotaped, or live performances of a child about age three, another child age four to five, and a third child age six to seven for periods of fifteen to thirty minutes. Describe the environment in which each child is performing and list each different motor pattern you observe. Compare the different environments. Compare the different motor behaviors, paying special attention to the quantity or emphasis and quality or maturity of the fundamental activities.

3
Select one fundamental motor pattern and teach it to a child you have previously observed and know to be physically capable of learning the pattern. Use the demonstration method of teaching so that the child may see the skill performed before attempting to execute it.

Readings

Arnheim, Daniel D., and Sinclair, William A. *The Clumsy Child, A Program of Motor Therapy.* St. Louis: Mosby, 1975.

Capon, Jack. *Perceptual-Motor Lesson Plans.* Alameda, Calif.: Front Row Experience, 1975.

Cratty, Bryant J. *Movement Behavior and Motor Learning.* 2d ed. Philadelphia: Lea & Febiger, 1967.

———. *Movement, Perception and Thought.* Mountain View, Calif.: Peek Publications, 1969.

Espenschade, Anna S., and Eckert, Helen M. *Motor Development.* Columbus, Ohio: Merrill, 1967.

Flinchum, Betty M. *Motor Development in Early Childhood.* St. Louis: Mosby, 1975. `

Frostig, Marianne, in assn. with Phyllis Maslow. *Movement Education: Theory and Practice.* Chicago: Follett, 1970.

Gerhardt, Lydia A. *Moving and Knowing.* Englewood Cliffs, N.J.: Prentice-Hall, 1973.

Godfrey, Barbara B., and Kephart, Newell C. *Movement Patterns and Motor Education.* New York: Appleton-Century-Crofts, 1969.

Harrow, Anita J. *A Taxonomy of the Psychomotor Domain.* New York: McKay, 1972.

Humphrey, James H. *Child Learning Through Elementary School Physical Education.* 2d ed. Dubuque, Iowa: Wm. C. Brown, 1974.

Latchaw, Marjorie, and Egstrom, Glen. *Human Movement.* Englewood Cliffs, N.J.: Prentice-Hall, 1969.

Scott, M. Gladys. *An Analysis of Human Motion.* 2d ed., New York: Appleton-Century-Crofts, 1963.

Sinclair, Caroline B. *Movement of the Young Child.* Columbus, Ohio: Merrill, 1973.

Singer, Robert N. *Motor Learning and Human Performance.* London: Macmillan, 1968.

Stone, L. Joseph, and Church, Joseph. *Childhood and Adolescence.* 3d ed. New York: Random House, 1973.

Wickstrom, Ralph L. *Fundamental Motor Patterns.* Philadelphia: Lea & Febiger, 1970.

Chapter V

Awareness of motion factors

People can best be trained to the performance of specific tasks in a manner most appropriate to the task and to their personal capacities when their understanding of the relationship and proportionality of motion factors is awakened.

Laban and Lawrence

■ Movement, whether patterned or unpatterned, simple or complex, exists in time and space. Time describes when it happens and for how long. Space is where it happens. The walk, run, skip, and other fundamental motor patterns exist only insofar as they actually take place in time and space. Even the written descriptions of these motor patterns refer to motion factors that distinguish them. Words like *fast, sideward,* and *uneven* specify space-time relationships.

Skill in the performance of motor patterns depends on the capacity of individuals to make subtle but precise adjustments in accordance with their "awakened" understandings of the "relationship and proportionality of motion factors."[1] Each skill is a harmonious composite of each motion factor, of time, of space, of weight (force). The blend varies continuously but is always correct for each step of the motor pattern forming the skill. In movements requiring extreme accuracy only a slight deviation in the effort rhythm can lead to a noticeable loss of control. However, motion factors should not be viewed only as utilitarian. Inner feelings and attitudes are revealed by the quality of movement. Movement is a form of nonverbal communication, sometimes performed consciously, but most often unconsciously.

■ Only a variety of stimulating environments will lead to the development of versatility in the use of the body as an instrument for movement. To assure appropriate emphasis and scope in the learning experience, the learner should acquire a complete movement vocabulary. It is the teacher's

The body as the instrument for movement

1 Rudolf Laban and F. C. Lawrence, *Effort* (London: MacDonald & Evans, 1947), p. 18.

role to guide learners through the movement learning experiences by offering them appropriate movement challenges that lead to development of efficient body management behaviors. The movement vocabulary described in this chapter, together with the fundamental motor patterns, form the foundation for a wide variety of specific motor skills and understandings that enable the student to think intelligently about movement and movement problems.

Awareness of **what** the body is doing (action), **where** the movement is going (space), and **how** the movement is going (effort quality)

Basic movement learning experiences emphasize the improvement of awareness of *what* the body is doing (action), *where* the movement is going (space), and *how* the movement is going (effort quality). Individuals with little feeling for these awarenesses are almost helpless in initiating the solution of common movement problems that face them in everyday life. Work tasks require efficient movement patterns; otherwise there is wasted effort for which the employer is understandably reluctant to pay. The increase in leisure time beckons the movement-oriented person to new adventures in activity that are risky for the poorly skilled or that require creative abilities dormant since preschool sandpile days. To physically educate means to movement educate. Movement education requires the application of thought to the process of learning. The first step is the development of the awareness of the *what*, the *where*, and the *when* of body, space, and effort. In addition, there are relationships between the self and space, objects, and other people. Movement, regardless of kind or quality, relates to its environment. Relationships also require awareness on the part of the mover. An outline of the content of these four aspects of movement awareness is shown in figure 5.1.

■ The four aspects of movement awareness can be identified in all voluntary movement situations. A child relates to a ball by manipulating it (relationship) with the hands (body) so that it goes up and down (space) with varying degrees of speed (effort). In addition, the child may be on the floor, next to a playmate, in the corner of the room—a further description of environmental relationship. The quality of manipulative actions varies as they are performed; sometimes the force used to move the ball is stronger as reflected by a sudden change in the distance of ball travel or its impact with the floor. Other parts of the body may be involved, too. They may enhance the primary action directly or in indirect ways such as when the legs bend and extend to help the hands and arms lift the ball or when the feet shuffle about to maintain a close relationship to the ball. All actions can be described using the movement vocabulary.

Four aspects of movement awareness

■ The force of gravity is responsible for body weight, a weight that resists being moved, altered in its direction once in motion, and being stopped in motion. To cope with this force of gravity, learners acquire a variety of abilities that permit them to carry out numerous motor behaviors in the satisfaction of individual interests and needs.

Body awareness

> The baby's pained surprise when he bites down on his foot, as though he hadn't expected it to hurt (or at least to hurt him), is one among many indications that knowledge of his own body is not given to the baby at birth, simply by virtue of its being an operating biological entity, but that the body, its extent and its capacities for feeling and action, is learned through a series of discoveries during a long apprenticeship.[2]

The acts of sitting up alone and of walking require the awareness of *balance.* Alignment of the body over its base makes it possible to balance. Traveling requires the mover to place body parts in position to receive the weight of the body as the line of gravity shifts from one base to another.

Balance must be felt. Its opposite, imbalance, must also be felt, and it usually is responded to reflexively by a contraction of muscles that causes body parts to shift the body back to a balanced state. A person demonstrates more conscious attention to balance when standing on a small body part or when traveling on a narrow surface, especially if it is raised above the ground.

The basis for guidance in the development of body awareness is often recognition of the body and its parts. Perhaps the first real awareness of the bodily self occurs very early when infants discover their feet and demonstrate their recognition of the feet as being parts of them.

Knowing where the parts of the body are, being able to identify them

2 L. Joseph Stone and Joseph Church, *Childhood and Adolescence,* 3d ed. (New York: Random House, 1973), p. 65.

Awareness of motion factors

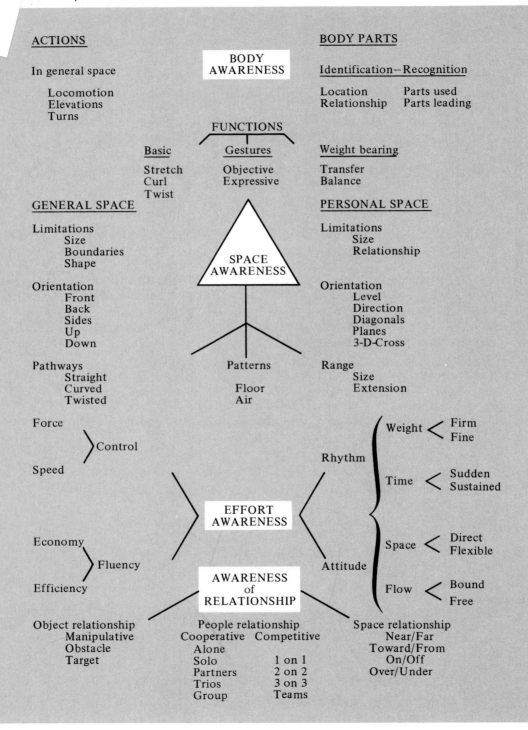

ACTIONS

In general space

    Locomotion
    Elevations
    Turns

BODY
AWARENESS

BODY PARTS

Identification–Recognition

    Location   Parts used
    Relationship   Parts leading

FUNCTIONS

    Basic   Gestures   Weight bearing

    Stretch   Objective   Transfer
    Curl   Expressive   Balance
    Twist

GENERAL SPACE

Limitations
    Size
    Boundaries
    Shape

Orientation
    Front
    Back
    Sides
    Up
    Down

Pathways
    Straight
    Curved
    Twisted

SPACE
AWARENESS

Patterns

Floor
Air

PERSONAL SPACE

Limitations
    Size
    Relationship

Orientation
    Level
    Direction
    Diagonals
    Planes
    3-D-Cross

Range
    Size
    Extension

Force

    Control

Speed

Weight   Firm
    Fine

Rhythm

Time   Sudden
    Sustained

EFFORT
AWARENESS

Economy

    Fluency

Efficiency

Space   Direct
    Flexible

Attitude

Flow   Bound
    Free

AWARENESS
of
RELATIONSHIP

Object relationship
    Manipulative
    Obstacle
    Target

People relationship
Cooperative   Competitive
    Alone
    Solo   1 on 1
    Partners   2 on 2
    Trios   3 on 3
    Group   Teams

Space relationship
    Near/Far
    Toward/From
    On/Off
    Over/Under

Child relates to ball by manipulating it (relationship) with his hands (body) so that it goes up and down (space) with varying degrees of speed (effort).

by name, and demonstrating to oneself what they can do enables the learner to participate intelligently in movement learning experience. Instructors often attempt to teach a particular skill only to realize that their students lack the necessary body awareness to follow their instructions. One example that occurs frequently is the overhand throwing lesson that leaves both the instructor and the student frustrated because of the student's inability to follow directions. The student is not aware of where the elbow is during the execution of the pattern.

Awareness of what the body can do is based on a general image of one's body. The sense of being, of existing within the corporate whole of a body that moves and has a variety of parts enabling it to move, to touch, to manipulate, to maneuver about in space is important for movement mastery. To feel keenly the location and relationship of each part of the body—the arms, the legs, the head, the trunk, and all of the smaller parts that make up these larger parts—gives one a greater sense of identification with one's bodily self. The capabilities for moving the body and its parts should be explored and developed as extensively as possible. The capability of the body to move and to make adequate adaptations to the special and general needs of daily living depends on the development of a wide

Awareness of
motion factors

117

array of movement patterns—from complete extension to complete curling and from twisting in one direction to twisting in the opposite direction.

Elements in body awareness

Proceeding from the simple to the complex, the teacher presents a series of challenges that focus upon a particular element of body awareness. In time, each of the five major divisions of body awareness is explored. The following explanation refers to figure 5.1 and should clarify the elements that constitute body awareness.

Division 1.0. Division 1.0 has been referred to already. After learners acquire an operational awareness and understanding of their bodies, they are able to undertake tasks requiring them to discriminate between body parts that are involved and uninvolved in an action. "Which parts of you are moving and which parts are still?" is a common question. Later questions are concerned with which of the moving parts is stressed the most or which part is leading the action. These questions are asked while children are performing all sorts of actions. Perhaps attention is focused on when the arms move during a standing broad jump, when one is balanced, or when one is hopping on one foot. The point of the questions is to help the child become sensitive to the movements of body parts. At the early stage the child has only a generalized awareness regarding movement, nonmovement, and the order in which parts move. Later, in other aspects, the learner will be aware also of the direction, speed, and force of these movements.

Division 2.0. Division 2.0 outlines the basic functions of the body and its parts. The stretch, curl, and twist functions are explored with the whole body as well as with all of its parts. Each function is worked to its maximum. Straightness is not enough. The body must be stretched to its utmost. The curl must be drawn as tightly as possible; the twist must rotate as far as possible. Only in this way is the complete feeling of the function experienced.

The term *gesturing* is not commonly used in this country except in the theater. Using one's hands to assist verbalization is common, and other parts of the body are used, too. The shoulders shrug, the eyebrows raise, the face grimaces, smiles, frowns, or shows surprise, and the feet shuffle, stamp, or kick. More subtle gestures are seen in finger tapping, slight shifts of weight, drooping shoulders, or a stiffening of the posture. All of these gestures communicate, consciously or unconsciously, feelings and attitudes. Other gestures are not intended to be expressive. The foot kicks at a rolling ball. The arm moves to counterbalance a sudden shift of weight in the opposite direction. Gesture for nonexpressive purposes is used to balance actions going on elsewhere in the body such as the swinging of the arms while walking or running or to manipulate anything from a pencil to a ball, from a bat to a sledgehammer.

A primary function of some body parts is weight bearing. Locomotion requires the use of body parts in a weight-bearing role. The feet customarily have that role, but other body parts can assume that function, too. As

> When the movement lesson focuses on what the body is doing, the emphasis is on the development of body awareness.

long as the principles of balance are observed and the strength is sufficient, almost any body part can support the body weight and function in locomotion. Learners should experience the effects of changes in the size of the base and the number of parts involved on the stability of balance. They should become aware of the moment when stability is lost and should position another part to assume the burden. At other times, learners should use different body parts to counterbalance shifts of weight in the opposite direction to avoid or postpone a loss of equilibrium.

Division 3.0. Division 3.0 was described in the previous chapter. The focus in awareness is not on learning specific patterns but on improving one's awareness of what the body is doing. The feel of the gallop is different from the feel of a run. Landing on the ball of the foot when running is different from landing on the heels. "What part is landing first?" or "When you perform your roll, which part of you touches the floor first? Last?" Different ways of traveling should be tried.

Elevation involves jumping or leaping. There are many possibilities for varying the jumps. One interesting task is to explore the possibilities for taking off from one or two feet and landing on one or two feet. The five resulting jumps are taking off from two and landing on two, taking off from two and landing on one, taking off from one and landing on two, taking off from one and landing on the same one, and taking off from one and landing on the other. These five forms of jumping are fundamental to sports, dance, and gymnastics.

Turns can be performed on different body parts like the feet, seat, and knees. One part may serve as the pivot while other parts push or pull. Traveling while turning can be quite a challenge.

Division 4.0. Division 4.0 involves movement within one's self-space. Actions such as reaching out into self-space, bending, swaying, swinging, and shaking should be explored to the fullest. Pushing, pulling, scattering and gathering, and raising and lowering are among the possibilities for additional movements in self-space. The body may rise and fall, or it may hold very still in a variety of shapes. Doing the same thing repeatedly or doing something different reinforces the development of essential concepts. Shapes, too, may be the same or different. The symmetry or asymmetry of bodily shapes should be noted.

The body is capable of moving in self-space and traveling at the same time. Attending to nonsupportive actions while traveling in different ways is an important part of the development of the mastery of movement.

Division 5.0. Isolated actions as well as those that occur in a series can be characterized as having a beginning shape or stance and an ending shape or stance. Between these two positions are the changing shapes of the action pattern. There is a sequence of individual actions involving certain parts of the body, main parts of the action, and secondary or supporting parts of the action. The total assembly requires the contribution, in proper proportion, of all primary and secondary actions from preparation to follow-through. Directed toward an objective, a target, or a focal point, the action becomes a fusion of separate actions into a harmonious whole.

Awareness of
motion factors

BODY AWARENESS

1.0 Awareness of the Parts of the Body

    1.1 *Recognition*: Demonstrating ability to match the observed body part with one's own body part

    1.2 *Identification*: Naming the body parts

    1.3 *Relationship*: Knowing where one part is in relation to other parts of the body

        1.31 *Location*: Being able to move the part identified or to find the body part on another person or picture

    1.4 *Use of body parts*: Knowing which parts are being used and which are not; identifying

        1.41 *Parts stressed* during an action

        1.42 *Parts leading or following* in the sequence of an action or actions

2.0 Functions of the Body and Its Parts

    2.1 *Basic action or function*: The body or its parts can *curl, stretch,* and *twist,* permitting execution of complex actions

    2.2 *Gestures*: Nonsupporting body parts can move functionally

        2.21 For *objective* purpose, to perform a task

        2.22 For *expressive* purpose, to communicate

    2.3 *Weight bearing*: The parts can be used to support the body

        2.31 To form a base for *static balance*

        2.32 To form new bases for *dynamic balance*

3.0 The Body Has Capabilities for Travel in General Space

    3.1 *Locomotion*: Different steplike or rolling actions for traveling are possible

    3.2 *Elevation*: Jumping actions put the body in flight momentarily

    3.3 *Turning*: The body may be rotated several ways to change its orientation

4.0 The Body Has Capabilities for Movement in Personal Space

    4.1 *Axial or nonlocomotor actions*: Stretching, curling, twisting, swaying, swinging, and turning actions lead to accomplishment of specific patterns in one's personal space

    4.2 *Stillness*: Awareness that the body or selected parts are not in motion

    4.3 *Shape*: Four basic body shapes are formed through movement of body parts: stretched *pinlike shapes,* stretched wall-like shapes, curled *round* shapes, and *twisted* shapes

        4.31 *Awareness of sameness and difference*: *Symmetrical* shapes and actions occur when one side of the body looks and performs like the other side; *asymmetrical* shapes result from differences in the appearance and behaviors of the two sides.

5.0 Contributions to the Total Assembly of an Action Are Made by Various Parts of the Body

    5.1 *Main parts of an action*: The beginning, the middle, and the ending of an action

    5.2 *The sequence of an action*: The correctness of a motor pattern depends in large measure on the proper sequence of body part involvement and proper proportion to the total assembly of the action

5.3 *Focus*: The projection of the whole body toward a particular place or in a particular direction called a focal point builds kinesthetic awareness of the attractive force

Deficiencies in body awareness

The following commonly observed deficiencies in body awareness indicate either perceptual motor problems or insufficient experience. Should the real deficiency be in strength, flexibility, or endurance, the problem is different and requires a different solution. Lack of awareness must be treated with patient questioning. Very young children show immaturity in their actions that, given opportunity, will grow to completeness as their awareness of what they are doing improves.

1 Cannot locate body parts without hesitation.
2 Cannot coordinate movement of arms and legs for traveling on all fours.
3 Does not complete the stretch of the legs when jumping.
4 Has difficulty completing an action like twisting.
5 Has trouble coming to a stop.
6 Does not operate arms in opposition with the legs in walking or running.
7 Lacks sensitivity to balance, even in simple balance problems.
8 Lacks movement memory as demonstrated by inability to recall a sequence or posture accurately.
9 Cannot tell which body part is leading the action.
10 Cannot sense body-part relationships required for a simple pattern; for example, does not realize that the feet are crossing.

Sample action themes for development of body awareness

First Stage of Movement Learning
1 Locating, naming, and moving body parts
2 Action and stillness: moving and stopping
3 Traveling in different ways
4 Performing different fundamental locomotor patterns
5 Collapsing and rolling
6 Jumping in different ways and landing safely
7 Taking body weight on the hands
8 Rising and falling
9 Forming round, narrow, wide, and twisted shapes
10 Combining different actions in a sequence

Second Stage of Movement Learning
1 Moving individual body parts, particularly by stretching, curling, and twisting
2 Traveling on the same and different parts in the same and different ways

Awareness of
motion factors

3 Taking body weight on different parts with emphasis on the sequence of weight transfer
4 Receiving body weight on different parts in succession
5 Exploring balance and losing balance
6 Beginning and ending action sequences, stressing clarity
7 Twisting and turning in different ways
8 Emphasizing gesture while traveling
9 Sequencing shapes, gestures, and locomotion
10 Performing sequences emphasizing inverted balances and rolling

Commentary on body awareness

Although themes as focal points for lessons in movement will be described in greater detail in subsequent chapters, the reader whose experience in physical education has been traditional will need some explanation now. Themes are ideas or actions that unify and give focus to movement lessons. They identify the thread that should tie together all of the concepts and actions in a lesson or sequence of lessons. *Action themes* stress motor pattern learning. *Idea themes* stress concepts affecting the direction, quality, and relationship of actions.

Another concept that requires explanation is that of the operational stages of movement learning. The reader should know that beginning movement learning experiences must be kept at simple action and conceptual levels until students demonstrate their ability to go on to more complex movement ideas. At the base of the operational stages is a proper learning environment—one that is safe for exploring, that takes into account individual needs and interests, and that is coordinated with essential lesson management rules. At the first level of movement learning, affective objectives are of primary importance. There is little point in attempting to teach movement behaviors to children who have poor listening skills, poor self-concepts, and poor social relationships. Action themes are kept simple, and improvement of affective behaviors is emphasized. Concepts of movement behavior will develop much more easily when the learning environment is comfortable for both teacher and children.

The action themes are related to different learning environments. As applied in apparatus environments, the ideas and actions must be modified or expanded on by the learner in adapting solutions to problems involving bars, climbing ropes, beams, trestles, and vaulting boxes. Other changes in the physical environment include the addition of balls, beanbags, hoops, ropes, or wands for manipulative or nonmanipulative movements in line with the selected theme. The addition of sound, like the beat of a drum, the clapping of hands, or the playing of an instrument, requires modification of the tempo and force of movement. Finally, the aquatic environment of a swimming pool would permit entirely different forms of exploration using the same themes, now with a different stress. How rich a background in movement learning beginners would have if it were possible to involve them in different physical learning environments for each theme!

Changes in the social environment should not be neglected either. Although individual solutions to movement problems are often emphasized, practice in relating effectively to others should not be neglected.

To give the reader a clearer picture of how action themes are related to different learning environments, figure 5.2 summarizes the application of themes from all four aspects of movement awareness—body, effort, space, and relationship awareness.

Fig. 5.2 Idea and action themes form the core of movement learning experiences in a variety of stimulating physical environments surrounded by progressive changes in the social environment

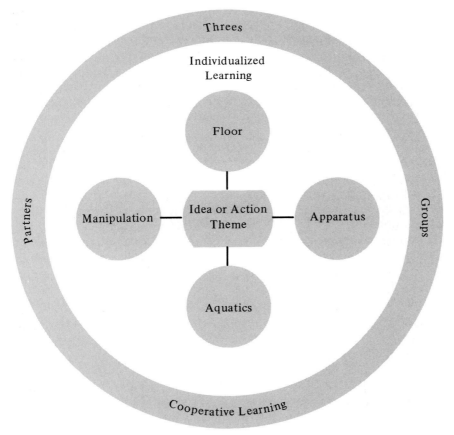

■ Spectators marvel at the expertise of the highly skilled performer. Such exclamations as "Elegant! Smooth! Beautifully executed! Expressive!" show appreciation for the quality of performance. These qualities may be appreciated quite apart from the action itself. One does not have to have technical knowledge to be moved by the artistry of the performer. One need only be reasonably sensitive to the harmonious flow of the actions,

EFFORT AWARENESS

Awareness of motion factors

123

whatever they may be. Awkward combinations and passages are recognized as lacking the rhythmical qualities that bring harmony to human performance. In this section on effort we will identify the components of movement that characterize its quality and that determine its accuracy and efficiency.

Human effort reflects itself in movement of all kinds—in gesture, work, play, or dramatic expression. The quality of a performance may range from bad to good or perfect. In a poor or bad performance movements are poorly articulated, out of harmony, inaccurate, and inefficient. Good to excellent performance is smooth, well articulated, efficient, and accurate. Because all movement shares common elements that determine the quality of performance, it is possible to develop learning opportunities that will add progressively to the desirable qualities of movement.

Granted that the combination of experience and maturation alone frequently results in improved performance and even attainment of mature movement, the time-consuming process of unguided trial and error leaves many failures in its wake. The development of desirable movement qualities should not be left to chance. Such neglect can only widen the gap between gifted performers and ungifted ones whose failures seem to confirm their status.

Rudolf Laban, a pioneer in research on human movement, developed the vocabulary that describes quality in terms of effort. Known mainly for his success in establishing movement principles through books published in Germany and in Great Britain, Laban has been the principle force in movement education in this country as well. His books and books by others based on his work are listed at the end of this and other chapters as the books relate to chapter content. Readers are urged to study thoroughly at least the basic works of Laban and to consider reading systematically all of his work, as well as the work of his associates and successors. Reading alone will not increase the depth of your understanding, however. You must participate in movement learning by moving, observing, and teaching. Patience, reflection, and continued effort in the analysis of movement will be rewarded by increased knowledge and ability, without which the teaching of movement is mere activity.

Elements in effort awareness

When the movement lesson focuses on how the movement is going, the emphasis is on the development of effort awareness.

Lessons on effort factors follow body awareness lessons. Each factor is introduced and then combined with previous material so that the link between awareness of what the body is doing and how the movement is going is firmly forged. Each factor consists of a pair of contrasting elements that are introduced and explored in tasks that focus first on one and then on the other element. *Quickness* is felt more clearly in the presence of its opposite, *slowness,* and the same is true with the elements of the other factors. The factors of effort are *TIME* with its elements of *quick* and *sustained; WEIGHT* with its elements of *firm* and *fine touch; SPACE* with its elements of *flexible* and *direct,* and *FLOW* with its elements of *free* and *bound.*

Rhythm in movement ties together the separate movements in a series. The parts are articulated to form a whole. Broken rhythms (those with start-stop-start patterns) differ markedly from continuous rhythms. It is this general rhythmic quality of effort that impresses the observer and that tells the performer when the sequence has been put together properly. It is not enough, however, for a teacher to instruct students to perform a pattern rhythmically without first instructing them in the character of rhythmic quality. Some students appear to select intuitively the right proportions of each effort element, while others exhibit various limitations as they struggle to attain the same degree of proficiency.

Division 1.0. The Division 1.0 factor, awareness of *time*, is described by the duration of movement. Quickness contrasts with sustainment. Speed varies from the sudden explosiveness of the jump or the race to the lingering sustainment of a balance or the slow stretching of the body. Some actions may be performed at different single speeds, while others require changes, often sudden, from one speed to another.

Balancing one block on another must be performed carefully and unhurriedly, lest the blocks tumble down through impatient haste. The practicing of athletic skills must be accompanied by continual adjustments in the tempo of the actions. Slow movements are speeded up until they can be performed at the tempo necessary for play. Some sequences appear unhurried, but they may be punctuated by sudden changes in direction or aggressive actions such as those performed when volleying a tennis ball against a wall.

Division 2.0. Division 2.0 describes the *weight* factor, the resistance to muscular force or tension. Touch typing requires a delicate or fine touch upon the keys much like the gentle action required in placing blocks upon one another, tapping a shuttlecock in badminton so that it barely clears the net, or delicately flicking a basketball toward the basket. The dynamic quality of movement is expressed through varying degrees of muscular exertion from a fine, featherlike touch to a firm, strong swing.

Division 3.0. Division 3.0 involves the *space* factor. In actions requiring the flexible use of space such as the overhand throw, the awareness of the spatial quality is clearly demonstrated by the action. The quick push of a basketball toward the basket has a distinctly different spatial character from the overhand throw. Direct rather than flexible is the appropriate space effort. To neglect the development of the essential spatial character of an action may lower learner performance. For example, attempts to throw overhand are often marred by problems with the spatial quality. The directness of the pattern results in a pushing action rather than a flicking or slashing motion. Time must be given to freeing the elbow from its anchor below the shoulder if more circular movement of the entire arm is to be attained. If learners fail to pay attention to the spatial characteristics or shape of a new pattern they may easily think they are performing correctly only to find that "the rhythm is fine but the shape of the pattern is off."

Division 4.0. Division 4.0 identifies the characteristics associated with

Awareness of motion factors

the *flow* of movement. Connecting the main actions of a new pattern together with small transitional movements often assures smoothness of performance. Jerky movement looks and feels uncoordinated. To smooth the pattern, the mover must eliminate the unessential, adjust the time factor, increase or decrease the tension during some particular part of the action, or modify the connecting movements. The result should be the appropriate amount of control, for overcontrol will cramp the action and undercontrol will destroy its accuracy. Each objective makes different demands on the character of the flow of action. The emotional state of the individual plays a large part in the selection of the appropriate degree of control. Caution, fear (especially of failure), distractability, and poor concentration are factors likely to influence the result.

Effort as a reflection of attitude

That the motion factors associated with an action also reflect the attitude of the mover can be substantiated through experiences common to everyone. From the examples that follow it should be apparent that teachers must observe children's natural inclinations with respect to effort qualities to provide sensitive lesson direction.

Among both children and adults there are those who either constantly hurry or resist efforts to hurry them. These exaggerated reactions give the appearance of a struggle, on the one hand, to race against time, and a yielding to time, on the other hand, as if it did not matter. Wives become annoyed when their husbands walk ahead of them. Unable to get their spouses to slow down, these wives may adopt a more hurried pace than they feel comfortable with. Then there are the students who work along as if they have all the time in the world. Nothing seems to speed them up, and the teacher reports that they never finish their work, although they are mentally capable.

Laban selected the term *struggling* to connote a stressed effort or fighting attitude and *yielding* to signify ease, absence, or indulgence in connection with effort.

> People moving with easy effort seem to be freer than those moving with
> obviously stressed effort. The latter seem to struggle against something.
> Against what they struggle we are unable to discover at once, though we
> can learn more if we observe subjective movements—that is, those which
> do not deal with objects and have therefore no outer cause for struggle.
> But there is an obvious struggle visible in the sometimes even painful
> deportment of a person.[3]

In addition to the fighters against and the indulgers in time, there are those who struggle or yield to the weight factor. They either appear to have an overabundance of bodily tension or a lack of bodily force. Again, quoting Laban:

> Force is another of the elements of which efforts are built up. It is the
> degree of energy spent in overcoming one's own body weight, or that of an
> object, which expresses itself in the attitude towards the weight effort.[4]

3 Laban and Lawrence, *Effort*, p. 54.
4 Ibid., p. 55.

The "bull in the china shop" quality that often characterizes the behavior of teenage boys clearly indicates their attitude toward the weight factor through their exaggerated use of force. The basketball coach is not always successful in converting boys who have just completed a football season into smoothly moving basketball players. The forceful, aggressive behaviors of football players, particularly linemen, are not always appropriate in basketball.

There are those individuals, too, who appear unable to exert themselves. They seem to lack the ability to apply force, a reluctance seen in their bodily carriage—a preference for yielding to rather than resisting the pull of gravity. Indifferent to the weight factor, their attitude is one of indulgence, and they appear to be lazy, weak, or heavy in their movements.

A highly visible attitude is reflected in movements associated with the space factor. The ease with which some people use their surrounding space is evidence of a yielding attitude toward the use of space. They enjoy it. Contrasting sharply with these indulgers in space are those who use space sparingly, whose movements are directed by economy, for whom the flexible use of space is a painful experience. These fighters against the use of space behave "as if they had an aversion against the manifold extension of space. This aversion does not manifest itself so much in a tumultuous struggle, but rather in a kind of restriction in the use of all too many space directions."[5]

Clearly, there are two distinct attitudes associated with space efforts. Physical education activities with any age group will reveal a range of attitudes toward space with the two extremes appearing in sharp contrast to one another.

> People who indulge in flow find pleasure in the unrestricted freedom of fluency, without necessarily giving much attention to the various shades of the time, the weight and the space development of movements.[6]

The *flow* factor is expressed by indulgers as freedom of movement, in sharp contrast to persons who hold the opposite attitude. Rather than permit movement to go on with little restraint, economizers overcontrol action. So bound is their flow that they can stop the action in an instant.

Laban's research and his unique ability to describe human movement, particularly the relationships of the motion factors of time, weight, space, and flow, are evident in the following passages.

> The richness of people's efforts consists just in the fact that their effort characteristics are an incredibly subtle mixture or compound of many degrees of attitudes towards several movement elements. They may indulge in several elements simultaneously, one equilibrating the other as well as possible. They often fight against the whole bunch of motion factors which nature has placed at their disposal. That both this great and unified struggle and its opposite, total surrender, are stimulated by experiences and circumstances, is a secondary consideration with which effort research has to deal.[7]

5 Ibid., p. 56.
6 Ibid., pp. 56-57.
7 Ibid., p. 58.

EFFORT AWARENESS

1.0 Attitude toward the Time Factor

    1.1 *Sudden*: Awareness of the quickness of movement resulting in a fast speed, expressing an attitude of urgency

        1.11 *Faster* means increasing the speed of a movement

    1.2 *Sustained*: Awareness of the slowness of movement resulting in a slow speed, expressing an attitude of indulgence

        1.21 *Slower* means decreasing the speed of movement

    1.3 *Neutral*: Not appearing to have any particular quality of time, or the time factor not being a major influence on the quality of the movement as a whole

2.0 Attitude toward the Weight Factor

    2.1 *Firm*: Awareness of tension or strength of movement resulting in a strong action, expressing an attitude of strength

        2.11 *Stronger* means increasing the firmness, strength, or tension of an action

    2.2 *Fine*: Awareness of the lack of tension or gentleness of movement resulting in a light action, expressing an attitude of lightness or softness

        2.22 *Gentler* means decreasing the tension or firmness of an action

    2.3 *Neutral*: Lacking in tension, not appearing to have any strength; weak or heavy

3.0 Attitude toward the Space Factor

    3.1 *Flexibility*: Awareness of the availability of space resulting in roundabout movement, expressing an attitude of openness

        3.11 *Lessened flexibility* shows only slight roundaboutness

        3.12 *Excessive flexibility* is exaggerated, not well controlled

    3.2 *Directness*: Awareness of space perceived narrowly resulting in straightness of movement, expressing an attitude of directness

        3.21 *Lessened directness* shows a deflection from straightness

        3.22 *Excessive directness* shows a very restricted use of space

4.0 Attitude toward the Flow Factor

    4.1 *Free flow*: Awareness of the fluency and ongoingness of movement, expressing an attitude of easiness

        4.11 *Reduced fluency* is shown by lessened freedom of flow

        4.12 *Increased fluency* is shown as excessive freedom with loss of control

    4.2 *Bound flow*: Awareness of fluency is limited to control or restraint, expressing an attitude of caution

        4.21 *Reduced boundness* shows lessened restraint

        4.22 *Increased boundness* results in very inhibited, cramped movement; overcontrolled

Deficiencies in effort awareness

Persons who have difficulty selecting the appropriate degree of each of the motion factors for the task at hand sometimes remark that they are uncoordinated, that they cannot manage the type of task involved. Imagine an individual accustomed only to strong, direct action attempting to thread a needle, or a person who never displays strength trying to pump up a tire, shovel snow, or hit a tennis serve. Effort deficiencies may be observed among children. Rather than ignore their deficiencies or comment negatively about them, the teacher should initiate corrective action to increase children's awareness of the range of their selection of motion factors and the different degrees of appropriate effort. Deficiencies are illustrated by the following behaviors.

 1 **Difficulty in controlling actions to avoid collision**
 2 **Difficulty in stopping, often resulting in a loss of balance**
 3 **Exaggerated efforts inappropriate to the task at hand such as using too much speed, force, or directness, or using too much control**
 4 **Lack of smoothness in fundamental movement patterns**
 5 **Heavy landings**
 6 **Stretch actions not reaching outward sufficiently, an indication perhaps of reserve in the maximum utilization of space**
 7 **Curved and twisted patterns, displaying insufficient flexibility in the use of space; too bound**
 8 **Failure to sustain action, tending toward inappropriate speed**
 9 **Too much tension or not enough tension to move or hold position**
10 **Failure to alternate tension and relaxation, or to relax completely**

Stages in the development of effort awareness

As in the development of basic movement patterns, there are discernible stages in the development of effort awareness. The first of these stages is gross awareness of the separate motion factors, *time, weight,* and *space,* in conjunction with either teacher- or learner-selected actions. Stage 2 includes the simultaneous awareness of two efforts in conjunction with free and bound flow. The final stage stresses basic effort actions and their derivatives.

Stage 1, Gross Effort Awareness. The emphasis at the beginning is merely upon the conscious performance of actions with each of the contrasting effort elements. The learner performs an action with a fine touch in contrast with one that is firm; an action that is fast in contrast with one that is very slow; an action that uses space directly in contrast with one that is more flexible. The flow factor is not stressed; it is merely observed as it appears in the separate actions being performed. Over a period of time, as inhibitions to move disappear, the flow of actions will change. Confidence will encourage a more fluent, flowing action. However, there are instances when individual children or even an entire class may be urged to "let the movement go." During manipulative lessons, when the problem of keeping the ball within assigned spaces is of uppermost concern, the word *control* is used to bind the flow and lead to the exercise of greater care. As control is established, greater fluency is encouraged once again.

"Letting go" is not done by command. It must be a conscious release of the self to the action. As children feel more and more at home in their exploration of effort possibilities with all kinds of actions, they will "let go." The flexible shaping of movements of the arms, the legs, the trunk, and

Awareness of
motion factors

combinations of these parts will contribute heavily to the development of fluency.

Stage 2, Awareness of Two Elements of Effort. This stage evolves out of the learner's demonstrated ability to express clearly the individually contrasting elements of the first stage. The reader is reminded that body awareness and effort awareness are exhibited in concert. Learners must also have an operational awareness of space. They must know where they are going, what their bodies are doing (at least in general), and how the movement is going with respect to at least one element of quality. When learners display their ability to manage these awarenesses in such typical movement problems as the following, it is time to engage them in the new challenges of this second stage.

1 The learners display ability to travel without collision at various speeds ranging from slow to fast.
2 The learners display ability to adjust to the strength requirements of tasks by selecting the appropriate degree of effort ranging from very fine touch to very firm touch.
3 The learners display ability to use either roundabout or direct ways of using space while moving in place or while traveling.

On entering into the second stage of effort awareness, learners are confronted with problems requiring them to attend to two motion factors simultaneously. Movement challenges may stress finding the contrast to two factors, as when changing from sudden-direct to slow-flexible. Or, they may be asked to change only one factor—sudden-direct to sudden-flexible, or sudden-direct to slow-flexible.

There are other possibilities for two-element tasks.

firm-direct to fine-flexible	(contrast in both elements)
firm-direct to firm-flexible	(change in the space factor)
firm-direct to fine-direct	(change in the weight factor)
or	
firm-sudden to fine-slow	(contrast in both elements)
firm-sudden to firm-slow	(change in the time factor)
firm-sudden to fine-sudden	(change in the weight factor)

Instructors are cautioned not to work too rapidly through lessons focusing on movement qualities because kinesthetic feeling and concomitant awareness of effort take time to develop. Lessons supporting the development of these awarenesses should take place in a variety of learning environments. As children develop control over their bodies through lessons and the reinforcement of play activities, they will demonstrate readiness to move on to greater challenges by the ease with which they manage the tasks requiring changes in the degree of effort demanded.

At the outset, the focus is on the ability to attend to two effort elements simultaneously. It is sufficient to be able to contrast the two elements and to show this ability in a variety of different movements, some performed in place, others in traveling. The actions themselves are of no importance, being merely the vehicles for expression of the qualities. A caution should be noted at this point. Movements involving objects such as ball handling or use of hoops, ribbons, and ropes will only obscure the major points of the lesson, which are not control of a ball or of anything else. Such actions distract the learner from the value of movement for its own sake. After basic awareness is established, the lessons may include use of apparatus or manipulative equipment. Sound may be used, however, to introduce or to reinforce the time-weight characteristics under study. A drum, tambourine, or triangle might be useful.

Stage 3, Awareness of Basic Effort Actions. The third stage completes the progression. When learners demonstrate their ability to attend to combinations of two elements of effort, attention is directed to the inclusion of the third element. Much more variation is possible. Eight basic effort actions, each capable of being performed with either free or bound flow, form the basis for this stage. Progression is demonstrated through the transitions of effort from one action to another, as shown in the following description, which is based on Laban's effort graph.

The flow of movement is represented by a horizontal line, the left end standing for free flow and the right end for bound flow.

free _____ bound

Bisecting the flow line is a vertical line representing the weight factor, varying from fine touch (gentleness) on the one end to firm touch (strength) on the other.

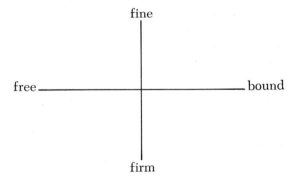

The space factor is indicated by a diagonal line, called the sign of effort, in the upper right angle of the axis. A right angle is used to represent flexible versus direct use of space.

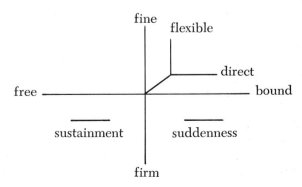

The time factor is graphically represented by two short lines, one on the left for sustainment and one on the right for quickness.

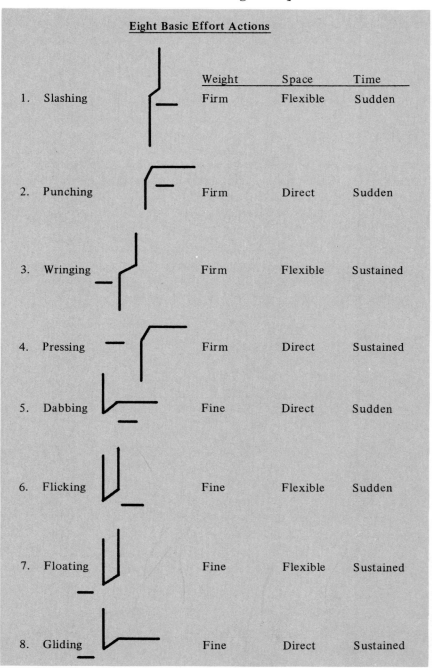

Eight Basic Effort Actions

		Weight	Space	Time
1.	Slashing	Firm	Flexible	Sudden
2.	Punching	Firm	Direct	Sudden
3.	Wringing	Firm	Flexible	Sustained
4.	Pressing	Firm	Direct	Sustained
5.	Dabbing	Fine	Direct	Sudden
6.	Flicking	Fine	Flexible	Sudden
7.	Floating	Fine	Flexible	Sustained
8.	Gliding	Fine	Direct	Sustained

The transition from one basic effort action to another is not easily made if all three, or sometimes just two, motion factors are involved. To smooth the transition, one factor at a time is changed.

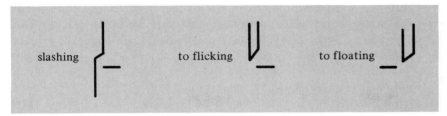

slashing   to flicking   to floating

The weight factor (W) is changed from firm to fine touch to achieve a flicking action. Time (T) is changed from sudden to sustained. Could the transition have been made by changing the time factor first? Yes, wringing could have been the transitional effort.

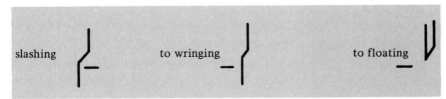

slashing   to wringing   to floating

Useful lessons can be built around effort transitions, but such lessons require that the learner have a mature learning attitude.

More difficulty arises when the challenge involves the change of all three motion factors. Slashing contrasts with gliding in weight (W), time (T), and space (S).

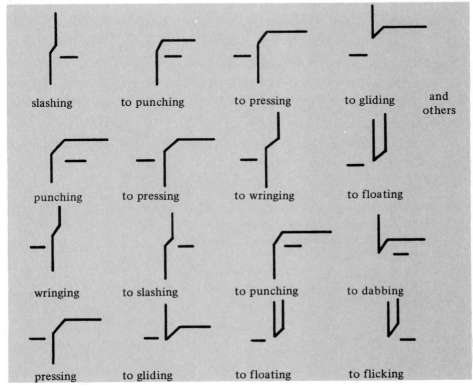

slashing   to punching   to pressing   to gliding   and others

punching   to pressing   to wringing   to floating

wringing   to slashing   to punching   to dabbing

pressing   to gliding   to floating   to flicking

When presented abstractly, each motion factor in a basic effort action receives as much stress or emphasis as every other factor. In practice, this rarely happens. Usually one or two motion factors are emphasized over the others. Further information on the subject of derivatives and effort actions may be found in Laban and Lawrence's book, *Effort,* from which the following quotation is taken.

> The reason for investigating a man's effort-balance is that he needs, apart from the capacity, skill and knowledge which enables him to do the desired operation once or twice excellently, other and frequently contrasting capacities in order to check and control his special habits or inclinations. Efforts which are mastered by a person must always be balanced by somewhat contrasting effort-capacities which allow for automatic compensation when the efforts in which his special gift lies are overstrained or overaccentuated by the extent of the work or adverse situations and conditions.[8]

In effect, this message to the physical educator says children should be encouraged to develop their full effort capacities—development that can occur only if education in basic movement is given a position of importance in the physical education program. If the football player can relieve the strong, quick action efforts required of him in his chosen sport by participating in dancing, ping pong, fishing, or other activities that require contrasting efforts, his movement life will be richer for it. So it is with every other facet of one's movement life at work and at play. Too much behavior of one type causes a lopsidedness in one's effort capacities, a condition that can be corrected only with difficulty.

Sample action themes for development of effort awareness
First Stage of Movement Learning
1 Contrasting fast and slow movements
2 Contrasting heavy and light movements
3 Making sudden or sustained changes in level, direction, or action
4 Contrasting quick starts and sudden stops
5 Slow rising and falling with quick changes of place
6 Using different speeds for different actions
7 Increasing and decreasing speed
8 Stressing feeling for straightness and curvedness of pathways
9 Gesturing with firm and fine touch in place and while traveling
10 Holding tension and then relaxing into a collapse with control
11 Strong jumping and light landing
12 Contrasting sustainment in weight transfer
13 Growing bigger to increase tension and smaller to decrease tension
14 Contrasting jerky and smooth actions
15 Exploring variations of weight/time factors
Second Stage of Movement Learning
1 Carrying out action sequences like jump, land, collapse, and roll, stressing appropriate changes in speed

8 Ibid., p. 36.

2 Contrasting attitudes toward the space factor, flexible/direct
3 Connecting points in space with straight and flexible actions while matching or moving in opposition to a partner
4 Refining newly acquired action sequences
5 Lengthening sequences with emphasis on the continuity of flow
6 Sequentially relaxing body parts, leading to total relaxation
7 Stressing space/time efforts
8 Stressing weight/time efforts
9 Stressing flow with changes in the weight factor
10 Stressing flow with changes in the time factor
11 Stressing flow with changes in the space factor
12 Exploring the eight basic effort actions
13 Working with transition from effort action to effort action
14 Changing two elements in an effort action
15 Contrasting effort actions in partner relationships

■ Spatial structure is based upon the awareness of the bodily self. The concept of space can be developed only through movement, according to Kephart, who says, "We have no direct information concerning spatial relationships in our environment. All of our information concerning spatial localization comes to us through some clue which has to be interpreted to give us concepts of space."[9] The kinesthetic sense, Kephart says, provides us with information about the amount of tension in our muscles, the movement of body parts, and their relationship to the body. All of the data must be interpreted, but gradually the amount of muscular movement required to reach an object is interpreted as distance. Kephart goes on to describe the process of transference to the visual sense, another learned ability that involves accurate interpretation of the size of the retinal image. The location of things in space in relation to oneself and in relation to other objects is learned through many experiences in which movement plays a large role. Movement permits the individual to check quickly to make sure that what the eyes see is really there.

Awareness of space depends on awareness of relationship. Things exist in relationship to other things.

> These relationships are maintained through the development of a space structure and through the use of space structure to maintain stable relationships between the objects which lie around us. Without such a space structure, we lose or distort many of these relationships and our behavior suffers from inadequate information.[10]

Physical educators, if parents have not done the job, can help young children greatly by encouraging them to perceive their own bodies accurately. The body has different parts—two legs, two arms, one head. It has a front, two sides, and a back. Things in general fall down. The feet are

Spatial awareness

> *When the movement lesson focuses on where the movement is going, the emphasis is on the development of spatial awareness.*

9 Newell C. Kephart, *The Slow Learner in the Classroom* (Columbus, Ohio: Merrill, 1960), p. 91.
10 Ibid., p. 114.

Awareness of
motion factors

Selecting the appro-
priate degree of effort

down; the head is up. The dominant side of the body may be right or left,
the nondominant side being the opposite.

The relationship of the body front to movement in which the body
front leads establishes the direction *forward*. (Young children sometimes
say *frontways. Backward and sideward* are learned in a similar fashion, but
sometimes not as clearly if the body is twisted during the action. Sideward
movement with a twist is not clearly sideward. It is partly forward. Backward movement with a twisted body is partly sideward. This condition
should be corrected.

The midline of the body separates the right side from the left side.
Awareness of laterality or sidedness is necessary in spatial orientation. Confusion between the left and right sides of the body causes confusion in the
space structure too. It is important for children to develop stability of
sidedness.

Movement through space leads to awareness of personal space, often
referred to as self-space. This space surrounding the body is used by various parts for movement. If self-space is limited by the body's being too
close to something else, then movement is limited too. The stance of the
body influences the size of personal space, because the larger the base, the
larger the space, and vice versa.

Outside the limits of personal space is the general or common space
into which one may enter only by changing one's stance through locomo-

Awareness of space
depends on awareness
of relationship.

tion. Its boundaries are variable, sometimes being the walls of a room, the area restricted by a fence, or the field of play. The larger the general space, the larger the amount of space for personal movement without risk of collision. To reduce the risk, a portion of the general space may be assigned as a place for each person involved. The imaginary boundaries extend halfway to every adjacent person.

Through space, whether it be personal or general, goes movement. Movements of gesture extend through personal space, while movements of locomotion cause the body to travel to different places. The pathways of either form of movement have shape, which may be described as angular, curved, or twisted. Movement shapes have direction, size, level, and form. The movement of a snake is characterized as low, twisted, narrow,

Movement shapes have
direction, size, level,
and form.

Awareness of
motion factors

and forward. The movement of the overhand throw is high, circular, rearward, upward, and forward, with variations in size depending on throwing distance and force.

Elements in spatial awareness

Division 1.0. Division 1.0 concerns the awareness of *general space,* its limitations in size and shape and its boundaries. Movement may go through general space to every part of it, or movement may be limited to a portion of general space through inhibition, lack of awareness, or imposed limitation such as the assignment to stay in one place. In square dancing, for example, when the front of the room is established, all other parts of the room are identified. When the square dance caller declares that the couple in each set with its back toward a certain wall is couple number one, all other couples in each set know which couple number they are immediately. All of the points in general space may be connected by straight, angular, curved, or twisted pathways.

Division 2.0. Division 2.0 involves awareness of *personal space,* called the kinesphere by Laban.[11] The size of one's personal space may vary in direct relationship to its base of support; its relationship to others, to objects, and to boundaries may vary as well. Movement through one's personal space may involve the limbs, the head, and other parts such as the lips, shoulders, sternum, and hips. Movement may be perceived as a sequence of extensions into and contractions out of surrounding space. In games and other tasks the extension of the body into space may even be increased by the use of implements. The baseball bat increases the potential size of personal space, a factor to be reckoned with in player safety.

Spatial orientation requires that one have a sense of direction. The body, or more precisely the body center, is the major reference point around which the sense of direction is built. A three-dimensional axis is formed by the lines connecting the six basic directions in personal space. One line runs through the body center from front to back, another from side to side, and a third from up to down. If you imagine the human figure standing in a box defined by the eight corners of its personal space, the diagonal lines connecting the opposite corners establish eight more directions or points in space (see fig. 9.4, p. 317).

right-forward-high to left-rearward-low
left-forward-high to right-rearward-low
right-rearward-high to left-forward-low
left-rearward-high to right-forward-low

Additional diagonal lines, called *diametrals* by Laban, connect the center of each line forming one side of the box or cube with its diagonally opposite member. High-right connects with deep-left (low-left), forward-left connects with rearward-right, and so forth. The reader is urged to consult

11 Rudolf Laban, *Modern Educational Dance,* 3d ed. (London: MacDonald & Evans, 1975), p. 85.

Awareness of personal space and its relationship to others, objects, and boundaries

Laban's *Modern Educational Dance*, now in its third edition, with revisions and additions by Lisa Ullmann, Laban's renowned former associate. Beautifully written and clearly illustrated, this book can serve as a reference work throughout a lifetime of teaching the art of movement.

The planes of personal space constitute another orientation toward personal space. Should the box or cube representing personal space be cut in half between its upper and lower parts, the cut would be made on a horizontal or tablelike plane. Were the cut made to separate the right from the left half of the body, the cut would occur along the saggital or wheellike plane. A third plane might be established by cutting the space to separate the front half from the back half, establishing the frontal or wall-like plane. Forward and backward movement occurs in the wheel plane, a concept which may be further clarified by rolling forward around a transverse axis corresponding to the directional line connecting the two sides of the body. Catrwheels occur in a wall plane, and spinning movements rotate around a vertical axis. For example, a skater spinning around maintains stability of the body parts in the table plane, a condition more easily recognized when the arms are extended horizontally and maintained in that position relative to the floor throughout the movement.

All movement has direction, both in relationship to one's own body and in relationship to external space. The gravity line extending along the vertical axis of the body establishes the location of up and down. Along this axis one may raise or lower the body. Lowering it takes one to a *low level*, raising it takes one to a *high level*, and taking a position anywhere in between establishes it at a *medium level*. The level is related to the distance from one's base of support. If the base of support is the rung of a ladder on which one is crouching, the level of the body is described as low or medium in relationship to the ladder rather than to the floor on which the ladder is standing. A child standing on a jungle gym six feet tall is high above the ground but stands at a medium level with respect to the jungle gym.

Direction can be confusing in another way. A child traveling in a straight line may turn about and continue in the same direction (pathway). The child started moving forward and is now moving backward. But, had the child turned and, instead of traveling backward, returned to place, the child would still be traveling forward. To change direction may mean to change one's path or direction, or to change the leading aspect of one's body. It is a distinction that makes a difference and should be taken into account when teaching direction.

Division 3.0. Division 3.0 describes the pattern of movement, its shape (straight, angular, round, or twisted), and its location (whether formed on the floor or in the air). Floor patterns are designs made up of the pathways followed by supporting body parts, while air patterns are designs formed by the gestures of the limbs, head, and lesser body parts. To understand the meaning and implications of the difference between floor and air patterns, imagine the movement of human shadows cast on a huge white curtain by a strong light. The viewer does not see the people, only the shadows that change shape with every movement of their bodies. Think about the shadow shapes of people who are crouching low or stretching upward, or whose arms are gesturing at various levels and in different directions. Could not the shapes be likened to the extensions and contractions of moving inkblots, without regard for the humanness of their source? Could one recognize a walking pattern, a throwing pattern, or any other familiar action pattern by observing only the projections and contractions of an inky blackness on a single plane? Of course such patterns can be recognized because they are familiar and do not need the embodiment of the person.

Going one step further, would it not be possible to differentiate between mature motor patterns and immature motor patterns given only the shapes of the actions? Again, the answer is yes. The spatial pattern of movement is one of its major characteristics. The other is the effort quality or rhythm. The effort produces and monitors the movement, which in turn produces the shapes in space. Each shape or pattern has direction. It goes somewhere. It has size, and it follows pathways. For a full description of the interaction of space and effort, see Lisa Ullmann's addition to the third edition of *Modern Educational Dance,* "Some Hints for the Student of Movement." Although it focuses on dance, it applies to all spheres of human movement.

SPATIAL AWARENESS
1.0 Awareness of General Space
   1.1 *Limitations:* The space through which all may travel has boundaries, is variable in size and shape
   1.2 *Orientation:* The establishment of front, back, and sides helps fix one's relationship to general space
   1.3 *Pathways:* General space is penetrated by the pathways of movement, categorized as straight, angular, curved, or twisted.

2.0 Awareness of Personal Space

2.1 *Limitations*: The size of one's base and ability to stretch the limbs determines the outer limits of one's personal sphere of movement

    2.11 *Size* varies according to the relationship of one's personal space to that of others and to the physical environment

    2.12 *Relationship* of personal space varies according to one's proximity to the personal space of others or to objects that, if close, restrict movement within that space

2.2 *Range*: The amount of space used by a movement varies from little to much according to such factors as physical ability, attitude toward space, and task requirements

    2.21 *Size* awareness is described by the terms *large* and *small*

    2.22 *Extension* of the arm through the use of an implement increases the range potential of a movement

2.3 *Orientation*: Awareness of where movement is going in relationship to the body

    2.31 *Level* means the relationship of one's self to the base of movement; it is *low* when movement is close to the floor, *high* when extended above it, and *medium* when somewhere in between

    2.32 *Direction* is related to an accurate representation of one's body; *forward* and *backward* relate to front and back, *right* and *left* relate to the sides, *down* relates to the feet, and *up* relates to the head

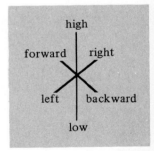

        2.321 *Diagonals* are combinations of directions that connect the four upper corners of one's sphere of movement with the four lower corners and intersect each other in the center of the body

        2.322 The *three-dimensional cross* represents the basic directions—forward and backward, up and down, and side to side—as they bisect each other; the axes of rotation are so identified, too

    2.33 *Planes* are dividers of space, the *wall plane* dividing front from back, the *table plane* dividing up and from down, and the *wheel plane* dividing right side from left side

3.0 Awareness of the Pattern of Movement

3.1 *Shape*: The spatial form of movement

    3.11 *Angular forms* are distinguished by straightness and by corners created by abrupt changes of direction

    3.12 *Rounded forms* curve gradually as they change direction around a single center

    3.13 *Twisted forms* curve gradually around one center and then reverse to curve around another center

3.2 *Floor pattern*: The pathways to be followed by the supporting body parts during locomotion; the pattern is two-dimensional

3.3 *Air pattern*: The pathways followed by nonsupporting body parts in the creation of three-dimensional shapes, although two-dimensional shapes are possible too

Deficiencies in spatial awareness
1 Crowding, colliding with others, and difficulty in controlling movements
2 Failure to travel throughout general space; remaining in a limited area
3 The child who is unable to get low enough may have a spatial awareness problem rather than a body awareness problem
4 Inability to change the direction of travel in time to avoid a collision
5 Underestimating the size of the space that the body is going through, resulting in bumps against the sides or top of the area
6 Standing up too soon after going under something, resulting in bumps to the back against the obstacle
7 Forming curved corners that should be angular
8 Lacking awareness of closeness to an object, leading to accidental contact; particularly seen in children who do not know that the wall behind them is there
9 Inability to vary the size of movements, making them larger or smaller
10 Failure to fit movement patterns into available space
11 Failure to make full use of available personal space under circumstances requiring broad gestures
12 Making limited use of any direction other than forward
13 Not seeing large spaces; tending to relate to people instead of space
14 Failure to make clear shapes, responding instead with vagueness
15 Getting "lost" in space; losing orientation in relationship to the floor, for example

Sample action themes for development of spatial awareness
First Stage of Movement Learning
1 Finding places away from people and things
2 Making big and small movements
3 Traveling without collision
4 Finding all the parts of general space
5 Exploring changes in level
6 Experimenting with changes in the direction of movement
7 Contrasting straight and curved pathways
8 Forming shapes of familiar things
9 Finding points in space surrounding the body and connecting them with straight or curved gestures
10 Changing the direction of the pathway, with and without change in movement direction
Second Stage of Movement Learning
1 Changing levels and direction along straight, curved, or twisted pathways
2 Designing space shapes by connecting specific points in space with gestures varying in shape

3 Maintaining spatial relationship while changing action and/or effort
4 Designing the floor pattern of an action sequence
5 Designing sequences that emphasize changes in level, direction, and range

Commentary on spatial awareness

Spatial awareness develops as the body is used for more diverse movements. However, instruction in spatial awareness does improve the child's ability to cope with a greater variety of problems than would otherwise be the case. Laban's organization of elementary movement themes implies that awareness of what the body is doing and how the movement is going relative to time and weight precedes awareness of where the movement is going. Experience bears this out. Nothing much is gained by offering "space lessons" for very young children prior to their having "doing lessons." The situation is different for older children.

Whereas initial movement lessons for preschoolers to second graders can profitably revolve around body awareness themes, lessons for third graders and older children should focus on the awareness of space, particularly general space. Combining awareness of space with gradations in speed and force permits older children to use their already developed repertoires of movement skills in a variety of spatial challenges simulating situations encountered in games. Spatial awareness lessons readily lead to games as relevant culminating activities.

Although the third grader still needs to improve in body awareness, such lessons should follow lessons in spatial awareness. Changes of pathway, direction, level, and to an extent range can be made meaningful when changes in speed and force are included in the lesson and when a partner relationship is added. We will dwell more fully on the progression of themes later. We mention it now to allay the concerns of the experienced reader who quite rightly cannot see the sense in having older children explore stretching, curling, and twisting movements or other beginning variations on the body awareness theme, even though they need it. Opportunities to explore the spatial domain more fully are in order. In later lessons it will be possible to go back to body awareness, but objectively oriented older children must perceive the relevance of their activities to a movement world that is quite different from the ego-oriented, movement-itself-is-fun world of young children.

Further comment is in order on the elementary spatial focus for the young child, who after all does move through space. Safety is of paramount importance. Learning where self-space is and learning that other children occupy their own space is a good first step. As children explore their environment, they can be encouraged to find new spaces, to go through or into these spaces. Apparatus is particularly useful in identifying more clearly where these spaces are. The natural boundaries made by the framework of apparatus makes windowlike openings suitable for exploration. Crowding is avoided by asking children not to go into the self-space of others an admonition they take quite seriously. Landing areas around the equipment from which children might jump are spaces for landings only, and children must walk around them to avoid collisions with jumpers.

Aside from the simple rule that they should respect each other's personal space, young children can experiment with and concentrate on action themes, or awareness of what the body is doing. When the challenges involve speed of action, remind them to take additional care to avoid collision. A self-testing, gamelike atmosphere is often encouraged at first. Later the work takes on a more serious tone, but should always lie within the realm of relevance to the child.

All games are space games. Offensive maneuvers attack space, while defensive maneuvers protect space. Lack of spatial awareness may result in balls and in players going out of bounds, not through lack of skill but as a result of disorientation. Players who are deficient in spatial awareness crowd together, mainly in the center of the field, collide with each other, kick or throw the ball in the wrong direction, and generally have difficulty scoring points or defending their goal. Without an adequate space structure amplified by knowledge and understanding of spatial concepts and relationships, students will have difficulty participating in games. Instructors have a choice. They can teach spatial awareness elements that have broad transfer value or they can train children to play the position of a specific activity, aware that there will be little, if any, transfer from that position to other positions or activities.

Relationship awareness

When the movement lesson focuses on self in relation to other people and objects, the emphasis is on the development of relationship awareness.

■ The question of *how* one is relating is the focus of relationship awareness in movement. This concept may also extend into the area of how other people and things relate to each other. Many movement relationships are spatial, which requires the learner to have a basic space structure. The self is perceived as being near, away from, on, or to the left or right of something or somebody. Parts of the body also relate to each other and to people and things. A movement pattern begins with a specific relationship, and then the initial relationship changes or is maintained as the pattern unfolds. For example, the hand starts with the fingers touching the *left* side of the bench and travels to the *right along* the bench until it goes *off* the *right*-hand edge.

Concepts of relationship are crucial for following directions in safety training, for academic education, in the arts, and of course in physical education. Learners relate to their environments of people and things in many different ways. In physical education there are movement problems to solve, skills to learn, and strategies to execute. Although precise awareness of relationship is important in learning complex skills, the process starts with gross motor behaviors and proceeds gradually to tasks involving finer discriminations.

Elements in relationship awareness

Division 1.0. Division 1.0 concerns the fundamental relationship to objects. The relationship may be manipulative or nonmanipulative. If it is manipulative, one can explore the specific ways in which handling the ob-

Relating to people
and things in many
different ways

Emphasis on
manipulation

ject affects relationship. For example, a learner may trap a ball *close to* the ground, catch a ball *above* the head, or carry a ball *away* from the body.

Nonmanipulative relationships are those that do not involve handling an object. If a child holds a hoop above and parallel to the ground for another child to jump into, the first child is manipulating the hoop by holding it while the other child is related to it nonmanipulatively. If a child stretches a rope along the floor in a straight line and then walks on it, is the child/rope relationship manipulative or nonmanipulative? Answer: nonmanipulative, while the child is walking on the rope. The floor supports the rope; the body is manipulated on it, just as if the rope were a balance beam.

Equipment of various kinds can be used in children's movement explorations. Concepts like *over, under,* and *around* are usually explored first. How children relate to the equipment will depend on where the space is and how strongly built the apparatus is. Some obstacles can be negotiated by going *under* only, while others may be managed by going *over* or *around.* With sufficient body management skill, children can explore *on, off, along,* and *around* in the wheel plane. They can hang from the apparatus, have some body parts on it and other parts off of it, or travel between and through the equipment. Exploring the many possibilities of relationship with objects adds to children's movement knowledge and skills.

Awareness of
motion factors

Child manipulating
hoop by holding it
while other relates in
nonmanipulative
fashion.

Supporting and
balancing

Target relationships are those with objects that are to be struck with something or pushed. People can be targets, too. When people are targets, they are treated as objects. In games like dodgeball one tries to strike people targets with a ball, in games like football people targets are blocked (a form of pushing) or tackled.

Division 2.0. Division 2.0 describes possible relationships with people. Children may perform alone to show a solution to a given movement problem or to demonstrate a skill, or they may perform alone in a crowd of other people. When everyone is engaged in "doing their own thing," aloneness signifies a mutual avoidance of one another. The objective in such a performance is to relate to available space rather than to other people. Young children and, to a limited extent, older children profit considerably from experiences requiring that they operate without distraction in alone-in-the-mass relationships.

Partner relationships offer various possibilities for exploration and for pursuit of common objectives. Two people doing something together can relate in various ways. They can be side by side, face to face, back to back, one high and the other low, and so forth. One can be still while the other is in motion, or both can remain in place or travel together. The space between them may remain relatively fixed or it may vary, the distance increasing or decreasing according to the requirements of their objective. Body parts may touch or link as part of the partner relationship. The result of relationship may be the creation of a design, or a balance and counterbalance, or a balance on top of a support.

Sometimes a partner relationship requires that one person lead and the other follow, if the two are to work cooperatively or to compete with each other. As they work together, their pathways may take them toward and away from each other—a meeting and parting relationship. One may go around, over, under, or past the other. At any one time, the particular relationship may be very complex. Teachers often fail to realize just how much they are asking of young learners. Games, dances, and gymnastic stunts are compounds of relationships that must be understood before effective action can be taken. Movement tasks involving partnerships help children develop a basic construct for understanding relationships.

Relationships of threes offer additional movement experience, particularly in triangularity of design. A group of three can form a triangle with or without contact. A noncontact relationship permits the triangle to expand or to contract. One person can pass between the other two and form a different triangle. One person can go around the other two or stop between them and form a line. A line relationship may be a *file* with one person standing in back of the other, or a *rank* with persons standing side by side. Of course, everyone could face a different direction, in which case neither term applies. In a competitive relationship involving three children, two may oppose one, while in an obstacle relationship one may be dodging balls thrown by the other two. The three group is a fundamental offensive set in many games. In working the ball toward an opponent's goal in games like soccer and basketball, the ball handler has more options in relation to two teammates than in relation to a partner only. It is easier for two teammates to free themselves for a pass than it is for a single player

Noncontact relationship

partner. In large-team games triangles of players form spontaneously to meet the needs of the moment. The ball handler should always be in a position to relate to two teammates, the two others in the triangle being determined by the direction in which the ball handler faces. More about player relationships later.

Other group sizes, like fours, are possible. Fours may come about when one partnership joins forces with another partnership. Cooperative efforts among fours may produce a rectangular or square formation, a triangle plus one inside or outside, or a line of some kind. In competition two can oppose two. Five or more people relate more easily in twos or threes from moment to moment. Trying to keep track of the spatial relationships of many persons is too much to expect. The larger the group, the vaguer the focus. Sixes form two groups of three for competition. Fours can join to make eights for the same purpose. Most elementary school games may be played by groups no larger than this. Children tend to lose strength of identity in larger groups, and the importance of their role in relation to the group's objectives is diminished or diluted by greater numbers.

Awareness of relationship in movement is important to the individual, for safety and for growth in knowledge and skill. Social competence is as important an objective in physical education as are movement skills and understandings. Values develop a sounder basis for decision making in socially satisfying environments than in those where the individual feels uncomfortable, alone, oppressed, and afraid to express himself positively.

RELATIONSHIP AWARENESS
1.0 Relationship to Objects
    1.1 *Manipulative relationship*: Awareness of the specific manner of relating to objects when manipulating them, such as throwing, trapping, turning, squeezing, carrying, and lifting

    1.2 *Nonmanipulative relationship*: Awareness of a rather specific spatial relationship to an object in stillness or in motion characterized by such terms as *on, toward, near, far, over, under, through, off, between* and *along*

        1.21 *Obstacle relationships* are those in which the object, either by design or by accident, lies in the path of the mover, thus requiring some kind of decision about subsequent relationships

        1.22 *Target relationships* are those in which the object (or person treated as an object) is subject to an action such as being struck or pushed by the mover

2.0 Relationship to People
    2.1 *Relationship to others*: Contact and noncontact relationships are possible and either approach or avoidance behaviors

        2.11 *Alone* in space is a solo event in which the mover is a performer for others to observe and react to

        2.12 *Alone in the mass* is a scatter formation in which the relationship is indifference or avoidance, whether the person is traveling or moving in place; the mover behaves as if others are not present

    2.13 *Partner* relationships are those in which two people form an alliance to pursue a common objective

    2.14 *Threes* relationships are those in which three people form an alliance to pursue a common objective

    2.15 *Small group* relationships are those involving four to seven or eight people in pursuit of a common objective

2.2 *Formational relationship*: The regularity of a geometric design or shape is evident in specific formations involving two or more people (either contact or noncontact)

    2.21 *Line* relationships (often called *rank* or *file* relationships) are characterized by persons being side by side, face to face, back to back, or one in back of the other

    2.22 *Triangular* relationships may involve three people relating to each other only or relating to those outside the triangle as well

    2.23 *Rectangular* relationships involve four people in a square or rectanglar formation, but may include relationships to others within the formation or outside of it

    2.24 *Circular* relationships involve three or more people relating to a common center by maintaining a constant radial distance from it in concert with other members of the circle; members may face the center or have their backs or sides to it

2.3 *Social relationship*: Members of an alliance may cooperate with each other to achieve a common objective or by agreement compete with each other to achieve opposing objectives

    2.31 *Cooperative* relationships are those that facilitate the attainment of a common objective through mutually helpful behaviors

    2.32 *Competitive* relationships are cooperative relationships in which the objectives are agreed upon and then pursued in opposition to others' attempts to prevent their attainment

2.4 *Spatial relationship*: The space between two or more movers may remain fixed or may change in size

    2.41 *Fixed relationships* are those in which the distance between the members of an alliance such as a triangle remains constant whether members are traveling or not

    2.42 *Variable relationships* are those in which the space between members decreases or increases, as in *meeting* or *parting*, *passing, going around, going over,* or *going under*

2.5 *Contact and noncontact*: The members of an alliance or temporary partnership may avoid touching each other or engage in specific contact relationships

    2.51 *Touching or linking* body parts may serve to establish and sometimes maintain a specific relationship

Awareness of motion factors

2.52 *Balancing or counterbalancing* requires two or more people to link body parts to assist each other in achieving a balance in relation to a common line of gravity

2.53 *Supporting and balancing* requires that cooperating members perform separate roles so that one or more can form a base to support others

Deficiencies in relationship awareness

1 Knows what he is or she is doing with an object but does not know the particulars of the relationship; that is, knows that he or she is holding a ball but not that the ball is being held over the head
2 Failure to realize that one is moving toward something
3 Lack of awareness of being *under* rather than *next to*
4 Lack of awareness that an object is approaching
5 Confusing relationship terms like *on, along,* and *off*
6 Failure to maintain a relationship such as *staying near* while doing something else
7 Difficulty in deciding how to go about relating to an object or obstacle
8 Failure to realize one is making contact with people or things
9 Relating to people instead of to space when the latter behavior is called for, such as when the mover travels to find big spaces
10 Failure to relate to an entire area, limiting one's movement to the center or edge instead
11 Difficulty in forming relationships with others; wanders off from a partner without realizing it
12 Failure to perceive geometric form of relationship with others
13 Lack of awareness of where one's partner is
14 Failure to maintain relationship to the center of a circle and to adjacent group members at the same time
15 Difficulty in maintaining a relationship to an opponent and to a given area at the same time

Sample action themes for development of relationship awareness
First Stage of Movement Learning
1 Finding places to go under, over, or around an object
2 Being on, over, and off an object
3 Staying with a partner
4 Exploring different ways to manipulate objects
5 Performing the same movements as one's partner (matching)
6 Maintaining the same relationship while traveling with a partner
7 Following a leader
8 Linking different body parts with a partner
9 Forming triangles, squares, and circles
10 Being near and away from an object
Second Stage of Movement Learning
1 Forming different triangular relationships
2 Forming contact and noncontact relationships with partners and in small groups

3 Supporting a partner in various balances
4 Two persons helping one
5 Meeting and parting from others
6 Passing and going around partners
7 Forming a variety of targets
8 Developing obstacle courses to explore going over, under, and around objects in different sequences
9 Working as a team with specific individual responsibilities
10 Exploring ways of working in the triangle plus one relationship

Commentary on relationship awareness

Awareness of relationship too often is taken for granted. It is often assumed that children understand the concepts of *over, under, left, top, side,* and other relationships so important to their ability to follow directions. Many children do not understand the concepts and consequently are not able to understand so-called simple directions. Relationship concepts are easily taught through simple movement lessons at the preschool stage and may be reinforced, if necessary, during the primary school years. True, the concept of left and right is not generalized early, but even little children whose mothers and fathers read to them know that their favorite stories start on the left and proceed to the right across the page. Whether one side is called the left, or the good side, or any other term makes little difference, as long as it has relational stability. Then it has value as a point of reference, a way of distinguishing one side from the other.

Relationship lessons may involve space, body parts, or abstract qualities such as force and time. Simple body awareness themes or space themes are made more challenging when partner relationships are included in the development of the lessons. Progression in developmental skills and games often follows a pattern of increasing the number of players per team, which is a way of increasing the complexity of the relationship to which players must respond in appropriate ways, whether they are on offense or on defense.

Because it is so important to learning in general, some emphasis is given to relationship awareness in every lesson, even when the focus is on other goals.

Summary

■ The four elements of movement awareness—body, space, effort, and relationship awareness—constitute the content of basic movement education. Each element may serve as the theme of one or more lessons, unifying the lesson by giving it focus and stimulating, developing, and refining some aspect of movement awareness. It may be awareness of *what* the body is doing as it moves, or *how* the movement is going with respect to its speed, force, use of space, and flow characteristics, or *where* the movement is going through space. The lesson may focus only on the relationship of the movers to their different environments or even to their own body parts, leaving them free to select different actions, efforts, and spatial designs that make up appropriate responses to particular facets of relationship. As learners progress from simple to complex lessons, they find

Awareness of
motion factors

themselves increasingly involved in tasks that draw on more than one aspect of movement at a time. Learners may travel in different ways, at different speeds, and at different levels with awareness of a partner or in a manipulative relationship to an object. They may be encouraged to design a floor pattern to the accompaniment of a musical selection and within a certain amount of space for the purpose of a solo performance or to design a pattern that simply includes several people in different ways, some in contact relationship and others in noncontact relationship.

The line between basic movement and developmental movement is thin. It is relatively easy to shift the focus from mere awareness of body, space, effort, and relationship to specific outcomes requiring the utilization of these awarenesses. In basic movement lessons the focus is strictly on heightening the awareness of the motion factors. One may turn right around and select from movement awarenesses just explored those efforts and shapes needed to improve a particular skill without detracting in the least from the purpose of basic movement itself. The person engaging in basic movement experiences, for the moment at least, enjoys the freedom of moving just for the sensations it provides, not caring whether some purpose external to it is achieved. The mover becomes immersed in movement and forgets that there is any such thing as a game, a dance, or gymnastic stunt.

Assignments

■ One should not limit one's experience in basic movement education merely to reading about it. The following general assignments suggest meaningful investigations for each of the four aspects of movement.

1
While sitting, reach into all surrounding personal space, carefully avoiding contact with other people or with things.
Question: How close can you come to people and things without changing your position of support and without making contact?

2
Traveling about the classroom or other room, go through all of the spaces while avoiding collision with things and people.
Question: Can you also give attention to variations in other variables such as speed of travel, level of space used, or travel action used?

3
Analyze the weight, time, and space elements of your preferred walking gait to determine your effort preference.
Question: After deciding your basic effort preference, can you determine the effort preferences of others by identifying their attitudes toward time, weight, and space as revealed by their normal walking patterns?

4
Relate to different things in as many different ways as you can.
Question: Can you differentiate between manipulative and non-manipulative relationships? Between target and obstacle relationships? Between various spatial relationships such as *on, over, toward,* and *away from*?

5
Find a space away from others and explore all possible uses of that space.
Question: Can you move while limiting your attention to one, two, three, or four variables from the same or from different aspects of movement?

6
Use a piece of apparatus and explore the spaces under, over, and around it.
Question: Can you find different ways to relate to spaces, using different parts of your body for support? Leading the movement with different parts of your body? Changing speed without loss of control?

7
Move different parts of your body in time with some music of your choice.
Question: What are the effort characteristics of the movements you perform to this music?

8
With a partner investigate ways of helping each other in balancing tasks.
Question: Can you counterbalance each other, in addition to acting as a support or base for one another?

9
In a group of three, form a triangle without contact and travel about in general space.
Question: Can you maintain the space intervals between yourself and the others without talking about or nonverbally signaling your intentions to change direction or stop?

10
By yourself, with a partner, or in a group of three test your ability to recall all of the elements of one aspect of movement by structuring tasks that focus awareness on all of the elements, either singly or in combination with one or two others.
Question: Can you identify by observation the specific movement focus of another person or group of people?
A final test of your basic movement is to list from memory the essential elements categorized under each of the four aspects of awareness—body, space, effort, and relationship. The effective teacher must be able to discern the presence or absence of these awarenesses to respond with appropriate lessons.

Kephart, Newell C. *The Slow Learner in the Classroom.* Columbus, Ohio: Merrill, 1960.

Laban, Rudolf *The Mastery of Movement.* 2d ed. London: MacDonald & Evans, 1960.

———. *Modern Educational Dance.* 3d ed. London: MacDonald & Evans, 1975.

Laban, Rudolf, and Lawrence, F. C. *Effort.* London: MacDonald & Evans, 1947.

North, Marion. *Movement Education.* London: Maurice Temple Smith, 1973.

———. *Personality Assessment Through Movement.* London: MacDonald & Evans, 1972.

Radler, D. H., with Kephart, Newell C. *Success Through Play.* New York and Evanston: Harper & Row, 1960.

Awareness of
motion factors

Chapter VI

First steps in teaching

Young children cannot untangle their feelings about themselves and their experiences and tell us clearly just why
things are going well or badly for them at school. On
such matters someone must speak for them.

Teachers of Louise Duffy School
West Hartford, Connecticut

■ The teachers of Louise Duffy School were presented the following
creed to express for all children their needs as young learners.

As a child, I feel—

The need to be myself—to be the person I am, rather than being pushed
into trying to be someone I am not.

The need for self-achievement—to be allowed to progress at my own speed
and within the framework of my own abilities.

The need for motivation—to have someone open the world of knowledge to
me through reading and books, and show me how to find answers to my
questions.

The need for time—time to learn at my own pace; time to spend by myself,
absorbing what I have been given to learn.

The need for freedom from labels—freedom to learn whatever I can learn,
without the handicap of being prejudged and placed in a stereotyped group.

The need for freedom from anxiety—so that my confidence in myself may
grow along with my ability to cope with the experiences that lie ahead.

The need for a picture of myself which I can like—the need to see myself as a person of worth, one whom other people accept and like.[1]

■ This statement aptly establishes as the central subject matter in education not the content of the basic movement program, nor the teacher, but
the children themselves. When the children "come to gym," what kind of

The child comes to gym

1 *Weekly Bulletin #9.* Series 1967-1968, November 2, 1967, Louise Duffy School,
West Hartford, Connecticut. Permission granted by Judson E. Marble, former
principal, Louise Duffy School.

Making decisions
together

environment will there be? Will they be accepted as individuals or treated as objects to be manipulated by those in charge? Will "coming to gym" be an actualizing experience or an experience that victimizes? Will it be a challenge or a threat? Those who teach or plan to teach should consider their answers carefully. Every decision made in the acts of planning lessons, teaching, performing certain housekeeping chores, and assessing results impinges on the relationship of teacher and child and expresses values that guide the teacher's behavior.

It is easy to outline a program of instruction and plan lessons. It is quite another matter to develop child-centered objectives. Program needs and child needs do not necessarily coincide, but they can. If the child is viewed as a learner on an educational ladder, the teacher will first assess the readiness level of each rung on the ladder before developing a course of study. What are the implications of readiness for physical education?

The assessment of readiness for movement learning

■ Readiness for movement learning assumes that children have had some experience in moving, feeling, and thinking and that they have reached some observable level of competence on which to base new challenges to move, to feel, and to think. Teachers must make reasonably accurate assessments of movement competence for both the class as a whole and each individual. They ask themselves, "What experiences do these children need? What experiences does this particular child need?" Teachers are concerned with five areas of student ability.

1 The ability to operate with consideration for the rights of others.
2 The ability to operate in a reasonably self-disciplined manner.

3 The ability to manage their bodies in a variety of environments, present and future.
4 The ability to operate at a level of physical fitness appropriate to personal needs in becoming fully functioning individuals.
5 The skill, knowledge, and ability to satisfy their special needs for involvement, challenge, and success, now and in the immediate future.

Assessment ends with the teacher establishing priorities for student experiences. The teacher says, "First of all, these children need . . ." or, recognizing that not all children begin at the same level, "This child has a special need for . . . ." The teacher is now in a position to plan movement lessons for priority objectives. "Coming to gym" should lead to positive development that builds on clearly defined stages of learner readiness.

The *operational stages of learning* in a movement-oriented program of physical education take into account the present level of learner ability and guide the teacher in the construction of program objectives to meet learner needs. An outline of the behaviors expected at each stage of development enables the teacher to match observations and expectations in determining "where we are" and "where we are going first."

■ The first operational stage of learning recognizes two levels of student behavior. Level 1.0 identifies behaviors that are necessary to any instructional endeavor—behaviors that indicate the student's attitudes toward others, toward the learning environment, and toward self. Level 2.0 is the first step in a program that systematically proceeds from simple to complex in the development of a movement vocabulary and eventually an understanding of the scientific foundations of movement. Level 1.0 objectives must be attained before serious consideration can be given to level 2.0 objectives.

Operational Stage I

Level 1.0 is a time for orientation, a period of indefinite length devoted to the preparation of children for self-directed, problem-solving movement experiences. Preschoolers may need to devote all of their time to movement learning experiences at this level. If they do, it is small matter. They have the time. Unfortunately, older children may have to spend considerable time at level 1.0, too, before they are ready to move on to the next level. However, patience and persistence pay off when children begin to increase in their ability to solve problems which is so important in movement education.

Affective objectives predominate at the first level. Only those cognitive and psychomotor performance objectives that complement the development of favorable attitudes are sought at level 1.0. The teacher is definitely in charge, but the atmosphere is friendly. The teacher frequently praises some or all of the children for having made some progress toward greater self-discipline, better listening skills, or greater consideration for others. The children are encouraged to experiment—to find new ways and to test or vary old ways. The children are frequently asked to distinguish between behaviors that are the *same* and behaviors that are *different*.

Safety training begins with having children watch for empty spaces to

First steps in teaching

Being different

avoid collisions, use apparatus carefully, land in proper landing spaces, and avoid movements that are just for showing off. There is a direct relationship between safe behavior and freedom to decide for oneself.

Learners are expected to achieve six program objectives at Stage I, level 1.0

1 Show consideration for others by sharing.
2 Demonstrate consideration for their own safety and the safety of others.
3 Listen to instructions carefully and follow them.
4 Demonstrate understanding of *same* and *different*.
5 Operate without excessive noise.
6 Recall rules for the use of a facility or of equipment by staying within authorized bounds.

The program objectives at this level are aimed at reducing the incidence of behaviors such as shouting and unruliness that restrain teaching and learning. Their purpose is to create an environment conducive to learning—a reasonably calm, friendly place in which children need not fear being different or failing. The common complaints about children voiced by teachers who have tried and failed in movement education are in themselves descriptions of children's behaviors at this level. Their children

- don't pay attention.
- exhibit little self-control.
- cannot remember from day to day the rules of acceptable conduct.
- show little individual initiative.
- lack consideration for the feelings of others.
- are overly competitive or aggressive.

- are too cautious and inhibited, unless expectations are thoroughly explained and demonstrated.
- are noisy; they shout, giggle, and scream.
- give up easily when they think they may fail or when things get difficult.
- copy others rather than doing their own thinking.
- continually ask, "Is this right?"
- mistake freedom for license.
- are easily distracted.

When children exhibit these behaviors in physical education class, the teacher's immediate concern is not movement education but creation of an environment that permits movement education to go on. Top priority must be given to the six objectives of level 1.0. There is no point in pursuing cognitive and psychomotor objectives with children who do not know how to pay attention, who push and shove, or who show little awareness of safety needs.

> *Planning Hint: Because learning objectives for beginners fall primarily in the affective domain, the teacher may choose content from all areas of physical education—games, gymnastics, dance, basic movement.*

Efforts to develop a proper learning environment should not be diluted by wasteful attempts to teach specifics such as ball handling, complex games, movement sequences, dances, or relays. Older children who associate physical education with playing a particular game at every session need to learn some activities that focus on individual behavior in small groups. Younger children need basic movement instruction with emphasis on listening behaviors. Actions are the vehicle, and a drum or other instrument may be used to control the tempo or to vary it. The sequence of activities does not matter yet. Gymnastics today may be followed by games or dances tomorrow.

Question: How does the teacher know when a child has attained program objectives?

Answer: By observing the student behaviors that indicate attainment of the desired objective.

Explanation: If the following program objective is being sought, the teacher will look for consistent performance of specific behaviors. These specific behaviors are identified in instructional, behavioral, or performance objectives.

Program Objective 3, Operational Stage I, Level 1.0
The children should be able to listen to instructions and operate within the limitations specified.

The program objective will have been attained when most of the children consistently perform the following behaviors.

First steps in teaching

Performance objectives

Stop and pay attention to the teacher when the appropriate signal is given.

Listen to directions and wait for the appropriate signal before starting to work on the movement problem.

Repeat verbally the sequence of directions when called upon to do so.

Follow the directions correctly.

There are instances when performance objectives may need to be divided into smaller units. Performance objectives also may have to be stated differently for different activities.

Sometimes children will respond appropriately when performing gymnastics but not when engaged in manipulative or rhythmic activities. In this instance children should be praised for showing proper behavior in gymnastics and encouraged to behave likewise under other circumstances. The same performance objective stated specifically for manipulative or rhythmic activities would then include a phrase such as "when using a ball" or "when engaged in a rhythms lesson."

Children who have learned to respond appropriately in words and body movements regardless of the type of activity they are engaged in have achieved Program Objective 3, Operational Stage I, Level 1.0. The teacher can predict their behavior under similar circumstances in the future. They have learned.

When most children in the class, 80 percent or more, attain all level 1.0 program objectives, they are ready to move on to level 2.0 program objectives—the acquisition of a movement vocabulary, certain specified psychomotor behaviors, and continued growth in desired attitudes.

Guidelines to the specification of performance objectives

■ Performance objectives are the province of the instructor or teacher. They are written for the moment of instruction, and they describe what learners will be doing when they are performing the desired behaviors. Banathy offers these guidelines for specifying performance objectives. The instructor describes:

1 *What* the learner is expected to be able to do by:
   a) Using verbs that denote observable action.
   b) Indicating the stimulus that is to evoke the behavior of the learner.
   c) Specifying the resources (objects) to be used by the learner and persons (if any, sic) with whom the learner should interact.
2 *How* well the behavior is expected to be performed by identifying:
   a) Accuracy of correctness of response.
   b) Response length, speed, rate, and so forth.
3 Under what circumstances the learner is expected to perform by specifying:
   a) Physical or situational circumstances.
   b) Psychological conditions.[2]

2 Bela H. Banathy, *Instructional Systems* (Palo Alto, Calif.: Fearon, 1968), p. 33.

Program objectives are met by students who successfully accomplish performance objectives. The teacher determines the performance objectives that demonstrate the behavioral competence described in the program objectives. Here is an example of a program objective and a performance objective written according to Banathy's guidelines.

Program objective: The learner should develop an understanding of personal space requirements to avoid collisions and to show consideration for others.

Performance objective: When free to choose where they will work on their movement problems, learners will consistently demonstrate awareness of space needs for themselves and others allowing enough space to avoid collisions.

This performance objective meets Banathy's specifications. It states the desired behavior, the conditions under which the behavior will be exhibited, and the acceptable performance standard.

Behavior: Awareness of personal space needs and the space needs of others

Conditions: Free choice of location for working on movement problems

Criterion: Consistently, that is, always, or 100 percent of the time

Practice in writing performance objectives to these specifications may be a useful exercise, but the procedure is time-consuming and uneconomical in its repetition of conditions and/or performance standards. A more practical method is to group behaviors.

On completion of this unit, learners will consistently demonstrate the following behaviors during free exploratory movement, regardless of the activity.
1 Find space suitable for their movement requirements.
2 Share the available space and equipment with others.
3 Avoid collisions by stopping, changing direction, or slowing speed.
4 Select the actions that they can manage safely.
5 Engage willingly in activity according to their different ability levels.
OR
On those occasions when the teacher instructs, questions, or requests pupil demonstrations of personal solutions, learners will respond as follows.
1 Listen attentively.
2 Make an effort to behave courteously when asked to show personal solutions to a problem.
3 Observe other pupils' demonstrations of solutions with no display of inconsiderate behavior.
4 Obey the signal to stop moving.
OR
On those occasions when apparatus is used, learners will consistently demonstrate the following abilities.

First steps in teaching

1 Follow instructions in securing and replacing all equipment.
2 Cooperate with others in carrying and placing equipment that is too heavy for individuals to manage by themselves.
3 Use equipment with consideration for its structural limitations.
4 Use the landing mats for landings only when the mats are properly positioned according to teacher directions.

OR

On those occasions when learners are manipulating equipment, they will demonstrate consideration for the spatial requirements of the task and the spatial needs of others.

1 Handle the equipment in such a way that they show awareness of the object's properties that affect performance (size, weight, composition, shape, and so on).
2 Avoid crowded areas that require more control of the object than they can exercise to prevent it from accidentally striking others.
3 Select actions that they know they can control with a reasonable degree of certainty.

Review of program objectives and performance objectives

■ Program objectives have been met when performance objectives, in the form of easily perceived behaviors, have been met. The program objectives for level 1.0 are stated broadly. Each asks, "How will the teacher know that this objective has been attained?" Banathy's specifications for developing performance objectives serve as a guide.

The specification of behaviors requires a description of overt actions, the way in which learners will perform at the end of the instructional period (or unit, or lesson). The specification of conditions or circumstances is a description of the situation in which learners will be when they behave in the desired manner. Criterion is the measure of acceptability or quality of behavior. It may also be a quantitative standard, for example, a minimum of three hits out of five attempts.

Just thinking about behavior in terms of performance helps the teacher focus on what learners will be able to do as a result of the teacher's having behaved in a certain manner. No longer will this teacher think of mere exposure of children to a particular activity as teaching.

The program objective of courteous behavior as the outcome of instruction will not be realized by the teacher's putting up cute cartoons about courtesy on a bulletin board. Nor will children necessarily behave courteously because the teacher says only courteous behavior will be tolerated. If the objective is courtesy, then courteous behaviors, those that demonstrate real concern for others, will be many. Just learning to say "thank you" under certain circumstances certainly is not enough to satisfy such a broad program objective. However, the instructor must decide if it is a step in the right direction.

Although program objectives are stated broadly, they should indicate clearly the type of behaviors being sought. Most program objectives will be described by more than one performance objective. Curriculum guides written in behavioral terms tend to follow a format like this.

Elementary school physical education: Operational Stage I
  Program objective 1.0 (description)
  Performance objective 1.1 (description)
  Performance objective 1.2 (description)
  Performance objective 1.3 (description)

■ As soon as learners demonstrate adequate concern for others, awareness of their own limitations, and acceptable listening skills, the teacher begins to stress performance objectives in the psychomotor and cognitive domains. From kindergarten to grade 3 or 4 it should be possible to introduce the subject of motion factors. Awareness of *what, how,* and *where* is emphasized through movement challenges, and the atmosphere is kept exploratory. For example, the teacher makes much out of all of the different ways people have found to move. Children are encouraged to look for differences, to experiment, to give new experiences a try. Their successes are exploited and their failures are ignored in the belief that once children lose their fear of being wrong the lessons can become meaningful adventures. Children can explore the world of human movement, using the motion factors as themes for actions and ideas.

With older children, those in fourth or fifth grade through eighth grade, the situation is different. Most of them have participated in either structured activities, with no instruction in the motion factors underlying all of the activities, or in semistructured recreational activities, with little or no instruction in skills. Both situations are difficult to correct, but the one that has neglected instruction in favor of play is the more difficult. These are common roll-out-the-ball activity periods that pass for physical education. Certain activities form the core of such a program, and there is great resistance to change. The children feel comfortable playing kickball, killerball, softball, football, or some other ball game from a limited selection of games. This seems to be all they want to do, but with a little investigation the teacher soon learns that these games offer some students important opportunities to succeed with the peer group. "Today, I might get a hit" is the feeling that group members have. It is a loser orientation in a society that values winning above all else. The activity is the only way some children have of coping with their peers. Change would put group leaders, who consider themselves winners, in the position of having to risk their status—an unhappy prospect and a step they often dare not take. Meanwhile, the rest of the class seems content to go on with the activity, playing out the hand so to speak, to maintain the status quo. Hungry for activity and hungry for recognition, they fear the loss of what they have and the unknowns that change would bring.

The new teacher with a movement orientation to physical education or the teacher who wants to change to exploration, problem solving, and analysis in physical education must approach these older children carefully. Sensitive preadolescent and adolescent egos require much teacher support and reinforcement through new successes. Little changes that do not upset the class social structure are made until the children are ready to try

**Level 2.0
involves
understanding**

First steps in teaching

something different in the main part of the activity period, which is gradually, perhaps ever so gradually, becoming a lesson.

Given the usual problems of children from kindergarten through third or fourth grade, motion factors are introduced in two stages. Up through second grade, a beginning lesson on movement emphasizes awareness of what the body is doing. Attention is focused on the actions, positions, body parts, and changes in body shape. After second grade, the child's orientation toward movement is strongly spatial. Although this may not be true of the girls, the boys through their growing interest in group games find exploration of space a more interesting challenge than exploration of the body. Consequently, to avoid upsetting peer group leadership by asking them to do what they might consider "baby stuff," the teacher structures lessons to emphasize where in space the body is traveling. Avoiding collisions is a great challenge to the beginner. Going over, under, and around is great fun, but the natural desire to check one's physical prowess can be used as the basis for activities exploring force, speed, balance, and skill in manipulation.

The first step in beginning movement education is to establish a functional movement vocabulary. Let us begin with Stage I. Suggestions for starting themes are listed in chapter 5. Children in kindergarten through second grade should start with lessons emphasizing *body awareness,* while those at upper levels should begin with *spatial awareness.*

The movement lesson

■ At the conclusion of this discussion on the format of a movement lesson, the reader should understand the relationship between lesson format and purpose.

Lesson format

A movement lesson introduces one or more concepts in the form of movement problems. The teacher begins the lesson with a simple activity that includes some element of the new concept or that establishes a situation in which some element of the new concept may be introduced. This is called the *Initial Task* or T^1. The term *movement challenge* might be used just as easily, but *task* connotes a problem that needs to be worked out, a job that needs doing. To manage the task, however, children need to understand all that is involved. Whether they understand or not will be evident from watching what they do, when they do it, with whom, and how. Any misunderstanding should be cleared up before proceeding to the next step. This process is called *Clarification* and is identified by the letter C on the lesson plan.

As soon as children demonstrate their understanding by solving the problems presented in T^1, the lesson enters the developmental phase. An additional movement challenge is presented to the children, which may take one of two forms. They may be asked to add some movement to what is already being done or to investigate some aspect of what is already being done. The new challenge is identified as D^1, and it includes the process of clarification. Remember that children's understanding is demonstrated by

Desire to check one's
physical prowess

Experiencing force,
speed, balance,
and unbalance

the manner in which they behave. It is what they do that counts. If they do not understand, the observant teacher will find a way to clarify matters. The teacher may ask for student demonstration of several acceptable solutions or discuss the task again directly. D^2, D^3, and any additional challenges follow the same pattern, challenge and clarify, until either the task changes or the sequence is brought to an end with a culminating activity, CA.

The CA may be an activity of the children's own creation that incorporates certain elements of the tasks that went before or an activity structured by the teacher to reinforce the previously acquired understandings. The activity may be competitive, exploratory, or creative. It may be individualized or cooperative. In any case, it must give maximum exposure to the new concepts. Otherwise, it is just random activity that takes up time but does little to further education.

At the very beginning of class, when the children first enter the gymnasium, they engage in *Preinstructional Activity,* or PIA. More than a warm-up, PIA includes dressing, getting on the floor, getting and distributing equipment, arranging the apparatus, and grouping, if grouping is called for in the general movement challenge.

When the children arrive on the gymnasium floor or outdoors, they are immediately challenged to find ways to move or warm up on their own. Young children are not concerned with warm up, but older children have some idea what that means and start doing jumping jacks or some other set exercise. No matter, it is a beginning. What matters is that children find themselves a space away from others. Formations should not be used ex-

First steps in teaching

cept in cases in which this has been the practice and the teacher fears that a sudden departure would lead to chaos. While older children may be finding different ways to do pushups and situps, the younger children are shifting their weight to different parts of the body, jumping in space, stretching in all directions, or twisting and curling in different ways. This preparatory period gives the teacher a chance to see what the students can do with their bodies when given the freedom to think for themselves. At first, the results are most discouraging, especially with other children who may have become so brainwashed by structured exercise that, given the opportunity to move freely, they resort to repetitions of set forms used by Little League coaches and other advocates of calisthenics for children.

The PIA period offers the teacher the best opportunity to assess learner competence and understanding of movement concepts. It is a period when children become increasingly free and creative, a time period that serves as a showcase for their learning. For the teacher-observer, PIA is the springboard to the lesson.

> *A teacher's first step in understanding and carrying out a movement lesson is knowing how to state a movement problem.*

The simplest way to begin a movement lesson is to ask questions that require movement answers.

> *Can you show me some different ways of jumping?*
> > *stretching?*
> > *turning?*
> > *balancing?*

> *Who can travel through all the spaces without bumping into anyone? Show me!*

This challenge is answered by a great variety of different actions executed while traveling in varied ways and avoiding collision. A number of alternative movements, like stopping in time, changing direction, and twisting away, are possible.

> *How can you move without traveling anywhere?*

The challenge includes a condition that limits the movement to personal space. All movement problems contain either implied or explicit limitations.

In formulating a movement problem, the teacher who in the past always told the children what to do finds ways of questioning that challenge children to think about the what, how, and where of their movements. Even if the children in the end do what they would have done under more explicit instructions, they have had to think about it first. This is the *Listen - Think - Do* process, rather than *Listen - Do* process that leaves the thinking to the teacher.

It is important to recognize the implicit and explicit limitations expressed in the movement problem.

> *Can you show me some ways of balancing?*

(Implied limitation: in your own space, without traveling.)

While staying in your own space, can you show me some different ways of balancing?

(Explicit limitation: while staying in your own space. There is no other option available. The condition under which exploration of balance is to be undertaken is clearly stated.)

When limitations should be stated explicitly is often obvious. If the teacher has made an error in stating the movement task, the error will soon be found out. When one teacher challenged children to find ways of balancing, they responded by climbing up the apparatus lining one of the walls. Anytime there is a possibility that children need explicit instructions, the movement task should include them.

Another situation involving implication is the teacher's request that children "Show me some . . . ." The children should respond not as if the request were a command but a question: "Can you show me . . ." or "Who can show me . . . ." Children should always know that in these situations they are being challenged to think and do, and if, at the moment, they cannot think what to do, they are not required to do anything. Doing nothing communicates to the teacher as effectively as doing something. The teacher may respond by rewording the task to make it clearer.

The *Initial Task* (T^1) of the lesson is the most important movement question because it starts the sequence of challenges that should lead to gains in awareness, ability, and understanding. Whether the question is vague, or inappropriate, or clearly stated will make a big difference in the response and in subsequent development through additional challenges. Vague questions are often unanswered, the response being no activity. At other times, children respond with meandering actions that seem to have no purpose. Inappropriate questions often lead to collisions, noise, and other problems associated with poor control. The children cannot respond properly to movement challenges that are not appropriate to their physical, mental, or psychological state.

Simple themes and objectives

There are two kinds of lesson themes. One gives attention to action— traveling, balancing, twisting and turning, and the like. The other stresses ideas or concepts that result in modification of actions. Fast and slow, heavy and light, roundabout and straight are examples of movement idea themes.

A theme gives unity to a lesson or sequence of lessons. The thematic emphasis in good lessons may be seen in the movements of the children. If actions are involved, these will be exhibited. If a movement idea is being stressed, the viewer will recognize the concepts, even though the actions are highly individualized. Alternations in slow and fast actions, for example, should be clearly expressed, even if some children are working with traveling actions while others are exhibiting nonlocomotor movements of the arms, legs, and head.

Themes may be stated first, followed by objectives to be realized in

Lesson theme on
actions—balancing and
traveling

the process of working through the theme. Or certain objectives may be
identified that lead to the formulation of an appropriate theme.

Theme: Identifying different body parts

Objectives: Presented with the problem of moving different body
parts, learners will demonstrate their understanding of *same* and *different* by moving different parts of their bodies.

Given the task of placing their weight on different parts of the body,
learners will select and name each different part as they solve the problem.

Given the name of a body part, learners will demonstrate their understanding by moving that part in the manner determined by the teacher
(stretching their arms, wiggling their hips, or turning their shoulders).

OR

Theme: Contrasting slow and fast movements

Objectives: Given the task of traveling while showing a change in
speed, learners will clearly display slow and fast speeds while traveling
in any manner they choose.

Given an action of the teacher's choice, learners will clearly illustrate
differences in fast and slow speeds while performing the action.

The teacher should be able to state learner objectives in behavioral
terms. For personal lesson plans, the teacher can short-cut the descriptions. The last two objectives might be written:

Show contrast while traveling.

Given action, show contrast in speed.

The environments in which the behaviors will be shown are determined or created by the teacher. Environment makes a difference. In the above examples, it is assumed that the environment is open space and that no social relationships are involved. Changing either the physical or the social environment affects the difficulty of the task, sometimes making it harder, sometimes easier.

A sample lesson

THEME: _Action and stillness_   **GRADE:** _1_

PROGRAM OBJECTIVE: _Body awareness: Control of starting and stopping actions_   **STAGE:** _1_

INSTRUCTIONAL OBJECTIVES: _Freeze after traveling; hold free body parts still while traveling; stop action of one part and start action with another_

INSTRUCTIONAL ENVIRONMENT: _Floor area_

PREINSTRUCTIONAL ACTIVITY: _In own space, move in different ways_

INITIAL TASK: _When I say "Go," travel in any way you choose; but stop moving and be like a statue when I say "Freeze!"_

CLARIFICATION: _"Freeze" means not only stop traveling, but also stop moving everything_

DEVELOPMENT 1: _In own space, move until I say "Freeze."_

CLARIFICATION: _Repeat until concept of freeze is demonstrated._

DEVELOPMENT 2: _You are a statue, but when I name a body part, move it until I say "Freeze" and name a different part._

CLARIFICATION: _Supporting parts, when named, can move and cause the person to travel, while other parts, when moved, produce gestures._

CULMINATING ACTIVITY: _Starting in own space, play Stop and Go either by moving and stopping different body parts while standing in place or by traveling to different places._

CLOSING ACTIVITY: _Observation of several individual solutions and discussion; dismissal._

The sample lesson is far more detailed than a real lesson plan for each day of every week would be. However, the lesson illustrates the relationship between program objectives and instructional or performance objectives. Note that the theme, action and stillness, focuses on the program objective, awareness of starting and stopping actions.

Assuming that the teacher has a curriculum for the elementary school physical education program, it is then the teacher's responsibility, to plan lessons that bring about the desired behaviors. The steps in planning are as follows:

1. Select the appropriate program objective according to guidelines set forth in the curriculum.
2. Decide the operational stage for each learner to determine which instructional objectives learners are presently capable of attaining.
3. Choose a theme that emphasizes specific ideas or actions.
4. Write instructional objectives for the learners.

To those unacquainted with movement-oriented physical education, it is the visible portion of the lesson that is of greatest interest. The lesson

First steps in teaching

itself starts with the preinstructional activity and ends with the culminating activity.

A short form of the sample lesson is illustrated here.

THEME: **ACTION AND STILLNESS**

Grade: 1 Stage: I (can be omitted if all classes operate at this level)

Objectives: Awareness of movement and nonmovement, in place and while traveling.

Area: Floor

PIA: Movement in self-space

T^1: Travel and freeze on command

C: Differences between stop and freeze

D^1: Gestures and freeze

D^2: Call out parts for movement and freeze

CA: Create own stop-and-go sequences in place and while traveling
Use show and tell to clarify and reinforce

This lesson plan provides all of the information in a simple form, one that can be read at a glance. It is up to the instructor to flesh out the plan through creative teaching. Clarification may require the instructor to adjust the plan. It may even be necessary to repeat parts of the lesson on the following day or to carry out half of the plan on one day and half on the next. How students respond will determine how the plan is executed. A lesson plan is only a possible plot. It assumes that all conditions will be favorable, but that is not always the case. The teacher who observes students and reads their behavior will adjust the lesson to present conditions. Experienced teachers are prepared for such departures.

Even though lesson plans are not always followed to the letter, the plan does ensure a more systematic approach to education than teaching "off the top of one's head." Program planning requires the teacher to think through the objectives and justify the inclusion of topics, actions, and ideas. Planning shows in writing how the teacher's instructional objectives are related to the program objectives of the system and the goals of education of the community.

Planning for apparatus, rhythm, and manipulation

The lesson plan format applies to areas other than the floor. The only additions that might be needed are descriptions of any equipment to be used and possibly a floor plan to illustrate arrangement of the apparatus.

There are two reasons for involving children in apparatus, rhythm, and manipulative activities. First, each of these areas is directly related to the major programs of dance, gymnastics, and games. Second, concepts introduced in a floor lesson can be reinforced and extended under different environmental circumstances. For the lesson theme, action and stillness, an introductory floor lesson might be followed by a manipulative lesson in which the children handle a ball while traveling or moving in place. Apparatus could also be used to reinforce the floor lesson, as well as to challenge learners to relate to a different environment. One rhythm adaptation to the theme would be to accompany action with the beat of a drum. Silence would mean stillness.

■ Managing the environment for physical education entails organizing both the physical and the human elements. In addition to housekeeping responsibilities to which every teacher is heir, the physical educator is responsible for deciding what kind of equipment to use, the amount to be used, how it is to be distributed or arranged, and how the children will relate to it. Use of space is another component of the physical environment. Indoor and outdoor spaces vary in size, floor or surface, shape or boundaries, and indoors, height.

Managing the environment

The human environment in physical education is also of concern to the teacher. Understanding the children and their characteristics, developmental patterns, needs, and interests are teacher responsibilities. Equipped with this knowledge, the teacher attempts to establish a warm, enabling, learning climate. The teacher also continues to observe the learners as they interact with the physical environment, with each other, and of course, with the teacher. It is the teacher who decides how the learners will be distributed in the learning environment and whether or not they have any say about it. Authoritarian practices, which are still quite prevalent in physical education, employ formations in which each student has a place. Movement from place to place is rigidly controlled, as are organizational patterns for various activities. Students make no decisions about who will be their partners. Some form of counting-off usually is used to determine that. Authoritarian teachers assume that they know what is right and that they are paid to make decisions. We obviously do not favor authoritarianism.

Discipline. When the subject of managing the human environment comes up, the word *discipline* always enters the discussion. But discipline means different things to different people. Rogers identifies three basic approaches to discipline.

1 Making children behave through the use of force
2 Inspiring them to behave through love for their teacher
3 Leading them to behave through the concept of self-responsibility[3]

Of course, there are combinations and variations on the three.

3 John R. Rogers, "Three Approaches to Discipline," *NEA Journal*, September 1958, p. 368.

Coercive discipline is probably the approach most typically used in American schools. That has been the pattern in the past, and it is one that the teachers themselves are most familiar with, having once been on the receiving end. Beating is almost a thing of the past, but there are forms of psychological coercion that can be just as damaging as physical punishment. Granted that children's immaturity may sometimes make compulsion necessary, the general attitude accompanying coercive pronouncements can do much to soften the impact. Children should be helped to understand that as they grow up they will assume greater responsibility for making decisions that are presently being made for them.

Some teachers will always seek to be idolized by their students. They use a form of love to control their subjects. It can work quite well in the lower grades, but as Rogers notes, "When the inevitable disillusionment comes, value systems suffer; children are often left with even fewer and weaker guidelines than they had in the beginning."[4] The child is unable to discipline himself, to make decisions about good and evil or right and wrong, because he has never been taught how to make these decisions for himself.

> If the goal of an individual's developmental task is that of becoming a worthy, responsible member of adult society, the essential weakness of the two previously discussed views of discipline is that each of them actually works toward the opposite goal of making children more dependent instead of less so. The most significant criterion of maturity is responsibility, and responsibility demands self-control. It does not come as a built-in feature; it must be learned. Here as elsewhere, children learn through doing; and if a discipline system is to be truly educative, it must place primary responsibility on the individual.[5]

Discipline, to be effective, must rest on self-discipline. In movement education self-discipline is essential to the fulfillment of all major learning objectives. Without it learning cannot be individualized.

Inclusion vs. exclusion. "Everybody needs to belong somewhere" is a cliché often used as a theme in popular songs. It expresses a need to identify with a place and, even more, with people who are friendly and behave like members of one's family. Children need to have this feeling in school, particularly in physical education, because it is so easy to be left out of some games and sports. The teacher must find ways to make every child feel wanted and to help all children understand this need in others so that they, too, will consider the feelings of the excluded child.

Children can make certain decisions for themselves about organizational patterns in physical education. There are times when children need to be in groups or on teams, and other times when they just need to be with a partner. Sometimes, all three patterns may be exhibited in the same lesson. This happens when some children are ready to test their skills in team competition while others are still working at the cooperative level. A few may work in partnerships or groups of threes, while others form larger

4 Ibid., p. 368.
5 Ibid.

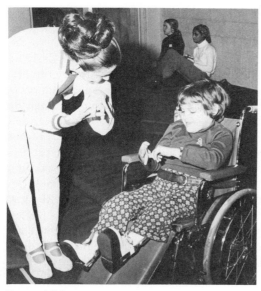

Every child can
participate in physical
education.

groups. The movement patterns may be like those exhibited in soccer or in basketball, so that children who are not ready for competition or do not want to compete are participating. They belong.

Competition does not have to be fostered in physical education to make the activities worthwhile. Manipulative skills are not limited to the competitive games. They belong in programs of gymnastics and dance as well. Why force children to withdraw from participation because they do not like to compete? Can't physical education offer alternatives to competitive social relationships?

Procedures for organizing children should be carefully considered. Left to their own devices, children will often exclude the child who talks, looks, or acts different, or is less skilled. Formal counting off is not an appropriate means either. Children should be guided in deciding who to buddy up with today. Starting at the earliest age in school, children can be encouraged to find a friend with whom to share a ball or a piece of apparatus. Sharing space and equipment is a big first step in understanding cooperation.

After children develop a few secure partner relationships, they can be encouraged to choose different partners, make new friends. When larger groups are needed, the teacher can ask partnerships to buddy up with other partnerships to make groups of four. If one pair is left over, give them the option of splitting up and joining different groups to make fives or staying together to make one group of six.

Beginning in grade 2 or grade 3, children may be organized three to a group. A threesome may operate as a partnership plus one, which is not a comfortable situation for the person left out. It should be a fully coopera-

First steps in teaching

tive relationship, with equal consideration being given to each member in the use of space and equipment. Threes joining threes form sixes, a good size for beginning team play in activities such as Keep Away.

As groups of various sizes are being formed, the values underlying membership are discussed. Children can be taught responsibility, obligation, consideration for others, sharing, trustworthiness, and cooperation in the context of meaningful social relationships. Physical education can do much to strengthen the foundations of civic responsibility and moral and ethical decision-making.

The voice and manner of the teacher. Children do not like teachers who scream at them, and they don't respond well to those who speak in a monotone. A firm, low-pitched voice, a ready smile, and approach behaviors are desirable. The approach behaviors are those that close the gap between teacher and child.

Male teachers should notice personal things about young children, such as new clothes, new shoes, a nice smile, a special monogram on the T-shirt. Their comments should often be accompanied by touching. There is nothing wrong with either a male or a female teacher giving children a hug that says "I like you," "I'm proud of you," or "I'm happy to see you back in school." Gushy, superficial, insincere, ingratiating speech turns children off.

Children read the movements of the teacher quite accurately, and they will not be fooled by speech patterns that conflict with the teacher's body language. Teachers who like children say so in the movement of their bodies. They get down to the level of the small child, display an open stance with all children, and move among them. Standing to one side with arms folded, eyes downcast or looking out over the children's heads, and a deadpan expression communicate a lot of negative feelings to children.

The child-oriented teacher will look directly at children, will say "Hi there" and mean it, will smile and laugh, and will try not to leave anybody out. He or she will be readily approachable any time during the day and will make time, if necessary, to talk to children who need private consultation. He or she will keep a confidence, "go to bat" for the child who needs special help, and speak plainly when it is necessary.

Children like teachers to dress properly. Clean, well-pressed clothing that is appropriate for the activities being taught helps to set an example— a role the teacher cannot and should not avoid. It is part of teaching.

Children like to know that their teacher is "smart," someone they can turn to for special help. The teacher, male or female, who cannot demonstrate how to throw a football or correct a front walkover will not stand as tall in the eyes of children as the one who knows everything or is willing to find out.

Children like teachers who are trustworthy. They also like teachers who are dependable. Missing appointments, breaking promises, and just plain forgetting tell children that the teacher does not really care about them.

Teachers who are always sick, who arrive just before classes start and leave early, who are always too tired or too busy stand little chance of making the child's hit parade. The teacher's voice and manner are most important personal characteristics. These are the channels of communication that run directly to the hearts of children.

The importance of observation. Management of the learning environment depends on the teacher's sensitive powers of observation. Lesson plans are mere projections, intentions to teach certain subject matter. They are based, in part, on observations of children's responses to previous lessons. But, to be effective, lesson plans should be considered guidelines rather than dictums. Each part of the lesson lends itself to particular kinds of observations.

Even before the preinstructional activity begins, the teacher may make some valuable observations. How the children enter class may indicate that a slight change in plans is necessary. Children kept in their seats, denied a supervised play break, or repressed in some other way will usually provide clear signals that they need release from a few tensions before they will be ready for a lesson. The preinstructional activity is not a time for the teacher to relax and just let the children play. The playing is all right, but what the children do, how they do it, and with whom or with what should be noted by the teacher. How do the children behave when given free choice? What apparatus do they prefer? What apparatus do they neglect? Where in the available space do the children go? Who seems to

Finding a space away
from others

be left out, who is a spectator rather than a participant? Are children applying principles taught in previous lessons? The answers to these questions will furnish strong direction for the lesson in progress as well as for future lessons.

The body of the lesson, the tasks that challenge the children to move, is another source for observations. Is the lesson fun as well as challenging? Are any children copying others instead of thinking for themselves? When asked to find a space away from others, do some children continue to stay near? The teacher can adjust the lesson to meet some of the children's special needs.

As the teacher observes children participating in the culminating activity, be it a game, dance, gymnastics sequence, or creative movement, it will be rather obvious from their behaviors how successful the lessons have been. This is when the teacher gets graded. Shortcomings on the part of the learner should be translated into future lessons. Are the children performing at an acceptable level? Do they use the organizational patterns offered them? Are there weaknesses in their cooperative behaviors that need immediate attention? Do the children apply their knowledge, understanding, and skills in appropriate ways? The instructor will use these observations to make changes, if necessary, in tomorrow's plans.

The flexible use of environments for lessons. Most basic movement lessons are best introduced as floor activities. However, teachers should consider other environments that might suit the purpose of the movement lesson better.

Draping a parachute over a piece of standard apparatus can create interesting spaces and tunnels for young children. Drum sounds or music may be used in conjunction with apparatus work or manipulative lessons. Through the creative use of materials, even just plain junk may make drab environments more stimulating.

Challenging the children to improve. Children want to grow and develop. They thrive on success and will work hard to improve themselves with very little urging. Challenging children to improve is part of the physical education lesson. To respond to the challenge, the child needs to know where he is in relation to where he is going. A teacher who keeps children posted on the progress they have made maintains continual motivation. Because improvement is a personal matter, the teacher must be able to evaluate individual improvement as well as improvement in group endeavors.

Deciding what to teach

■ Many beginning teachers are concerned about what to teach. Physical education activities are most often viewed as games—organized, structured activities that include every child in the class in some formation. Organized games for children often are a waste of time because they provide little activity for most of the children most of the time. In circle games, only two or three children are active at any given time, yet these games are the most popular with teachers who like to exercise rigid control. Relay races are popular also, but they test both the skilled and the unskilled children in pursuit of the same objective: to win the race.

Showing consideration
for others

Playing games will not solve the problem of what to teach beginning students in a movement-oriented physical education program. There is a host of alternatives that will help the teacher develop primary, affective program objectives. Children need to learn how to approach a task, how to listen, how to show consideration for others, and how to operate in a safe manner. Games test skills; they have limited value in teaching. To learn, children must have countless experiences that structured games do not provide. The teacher must look to other activities for movement-oriented lessons that are appropriate for beginning students.

Children at play exhibit four kinds of activity.

1 Exploratory movements help children adapt themselves to different surfaces, to overcome obstacles, to test ability to manage objects, and to relate to partners or groups.

2 Skilled movements of set form are executed by children to achieve greater skill or to test themselves—those that demonstrate how far, how high, or how accurately they can perform.

3 Competitive play tests the skills of individuals in partnerships or groups to see who is the best, the fastest, the strongest—who is the most highly skilled.

4 Creative movements, structured by fantasy and imagination, range from "let's pretend" activities to all kinds of improvisational playing, singing and dancing, chanting, and rhyming.

Lessons built around these four categories of activity find ready participants. Affective objectives are given full range as the teacher interacts with the children during the lesson. Learning to play together, to move for the fun of moving, to explore and savor the satisfaction of doing some-

First steps in teaching

thing different or mastering a new skill are important to these lessons because they are meaningful objectives for children. As children gain mastery over themselves through movement, the teacher will find them increasingly responsive to further exploration, to new situations with new problems, and to reinvestigations of the familiar in different settings.

Options for the outdoor lesson. Lesson ideas may develop from the natural urge to explore one's environment. The school grounds often remain unexplored by children who arrive and leave by bus. There may be grassy areas, hills, trees, hardtop surfaces, and sand. In these settings, children may be challenged to

1 show how they perform different actions, such as running, jumping in different ways, climbing, swinging, and rolling.
2 show how they can manipulate different objects, such as balls, ropes, and hoops.
3 show how they can improvise activity in pairs or small groups.
4 practice skills of their choice, such as throwing and catching, batting and fielding, shooting baskets, jumping rope, hand balancing, or high jumping.

There is no format or rule for these lessons. Teachers need to respond on the basis of their observations. The guidelines are simple. Encourage self-expression, observe and respond with praise to successful performances, and further urge children to improve on quality, to find other ways, to develop sequences or patterns. One of these responses usually will lead children into another round of activity. When in doubt, ask the children. Let them suggest activities and find ways to carry out all suggestions within any limits that the teacher feels must be imposed.

Options for the indoor lesson. It is important to have full-sized gymnasiums in elementary schools where children can have enough space to exercise their bodies through a variety of movements. Large-muscle activity, so important to growth and development, requires a spacious environment. Most elementary schools have limited indoor space. Some offer combination cafeterias and gymnasiums (sometimes even auditoriums), while others have nothing but hallways and classrooms for indoor activities.

However, the teacher should be able to find ways to adapt the following activities to the amount of space available by imposing specific limitations to avoid damage to property or person. The teacher may challenge the children to

1 show different ways of performing actions, such as jumping, sliding, and skipping around obstacles (chairs and tables, rug samples or plastic containers scattered about).
2 show different ways of handling a ball so that it does not touch the furniture by carefully controlling its rolling or bouncing motions.
3 create simple action patterns to the accompaniment of folk music, the sound of a drum, or the clapping of hands or other body parts.
4 make up simple target or accuracy games using paper cups and plates, yarn balls and wastebaskets, homemade quoits, or other improvised equipment.

Using ropes to mark
the boundaries

5 make up games using the squares of the tile floor, lines or other floor markings, or ropes stretched to make spaces and places.

6 work with a partner in activities such as balancing, pulling or pushing contests, doing same or opposite actions; play Follow-the-Leader in creatively self-structured play forms, for example, when one is a mouse, the other is a cat, or when one is the horse, the other the rider. (But let the children decide for themselves. They may have other ways of perceiving the relationships.)

■ If, throughout the previous discussion, you have been thinking in terms of specific lesson outcomes such as learning to play a particular game or execute a particular skill or dance step, this section should remind you that activities are merely vehicles. The beginner is not ready for systematic learning experiences in either psychomotor or cognitive activities. True, psychomotor and cognitive activities are employed; but the desired outcomes are better listening skills, improved consideration for the rights of others, and ability to carry out activities without being easily distracted or showing off. When these objectives are attained, emphasis shifts to cognitive and psychomotor outcomes, and not before.

Beginning lessons are means to affective objectives

Maintaining one's perspective

Children differ as much in their learning styles as they do in their temperaments. Physical education can put great strain on young children when the activities are too highly structured, too demanding for their ability levels, or too free, requiring decision-making skills they have not yet developed.

Not all children are agreeably cute, clean, and sweet talking. Not all children listen intently, operate without distraction, show persistence, or

First steps in teaching

move eagerly from activity to activity. Yet the teacher must relate to all children—those with clean shiny faces and those with runny noses, those with nice new clothes and those with worn, patched clothes. Some children may even speak a language foreign to the ear of a middle-class teacher whose upbringing has not only taught the teacher values that make certain behaviors of the children confusing or conflicting but also protected the teacher from the kinds of experiences that the children discuss so glibly. Still, the teacher is a teacher of all of the children.

The teacher's first objective should be to establish a learning environment in which all of the children can function comfortably, in which every child is valued, every child has a chance to move forward toward self-chosen goals, however vague and nebulous they may be to begin with. Looking at physical education from the perspective of self-achievement rather than winning and losing games is an important first step in movement learning and one that needs to be amplified and followed through on by every teacher.

The transition from level 1.0 to level 2.0

■ The transition from Level 1.0 to Level 2.0 objectives is not marked by a sudden change in lesson emphasis. Changes occur slowly. One class here and another there in a school in which all begin at the first level will demonstrate their readiness to learn movement vocabulary and begin development of body management skills in games, dances, gymnastics, and the like. As you become aware of positive changes in listening behaviors and in following directions, you begin to structure the lessons to accomplish objectives that require these abilities. Present the children with interesting movement problems and different game, dance, or self-testing activities. Successful accomplishment will be a reward for the good listener. The good listener has more fun and does more in a class period. As children become

Demonstrating
cooperation with
a partner

aware of the good things that happen to good listeners, they become even better listeners.

When children demonstrate cooperation, consideration for others, and concern for safety, similar changes in movement challenges may follow. Cooperation and consideration for others may lead to more opportunities for free exploration or for repetition of a favorite activity. Consideration for others also may lead to challenging space relationship activities, more opportunities for ball handling perhaps, and time to do things with partners. Concern for one's safety is a particularly important prerequisite for increased challenges using apparatus.

Operating safely
within limitations

■ Experienced teachers know that upper-level classes in elementary school are not always ready for upper-level objectives. Inadequate or poor foundations for advanced physical education, whatever the reason, can leave children in the upper grades unprepared for the responsibilities required of them. Poor listening skills are often accompanied by unruly behavior, unwillingness to try anything new or different, and inconsiderate, discourteous behavior to others. The temptation to be "tough on them" is strong, but that does not work. True, the reins have to be pulled in tight, but what these children need is activity, lots of it.

The teacher who can say "C'mon kids, let's go" and lead them in a brief run, in some one-on-one games, or in some prowess challenges will probably do a better job than one who stands back and gives orders. Level 1.0 objectives have priority. Whatever activities are used, they are vehicles for the achievement of the number one program objective—to establish an en-

Level 1.0 objectives for upper-level classes

First steps in teaching

vironment conducive to learning. There are many ways to approach this objective. "Let's go out and play *together*" is the first step. The second is, do it and use the opportunity to let the children know their physical education teacher is interested in them, first as people and then as students. Opportunities to teach will follow in due time. Teach minilessons during parts of class periods in which a few members of the class participate in instruction while others cling to their games or random activities like security blankets. If these activities were not important to them, they would not be so insistent on sticking to the old in preference to the new. Play the game or games with them is our best advice. It is too late to change their behaviors dramatically. Patience will be rewarded with change quicker than sudden installation of new programs. In time the children will come to trust you, to respect your decisions, and to depend on you for guidance in learning as much as possible, now that they know they can learn, that they have possibilities, and that they do not all have to learn the same thing to the same level of competence to "pass."

Fear of failure is strong among the upper-level classes in so many schools. Children seem to want to know where they stand and at the same time to fear that that knowledge will hurt them. A positive, no-nonsense approach is to say, "You have the potential to learn. You can do it, and I am going to do my very best to help you." Such an attitude will help these children become good listeners, avoid inconsiderate behaviors in the interest of cooperation, and stop displaying attention-seeking conduct that disrupts learning. Once they have achieved these Level 1.0 skills, they are ready to learn the second-level cognitive and psychomotor skills that are so important to them when they are about to enter the junior high school years.

Remember: Let's go out and play together is the first step.

Assignments

1

Visit a local elementary school to observe physical education instruction. Identify the following:
a. The program area (movement, games, dances, gymnastics).
b. The operational stage of the children (level 1.0 or level 2.0).
c. The primary teaching style of the instructor (command- or guidance-oriented).
d. Observable objectives of the lesson.
e. Ability of the children to manage lesson objectives.
f. The culminating activity.
g. Management behaviors of the teacher (organization of the class for instruction; procedure for getting, distributing, and returning supplies and equipment; discipline problem management; dismissal procedures).

2

Observe a group of children at play in either a formal or informal situation, and identify instances in which individual children are clearly behaving in any of the following ways:
a. Showing consideration for other's space or equipment needs by sharing or moving out of the way.
b. Showing self-discipline by working on a problem independently.
c. Making decisions about what to do on a piece of apparatus and demonstrating concern for his and others' safety.
d. Practicing or repeatedly using one or more skills in an appropriate manner.

3

Write performance or instructional objectives according to Banathy's guidelines for the following:
a. Learning basketball skills.
b. Rolling to prevent injury after a fall.
c. Balancing in different ways.
d. Getting a piece of equipment and returning it to place.

4

Write one performance objective for the following program objective: At the conclusion of primary level instruction, children should demonstrate competency in the execution of fundamental locomotor patterns.

5

Using the format for a movement lesson described in this chapter, write a lesson plan for primary children on the theme, Listening and moving.

6
Present the following movement as problems in question form:
a. Skipping.
b. Getting from one place to another.
c. Changing the shape of the body.
d. Avoiding collision while running.
e. Using all of the space.
f. Using the space in the corners.
g. Changing speed.
h. Experiencing sustainment.
i. Doing something with a partner.
j. Getting balls out of a container in an orderly fashion.
k. Finding a place to put one's shoes on.
l. Throwing overhand at a target.

Readings

● Beginning teachers or experienced teachers in search of a fresh approach will find good ideas in the following books.

Braley, William T.; Konicki, Geraldine; and Leedy, Catherine. *Daily Sensorimotor Training Activities.* 1968. Educational Activities, Freeport, N.Y. 11520.

An activities book designed for teachers and parents of preschool children, it has lots of ideas for body management lessons that can be converted to problem-solving tasks. Specific suggestions with illustrations are given for activities to enhance body image, space and direction awareness, balance, coordination, form perception, and other similar activities.

Clark, Carol E. *Rhythmic Activities for the Classroom.* 1969. The Instructor Publications, Dansville, N.Y. 14437.

Ideas for movement exploration, singing games and folk dances, creative rhythms, relaxation, and resources.

Cratty, Bryant J. *Active Learning.* 1971. Prentice-Hall, Englewood Cliffs, N.J. 07632.

Aimed at enhancing academic abilities through games, many of the activities are adaptable as culminating activities to movement learning lessons using a problem-solving approach. Classroom teachers will find this book an invaluable aid to lesson planning for children experiencing difficulties in the academic areas.

Diem, Liselott. *Who Can . . .,* American Edition, 1965. Wilhelm Limpert, Publisher, Frankfort A.M./ Germany.

A simple booklet with a host of good ideas for the development of body management and manipulative skills. Activities with balls, hoops, wands, ropes, ladders, boxes, beams, and partners. Well illustrated, this booklet presents movement challenges for children at all levels and stages of development.

Hackett, Layne C. *Movement Exploration and Games for the Mentally Retarded.* 1970. Peek Publications, 164 E. Dana St., Mountain View, Calif. 94040.

With a foreword of appreciation for the practicality of the book by Julian U. Stein, the book presents movement exploration as a problem-solving approach to activities for the mentally retarded, both trainable and educable. Excellent ideas for movement challenges for other academic ability levels are recognized in the easy to read instructions. Includes a rationale for movement exploration as a method of teaching the retarded.

———, and Jenson, Robert G. *A Guide to Movement Exploration,* 1966. Peek Publications.

A booklet that presents many excellent ideas for activities utilizing the problem-solving approach. Includes hints for the teacher on classroom management techniques, the phrasing of questions, discipline, and lesson plans.

Joyce, Mary. *First Steps in Teaching Dance.* 1973. National Press Books, 850 Hansen Way, Palo Alto, Calif. 94304.

An excellent first book in dance with lots of ideas related to exploration. A complete book; chapters are devoted to such topics as theory, method, and lessons, with concluding notes on resources.

Kirchner, Glenn; Cunningham, Jean; and Warrell, Eileen. *Introduction to Movement Education.* 1970. Wm. C. Brown Co. Publishers, Dubuque, Iowa 52001.

Well illustrated, thorough in the primary elements of movement education, the book demonstrates the authors' broad background in using the challenge approach to movement in physical education. Instructional methods, curricular ideas, and a discussion of the values of movement education are followed by lesson plans using themes for primary and intermediate grades. Includes an excellent appendix on resources and construction ideas.

Rowen, Betty. *Learning Through Movement.* 1963. Teachers College Press, Teachers College, Columbia University, New York, N.Y. 10027.

One of the earliest American text books on movement, it is heavily oriented toward dance but includes interdisciplinary materials in the areas of math, science, and language. Suited more to the classroom teacher or the music specialist, the book does contain some meaningful material for the specialist in physical education, particularly the beginning chapters on creativity, language, and movement.

Taylor, Carla. *Rhythm, A Guide for Creative Movement.* Peek Publications, 1974.

Easy dance steps are well described in this book for the classroom teacher or specialist with limited background in creative dance for children. The introduction is especially helpful, but the reader will not be able to stop there.

First steps in teaching

Chapter VII

Movement learning lessons

Classrooms themselves must be
"good societies" on a small scale.
The school must emphasize sharing and
helping in an atmosphere of mutual trust
where everyone can experience a
feeling of oneness.

*Perceiving, Behaving,
Becoming*
ASCD Yearbook 1962,
p. 166

■ It is hard to establish a working atmosphere in the physical education laboratory without certain frustrations and disappointments. Children are not predictable. Just when everything seems to be working right, they have a "bad day." It is just like starting over from the beginning; the fact that it is not a beginning, but just a different set of circumstances, sometimes makes it easier for the teacher to manage. Then they move forward again for a few days or a week until there is another relapse. It is all part of the process.

Another frustration, oftentimes all too evident, is the reluctance of the school principal to accept change. If the present physical education program emphasizes competition and games, the principal may not look with favor upon a less authoritarian structure. The idea that children can solve problems in physical education may not seem feasible to an ex-athlete who never clarified the distinction between athletics and physical education and who accepted submissiveness to authority as part of the "game." Goals other than striving to win may seem out of place to a person who equates physical education solely with activities on the playing field. To replace that frame of reference with one that insists that awareness of motion factors, cooperative learning, and problem solving are at the heart of physical education may take awhile. The easiest route may be to convince the principal that many more children will turn to athletics when they discover their movement potential and that others will gain a deeper appreciation of movement through learning how to move more efficiently.

Classroom teachers often consider themselves to be the school custodians of all things intellectual. After all, they have the textbooks and workbooks that purport to be the instruments for learning about science,

Learning how to
move efficiently

mathematics, geography, and other interesting subjects. And they are right, up to a point. But learning takes place in any environment that facilitates thinking, including the environment of playground and gymnasium.

**Stage I,
level 2.0
objectives**

■ To learn the vocabulary associated with movement is the first goal. Thinking is facilitated through the ability to manipulate symbols, and the symbols of movement express actions or ideas associated with the direction and qualities associated with action. Communication between teacher and child, between child and child, and between the child and his own personal understanding requires mental images that are fairly fixed as verbal expressions. The greater the experience with a given verbal expression, the more significant the meaning attached to it becomes. Developing these cognitive images of action, space, and effort relationships is the major goal of a well-conceived movement education program. The images formed become part of a totality seen in the mind and felt in the body, a oneness of understanding that contributes to further understanding as words and actions clarify the direction of the learning sequence.

Chapter V identified and defined the essential words in the vocabulary of movement under the four aspects of awareness of body, space, effort, and relationship. Before proceeding any further in the direction of the understandings essential to basic movement or movement-oriented physical education, a brief description of the cognitive domain is in order so that the reader will have an operational definition of the relationship between content and thinking behaviors.

Balancing on three
body parts

■ The *Taxonomy of Educational Objectives, Handbook I: Cognitive Domain*, edited by Bloom, identifies six categories of thinking behaviors in a hierarchy of educational goals. Each of the classes of behaviors is identified below, along with a brief description of thinking abilities and skills as described in the taxonomy.

Knowledge

Knowledge as defined here, involves the recall of specifics and universals, the recall of methods and processes, or the recall of a pattern, structure or setting. . . The knowledge objectives emphasize most the psychological processes of remembering.[1]

This category includes knowledge of specifics, terminology, facts, methods of inquiry, correct technique (conventions), sequence, the arrangement of participants, criteria used for judging, high levels of abstraction, and principles and generalizations.

The other five categories, according to the authors of the *Taxonomy of Educational Objectives,* are classed as "abilities and skills."

Abilities and skills refer to organized modes of operation and generalized techniques for dealing with materials and problems. The materials and problems may be of such a nature that little or no specialized and technical information is required. Such information as is required can be assumed

---

1 Benjamin S. Bloom, ed., *Taxonomy of Educational Objectives, Handbook I: Cognitive Domain.* (New York: McKay, 1956), p. 201.

to be part of the individual's general fund of knowledge. Other problems may require specialized and technical information at a rather high level such that specific knowledge and skill in dealing with the problem and the materials are required. The abilities and skills objectives emphasize the mental processes of organizing and reorganizing material to achieve a particular purpose. The materials may be given or remembered.[2]

Abilities and skills include the following objectives in hierarchical order.

Comprehension

This is the lowest level of understanding, that requires apprehension of what is being communicated and the ability to make use of the material but not how it relates to other material.

"Comprehension" includes the abilities to translate movement vocabulary into appropriate actions and vice versa; to interpret a communication (for example, a poem) through movement; to extrapolate the consequences of a sequence of actions or strategies in gymnastics, dance, or games or to grasp the theme of an interrelated group of actions.

Application

The use of abstractions in particular and concrete situations. The abtractions may be in the form of general ideas, rules of procedures, or generalized methods. The abstractions may also be technical principles, ideas, and theories which must be remembered and applied.[3]

"Application" includes the ability (1) to apply rules to a game or other competition; (2) to apply principles of movement to solution of movement problems; (3) to apply the laws of motion to experimental and pragmatic situations in sport, dance, and gymnastics; (4) to employ experimental procedures to problems in moving under adverse physical, social, or psychological conditions; and (5) to apply "principles of democratic group action to participation in group and social situations."[4]

Analysis

The breakdown of a communication into its constituent elements or parts such that the relative hierarchy of ideas is made clear and/or the relations between the ideas expressed are made explicit. Such analyses are intended to clarify the communication, to indicate how the communication is organized, and the way in which it manages to convey its effects, as well as its basis and arrangement.[5]

"Analysis" includes the ability (1) to identify or classify the elements within an activity, movement pattern, or skill and (2) to identify the relationships in competitive and noncompetitive activities; between major parts of an activity, pattern, or skill; or between elements and the main theme or purpose. It includes, also, the ability to perform an analysis of

2 Ibid., p. 204.
3 Ibid., p. 205.
4 Ibid., p. 124.
5 Ibid., p. 205.

organizational principles, such as identifying the structure of a dance composition or the underlying principles of offense and defense in a single game or a series of contests.

Synthesis

The putting together of elements and parts so as to form a whole. This involves the process of working with pieces, parts, elements, etc., and arranging and combining them in such a way as to constitute a pattern or structure not clearly there before.[6]

"Synthesis" includes creative behavior "within the limits set by particular problems, materials, or some theoretical and methodological framework."[7] Involves drawing together elements from various sources to put together a composition, pattern, activity, or other structure not clearly in evidence before. Products resulting from synthesis range from unique combinations of elements carried on for their own sakes to instructional plans to carry out such operations as learning new gymnastics skills, dance steps, and other skills in pursuit of specific goals to the highest level of creative expression, in which the student produces or derives a set of abstract relationships such as might occur in the creation of original compositions in dance based upon principles abstracted from nature, technology, the arts and other forms, properties, or constructions.

Evaluation

Judgments about the value of material and methods for given purposes. Quantitative and qualitative judgments about the extent to which material and methods satisfy criteria. Use of a standard of appraisal. The criteria may be those determined by the student or those which are given to him.[8]

"Evaluation" is the terminal level of cognitive behavior because, to a certain extent, it involves the use of the preceding thinking skills. Sometimes evaluation is an earlier step; for example, it may precede analysis. Evaluations are often merely opinions and judgments given with little consideration for criteria. "For purposes of classification, only those evaluations which are or can be made with distinct criteria in mind are considered. Such evaluations are highly conscious and ordinarily are based on a relatively adequate comprehension and analysis of the phenomena to be appraised."[9] This may sound as if opinions do not count. As a matter of fact, the purpose of education is to enlighten, to broaden the bases upon which judgments are made.

Included in the category of evaluation is the ability to apply given criteria (1) to a composition in dance or gymnastics, (2) to offensive or defensive team play, (3) to specific performances relative to certain standards or principles, (4) and to movement behaviors purporting to increase

6 Ibid., p. 206.
7 Ibid., p. 162.
8 Ibid., p. 207.
9 Ibid., p. 186.

efficiency, promote well-being, or prepare the individual for future endeavors. Evaluation also includes the ability to apply internal standards to such work as a dance composition, in which logical relationships present themselves in an effort to communicate with the viewer. Is it accurate, *carefully done,* consistent? How?

Suggested objectives

Identification of attainable cognitive objectives is important. Major areas in which objectives appropriate to Stage I movement learning experiences may be found are indicated by the general statements of program objectives listed below. The instructor should find it relatively easy to design instructional objectives for physical education lessons that lead to acquisition of the behaviors described.

A learner who has successfully completed Stage I in movement learning exhibits these behaviors.

1 Knows or understands and responds appropriately to
  Directions for listening
  Words denoting place in space (relationship)
  Basic movement terminology (from the four aspects)
  Fundamental movement terms (i.e., walk, hop, swing)
  Rules of games and other activities
  Teacher-imposed restraints to ensure safety and a disciplined learning environment
2 Demonstrates understanding of
  Same and *different*
  Basic concepts of pattern and sequence
  Principles of balance and unbalance as related to the learner's own action or stillness behaviors
  The creation and dissipation of force through muscular activity
  Basic principles related to the characteristics and/or flight of an object (i.e., thrown ball, trajectory)
  Terms and fundamental patterns or sequences associated with games, dance, gymnastics, and aquatics (concept of offense, steps, stunts, strokes)
  The relationship of environmental conditions to activity (temperature, size of group, height of apparatus, type of surface, boundaries)
3 Generalizes understandings of movement terms and restraints to movement conduct by
  Applying movement terms learned in one environmental situation to other environmental situations (space concepts in a floor environment applied to an apparatus environment, for example)
  Applying rules of play or directions from one activity to another similar activity (application of offensive concepts in soccer to offense in basketball, of circling in folk dance to circle activity in square dance)
4 Operates subjectively in basic movement by
  Applying basic movement concepts to movement problem-solving situations (increases force if necessary; changes level, direction, or re-

lationship; manipulates other variables appropriately in efforts to achieve a satisfactory solution)

Identifying the what, where, and how characteristics of another learner's movements, either through words or with a matching presentation

Being able to discuss what one is doing, where in space the movement is going, and the qualities of the action

5 Operates objectively through purposeful movement in a manner that demonstrates knowledge and understanding by

Playing according to the rules of a game the learner has created or one created by another student or the teacher

Executing actions that denote understanding of offensive and defensive strategy affecting the spatial relationships of the activity

There are other possible objectives. But these five impress us as being of prime importance. The preceding list is meant to serve as a guideline not only to the preparation of instructional objectives but also to the possible inclusion of other program objectives.

Objective 1 aims at satisfying the question, "What is the least the learner should know by the end of the first stage of movement learning?"

Objective 2 emphasizes understandings that the learner may not be able to verbalize but that may be demonstrated through movement. For example, a child throws a ball at a certain angle to achieve a desired distance. When a set of movements is shown to children, such as walk, jump, cartwheel, they can identify similarity and difference; that is, the first two require the feet alone and the latter also requires use of the hands for support. As children catch a heavy ball, their hands give with the object to absorb the force; if their throws do not reach the target, they find a way to increase the force behind the throw. Children's participation in activity is governed by their understandings of concepts appropriate to the activities.

Objective 3 demonstrates the generalized understanding of the learner. Instead of having to be told the specific concepts that apply to each new environmental circumstance, the learner demonstrates understanding by applying spatial or other concepts learned in one area to another area. Children perceive space as having three dimensions, as surrounding objects as well as their own bodies, as being capable of transformation into various shapes through the manipulation or placement of their bodies, the bodies of others, or objects. When a rule for one activity is learned, it is applied in appropriate circumstances to a similar but different activity.

Tagging behaviors, for example, are covered by rules to protect the tagger and the person being tagged; these rules apply regardless of the game. The "keep-away" concept of soccer offense applies to basketball, also, despite the fact that different skills are employed under quite different environmental circumstances. Relationship and formation concepts in structured forms of dance are generalized, so that terms learned in one dance are carried into later dances where additional concepts are learned. In gymnastics there are similar generalized concepts. The roll on the balance beam is similar conceptually to the roll on the mat, although much more difficult: weight is transferred to the adjacent body segment along a curved back with other body parts providing support or counterbalance when required. The concept of a swing is generalized to include a swing from suspension as well as from support.

Objective 4 is subjectively oriented. The concepts are flavored by personal bias and students' emotional backgrounds. Concepts of time, weight, and space are applied in a literal representation of the students' comprehension. They discuss movements in terms of their own feelings, their perceptions of the nature of the movement problem, or what they consider to be important. While viewing another's movements, students are able to translate these movements quite accurately into words or, if called upon, into matching actions.

Objective 5 has an outward focus. Children are able to deal with concepts relevant to what is happening outside their own bodies. They are able to comprehend changes in relationships, action qualities, and movements as exhibited by the play of others and the movements of objects. They can structure activities for themselves (or include others) and operate within the framework of the rules created. If necessary, children can change the rules to better meet the objectives of the activity. At this stage, children are beginning to make moderate application of their understandings.

To summarize briefly, Stage I of movement learning operations consists of acquiring ways of thinking about movement and movement problems as well as specifics of movement terminology and the terminology associated with relevant activity. Important to the first stage of learning is acquisition of knowledge that enables the child to become a learner. Learning how to follow directions must have priority over the demand that directions be followed.

Learning to follow
directions

■ Level 1.0 objectives do not include psychomotor or cognitive objectives beyond those essential to the establishment of a proper learning environment. Each instructor will have to decide which instructional objectives have priority. What rules, if any, does the learner have to remember? What motor behaviors, if any, are immediately important?

In some physical education situations, it may be very important for children to learn and abide by rules meant to assure minimal interference with neighboring classes. In addition, many playrooms and gymnasiums are quite unsafe for active play. Windows with breakable glass, posts in the play area, painted concrete or tile floors, boundary lines close to walls, and equipment left along the walls because of lack of storage space require establishment of appropriate rules and movement modification. Quick stopping skills, modified throwing patterns, and careful changes of direction may be important to learn.

Level 2.0 objectives include the following from the psychomotor domain.

1 Control of starting and stopping actions.
2 Ability to land properly with flexion to absorb shock.
3 Safety rolling in all directions after landing from a fall or unbalanced landing to dissipate the force.
4 Ability to "give" with the hands in catching an object to absorb the force of throw or kick.
5 All fundamental locomotor, nonlocomotor, suspension, and manipulative patterns corresponding to the present developmental stage of the child. (Preschoolers, primary, intermediate, and junior high age groups have different needs.)
6 Specific tool skills that enable children to function effectively or efficiently in activities appropriate to their age group and relevant to the cultural bias in sport and dance or other play forms. In general, provision must be made for children to learn the correct forms of skills most highly valued by the peer group which the child is about to enter. In some locations great value is placed upon the ability of boys to throw, catch, kick, and bat, whereas in other locations skating and skills associated with hockey are important. With the increasing interest in sports for girls, attention should be given to early and proper instruction for sports-minded girls. If taught properly, folk dances and square dances add fun and opportunities to strengthen relationship concepts while acquiring specific footwork and pattern skills.

■ When the affective, cognitive, and psychomotor objectives for Stage I are attained, the learner is able to go to the Stage II tasks, which require a more sustained ability to apply the principles of movement to the solution of problems than was previously necessary. Before children proceed to the second stage, they must first demonstrate the following traits and abilities as learners.

1 Self-discipline, respect for the rights of others and a positive attitude toward learning.

Decision making

2 A clear understanding of basic terminology and related concepts as demonstrated by the accuracy with which they employ their knowledge in solving problems presented by the instructor.

3 Functional fitness and safe self-management in a variety of environments, including apparatus and objects difficult to control, such as a ball.

These children are good movers and are ready to proceed to the more complex challenges of the next stage of movement learning. This stage, identified as Stage II, consists of three levels of work within each lesson. Stage I, level 2.0, explores the possibilities for movement without concern on the part of the instructor for refinement of whatever has been discovered. It is enough simply for the child to enjoy his newly found movement possibility. Having finally discovered how to jump with two feet from a small box, it is enough for the elated preschooler to have the opportunity to repeat it many times without being concerned with efforts to make it more efficient or attractive. Even older children need time to enjoy the fruits of simple discoveries or they will lose their spontaneity of movement, and their enjoyment of "going to gym" will diminish. At the Stage II level, however, children want to be engaged in something more than mere exploration.

The ESR process

Stage II lessons consist of three steps that may take a number of lesson episodes to complete before moving on to a new theme.

1 New ideas or actions are *explored* to discover as much about them as possible. The previously acquired understandings are used to increase the absorption of new understandings. When the instructor is satisfied that children have had sufficient time to explore the possibilities, the next step is taken.

2 The *selection and sequencing* of desired ideas or actions are stimulated through appropriate instructor-given challenges. In the process, the

learner discards some ideas or actions and retains others. The end product is a sequence ready for the next step.

3 *Refinement* through repetition, changes and additions, and efforts to smooth out the sequence is the final step. The end product is, at the very least, a movement phrase with a clear beginning and a clear ending. It has an appropriate rhythm and spatial design.

The ESR (Exploration—Selection—Refinement) process that results in sequences is employed for all learning environments. Sequences on the floor by one's self or with partners; using light equipment, apparatus, or objects; and in relation to sound lead to increasingly longer sequences with more complex shapes and dynamic qualities. Some sequences may be completely creative, while others utilize traditional skills in either expressive or efficient ways.

Learners who undergo this type of learning experience may attain sufficient competency to move on to Stage III, at least in certain areas of interest. Stage III learners are those able to operate without the direct assistance of the instructor. In fact, they are at the stage where they perceive movement problems that need solution and go ahead with the ESR process without instructor intervention. Lessons that are student planned (in part at first, and increasingly more so, until entire lessons are under control of the students) lead to Stage III behavioral competency. Of course, some children will operate in this fashion outside of the regular instructional periods and should be encouraged to do so. Intramural activities offer opportunities for the development of Stage III competencies.

ESR in evaluation

The ESR pattern of instruction provides a built-in method of evaluating the instructional program. The sequences are developed within the limitations presented by the instructor at Stage II and by the learner at Stage III. It should be noted that when the psychomotor outcomes of instruction in the developmental movement track are compared with the cognitive outcomes of the basic movement track, *the common denominator is a movement sequence.* The sequence in basic movement demonstrates awareness and/or knowledge of certain elements, while sequence in developmental movement demonstrates skillful use of the body as the instrument for movement.

A useful schematic to clarify the relationship of all the factors relevant to ESR is shown in figure 7.1.

Another useful relationship may be observed in figure 7.2, in which the initial theme for work with young children is often action and stillness. These early lessons foster awareness of the difference between movement and nonmovement and lead to the related concepts of beginning, or start, of a movement and ending, or stop, of a movement. In between the start and the stop is the action of the movement, whatever it may be. This simple framework is the same one that the concept of sequence is built on. A sequence is a simple movement phrase of at least two actions. Initial steps in progression involve increasing the length of the sequence. Hitching

Fig. 7.1

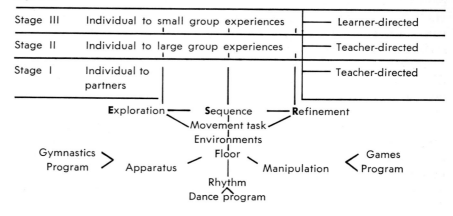

Stage III	Individual to small group experiences	—— Learner-directed
Stage II	Individual to large group experiences	—— Teacher-directed
Stage I	Individual to partners	—— Teacher-directed

Exploration —— Sequence —— Refinement
Movement task
Environments

Gymnastics Program > Apparatus — Floor \ Manipulation < Games Program

Rhythm
Dance program

Fig. 7.2

Action

```
S        S                                    S        S
T        T                                    T        T
I        A _____ O      I
L        R                                    P        L
L        T                                             L
N                                                      N
E                                                      E
S                                                      S
S                                                      S
```

STILLNESS .... STILLNESS

SEQUENCE   MODIFYING ELEMENTS

Skills,   Space: Direction, level, pathway
composition or   Effort: Speed, force, rhythm
play patterns

sequences together, specifying pathways, and eventually constructing a complete pattern, routine, or composition are future steps to take.

The following section describes lesson modules—time blocks—that may be linked to form a lesson composed either of different learning environments for the basic movement track or of different programs within the developmental movement track, or that may be a combination of both tracks. Such a format is a useful scheme for accomplishing objectives not feasible under more traditional lesson planning procedures, but it is not suitable for the kindergarten or the first half of first grade.

The modular lesson plan

■ Two or more time periods may be linked together to constitute a lesson. It is recommended that two modules form the lesson plan in basic movement education. The theme's concepts are introduced and then developed in the first part of the lesson, using only the floor surface. In the second part of the lesson, the very same concepts are explored again and developed in relation to a different physical and/or social environment. A change in the physical environment is most often recommended for children up to grade 2. Apparatus, sounds, or objects to manipulate will stimulate additional exploration of a concept along the same lines as when only the floor surface was involved.

Stage I children focus mainly on exploration until they demonstrate their readiness for tasks that require selection and organization of movement ideas, actions, or a combination of both. The modules of their lessons permit a wide variety of exploratory experiences.

Stage II children explore, select and sequence, and finally refine their ideas or actions. Rather than exploring different environments every time they come to physical education, the first three days of exploration may be repeated to provide time for sequencing and refinement. Under these circumstances, the shortest instructional unit would be nine lessons long (fig. 7.3).

Fig. 7.3

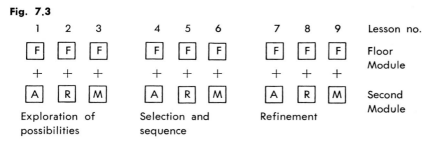

The second module rotates three environments, apparatus, rhythm, and manipulation. In Stage II lessons these environments are not changed until the selected sequences have been refined to the satisfaction of the teacher.

Beginning lessons, those characteristic of Stage I, usually have just one major objective and several subordinate objectives. After the preinstructional activity (PIA), during which the instructor notes the learners' readiness for the proposed lesson, a sequence of tasks is introduced. On the lesson plan, this initial task is identified by T^1. A succession of additional tasks belonging to the same sequence may be identified as developmental steps (D^1, D^2, and so on). At the end of this portion of the lesson there may be a culminating activity to provide additional experience with the concepts or actions developed, or there may be a second module with a change in the environment but no change in the theme. As illustrated on the following pages, T^2 identifies a second sequence of tasks. Additional modules continue the practice of identifying the task sequence in the manner described. When the theme has been sufficiently explored, it is changed and new task sequences are planned. The letter C stands for clarification, a practice engaged in by the instructor to make certain that essential concepts are clearly understood. The following is a floor module.

    PIA Free limbering activities on the spot.

      T^1 Travel with emphasis on curved pathways.

      C Identify difference between curved, straight, and twisted.

D¹ Travel using straight pathways only. Use different ways.

D² Sometimes use straight, other times curved, pathways. Go from one to another.

D³ On the spot, use gestures to form straight and curved air pathways.

CA Experiment with both floor and air pathways, perhaps doing one or both at the same time.

Only the floor space is required for this lesson. If time does not permit, the lesson is terminated after the CA. If the lesson is followed by a change to apparatus, rhythm, or manipulation, the same concepts are stressed again. Although short, the above lesson is complete, in that it includes all instructional elements from the initial task to the culminating activity. In the modular plan, the lesson would be extended to include other environmental relationships.

Extensions into other environments

Apparatus environment. Ladders, trestles, beams, and benches or boxes arranged to permit traveling under, on, over, and around.

PIA Children arrange the apparatus as instructed by the teacher.

T² Find ways of traveling in relation to the apparatus, using only curved pathways.

C The curves of the pathways may be in the horizontal or other plane.

D¹ Using the apparatus, travel in straight pathways only.

D² Combine straight and curved pathways.

D³ Start on the floor away from the apparatus. Use a straight pathway to the apparatus; travel in a curved pathway on, under, or around it; and return to place using a curved pathway.

CA Starting from the same place, use either or both shapes of pathways and find other pieces of apparatus to which to relate.

Note that in this extension of the lesson into the apparatus environment no use of air pathways was made. The problems of relating to the apparatus are considered to be enough at this point.

The use of manipulative objects permits extending the concept of pathways to take on additional dimensions. For example:

Manipulative environment. An 8½-inch playground ball or its equivalent for every child.

PIA Children travel while controlling the ball in any way they can.

T³ Select one way of controlling the ball and use it while traveling only in straight pathways.

C The necessity of pausing to change direction without losing control of the ball may need clarification. Also, the possibility of traveling sideways to change direction while maintaining a straight pathway may need to be explored.

D¹ Travel in curved pathways only.

D² Travel around others who are also traveling.

D³ Travel as directly as possible from end to end or side to side of the general space but use the curved pathway if possible to avoid having to stop until finished.

CA Choose a partner. One leads and the other follows along the same pathway while controlling the ball in the same manner. Change places every minute or so. Try to use both straight and curved pathways.

None of the lessons has been elaborate. Each really repeats the theme but in relation to a different environment. That is where the challenge really lies. In the case of the manipulative environment, the teacher is able to continue the search for new meanings by using ropes, hoops, wands, or any other kinds of manipulative equipment. A different challenge is presented merely by changing the object. Later, of course, the child will be ready for more sophisticated challenges.

Changing the environment once again, the child is now required to think of pathways, curved and straight, while responding to the sound of clapping hands, beating drums, or a record player.

Rhythm or sound environment. A dance drum and floor space.

PIA The teacher or a child beats fast and slow patterns alternately while the children explore movements in place to the tempos heard.

T^4 As the drum sounds, travel in very straight pathways. (Drum sounds an even pattern: - - - -/- - - -/- - - -/.)

C Change direction with sharp turns if necessary. Make sure that the feet keep time.

D^1 As the drum sounds, travel in curved pathways. (Drum sounds an uneven tempo: -../-../-../-../-../-../.)

D^2 Change the shape of the pathways according to whether the sound pattern is even or uneven.

D^3 Choose a partner. One partner claps a pattern for the other to use for straight air pathways of the limbs and a different pattern for curved air pathways. Change places and repeat.

CA Put it all together. Travel while using straight pathways on the floor and in the air to the sounds made by the partner. Do the same for curved pathways. Try doing one and then the other. Be prepared to show your finished product to others.

Procedures for linking module. The PIA (preinstructional activity) are not always maintained in each of the linked modules. If the daily lesson consists of two modules, each about fifteen minutes in length, the first module may contain the PIA and no CA, while the second contains no PIA but a CA to climax the lesson as a whole.

The lesson	
Floor module	**Apparatus module**
PIA	T^2
T^1	D^x
D^x	CA

In this lesson, the concepts of the floor module are carried over to the apparatus module, the whole lesson ending with a culminating activity to tie both modules together. This is relatively easy to do. In fact, it is the most practical way of handling the matter of culminating activities. However, there are times when it is necessary to culminate the first part before moving on to the second part of the lesson. The option is available, depending upon the needs perceived by the teacher.

Themes and subthemes

■ The theme is the movement idea or action stressed in a lesson or sequence of lessons. It is generally the practice to make themes broad enough to last from one week to as many as six weeks. Often, the main idea or action is stated by itself with supporting ideas and actions listed separately as subthemes. For example:

Main theme: Traveling in curved and straight pathways.
Subtheme: Changing direction.
Subtheme: Changing speeds.

Why subthemes?

Working with a main theme and subthemes has the advantage of permitting instructors to operate with more flexibility than when the main theme includes all ideas and actions. The entire lesson given as a single main theme might take the following form:

Main theme: Traveling in curved and straight pathways with emphasis on change in direction and speed.

Stated in this fashion, the implication is that change in speed and direction is the main idea, rather than the supporting concept. Less direction is given to the new teacher, for whom such a theme might seem quite a large undertaking. The modular concept of lesson planning utilizes subthemes to identify the special additional emphasis each module needs to clearly identify its role in securing the objectives of the lesson.

Main theme: Traveling in curved and straight pathways.
Subtheme for apparatus: Pathways under, over, and around.
Subtheme for manipulation: Using curved and straight pathways to avoid collision.
Subtheme for rhythm: Changing movement direction along pathways.

Environmental subthemes

Subthemes enable instructors to select an emphasis suited to a particular type of environment. This has the effect of making the main theme more relevant to the child's experience.

Main theme: Contrasting fast and slow.
Subtheme for apparatus: Selecting appropriate speeds for work on the apparatus, with emphasis on safety.

No danger exists when speeds are contrasted while using balls, hoops, or ropes or when moving to the beat of a drum. However, the risk of having children travel too fast for safety on apparatus is reason enough to adopt a special subtheme that focuses attention directly on this problem. There are many reasons other than safety for the inclusion of specific environmental subthemes.

The rhythm area by its very nature places great stress on the qualities of movement. Slow, fast, light, heavy, smooth, and jerky can make suitable subthemes after these qualities have been the subject of a main theme. Admirable subthemes for rhythm are listening skills, changes in tension from strong to complete relaxation, sequence, design, shapes, relationships to others, and changes in the size of space or the directions of movements through space. Consider, also, the possibility of working with accents in movement patterns. Play action rhythms and the rhythms of work tasks have their special accents, which can be explored further or used as the basis for investigations bordering on the dance area.

The manipulative area is suited for subthemes on relationships, changes in level and direction of objects, sequence, speed, and formational designs or shapes. How a main theme relates to a specific environmental circumstance (for example, the manipulative area) depends in large measure on the subtheme. Awareness of direction when concerned only with one's self is different from awareness of direction associated with the movement of an object. The former is primary, the result of having a stable perception of structured space, an internal space structure. Object direction is perceived in terms of the self. An object moving away from in front of the body is translated as traveling in a forward direction. An object thrown away from and above the head travels up. It is possible for the body to be traveling up to meet a ball coming down, to be traveling backward to receive a ball thrown forward by a partner, or to travel to the right to throw a ball forward and to the left.

The apparatus area provides a rich source of variety in space relationships. Apparatus has surfaces for supporting weight on different parts at various levels. Children experience changes in body shapes while traversing the shapes of spaces formed by the apparatus. Control is essential to safety in relationship to apparatus. Failure of control can mean considerably more than the bump that might occur when control is lost on the floor. Children's awareness of their positions in relationship to others who might be above or below them, who might be swinging and thus in need of more than the normal amount of space, or who might be upside down and, therefore, more vulnerable to injury is urgently needed when engaged in an apparatus lesson.

Write a subtheme for a module if the environmental relationship requires a special emphasis, such as self-control, or when the main theme needs special clarification, such as when object direction and self-movement direction are involved at the same time. Safety and clarification are the two major reasons for using subthemes. It is perfectly all right not to use them. Experience will usually dictate the use of subthemes to help make the lesson go smoothly.

Writing themes

Although it is quite possible to select a theme from a book or list of some kind, many instructors prefer to write their own. It is not difficult to do and should be practiced for those occasions when a theme tailored to the needs of the class is required. The following steps will help.

1 Observe the class and list the movement deficiencies.
   a) What are the body awareness problems?
   b) What problems exist with control or the quality of expression?
   c) What are the spatial problems?
   d) In what way are physical or social environmental problems manifested?
2 Arrange the list in order of priority.
3 Select the movement idea or ideas.
4 Write the theme as a simple statement with any supporting ideas either incorporated in the body of the theme or as a subtheme.
   a) Example: Traveling in a variety of ways with emphasis on change in level, direction, and speed.
   b) Example: Traveling in a variety of ways.
      Subtheme: Change in level, direction, and speed.
5 Write subthemes, if needed, for different learning environments, i.e., apparatus, manipulation, rhythm.

Linking modules

■ Lesson modules are easily linked, as illustrated by the diagram of the floor and apparatus lesson in figure 7.4. This section will illustrate a more extensive use of linking to clarify progression. A sample weekly plan for a system that schedules daily physical education might look like that illustrated in figure 7.4.

Each module is linked with the main theme, traveling in different ways, and with each other through the main theme and the subthemes. The entire sequence of modular links is like a paragraph, each sentence supporting the main thought.

Periods of forty or forty-five minutes may employ three modules (fig. 7.5). This division into three modules allows children to have greater variety within the lesson and to have more repetition during the course of a week's lessons.

The progression of concepts should be not only from one portion of a lesson to another but also from lesson to lesson. All like modules are linked through the environments they represent (fig. 7.6). Within these progressions there are often progressions into different social environments: partner and small-group relationships; single and mixed sexes within these relationships. These relationships might involve contact or noncontact and various levels of cooperative endeavor from simple to complex.

From general to specific

Progression of instructional materials and concepts from the broad awarenesses of basic movement education to more specific competencies in body management, expression, and competition leads to gymnastics,

Fig. 7.4

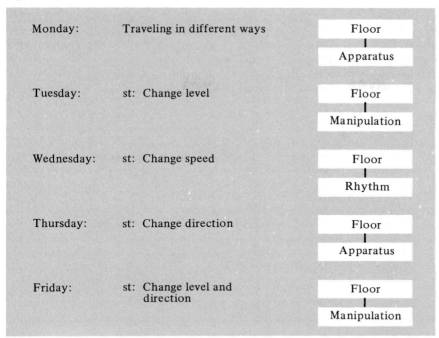

Monday:	Traveling in different ways	Floor — Apparatus
Tuesday:	st: Change level	Floor — Manipulation
Wednesday:	st: Change speed	Floor — Rhythm
Thursday:	st: Change direction	Floor — Apparatus
Friday:	st: Change level and direction	Floor — Manipulation

Fig. 7.5

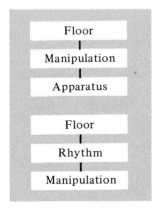

Floor — Manipulation — Apparatus

Floor — Rhythm — Manipulation

Fig. 7.6

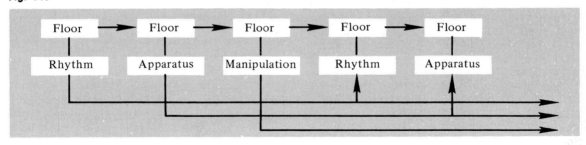

dance, and games. The rate of progression is determined entirely by learner readiness and is handled through an exploratory approach by the teacher. By the time most children have reached the third grade, the curricular progression takes on the character of the developmental track. The modular structure is retained.

Broad themes covering different learner environments are now discarded in favor of themes specific to each separate area of learning, as in-

Fig. 7.7. Thirty-minute daily lessons

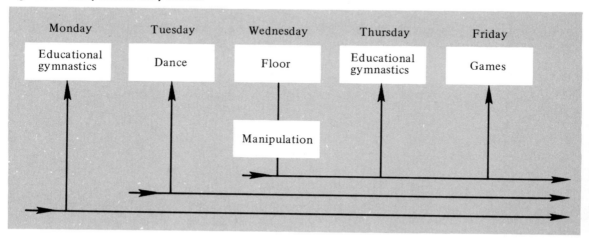

Fig. 7.8.

Main theme at beginning	Six Week Time Block: Three to five lessons per week.				
	Subtheme	Program	Activity	Theme
3's Relationships				
Floor | Rhythm	Design	→ Dance	Modern	Meeting and Parting
Floor | Apparatus	Pattern	→ Gym.	Ed. Gym	Observe, Analyze, Improve
Floor | Manipulation	Foot control	→ Games	Soccer	Three/on/Three
Floor | Hoops	Jumping patterns	→ Games	Self-testing	Leader and Follower
Floor | Ropes	Jumping and turning	→ Games	Contest	Rope Jumping

dicated in figure 7.7. Themes for educational gymnastics do not give direct support to the dance program, which has its own theme. However, a good teacher will keep them closely related in areas where learners need additional reinforcement. The floor module followed by manipulation is connected to a games lesson, which indicates progression from cooperative relationships to some kind of competitive relationship.

The curriculum may be structured in many ways to suit the facilities, time allotment, and other important areas of consideration. Arguments against the unit block in which six or eight weeks are spent on one activity will be presented later. For now, a preview of a multiactivity program built around relationships in threes is illustrated in figure 7.8 as an alternative to the commonly accepted single-program offering.

The lesson modules that enable the instructor to structure learning experiences that lead learners from the general theme of relating in threes to specific program area themes may be grouped at the discretion of the instructor within the constraints of time, space, learner readiness, and so forth. As long as the instructor does not expect children to handle complex material in a short period of time, it is quite possible for them to engage in unrelated activities within the same lesson time period. In fact, it is often lots of fun.

For example, one possible program (also using the theme of threes relationships) is shown in figure 7.9. In some cases the floor lesson introduces concepts and actions common to the environmental changes to follow; at other times, it is best to return to the floor for a specific subtheme. Threes relationships on apparatus at the beginning of the lesson may not focus sufficiently on the specifics of concepts and actions related to soccer in the second part of the lesson. A subtheme such as working in triangles would be appropriate.

The lessons near the end of the time block have the characteristics of lessons within lessons. Gymnastics may shift to dance; each activity with its own theme. The same is true of the other lessons. Well-organized classes will put equipment away and prepare the new environment with whatever else is needed for the next lesson. Time blocks of at least fifteen minutes are needed for most lesson modules, but even this aspect of a lesson can be modified (fig. 7.10).

The case for multiactivity progression

This lesson eventually takes on the characteristics of a warm-up that uses the floor and apparatus agilities of the educational gymnastics program. It then goes directly into cooperative team and then to competitive team relationships and skills involving the game of soccer. Why mix up the lesson in this way, the reader may ask? Is it really important to have a multiactivity progression?

The question may be answered by referring to the situation in the academic classroom. Does the classroom teacher spend the time devoted to academic pursuits solely on reading for six weeks, perhaps followed by six weeks of mathematics? Of course not. It would be ridiculous to expect

Fig. 7.9

Lesson at beginning of time block	Lesson near end of time block
Floor | Apparatus | Rhythm	<u>Educational gymnastics</u> + <u>Modern educational dance</u>
Floor | Rhythm | Apparatus	<u>Modern educational dance</u> + <u>Educational gymnastics</u>
Floor | Manipulation–hoops | Rhythm	<u>Self-testing</u> + <u>Modern educational dance</u>
Floor | Manipulation–hoops | Manipulation–ropes	<u>Self-testing</u> + <u>Contesting</u>
Floor | Apparatus + Floor | Manipulation	<u>Educational gymnastics</u> + <u>Soccer</u>

children to concentrate their learning on just one subject and then leave it until the following year. Yet, this is what happens in physical education. The basics of movement learning as well as the basics of academic learning must receive a continuing emphasis until the foundations of concepts and skills are well established. Then, and only then, is the learner ready to undertake short-term concentration on such subject matter as ancient history, handball, tennis, Elizabethan literature, typing, and any number of other courses of instruction designed to develop a specific competency.

The games program is tremendously varied when viewed from a universal perspective. There are games indigenous to every culture in the world and even to sections of countries. Games serve purposes beyond the objectives of the game itself. Games are vehicles for the development of social skills, for the reinforcement of the ego, and for the development of

Fig. 7.10. Thirty-minute lesson

Preinstructional activity	Traveling over and under through the apparatus with emphasis on agility
Floor task	Grouped in threes, stay in triangular formation while traveling in small area
Development	One goes between the other two or around one of the other two to form a new triangle
Manipulative task	Using soccer skills, maintain triangular relationships while keeping the ball moving
Culminating activity	Three-on-three game of keepaway

certain appreciations. Skills are often only the tools through which other, more important, abilities are developed. In such a case, almost any game will serve the purpose.

If this is true, why has soccer been singled out so early in the program? Soccer is used because it permits progression both in game skills and concepts and in the application of broad spatial concepts, cooperative and competitive relationships, and restrictions of rules upon play. A great deal of initial skill is not required for a child to participate successfully. Soccer is fun, challenging, and exciting, and at the same time it leads participants to (1) increased levels of cardiovascular endurance through running, (2) skill in dealing with the emotional aspects of competition, and (3) increased feelings of competence and the assurance of belonging, of being a part of a common effort. We highly recommend that soccer precede basketball, football, and all other team sports as the vehicle to success not only in future soccer play but also in all games involving running and spatially oriented strategies.

■ We conclude this section with a list of the six competencies that are the goals of the total program. These competencies serve as the basis for evaluation of student progress, which is discussed in chapter XV.

Six learner competencies

1 *Self-management behaviors.* The learner demonstrates ability to operate in a self-controlled manner.
2 *Social behaviors.* The learner demonstrates ability to relate effectively to others.
3 *Body management behaviors.* The learner demonstrates ability to utilize fundamental movement abilities effectively in a variety of physical environments.
4 *Functional fitness abilities.* The learner demonstrates physical fitness to participate in activities important to his growth and development.
5 *Activity skill behaviors.* The learner demonstrates ability to perform with acceptable skill in the areas of dance, gymnastics, and games (aquatics, also, if possible).
6 *Knowledge and understanding behaviors.* The learner demonstrates the ability to recall and apply properly information essential to successful participation and a reasonable command of fundamental processes leading to the solution of movement problems and the creation of new problems and solutions.

Objectives of a movement education program

■ The identification of these six competencies sheds some light on the overall objectives of the movement-oriented physical education program, objectives that may still be somewhat obscure to the reader. A further discussion of objectives can now take place.

There are two kinds of objectives to which attention will be given when designing a curriculum. Objectives that describe what the program is supposed to accomplish are called *program objectives*. They describe how the learner should behave as a result of having undertaken the program of instruction.

Instructional objectives

These describe explicitly how a learner will, not should, behave. They are written for the moment of instruction and subscribe to three criteria, (1) an exact description of the behavior to be observed or product to be produced, (2) the circumstances under which the behavior is to occur, and (3) the minimum standard of acceptability. Instructional objectives are sometimes called performance objectives, behavioral objectives, or behavioral outcomes. They all mean the same thing. But there are two types of instructional objectives, *terminal* and *enabling*.

Terminal objectives. These objectives describe the end products of instruction. Here are some sample terminal objectives.

1 The learner will perform a minimum of six of ten listed tumbling skills with an instructor rating of 6.0 out of a possible 10.0 points.
2 Given a ball to handle within the confines of a ten-foot-square area, the learner will demonstrate ball control using basketball dribbling skills while continuously traversing the area for a period of thirty seconds with no errors.
3 Given a ball, a hoop, and a wand, the learner will demonstrate ability to create a game for four people by designing objectives and describing the manner in which the implements are to be used and the players are to behave. A five-minute time limit will be followed by actual play to prove the feasibility of the activity to the satisfaction of the players and the instructor.
4 The learner will demonstrate consideration for others by avoiding collision during general spatial movement generated by instructor direction during physical education with a maximum error rating of one collision per week of instruction.
5 Asked to name the body parts indicated by the instructor, the learner will correctly identify nine out of ten.

Enabling objectives. Terminal objectives are attained by way of enabling objectives. If a terminal objective is performance of a headstand, an enabling objective might be the ability of the performer to balance in some fashion with the head assisting in support of the body. The ability to break a terminal objective and large enabling objectives into very small enabling objectives is the mark of a skilled instructor. Progression for learners means assimilating new material, moving from what is known and from what they can do to what they do not know or cannot do. If the step into the unknown is too big, the learners fail. Each step qualifies as an enabling objective only if it serves the purposes of learners or the instructor acting for learners. Learners must be able to attain enabling objectives; without this attainment they cannot achieve the terminal objective. The following breakdowns of terminal objectives illustrate some of the possible enabling objectives.

Terminal objective: To play three-on-three soccer acceptably

Enabling objectives:
1 Dribble a soccer ball in a one-on-one situation and progress toward the goal or keep ball from opponent.
2 Trap a soccer ball using the sole or the inside of the foot. A medium-speed ball kicked by another learner will be trapped four out of five times.
3 When not in possession of the ball, run to an open space and position self for a pass during triangle passing drills.
4 Receive properly and pass the ball a distance of twenty-five feet to a partner traveling right or left in three out of five tries.

Terminal objective: To travel with steplike actions on the balance beam set at a height of four feet.

Enabling objectives:
1 Get on and off the balance beam set at eighteen inches high.
2 Step on and off the eighteen-inch-high beam with landing control.
3 Walk from end to end on the eighteen-inch-high beam.
4 Get on and jump from the three-foot beam with good landing control.
5 Start to walk on the three-foot beam and jump either to right or left with good landing control.
6 Walk from end to end on the three-foot-high beam.
7 Repeat steps 4 and 5 on the four-foot-high beam.

Terminal objective: To travel without collision with change in direction

Enabling objectives:
1 Come to a stop on command, "freeze."
2 Start and stop quickly under self-direction.
3 Travel slowly between and around people without collision.
4 Slow down or stop to avoid collision when intersecting the path of another.
5 Travel sideways without collision.
6 Travel backward without collision.
7 Travel in a crowded situation without collision.
8 Travel with change in direction while traveling quickly in crowded circumstances without collision.

Movement learning
lessons

Terminal objective: To listen to and follow directions.

Enabling objectives:
1 Look at the instructor when directions are given.
2 Repeat the directions given without error.
3 Follow the directions in correct sequence.

Enabling objectives should be individualized to match a child's abilities. Some children will need many little steps between present status and the desired terminal behavior. There are differences in intellectual, perceptual, integrative, and performance abilities. Children vary in physical qualities (size, speed, strength, flexibility, and endurance) and in psychological qualities (frustration tolerance, concentration, feelings of worth, temperament, and willingness to achieve). In addition, social variance may be a factor to consider, with some children remaining in partner relationships longer than others, who feel comfortable in moving on to more challenging small group situations.

When children have mostly positive attributes, it is possible to plan enabling objectives quite accurately. However, when children have many negative attributes, the teacher must be prepared to adjust the program to the special needs of these children. In practical ways, this means adjusting the height of equipment, the size of a ball, the weight of an object to be handled, the amount of space, the tempo of the music, the number of variables within the task to which the child must consciously attend. It means allowing extra time and giving extra praise to reinforce progress.

Process objectives

Some of the objectives children work to achieve should be regarded as process objectives. Learning how to go about solving a movement problem may be a more important accomplishment than the actual solution to the problem. Looking at the end result for the purpose of evaluation does not always provide a complete picture of a child's accomplishments. A good example of the importance of process is seen in the young child who finally accomplishes a head and handstand balance by adjusting the size of the base and the position of the body's center of gravity over it. The child discovers that when head and hands are positioned in a straight line, achieving forward and backward stability is difficult. When head position is adjusted to form a triangular base the child achieves a stable position. The product is an important accomplishment because it signifies, in this instance, the achievement of a process objective. A principle has been learned, also.

Process objectives are important because they often signify important cognitive behaviors that would otherwise go unnoticed in any statement of objectives. To reinforce this point: the means may be as important or more important than the ends of the learning sequence. Enabling objectives are not just means to attain ends.

The lesson plan objectives will most often be enabling rather than terminal. During the instructional process, modifications of enabling objectives will be made to accommodate individual learners. In many cases, learners can be helped to structure their own enabling objectives once they have a clear picture of where they are headed.

■ A good movement education program is one that blends the general objectives of the basic movement track with the specific objectives of the developmental movement track. As soon as children have acquired the important affective objectives of Stage I, Level 1.0, Level 2.0 objectives are given priority. These objectives should include not only the understandings associated with basic movement education but also those fundamental to the attainment of certain specific skills.

There are two fundamental ways of learning how to perform a particular movement pattern skillfully. Discovery learning is one way, either through student exploration or through teacher guidance. A second way is through directed experience, often called the command or authoritarian teaching style. Either way can be effective in attaining the terminal objective, the specific skill.

When skill attainment is the important objective, some form of directed teaching is superior to the exploration-discovery method. In other words, there are times in a good movement education program when the teacher tells and shows the children so that they may reach a desired objective. However, telling and showing in a movement education program differ from the same instructional behavior in traditional programs.

Directed teaching aimed at movement-oriented students draws upon a reservoir of understandings and experiences that enable students to accomplish the directed task successfully. The language of the task is the familiar language of basic movement. The skills are specified shapes and rhythms directly related to generalized shapes and rhythms learned under different circumstances.

Every instructional effort should be made to guide children's acquisition of skills essential to their welfare. Directed teaching methods should be utilized to assure accomplishment of this goal.

The following skills are essential to the development of most young children. Beyond the third grade, other skills make themselves known to the observant instructor. Children may speak up and tell the instructor what they want to learn.

Fundamental aspects of the developmental track

Fundamental skills that children should acquire by grade three

Pattern	Skill
Walk	Conventional walk, erect body, opposition of arms to legs
	Walk on balance beam, arms sideward or low
Run	Sprint run, body erect, arms bent and in opposition, drive off ball of foot.

Movement learning
lessons

Pattern	Skill
	Distance run, body erect, arms bent and in opposition, landing on almost flat foot, push off ball of foot
Gallop	Lead with either foot and change without stopping
	Travel backward with either foot leading
Sliding	Travel left and right with quick change in direction
Hop	Consecutive hop on either foot in place or while traveling with ability to change direction at will
	Run and hop: travel several running steps and take a hop off either foot, continue with run or step into some other pattern (such as a cartwheel or roundoff)
Jump	Standing broad jump with arms swinging upward on extension and downward upon landing
	Run and jump (long jump) with appropriate arm action; run action should use sprint form
	Run, jump, and grasp a bar, climbing rope, or pole
	Run, hurdle jump, and rebound off both feet to grasp overhead bar, rope, or pole, or to mount or vault an object like a box, beam, or vaulting horse
Leap	From a run, leap onto either foot and continue in stride
	From a stand, leap in different directions consecutively
Turn	Turn in the air during any form of the jump and land in balance
	Turn on either foot (pivot) as a way of quickly changing direction
	Turn on both feet when on a balance beam
Roll	Collapse and roll upon landing from a jump or suspension
	Diagonal forward and backward rolls upon landing
	Roll forward to safely transfer weight from the hands
Cartwheel	Transfer weight sideways from foot to hand, to hand, to foot and repeat or continue with running action
	Run, hop, (hurdle) cartwheel, and run without hesitation
Support	Support the body in the bridge position both on the front and on the back
	Support the weight of the body on the hands and return the feet to the floor with good control
	Jump to support on a bar and turn forward to a controlled landing

Pattern	Skill
	Jump to support and step on bar to outside of hands to continue forward to dismount
	While in support on a horizontal bar, swing the hips away from the bar to momentary free support
	Travel on the hands with the body in support between two parallel bars
	Take the weight on the hands to mount or vault a box, beam, or vaulting horse
Throw	Overhand throw of small ball with underhand preparatory action (outfielder's throw or pitch)
	Overhand throw of large ball, with overhand preparatory action (peg pass or catcher's throw)
	Underhand throw of large ball (underhand foul shot action)
	Underhand throw to roll ball (bowling action)
	Underhand throw of small ball (softball pitching action)
Catch	Two-handed catch of direct, overhead, or below-waist throw or rebound with proper hand position and "give" of arms and wrist.
Dribble	One-handed dribble of large ball in place or while traveling
	Soccer dribble using either foot
	Dribble tennis ball by using a paddle
	Air dribble a tennis ball by using a paddle
Strike	Kick a ball rolling toward the kicker using either the toe or the instep
	Dribble and kick using either the instep or the inside of the foot (control and pass)
	Kick a ball dropped from the hands using a step-kick rhythm (punt)
	Punch a dropped ball using an underhand swing with a closed fist or flat hand
	Punch a tossed ball using an overhand action similar to a peg pass
	Bat a ball off a tee using either a wooden or plastic bat and a two-handed grip

Are there other skills that should be learned by third grade? Yes, but it depends on the location of the school. Some youngsters are playing street basketball by grade three. Others are playing ice hockey or soccer.

Movement learning
lessons

Girls need skills, too

Should girls be expected to achieve the same degree of proficiency as boys? Yes. If it is important for girls to acquire skills, it is just as important for them to execute them properly. Bad habits are difficult to break. Bad fundamentals weaken the foundation of the developmental movement education program. It is not possible to predict which boy or girl will use the fundamental skills to the greatest advantage; this makes it necessary for all children to have a common foundation of properly learned skills. Manipulative skills for girls may not develop as rapidly as they do for boys, simply because the cultural climate does not encourage girls to participate in competitive sports. This can be overcome by deemphasizing the competitive aspect until later, when girls are motivated to compete. In the meantime, rhythmic gymnastics and cooperative tasks that stress self-testing rather than competition will serve their interests better.

Fundamental skills should be demonstrated with acceptable form and control of beginnings and endings. They can be taught within the context of body management and manipulative lessons through tasks aimed at leading or guiding learners to specific motor patterns. The specifics of teaching skills will be developed in chapter X.

Episodes of the Modular Lesson

■ The purpose of this section is to further clarify the role of the modular lesson plan format in the instructional program of physical education. Reading this section should give a clear understanding of four aspects of the modular lesson plan.

1 The modular lesson plan can be taught in episodes rather than all at once.
2 Modules from the same or different programs may be included in the same lesson plan.
3 Modules of the same course of instruction are linked either by a common theme or by a specific instructional purpose.
4 The modular lesson plan is part of an instructional unit.

Learning episodes

Once a lesson plan is prepared, there is no rule that requires the contents of the plan to be taught during a single instructional period. From the standpoint of the learner, it is not reasonable to expect much to be accomplished in the ten or fifteen minutes devoted to instruction in a concept or action. It may take several episodes before the desired objectives are attained at the minimum acceptable level of learner proficiency. Consider the following plans, one for basic movement, the other for developmental movement objectives. Observe the similarities and differences. Note how episodes of learning simplify the planning process by permitting the instructor to utilize the same plan several days in succession. Finally, take into consideration the fact that the concept of learning episodes permits adjusting the program to the learner because the plan is structured toward individual learner requirements at the outset.

Lesson plan

Operational Stage I   Level 2.0   Grade 3
Theme: Traveling through general space with emphasis on curved,
        twisted, and angular pathways.
Subthemes: Change in direction
           Different locomotor patterns
Objectives: The student will achieve minimal standards of competen-
            cy in being able to:

1 Create his own design of curved, twisted, and angular pathways by
  traveling through the general space.
2 Perform at least ten different locomotor patterns or combinations of
  patterns while contrasting the shapes of his pathways.
3 Demonstrate change in the direction of his movement without confusing the shape of the selected pathway.
4 Perform his design so that his partner, other children, or the instructor
  can evaluate the level of its acceptability, using an instructor-given
  rating scale of: Needs to improve, a score of 1; Satisfactory, 3; Outstanding in comparison to others, 5.
5 Participate in analysis of outstanding student performances by contributing to the discussion verbally or by demonstration, in a constructive manner.

There is no set starting point for this lesson plan. The statement of objectives includes both the psychomotor and the cognitive domains, with
strong support of affective behaviors. These are the desired outcomes. Instructional methods have to be selected that will assure attainment of these
objectives. Task sequence can vary widely. It is up to the instructor.

The floor lesson on day 1 may be able to achieve progress in the variety
of locomotor behaviors performed along either curved or twisted pathways. That may be enough, because there is a lot of room for learner innovation if children are given time to explore.

Episode 1 is the floor lesson.
T¹   Travel in general space along curved pathways.
PIA Practice the design of the previous CA.
D¹   Practice different locomotor patterns.
D²   Connect one pattern with another along segments of a curved
     pathway.
D³   Change the direction of the curve to twist the pathway while per-
     forming various locomotor patterns.
CA   Make up a design consisting of two curved pathways and one
     twisted pathway to show to a partner.

Episode 2 might continue the floor lesson in this way.
PIA Practice the design of the previous CA.
T²   Travel only in straight pathways while using different locomotor
     patterns.

D¹   Make sharp corners or angles to change the direction of the straight pathway.

D²   Connect a curved pathway to an angular pathway. Repeat in different ways.

D³   Change the curved pathway to a twisted pathway and repeat several times.

CA   With a partner, play a simple game in which one shows the other a design that consists of three differently shaped pathways and uses various movements that the partner must match. Reverse roles. Discuss results.

Episode 3 should introduce change in movement direction and generate discussion concerning the difference between change in pathway and change in movement of the body. The CA should reflect the ability of learners to assimilate this addition.

Episode 4 might start the process of student evaluation, with partners evaluating each other according to criteria given by the instructor. Allowances for student input in formulation of criteria should be made for classes where such activity would be fruitful. Pairs of children could evaluate other pairs, with the instructor serving as guide for those children unable to reach agreement.

Episode 5 would be the "wrap-up" session that concludes the module. All objectives should be attained by at least 80 percent of the students. If this standard cannot be met, the instructor must decide whether to continue the lesson with additional episodes or to return to the lesson at a later time.

When one class of a grade is slow in attaining minimum performance standards, the instructor may move more slowly with this class while giving the faster-moving classes more time with a different environmental module, such as apparatus, or by enriching the floor lesson. The latter may be accomplished by adding a subtheme, changing the level or tempo, emphasizing elevation or rolling, or use of other appropriate variables. The instructor may add an enriching experience by providing the faster-moving class with an opportunity to utilize rhythmic instruments in conjunction with the designs they have created or by adding a graphic art experience. As stated previously, there is no one way to achieve the objectives. Teacher creativity is to be encouraged.

Only the floor module for each of the five learning episodes has been described. *Because the potential of environmental change should not be denied children, the floor module should always be supplemented by at least one other module.* Some children will gain the concepts better in one environment than in another. The opportunity to expand concepts introduced in a floor setting should not be overlooked. Here are some ways of linking the floor module to the other modules.

Subtheme for apparatus:
Incorporating the pathways through apparatus within the larger floor design
or

Emphasizing different locomotor patterns along pathways appropriate for various apparatus arrangements

or

Emphasizing going over and under (twisted, curved, and straight pathways are assumed from the theme statement)

Subtheme for rhythm:
Emphasizing strong or light movement

or

Changing and maintaining the tempo of movement

or

Accompanying a partner through percussion (clapping, beating a drum, etc.)

Subtheme for manipulation:
Tossing, catching, and handling a ball (hoop or rope)

or

Creating manipulative patterns with selected objects

or

Handling a ball (hoop, rope, wand) in different ways

Sometimes the number of learning episodes depends on the emphasis given to the environmental subtheme. If children demonstrate a need for more opportunity to develop desired competencies in a particular environment (or several environments, for that matter), additional episodes are included and the modular plan may be stretched out over a two-week period. As a rule of thumb, if the objectives of the module cannot be achieved within a week, the module is too complicated. Decreasing the number of objectives and their complexity will alleviate the problem. Long periods of time spent on pursuit of the same objectives soon become counterproductive as children become bored doing what appears to them to be the same thing. *The main theme does not have to be changed,* only subthemes and objectives. A main theme can be effective over a period of several weeks or more, depending on the learner and the teacher, their combined innovativeness, and their mutual struggle to dig deeply into possibilities for exploration and discovery.

Mixing and matching modules

One of the advantages of the modular lesson plan is the flexibility of its structure. A multiactivity program for the daily physical education program was illustrated earlier in this chapter. The experienced physical education teacher should be able to conduct multiactivity programs in the same lesson time period (fig. 7.11). This is particularly advantageous when the number of lessons per week is limited to just one, two, or three, and when at least thirty minutes of instructional time is provided. In some situations, the classroom teacher is able to follow up with further development of the module introduced by the physical education teacher.

Matching modules have the same main theme but vary in subthemes and/or environmental circumstances. These are the floor, apparatus, rhythm, and manipulation environments described so far. Learners are directly reinforced in their development of new concepts and actions by the mutual relationship of main theme and environment. There is no major conceptual change to which they must accommodate themselves, even though environmental circumstances are different. It has been demonstrated over and over again by learners in classroom situations that they are perfectly capable of stopping one activity and starting another that is completely different. Learners function just as well when such changes are made in the physical education setting.

Fig. 7.11

Matching modules in a lesson episode

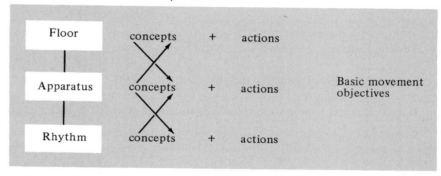

Mixing modules in a lesson episode

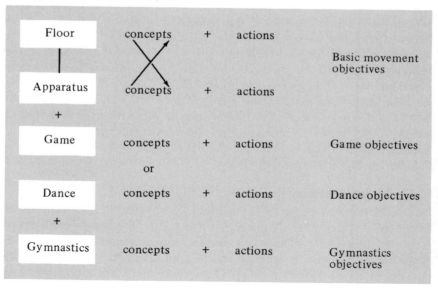

Summary

■ Level 2.0 cognitive and psychomotor objectives complete the description of Operational Stage I. Knowledge objectives stress recall of the movement vocabulary, fundamental principles of movement, and rules of play or directions for an activity. There are objectives requiring thinking skills, also.

The major intellectual ability sought by the first stage is that of comprehension. Other abilities that may be included in statements of objectives are the ability to apply information, such as directions, rules, and simple principles; the ability to analyze at a beginning level, to structure elements in new combinations; and the ability to apply given criteria in making value judgments relative to movement experiences paralleling learning, like evaluation of a partner's performance.

Psychomotor objectives vary considerably according to the age and motor ability of the learner. Even young children should learn certain skills in preparation for the next stage of their development. Skills fundamental to present and future achievement should be identified and taught.

At the conclusion of the first stage of learning, the learner should be self-disciplined, knowledgeable about movement terminology and basic processes, and functionally fit, with body management skills that enable him to operate safely in a variety of environments.

The modular lesson plan is a useful format for structuring the movement learning experience, whether it is basic or developmental. Each module can stand by itself, with preinstructional activity, tasks, and a culminating activity. Linking modules to enrich the learning experience or to reinforce concepts makes for great variety within a lesson, even though the concepts are minimal in number. It is the usual practice to begin the movement lesson with a floor module and to follow with one or more modules stressing a different environmental relationship. This depends on the length of the learning episode, a term used to describe each of the periods devoted to acquiring the lesson objectives.

To assure attainment of fundamental skills by grade three, the teacher must know what they are and how to teach them. Two methods are suggested, the direct method, which assumes that the learner is able to handle very specific directions, and the indirect method, which guides the learner to a solution. More specific information is found in chapter XII on skills instruction.

The modular lesson plan structure permits the instructor to carry on several programs at the same time. One way is to vary the daily lesson episode to provide a multiactivity program. Another way, when only two or three periods of thirty or more minutes of instructional time per week are provided, incorporates the multiactivity program within the modular structure of each lesson episode. The procedure for linking and conducting the modular multiactivity lesson episode is the same as for a single module used for an entire episode. Modifications to PIA and CA are made, depending on what kind of instruction has preceded or will follow.

PIA May or may not be needed to bridge the modules of either two similar or two different environments, themes, or activity purposes.

T Tasks that initiate the learning experience of each module, whether alike or different, are specific to the objectives and the environmental circumstances relevant to each module.

C Clarification of each initial or developmental task that follows is automatic, a condition under which the lesson proceeds. Lack of clarity means lack of understanding on the part of the learner, whose clarity of understanding is demonstrated by the clarity of his or her response.

D   Developmental tasks are those that follow a satisfactory solution of the initial task (T). There may be several of these steps, each one introducing a slight change in the movement challenge, so that the learner solves problems with only a few additional variables to consider. Little developmental challenge steps are met with greater success than are big steps that leave many children frustrated.

CA   The culminating activity wraps up the lesson module when it is the final module of the lesson episode or when the module to follow will engage the student in different objectives. When two or three modules that use the same theme are linked, the final module is often closed with a culminating activity that pulls all three modules together in a common wrap-up. The instructor's decision is based on the needs of the children.

The first operational stage of learning is usually the only stage experienced by students in the primary grades (and, often, by students in the upper elementary grades as well). Stage II will be emphasized in the following chapter as a program aim for all elementary school children.

Assignments

1
Write theme statements that incorporate
a. Balance, shape
b. Weight of the body, body parts
c. Pathways through space
d. Levels, direction
e. Time, weight
f. Flow, action
g. Contact and noncontact relationships
h. Partner relationships
i. On, over, under and other "space" words.

2
Select one of the theme statements that you wrote for assignment 1 and write a subtheme for
a. An apparatus environment with an arrangement that encourages climbing, hanging, swinging, and jumping behaviors.
b. A rhythm environment in which a record player and children's folk-dance music is used.
c. A manipulative environment with a jump rope for every child.
d. A manipulative environment in which a ball is available for one third of the group, a wand for another third, and a hoop for the last third.

3
Select a grade previously visited and observed in physical education and write three cognitive objectives with a rationale to explain the purpose. Cite behavior, circumstance, and quality standard for each objective. Consider yourself as the teacher when writing the objectives for any program of your choice.

4
Write a modular lesson plan that focuses primarily on one of the four aspects of movement—body, space, effort, or relationship—with attention to
a. Theme statement
b. Subtheme from one other aspect of movement
c. Cognitive and psychomotor objectives
d. Floor module linked to either apparatus, rhythm, or manipulation with appropriate subtheme, PIA, tasks, initial and developmental and CA.

5
Exchange modular lesson plans with a partner. Complete the module by writing subthemes for the two remaining environmental areas, along with projected lesson descriptions.

6
Observe a group of elementary school children participating in a game, and prepare a written analysis of their fundamental skills as described in this chapter for the purpose of making program recommendations. *Note*: The children may demonstrate good skills and the need to engage in more challenging activity in the future, or they may reflect a need for some immediate instruction in proper techniques.

■ In addition to the books listed at the end of chapter 6, the following are recommended for additional ideas for lessons. The modular format can be used for any of the material presented.

Boorman, Joyce. *Creative Dance in the First Three Grades.* New York: McKay, 1969.

An excellent book with pictures, sample lesson plans, the use of stimuli, and a chapter on the observation of movement, that will give readers ideas to last for a long time.

———. *Creative Dance in Grades Four to Six.* Don Mills, Canada: Longman Canada Limited, 1971.

A much-needed book that contains interesting material and lesson plans for those interested in going beyond the material presented in Boorman's first book or for beginning creative dance in the upper grades. The author puts into practice many of the more elusive ideas of Rudolf Laban.

Dauer, Victor P. *Essential Movement Experiences for Preschool and Primary Children.* Minneapolis: Burgess, 1972.

Many readers would disagree with the rigidity of lesson structure suggested by the contents of this book, but it does present many good ideas as the basis for problem-solving movement experiences.

Dauer, Victor P., and Pangrazi, Robert P. *Dynamic Physical Education for Elementary School Children.* 5th ed. Minneapolis: Burgess, 1975.

A comprehensive book on everything from the historical to the practical with a chapter on every major activity worthy of inclusion in the physical education program except basic movement education. Useful particularly as an activity reference.

Dimondstein, Geraldine. *Children Dance in the Classroom.* New York: Macmillan, 1971.

Concepts and movement elements are the focus of each creative dance experience presented, along with a rationale both for dance and for the teacher as a dance educator. A well-conceived and practical approach, the material is valuable to classroom teacher and physical educator alike.

Kirchner, Glenn. *Physical Education for Elementary School Children.* 3rd ed. Dubuque, Iowa: Wm. C. Brown, 1974.

Similar in scope and emphasis to Dauer and Pangrazi, the author provides a more comprehensive movement education program description and an educational gymnastics program not included in other textbooks. An excellent resource for the development of a physical education curriculum.

Additional references

■ The following books are additional references for persons interested in improving understandings of educational objectives.

Association for Supervision and Curriculum Development. *Perceiving, Behaving, Becoming.* Yearbook 1962, Arthur W. Combs, chairman. Washington, D.C.: National Education Association, 1962.

Bloom, Benjamin S., ed. *Taxonomy of Educational Objectives, Handbook I: Cognitive Domain.* New York: McKay, 1956.

Gerhard, Muriel. *Effective Teaching Strategies with the Behavioral Outcomes Approach.* West Nyack, N.Y.: Parker, 1971.

Harrow, Anita J. *A Taxonomy of the Psychomotor Domain.* New York: McKay, 1972.

Krathwohl, David R.; Bloom, Benjamin S.; and Masia, Bertram B. *Taxonomy of Educational Objectives, Handbook II: Affective Domain.* New York: McKay, 1964.

Kryspin, William J., and Feldhusen, John F. *Writing Behavioral Objectives.* Minneapolis: Burgess, 1974.

Lee, Blaine Nelson, and Merrill, M. David. *Writing Complete Affective Objectives: A Short Course.* Belmont, Calif.: Wadsworth, 1972.

McManama, John. *Systems Analysis for Effective School Administration.* West Nyack, N.Y.: Parker, 1971.

Mager, Robert F. *Developing Attitude Toward Learning.* Belmont, Calif.: Fearon, 1968.

———. *Preparing Instructional Objectives.* Belmont, Calif.: Fearon, 1962.

Tyler, Ralph W. *Basic Principles of Curriculum and Instruction.* Chicago: University of Chicago Press, 1949.

~~~~~~

Chapter VIII

Units of instruction: themes i to v

The most useful form for stating
objectives is to express them in terms
which identify both the kind of behavior
to be developed in the student
and the content or area of life in which
the behavior is to operate.

Ralph W. Tyler,
*Basic Principles
of Curriculum and
Instruction,* p. 46

■ The quotation from Tyler aptly defines the problem that was for quite some time characteristic of many instructional programs conducted in the public schools. Objectives were stated in such general terms that almost any behavior within remote range of the objective could be considered acceptable. Such generalities have come under attack in recent years, hence the reason for stating objectives in behavioral terms.

A unit of instruction is a sequence designed to lead to specific instructional outcomes as part of a larger purpose or objective. The length of a unit varies from one week to six or more weeks depending on its purpose and the number of instructional periods available. When grading periods are used throughout a school system, instructional units are generally planned to coincide with the length of such time blocks. A grading period of six weeks accommodates a unit of six weeks or a combination of units totaling six weeks.

Objectives

■ The lesson plan and the unit plan both have specific objectives. Being of shorter duration, the lesson is aimed at fewer and more immediately attainable objectives. The unit focuses on a relatively large body of information and skills. The teacher designs instructional sequences that will meet the immediate objectives of the unit. One such objective might be for the children to successfully play some form of soccer such as Four-on-Four Soccer.

Unit objectives also are classified as program objectives because they describe what the learner should be able to do by the end of the unit of instruction. Each program objective is further described by one or more instructional objectives that state as specifically as necessary the actual behaviors of the student in the psychomotor, cognitive, and affective domains.

The instructional objective is always prefaced by the words "the learner *will*," as opposed to "the learner *should*," which is the wording for program objectives.

Program objectives (an example)

Program objective for team sports. The learner should be able to perform capably, according to the standards of his peer group, in at least one team sport.

Program objective for soccer. The learner should be able to employ offensive skills in a manner appropriate to the game of soccer. The learner should be able to perform actions that show understanding of player position when a teammate has the ball as well as when the learner controls the ball. In actual play, one should demonstrate one's understanding of the proper interrelationship of players in accordance with at least one style of offense such as the W form of attack.

Program objectives for a third-grade unit on Four-on-Four Soccer. On completion of the unit, the learner should be able to demonstrate ability commensurate with maturity in the cognitive, psychomotor, and affective components of Four-on-Four Soccer by:

1 Using either foot to dribble the ball to advance it or to control it when opponents have blocked advancement.
2 Trapping the ball with the sole and the inside of either foot.
3 Push-passing with different parts of the foot.
4 Shooting a dribbled or passed ball for goal using any basic kick.
5 Demonstrating knowledge of the principle of applying force to a specific part of the ball to vary its elevation.
6 Demonstrating knowledge of the principle of "giving" with the ball to absorb its force or soften the impact.
7 Demonstrating by movements in relation to partners and opponents awareness of the spatial factors governing passing and receiving the ball.
8 Demonstrating the defensive principle that the player on defense is responsible for protecting space against the offensive actions of opponents.
9 Acting in accordance with agreed upon rules of play.
10 Accepting the necessity for cooperating with teammates to achieve the purpose of Four-on-Four Soccer.

Program objectives 1-4 are psychomotor, 5-8 are cognitive, and 9 and 10 are affective. Additional program objectives may be listed for skills such as goaltending, problem solving in the developmental stages of rule making, and ethical decision making in the formation of teams or the conduct of tournaments.

Instructional objectives

Given the above set of program objectives for the soccer unit, Four-on-Four Soccer, how does the teacher design appropriate instructional objectives? Designing instructional objectives is relatively simple after the program objectives have been described. A sequence of enabling objectives for achieving specific terminal objectives are created for each program objective. If a visiting supervisor asks, "Mr. Jones, how will you know if Johnny or Mary has learned to trap the soccer ball?" the answer should be a description of the behaviors Johnny or Mary exhibits in demonstrating the skill.

Instructional objectives for trapping the ball in soccer. During a one-minute session of continuous passing and trapping with a cooperative partner, the learner will demonstrate correct technique in the following skills.

1 Using the sole of the foot, the learner will trap the ball successfully at least once when it is passed to the right, to the left, and directly toward the learner for a minimum of three correct demonstrations.

2 Using the inside of either foot, the learner will trap a ground ball passed to the right, to the left, and directly toward the learner and will return the pass.

Teacher A and teacher B may differ in designing instructional objectives. The circumstances under which tests of skill are undertaken and the criteria of quality or quantity may vary from instructor to instructor, but the actual behavior should be clear to the observer. Under some circumstances, competition is required as a proper test of learning. Distance may be specified as thirty feet; accuracy may be specified as a minimum of seven out of ten tries. Technique or skill should be understood to mean a standard of acceptability agreed upon by those knowledgeable in the field. Soccer experts, assisted by research in biomechanics, are the people qualified to describe the proper patterns of execution. Instructors may need to review modern techniques occasionally to update their knowledge of instructional objectives so that program objectives may be met adequately.

Procedures for developing instructional units

■ Activity titles like soccer, folk dance, and swimming are immediately associated with specific subordinate activities such as lead-up games, drills, and skills, and with related cognitive elements such as rules and strategies, directions for dances, and stroke mechanics. Instructional units are easily determined because the limitations of subject matter are recognized by anyone who is acquainted with these activities. The objectives appear to be obvious.

Not so with education in *basic movement* and in *fundamental activities* that are not directly related to specific sports, games, dances, and aquatic events. The general psychomotor competencies that develop as a result of participation in these programs are not so easily classified, but the rationale for giving such activities titles to avoid lengthy descriptions points to a solution for the problem as shown by the following activity titles.

The title of a unit on soccer should be specific about the form of the game: Modified Regulation Soccer, Eight-Man Soccer, Three-on-Three Soccer, and so forth. Folk dance units should be clearly described by title: Children's European Folk Dance, Elementary Scandinavian Folk Dances,

Units of instruction: themes i to v

225

English Country Dance for Children. Swimming activity titles should be modified by adjectives such as elementary, beginning, intermediate, or advanced. Titles such as Drownproofing. Elementary Water Stunts, and Recreational Aquatic Games for Six-to-Eight-Year-Olds are succinct descriptions of other water activities. Each specific title helps the instructor select and develop appropriate supportive objectives. Subordinate activities are chosen and arranged in a progressive sequence from simple to complex, each with its own instructional objectives. The sequence terminates with the attainment of the objectives defined by the title of the unit of instruction.

For example, the instructional objectives for a unit on Four-on-Four Soccer might be developed as follows.

Complete the statement, "The student should be able to, . . ." with

1 a description of the activity the student should be able to manage with a minimum acceptable level of competence.
2 a description of the kinds of skills the student should be able to display while participating in the activity.
3 a description of the facts, rules, directions, and/or principles associated with the minimum acceptable level of knowledge relevant to the activity.
4 a description of the process behaviors the student should acquire and use in learning the skills and in participating intelligently, including solving problems relevant to distance, direction, speed, and spatial relationships of offensive and defensive players or other participants.
5 a description of conduct associated with participation such as aggressiveness within the limits of fair play, cooperative relationship with teammates, and appreciation of the need for equal distribution of athletic talent to make competition equal.

Procedures to be used in evaluating unit objectives should be clearly spelled out. Student progress reports should indicate which physical education goals have been attained in each unit. Each program objective, when converted to specific instructional objectives, may be used as the basis for grading performance. A scale may be used to rate the learner either against his own previous standard of performance or against the standard of his group, class, or grade level. One such scale might be 1—needs to improve; 3—satisfactory achievement; 5—outstanding accomplishment. Instructors usually are more interested in how well children perform in relation to their previous performances, while parents usually want to know where their children stand in relation to others.

Instructors today try to evaluate skill in the setting in which it is employed rather than in some isolated situation. Passing and kicking the soccer ball in an appropriate manner at the proper times is often viewed as a better criterion of learner performance than merely being able to kick the ball with the instep. Such skill tests, when used, should be followed up by observations of play behaviors to assure that the skill is used adequately at the proper time.

Subordinate activity titles are listed for each unit of instruction. These activities divide the broad unit objectives into smaller, more manageable, instructional objectives. Four-on-Four Soccer is arrived at through a sequence of lessons, each of which aims at the accomplishment of objectives related to a specific subordinate activity.

Subordinate activities in order of difficulty for a unit on Four-on-Four Soccer might be:

1 one-with-one dribbling, passing, and shooting.
2 two-on-two keepaway.
3 one-on-one play plus a goalie.
4 two-on-two play plus a goalie.

Each subordinate activity is supported by appropriate instructional objectives. These objectives describe as clearly as possible the desired behavior, whether psychomotor, cognitive, or affective, the circumstances under which the behavior is to occur, and the standard of acceptable performance. Subordinate activities may be suggested in a unit description, but instructors should be permitted to make the final decision. Only the instructor writes the instructional objectives. Such latitude is necessary if the instructor is to individualize or tailor programs through instructional objectives to the needs and interests of the learner.

Fundamental movement activities are grouped according to the purpose of the activity. For example, Recreational Indoor Games for the Primary Grades is a title that provides reasonably clear direction to the program planner. A unit entitled Circle Games Stressing Chasing and Fleeing would not include such subordinate activities as Dodgeball but would include such activities as Duck, Duck, Goose and Beater Goes Round. Eliminating the emphasis on chasing and fleeing or substituting a different emphasis changes the nature of the subordinate activities but does not change the circular formation of the activity. Should the unit require a variety of formations, a more suitable title must be chosen.

The title Chasing-and-Fleeing Single-Goal Games eliminates those games in which children may run to two or more bases or places to avoid capture. In this case, formations are optional; circles, lines, and scattered formations may be employed.

Noncompetitive activities also are grouped according to purpose. Balancing Stunts in Twos and Threes, Hitting Targets of Different Sizes and Shapes, Beginning Roller Skating, Cycling, Rope Jumping, and Frisbee Throwing are some sample titles.

Beginning units

■ Operational Stage I, level 1.0, consists of instructional units designed to achieve the major affective objectives previously identified. Subordinate activities with very specific instructional objectives are structured to meet the specific needs and interests of the group in question. *Basic movement* makes good subject matter for exploration of actions, efforts, space, and relationships in different physical and social environments. Children in grades up to 3 or 4 should be involved in sequential instructional units emphasizing exploratory movement experiences. This does not rule out the use of games or gamelike activities as culminating activities when the sub-

Units of instruction: themes i to v

ject matter being explored has been properly developed. *The affective objectives are the main target of instruction at this stage and level.*

Older children usually prefer activities having more specific purposes from the outset of the lesson. One way to achieve level 1.0 affective objectives with older children is through games and contests in which all children win if they follow directions, employ the proper skills, or cooperate thoughtfully with each other. Large group games in which few children handle the ball or perform important actions are not appropriate in an instructional program. Subordinate activities for the upper levels of instruction, when the objectives are still in the affective domain, are kept simple until the children demonstrate their readiness to move on to level 2.0 psychomotor and cognitive objectives. The shift in emphasis is evident from the titles of the units, which describe the content in more specific terms than is possible or necessary for Stage I, level 1.0 activities.

Themes as basic movement units

■ Units of instruction in basic movement education rely largely upon the work of Rudolf Laban, particularly his *Modern Educational Dance.*[1] Of the sixteen movement themes he describes, the first eight and some parts of the other eight are especially helpful in identifying appropriate basic movement content.

Each theme focuses on certain elements, but each theme is broad enough to provide ideas for many lessons when it is divided into smaller parts suitable for unit level themes. Each unit theme describes the purpose of the supporting activity and provides direction for the selection of more specific lesson themes, which operationalize the unit theme. Unit level program objectives are described, but lesson themes replace the subordinate activity titles mentioned previously. Again, instructional objectives are written for each lesson theme to assure attainment of unit level program objectives.

A most helpful supplement to Laban's book is that of Valerie Preston-Dunlop, *A Handbook for Modern Educational Dance.*[2] She breaks down each of Laban's movement themes into many smaller, more operational themes, which the authors of this book have categorized and modified for ease in constructing unit and lesson plans for basic movement education.

Clearly designed, progressive, instructional sequences in basic movement education now lie within the reach of all elementary school physical education teachers and interested classroom teachers with physical education responsibilities. Instead of picking lessons at random, with no consideration for what went before or what is to follow, instructors in basic movement now can design instructional units selected from a recognized series of major movement themes that constitute the required grammar of movement learning experience and the foundation of a movement-oriented physical education program.

1 Rudolf Laban, *Modern Educational Dance,* 3d ed. (London: MacDonald & Evans, 1975).
2 Valerie Preston [-Dunlop], *A Handbook for Modern Educational Dance* (London: MacDonald & Evans, 1963).

Body awareness
activities

The major movement themes introduced by Laban are designated by Roman numerals. Each is elaborated in the manner of Preston-Dunlop to clarify the content. Unit and lesson themes follow.

Each part of this Theme is based on particular manners of moving which co-ordinate the bend, stretch and twist in different ways. Each is also designed to encourage an awareness of the relationships between the different parts of the body so that they can work together and assist one another in producing harmonious movement.[3] Bodily coordination or lack of coordination as revealed through the kinesthetic sense are central to body awareness.

Theme I:
Body awareness

The six unit level themes under body awareness are aimed at making the individual more responsive to the kinesthetic sense, at awakening the body to the feeling for motion within the body. Suggestions for lesson themes are offered, but experienced teachers are encouraged to devise their own lesson themes from the content. Additional unit level themes will be suggested.

1.0 The Body as a Unit in Motion and Stillness

1.1 *Actions Using the Whole Body*: A lesson theme that is easily expanded to the unit level. Whole actions of the body are emphasized with all parts of the spine, the trunk, the head, and the appendages being active.

    1.11 *Opening and Closing*: Actions in which the body widens or narrows by gathering itself together. Maintaining one position as well as alternating positions are possible actions.

3 Ibid., p. 3.

Actions using
the whole body

Twisting and turning

1.12 *Twisting and Turning:* A popular theme that leads to such concepts as twists resulting in turns. Twists differ from turns in that they do not involve complete rotation. All parts of the body may be twisted, but only the whole body is capable of a complete turn.

Finding ways to
run and jump

1.13 *Rising and Falling*: Pushing downward against the pull of gravity raises the body, while giving in to gravity causes the body to fall. Rising and falling, used in combination with actions such as twisting and turning, are especially stimulating for young children.

1.14 *Locomotion or Traveling*: Getting from one place to another may take many forms. Walking, running, jumping, hopping, leaping, skipping, galloping, sliding, rolling, crawling, creeping, and hitching are ways children will find to travel.

1.2 *Action and Stillness*: All kinds of actions may be combined with awareness of stillness which is accomplished by holding a position upon completion of an action. Holding various postures before and after action is particularly useful in developing awareness of position. Muscular tension holds the parts against gravitational pull in a frozen state. Some teachers prefer to start with this theme to teach the concept of freezing. Level 1.0 lessons give considerable emphasis to starting and stopping behaviors. The command "Freeze!" is used in place of the often overused whistle signal. Apart from its application in class control, stillness is valuable in the "education of the kinesthetic sense."[4]

4 Ibid., p. 4.

1.21 *Going and Stopping*: Self-starting and stopping teaches learners to feel the difference between the two behaviors and to know when the body is absolutely still before resuming motion. "Going" can mean traveling or movement while remaining in one place.

1.22 *Stillness to Stillness*: This theme stresses held positions and motions used to change to different held or frozen positions. It is used mainly as a subtheme because children are not able to engage in an entire lesson devoted to such limited exploration.

1.3 *Sequences of Whole-Body Actions and Stillness*: This is an adjunctive theme, one that may be used to climax a series of themes involving use of the body. The concept of sequence must be taught through experiencing the beginnings, middles, and endings of actions. This is where awareness of stillness enables the learner to develop clarity in a sequence of same or different actions.

1.31 *Combining Rising and Falling and Twisting and Turning*: Developing sequences of four actions, such as a turn followed by a fall, a twist, and a rise. These and other combinations should show stillness at the beginning and at the ending so that the movement phrase stands out clearly. Children should be able to verbalize as well as perform the sequence.

1.32 *Combining Traveling with Rising and Falling*: Falling into a roll, rising to a run, and all sorts of other combinations are possible. Sequences can be complicated even more by adding twisting and turning.

1.33 *Opening and Closing into Twists and Turns*: This theme is self-explanatory. Closing while turning on one foot speeds up the action and heightens the sense of instability, while opening slows the turn—a useful principle for later participation in gymnastic activities such as tumbling, turns on the apparatus, and somersaults on the trampoline. With the addition of content from other themes, a wide range of possible explorations and sequences emerges.

2.0 Symmetric and Asymmetric Use of the Body

2.1 *Asymmetry and Symmetry Contrasted*: First, positions of stillness are used to help learners sense the equality or inequality of the two sides of the body. Then learners perform movements, focusing their awareness on whether the two sides of the body are acting together or not. When the actions are together, there is an accompanying sensation of balance. Instability, or the sensation of imbalance, is experienced when one side of the body is stressed over the other.

The free flow of one gesture into another is more easily felt in asymmetry where turning and traveling naturally occur. Turning, particularly, brings the sensations of unbalance and mobility one can feel the continuation of the spinning quality after the body has come to rest. Symmetry has a more solemn quality because of its balance and stability, the flow of such movements being naturally more restricted and bound together.[5]

5 Ibid., p. 4.

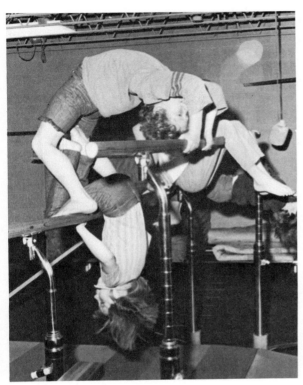

Sequences of whole
body actions
and stillness

Combining rising and
falling, twisting
and turning

Balancing, using
all the space

Using the legs in
different ways

2.2 *Symmetry and Asymmetry in Locomotion and Stillness*: The learner is ready to explore a little further the feelings of symmetry and asymmetry experienced in locomotor activities. Immediate stillness after such actions helps focus attention even more clearly on the equality or inequality of the two sides of the body.

3.0 Emphasis on Areas of the Body

3.1 *The Lower Body Parts Assume the Major Role*: From the hips and the center of gravity down to the toes, each body part can be emphasized in a supporting role in balancing, stepping, or leaping, or as a gesture into various parts of surrounding space.

3.11 *Using the Legs in Different Ways*: Parts of the legs are identified and used in movements on the spot or in traveling. Sometimes the entire leg participates in an action, while at other times a single leg part leads while other parts follow.

3.12 *Lower Body Parts for Support and Traveling*: Specific roles are given to various parts of the lower half of the body. Support on one foot or even the right foot and the other knee may be followed by a change to two different parts of the legs or hips. Although

Emphasis is given to
what the lower body
is doing.

Upper body parts
assume the major role.

the upper parts of the body participate in these movements, emphasis is given to what the lower half of the body is doing.

3.2 *The Upper Body Parts Assume the Major Role:* Although the legs may be used for support, the emphasis is on what the upper parts of the body are doing. These parts can gesture in all directions, take the weight of the body, and pull or push to make the body go.

    3.21 *Using the Arms in Different Ways:* Careful attention is given to the names and actions of the upper parts of the body.

    3.22 *Upper Body Parts for Support and Traveling:* Learners explore the ways in which the upper body parts may take the weight of the body and cause it to travel, alone or in combination with the legs.

3.3 *Coordinating the Upper and Lower Parts of the Body:* After exploring movements of the lower and upper halves of the body, learners may coordinate the two halves in a variety of ways. The two sides of the body and the two halves of the body make up four quarters, each of which may be moved separately, in sequence or in combination with any other quarter. Each quarter consists of various body parts which support the role of the body area as a whole.

    3.31 *Emphasizing Single Areas of the Body:* Each body area performs major movements while other body areas perform some necessary supporting function. The right leg, arm, and hip may support the body while the left arm, shoulder, and head perform a variety of different actions. Changes in position permit other areas to function in similar ways. Stillness should be included as a possible action. "Each limb can take the solo part so that the four

Upper body parts for
support and traveling

quarters of the body 'sing' one after the other either in motion or in stillness."[6]

3.32 *Stressing Sameness and Difference in Areas of the Body*: Having the right side of the body match the movements of the left side, the upper right, the lower left, and so forth, not only helps the learner articulate the body parts, but also helps the learner identify what is the same and what is different about the specific actions. Stretching, twisting, and curling, raising and lowering, or widening and narrowing may be the focus of various explorations.

3.33 *The Trunk Leads the Body*: Here emphasis is given to the trunk's leading the body into various contractions, extensions, twists, and elevations.

4.0 Leading the Movement with Specific Body Parts

4.1 *Leading with Specific Parts of the Limbs*: The arms may be differentiated into hands, wrists, and elbows, and further into the palm, the back of the hand, and the little finger or thumb side. The legs are made up of toes, foot, heel, and knee, or further, ball of foot, outer and inner sides, instep, and arch. Any of these parts may be singled out to lead an action.

4.2 *Leading with Specific Parts of the Trunk*: Upward movements, as in rising, may be led by the chest when support is to be on the feet or on the hands and feet. The hips may lead when support is to be on the

6 Ibid., p. 5.

Units of instruction:
themes i to v

Emphasizing single areas
of the body

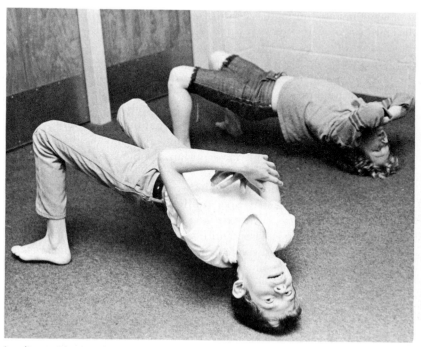

Leading with specific
parts of the trunk

hands. Elevations should stress the chest leading as the center of lightness. Downward actions are often lead by the pelvis, either one hip or both hips.

4.3 *Leading into Weight Transfers*: Specific body parts lead the body into steps or rolls.

4.4 *Leading into Turns and Elevations*: A variety of turns and jumps grows out of explorations in using different body parts to lead into important actions.

4.5 *Sequences of Leading and Following Actions of the Body*: A specific part may start a sequence of actions by taking the lead, only to have another part assume the lead. Attention is given to the order in which the different parts follow.

5.0 Transfer of Weight and Gesture

5.1 *Transferring the Weight of the Body in Different Ways*: Various ways of transferring the weight of the body have specific names such as walking and rolling. Awareness that each of these ways may be different from all other ways of transferring weight is emphasized.

    5.11 *Transferring the Weight in Steplike Actions*: Awareness of which part of the foot or hand, for example, the weight is on at the beginning of support and at the end of support. As the weight

Leading into
weight transferences

Sequences of leading
and following actions
of the body

of the body is received, which part in involved? Where does the weight go next?

    5.12 *Transferring the Weight in Rolling Actions*: The difference between steplike and rolling actions is perceived as intermittent transfer in the former and continuous transfer to adjacent areas in the latter. The curved shape assumed by the body to facilitate weight transfer initiates development of more advanced concepts and awarenesses concerning the shift of the body's center of gravity in rolling actions.

5.2 *Balance and Imbalance*: The use of gesture to balance and unbalance the body is explored. Shifting the hips in various directions with no counterbalancing movements of the shoulders or arms leads to imbalance.

    5.21 *Static Balance in the Upright and Inverted Positions*: Maintaining balance by using the parts of the body not being used to support the body.

    5.22 *Dynamic Balance and Gesture*: Exploring the use of free body parts to help balance the body while traveling or turning. Shifting the weight from a high to a low position when coming to a stop or changing direction is recognized as one way to increase the stability of the action.

    5.23 *Sequences of Balance and Imbalance*: Balancing and unbalancing into a new balance. The same balance may be used and different ways of unbalancing, ending up with the same balance, may be explored.

5.3 *Creating Sequences of Balance and Transfer*: Different weight transfers and balances may be sequenced. A sequence may begin with a balance, be followed by imbalance into one or more ways of transferring weight, and end with another balance or the same balance.

6.0 Parts of the Body in Contact

6.1 *Awareness of Contact and Noncontact*: Body parts are brought together to near-contact or touch. Parts try to make contact or to avoid contact. One part may surround another part, link with it, or intertwine with it.

    6.11 *Parts in Contact*: Different ways in which body parts may contact each other are explored. Older children particularly enjoy development of this theme in partner relationships. There are many ways of linking and intertwining body parts.

    6.12 *Changing Relationships of Body Parts*: Parts of the body can go toward, away from, next to, and around without making contact with other parts.

6.2 *Creating Sequences of Contact or Noncontact*: Going from contact to contact or from contact to noncontact with various body parts leading the action makes for interesting sequences involving motion and stillness.

    6.21 *Meeting and Parting or Passing*: Gallops and slides are meeting and parting noncontact body-part relationships, while walking and running are meeting and passing noncontact relationships.

Static balance in
contact with
different surfaces

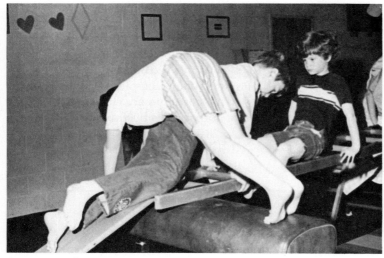

Awareness of contact
and noncontact

The feet may part and come back together during a jump. Knees, elbows, head, and other parts may be used in the formation of sequences.

6.22 *Improvisations on Contact or Noncontact*: Teachers or children can single out parts of the body and relationships for improvisations in creating interesting sequences. The use of stillness helps create a dramatic effect.

Improvisations on
contact or noncontact

A sample unit is provided for each major theme to illustrate how the material may be processed for both unit and lesson plans. Also shown is a method for identifying the unit for further reference, for placing it in a curricular sequence, and simply for purposes of illustrating development of a coding procedure.

Sample Unit: Theme I

Theme: I Body Awareness

Unit: 1.0 The Body as a Unit in Motion and Stillness

Instructional level: Grade 1   Operational stage: I, level 2.0

Program objectives: On completion of this unit, the learner should
1 Be able to identify and name correctly instructor-selected whole-body movements involving traveling or nonlocomotor actions;
2 Demonstrate through motor behaviors a general understanding of whole-body actions in place and while traveling;
3 Be able to start and end whole-body actions with stillness.

Suggested lesson themes:

The following lesson themes have been selected as the means for securing the program objectives. Each theme and subtheme is supported by appropriate instructional objectives in modular lesson plans, using floor, apparatus, rhythm, and manipulative environments.

1.1 Actions Using the Whole Body
    1.11 Opening and Closing
    1.12 Twisting and Turning
    1.13 Rising and Falling
    1.14 Locomotion
1.2 Action and Stillness
    1.21 Going and Stopping
    1.22 Stillness to Stillness

Notes on sample units

Given this unit, teachers are free to exercise one or more options. They may elect to use the suggested themes; restate the themes or regroup the content; or reorder the themes suggested.

Teachers may *not* decide not to teach the unit because it is an administrative directive that they teach it. Program objectives have been decided on by a curriculum committee. The teacher's role is to pursue these objectives with the students through the themes suggested or in some other way. No administrative decision is indicated for the amount of time to be spent on the unit. Therefore, teachers may spend as much or as little time as they feel will make the unit profitable to learners. They may even go beyond the program objectives.

This unit, The Body as a Unit in Motion and Stillness, can be used in future lessons during the same year. Subthemes in this unit may be used as themes for more in-depth work in other units. Other themes also may be added. The time between repetitions of a single theme is rich in the introduction of new concepts and the development of deeper understanding of concepts already acquired. A return to an old theme is accompanied by perceptions of new possibilities for exploration and further discovery. Learners can be challenged to seek higher levels in thinking behaviors as well as movement behaviors. Shifting the emphasis in the statement of objectives from comprehension to application, and eventually to creation of new and different structures, concepts, and ideas greatly changes the lesson for the learners. It is not "old stuff" unless the teacher lacks the understanding and imagination needed to revitalize the content. Theme revisitations enable teachers to add subthemes from other units. After all, the final product—learners graduating from the physical education program—are a blend of all of the units of instruction through which they have passed and from which they have learned. At each step along the way, learners exhibit both what they have learned and what they have not learned. We can only guide the teacher in planning lessons that meet the needs of individual learners.

Theme II: Awareness of weight and time

■ No clearer explanation of this theme can be had than that supplied by Preston-Dunlop.

> This Theme is the first of several dealing with the quality of movement. Quality and quantity of time and weight are sometimes confused. There is a "weight-quantity" which can be measured in pounds or grams, and a "time-quantity," which can be measured in seconds and speeds. There are also weight and time qualities, and they are not measurable, but a question of attitude. One talks of having a "strong desire" to do something, or a "sudden urge," and these are weight and time qualities, or attitudes to weight and time. The movements which result from such attitudes are the outward expression of an inner drive. In exercising these qualities in movement, psychosomatic education is attempted.[7]

There is much food for thought in this quotation. The concept of weight and time quality is new to American physical education and to American readers who tend to think quantitatively. It is essential that the teacher focus on the qualitative aspects of this theme, which may require some learner reeducation when older students are involved.

Combine work on this theme with themes previously studied. In this instance, explore thoroughly the weight and time qualities of whole-body actions and stillness studied in the previous unit until children can articulate the movement phrases with clarity of attitude. Stillness should be held for varying periods of time from very briefly (while a previous action is still felt, even though it has ceased) to a long time (long enough for the feeling of the previous action to dissipate completely and for the mover to give complete attention to the state of nonmovement).

Strong and gentle whole-body actions express different feelings, as these terms imply. Although introductory lessons merely focus on new material and bring some basic concepts into the learner's growing vocabulary of movement, continued refinement of the learner's attitudes toward the motion factors is necessary. The theme of weight and time should be reviewed many times to enhance the learner's concept of effort.

The five parts of the weight and time theme are progressively ordered. Here it is better to follow the suggested sequence rather than to skip around, which is possible with some other themes. Awareness of the separate elements of weight and time is followed by work on awareness of an element from each factor at the same time.

Parts 4.0 and 5.0 follow as outgrowths of work on phrasing of movements. Meter arranges time into units that can be heard in music or in the measured beats on a drum, cymbal, or triangle. Short, long, even, and uneven time units may be repeated in all movements. The final part of Theme II is devoted to specific aspects of rhythm.

The capacity to use and to discern slight differences in time duration and weight accent is directly related to the development of efficient motor

7 Ibid., p. 9.

Firm touch quality
in action

patterns. It is the sense of proportion that enables the learner to acquire the
level of skill needed to perform a given action.

The modular adaptation of the theme of weight and time is directed
toward awareness of rhythm and control in work with apparatus and in
manipulative work, and toward freer expression in rhythm and dance.

1.0 Weight Qualities—Firm and Fine Touch Movement

1.1 *Contrasting Firm and Fine Touch Qualities*: The quality of firmness
is felt as strong tension, which produces a forceful action or holds a
firm position. Fine touch is delicate, light, and airy with only slight tension. The actions of the unit on body awareness can be gone over in
their entirety, this time with the focus on touch qualities.

   1.11 *Stressing the Participation of the Whole Body*: The whole body
rather than smaller body areas or body parts is used to explore
the weight quality.

   1.12 *Stressing the Participation of Isolated Parts*: Areas of the body
and separate body parts are moved with attention to the weight
factor.

   1.13 *Attitude versus No Attitude Toward Weight*: Firm as a weight
attitude may be contrasted with heavy as an absence of attitude,

and fine touch may be contrasted with heavy touch to achieve mastery of these qualities.*

1.2 *Changing the Degree of Tension Along the Continuum*: Slight tension can be increased gradually until the strong tension is achieved; then the process can be reversed. Degrees of tension along the continuum can be felt and held. Some learners will tend toward a firm touch while others will lean toward a fine touch. The appropriate degree of tension can be decided upon in such actions as holding the abdomen flat, walking erect without being stiff, maintaining slight tension in the arms while running, and preparing for a vertical jump in contrast with the actual jump. Body mechanics, sports, and other activities may be explored by learners to increase their sensitivity to the most appropriate degrees of effort to be used in relation to the tasks presented.

2.0 Time Qualities—Sudden and Sustained Movement

2.1 *Contrasting Sudden and Sustained Movement*: Sudden movement is sharp, quick, or instantaneous. The quality may be exhibited at the beginning, the middle, or the end of an action, as well as throughout the movement. Sustainment is a quality of lingering, prolonging, slow, or unhurried motion, or pauses between actions. The full range of actions experienced previously may be explored again with this new focus.

    2.11 *Stressing the Participation of the Whole Body*: The whole body rather than smaller body areas or body parts is used to explore the qualities of time.

    2.12 *Stressing the Participation of Isolated Parts*: Areas of the body and separate body parts are activated in exploration of time quality.

    2.13 *Attitude versus No Attitude Toward Time*: This is a most difficult theme because learners are asked to contrast feelings of urgency and sustainment not with each other but with feelings of neither urgency nor sustainment. In some actions, the attitude toward the time factor is not at all important.

2.2 *Stressing the Dramatic Qualities of Time*: *Surprise, boredom, vibration, shaking, waiting, stalking,* and *patience* are among the words that can be explored for dramatic impact in a variety of situations.

3.0 Time and Weight Qualities

3.1 *Exploring the Combinations of Weight and Time*: The four combinations are sustained-fine touch, sudden-fine touch, sustained-firm touch, and sudden-firm touch.

3.2 *Sequencing Phrases of Different Weight-Time Qualities*: The first step is to recognize similarities and differences among several phrases when only weight-time qualities are observed. One phrase can follow a different phrase, with clarity of ending and a pause helping in the

---

* Readers with a special interest in the psychological factors surrounding the qualities of effort should read *Personality Assessment Through Movement* by Marion North (London: MacDonald & Evans, 1972).

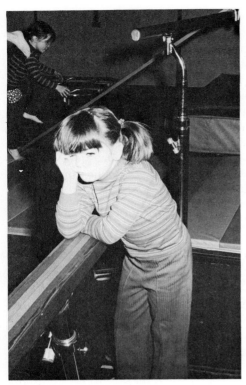

Stressing the dramatic
qualities of time

transition. Powerful action phrases can end in contrasting gentle phrases. All parts of the body should experience the weight-time qualities, either as the leader of movement or as the supporter of weight. Subthemes involving use of percussion are most helpful.

4.0 Meter—The Division of Time into Measurable Units

4.1 *Translating Meter into Movement*: The short and long units of time are listened to and repeated in movements.

4.2 *Forming Repeatable Metric Phrases*: Given possibilities for combining time units, children explore the formation of phrases they can repeat and perhaps show others, or contribute to a group endeavor.

5.0 Rhythm—The Fusion of Time and Weight

5.1 *Contrasting Metric and Free Rhythms*: One rhythm obeys the principle of metric time while the other is free to change at will. Feet customarily are used for metric gestures more often than other body parts. Free rhythms abound in sports and gymnastics, whereas dance may involve either metric or free rhythms.

   5.11 *Placing Strong or Light Accents in Different Parts of a Movement Phrase*: Accents may be placed at the beginning, middle, or ending of a movement phrase.

   5.12 *Placing Both Strong and Light Accents in the Same Movement*

Phrase: Strong and light accents may be used in the same movement phrase. Recognizing and creating movement phrases with accents of varying intensity helps sensitize learners to rhythm. Movement patterns with a sports motif, particularly ball handling, may be analyzed for their use of accents.

5.2 *Performing Metric Rhythms with Variations in Weight Stress*: Different beats in measured time units may be accented. Long phrases may show accents of different intensity; for example, the first and fifth beats of an eight-count phrase may be stressed differently.

    5.21 *Movement Phrases in Legato (Sustained Manner) and Staccato (Sudden Manner)*: The weight stress remains the same, but the time units vary greatly in length.

    5.22 *Changing the Quality of Time While Maintaining the Tempo*: Double-timing and half-timing are common ways in which the quality of time is changed. Movement may change to sustainment or to urgency without change in the metric measure of time.

5.3 *Fitting Free Rhythms into a Metric Framework*: Free rhythms based on weight-time changes are created and adjusted to a metric structure.

Sample unit: Theme II

Theme: II Awareness of Weight and Time

Unit: 3.1 Exploring the Combinations of Weight and Time

Instructional level: Grade 2   Operational stage: I, level 2.0

Program objectives: On completion of this unit, the learner should

1 Be able to demonstrate clearly the differences in the weight-time qualities of selected movement phrases or patterns such as walking, running, and skipping.

2 Be able to perform simple phrases of movement that show a given quality of weight and time such as sustained firmness.

3 Be able to recognize and name the different weight-time qualities in a simple series of movements.

Suggested lesson themes:
The following lesson themes have been selected as the means for securing the program objectives. Each theme and subtheme is supported by appropriate instructional objectives in modular lesson plans, using floor, apparatus, rhythm, and manipulative environments.

3.1 Exploring the Combinations of Weight and Time
    3.11 Discovering the Combinations of Weight-Time Qualities
    3.12 Changing One Quality While Maintaining Another
    3.13 Contrasting the Weight-Time Quality of Movements

Notes on the sample unit for Theme II

This sample unit illustrates some ways in which the thematic sequence may be adjusted to suit the needs of the program and the children it is to serve. Note that the title of the unit is repeated in the suggested lesson themes, but that this larger theme is divided into smaller, more manageable themes. The instructor is free to use suggested themes as main themes or as subthemes.

The main theme might be 3.11, Discovering the Combinations of Weight-Time Qualities. Realizing that children will have little difficulty with this aspect of the work, the instructor might include as a subtheme, 3.12, Changing One Quality While Maintaining Another. This or any other combination or reordering is acceptable. Experienced instructors will add subthemes of their own.

Program objective 1 says that the learner should be able to demonstrate differences in weight-time qualities of selected movement phrases or patterns such as walking, running, and skipping. First, how might walking demonstrate differences in weight-time qualities? What are the possible combinations of these two factors? How can these four combinations be shown through walking? Through other patterns?

Obviously, before children can distinguish the different weight-time qualities of a movement pattern, they must know that it is possible for these two qualities to exist in different combinations. What better way to arrive at the answer than through discovery? Having found the answer in one environment and repeated the process in another, such as in apparatus work, ball handling, or movement to the sound of a drum, learners should be able to use this understanding in different ways to solve new problems.

Is it possible to maintain one quality and change the other? Can a sudden-strong action become sudden and gentle? Can a sustained-light movement become sudden and light? Various whole-body actions, which should be very familiar to the children by now, can be used in the discovery of answers to these and other questions about the relationships of weight and time to movement.

A final note before leaving this sample unit. The unit theme is numbered 3.1, because the theme involves elements and combinations of two motion factors, weight and time, and it is assumed that these factors have been the subjects of previous work. If that is the case, children should have no difficulty with this unit.

■ The environment of space is the focus of this theme—where the movement goes, rather than what is moving or how it moves. As the elements of spatial awareness are introduced, learners merge their understanding of Themes I and II with these new experiences. Mastery of spatial awareness

**Theme III:
Awareness
of space**

Using all available space

is essential, for "the mover must be at home in it if he is to fully develop his movement potential and be independent."[8]

Thematic progression generally follows the sequence from 1.0 to 5.0, after which themes are selected on the basis of need until full comprehension is achieved. The full impact of moving through space is best felt when no stress at all is placed on the action or the quality. Attention to space gives movement an outward focus.

You might wonder why more attention has not been given to space in the sequence of basic movement themes up to this point. The abstractness of space for small children makes it difficult for them to divorce their great interest in what they are doing from where they are doing it. There is considerably more to spatial awareness than "finding a big space away from other people." One of the first major concepts to be learned is the difference between general space, a place in general space, and one's personal space. These spaces are different, but the difference is not readily apparent. Rather than present young children with facts they are not yet ready to assimilate, introduce only the information essential to their safety and within the purview of their understanding, using it as a subtheme to body awareness or to concepts of weight and time.

1.0 General Space

1.1 *Using All Available Space*: The concept of "all available space" is not easy for beginners to grasp. Interest in what the body is doing and how the movement is going detracts from awareness of precisely where in general space the learner is traveling. A different looking environment, such as one encompassing apparatus, brings space into focus by helping children see more clearly where they have or have not been.

8 Ibid., p. 15.

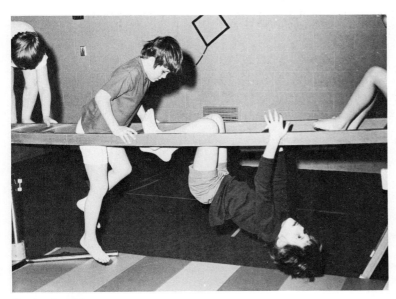

Contrasting big
spaces with
small spaces

    1.11 *Finding Big Spaces to Travel Through*: This very limited space
theme is excellent for beginners with learning difficulties. Being
able to distinguish big spaces from small spaces, to select a big
space quickly, and to travel through one big space while looking for another big space is quite a lot for some children to handle.

    1.12 *Contrasting Big Spaces with Small Spaces*: Children experience
big space when it is uncrowded by people or things and small
space when it is so crowded they have great difficulty avoiding
contact. The major objective is being aware of the size of surrounding space while in motion or at rest.

1.2 *Movement Relative to Space*: The body takes up space, penetrates it,
surrounds it, and retreats from it.

    1.21 *Penetrating Contrasted with Filling Space*: The feelings asso-
ciated with going through space in a narrow, penetrating way, as
if to use as little of it as possible to achieve one's objective, is
contrasted with using space as generously as possible, filling it
up with one's self.

    1.22 *Surrounding Contrasted with Repulsing Space*: The feelings of
surrounding or engulfing space with various parts of the body
are contrasted with those of repulsing or moving away from
space. One is approach behavior, the other avoidance behavior.

2.0 Spatial Areas around the Body

2.1 *Levels of Space*: The high level of space is contrasted with the deep
or low level of space, requiring that the body be used in different ways
to experience these different areas. The medium level of space sur-

Units of instruction:
themes i to v

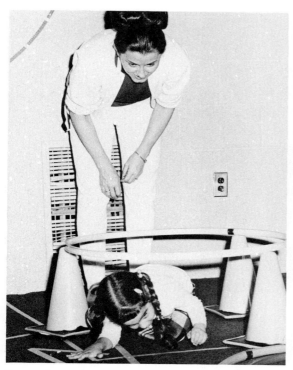

Penetration rather
than filling of space

Surrounding rather than
repulsing space

rounding the body is experienced more through horizontal movement than through vertical movement.

2.11 *Changing Levels*: Going from one level to another and becoming aware of rising as the action associated with changes from low or medium level to high level and of lowering as the action associated with changes to low level. Movement in the medium level requires maintaining the action in the area between the upper and lower levels.

2.12 *The Spatial Areas of the Body*: High level is associated with movement that takes one in an upward direction. The ceiling relates to high level; it is above the medium level. Low level is downward; it is associated with the floor. Low level is located below medium level. Surrounding the medium level space are real or imaginary walls or boundaries located in front of, in back of, to the right of, or to the left of the body. These are the six spatial areas surrounding the body.

2.2 *The Directions of Movement*: It is easier to understand direction when the concept of *forward* is related to the space *in front of*, first in relation to one's own body and later in relation to another person's body. Backward, to either side, up, and down are the other five fundamental directions easily developed as an outgrowth of the spatial

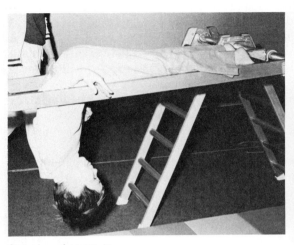

Stressing changes in
level while using
whole-body or
body-part actions

Changing levels

areas surrounding the body. This linking of the concepts of space and direction in relation to the body later helps young children grasp even more abstract concepts associated with general space.

2.3 *Combining Whole-Body and Body-Part Actions with Spatial Area Concepts*: Theme I awarenesses are combined with the fundamental awarenesses of level and direction.

    2.31 *Stressing Changes in Level While Using Whole-Body or Body-Part Actions*: Body parts leading the body into the different levels of space is the theme focus. Twists, turns, stretches, curls, pushes, and pulls take on additional meaning here.

    2.32 *Stressing Changes in Direction While Using Whole-Body or Body-Part Actions*: Changes in direction of forward, backward, to either side, up, and down may be added to changes in level, in leading parts, and in types of actions involving body parts as well as the entire body. Hands lead the body upward to high level. The hip leads the body backward and downward to the floor where a backward roll is executed at a low level. Skipping backward and combining forward and backward steps to cause turning with the addition of a slight change in the sideward direction augments the movement possibilities of Theme I.

2.4 *Combining Weight-Time Qualities with Spatial Areas*: The addition of weight and/or time qualities to movement in relation to spatial areas

Units of instruction:
themes i to v

253

requires that the learner be aware of the what, how, and where of body movement at the same time. The addition of weight-time qualities to the spatial dimension greatly increases children's capacity for inventiveness.

    2.41 *Stressing the Qualities of Weight with Spatial Areas*: Strong or light actions performed at various levels or in various directions. Whole-body and body-part actions can be specified.

    2.42 *Stressing the Qualities of Time with Spatial Areas*: Sudden or sustained actions leading or taking the body in various directions on various levels. Numerous combinations and sequences can be explored.

    2.43 *Stressing the Qualities of Weight and Time with Spatial Areas*: The full range of four fundamental attitudes toward weight and time are related to the six spatial areas in terms of level and direction.

2.5 *Movement Sequences Stressing Spatial Areas*: This is a culminating theme, combining the concepts acquired through work with Themes I and II. The learner must apply cumulative knowledge in the creation of new and different movement sequences, giving clear expression to differences in action, quality, and spatial area.

3.0 Personal Space or the Kinesphere

3.1 *Personal and General Space Contrasted*: A general distinction between personal and general space can be made quite early. "My space is where I can reach all around me" is the initial personal concept that goes with the thought, "When I travel, I take my personal space with me." When the children are ready for related concepts, use the following themes.

    3.11 *The Size of the Kinesphere Changes with the Base of Support*: Widening the base of support enlarges the space through which the body parts can extend. A smaller kinesphere accompanies a decrease in the base of support. Various parts of the body may be used for support to enable free parts to use all personal space made available through gesture.

    3.12 *The Limits of the Kinesphere in All Directions*: Body parts may be stretched out in all directions from various bases of support to define the outermost edges of personal space. Loss of balance requires that one establish a new base of support, with a consequent change in personal space.

3.2 *The Zones of Body Parts*: Within the kinesphere are zones of space associated with the normal range of movement of body parts. Normally, the legs and arms have separate zones, but each can invade the zone of the other in the exploration of new movement ideas. First, the normal zones are identified through movement of the legs and the arms. Then these body parts cross into other zones and areas of zones that are easily reached. Accompanying shifts in the center of gravity or in the base of support during these explorations should be noted.

4.0 Extensions in Space

4.1 *Focus on the Near and Far Aspects of Movement*: Although the body may stretch to reach far away from the body center or curl to bring the gesture into the body, the focus here is on spatial factors, not on what the body is doing. Actions that extend far into space or draw near into the space around the body are associations of *outward* with *far* and *inward* with *near*. Movements with an outward focus generally move into the farther reaches of space, whereas those with an inward focus are directed in toward the body.

  4.11 *Changing the Focus from Self and Near to Outward and Far*: Ideas for movement are stimulated through changes in the focus of movements.

  4.12 *Countertensions of Focus and Extension*: Experience and maturity are required in work with this theme. Movements of extension are accompanied by an inward focus and movements of contraction are accompanied by an outward focus.

4.2 *The Elementary Shapes of Large and Small*: Accompanying extension into space is an increase in the size of the body. The body occupies more space in its extended state. Contractions that bring body parts closer to the body center reduce the size of the body and the amount of space it occupies.

  4.21 *Growing and Shrinking*: Body parts as well as the whole body can be made to grow or to shrink, with accompanying changes in the amount of space occupied. This is a suitable theme for small children.

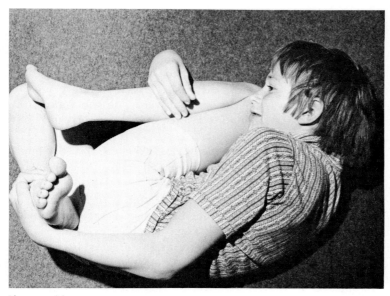

Shapes of large
and small

4.22 *Simultaneous or Sequential Growth and Shrinking*: Older, more experienced children might explore movements of body parts extending some to more space while contracting others to use less space. The action may be simultaneous, or it may be sequential, with first one part growing and then a different part shrinking.

5.0 Spatial Relationship

5.1 *Space Words*: Learning meanings for *on, over, under, through, between, toward, away from, next to,* and *along* through actions in relation to people or objects is the purpose of this theme. The theme is most useful for beginners of all ages who enjoy the feelings associated with changing relationships.

5.2 *Sequencing Space Words*: The teacher or learners may develop tasks requiring students to sequence actions in which the relationship remains the same (like *on*) but the actions, qualities, or spatial areas change, or the relationship changes but the action, quality, or spatial area remains the same.

5.21 *Maintaining a Spatial Relationship While Changing Level or Direction*: Remaining *next to* or *far from* while changing some spatial area is emphasized. Little sequences of movement can be developed in which the spatial relationship is constantly and clearly maintained.

5.22 *Maintaining the Action or Effort While Changing Spatial Relationship*: The tempo of action changes, but the relationship remains the same. Actions change but not the relationship. Numerous sequences can be developed.

6.0 Linking the Aspects of Space

6.1 *Simultaneous Awareness of Personal and General Space*: Changes in the size of personal space as the body travels into crowded general spaces have implications for extension and contraction in surrounding space. This is the first of the linking themes that can be used after the basic concepts of personal and general space have been established.

6.2 *Spatial Orientation in General and Personal Space*: Body parts can move upward, downward, to either side, forward, and backward within personal space while the body is traveling in the same or a different direction through general space.

6.21 *Awareness of Direction in Personal and General Space*: Simultaneous awareness of same or different directions in movements in both spaces.

6.22 *Awareness of Change in Level and Direction with Movement in Personal and General Space*: The body may change level while traveling forward with a simultaneous change or with no change in the level of the arms. Many interesting sequences are possible.

6.3 *Changes in Spatial Relationship and Orientation*: Awareness of change in orientations such as level, direction, and relationship to people or objects is stressed. Extensions in space that increase or decrease the size of the body may be included or substituted.

6.31 *Growing and Shrinking in Different Relationships*: The size of

Learning the
meaning of **on**

the body may change or remain the same with changes in relationship. Contracting the body while going around something, extending it while going under it, or using a body part instead of the whole body in similar movements requires simultaneous awareness of the interrelationship of different aspects of space.

6.32 *Direction, Level, and Relationship Variables*: Exploration of various actions accompanied by systematic changes in direction, level, and relationship may lead to creation of new sequences or other movement possibilities.

6.4 *Linking Aspects of Space with Body Awareness and Awareness of Weight and Time*: Numerous culminating activities linking Themes I, II, and III can be devised.

Notes on the sample unit for Theme III

Space units change the learners' focus from themselves and what or how they are doing to a focus outside of or away from themselves. The teacher must be careful not to go too fast with children who are exploring a space theme. Children need lots of time to develop full understanding of each space theme before going on to new spatial concepts. Children who almost unconsciously copy others and thereby retain their dependency should be helped. Independence of movement is achieved through self-directed activity with full awareness of where the action is going.

Changes in spatial
relationship and
orientation

Elements of spatial awareness can be introduced quite early with young children, but students will need to review and expand their concepts continually to establish links between the various elements and between spatial concepts and the concepts of weight, time, and action previously developed. Most of the work in the basic movement track for kindergarten through grade 2 is confined to the first three themes.

Sample unit: Theme III

Theme: III Space Awareness

Unit: 3.0 The Kinesphere

Instructional level: Grade 2   Operational stage: I, level 2.0

Program objectives: On completion of this unit, the learner should
1 Demonstrate awareness of the size of personal space by operating within its limits while traveling or moving on the spot.
2 Know that the size of the kinesphere is limited by the base of support and demonstrate this knowledge through appropriate adjustments in movement.

3 Be able to adjust the base of support and shift the center of gravity appropriately when extending body parts through adjacent zones of space.

Suggested lesson themes:
The following themes have been selected as the means for securing the program objectives. Each theme and subtheme is supported by appropriate instructional objectives in modular lesson plans, using floor, apparatus, rhythm, and manipulative environments.

3.1 Personal and General Space Contrasted
    3.11 The Size of the Kinesphere Changes with the Base of Support
    3.12 The Limits of the Kinesphere in All Directions
3.2 The Zones of Body Parts

■ This long theme completes the introduction of weight, time, space, and flow factors in motion and adds new material on learning to integrate the movements of the body. The flow factor, alone and in combination with other factors, is given greatest emphasis. Its integrative nature is recognized in all movements, especially when it is needed to coordinate actions that do not connect smoothly or to free an action that is too bound. One does not need to have specific knowledge of flow in motion, only sensitivity to the presence or absence of flow in the action being observed.

The space factor is the learner's "bodily attitude of directness or flexibility, which reflects mental directness or flexibility; and not the shapes or directions of his movement."[9] Like other effort factors, space effort is an attitude that may or may not be present in movement. In spatial awareness, it is psychosomatic space, and not measurable size, shape, or design that is important. It is what North calls "a subjective qualitative aspect,"[10] or as the theme states, "Awareness of the Flow of the Weight of the Body in Space and Time."

The range of awareness of each of the four motion factors—weight, time, space, flow—can vary greatly. It is important for learners to develop the capacity to alternate between the opposite attitudes expressed by each of the four factors. The ability to alternate attitudes prevents students from developing an unbalanced effort character such as that displayed by persons who cannot operate with a fine touch, or with sustained effort, or with flexibility. The teacher should assure children the opportunity of developing the capacity to alternate between opposing attitudes by having them move between "sensitivity and firmness; leisureliness and urgency; flexibility and directness; free and bound flow,"[11] a capacity that North goes on to state "shows a developed use of elements, which by no means everyone acquires."[12]

Theme IV: Awareness of the flow of the weight of the body in space and time

9 Marion North, *Movement Education* (London: Maurice Temple Smith, 1973), p. 157.
10 Ibid.
11 Ibid., p. 162.
12 Ibid.

Lessons on smooth flow, while helpful, are not enough. The teacher should return to this theme again and again so that children can experience the interrelationships of the elements of effort, without which full expression of the self or the mastery of movement is not possible.

Marion North describes alternative stresses for each motion factor. She has had extensive experience in the study of movement, particularly in the assessment of personality. Her work with children, her research into the psychological development of the handicapped child as well as the normal child, and her ability to write about her experiences with insight into their importance for movement education should be recognized in this country, too. According to North,[13] a person's attitude toward the weight of body, time, flow of movement, and space may be illustrated along separate spectrums running from one extreme to the other. In each case the midpoint of the spectrum denotes the moment of change from one attitude to another.

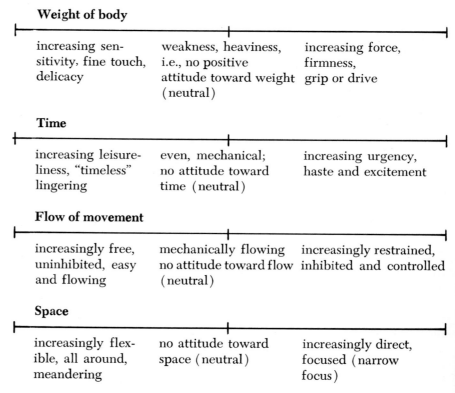

Weight of body

| increasing sensitivity, fine touch, delicacy | weakness, heaviness, i.e., no positive attitude toward weight (neutral) | increasing force, firmness, grip or drive |

Time

| increasing leisureliness, "timeless" lingering | even, mechanical; no attitude toward time (neutral) | increasing urgency, haste and excitement |

Flow of movement

| increasingly free, uninhibited, easy and flowing | mechanically flowing no attitude toward flow (neutral) | increasingly restrained, inhibited and controlled |

Space

| increasingly flexible, all around, meandering | no attitude toward space (neutral) | increasingly direct, focused (narrow focus) |

Observations of children working on various tasks will reveal how much more work they need on a particular effort characteristic. Individual children who have problems alternating particular effort factors can be given special help and encouragement to correct any imbalance. If an imbal-

13 Ibid., pp. 158-61.

ance cannot be corrected, a psychologist should be consulted for help in getting at the underlying problem.

1.0 Successive and Simultaneous Body Flow

1.1 *Contrasting Successive and Simultaneous Flow*: To experience simultaneous flow, all parts of an action must occur at the same time rather than one after the other. Going from the curled to the extended state of the body in simultaneous flow requires the arms, head, trunk, legs, and feet to move at the same time and to stop together when the stretched body posture is attained. Successive flow from curl to full extension might begin with opening of the fingers, followed in order by extension of the hand, arm, head, trunk, upper leg, lower leg, and finally the foot.

1.2 *Experiencing Successive and Simultaneous Flow in Conjunction with Another Effort Factor*: Firm and fine touch qualities, sudden and sustained time qualities, and directness of focus or lack of spatial focus can be combined with successive and simultaneous flow in actions ranging in size from large to small, occurring on the spot or while traveling.

  1.21 *In Conjunction with Firm and Fine Touch Qualities*: Emphasis is given to the strength of the action.

  1.22 *In Conjunction with Sudden and Sustained Qualities*: Emphasis is given to quickness or to sustainment of the action.

  1.23 *In Conjunction with Directness and Flexibility*: The action may be narrowly or flexibly directed through space. It may have a specific focus and move toward some point in space, some object, or some person.

  1.24 *In Conjunction with Large and Small Actions*: Movements of body parts as well as movements of the whole body may be used.

  1.25 *In Conjunction with Movement on the Spot or While Traveling*: On-the-spot actions may precede the same actions performed while traveling with either successive or simultaneous flow.

1.3 *Sequences of Successive Body Flow Involving Particular Parts of the Body*: Specific body parts are the focus for practice in successive flow in various directions.

  1.31 *Shoulder, Elbow, Wrist, Fingers*: Either the fingers or the shoulder may begin the action and lead. The left and the right sides of the body should be involved alternately.

  1.32 *Hip, Knee, Foot*: The hip should lead the action in this sequence. The application of this sequence in such activities as shot-putting, discus throwing, and kicking should be obvious.

  1.33 *Knee, Hip, Chest, Head*: The successive flow of movement from knee to head produces a body wave.

  1.34 *Less Usual Body Parts*: Encouraging children to identify different body parts to use successively is one way to sensitize them to the variety and the limitations of successive flow.

  1.35 *Finger Play*: Movements of the hands and fingers are stressed in activities involving successive flow, but activities involving simultaneous flow may be used also.

2.0 Free Flow and Bound Flow Qualities

2.1 *Contrasting Free and Bound Flow*: There are four ways to stress flow quality: free flow while moving, free flow while pausing, bound flow while moving, bound flow in stopping.

    2.11 *Contrasting Free and Bound Flow While Moving*: Free flow movements are difficult to stop, whereas bound flow movements are always ready to stop.

    2.12 *Contrasting Free and Bound Flow While Stopping*: The sensation of free flow is experienced in a pause that follows freely flowing action. Held, statuelike positions show bound flow. Coming to a stop with bound flow after a freely flowing or bound flow action offers additional experiences with these two flow qualities.

2.2 *Sequential Phrases of Movement Involving Free and Bound Flow*: Phrases connected by brief pauses lead to the development of movement sentences.

3.0 Flexible and Direct Space Qualities

3.1 *Contrasting Direct and Flexible Movement Qualities*: Direct movement has a narrow focus, uses space sparingly, and has a nondeviating path. Flexible movement may be described as roundabout, plastic, wavy, and meandering. The attitude toward space expressed by flexible movement is generous. Direct movement avoids use of space while flexible movement indulges in it.

3.2 *Experiencing Direct and Flexible Movements*: This effort theme focuses on the development of direct and flexible qualities through a variety of movement tasks.

4.0 Flow-Space Qualities

4.1 *Contrasting Flexible-Free and Flexible-Bound Qualities*: The space quality is maintained, but the flow factor is changed to stress the difference. Freely twisting, turning, and undulating movements retain their flexibility but become restricted in their flow quality.

4.2 *Contrasting Direct-Free and Direct-Bound Qualities*: The space quality is maintained, but the flow factor is changed to stress the difference. Freely directed, aimed, straight movements become restricted, limited, and increasingly controlled as the flow factor is restricted.

4.3 *Creating Transitions from One Space-Flow Quality to Another*: The teacher or the student creates different transitions from one space-flow quality to another. Flexible-free to flexible-bound requires only a change in the flow factor, but if the change is to direct-bound, use of a flexible-bound movement may be necessary to achieve control before the space factor is changed.

5.0 Flow-Time Qualities

5.1 *Contrasting Sudden-Bound and Sudden-Free Qualities*: Quick movements stop suddenly and appear jerky and disjointed, whereas the quality of suddenness with free flow appears bouncy, shaky, and, if exaggerated, vibratory.

5.2 *Contrasting Sustained-Bound and Sustained-Free Qualities*: Slow, stalking, cautious movements are contrasted with continuous, never-ending, timelessly free, unhurried movements.

5.3 *Creating Transitions from One Flow-Time Quality to Another*: The teacher or the student creates different transitions from one flow-time quality to another. Sudden-free to sustained-bound may require the transition to sustained-free quality before the flow is bound.

6.0 Flow-Weight Qualities

6.1 *Contrasting Firm-Bound and Fine Touch-Bound Qualities*: The quality ranges from cramped movement with a great deal of tension to delicate, sensitive, careful movement.

6.2 *Contrasting Fine Touch-Free and Firm-Free Qualities*: Strong, flowing movements, perhaps of the swinging or pendular type, are contrasted with light, airy, buoyant movements.

6.3 *Creating Transitions from One Flow-Weight Quality to Another*: The teacher or the student creates different transitions from one flow-weight quality to another by changing one element at a time.

7.0 Weight-Space Qualities

7.1 *Contrasting Firm-Flexible and Firm-Direct Movements*: Strong twisting actions that make generous use of space are contrasted with firm-direct, aimed actions.

7.2 *Contrasting Fine Touch-Flexible and Fine Touch-Direct Movements*: Gentle, twisting, spiraling, fine touch actions are contrasted with gentle, straight, threadlike, pointed actions.

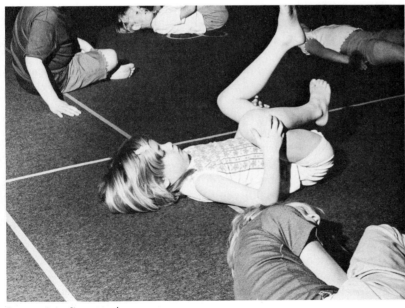

Contrasting fine touch-flexible and fine touch-direct

Creating transitions
from one space-time
quality to another

7.3 *Creating Transitions from One Weight-Space Quality to Another*: The teacher or student creates different transitions from one weight-space quality to another, such as firm-flexible to fine touch-flexible or firm-flexible to fine touch-direct.

8.0 Space-Time Qualities

8.1 *Contrasting Direct-Sudden and Direct-Sustained Qualities*: Tapping, pouncing, sharp actions are contrasted with straight, smooth, gliding actions.

8.2 *Contrasting Flexible-Sudden and Flexible-Sustained Qualities*: Contrasting whirling, flicking, whiplike actions of short duration with twisting, spiraling actions of long duration.

8.3 *Creating Transitions from One Space-Time Quality to Another*: The teacher or student creates different transitions from one space-time quality to another, such as direct-sudden to flexible-sustained with an intermediate action like direct-sustained or flexible-sudden.

9.0 Phrasing and Punctuation

9.1 *Phrasing with Clarity of Quality*:

A phrase must contain a main action which is done with clear quality and have either a preparation, a result or both. Running into a leap and landing could constitute a phrase but it says too little to be expressive. Much more is said if the run is speedy, the leap high and wide and the landing strong and bound. This is worth saying because it feels good to do; there is sufficient in it to make the mover want to participate with his whole being.[14]

The flow of movement is experienced in meaningful phrases that have what Preston-Dunlop calls "a preparation-action-result rhythm."[15]

9.11 *Emphasizing Preparations and Endings to Main Action*: Starting and ending positions help clarify the main action of short movement phrases and prepare the learner for the construction of longer phrases and movement sentences.

9.12 *Connecting Short Phrases*: Two or three main actions constitute a similar number of phrases, each with appropriate preparatory movements. The endings of all but the final phrase do not come to a full stop, being a pause still carrying the sensation of flow so that the preparation for the next action is carried out without interruption. A full stop at the end terminates the sequence.

9.2 *Integrating Previous Work with the Concept of Phrase*: All themes previously introduced under Themes I, II, or III may be restructured slightly to emphasize phrasing with clear expression of body flow and beginnings and endings, and with awareness of sequence within each phrase.

9.21 *Integrating Body-Action Ideas with the Concept of Phrase*: Whole-body actions, leading and following actions, the sequence of different locomotor or nonlocomotor actions are subjects for phrasing. Awareness of the flow factor provides appropriate control while connecting the separate parts.

9.22 *Integrating Rhythmic Ideas with the Concept of Phrase*: The strong and light accents of individual actions are used to form rhythmical phrases, or the desired rhythm is first identified and then used to structure different actions. Accompanying the accents are movements of varying degrees of flexibility or directness, and fluency.

9.23 *Integrating Spatial Ideas with the Concept of Phrase*: Incorporating ideas of level and direction, the phrases can use various movements to integrate spatial concepts with those of body flow. Additional meaning can be given to spatial concepts within the structure of phrase when spatial attitudes toward flexibility and directness are given attention also.

9.3 *Punctuating Movement Sentences*: A more advanced concept of phrase includes investigations of the nature of the stop after an action. Is it a pause with expectation? Is it a question or an exclamation? Working with partners and later in threes or fours, students can try their movement sentences on each other and eventually build a sequence of sentences. The end product may be a brief, dancelike composition, a short routine of stunts or tumbling actions, or an exercise

14 Preston, *Handbook*, p. 27.
15 Ibid.

Connecting short
phrases

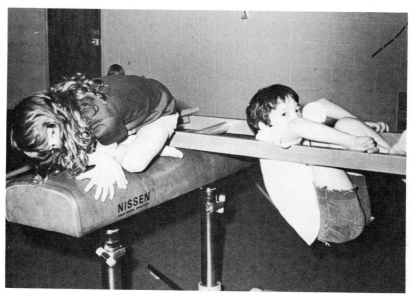

Punctuating movement
sentences; creating
apparatus routines

involving the use of manipulative objects. Simple apparatus routines also are possible outcomes. Awarenesses rather than actions should be given main emphasis. Actions should be viewed as vehicles for expression.

Theme IV, Awareness of the Flow of the Weight of the Body in Space and Time, incorporates essential elements of efficient or expressive movement and must not be glossed over in an effort to move on to other themes. The integrative nature of Theme IV should be recognized and used again and again to secure sensitive movement behaviors. Mastery of this theme assures that those children who are seriously interested in learning particular skills have acquired the necessary awarenesses of the elements that constitute those skills. This theme may be directly applied to skill learning, but such application should not be emphasized with young children, who will develop in a more natural way if they are allowed to apply the awarenesses gradually. Older children will need more direction in the application of these awarenesses to skills. The instructor, therefore, might elect to follow modules on flow, phrasing, or other content with modules on ball-handling skills, the construction of routines in gymnastics, and the like.

Sample unit: Theme IV

Theme: IV Awareness of the Flow of the Weight of the Body in Space and Time

---

Unit: 9.0 Phrasing and Punctuation

Instructional level: Grade 3   Operational stage: I, level 2.0

Program objectives: On completion of this unit, the learner should
1 Be able to identify correctly the main actions in a sequence of actions and the preparatory and ending movements.
2 Be able to construct a sequence of two or three short movement phrases with appropriate pauses and stops.
3 Be able to construct an appropriate sequence, given one to three main actions, using body flow to integrate the actions into a phrase.

Suggested lesson themes:
The following themes have been selected as the means for securing the program objectives. Each theme and subtheme is supported by appropriate instructional objectives in modular lesson plans, using floor, apparatus, rhythm, and manipulative environments.

9.1 Phrasing with Clarity of Quality
   9.11 Emphasizing Preparations and Endings to Main Actions
   9.12 Connecting Short Phrases

**Theme V:
Adaptation
to a partner**

■ With this theme the environmental circumstance shifts from the physical to the social. The learner is now involved in learning how to operate with someone. Performing movements together involves sharing, cooperating, communicating, even sacrificing.

Movement lessons with preschoolers and kindergartners involve children in a physical environment with other children but with little interaction beyond sharing space and equipment, or the teacher's attention. This is because young children are not ready to move in relation to one another while simultaneously learning awareness of what they are doing, how they are doing it, and where the action is going. Young children should be permitted to develop some movement mastery and understanding before they are required to relate their movement ideas and actions to those of another. Initial experiences with this theme may be limited to simple themes—doing something together, observing one another, and so on. It takes time for children to learn to work with a partner. In work with familiar tasks, they will gradually improve the standard of their performance after an initial breakdown when they find it difficult to relate and to perform at the same time. Many effort and spatial adaptations must be made for which both time and guidance are needed.

Older children can work immediately with this theme in most cases. In

Learning to move in
relation to another

fact, the sooner they work with another person the better. They often find it difficult to operate alone, so short periods of working alone followed by work in partner relationships will help improve the quality of both situations, provided the teacher makes it important enough by talking about it. What are the implications of working alone? Self-discipline? Independence? Concentration? What are the implications of working with a partner? Leadership and followership? Cooperation? Competition? Helping? Sacrificing? Fun? Understanding? Tolerance? Interdependence?

In partner relationships the individual's main interest must be the partner. Looking at each other, knowing where the other is at all times, being careful of each other, being nice to each other, and helping each other are visible signs of a meaningful relationship between partners. With young children simple partner themes should emphasize the partner relationship, and little attention should be given to the actions as long as they are appropriate to the intent of the lesson. Older children, those in grade 2 and beyond, should move from simple themes to more complex relationships incorporating awareness of the movement ideas and actions being carried out by the partnership.

Operational Stage I emphasizes beginning or introductory concepts focusing on comprehension. Theme V lessons must be kept simple at this stage of movement learning. Instructors are cautioned not to expect older beginners to manage more than the introductory ideas of this theme. With Theme V it is easier to get involved with analysis and synthesis before learners are ready than it has been with previous themes. However, make note of the following point.

> *When children demonstrate their ability to operate comfortably with partners in a variety of movement learning situations, they invariably demonstrate their readiness to take on higher level cognitive functions.*

The shift from Stage I to Stage II operations is not an abrupt one. In Stage II, children are introduced to new thematic content as if they were still at Stage I. That is to say, even when they are able to analyze, to apply movement principles in different situations, to construct new combinations, and to refine them, they should be introduced to new material with simple themes just as if they were still operating at the first stage of movement learning. In this way understanding is given priority over integration of new concepts with all facets of previously acquired knowledge. Children who are ready to operate at the second stage will develop lesson content further and look for additional challenge not only in their psychomotor behaviors but also in their intellectual behaviors.

Although this theme will mark the transition from Stage I to Stage II for many children, the sample unit for this theme and the remaining themes will continue to aim at Stage I program objectives.

1.0 Doing the Same

The themes suggested in this section are generally introductory themes and therefore are suitable for use even with some young chil-

Relating to same piece
of apparatus while
being together

Partner relationship,
traveling from place
to place

dren. They help the learner focus attention on what a partner is doing and respond by copying. This elementary relationship requires learners to take turns, to wait until a partner has completed a movement. It begins with sharing space and equipment.

1.1 *Being Together*: Accepting a partner relationship for even a brief period of time and doing something (anything) together. Traveling together, carrying, lifting, pulling, relating to the same piece of apparatus with or without direct physical contact with each other.

   1.11 *Going Together*: Traveling from place to place in simple partner relationship.

   1.12 *Sharing*: Simple sharing of space or equipment.

   1.13 *Taking Turns*: Waiting until one's partner has finished before commencing one's own turn.

1.2 *Copying*: Keen observation is required if a child is to copy the details of a partner's movements. Previous themes provide the required foundation.

   1.21 *Copying the Body Shape of Another*: Observing and reproduc-

Learning to share
the same space

Copying the
body shape of another

ing twisted, wall-like, arrowlike, and ball-like shapes of the whole
body or its parts as formed by another.

1.22 *Copying the Sequence of Levels of a Movement Phrase*: Paying
attention to the beginning and ending of a phrase along with all of
the changes in between.

1.23 *Copying the Sequence of Qualities Demonstrated*: Clarity of expression is a prerequisite for this theme, which calls for the partner to observe and reproduce weight, space, time, or flow qualities. Single motion factors such as time should be handled first: a
quick action is followed by a lingering movement, and then by
three quick actions, or a direct action is followed by a flexible
movement, ending with a direct thrust. Sometimes the partner
will respond to the weight quality rather than the time quality,
or the time quality rather than the flow. Clarity of expression is
important, particularly when two or more qualities occur in the
same sequence.

1.24 *Copying the Rhythm of Another's Movement Phrase*: The duration and accents of the parts of a metric or nonmetric phrase are
copied. Movements do not have to be the same, but the rhythm
must be; that is, a sequence of steps might be reproduced rhythmically by the clapping of hands.

1.25 *Copying the Action*: The sequence and importance of each action is observed and reproduced. The observer must take care to
distinguish which body parts are performing the main actions
from those performing either supporting or nonessential actions.

2.0 Replying with Movement

The following themes lay the foundations for all partner relationships in which observation is followed by a movement behavior different from but appropriate to the observed behavior.

2.1 *Responding to the Final Position or Shape of the Partner*: After one partner concludes a movement and holds a position, the other assumes a position; for example, partner A moves and ends in a wide position; partner B moves and ends in a round shape. Opposites are easily learned and used by children for this theme.

2.2 *Responding to the Change in Level of a Partner*: As one partner moves, the other avoids being on the same level, or when one performs a sequence like high-low-high, the other responds with low-high-low.

2.3 *Contrasting the Qualities of Movement*: One partner performs a strong, flexible action to which the partner responds with a light, direct movement. All ways of combining and contrasting qualities may be explored.

2.4 *Responding within a Metric Framework*: One partner moves to the first half of a metric phrase, and the other responds during the second half. For example, the first four counts may be an opening action by A, which B follows with a lowering and raising action. Manipulative actions are particularly suitable for this theme.

3.0 Moving Together

Moving at the same time, either because of a common purpose or because the presence of others or their actions require it, is the emphasis of this theme.

3.1 *Meeting and Parting*: This theme has many possibilities. The approach to a partner can be followed immediately by parting, by parting after doing something together, by passing or going around each other, or by one going over the other. "*Approaching* can have many expressions, being done with fine touch or firmly, sudden-directly or in a roundabout way, thus giving a tentative, overwhelming, straightforward or surreptitious expression."[16] Various rhythms, patterns, body parts, levels, and directions can be stressed during the approach, the meeting, or the parting.

3.2 *Meeting Different Partners*: All of the ideas and actions in 3.1 can be employed with this theme, but after the phrase is completed, the parting is followed by movement toward a different person. The exchange of partners may be structured (within a small group) or free (with anyone anywhere).

4.0 Discovering the Properties of Small Group Relationships

New actions are possible in small groups. Formations other than lines are possible. Partners may work in opposition to one or more persons. A single person may be confronted by two or more persons. After partner relationships have been thoroughly explored, the addition of one more person requires exploration of new properties. Each additional person changes the properties of the whole group relationship.

Units of instruction:
themes i to v

16 Ibid., p. 33.

A relationship of
three being different

4.1 *Trios or Threes Relationships*: Three people form a group with action and relationship possibilities different from a partnership.

    4.11 *Orienting Movement to a Circle and Its Center*: Threes can make a circle and relate to the center by moving toward it, away from it, or around it. Various effort actions, rhythms, patterns, and spatial relationships can be explored in phrases and movement sentences.

    4.12 *Splitting or Passing Between or Around*: Triangles can be of different sizes and shapes and still be triangles. One member of a triangle may pass between the other two members, or go around one member and form a new triangle. Efforts, actions, and spatial relationships may be added. Manipulative patterns show a give-and-go sequence.

    4.13 *Formations in Threes*: A group of three can form a circle, a triangle, or a line. The members of the group can face in various directions and vary the distances between themselves. The formation can perform actions in place or while traveling and avoid other threes or relate to different physical environments.

    4.14 *Two and One*: A two-and-one relationship is one in which two persons help the one person or act against the one person. Contact and noncontact and manipulative and nonmanipulative relationships may be explored.

4.2 *Quartets or Fours Relationships*: Four can move together by two and two or three and one. Circles, squares, rectangles, and triangles plus one are possible formations, in addition to lines and files.

4.21 *Two and Two*: Two may help two or be against two. Meeting and parting, going between or around, leading and following are possible themes, along with all previously explored efforts, actions, and spatial relationships.

4.22 *Three and One*: Three may help one or be against one. Contact and noncontact, manipulative and nonmanipulative relationships may be explored, along with previously explored efforts, actions, spatial relationships, and formational changes.

4.3 *Quintets or Fives Relationships*: Interesting possibilities are offered by fives, with all previous relationships providing foundational concepts.

4.31 *Formational Changes in Fives*: Lines, circles, triangles, and rectangular formations are possible. Fives can form a wing shaped like a "W," which is also a combination of three triangles.

4.32 *Groups and Subgroups*: The group of five can be split in a variety of ways that have been previously explored with other groups.

Sample unit: Theme V

Theme: V Adaptation to a Partner

Unit: 2.0 Replying with Movement

Instructional level: Grade 3   Operational stage: I, level 2.0

Program objectives: On completion of this unit, the learner should

1 Be able to relate to a partner while emphasizing given effort, action, and spatial concepts, patterns, or ideas.

2 Be able to use different combinations of beats in a metric framework while relating to a partner.

3 Use a variety of previously learned actions, efforts, and spatial relationships in observing and responding to movements within the framework of a partner relationship.

Suggested lesson themes:
The following themes have been selected as the means for securing the program objectives. Each theme and subtheme is supported by appropriate instructional objectives in modular lesson plans, using floor, apparatus, rhythm, and manipulative environments.

2.4 Responding within a Metric Framework
  2.41 Working with a Four-and-Four Phrase
    2.411 Stressing Change in Level and Direction
    2.412 Stressing Whole-Body and Body-Part Actions
    2.413 Stressing Variations in Sustainment with the Four Available Counts
  2.42 Working with Different Combinations of Beats within the Eight-Count Phrase

Summary and comment

■ The concept of instructional units is familiar to most students of physical education. However, students may not have learned the related concepts of program and instructional objectives from their own experiences in activities such as soccer, gymnastics, and dance. Hopefully, the reader is now in a position to apply the following concepts to the design of instructional units.

1 Program objectives are written by program planners to describe the purposes of an instructional program. The outcomes are identified by statements describing what the learner *should* be able to demonstrate as a result of having had the program.

2 Instructional objectives are written by instructors to describe specifically what the learner *will* be able to do as a result of having received instruction. The outcomes are written as behaviors to be observed in various situations or circumstances, and these objectives are to serve as tests of competency. Instructional objectives take the individual differences into consideration by detailing the quality or the quantity of the expected performance. An example of an instructional objective in kickball is, learners will kick a ball traveling at moderate speed toward them so that the ball enters the field of play on three out of four tries.

3 Units of instruction are designed to attain the objectives of larger programs of instruction, sometimes called courses of instruction.

4 Activity units in physical education describe the purpose of a specific activity within the developmental movement track such as Four-on-Four Soccer in the course of instruction on soccer.

5 Themes are used to describe the units of instruction in the basic movement track such as Action and Stillness in the course of instruction on body awareness.

6 Instructors design units or adapt materials to meet the specific needs of the learners. Comment: If a school principal or director of physical education gave a physical education teacher a curriculum guide describing the general outcomes to be attained through a course of instruction in movement education, the instructor would have to outline the units of instruction needed to fulfill the program expectations. The specific details of unit construction can only be written by the instructor or the person who knows the limitations of facilities, instructional time, and the learners. Units of instruction for slow or inexperienced learners will be quite different from those for fast or experienced learners.

This chapter starts the reader on the road to curriculum construction. Themes as units of instruction, first in basic movement and then in dance and gymnastics, will have to include units on specific instruction in game skills and other competitive activities. A form for preliminary work on instructional objectives for a unit is given in figure 8.1.

The beginner in curriculum writing may be an experienced teacher or a recent graduate. Each has the problem of deciding what to write on paper. We feel that physical educators find it easier to begin with what they know best, the activities, rather than the educational goals. Although this may seem to be a backward approach, it produces tangible results imme- diately simply because every decision about the selection of themes, activi- ties, objectives, and their sequence reflects the curriculum writers' pre- viously unverbalized values. The writers can eventually state these values as beliefs and formalize them in goal statements. A complete curriculum guide should not emerge from a first series of meetings. Completion should be left for later, when unit content and sequence have been thoroughly field-tested.

Here are the steps in initial curriculum construction.

1 List the major activities for upper grades 5 and 6. This is usually the easiest place to start. Follow with activities for grades 3 and 4. These will usually be lead-up activities to the upper level program.

2 List the themes in their major headings for the K-2 program. Action and Stillness may be the first theme, followed by Whole-Body Actions, Fast and Slow, and so forth. Consider basic movement units first.

3 Examine each theme and activity for the purpose of identifying objec- tives. Start with the most obvious such as psychomotor objectives for the games unit and cognitive objectives for the basic movement unit. Write down the objectives to clarify the rationale for including the unit in the first place.

4 Consider the learners. If they are at the first operational stage, it will be important to emphasize affective outcomes. Write down the impor- tant affective objectives such as development of courteous behavior, good listening skills, attentiveness to directions, and positive attitudes toward participation.

5 Basic movement instruction results in development of general motor competency or the ability to cope with various problems inherent in the physical, instructional environment. Ability to manage one's own self should be an expected psychomotor by-product. Write a statement that includes this objective.

6 Developmental units for skills and activities should include cognitive objectives. Mechanical principles, laws of motion, the principle of of- fensive relationship to opponents, targets, boundaries, rules of play, and many other understandings important to full realization of feasible cog- nitive objectives should be examined for each activity unit. For exam- ple, what may the fifth grader learn about balance, both dynamic and static, in a unit on soccer? When guarding an offensive player without the ball, what principle involving space will help the learner make ap- propriate movement decisions?

7 While writing objectives for basic movement units or units in the de- velopmental track be on the lookout for those that are too narrow and would therefore be better for lesson plans. List them under the title of a unit to which they belong or gather them together with similar ob- jectives and assign them to a new instructional unit. For example, ac- tivities like tetherball, Four Square, Hopscotch, and similar games are best considered under a unit titled Activities for the Hardtop Surface or Recreational Games. Activities for the Fast and Slow theme might be

Units of instruction:
themes i to v

listed in a unit on Weight-Time Relationships. Field testing will help in the final determination of where a theme or activity belongs.

8 Review all instructional units, their titles and objectives, making sure that basic movement units are together and developmental units are together.

9 Sequence the basic movement units along with any subordinate lesson plan themes, and then do the same for the developmental movement program. Do this for grades K-2 in basic movement and grades 3-4 and 5-6 in developmental movement education.

10 Wherever possible, assign a grade level and, in the developmental track, a season for the activities (for example, some games are best played outdoors in the fall).

Following these ten steps will produce a rough outline of the curriculum. Many parts are still missing and will be included as they are identified. These additional curriculum concerns may be relevant.

11 Basic movement units for the upper grades, particularly for grades 3-4, may need to be developed. (Note: Fifth and sixth graders work best only with those elements of basic movement that seem related to specific activities with which they can readily identify, such as quick movements through spaces while avoiding collisions.)

12 Developmental skills and related activities should be planned for in K-2. To make the transition from a basic movement emphasis to specific game skills, learners should develop certain abilities. It is important that they know the fundamental motor patterns by the end of grade 2. Any delay will be accompanied by a certain unpleasantness as children discover they are inadequately prepared for games and other desirable activities. Use guided discovery and directed teaching to develop these essential skills rather than wait for unguided discovery to produce the results desired.

13 As objectives emerge, value statements of rationale and purpose for each program division and each unit of instruction may be written. This will come after field testing. In some instances activities may be eliminated because they do not serve an educational purpose, as demonstrated by the behavior of the children.

Elements missing from the curricular sequence are gradually identified and inserted in their proper places. Field testing is important and should be done as part of regular instruction over the course of at least a year.

Changes in objectives, deletions of material, and additions of new activities, skills, and themes are made either during field testing or between school years. If two or more instructors are involved, regular meetings should be held to consider various points and arrive at mutually satisfying statements. Eventually, the educational goals will emerge.

A curriculum guide is only as good as the teachers who use it. Consequently, it should never be treated as permanent. Instructional materials will be continually revised to make them relevant to the needs and interests of learners. As new equipment is purchased, new programs may be instituted. These will be experimental until instructors have developed sufficient expertise.

The sample form for describing an instructional unit will guide the teacher and curriculum writer in the formulation of units and program objectives. Also completion of the following assignments will help the learner considerably.

All themes identified in this chapter may be used in gymnastics and dance programs, either to familiarize learners with new concepts or to help them develop specific skills. Many of the themes will be useful, even in the games program, particularly those involving general space and relationship to others—two areas producing problems that might otherwise go unsolved by the learners and thus handicap their development as players.

A sample unit form

PHYSICAL EDUCATION INSTRUCTIONAL UNIT

Course of instruction:_____
(Indicate Theme Category or Activity Category)

Unit title:_____
(Indicate Instructional Theme or Activity)

(Indicate grade, group, and competence level such as Beginning, Stage I, level 1.0 or 2.0)

Program objectives outlined: _____
By the conclusion of this unit, the learner should_____
(List briefly the desired competencies under each or any of the educational domains listed)

   Affective outcomes:
   (Identify behaviors that demonstrate the attainment of desired attitudes)

   Cognitive outcomes:
   (Identify behaviors that demonstrate the attainment of desired facts or thinking skills.)

   Psychomotor outcomes:
   (Identify desired motor behaviors or skills)

Suggested lesson themes or activities:_____
(List the themes that have been selected along with any subthemes that will make for good learning progression in basic movement or modern educational dance or gymnastics OR list the subordinate activities that will make for good progression towards the desired competency in the specified activity.)

Resources:_____
(List written material and source or the names of people that will make good references for additional assistance)

Assignments

■ The following assignments are aimed at improving the student's understandings of program unit construction. Variations of the assignment are easily made to meet the specific needs of the student.

1

Write a specified number of program objectives for a unit of instruction in developmental movement education.

Explanation: The learner may feel most comfortable using a familiar activity for the purpose of developing competency in writing program objectives.

2

Select one of the program objectives developed in assignment 1 and write an instructional objective for each educational domain—affective, cognitive, and psychomotor.

Explanation: The learner should be able to specify the behavioral outcomes that will demonstrate learning (the acquisition of the desired program objective).

3

Using the format for program units given in this chapter, outline one instructional unit for each of Themes I through V.

Explanation: The learner should be able to select a theme from those given under each category and to write appropriate program objectives at the unit level of instruction. Sample units may be used as models.

4

Select any operational theme (as opposed to theme category like body awareness) and rewrite it to suit the purpose of a lesson or series of lessons in a specific learning situation.

Readings

■ The following books provide indirect help in the construction of lesson themes through the manner in which the authors have written on basic movement, dance, and modern educational gymnastics.

Briggs, Megan M. *Movement Education, The Place of Movement in Physical Education.* Boston: Plays, 1975.

Buckland, Don. *Gymnastics.* London: Heinemann, 1969.

Gilliom, Bonnie Cherp. *Basic Movement Education for Children: Rationale and Teaching Units.* Reading, Mass.: Addison-Wesley, 1970.

Kirchner, Glenn; Cunningham, Jean; and Warrell, Eileen. *Introduction to Movement Education.* Dubuque, Iowa: Wm. C. Brown, 1970.

Morrison, Ruth. *A Movement Approach to Educational Gymnastics.* London: J. M. Dent, 1969.

North, Marion. *Body Movement for Children.* Boston: Plays, 1972.

Tyler, Ralph W. *Basic Principles of Curriculum and Instruction.* Chicago: University of Chicago Press, 1949.

Williams, Jean. *Themes for Educational Gymnastics.* London: Lepus Books, 1974.

Winters, Shirley J. *Creative Rhythmic Movement for Children of Elementary School Age.* Dubuque, Iowa: Wm. C. Brown, 1975.

Chapter IX

Units of instruction: themes vi to xi

Those who teach games, gymnastics and
agilities do admirable work in their field
but their teaching does not provide
a comprehensive movement education.

Marion North
Body Movement for Children, p. iv

■ This statement by Marion North from the introduction to her book, *Body Movement for Children,* should no longer shock the reader who has a developing concept of physical education. It should serve as a reminder, rather, that there is much to learn and to do in the struggle to achieve competency as teachers of physical education. Through movement education, with its emphasis on knowing the vocabulary of basic movement, physical education can orient its content around the universal principles of human movement that Rudolf Laban developed and that are the basis for the dual-track physical education program described in this book.

After a suitable period of work with the content of Themes I to V, the students, as well as the teacher, should be ready to take on the more demanding work of Themes VI to XI. Exploratory efforts through certain lesson themes can be made to determine whether the children and the teacher are, indeed, ready.

■ Theme VI is an extension of Theme I and focuses the learner's attention more specifically on what the body is doing. Preston-Dunlop describes the theme.

Theme VI: The instrumental use of the body

The purpose here is to further the general awareness gained through Theme I by differentiating movement into activities which can be recognized and by learning how the parts of the body have clear roles to play in the mastery of movement. This is done through looking at the movements the body can do when acting as an instrument and secondly by building up a technical vocabulary through the practice of different activities.[1]

1 Valerie Preston [-Dunlop], *A Handbook for Modern Educational Dance* (London: MacDonald & Evans, 1963), p. 31.

The importance of the work on Theme VI cannot be overemphasized. It is the link between the large muscle activity or gross motor skills with which movement life starts and the fine motor skills that enable the individual to fulfill intellectual, aesthetic, and recreational pursuits. Young children can be led to the achievement of finer muscle control so necessary to their growing need for movement specificity. Older children who have difficulty coordinating the skill patterns in games, dance, and gymnastics need the activities of this theme to bridge the gap between their present status and the skill level to which they are aspiring. Coaches and experienced teachers of skills will recognize the importance of developing the body's instrumental functions through the activities of Theme VI.

1.0 Exploring the Meaning of Instrumental Use of the Body

Introductory themes involving the use of the hands and how they function instrumentally are followed by themes that extend the concepts and awarenesses to other parts of the body and to the body as a whole.

1.1 *Instrumental Use of the Hands*: Hand actions such as striking, scooping, carrying, gripping, pinching, pushing, pulling, and throwing are explored in mimetic form to clarify the actions as much as possible. The application of these actions to movement tasks in other environments is important so that the objective as well as the expressive purposes of the movements can be practiced.

1.2 *Instrumental Use of the Feet*: Actions limited to the feet are explored —kicking, stamping, and gripping. Using the feet to grip the apparatus, to pick up small objects, to kick a ball are objective movements with a specific purpose.

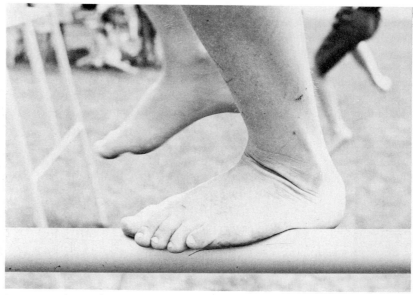

Instrumental use of
the feet—gripping

1.3 *Coordinating the Feet and Hands with Large Actions of the Body*: Rising and reaching to grasp, stepping and kicking, and bending and scooping are examples of activities within the purpose of this theme. All manner of instrumental uses of the hands and feet are coordinated with previously learned actions of the body as a whole. The lower half of the body may perform supporting or traveling actions that permit the hands to lead the upper body into a specific instrumental use.

1.4 *Instrumental Use of Other Body Parts and Their Coordination with the Body As a Whole*: The head can strike or push. In cooperation with one shoulder, it can grip. Hips, knees, and elbows can strike, as can the forearms and wrists. They can push, press, and, in cooperation with adjacent parts, grip. Many instrumental actions are possible without the use of hands or feet. The whole body can be used in both preparatory and helping actions.

1.5 *Gathering and Scattering Actions*: A gathering action is a large gripping action of the whole body toward a specific point. For gathering, the easiest of such points is in front of the body. The hands and arms reach out and gather together with assistance from the spine, which bends forward. Releasing causes a scattering movement. All parts of space within the kinesphere are subject to gathering actions and, al-

Coordinating the feet and hands with large actions of the body

Gripping actions of body parts and their coordination with the body as a whole

though the arms are the most common means of gathering, the feet and legs can also participate in this action. Coupled with jumps and turns, the action of gathering is basic to dance and to the objective purposes of games in which balls are gathered in and released through a sophistication of the scattering action called throwing.

2.0 The Five Body Activities and Stillness

Each of the five body activities is a category of activities, as is stillness. The aim of the following themes is to differentiate them and their content as clearly as possible. Each activity within a category is similar to and, at the same time, different from every other activity within the category. These similarities and differences should be noted and felt by the learners.

2.1 *Gestures*: This category of movement activity includes all actions not concerned with the support of the weight of the body. Gestures may have an expressive purpose—an aim to communicate—or an objective purpose such as an instrumental use. Both supporting functions and gesturing functions should be explored and clarified, with the body in all kinds of supporting positions, so that the difference in meaning and feeling between body parts functioning to support and those functioning to gesture is fully clarified.

2.2 *Stepping*: All weight transfers are included in this category. Steps can be taken by parts of the body other than the feet, a fact that should

Transferring the weight
from feet to hands
to feet

be given considerable attention particularly with younger children. Transferring the weight from feet to hands to feet as in walkovers, tinsicas, and cartwheels is a specific gymnastic outgrowth of stepping activities for some children.

2.3 *Locomotion*: The locomotor forms learned through exploration, discovery, and guidance in Theme I are expanded to include all kinds of traveling, even on body parts not usually associated with locomotion. Various kinds of rolling, sliding, creeping and crawling, hitching, walking, and running are the subject of experimentation so that a base for future activities with specific expressive or objective purposes may be formulated.

2.4 *Jumping*: It is seen that jumping involves two main parts, the takeoff and the landing. Each part utilizes the feet in some particular way that forms the basis for the differentiation of jumping into the five basic jumps. Jumping has a variety of instrumental uses such as for jumping high or for jumping long, for reaching, for rebounding, and for imaginative, creative activities. In the following list, each jump is given its English name, if one applies, and its classical ballet name.

From one foot to the same foot (hop): temps levé
From one foot to the other foot (leap): jeté
From one foot to both feet: assemblé
From both feet to both feet: sauté
From both feet to one foot: sissonne

The jumps can be used in combination with steps and other jumps. Dance steps and athletic events in track and field are among the specific activities to which these jumping activities point. Gymnastics work in floor exercise and balance beam is another important area in which these jumps are used with variations in combination and gesture. Exploratory themes should aim at acquiring the basic jumps and combining and varying them as much as possible. Concurrent work in developmental activities may be employed with older children.

2.41 *Different Takeoffs and Landings*: Emphasizing the five basic jumps, special attention is paid to their differentiation.

2.42 *Taking Off on One and Landing on Two*: Special attention is given this jump because of its prevalence in all manner of activity. It is used in a sequence such as run, jump, land, roll. In an apparatus environment it is used for mounting various pieces of equipment.

2.43 *Combining Jumping in Different Ways*: Jumps can be combined with connecting steps to form a variety of patterns. Run, hop, step, jump is an example of a form made popular by the triple jump of track and field. Other possibilities include ways of combining all five jumps in a sequence with no steps or repetitions.

2.5 *Turning*: All movement involving a change of front results in a turn. Spinning, whirling, changing levels, and learning to focus on a new front are among the activities that help to introduce the turn and the

Different ways to jump

Different takeoffs
and landings

Turning on various
parts of the body

special feelings that accompany turning. Gathering and scattering gestures can affect turns by helping to initiate them and to control their speed. Turns can be made on various parts of the body.

2.51 *Turning on Different Body Parts*: With different parts of the body serving as the pivot, other parts are used to initiate and control the turn.

2.52 *Turning with Changes in Level*: Spiraling actions result as the level is changed during a turn. A downward spiral may end with a roll or a change to a different body part as the pivot for another turn, while an upward spiral may end with a pivot high on the ball of one foot or even with elevation.

2.53 *Turning to Avoid Contact or to Lead with a Different Body Part*: Traveling through crowded places provides opportunity to twist and turn the body in order to avoid contact with the people or things crowded in the space. A partial turn may be made to change bodily direction or front so that the back rather than the front of the body is leading.

2.6 *Stillness*: The first association of stillness was as a stopping action, a way of bringing a moving action to a halt. The body does something to accomplish this important action, and so it was introduced in Theme I. Later, in Theme IV, stillness was viewed in connection with the flow factor. A pause in stillness carries with it the sensation of the previous movement. This can be experienced most readily by stopping after whirling around; one continues to feel the sensation of whirling as a suppressed flow with the body. Maintaining stillness obliterates the sensation of the previous action and brings with it a sensation all of its own, balance, achieved by the tension of muscles needed to hold body position against the pull of gravity. The feelings of balance and imbalance and the awareness of the relationship of the body parts to each other and to the center of gravity can be explored to help the learner deepen his appreciation of the concept of stillness.

2.61 *Stillness and Balance*: Stillness is achieved with certainty by accurately controlling the position of counterbalancing body parts. This is done by placing the center of gravity over the support. The muscular tension required to achieve and hold a position of balance is an important awareness to achieve.

2.62 *Holding Difficult Balances*: Balancing on one body part, elevating the center of gravity as much as possible to increase the difficulty of balancing, and balancing on smaller body parts are challenges for increasing the learner's awareness of balance and stillness.

Holding difficult
balances

3.0 Combining the Five Body Activities

The five body activities listed in the previous section may be combined in a number of different ways, each of which is capable of considerable exploration to differentiate the possibilities even further.

3.1 *Gesturing While Stepping*

3.2 *Weight Transference to Achieve Locomotion*

3.3 *Traveling While Turning*

3.4 *Turning Jumps*

3.5 *Gestures during Jumps and Turns*: The legs may be tucked, piked, held stretched, or formed into combinations of shapes. Arms are frequently used for gesturing, often to counterbalance the body and to help give impetus to the lift in jumping.

3.6 *Gestures and Locomotion*: Both expressive and objective gestures may be used. Manipulative actions can occur while traveling.

3.7 *Traveling Jumps*: Running and jumping, round offs, and springs from the hands, or feet to hands, are possible outcomes of practice in this area.

3.8 *Step Jump Rhythms*: A variety of ways for combining a step into a jump to form a rhythmic pattern can be found.

3.9 *Stepping during Turns*: Steps during turns may help to prolong the turns but require considerable attention to the placement of the stepping part so that dynamic balance is maintained.

4.0 Sequence of Activities

"Bodily skill is increased by the practice of sequences consisting of transitions from one body activity to another. The ability to change from one to the other in a skilful manner constitutes body technique."[2] Skill learning is essential to a physical education program. The themes in this section aim at the improvement of skill by making the learner aware of what the body is doing as various actions are sequenced and what is needed in order to control the sequence. Large actions follow each other with appropriate transitional movements. Direct application to games, dance, gymnastics, and aquatic activities can be made as long as not too great a degree of refinement is expected immediately.

4.1 *Action Motifs in Increasingly Complex Situations*: A large action like jumping is selected and practiced on the spot, while traveling, with a turn, or in combination with collapsing and rolling. All kinds of actions can be selected. Note how easily catching and throwing can be developed in a similar fashion. Children, when capable, should be allowed to present increasingly more difficult situations to themselves, a partner, a group, or the entire class.

4.2 *Adding Actions*: The emphasis of this theme is on stimulating children to think about sequences by taking an action and adding another and another until a climax is reached. Run, jump, turn, land, roll, balance is one such sequence. Jump, fall, roll, spin, sprawl is another. Pres-

2 Ibid.

ton-Dunlop suggests the following list as a starter but admonishes the reader to be careful when putting them into a sequence so that the flow of the action is not hampered by poor combination. The children may add to the list, of course.

Flying, whirling, pouncing, hovering, creeping, dangling, sprawling, darting, twisting, precipitating, falling, shivering, drifting, spinning, tossing, curling, sinking, collapsing, overbalancing, crawling, bowing, rising, opening, closing, bursting, exploding.[3]

Sample unit: Theme VI

Theme: VI The Instrumental Use of the Body

Unit: 2.4 Jumping

Instructional level: Grade 2   Operational stage: I, level 2.0

Program objectives: On completion of this unit, the learner should
1 Be able to differentiate the five basic jumps by describing each one and by performing each one.
2 Know that the beginning of a jump involves a takeoff and that the ending involves some form of landing, each of which may be varied or adjusted according to the purpose of the jump.
3 Be able to connect a run with a hop or with a leap without error.

Suggested lesson themes:
The following lesson themes have been selected as the means for securing the program objectives. Each theme and subtheme is supported by appropriate instructional objectives in modular lesson plans, using floor, apparatus, rhythm, and manipulative environments.

2.4 Jumping
    2.41 Different Takeoffs and Landings
    2.42 Taking Off on One and Landing on Two
    2.43 Combining Jumping in Different Ways

Theme VII: Awareness of basic effort actions

■ Theme II introduced awareness of weight and time, the components of rhythm, and Theme IV did the same for space and flow with an additional emphasis on two effort combinations. Progression to the consideration of weight, time, and space within the same action leads to the study of the eight basic effort actions. In this theme the learner will analyze movement for its effort rhythm and for structuring the parts of a sequence to achieve desired levels of expression or efficiency.

The flow factor is not considered directly with the content of this theme. Each of the eight basic effort actions and their derivatives may be

3 Ibid., p. 43.

performed with either free or bound flow, although one is usually more commonly experienced or observed than the other.

Chapter V described the basic effort actions and the steps that might be taken in making the transition from one effort action to another. This chapter suggests unit and lesson themes aimed at identifying the eight effort actions and at developing concepts essential to analysis of effort requirements and capacities.

As has been stated previously, mastery of basic effort actions is essential to performance of the highest order. Teaching basic effort is not easy for teachers whose physical education background has emphasized the teaching of skills so the learner can play games. Such teachers are at a disadvantage; they have experienced only the development of action ability and have paid little, if any, attention to the development of feeling capacities, the fusion of which gives the performer kinesthetic mastery of movement learning.[4]

The instructional unit on basic effort actions may be handled in one of two ways or a combination of the two: (1) through the mood and actions of an effort and its opposite, or (2) through building up the properties of each of the effort actions—its attitude toward weight, time, and space.

1.0 Eight Basic Effort Actions

The emphasis of these themes is on discovering the eight basic effort actions by analyzing familiar actions.

1.1 *Thrusting and Slashing Efforts*: Familiar actions such as chopping, throwing, fencing, and boxing are analyzed for the purpose of isolating the common attitudes toward weight, time, and space factors.

    1.11 *Gliding and Floating Efforts*: The thrust and the slash are contrasted by the glide and the float, which are used as recovery actions.

1.2 *Wringing and Pressing Efforts*: Familiar actions such as gathering, twisting, pushing, and shoving are analyzed for the purpose of isolating the common attitudes toward weight, time, and space factors.

    1.21 *Dabbing and Flicking Efforts*: The wring and the press are contrasted by the dab and the flick, which are used as recovery actions.

1.3 *The Four Strong Efforts and Their Contrasting Efforts*: Strong actions are explored for the purpose of categorizing the thrust, slash, wring, and press effort actions. With the weight, time, and space attitudes identified for each, the opposite effort is arrived at by contrasting the attitudinal factors. For example, float is discovered to be the opposite of thrust because its attitudinal properties are to space, flexible, to weight, fine touch, and to time, sustained.

1.4 *The Four Sudden Efforts and their Contrasting Efforts*: Here the approach to discovering the eight basic effort actions is through the time factor. Thrusting, slashing, dabbing, and flicking actions are experi-

4 Ibid., p. 48.

enced through a variety of familiar activities, each of which is contrasted by its opposite, arrived at by identifying and contrasting each attitudinal property.

2.0 The Properties of Basic Effort Actions

The separate properties of effort are worked on and combined for the purpose of feeling the difference between a given effort action and others with different properties.

2.1 *Additions to the Weight Factor*: Either firm or fine touch is selected, worked with to clarify the difference, and added to from either the space or time factor. Firmness is experienced, for example, in conjunction with sudden change and sustainment. Fine touch is considered in the same way. To the four dual property combinations discovered—firm-sudden, firm-sustained, fine touch-sudden, and fine touch-sustained—are added the space factor. Firm-sudden becomes firm-sudden-direct and firm-sudden-indirect. Firm-sustained becomes firm-sustained-direct and firm-sustained-flexible. The other four basic effort actions are achieved by changing the weight factor of these four to fine touch.

2.2 *Additions to the Time Factor*: Time qualities of movements are explored and further differentiated by giving attention first to the weight factor accompanying each and then to the space factor in the same manner as above.

Wringing efforts

Notes on Theme VII

Only the simplest ideas associated with basic effort actions are suitable for children at Operational Stage I. The effort actions can be introduced in the manner suggested by the sample unit. A fuller treatment of the content of this theme should await the attainment of maturity and learning ability of learners at Stage II.

The teacher who is able to develop a program of modern educational dance can give Theme VII the special treatment it deserves. Both metric and nonmetric rhythms may be used, along with all kinds of action and mood words aided by various dancelike compositions.

To meet the general objectives of the basic movement education program, children should have the understandings of the movement vocabulary that articulate readily with the understandings associated with the developmental track as a whole. Basic movement education is the foundation upon which to build additional understandings such as those demanded by modern educational dance, modern educational gymnastics, and games. The more specific requirements of dance require some differences in approach because of the difference in objectives.

Sample unit: Theme VII

Theme: VII Awareness of Basic Effort Actions

Unit: 1.0 Eight Basic Effort Actions

Instructional level: Grades 4, 5, 6   Operational stage: I, level 2.0

Program objectives: On completion of this unit, the learner should
1 Be able to perform each of the basic effort actions with either functional or expressive gesture.
2 Be able to select the appropriate compensatory effort for a main effort action.
3 Be able to identify correctly the basic effort actions when demonstrated by the instructor or another student.

Suggested lesson themes:
The following lesson themes have been selected as the means for securing the program objectives. Each theme and subtheme is supported by appropriate instructional objectives in modular lesson plans, using floor, apparatus, rhythm, and manipulative environments.

1.0 Eight Basic Effort Actions
1.1 Thrusting and Slashing Efforts
    1.11 Gliding and Floating Efforts
1.2 Wringing and Pressing Efforts
    1.21 Dabbing and Flicking Efforts

**Theme VIII:
Occupational
rhythms**

■ Although the intent of Laban's Theme VIII is the study of occupational rhythms common to the work of adults, the area of professional sports should not be left out. It has become a legitimate part of the entertainment world and provides a wealth of interesting subject matter. Because the principles that govern working actions also govern expressive movement, the work of this theme also extends into dance. This theme links the previous themes, particularly V, VI, and VII, and forms a vital bridge to the content of Theme X.

1.0 Miming Working Actions

The subject matter is the action associated with the kinds of work performed in the adult world. Trades such as carpentry and construction, professions such as medicine, and professional sports, among other possibilities, should be explored thoroughly. Preston-Dunlop[5] suggests that the following points be considered in clarifying the actions emphasized:

a) the shape of the hand, how an object is held, the shape of the object and its size;
b) the rhythm that evolves from repeating the action;
c) the weight, time, and space qualities of the action;
d) the quality of the transition between each action;
e) how much of the body is involved in the action.

Not all of these points are pertinent in the same lesson, but they should certainly be considered during the course of the work so that the results are clearly demonstrated. For some classes, it would be appropriate to use one or more of the points as subthemes to the main thrust of the lesson.

1.1 *Miming Simple Repetitive Actions:* Certain kinds of work require rhythmic repetition of specific actions. Sawing wood is a prime example. Hammering, pounding, kneading, ironing, and typing are other examples. There are the repetitive actions of assembly-line workers, fruit pickers, farmers harvesting hay or grain, and so forth. There is almost no end to the possibilities, but the perspective of the learner may have to be enlarged through film and television.

1.2 *Miming Simple Sequences of Actions:* In some lines of work, even those listed above, several main actions are sequenced in order to carry out the objective. Objects are picked up and carried, thrown, or placed. The entire sequence must be recalled and each action clarified separately and in conjunction with appropriate transitional actions. The quality of the actions within the sequence may change, an important aspect of study, and the transitional actions assist in making the entire sequence a coordinated whole. Sports actions, particularly in baseball, are especially useful in studying the sequence of actions.

5 Ibid., p. 60.

2.0 Working in Pairs or Groups

Certain actions are best performed by two or more people working together. For example, a large saw requires two people. Some objects are too heavy for one or even two people to lift or carry. Certain occupations require the cooperative physical behavior of two or more people, each of whom utilizes different actions as a contribution to the group's objective. Teamwork in various occupations as well as in sports may be drawn upon for study.

2.1 *Working with a Partner in Miming Actions*: Partner relationship includes working together rhythmically to achieve a common purpose. Pulling together to haul an object, making a bed, sawing wood, loading a truck, pitching and batting, and serving and returning are among the endless examples. The actions and rhythms should be carefully worked out so that the partnership works together in a coordinated manner.

2.2 *Working in Small Groups in Miming Actions*: Relating to more than one person while performing job actions is required by this theme. Pitcher, batter, and catcher make a threesome, to which could be added other members of the infield if the group demonstrates its ability to integrate additional personnel. Assembly lines that put automobiles together require several persons working together. Construction workers demonstrate commonality of purpose with each performing a different sequence of actions aimed at accomplishing the mission of the group. Farming and fishing suggest similar teamwork.

Pulling and pushing
with a partner

Groups of more than
three working

2.21 *Working in Threes*: The group is limited in size. Each person should participate with clarity of action and purpose.

2.22 *Working in Groups of More Than Three*: Groups larger than three require more analysis of the part each member is to play and how each is to relate to the others and to the purpose of the group. Coordinating the rhythms of a number of people is required.

2.23 *Miming Industrial Actions*: The children work in groups of various sizes while miming actions typical of industry. This theme might be selected because of its relevance to a social studies unit or because the parents are engaged mainly in occupations such as mining, manufacturing, and distribution that are related to industry.

2.24 *Miming Commercial Actions*: The children work in groups of various sizes while miming actions typical of commerce. This theme might be selected because of its relevance to a social studies unit or because the parents work in such commercial jobs as bookkeeping, shipping and transportation, banking, and postal services.

2.25 *Miming Farming Actions*: The children work in groups of various sizes while miming actions associated with farming or ranching—in fact, with any of the food-producing occupations. This theme might be selected because of its relevance to a social studies unit or because the parents work in such occupations. Riding, roping, branding, sowing, and harvesting are among the activities included in the commonly recognized food-producing occupations, to which fishing and hunting might be added in certain geographic locations.

2.26 *Miming Professional Sports and Recreational Activities*: The children work in groups of various sizes while miming sports and recreational activities.

3.0 The Rhythm of Action

Each action has three parts—preparation, main action, and recovery, sometimes called beginning, middle, and ending. In a sequence of actions, the preparatory action may be for the entire sequence as well as for all the main actions to follow: preparation, main action, recovery, main action, recovery, main action, recovery. These subthemes require the learner to analyze movement efforts.

3.1 *Miming the Three Parts of Action*: The three parts of an action are analyzed and reproduced. Comparisons of the analysis are made, and any personal effort rhythms that may be included are identified. Batting a ball probably displays the greatest individual variation. Hammering, sawing, lifting, and similar actions reveal personal effort preferences.

3.2 *Miming the Three Parts in a Sequence of Actions*: A sequence of actions is first analyzed to determine the placement of preparation, main action, and recovery. The sequence is then mimed in its entirety, and comparisons are made to determine the inclusion of personal effort preferences.

Sample unit: Theme VIII

Theme: VIII Occupational Rhythms

Unit: 1.0 Miming Working Actions

Instructional level: Grade 2   Operational stage I: level 2.0

Program objectives: On completion of this unit, the learner should
1 Be able to mime selected work actions clearly, showing the appropriate rhythm and body action.
2 Be able to identify verbally and repeat in mime the weight, time, and space qualities of actions being mimed.
3 Be able to shape the hand so that it clearly shows how the object is held, the shape of the object, and its size.

Suggested lesson themes:
The following lesson themes have been selected as the means for securing the program objectives. Each theme and subtheme is sup-

ported by appropriate instructional objectives in modular lesson plans, using floor, apparatus, rhythm, and manipulative environments.

1.1 Miming Simple Repetitive Actions
    1.11 Miming the Rhythms of Work Actions
    1.12 Recognizing and Miming Weight, Time, Space Qualities of Work Actions
    1.13 Clarifying the Use of the Hands in Miming Work Actions

**Theme IX:
Awareness
of shape
in movement**

■ Shape in movement is seen in body shapes and in floor and air patterns. Shape concepts are most important to both academic and movement education. Young children learn to identify simple geometric shapes in preparation for school achievement. They learn about circles, squares, triangles, and rectangles before first grade, and somewhat later they are able to identify diamond shapes. Kephart[6] writes about the research supporting the development of form perception—how the infant's undifferentiated, primitive form perceptions are refined, by learning and development, to particular forms, which he calls constructive form. A number of the tests he describes require visual discrimination to determine a child's perceptual motor development.[7] The visual-motor associative processes are strongly emphasized in this theme. Awareness of these processes is an outgrowth of the body awareness exercises relating to large and small—a more primitive concept of shape—experienced in Theme I.

6 Newell C. Kephart, *The Slow Learner in the Classroom* (Columbus, Ohio: Merrill, 1960), pp. 71-89.
7 Ibid., pp. 150-55.

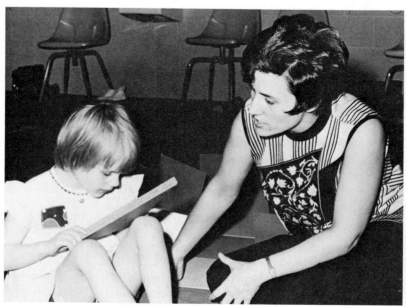

Identifying geometric
shapes

1.0 Basic Space Patterns

There are four basic space patterns. The first is *straight,* such as the pattern found in certain numbers and the letters l, X, and H. The feeling of straightness is associated with a straight line. An *angular* pattern is formed when straight lines change direction, as in the number 7 and the letters Z, L, and N. *Rounded* patterns have no corners and can form simple curves, circles, spirals, and repeating curves in a smooth and flowing manner. The last of the four shapes is a *twisted* pattern created by changing the direction of a rounded pattern. The letter S is an example. Twists can be simple, or composed of repeating twists, or spiraled.

1.1 *Contrasting Straight and Rounded Patterns*: The floor and air space are used to acquire (1) the concept of straightness and its associated feeling of directness and (2) the concept of roundness and its associated feeling of smoothness and flexibility. When straight lines change directions, they form angles. Rounded patterns that change directtion form twisted patterns. To identify the patterns, the student may use all kinds of movement in traveling and gesturing, either individually or with a partner.

   1.11 *Emphasizing Circles and other Rounded Patterns*: Rounded or curved pathways may be traveled on the floor. The same path-

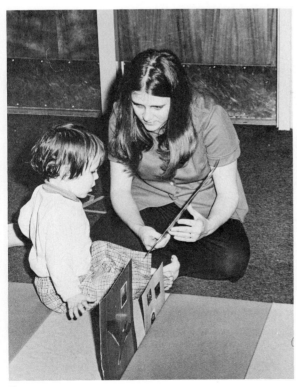

Shape concepts
important to movement

Contrasting straight
and rounded patterns

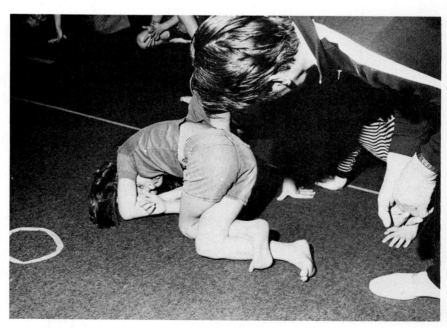

Emphasizing the
twisted pattern

Combinations of
straight and curved

ways may be indicated on the floor with ropes or drawn on paper or chalkboard. Circles and ovals may result from continuing curves. Spiraling patterns are most easily experienced by swirling a long ribbon, by gestures of the hands, or by rising and falling while turning.

1.12 *Emphasizing Straight and Angular Patterns*: Traveling in straight lines, one experiences the angular pattern when directions are changed at an angle to the original direction of travel. The angle has to be less than 180 degrees or the same pathway will be used. Gestures in straight pathways and line formations help to reinforce the concept. Drawing the pathways is especially helpful.

1.13 *Emphasizing the Twisted Pattern*: When one is traveling in a rounded pattern, changing direction will produce the twisted pattern. A long ribbon held in the hand is useful in demonstrating the twisted shape. As the body changes direction through rapid movements back and forth while the ribbon is moved upward and downward, the ribbon will take on a twisted pattern.

1.2 *Combinations of Straight, Curved, and Twisted Patterns*: The four basic patterns can be combined in a variety of ways to enhance the concept of action sequence. Simple combinations such as an angle with a curve, or a curve plus an angle plus a curve provide more than enough challenge when combined with different actions. For variation, the arms may gesture in a similar manner. Different points in surrounding space may be connected by straight or curved lines.

Units of instruction:
themes vi to xi

301

2.0 Body Shape and the Size of Movement

The elementary body shapes of large and small explained in Theme III are expanded into concepts of elongated, wall-like, round, or twisted shapes.

2.1 *Stretched and Rounded Shapes*: Stretching the limbs away from the body center can produce either a long, pinlike shape that is narrow or a wide, wall-like shape. Rounding the body brings the limbs together and toward the body center. The extended shapes are always two dimensional.

　2.11 *Expanding the Concept of Large and Small*: *Long* is a term for large in length. *Wide* means large in breadth, a different dimension. Small in breadth equals narrow in width. So it is possible for the body to be large in one direction and small in another. The relationship of the two dimensions determines the shape.

　2.12 *Awareness of the Stretch*: The focus is on shaping the stretch, moving the limbs away from the body center to show clearly the pinlike shape. The narrowness should be felt as a compression of legs against each other and arms against the head. The relationship of the arms and legs changes to "away from" when the wall-like shape is assumed, but the stretch remains the same. Legs

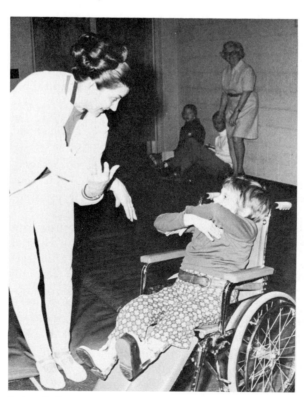

Twisted shapes

Curved, straight, and
round shapes

With a partner,
demonstrating long
and wide shapes

Two body
parts twisted

Two body
parts stretched

may be elongated while the arms are spread wide apart, and vice versa. One arm or leg may remain aligned with the trunk while its opposite member moves laterally to form a shape similar to the letter K.

2.2 *The Twisted Body Shape*: The lower and upper halves of the body rotate in opposite directions around the long axis of the trunk. Arms and legs may be stretched or curled while participating in the expression of the twist in screwlike shapes of the body.

2.21 *Twisting Areas of the Body*: Specific sections of the body such as the shoulders, arms, hips, or legs are twisted with other parts assuming distinct curved or stretched shapes.

2.22 *Twist to Twist*: The twisted shape of the body or part is changed to a different twist, usually by rotating in the other direction or by varying the twist. Extended twists show the body parts in close proximity to the long axis around which the twist occurs, as in twisting jumps or in the multiple twists of advanced tumbling and diving. A shortened, broader, and deeper shape is displayed when the body is semicurled and twisted with the limbs apart, held far from the body, and shaped in curves, stretches, or twists. Grotesque shapes may be explored. The discus thrower or the shot putter preparing to throw may be mimed.

One leg curved,
one leg straight

Notes on sample unit: Theme IX

The teacher has available a vast array of stimuli for developing shape awareness. As children are observed in free play, in preinstructional activity, and in movement problem solving, they usually display little variation in the shaping of their bodies until other possibilities are explored. Initial lessons should attempt to awaken the learner's awareness to differences in the shapes of objects, in body shapes, in the shapes of pathways on the floor or in the air, and in those made graphically in the formation of letters, numbers, or simple pictures on the chalkboard or paper.

Not only is it important for learners to acquire concepts of shape so that they can distinguish one from the other by its "signal qualities," as Kephart expresses it,[8] but they must also feel the shape in their own bodies. Imaginative ways of stimulating children to explore in depth must be found. It has been observed that teachers are often too quick to abandon themes on shapes simply because the children have learned the difference between lines, circles, triangles, and other geometric and letter shapes.

Simple shapes with many variations should be encouraged in the use of the body. Designs employing the basic shapes in floor and air patterns can utilize graphic arts. Body shapes may be extended into sculptured forms, using clay, papier-mâché, or add-on forms in which shapes of various kinds are stuck together. The extension of movement into the arts does not mean shifting the emphasis from movement objectives to other art forms. The intention, rather, is to relate the kinesthetic feeling of movement shape to visual images. The use of sounds to accompany or to stimulate movement adds another dimension to the concept of shapes in movement.

Sample unit: Theme IX

Theme: IX Awareness of Shape in Movement

Unit: 2.0 Body Shape and the Size of Movement

Instructional level: Grade 3   Operational stage: I, level 2.0

Program objectives: On completion of this unit, the learner should
1 Be able to demonstrate adequately the difference between the basic body shapes and how they may be combined through shaping separately the different areas of the body.
2 Be able to hold a given body shape during such actions as flight, balance, turns, and rolls.
3 Be able to relate effectively with a partner or small group for the purpose of experimenting with concepts of shape.

8 Ibid., pp. 73-75.

Suggested lesson themes:
The following lesson themes have been selected as the means for securing the program objectives. Each theme and subtheme is supported by appropriate instructional objectives in modular lesson plans, using floor, apparatus, rhythm, and manipulative environments.

2.1 Stretched and Rounded Shapes
    2.11 Expanding the Concept of Large and Small
    2.12 Awareness of the Stretch
2.2 The Twisted Body Shape
    2.21 Twisting Areas of the Body
    2.22 Twist to Twist

■ Mastery of change between effort qualities is the purpose of this theme. In all probability such mastery is beyond the reach of most elementary school physical education teachers, not because they lack ability but because time and opportunity are lacking for the pursuit of excellence. The reader who finds this theme inadequately treated is urged to consult Preston-Dunlop's *Handbook for Modern Educational Dance,* from which we have drawn so liberally. Teachers whose responsibilities do not include instruction in sport skills and games, who work almost exclusively in basic movement or dance, should have this book for the wealth of stimulation it provides.

Theme X: Transitions between the basic effort actions

All the work in Themes II, IV, and VII has been of an introductory nature, dealing first with the awareness of single motion factors in an effort action, then with combinations of two factors, and finally, in Theme VII, with all three factors in combination. The focus now shifts to change of quality within a movement. There are three levels of change: (1) gradual change, in which one motion factor is altered; (2) less gradual change, in which two factors are altered; and (3) abrupt change, in which all three motion factors are altered to produce a contrasting effort quality.

The table of levels of transition taken from Preston-Dunlop's book (Table 9.1) illustrates what may occur as a result of change in quality at the three levels. To appreciate fully the significance of these changes, the reader is asked to go beyond reading about them by experiencing them in actions of the arms, legs, or trunk.

As indicated in the table, a basic effort action, changing one quality at a time, becomes its opposite in gradual steps.

Float with change in time becomes flick.

Flick with change in weight becomes slash.

Slash with change in space becomes thrust.

The blending of actions to achieve coherent expression or to perform skillfully requires the appropriate use of transition. Sometimes the changes are subtle, at other times more abrupt. Although dance is often looked upon as the most natural vehicle for gradual and abrupt transitions, these transitions may be found in abundance in such activities as

swimming, during the recovery of the arms, the turn on the wall;

Table 9.1 Three levels of transitions between basic effort actions

1 Gradual

	Time change	Weight change	Space change
Float	Flick	Wring	Glide
Thrust	Press	Dab	Slash
Glide	Dab	Press	Float
Slash	Wring	Flick	Thrust
Dab	Glide	Thrust	Flick
Wring	Slash	Float	Press
Flick	Float	Slash	Dab
Press	Thrust	Glide	Wring

2 Less Gradual

	Weight-Time	Time-Space	Space-Weight
Float	Slash	Dab	Press
Thrust	Glide	Wring	Flick
Glide	Thrust	Flick	Wring
Slash	Float	Press	Dab
Dab	Press	Float	Slash
Wring	Flick	Thrust	Glide
Flick	Wring	Glide	Thrust
Press	Dab	Slash	Float

3 Abrupt

Space-Weight-Time changes, or complete contrast

Float	to	Thrust
Thrust	to	Float
Glide	to	Slash
Slash	to	Glide
Dab	to	Wring
Wring	to	Dab
Flick	to	Press
Press	to	Flick

From Valerie Preston [-Dunlop], *A Handbook for Modern Educational Dance* (London: MacDonald & Evans, 1963), pp. 71-72.

diving, in the preparation phase, in the execution followed by the entry;
softball, in fielding and throwing to a base, in batting and running, in
    catching and tagging, and in pitching and fielding;
vaulting, in running and hurdling, in preflight and repulsion, in after-
    flight and landing.

Basic effort action studies of all kinds can be undertaken by students
with the interest and the motivation. The teacher can provide specially
created sequences that will enable the students to develop the awareness
of transition. It takes concentration and familiarity with previous themes
on effort. Only the first of the themes in this section is appropriate for a unit
on transition for children in the first stage of movement learning. For them
it is enough to experience the concept of transition. More serious study can
come later.

1.0 The Sensation of Acceleration and Deceleration

The learner is asked to concentrate on the increase or decrease in one
factor while maintaining the stress on the remaining two. Initial themes
are concerned mainly with developing the general awareness of the

Sensation of acceleration
and deceleration

sensation of acceleration or deceleration. Familiar actions are used to transmit the concepts and the experience of change in a particular factor. Change in the other factors may have to be overlooked at first.

1.1 *Faster and Slower:* This theme introduces the concepts and awarenesses associated with change in the time factor. Familiar actions such as running and walking, spinning, and opening and closing are begun at a normal tempo and then made to go either faster or slower to the furthest possible extent. All sorts of actions are used to differentiate between faster, slower, and staying the same.

1.2 *Changes in Efforts through Change in Time:* A more sophisticated form of the same theme reveals the change from one effort to another: for example, from dabbing, as in light skipping, to gliding, as in sustained walking; or from pushing to punching; or from flicking to floating. The intensity of the time factor—either in its sense of urgency or in its timelessness—may be felt by the exaggeration of speed. An action that requires speed can be speeded up to its ultimate end, and the same or a different action can be slowed down to a stop.

2.0 Weight or Space Factors in Transitions

Themes based upon change in either the weight factor or the space factor may be developed to heighten the sensation of change.

2.1 *Experiencing Change in the Space Factor:* Actions stressing flexible use of space, as in floating or wringing, are given exaggerated emphasis to help the learner fully experience the quality of space before reducing the use of space to the point where the contrasting efforts of gliding or pressing are felt. Slashing wildly in all directions gradually changes to more controlled slashing and then becomes more and more thrusting in its spatial quality. Flicking changes to dabbing in the same manner. Manipulative objects like fleece balls and plastic wands help to clarify many of these effort changes.

2.2 *Experiencing Change in the Weight Factor:* Increases and decreases in the intensity of actions change the effort qualities. Exaggeration of the weight factor is experienced in such actions as strong steps and vigorous gestures that gradually soften to gliding, floating, flicking, or dabbing. Gentle movements are increased in the strength factor until they are no longer gentle, and the power exerted is felt to be responsible for the change in the effort action.

3.0 Transitions Involving More Than One Quality of Effort

3.1 *Making Gradual and Abrupt Changes from One Effort to Another:* For the more advanced students there is fun in experiencing the changes that occur in a sequence of effort actions. Slashing into wringing, followed by floating, gliding, and dabbing. Wringing into slashing, followed by gliding and ending with wringing. Gestures, rising and falling, opening and closing, locomotion at different levels in various directions can be utilized to experience the changes. Another, and often simpler, way to begin this theme is to let the children change the qualities one at a time at will and then identify the resulting sequence of basic effort actions. One may start with slashing, change the weight factor to flicking, the space factor to dabbing, the time factor to gliding, and so forth. The sequence may start with fast, strong actions; change to gentler, more sustained actions; and become stronger and faster before dissolving into stillness.

3.2 *Transitions from One Effort Action through the Other Seven*: Starting with any of the eight basic effort actions, the learner changes one element at a time until all the basic efforts have been displayed and the original action is regained.

3.3 *Transitions Involving Two Efforts*: Short sequences of basic effort actions are developed in which the transition from one to another requires changing the quality of two factors. A pressing effort may change abruptly to a flicking action, followed by a glide (change in weight-time and then in space-time). Slashing could be followed by floating (change in weight-time), then pressing (change in space-weight), and then become slashing again (change in space-time).

Operational Stage I themes can focus only upon changes in the time factor. These changes are relatively easy to incorporate into lessons involving all kinds of actions. When the learners reach the stage where movement analysis becomes increasingly important to their acquisition of skilled

Experiencing
effort changes

Units of instruction:
themes vi to xi

movement behaviors, lesson themes involving transitions in effort actions are important.

Consider the transitions, sometimes abrupt, sometimes gradual, in sport skills as the sequence of actions unfolds. The infielder uses rapid steps (dabbing) to field (thrust or dab) and follows with a wringlike preparation for a slashing throw. The foul shooter's action may be analyzed to determine the appropriate sequence of efforts and to see how these efforts differ from the main effort actions of shooting during play. Gymnastic routines, particularly floor exercise and balance beam, offer many opportunities for the display of a great variety of basic effort actions through tumbling, dance, and acrobatic movements. Single skills may be analyzed to determine whether the transitions from one effort to another are being made in a manner that facilitates the execution of the skill. The mill circle on the bar should be a pressing lift, a gliding forward rotation, ending with a slight increase in the weight factor—almost a press—to achieve the final position as the press quickly dissolves into a wringing effort to control the ending. The cast to back hip circle from front support involves preparation, a wringing pike, and lowering of shoulders, followed by a slash of the legs and thrust of the arms to achieve free front support (a rapid dissolving to float and stillness). As the body moves toward the bar, the floating quality seems to shift quickly to gliding, which, in turn, increases in speed and intensity as the hips approach the bar, becoming pressing and thrusting in order to achieve the body position and the power for the rearward rotation. To achieve control of the ending, the performer extends the body, which has achieved a slight pike, and quickly extends the shoulders and arms toward the bar. This thrusting action brings about the desired control of the ending as it quickly changes to pressing, an action that brings about stillness momentarily until either the entire action is repeated or a different one is added.

It is hoped that these comments will alert the reader to the limitless opportunities for utilizing the concepts and awarenesses gained through basic movement education in the development of the highest order of personal skill and knowledge. Further reference to the analysis of skills will be made in other parts of this book so that the bridge between the basic movement track and the activities in the developmental track will be clearly understood.

Sample unit: Theme X

Theme: X Transitions between the Basic Effort Actions

Unit: 1.0 The Sensation of Acceleration and Deceleration

Instructional level: Grade 2   Operational stage: I, level 2.0

Program objectives: On completion of this unit, the learner should

1. Be able to accelerate and decelerate smoothly actions of his choice or the selected actions of the instructor.
2. Be able to accelerate to a given quickness, maintain the tempo an appropriate length of time, and decelerate to stillness, using actions such as running, skipping, galloping, and sliding.
3. Be able to observe the actions of others and identify where in the sequence there is acceleration or deceleration and where the tempo is maintained.

Suggested lesson themes:
The following lesson themes have been selected as the means for securing the program objectives. Each theme and subtheme is supported by appropriate instructional objectives in modular lesson plans, using floor, apparatus, rhythm, and manipulative environments.

1.0 The Sensation of Acceleration and Deceleration
1.1 Faster and Slower
1.2 Changes in Efforts Through Change in Time
    1.21 Dabbing, Gliding; Slashing, Wringing
    1.22 Floating, Flicking; Thrusting, Pressing

Theme XI: Orientation in space

■ Themes III and IX dealt with the general ideas of space. Personal and general space have been identified. *Place* is understood to be an area within the general space, like a spot on the floor, or a larger space within which one must remain. *Level* identifies the relationship of space above the floor (or whatever one is on) to above the head. *Low, medium,* and *high* are terms that describe this relationship. (The term *deep* is often used in place of *low.*) The terms *size of movement,* referring to the amount of space used, and *direction,* so far experienced only with reference to primary directions, complete the spatial terminology acquired through previous themes.

"The objective word for this Theme is *where,* into what direction do I move the different parts of my body and how are these directions related?"[9] With this question Preston-Dunlop opens a fascinating analysis of direction, far beyond the purview of this text but of substantial importance. Only those aspects of spatial orientation relevant to basic movement education are being considered here.

The primary directions forward and backward, side to side, and up and down, when radiating outward from the body center, form a three-dimensional cross (fig. 9.1).

The three dimensions—up-down, left-right or sideways, and forward-backward—pass through the body center. Superimposing the drawing of a person on this figure helps to make this point clearer (fig. 9.2).

This body center is also called the center of gravity, but it is more accurate to say that the center of gravity and the body center coincide when

9 Preston [-Dunlop], *Handbook,* p. 78.

Orientation in space

Fig. 9.1 The three-dimensional cross

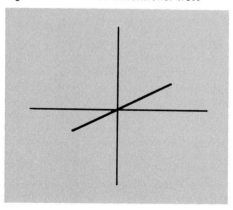

the body assumes an erect stance. A change in posture causes the center of gravity to shift, but the body center remains fixed.

The six directions established by the dimensional cross are upward, downward, right, left, forward, and backward. Movements that follow these directions are rising and falling, opening and closing, and advancing and retreating. Quite a variety of movements are possible along this *dimensional scale*.[10] Various parts of the body can lead movements into the six directions. Steps and jumps of all kinds can be used also.

Movements traveling outward along a line coincident with each of the

10 Ibid., p. 79.

Fig. 9.2   The three dimensions in relation to the body center

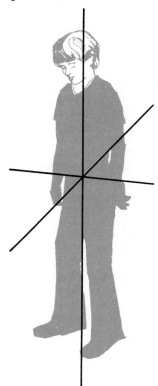

Fig. 9.3   The octahedron: Central and peripheral pathways

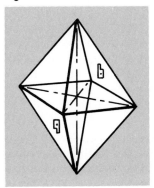

six directions and back toward the body center are spokelike and involve extension and curling actions. Another way to treat movement in relation to the three-dimensional cross is to connect the ends of each dimensional line of the cross so that movements may follow a peripheral pathway, as shown in figure 9.3.[11]

11 Ibid., p. 81.

The ends of the dimensional scale may be considered points in space, one each for high, low, right, left, forward, and backward. These points can be connected by movement.

To make this clear, the reader is asked to hold the right hand directly upward. The point to be connected is *forward*, which is attained by moving the hand in its extended position until the forward point of the forward-backward dimension is reached. Proceed to connect the other points of the dimensional scale described. These peripheral movements contrast with actions that move outward to a point in space and return to the body before moving to another point in space. Consider the application of these transitional awarenesses by the balance beam performer as, with the arms leading and the body accompanying the efforts, the performer moves along the dimensional scale in a variety of dance and acrobatic movements.

Looking ahead to other applications of the awarenesses fostered by this theme, one is struck by the number of skill learning situations that require accuracy in linking points in space within the kinesphere. The forehand and backhand strokes in tennis use the peripheral pathways of *right* to *forward* and *left* to *forward*. Or consider the breaststroke or the crawl in swimming, the volleyball serve, or the football pass. Volleyball utilizes both the spokelike or central transitions and the peripheral transitions.

However, the six points in space of the dimensional scale are too limiting. A need for additional points in space is established early in the learning sequence. The diagonal scale with its eight additional points in space comes about when one considers the kinesphere to be boxlike. Radiating outward from the body center are spokes directed toward the corner of the box. Figure 9.4 illustrates the diagonal cross.[12]

Movements along the diagonal scale connect high and low corners of surrounding space. Each point in space is a combination of three directions. High-right-forward to deep-left-backward is shown in figure 9.5.

As experienced earlier with the dimensional cross, the eight diagonal directions can be linked peripherally. Such movements avoid the body center, while linking the corners either by following the edges of the box or by traveling kitty-corner over the sides, called planes. Figure 9.6 illustrates one example each of central, overedge, and overplane transitions.[13]

Greater mobility is required when exploring the possibilities of diagonal transitions than when the dimensional scale is used. A brief exercise in which the points of diagonal directions are contrasted with those of dimensional direction will illustrate that central and peripheral transitions are more easily made dimensionally than diagonally. Bending and twisting is required when diagonal directions are used.

Another set of reference points may be located when the three planes of movement referred to in chapter V are analyzed. The wheel, or sagittal plane, dividing the body into right and left halves, has four corners: forward-high, forward-deep, backward-high, and backward-deep (fig. 9.7).[14]

12 Ibid., p. 87.
13 Ibid., p. 88.
14 Ibid., p. 94.

Fig. 9.4 The diagonal cross: Eight points in space

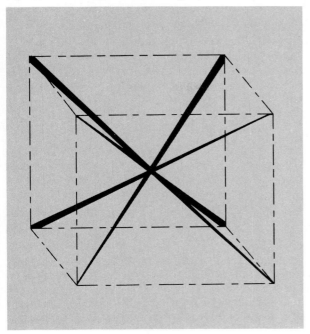

Fig. 9.5 A diagonal: High-right-forward to deep-left-backward

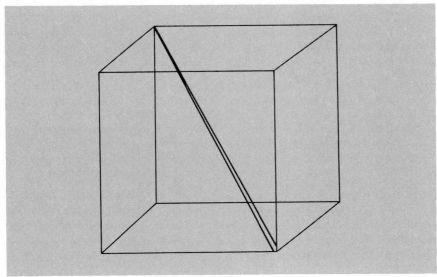

The wall, or frontal, plane's corners are high-right, high-left, deep-right, and deep-left. Those of the table, or horizontal, plane are right-forward, right-backward, left-forward, and left-backward.

Peripheral transitions using the twelve points of the three scales join

Fig. 9.6 Central, overedge, and overplane transitions

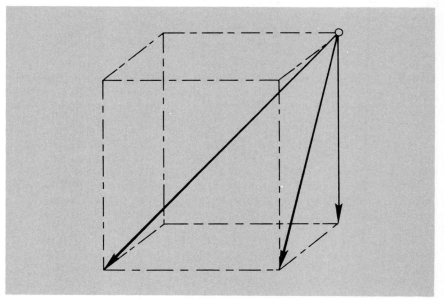

adjacent points on the same plane or another plane. Transversal transitions are those that pass through another plane to reach a planetary direction further away (fig. 9.8).[15]

Central transitions connect the diagonally opposite corners of the planes while passing through the center of the body. Standing with arms at high-right and left and legs at deep-right and left describes a shape in which opposite arms and legs connect the diametral points of the wall plane (fig. 9.9).

> The planes are linked with the actions of traveling, turning, and jumping. Movements in the door plane are primarily rising and falling, which leads into elevation; movements in the wheel plane are advancing and re-treating, which leads into traveling; and in the table plane movements are opening and closing, which leads into turning. Students should be given experience in these planes by stressing the dimensional origin and the link with traveling, turning, and jumping, by giving sequences based on this, and by encouraging experimentation.[16]

Preston-Dunlop offers a sound suggestion, one that helps to clarify the purpose of the exploration-discovery process in spatial orientation. She states that "it is best to proceed in two ways; firstly, to improvise shapes around the body freely and then recognize the points through which they have passed; and secondly, to consciously join the points and then recognize the shapes which have been created."[17]

15 Ibid., p. 96.
16 Ibid., p. 92.
17 Ibid., p. 96.

Fig. 9.7 The three planes of movement

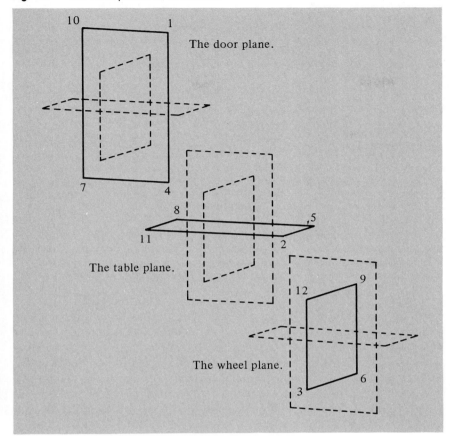

The door plane.

The table plane.

The wheel plane.

Fig. 9.8 Peripheral and transversal transitions

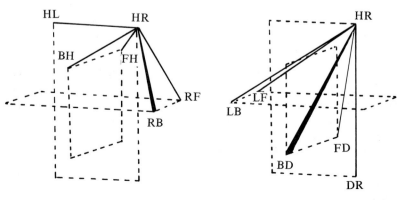

The peripheral transitions
from high-right

The transversal transitions
from high-right

Fig. 9.9

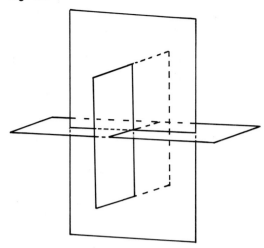

Further elaboration and explanation of movement theory and practice involving spatial orientation may be obtained from a thoughtful reading of the pertinent materials in Preston-Dunlop's book and in Laban's Choreutics. Mastery of movement involving the transitions between the twenty-seven points in space must await individual research and practice. Knowledge of dimensional, diagonal, and diametral points in space helps the learner of movement develop versatility in the utilization of the kinesphere. Such heightened awareness of movement possibility, accompanied by appropriate vocabulary, permit direct application to skill learning in all activities. (See readings at end of this chapter.)

1.0 Establishing the Dimensional Cross

The six directions of the dimensional cross are emphasized.

1.1 *Movement Variations Based on the Dimensional Cross*: Forward, backward, upward, downward, right, and left movements are explored. These primary directions may accompany both locomotor and nonlocomotor actions. Traveling in different directions and gesturing, also in different directions, are important features of many creative activities like floor exercise, balance beam, free skating, and dance.

1.2 *Dimensional Step Patterns*: Traveling actions of all sorts are explored. The child should learn that dimensional directions are determined by the front of the body, not the front of the activity or classroom.

1.3 *Central and Peripheral Transitions*: The octahedron may serve as a model to depict the pathways that follow the edge of the body and those that travel through its center. Jumping, turning, and traveling actions of all kinds may follow peripheral transitions such as *deep* to *forward* to *high*, leading to a jump; *forward* to *right*, leading to a turn; or *high* to *forward*, leading to a forward roll.

1.31 *Sequencing Transitions with the Dimensional Scale*: Spokelike movements toward and away from the body center are connected to peripheral transitions with their emphasis on extension. The pathways of the octahedron are explored in a variety of ways, with various body parts leading the actions as both the central and peripheral transitions are combined.

1.32 *Turning, Jumping, and Traveling from Peripheral Transitions*: The peripheral transitions of the dimensional scale are accepted with this theme. All known locomotor actions are explored, as well as turns at different levels and elevations, with appropriate peripheral transitions leading the actions.

1.33 *The Dimensional Scale with Partner Relationships*: All of the partner relationships of Theme V are reexamined with the stress placed upon the dimensional scale. Working together, working in opposition, complementing each other, or making adaptations with countertension are enhanced through careful use of dimensional transitions.

2.0 The Diagonal Cross

Movements involving diagonal directions through the body center are explored after the diagonal cross has been established. There are four possibilities.

high-right-forward to deep-left-backward
high-left-forward to deep-right-backward
high-left-backward to deep-right-forward
high-right-backward to deep-left-forward

Standing in the center of the room, the diagonals can be perceived as passing through the body while connecting the diagonally opposite corners of the room. Movements along the diagonal are more difficult to master than those of the dimensional scale because directions are combinations of the primary directions.

2.1 *Movements along the Diagonal Scale*: Exploration is confined to movements following the diagonals. Sequences of possible transitions can be led by different parts of the arm and hand, even the elbow.

2.2 *Variations on the Diagonal Cross*: In addition to central transitions, movements may follow peripheral pathways. When the four directions of the diagonals are connected, a cube is formed. Movements along the edge of the cube are called overedge transitions. Those that connect across the side of the cube are called overplane transitions. All, of course, avoid the body center.

3.0 Establishing the Three Planes

The four corners of each plane are located. Each is connected with the others kinesthetically and linked peripherally and transversely.

3.1 *Orientation to the Door Plane*: High-right, deep-right, deep-left, and high-left are the directions. Closing and opening actions resulting in lifting and lowering, lateral bending, sideward stretching, and wheeling are possible.

3.2 *Orientation to the Wheel Plane*: Forward-high, forward-deep, backward-high and backward-deep are the directions. Advancing and retreating, lifting and lowering, bending forward and backward, backward and forward rolling, and certain more advanced acrobatic and tumbling movements are possible.

3.3 *Orientation to the Table Plane*: Left-forward, right-forward, left-backward, and right-backward are the directions. Note that the directions left and right are stated first because they are mainly left and right and only a little bit forward or backward. Actions are trunk twisting, opening, closing, and turning.

3.4 *Central and Peripheral Transitions*: Central transitions travel from the body center to any of the twelve points of orientation created by the three planes. A variety of body parts can perform the actions. Peripheral movements proceeding from one point of orientation may make five different transitions, two each going to a different plane and one going to a different point on the same plane.

3.5 *Transversal Transitions*: Only transversal transitions travel between the body center and peripheral points of orientation. These transitions cut directly through the kinesphere, rather than following the outlines of the periphery.

Notes on sample unit: Theme XI

Because Theme XI appears to the uninitiated physical educator (whose concepts of space and direction have largely been limited to simple changes in directions or changes of front) to be an arrangement of rather complex spatial concepts, a few comments are in order. Accuracy in the direction that body parts take while performing complex skills determines in large measure the success of the performance. Generalized concepts of direction are not enough foundation with which to proceed into the very specific spatial realm of skill learning unless one is content to have many children doomed to failure.

Awareness of the shapes made by the body or its parts as it moves through space is a helpful, almost essential, aspect of the analysis of motor performance. The teacher, the coach, and the student observer are more likely to compare observed performances with a composite mental picture of many previous examples of good technique than to make a kinesiologic analysis involving levers and other mechanical principles, important as they are to a complete study. To be able to distinguish, with attention to the minutest spatial detail, the difference between perfect and not so perfect is one of the objectives of a quality based learning sequence. High levels of a skill cannot be learned by performers whose concepts are not adequately developed. Frustration results when learners repeat the same errors because either the instructor or the learner (or both) have inadequate spatial concepts. The teacher should begin early to lay the foundation for future skill analysis.

Sample unit: Theme XI

Theme: XI Orientation in Space

Unit: 1.0 Establishing the Dimensional Cross

Instructional level: Grade 2   Operational stage: I, level 2.0

Program objectives: On completion of this unit, the learner should
1 Be able to travel accurately in forward, backward, and sideward directions with a variety of step patterns.
2 Be able to demonstrate clearly actions of raising and lowering, and other gestures in upward and downward directions.
3 Be able to demonstrate through appropriate gesture his understandings of central and peripheral transitions involving the dimensional points of orientation.

Suggested lesson themes:
The following lesson themes have been selected as the means for securing the program objectives. Each theme and subtheme is supported by appropriate instructional objectives in modular lesson plans, using floor, apparatus, rhythm, and manipulative environments.

1.0 Establishing the Dimensional Cross
1.1 Movement Variations Based on the Dimensional Cross
   1.11 Combining Change in Direction with Change in Level
1.2 Dimensional Step Patterns
1.3 Central and Peripheral Transitions
   1.31 Sequencing Transitions with the Dimensional Scale

Addendum

■ No significant purpose would be achieved by providing written assignments for this chapter. One more chapter on themes follows. Because it consists of the most complex of all Laban's movement themes, it is doubtful whether many physical educators will make regular use of it. However, the material is useful for those interested in seeing how the major principles of movement interrelate. What is important is not so much being able to use the material as simply knowing that it is there.

Readings

■ In addition to the following books referred to in this chapter, see the list of readings at the end of Chapter VIII for help in the construction of lesson themes.

Kephart, Newell C. *The Slow Learner in the Classroom.* Columbus, Ohio: Merrill, 1960.

Laban, Rudolf. *Choreutics.* London: MacDonald & Evans, 1966.

North, Marion. *Body Movement for Children.* Boston: Plays, 1972.

Preston [-Dunlop], Valerie. *A Handbook for Modern Educational Dance.* London: MacDonald & Evans, 1963.

◆◆◆◆◆◆◆◆◆◆◆◆◆◆◆◆◆◆◆◆◆◆◆◆◆◆◆◆◆◆

Chapter X

Units of instruction: themes xii to xvi

As teachers, we should first try to make everyone confident and secure through their own greatest gifts, and gradually lead them to a wider variety of movement.

Ruth Morison
A Movement Approach to Educational Gymnastics

■ The teacher will find selected aspects of the final group of themes very useful in helping to attain certain cognitive objectives. Concepts relevant to shapes and efforts will apply to the analysis of skills. Formational concepts relate to the shapes of groups, for example, circle, line, and square. The material should be studied with an effort toward integrating one's concepts of movement, dance, games, and other aspects of physical education.

In several places within this chapter, reference is made to the application of a particular concept to learning in other areas of physical education. We hope our readers will be able to see additional ways in which material in this and in previous chapters relates to learning in all areas of physical education. For physical education to become movement oriented, its teachers must be well grounded in both the theory of movement and the art of teaching. Smiles and words of encouragement are not enough. The teacher must know the subject and must be able to analyze. With that consideration in mind, attention is now turned to the content of the final group of Laban's themes.

Theme XII: The combination of shapes and efforts

■ This is a study of the two major aspects of human movement—the shape of action as it carves its way through space and the efforts required to produce and control it. Preston-Dunlop calls it "the first Theme in which the concept of wholeness is encountered, . . . the culmination of individual technical ability."[1] Although what Preston-Dunlop has in mind is choreography for modern educational dance, the implication for skill learning

1 Valerie Preston [-Dunlop], *A Handbook for Modern Educational Dance* (London: MacDonald & Evans, 1963), p. 103.

in all activities is inescapably clear to those whose backgrounds include performance and coaching of such technically involved sports as gymnastics, track and field, and the individual and group patterns of team sports. Shape and effort analysis offer the student of physical education and the coach exciting prospects for growth in analytical competence.

> A parallel can be drawn in the teaching of Art in that the patterns and forms of the painting (shape in movement) and the colour and texture (effort and rhythm in movement) are looked at and worked on together, and the relationship between the two studied. In music a similar parallel can be drawn, i.e. the melody and pitch (shape and orientation in movement) and the harmony, rhythm, tempo and volume—(effort and rhythm in movement) are integrated and studied.[2]

Are there any who would argue that there are no parallels? Surely there is a way here for the teacher of physical education to become expert in teaching movement for activities ranging from simple games, dances, stunts, and fundamental skills to the highest levels of motor performance in areas of the instructor's choice. Becoming skilled as a teacher of movement should be an objective of every prospective and beginning physical educator. This editorial effort to motivate readers to pursue the study of human movement is inserted into a description of this major contribution of Laban for the purpose of stimulating them to go beyond the words of this theme, beyond the descriptions, into the realm of future teaching and coaching possibilities.

Only the beginning of Theme XII has application to the beginning student of movement (at Operational Stage I, level 2.0). Certain lesson themes can be developed for children with sufficient background in fundamental concepts and their associated motor behaviors. Effort qualities and basic effort actions should be clearly expressed in a variety of actions and in relationship to different physical as well as social environments. The complexity of Theme XII and the advanced level of work required to master its content place the subject matter in Operational Stage II. Therefore, only a cursory explanation of those aspects of the content that are applicable to basic movement education will be given.

1.0 Forming the Effort

Having a certain mastery of movement qualities as expressed through effort rhythms in movements performed by different body parts, the learner is ready to combine awareness of the shape of action with the effort.

1.1 *Space Patterns and Effort*: The focus is on association of the basic space patterns (straight, angular, rounded, and twisted) with effort. There is a tendency for basic effort actions to be associated more with one particular pattern than another, although the other is not entirely excluded. Slashing is usually found with rounded or twisted shapes, gliding with straight or angular shapes and so forth. These pairings are generally seen as a match between the space attitude and the space

2 Ibid., p. 103.

pattern. Directness is more apt to be related to straight or angular patterns than to twisted or rounded patterns. Flexibility is generally associated with twisted and rounded patterns. The stress of this theme is upon performing clear basic space patterns with clear basic effort actions, no more and no less.

1.2 *Floor Patterns and Effort*: Straight, angular, rounded, or twisted floor patterns are decided upon first, after which various actions are performed sequentially from beginning to end of the pattern. Children should discover that actions using space flexibly can be performed along a straight pathway; that direct actions, such as gliding and thrusting, can be performed while following a curved pathway; and that both direct and flexible actions, regardless of their order, may be utilized in patterns made up of combinations of differently shaped pathways. Turns, rolls, jumps, and traveling actions can be performed as main actions or transitions between main actions.

1.3 *Air Patterns and Effort*: The shape of air patterns may be rounded, twisted, or straight (angular is a composite of straight lines). Flexible efforts usually produce curved shapes; direct efforts, angular shapes. Although the arms are generally used to create air patterns, the legs can produce a variety of shapes also. "Any effort can be used to come into a position with shape content, for example, pressing into a spread body shape, wringing into an elongated position, flicking into a rounded body shape. Such movements can be made in a sequence, one leading on from the other."[3]

2.0 Integrating Shape and Effort

Natural and contrived rhythms can be used in the process of integrating shape and effort.

2.1 *The Natural Rhythms of Common Actions*: The natural shadings of effort in such actions as are found in gymnastic, game, and dance skills or those fundamental to simple play and work. Weight, time, and flow changes are clarified.

2.2 *Creative Forms and Contrived Rhythms*: Angular, circular, and twisted forms may be variously combined with given rhythms. Accents may be placed at the beginning, middle, or ending; when a direction is changed; or to punctuate a change in level. Time and flow changes may also be made at the whim of the mover.

Notes on sample unit: Theme XII

Theme XII is not for beginners. Its value lies in its application to analyses of all kinds of motor patterns, from simple to complex, from gymnastics to games, dance, and aquatics. Just how this is done will be explained in detail in succeeding chapters, but the general idea will be presented at this point.

All movements carve themselves into space, making a great variety of shapes that usually go quite unobserved until special attention is drawn to

3 Ibid., p. 105.

them in mime, dance, figure skating, gymnastics, and certain specialized patterns, such as the foul shot in basketball. To the expert observer in any field, there is a correct form (or shape) for an action being observed. However, if its form is mainly an expression, there is great latitude governed by cultural acceptance of style. The foul shot, handstand, pas de chat, or back handspring carve pathways through space that, if well performed, match the shapes of the same movements performed by individuals whose technique is considered to be correct. The teacher or coach must be able to ascertain what is wrong with an action sequence; that is, able to discern incorrect from correct shapes and deduce that a particular part of the body, for example, is moving in the wrong direction.

The correct handstand is an inverted elongated shape with no accentuated curvature of the spine. Until a few years ago, however, a moderate curvature was accepted as proper. Then scientific investigations disclosed the difficulty of performing twisting movements or turning actions when the body is not held perfectly straight either while supported on the hands or while rotating freely around the long axis. It was necessary, therefore, to change the shape of the handstand and to educate the gymnasts of the world to the new concepts and the new shape so that they could progress in areas previously denied them by faulty technique and inadequate understanding of the relationship between the long axis of the body, the center of gravity, and dynamic balance.

Basketball coaches often will insist that their foul-shooting practices follow certain principles. The foot is to be placed on a particular spot in relation to the foul line, the body parts primarily involved in shooting are lined up in relation to an imaginary line from the eye of the performer to the rim of the basket. All of the action is to be performed in relation to that "line," including the follow-through. The expert eye of the coach immediately detects when the shape of the action or the beginning or ending positions are contrary to form.

All movement patterns make shapes through space. To physical educators interested in the proper education of their students, the shaping of movement patterns and the related understandings play an important part in instruction. Teachers who want their students to become analysts of movement so that the students can help each other make corrections in technique or improve messages transmitted through movement will engage them in activities that deepen their awareness and heighten their understandings of movement shape and effort.

Efforts that initiate, sustain, or end movements, or that hold the body in various postures, are clearly observable to both trained instructors and performers. Correct actions have correct shapes and correct effort rhythms. An inappropriately placed accent may destroy the timing of an entire sequence. Teachers or coaches who engage in effort-shape analysis draw upon their abilities to retain the image of correct form and correct effort rhythm and thus determine the faults, if any, of learner motor behavior.

Serious study of Theme XII will not be feasible until the later elementary school years, junior high school, or senior high school. Both maturity and experience are required before the content of this theme can be explored and applied, even in the shortened version presented here. More extensive work, particularly in dance, will call attention to all directions of the previous themes and their relationships to basic effort actions. Basic effort actions should be directed toward a variety of objectives for the purpose of developing associations between the shapes formed and the efforts expressed.

Sample unit: Theme XII

Theme: XII The Combination of Shapes and Efforts

Unit: 2.0 Integrating Shape and Effort

Instructional level: Grade 6   Operational stage: II

Program objectives: On completion of this unit, the learner should
1 Demonstrate ability to integrate the shape of a given action with various efforts and select the effort rhythm most suitable to the form according to criteria given by the instructor.
2 Be able to differentiate between changes in form or shape of a given action and the correct form and between the correct effort rhythm of a given action and the correct rhythm.
3 Be able to develop a sequence of actions using either air or floor patterns or both with harmonious use of effort.

Suggested lesson themes:
The following themes have been selected as the means for securing the program objectives. Each theme and subtheme is supported by appropriate instructional objectives in modular lesson plans, using floor, apparatus, rhythm, and manipulative environments.

2.0 Integrating Shape and Effort
2.1 The Natural Rhythms of Common Actions
    2.11 Exploring Locomotor Patterns
    2.12 Exploring Gymnastic Patterns
    2.13 Exploring the Patterns Associated with Games
    2.14 Exploring Patterns Associated with Dance

Theme XIII: Elevation

■ The subject of this theme is more than merely the action of jumping. It is to elevate, to suspend as if free from the force of gravity. This temporary freedom can only be achieved by those strong enough to jump high enough to permit them a moment of release from the downward pull of gravity. Such aids as trampolines, trampolettes, takeoff boards, and artificial or natural ramps or inclines leading to soft landings help less-able students feel these moments of freedom.

Units of instruction: themes xii to xvi

Theme I, Body Awareness, introduced learners to all manner of large body movements aimed at taking them from one place to another. Jumping actions were learned in reference to takeoffs and landings on either one foot or both feet. This theme is an extension of that work.

1.0 Getting Away from the Floor

The objective in elevation is, in part at least, to get away from the floor. The physical aspect of pushing off is the aim of this theme.

1.1 *Taking Off in Different Ways or with Repetition*: The focus is simply on getting off the floor by means of vigorous jumping actions, sometimes by performing a series of different jumps and other times by repeating the same jump to concentrate on the explosiveness of the force.

1.2 *Jumping Phrases with Variations in Intensity*: Small jumps and big jumps are phrased so that the intensity of the action builds to a climax. Explosive power upon takeoff and the reduction of tension while airborne are stressed. There should be no observable tension, especially in the upper half of the body, and that in the lower half should be only enough to maintain the shape of the body.

2.0 Leading with Particular Parts of the Body

The top of the head is an especially good part of the body to concentrate on as the leader of the jumping action. When the head leads, all other body parts follow along the same pathway. Accurate elevations are especially important in such activities as gymnastics, figure skating, diving, and dancing. The jump shooter in basketball requires accuracy in his jump to reduce the variables that may affect his shooting. The jumping patterns associated with Theme VI are reexplored with a variety of body parts leading the actions of jumping. Care must be taken that only skilled performers lead with body parts that are liable to cause forward, backward, or sideward rotation while in flight. Unless the rotation is completed, the performer will not land on his feet.

2.1 *Elevations Stressing the Head as Leader*: The top of the head leads all the different jumping patterns. Turns in the air may be executed for variation but not until the body is properly aligned and the eyes focused directly forward.

2.2 *Elevations Led by Different Body Parts*: Depending on the skill of the learner, a variety of different body parts may be used to lead the actions of elevation.

3.0 Shapes and Elevation

Elevated positions with the body assuming different momentary shapes, such as those described in Theme IX, are the focus of this level of Theme XIII.

3.1 *Emphasizing Stretched Body Shapes in Flight*: The stretched body shape may be narrow or wide. The former is emphasized as the primary "stretch."

3.2 *From Stretch to Curl to Stretch in Flight*: A strong jump leading into a fully stretched body shape that immediately curls and then returns to stretch is stressed. Storming planks, boxes, beams, trampolines, and other kinds of apparatus can be used indoors or outdoors to supplement natural or created terrain that invites jumping and aids the development of moments of suspension of sufficient duration to be felt and to permit the execution of changes in shape.

3.3 *Variations of the Body Shape While Elevated*: More creative shapes are elicited by use of this theme. Some of the shapes demonstrated will aid the feeling of elevation, while others will hinder it. Unless the landing area is soft, all shapes should return to a reasonably good form of the stretch before landing.

4.0 Effort and Elevation

Elevation is generally associated with sudden effort. It takes quickness to get away from the floor. However, the body can experience a floating or gliding sensation while in suspension. It can also experience pressing and wringing efforts either in preparation for or upon landing.

4.1 *Sudden Efforts on the Spot or While Traveling in Elevation*: Thrusting, slashing, dabbing, and flicking effort qualities are experienced in large and small jumps, on the spot, while traveling, and in turning jumps.

4.2 *Floating and Gliding Sensations and Elevation*: Only extremely powerful jumpers will experience these sensations, unless apparatus is used. Correct technique in split leaps leads to these qualities of elevation also.

4.3 *Effort-Elevation Phrases*: A sequence of actions with emphasis on elevations utilizing different effort qualities is the main thrust of this theme. The greatest intensity of the elevation may be in the beginning, the middle, or the end of the sequence. Turns, either on the spot or traveling, may be selected.

5.0 Landing

Three possibilities for landing exist: landing followed immediately by elevation; landing with dissipation of force; landing with the sensation of elevation retained. Young children will demonstrate the first two by bouncing about or by collapsing completely. The third form of landing requires great strength in the legs and back and great control, so that the mover is able to connect the landing to actions other than those with a downward direction. Gymnasts in their floor exercises, figure skaters, and dancers exhibit this quality of landing skill, without which they could not perform properly the many leaps, jumps, and elevated turns so important to the full expression of their movements.

5.1 *Rebounding*: The emphasis of this theme is upon preparation to go up again before one has landed. The legs thrust quickly, the ankles remain firm, and only the ball of the foot makes contact with the floor or landing surface. In gymnastics, this landing is called a "punch" and is used to direct the body upward for vaults and somersaults in floor exercise or tumbling. However, whole-foot landings, which are softer, are required for some jumps, such as those in trampolining and diving.

5.2 *Absorbing the Force of the Body upon Landing*: Soft landings in which the tension of the body is released and gravity is allowed to take over are emphasized. Learning to "give" at the joints of ankle, knee, and hip is especially important, particularly for individuals who tend to be tense or fearful of landing from heights. Accident prevention in the early grades, as well as in upper grades where apparatus of greater heights is used, demands continual emphasis upon the proper absorption of force when landing.

5.3 *Retaining the Sensation of Elevation upon Landing:* This very difficult theme requires the performer to use the legs for firm, controlled landing without collapsing the body "so that the next movement can be of any character he chooses; it does not make it necessary to either jump or collapse."[4]

Sample unit: Theme XIII

Theme: XIII Elevation

Unit: 5.0 Landing

Instructional level: Grade 5   Operational stage: I, level 2.0

Program objectives: On completion of this unit, the learner should
1 Demonstrate improved performance in ability to absorb the force of the body upon landing from various learner-selected heights and from jumps from the floor.
2 Be able (a) to rebound when landing on such different surfaces as the floor, takeoff board, trampoline, and trampolette and (b) to explain the difference in effort when taking off from resilient or nonresilient surfaces.
3 Be able to land and retain the ability to travel with control after jumps with and without turns in elevation.

Suggested lesson themes:
The following themes have been selected as the means for securing the program objectives. Each theme and subtheme is supported by appropriate instructional objectives in modular lesson plans, using floor, apparatus, rhythm, and manipulative environments.

5.0 Landing
5.1 Rebounding
    5.11 Emphasizing Stretched Rebounds
    5.12 Turning Rebounds
5.2 Absorbing the Force of the Body upon Landing
5.3 Retaining the Sensation of Elevation upon Landing
    5.31 Connecting Movements to Landings

---

4 Ibid., p. 115.

■ A common interest is the usual reason for people forming some kind of group relationship. In physical education there are many activities that bring people together, but the specifics of their relationships are not all the same. In some activities leadership is bestowed upon one individual, in others it shifts according to changes in the situation, and in certain activities it is difficult to tell who is leading (although someone must be). Developing awareness of a need for group feeling is one way an instructor can make an important contribution to the sensitivity needed for effective and efficient team or group work. The activities suggested by this theme are aimed at arousing group feeling. Imaginative use of the ideas presented will be rewarded through application of the principles to all manner of activity within the physical education spectrum.

1.0 Leading and Adapting

Leading and following behaviors are explored and analyzed to determine the special responsibilities associated with each of them.

> The leader's role: to make a clear pathway, to stay in each direction sufficiently long for the group to be able to respond to it, to keep a speed which is possible for all with special regard for the last person in the row, to make each level change gradual but definite and to watch his group reactions to his leadership. The follower's role: to watch the leader and respond without delay, to see that his own movements are sufficiently clear so that the one behind him can easily follow.[5]

These responsibilities, so easily identified when a file formation is employed, are readily adapted to other situations as well. Little by little, the teacher helps learners understand that the roles of the follower and the leader are mutually dependent. Leaders cannot lead without followers; followers cannot follow if leadership is absent.

1.1 *Sensing Leader-and-Follower Relationships:* The aim of this theme is to sensitize movers to nonverbal behaviors that communicate changes in speed, level, or direction. Partner and small-group relationships are used with such tasks as traveling from place to place, traveling around or through obstacles, or changing the size of the group. Instructors often serve as leaders until the basic concepts are understood; however, this is not always necessary. When tasks are performed in small groups, each facing a common center, the leadership role may be assumed by anyone, with the others following to avoid collisions with other groups or simply to develop mastery over this type of problem.

1.2 *Communication Through Physical Touch:* A group with members facing in opposite directions but touching each other lightly responds to signals of various members by adjusting positions in an appropriate fashion. Simple back-to-back activity may be used, partner stunts of all kinds, and activity akin to pyramid building. Rather than touching

5 Ibid., p. 119.

each other, the members may touch or hold something, such as a rope, hoop, or pole. Carrying large objects through small places and around obstacles requires the kind of cooperation sought by this theme.

2.0 Mimetic Group Action

Self-conscious individuals who might fail to develop ideas of their own can be helped through mime. Small groups are formed, and each works out the rhythms of one facet of a larger operation engaged in by the class as a whole. The construction of large buildings; the assembly of motor cars; mining, hauling, and storing; and many other occupations can form the subject of the study. Movements are repeated to develop a rhythm. Although each group may operate independently of the others at first, the groups are gradually brought together so that one group may respond to another in a cooperative manner.

2.1 *Work Actions in Groups*: The children select from various occupations the particular actions corresponding to an occupation and evolve the rhythm, tempo, spatial patterns, and interrelationships required.

2.2 *Play Actions in Groups*: Games of all kinds are used to develop interesting group rhythms. Ideas for offensive or defensive movements in response to the situations created make for challenges that evoke a wide range of group responses.

3.0 Time Relationships

The special feature of time relationships is the synchronization of movements, which occurs when the group feels together the movement when an action should occur.

3.1 *Synchronizing without Outside Help*: Partners first and then small groups perform actions in which there are sudden changes in time factors (for example, moving toward slowly and away from quickly), in level, and so forth. Body parts can move toward and away from each other, shapes can change, all manner of movements are possible; the objective is for the group to sense, as a group, when the sudden change should occur without any kind of outside assistance.

3.2 *Common Effort Rhythms Synchronized*: A sequence of effort rhythms starting with preparation and ending with recovery is given the class; for example, preparation, punch, wring, slash, recovery. All may be started together, either in response to a chant by the teacher or to the sound of some other accompaniment. Gradually, the accompaniment is withdrawn. The class continues to respond with effort synchronization without need for an audible rhythm simply because they are aware of each other. This theme is difficult for many because concentration must be on the effort action rather than on a specific motor action. The effort action may be directed along many different paths, whereas a specific motor action has a specific shape, a factor that would make synchronization much easier to achieve.

4.0 Weight Relationships

The expression of the weight relationship is called *consolidation*.[6] It is a relationship based on degrees of physical contact, ranging from firm touch to weak contact.

6 Ibid., p. 122.

4.1 *Circles with and without Contact*: Children are linked by hands, by fingers, or by a gentle touch upon the shoulders to describe relationship among members of a circle. The physical bond is experienced as strong or light. The solidarity of the circle may be broken by breaking or weakening the physical contact. Those on the end of the line where the break occurs sense a loss of security, which is remedied when the ends are reunited. Traveling about, moving into the center and away from the center, and trying to maintain a circle without contact are some of the experiences that will help to establish the feeling for consolidation, for a weight relationship.

4.2 *Group Expression in Weight Relationships*: Preston describes three categories of expression that may be expressed by group action: (a) "we are a solid group," (b) "we are a tentative group," and (c) "we have no contact."[7] Working with different efforts while using the same pattern will demonstrate that the weight factor is important in the expression of these feelings, according to Preston.[8]

5.0 Flow Relationships

As has been said, flow means the change between going and stopping, between being ready to pour out or withhold movement. This is the very stuff of relationship, and of all kinds of contact this is the most important.[9]

The strength of this comment by Preston-Dunlop is more keenly felt when the flow relationship is expressed as *communication*. Individuals with bound flow do not communicate well. It is as if they prefer to lose contact with others, to withdraw. As partners in activities such as dance they are especially difficult, but one may recognize the symptoms in manipulative activities and gymnastics that require group relationships. Themes to improve flow relationship require learners to experience contrast so that desired concepts and feelings are more easily clarified.

5.1 *Passing a Movement on to Others*: A loose group is used. Individuals take turns initiating a movement, which is picked up and passed from one to another until it is returned to the initiator. Preston-Dunlop suggests trying free flow first, "entering into the movement with the whole body and then with bound flow, withholding the centre of the body. The expression 'I wish to communicate' and 'I am reluctant to communicate' will be experienced immediately."[10]

5.2 *Increasing and Decreasing the Flow to Experience the Contrast in Relationship to Others*: Groups may start a rhythmic pattern that is passed across to another group and then back again. The increase in the flow factor makes it possible. Restraining the flow will cut off communication. Individuals can experience the same phenomena through free movement in the common space that becomes restrained in its flow.

---

7 Ibid., p. 123.
8 Ibid., p. 123
9 Ibid., p. 123.
10 Ibid., pp. 123-24.

Sample unit: Theme XIV

Theme: XIV The Awakening of Group Feeling

Unit: 1.0 Leading and Adapting

Instructional level: Grade 5 or 6   Operational stage: I, level 2.0

Program objectives: On completion of this unit, learners should
1 Demonstrate by the responsiveness of their behaviors to the movement needs of others in a group relationship that they understand the mutually dependent relationship of leader and follower roles.
2 Be able to explain satisfactorily how in different situations under different circumstances the leader and followers may communicate nonverbally without physical contact.
3 Create various group relationships, both contact and noncontact, in which nonverbal communication is used to permit individual members to make appropriate adaptations to the group effort or to cooperate in assisting an individual effort.

Suggested lesson themes:
The following themes have been selected as the means for securing the program objectives. Each theme and subtheme is supported by appropriate instructional objectives in modular lesson plans, using floor, apparatus, rhythm, and manipulative environments.

1.0 Leading and Adapting
1.1 Sensing Leader-and-Follower Relationships
1.2 Communication through Physical Touch

**Theme XV:
Group formations**

■ Sports, games, dances, and gymnastics are liberal in their use of formations. Some formations are fixed in a particular shape, while others change and then regain their original shape later on. The severest problems that individual learners encounter in many physical education lessons are not those related to skill at all but those that are closely associated with their relationships to others. Position play and dancing to position depend upon the understandings of formation relevant to the activity being performed. It is the concept of formation and the variability of formation that are of interest in this theme.

Formations act as units. When people in a group act in formation, there is a sharp distinction between them and another group of people who may be together but who show no leader-follower relationships. Formations vary in their shape, some regular, others irregular. Their size may vary with the number of people involved and their proximity to one another.

1.0 The Group Acting as a Unit
Three different forms of group action are explored through this theme. The purpose is to learn how to respond to a situation in which the

group acts like a unit. This calls for individuals to adapt movements, efforts, and relationships so that the purpose of the group can be fulfilled.

1.1 *Group Focus outside the Group*: The movements of the group are directed toward a focal point outside the group. Movements of the same or different body parts may be aimed at the focal point. The group shape may reflect that of a single individual focused upon a spot.

1.2 *Group Focus within the Group*: The center of the group, some person or persons, is the focal point with all movement and positions related to this point. The action may be away from the focal point or toward it, moving in any direction desired with the central point remaining stationary.

1.3 *Group Focus upon a Moving Central Focus*: The focus of the group is toward a central point or person. As this focal point moves, so do the members of the group. If the central point rotates, the entire group rotates so that the relationships are not disturbed. Group members reinforce the aim of the central focus by various supporting actions.

2.0 Linear Group Formations

This theme explores events that occur when members of a group travel in lines. The position of the leader determines the action in some situations, while the shape of the formation determines the action in other situations.

2.1 *Lines*: When children form files (a line in which one child is behind another), the child in front is the leader. The pathways followed may be either straight or curved. If the children stand side by side, there is no leader; the formation is wall-like. If a leader in the center of the line is chosen, the group no longer acts together as a wall but attains a V-shape, either in front or in back of the leader. Walls are solid and travel forward and backward. V-shapes are more flexible but not as easily moved as files.

2.2 *Circles*: When wall-like formations are bent around, a circle is formed. A circle may also be formed when a file travels in a curved pathway until the leader ends up behind the last person. Circles have no leaders. The focus is upon the center of the circle toward and away from which the members of the circle may travel. There can be circles within circles at the same or different levels or traveling in opposite directions. Maintaining the circular shape while traveling is a particularly difficult task.

3.0 Geometric Group Formations

Geometric and letter shapes are explored so that the character of each shape can be understood. The purpose of this theme is not so much to establish an awareness of relationship to other group members (as in Theme XIV) but to understand the similarities and differences of formation in regard to the feelings associated with them. The major difference between a square composed of a compact group and a square composed of four people separated by space is one of solidarity compared to porosity. Triangles are wedgelike and seem suited for attack, whereas side-by-side lines resemble walls that can defend. Cir-

Geometric group
formations

cles may be complete or half moons. Lines may zig-zag, like Zs and Ws. The previous work of Theme V is expanded upon so that the special features of each formation can be better understood.

3.1 *Triangles and Squares Contrasted*: Triangles and squares are similar in some respects and different in others. Open triangle and square formations have corners with each person who occupies a corner capable of being the leader at any time, depending on the situation. Solid groups of people in triangle or square formations present participants with different problems along with differences in the character of the relationship. In the square formation, each side is a solid line of people all of whom are leaders capable of moving forward and backward as a solid wall. The triangle presents some different problems when it comes to locomotion. Triangles require as few as three people and are recognized more easily within larger formations, such as a W, which may be viewed as three triangles formed by five people. A pentagon looks like a box or square with a triangle on one side formed by the addition of one person.

3.2 *Circular Shapes*: Circles can enclose other shapes and can vary in shape to the extent that they may be oval- or egg-shaped. Half circles or broken circles have different characteristics because the people at each end are next to only one person instead of two. Under this circumstance, the end people may have leadership roles to fulfill.

4.0 Irregular Group Formations

Group shapes do not need to be regular or geometric in form. Irregular group shapes encourage more individual spontaneity.

4.1 *A Member of the Group as the Focus of Response*: ". . . one person makes a movement of clear character, rounded and soft, angular and hard, pointed and spiky, or broad and steady. One after the other each member attaches himself to the focal figure, keeping in character with him but with personal choice of movements, until a shape is formed."[11] One may follow the other into the final form or the group may respond simultaneously.

4.2 *Employing a Focus outside the Group*: A focal point outside the group, on the wall or floor, may attract or repel the individual members of the group and lead to interesting formations. A change in the focal point creates additional interest and unexpected relationships.

To summarize Theme XV, formations are of particular significance in group relationships. A focus is necessary, but the formation may take many forms, some regular, others irregular. Leadership and followership are established nonverbally by whatever the purpose of the moment may be.

Consider the leadership and followership demonstrated nonverbally by a basketball or a soccer team. How about the defensive secondary's reaction to the run or a pass? There seems to be ample reason to help children acquire sensitivity to group relationships in which the character of the formation and its responses are explored. Applications of formation concepts are easily transferred to games, dance, gymnastics, and aquatic situations.

Sample unit: Theme XV

Theme: XV Group Formations

Unit: 3.0 Geometric Group Formations

Instructional level: Grade 5 or 6   Operational stage: I, level 2.0

Program objectives: On completion of this unit, the learner should
1 Be able to assume leader or follower roles when working with geometric formations requiring leadership.
2 Be able to work cooperatively with other members in a variety of geometric formations.
3 Demonstrate significant improvement in the ability to respond spontaneously to nonverbal leader communication.

Suggested lesson themes:
The following themes have been selected as the means for securing the program objectives. Each theme and subtheme is supported by appropriate instructional objectives in modular lesson plans, using floor, apparatus, rhythm, and manipulative environments.

11 Ibid., pp. 127-128.

3.0 Geometric Group Formations
3.1 Triangles and Squares Contrasted
3.2 Circular Shapes

Theme XVI: The expressive qualities of movement

■ This is the last of Laban's movement themes. Work on this theme can be attempted only by those who have been well grounded in the preceding themes. There is no point, therefore, in developing the ideas of this theme because few people outside of those involved in such creative efforts as dance, figure skating, or rhythmic gymnastics will put it to use. Preston-Dunlop expresses it thus:

> The aim of work in this Theme is to integrate the movement ideas of the preceding Themes and bring about an awareness of the meaning of these as a form of human expression. The expressiveness may be further developed into the Art of the Dance. This is part of the work in Theme XVI but the inclusion of it in a course of study will depend on the interest and the time available. In order to do this a reasonable mastery of personal movement and social adaptability is required: that is to say the preceding Themes must have been fully worked . . . . An audience of some kind is needed to put the powers of expression to the test.[12]

Preston-Dunlop amplifies further by stating that "Modern Educational Dance is nearer the life situation than the art situation, for every human being is constantly trying to make himself clear to his neighbours, by words and gestures, which convey his needs, his moods and himself, or to understand someone else."[13]

This final theme raises a point that may have occurred to some readers by this time. Basic movement education and modern educational dance are closely related, so closely, in fact, that there may be some question as to how one tells them apart. Theme XVI is strictly a theme for modern educational dance. Its requirements take it well beyond the understandings sought in basic movement education. In previous themes, we utilized Preston-Dunlop's work to maintain a close alliance between the thematic development of modern educational dance and basic movement education. It appeared foolish to attempt to separate the content of the two when separation was not in the best interests of the learner. On the other hand, the stress in basic movement education is simply the awakening of awareness of movement and the motion factors relevant to basic movement education. There is knowledge associated with this awakening and with the ability to communicate both verbally and nonverbally. The end product of basic movement education is a body ready to learn and a mind that understands and has a certain mastery over the body. It takes very little effort on the part of the teacher to shift the focus of a lesson in basic movement to specific movements associated with dance, sports, and gymnastics.

The unity of all human movement is well understood. However, the relationship to basic movement as expressed by the work of Laban is still

12 Ibid., p. 130.
13 Ibid., p. 130.

not fully understood. It is only when teachers work closely with children and the work of the themes presented that this interdependence is realized. The basic movement track exists only as a pedagogic instrument that enables teachers to help children develop the foundational awarenesses necessary to all skill development.

Readings

■ In addition to the following books referred to in this chapter, see the list of readings at the end of Chapter VIII for help in the construction of lesson themes.

Morison, Ruth. *A Movement Approach to Educational Gymnastics.* London: J. M. Dent, 1969.

Preston [-Dunlop], Valerie. *A Handbook for Modern Educational Dance.* London: MacDonald & Evans, 1963.

Units of instruction: themes xii to xvi

Chapter XI

Division of the program

The drive among all people to build
new structures, to develop new plans,
to organize for new ends arises out of
their desire to make practice conform
to ideas, needs, or nature.

Jesse Feiring Williams
The Principles of Physical Education, p. 197

■ A few important points are recalled to clarify the relationship among the various parts of the total instructional program in physical education.

The general plan

The dual-track concept

The first point is the dual-track program concept of organization and instruction.

There are five major characteristics of the basic movement track.

1 The requirement that all lessons be organized around themes that have either an action or a movement idea orientation
2 Spiral progression of all lessons with the content of each linked to the material assimilated through previous work
3 A major focus on discovery learning utilizing, whenever possible, an individualized learner approach to movement problem solving
4 Enrichment of concepts, action, and qualities, through change in either the physical or the social environment or in both environments of the movement learning situation
5 Generalized outcomes, such as improved awareness of self in space, in relationship to others or to things, and general motor efficiency that serves as a foundation for specific skill learning or that enables the individual to make rapid adaptations to new movement challenges

The sharp contrast between the characteristics of the basic movement track and those of the developmental movement track, listed below, is clearly in evidence. The major characteristics are as follows.

1 All lessons are organized around specific activity objectives, either in skill or in concepts.

2 Learning progression is from the simple to the complex terminating with a specific skill or understanding.

3 Skill and understanding tend to be specific rather than general.

4 Directed learning experiences are the rule, although on some occasions experimentation is encouraged.

5 Proficiency tends to be specific with learners being on different skill levels, particularly in the four major areas of games, gymnastics, dance, and aquatics.

Modular lesson organization

The second point to recall is that lessons are organized around the concept of modules, each of which consists of a time period of ten to fifteen minutes for basic movement lessons and beginning lessons in developmental movement patterns. Modules are longer for older, more experienced children.

Each module aims to accomplish specified program objectives through the attainment of related instructional objectives. Basic movement modules link (1) with other modules pursuing the same theme but in a different physical or social environment or (2) with closely related game, dance, or gymnastics modules. Developmental movement modules are separated from other modules by the singularity of their purpose. The reasons for the flexibility of basic movement modules are easily understood, as are those for the structural rigidity of the developmental movement module.

Basic movement lessons seek to enhance or develop the learner's awareness of *what, where,* and *how* the body moves. Because specific skills are not at issue, the learner is encouraged to adapt his movements to a variety of environmental circumstances. Floor modules link very comfortably to apparatus, rhythm, or manipulative modules that stress the same theme.

Developmental movement lessons seek to attain objectives that should not be diluted by environmental variety. Skill objectives are specific and include the environmental circumstances. The physical and social aspects of a skill-learning situation are important to attainment of the desired objectives.

A major need of children

The third and final point that is important to recall is that basic movement education is the major need of young children, preschoolers through second grade. Developmental movement education is increasingly important as skills are needed to participate in games or to acquire desired levels of competency in any area of physical education. Program planning for the physical education experience from kindergarten through the sixth or eighth grade takes these needs into account by assigning increased amounts of time to the developmental movement track and less time to basic movement education.

The shift from the conceptual content of a basic movement program to the psychomotor emphasis of the developmental track does not signal an end to creative or innovative learning experience. It does not mean the end to an emphasis on student thinking behaviors. On the contrary, the shift from basic to developmental movement education continues the emphasis on the cognitive domain for the purpose of attaining the most significant learner progress possible in the development of psychomotor competence. Problem solving, new games, creative dance, unique ways of engaging in gymnastics activities, and other similar behaviors should characterize the developmental movement experience, as sensitive teachers guide children toward skilled movement behaviors amid thought-provoking tasks. The major shortcut to the acquisition of skills by elementary school children is through initial command of the basic movement vocabulary.

Curriculum-building options

There are varying philosophies of physical education curriculums in professional preparatory courses. Some take the position that the skills of conventional activities have no place in a movement education program. Others have yet to discover the concept of movement education. Some reflect the belief that movement education belongs in the lower grades. All this means that curriculum content depends upon the philosophy of the builder. In the absence of research-supported evidence, there is room for all points of view. The format presented in this text can be adapted to any of the philosophical positions, although it probably works best with the dual-track concept. It is important to get on with the work of building curriculums that will function as experimental models for testing physical education and determining the degree to which the objectives support educational goals.

The curriculum builder of the developmental track has four types of culminating activities from which to choose.

1 Teacher described and directed in accordance with predetermined rules, i.e., basketball according to a guidebook
2 Teacher designed, possibly with learner assistance, with the form or rules being modifications of existing rules
3 Teacher designed, possibly with learner assistance, that aim to tie concepts and skills together in meaningful ways
4 Learner-designed games, dances, and gymnastics routines that reflect imaginative and creative use of materials, concepts, and participants

We take the position that there is room for all four options. Some children need or want structure; others want only the chance to create. The former need to learn how to be creative, while the latter need to accept the imposition of structure. If education is preparation for the future, this argument has merit.

To accommodate the curriculum planner who wants to make sure that both teacher-designed and learner-designed activities are included, we suggest that activities be categorized in accordance with the emphasis of the instructional unit.

Teacher-designed activities might include one of the following:

Dance that stresses partner relationship

or

Dance that stresses design and partner relationship
or (even more specifically)
Dance that uses folk music and stresses design and partner relationship

The most specific form approaches folk dance, whereas the first two allow greater flexibility. In all three cases, however, the teacher structures the dance through tasks that place limitations on the outcomes.
Learner-designed activities follow the same pattern.

Game with partner or small group that uses one or more manipulative objects
or
Group game that uses a learner-selected object with emphasis on striking patterns
or
Small group game that stresses batting skills
or
Group game of the softball type

As these examples show, there are ways of describing curricular content to direct the instructor toward production of desired outcomes. Although some teachers might resent such "interference" with instructional options as infringements upon their "academic freedom," others would welcome the guidance. No designations have been used in describing activities in this book. All four options have been left open to teachers, who may add appropriate descriptions. A *statement of rationale and purpose* preceding course descriptions of all developmental program activities is a way to assure understanding of both intent and content.

Program areas

■ Chapter III described the general characteristics of the two movement learning tracks. By this time, you should be thoroughly familiar with these tracks. This section is an elaboration of the program area's relationship to the structure of these learning tracks.

There are five program areas in the two movement tracks: (1) basic movement in the basic movement education track; and (2) games, contests, and sports; (3) gymnastics; (4) dance, and (5) aquatics in the developmental movement track. The divisions of the basic movement program constitute levels of understanding and experience much like the *operational stages* used to designate general learning competency. No effort is made at this time, however, to predetermine categories of any kind for this learning track. It is not now and may never be feasible or even desirable. The entire basic movement program will be treated as one category, along with three of the four areas of the developmental track (omitting aquatics).

Basic movement
Instructional courses
1 Beginning movement themes
2 Elaboration and enrichment via apparatus

rhythm ("sounds" may be more accurate)
manipulative objects
water (wading or swimming area)
3 Intermediate movement themes
4 Advanced movement themes

Explanation. Beginning movement themes are meant to introduce children to the fundamental concepts of body, effort, space, and relationship. The cognitive objective is understanding, pursued through elaboration and enrichment of the learning environment. Lessons are introduced in a *floor environment,* following which the environment is changed to one of the media areas—apparatus, rhythm (sound), or manipulation. (Water, while a marvelous medium, is available in only a few school situations and will not be mentioned further.)

Intermediate movement themes require comprehension of fundamental concepts and problem-solving methodology because the ideas and movements being explored involve the addition of new or related concepts. If a beginning class in basic movement were exposed to an intermediate theme, the children would probably respond poorly. The teacher would recognize that the reason for the poor response is the children's lack of essential understandings. They have not yet explored elementary movement themes and learned their concepts. Therefore, the learners are unable to proceed to more complex understandings.

Advanced movement themes are selected from Themes IX to XVI for learners who have acquired the concepts of Themes I through VIII. As greater effort toward systematic progression is made by an ever-increasing corps of experienced teachers, the day will come when entry into advanced themes is made by fourth grade.

Games, contests, and sports

Instructional courses
1 Games
2 Contests
3 Sportslike activities
4 Individual and dual sports
5 Team sports

Explanation. Games are activities with a wide range of complexity and great variation in the number of required skills, just like established sports. Even within a single school, the mode of play, rules, number of participants, and the length of the activity may vary considerably. Uniformity, therefore, is not a requirement, although a particular mode of play may be strongly entrenched in some places. For example, kickball is played "to the mound" rather than the ball being thrown to the bases; or Hill Dill is played until everyone is eliminated except the last person, who becomes "it" for the next game.

Contests include relays; tug-of-war and other combatives; and activities that attempt to determine who can do the most, such as shoot the greatest number of baskets using a softball or put the greatest numbers of darts into the bull's-eye.

Sportslike activities are modifications of established sports or new activities that have the characteristics of sports, that is, definite rules, objectives, and mode of play. Floor hockey is an example. Rules may be selected from those provided by the manufacturer of the product being used; from outside sources, such as books; or may be teacher- or learner-designed, with the purpose being to establish rules that all will follow, at least for one season.

Individual and dual sports are the familiar activities of tennis, paddle ball, golf, wrestling, and archery. Team sports are soccer, touch football, basketball, volleyball, and softball or baseball. Track and field, although it uses an aggregate of points from various events to determine a team winner, is an individual sport. Competitive gymnastics is an individual sport, also; however, it is usually not included in the elementary school program, although its elements may be taught in the gymnastics program area.

Gymnastics

Instructional courses

1 Modern educational gymnastics
2 Modern rhythmic gymnastics
3 Exhibition gymnastics
4 Olympic (artistic) gymnastics

Explanation. Modern educational gymnastics is a direct outgrowth of the process of elaborating or enriching basic movement concepts by changing the environment to one that includes apparatus. The purpose of modern educational gymnastics is different from that of basic movement education, although both utilize themes and the same floor and apparatus environment. Modern educational gymnastics aims at developing a general competence in body management, adaptability to different environmental circumstances, and competency in safety controls. In modern rhythmic gymnastics, the student aims at combining flexible, strong use of the body with manipulation of an object, such as a wand, ribbon, ball, or hoop. Music is used to blend the areas of manipulation, dance, and gymnastics into a single expression of control and design.

Exhibition gymnastics is performed for an audience. It includes stunts, pyramids, and routines, either by individuals or by gymnasts working in pairs, threes, or small groups. Formation marching, rhythmic gymnastic routines, or artistic (Olympic) gymnastic routines may be included. The Olympic or artistic, gymnastics program, as some prefer to call it, is oriented toward the development of skills and exercises (routines) that are characteristic of women's or men's gymnastics. United States Gymnastics Federation age-group gymnastics, Junior Olympic gymnastics, or the Y program, all of which relate in some way and aim toward competitive goals, may be utilized as the framework for participation, even though no competition in the school setting is included. Because of the great specificity of skill required for this program, it is doubtful that boys and girls should be required to engage in efforts to achieve its objectives, except for certain fundamentals. It would be like requiring everyone to engage in baseball or tackle football. Olympic gymnastics will remain the province of the few who are gifted enough physically and dedicated enough to work the long hours it takes to achieve mastery of even the fundamental skills of the various events. After-school clubs are a better utilization of time than the physical education period.

Dance

Instructional courses

1 Modern educational dance
2 Folk dance
3 Square dance
4 Creative dance
5 Round dance
6 Contemporary dance

Explanation. Modern educational dance is an outgrowth of the basic movement enrichment of floor work combined with sound or rhythm in which the objective is the expression of feelings, moods, and ideas through individual, partner, small-group, and large-group movement design. The same themes used in basic movement education may be used, but the environment remains the floor, with occasional uses of sound. Skilled teachers will conduct modern educational dance side by side with basic movement education, with the only difference being that when the lesson focus is on basic movement it extends to apparatus and/or manipulative experiences that use the same theme or subthemes. When the focus is dance, the teacher is apt to be more conscious of expression and focus than when basic movement education is stressed. Awareness is the emphasis of one, and dance is the objective of the other. Anyone who has not worked with both types of lessons may find it hard to believe that what looks so much alike can be quite different, both to the instructor and to the learner.

Folk dance for young children often includes the play-party games, the dances that were accompanied by song in the early history of some parts of this country to avoid the designation "dance," which was a forbidden activity. Simple or elementary folk dance involves many of the favorite Scandinavian dances and some from other parts of Europe. The rhythms and phrases are easy to follow. Israeli dances, African dances, English country dances, and Slavic or Russian dances are intermediate to advanced and must be carefully chosen.

American square dance, with either singing or patter calls, ranges from the simple New England visiting couple dances to the complex western style dances with almost everyone active all of the time. Beginning or elementary square dance usually gets no more complicated than a grand right and left.

Creative dance differs from modern educational dance in that it consists of such activities as mime, interpretation, and other fun-type dance activities. All kinds of props may be used to stimulate ideas.

Round dance refers to structured couple dances. Walking steps, two-

Division of the program

Fig. 11.1 The yearly physical education plan

Instructional level: _____

Basic movement track			**Developmental movement track**	
Time	Description	Code	Description	Code
September				
October				
November				
December				
January				
February				
March				
April				
May				
June				

steps, schottisch, polka, and waltz steps are combined in a variety of patterns. Simple round dances (for example, The Salty Dog Rag, Boston Two-Step, and Laces and Graces) are still complex enough to warrant thoughtful consideration before including them in the dance program below grade six.

Contemporary dance is the dance of the day and the recent past. Certain dances, such as the Twist, have retained their popularity. Children enjoy doing them, along with such favorites as the Bunny Hop and Charleston.

■ The yearly program plan is a proposed sequence of instructional units in either basic movement or developmental movement or both for each instructional level. It is an outline of what the physical education program is all about, insofar as major themes and activities are concerned. Little detail is supplied in this one-page overview of each instructional level's program. This is left for the unit descriptions to follow. A program plan for physical education would look like this in a table of contents.

Yearly program plans

Yearly Program Plan for Grade 1 (or 1 and 2 or *x*)
    Major themes of study in basic movement education
    Major activity emphasis in developmental movement education

Basic Movement Education Units
    Theme I: Body Awareness
    Theme II: Awareness of Weight and Time
    Theme III: Space Awareness
    Selected Additional Themes

Developmental Movement Education Units
    The Games Program
    The Gymnastics Program
    The Dance Program

Figure 11.1 illustrates a format for the yearly plan. The time periods may be omitted by program planners who fear that the imposition of structure upon the teacher will stifle development of the most creative or progressive sequence for the individual school situation. Space is left for abbreviated descriptions of themes or activities for the two learning tracks. Where reference codes are used for storage and retrieval of information relevant to curriculum, space beside each description facilitates the use of a code, such as the one described in table 11.1. Each unit of instruction will tie its content to specific courses of instruction in each program area.

The addition of aquatics and outdoor education to the list of developmental movement education program areas is made to answer any question concerning their inclusion in the physical education program. Subordinate activities for games, gymnastics, and dance programs will be described in the following chapters, along with their places in the yearly program for each instructional level. Suggested themes for the basic movement track for each instructional level are listed in the following section of this chapter.

Division of the program

Table 11.1

Course of instruction	Theme/Activity Focus	Unit
Basic movement	16 major themes	Themes
Code no. 1	Code no. 01-16	Code no. 100-999
Games, contests, sports	5 or more activities	Subordinate activities
Code no. 2	Code no. 01-?	Code no. 100-999
Gymnastics	4 or more activities	Subordinate activities
Code no. 3	Code no. 01-?	Code no. 100-999
Dance	6 or more activities	Subordinate activities
Code no. 4	Code no. 01-?	Code no. 100-999
Aquatics		
Code no. 5		
Outdoor education		
Code no. 6		

Example: Code no. 101110 stands for Basic Movement, Theme I; Body Awareness (01); Actions Using the Whole Body (110).

Preschool swimming

Use of flotation devices

■ Progression in basic movement education is dependent on many factors, not the least of which is the skill of the teacher. There are also such variables as the abilities of the learner, the amount of time, the facility, and the equipment. Support by the classroom teacher makes a difference, also. We feel that the suggestions by Preston-Dunlop have merit.[1] Our own experience parallels the progression shown in figure 11.2.

Following this guide, it is possible to schedule unit level themes for each level of instruction. The instructor's task is to select appropriate lesson themes to support the unit themes in a manner similar to the examples given in the previous three chapters.

1 Valerie Preston [-Dunlop], *A Handbook for Modern Educational Dance* (London: MacDonald & Evans, 1963), p. 156.

Fig. 11.2

Grade					Themes							
K	I	II	(III)									
1	I	II	III									
2	I	II	III	(IV)	V							
3		II	III	IV	V	VI						
4			III	IV	V	VI	VII					
5				IV	V	VI	VII	VIII				
6					V	VI	VII	VIII	IX			
7									IX	X	XI	
8									IX	X	XI	XII	XIII

Grade	Theme course of instruction	Unit themes	
K	I: Body Awareness	1.1	Actions Using the Whole Body
		1.2	Action and Stillness
	II: Weight and Time	1.1	Contrasting Firm and Fine Touch Qualities
		2.1	Contrasting Sudden and Sustained Movements
	III: Awareness of Space	1.11	Finding Big Spaces to Travel Through
		2.1	Levels of Space
		3.1	Personal and General Space Contrasted
1	I: Body Awareness	1.11	Opening and Closing
		1.12	Twisting and Turning
		1.13	Rising and Falling
		1.14	Locomotion and Traveling
		1.2	Action and Stillness
		1.3	Sequences of Whole Body Actions and Stillness
		2.0	Symmetric and Asymmetric Use of the Body
	II: Weight and Time	1.11	Stressing the Participation of the Whole Body
		1.12	Stressing the Participation of Isolated Parts
		2.11	Stressing the Participation of the Whole Body (Time)
		2.12	Stressing the Participation of Isolated Parts

Grade	Theme course of instruction	Unit themes	
		2.2	Stressing the Dramatic Qualities of Time
		3.1	Exploring the Combinations of Weight and Time
	III: Awareness of Space	1.1	Using All the Available Space
		1.12	Contrasting Big Spaces with Small Spaces
		2.1	Levels of Space
		2.2	The Directions of Movement
		2.31	Stressing Changes in Level While Using Whole Body or Body Part Actions
		2.32	Stressing Changes in Direction While Using Whole Body or Body Part Actions
		3.11	The Size of the Kinesphere Changes with the Base of Support
		3.12	The Limits of the Kinesphere in All Directions
		4.2	The Elementary Shapes of Large and Small
		5.1	Space Words
2	I: Body Awareness	1.3	Sequences of Whole Body Actions and Stillness
		2.2	Symmetry and Asymmetry in Locomotion and Stillness
		3.0	Emphasis on Areas of the Body
		4.0	Leading the Movement with Specific Body Parts
		5.1	Transferring the Weight of the Body in Different Ways
		5.2	Balance and Unbalance
		5.3	Creating Sequences of Balance and Transfer
		6.1	Awareness of Contact and Noncontact
		6.2	Creating Sequences of Contact and Noncontact
	II: Weight and Time	3.2	Sequencing Phrases of Different Weight-Time Qualities
		5.11	Placing Strong or Light Accents in Different Parts of a Movement Phrase
	III: Awareness of Space	1.2	Movement Relative to Space
		2.4	Combining Weight-Time Qualities with Spatial Areas
		3.2	The Zones of Body Parts
		4.1	Focus on the Near and Far Aspects of Movement
		5.2	Sequencing Space Words
	IV: Flow of the Weight of the Body in Space and Time	1.1	Contrasting Successive and Simultaneous Flow
		2.1	Contrasting Free and Bound Flow
	V: Adaptation to a Partner	1.1	Being Together
		1.11	Going Together
		1.12	Sharing
		1.13	Taking Turns
		1.2	Copying
		3.0	Moving Together
3	II: Weight and Time	3.2	Sequencing Phrases of Different Weight-Time Qualities
		5.11	Placing Strong or Light Accents in Different Parts of a Movement Phrase
	III: Awareness of Space	5.21	Maintaining a Spatial Relationship While Changing Level or Direction
		5.22	Maintaining the Action or Effort While Changing Spatial Relationship
		6.1	Simultaneous Awareness of Personal and General Space

Grade	Theme course of instruction	Unit themes
		6.2 Spatial Orientation in General and Personal Space
		6.31 Growing and Shrinking in Different Relationships
		6.32 Direction, Level, and Relationship Variables
	IV: Flow of the Weight of the Body in Space and Time	1.0 Successive and Simultaneous Body Flow
		2.0 Free and Bound Flow Qualities
		3.0 Flexible and Direct Space Qualities
	V: Adaptation to a Partner	3.1 Meeting and Parting
		3.2 Meeting Different Partners
		4.1 Trios or Threes Relationships
	VI: Instrumental Use of the Body	1.1 Instrumental Use of the Hands
		1.2 Instrumental Use of the Feet
		1.3 Coordinating the Feet and Hands with Large Actions of the Body
		1.4 The Instrumental Use of Other Body Parts
		1.5 Gathering and Scattering Actions
		2.0 The Five Body Actions and Stillness
4	III: Awareness of Space	6.4 Linking the Aspects of Space with Body Awareness and Awareness of Weight and Time
	IV: Flow of the Weight of the Body in Space and Time	4.0 Flow-Space Qualities
		5.0 Flow-Time Qualities
		6.0 Flow-Weight Qualities
		7.0 Weight-Space Qualities
		8.0 Space-Time Qualities
	V: Adaptation to a Partner	4.12 Splitting or Passing Between or Around
		4.14 Two and One
		4.2 Quartets or Fours Relationships
	VI: Instrumental Use of the Body	2.4 Jumping
		2.5 Turning
		2.61 Stillness and Balance
		2.62 Holding Difficult Balances
		3.0 Combining the Five Body Activities
		4.0 Sequence of Activities
	VII: Awareness of Basic Effort Actions	1.0 Eight Basic Effort Actions
5	IV: Flow of the Weight of the Body in Space and Time	9.1 Phrasing with Clarity of Quality
		9.11 Emphasizing Preparations and Endings to Main Actions
		9.12 Connecting Short Phrases
		9.2 Integrating Previous Work with the Concept of Phrase
	V: Adaptation to a Partner	4.21 Two and Two
		4.22 Three and One
		4.31 Formational Changes in Fives
		4.32 Groups and Subgroups
	VI: Instrumental Use of the Body	4.1 Action Motifs in Increasingly Complex Situations
	VII: Awareness of Basic Effort Actions	1.3 The Four Strong Efforts and Their Contrasting Efforts
		1.4 The Four Sudden Efforts and Their Contrasting Efforts
	VIII: Occupational Rhythms	1.0 Miming Working Actions
		2.0 Working in Pairs or Groups

Grade	Theme course of instruction		Unit themes	
6	V:	Adaptation to a Partner	4.1	Trios or Threes Relationships
			4.2	Quartets or Fours Relationships
			4.3	Quintets or Fives Relationships
	VI:	Instrumental Use of the Body	4.1	Action Motifs in Increasingly Complex Situations
			4.2	Adding Actions
	VII:	Awareness of Basic Effort Actions	2.0	Properties of Basic Effort Actions
	VIII:	Occupational Rhythms	3.0	The Rhythm of Action
	IX:	Awareness of Shape in Movement	1.0	Basic Space Patterns
			2.0	Body Shape and the Size of Movement

Commentary and conclusion

■ Not everyone will agree with the selection of themes, even if there is no admonition to follow a specific sequence. Some may feel that there are too many themes; others, too few. There will be a temptation to select theme ideas from upper-level theme courses, which is perfectly all right as long as the children have had adequate preparation. There is no rush. Each conceptual brick must be laid on or linked with those that are already there. Gaps in knowledge or awareness must be quickly ascertained and evaluated to determine as quickly as possible whether the gaps must be filled immediately or can be left until later. Themes are selected according to the needs of children, not of the curriculum. That means making adjustments annually to bring the curriculum in line with the learners' needs and interests.

Teachers of kindergarten may wish to leapfrog over Theme IV to Theme V to emphasize aspects of the themes on sharing and taking turns. Introductions like this to upper-level themes are in order if the children are ready, a determination the instructor must make. Theme IX also contains elements that may be used at the primary level. Any material may be adapted to the needs of younger children when the instructor understands the subject matter and is able to structure it in an appropriate manner.

Chapters XII, XIII, and XIV, on the program areas of the developmental track, contain material familiar to most readers. We hope that by this time the importance of the basic movement track has been made clear. Discerning students may have already discovered that the sequence of themes presented may be used, with the addition of the appropriate emphasis, by the modern educational dance program and the modern educational gymnastics program of the developmental movement education track. The matter will be discussed in the relevant chapters.

Practice in writing objectives for the themes selected for each instructional level will make the content of this chapter more meaningful. If the opportunity presents itself, practice teaching to secure selected instructional objectives relevant to the program objectives of a theme should be employed. This activity will clarify the role of the basic movement track while giving valuable experience in wedding theory to practice.

1 Select a unit theme for any grade level.

2 Write appropriate program objectives.

3 Write a modification or adaptation of the unit level theme, or select a subtheme for a basic movement lesson.

4 Write appropriate instructional objectives for the floor module and for the three major media or environmental circumstances—apparatus, sound or rhythm, and manipulative objects.

5 If possible, teach a class at least one episode of the lesson, i.e., the floor module plus one of the other three environmental modules.

Assignments

1
Research books containing basic movement themes and fit them into the thematic sequence presented in this and the three previous chapters.

2
Find three themes in the sequences given that might be broken down into simpler themes. Offer some ways in which this could be done.

3
Select one grade level or instructional group and prepare a set of lesson themes for a minimum of three unit themes. Include subthemes for the three environmental media in addition to the floor.

4
Select one grade level and write program objectives for each of the unit themes proposed in this chapter.

Readings

Preston [-Dunlop], Valerie. *A Handbook for Modern Educational Dance*. London: MacDonald & Evans, 1963.

Williams, Jesse Feiring. *The Principles of Physical Education*. 5th ed. New York: Saunders, 1949.

The games program

One of the great contributions that
physical education can make, to the
enrichment of personality, to happy and
joyous living in childhood, is
the development of play skills.

Dorothy La Salle
*Guidance of Children Through
Physical Education*, p. 9.

What are games?

■ According to Hunt, "Games are crystallized forms of play patterns . . . ways of behaving in play that tend to conform to patterns that are generally experienced and shared by several individuals."[1] Mauldon and Redfern have a more restrictive definition. They call games "an activity in which a minimum of two people, themselves on the move, engage in a competitive play with a moving object within the framework of certain rules."[2] The following description both combines and clarifies these definitions.

A game is a competitive activity governed by rules, in which two or more people engage for the purpose of determining superiority. The composition of the rules vary from the simple to the complex, from those that permit self-government to those requiring the assistance of officials.

Game skills and strategies vary from simple avoidance behaviors utilizing quick changes of directions to highly skilled manipulative patterns employed in complex or difficult tactical situations. The psychological characteristics of play range from the concentrated determination of the archer to the aggressive contact of football. Social factors, also, enter into the composition of games play because competition requires the participation of at least two competitors and such adjuncts as player role, responsibility, and, in organized groups, position or teamwork requirements.

As mentioned in Chapter XI, games may be structures imposed upon children or self-imposed, learner-designed activities. Many teachers of movement education prefer to challenge children to create their own

1 Sarah Ethridge Hunt, *Games and Sports the World Around*. 3rd ed. (New York: Ronald, 1964), p. 3.
2 E. Mauldon and H. B. Redfern, *Games Teaching* (Old Woking, Surrey, England: Unwin Brothers, 1969), p. vi.

The successful game
takes cooperation

Learner-designed
activities

games out of the concepts, materials, participants, and space available.
The educative role of games would seem to be most clearly served by
skillfully planning tasks aimed at culminating in development of the creative process and all subprocesses required to develop one's own games.

While this may be so, more conventional teachers will argue for the place of organized play that leads to the development of sports skills and game forms that closely approximate the adult forms of activities.

Whether or not adult games have a place in the elementary school curriculum will not be argued here. The attitude, however, is that there is merit in teacher-designed games, as long as teachers remain flexible and use their powers of observation to modify activities. Better yet, if teachers follow up their observations and practice of listening to children with offers to assist children in modifying games they would like to play but that are not working out in their present form, the teachers will be helping children to apply thinking behaviors to the games programs as they did to the basic movement program. Doing what the coach says may fulfill some requirement that the coach perceives as important. It does not, however, lead to the growth of independent, responsible behavior on the part of participants. This does not say that teachers should give no directions or structure no games or gamelike activities at all. But the command style of teaching should be recognized as one that leaves few decisions to the learner.

Another, and perhaps a more satisfactory, definition of games may be derived from an examination of man's desire for play, as defined by Johan Huizinga.

> . . . a free activity standing quite consciously outside "ordinary" life as being "not serious," but at the same time absorbing the player intensely and utterly. It is an activity connected with no material interest, and no profit can be gained by it. It proceeds within its own proper boundaries of time and space according to fixed rules and in an orderly manner.[3]

The expansion of this concept of play by Roger Caillois identifies games as a form of competitive play activity, some of which evolve into the sports of adolescence and adulthood. Caillois's description of *agon* defines the characteristics of the games program.

> *Agon:* It is therefore always a question of a rivalry which hinges on a single quality (speed, endurance, strength, memory, skill, ingenuity, etc.) exercised within defined limits and without assistance, in such a way that the winner appears to be better than the loser in a certain category of exploits.[4]

Caillois perceives play as ranging along a continuum from the spontaneous, improvised, unsophisticated forms characteristic of young children (*paidia*) to the highly restricted, sophisticated, complexly governed sports of the varsity or professional level of the adult world (*ludus*). As Siedentop views Caillois's typology of play, "*ludus* contributes increasing meaning to play,"[5] which implies the necessity for skills instruction to increase competency as one progresses in the games program.

3 Johan Huizinga, *Homo Ludens: A Study of the Play Element in Culture* (New York: Roy, 1950), p. 13.
4 Roger Caillois, *Man, Play, and Games* (New York: Free Press, 1961), p. 1.
5 Daryl Seidentop, *Physical Education, Introductory Analysis* (Dubuque, Iowa: Wm. C. Brown, 1970), p. 189.

The games program

Practicing correct
techniques

Practicing fundamentals

Figure 12.1 depicts sport at the peak of the games program. It is shown as an outgrowth of basic movement lessons whose culminating activities are learner-improvised games. This phase of the games program, while serving the learner as a means for applying newly acquired concepts to competitive activity, may be considered to be the *paidia,* the unsophisticated end of the continuum that leads eventually to *ludus* within the Caillois category of play, *agon.*

Evolution of the *paidia* in basic movement

Basic movement education, as we have said before, is movement that is an end in itself, an exploration of possibility with no immediate concern for application. It operates in the same way as basic research in any scien-

Fig. 12.1 Progression through basic movement program to **paidia,** through developmental program to **ludus**

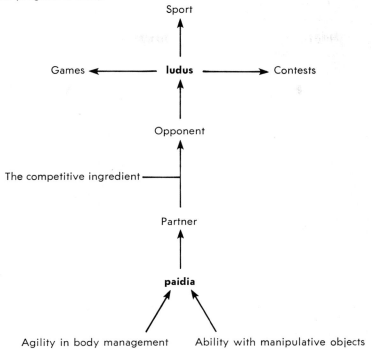

Sport

Games ◄——————— **ludus** ————————► Contests

Opponent

The competitive ingredient ———————

Partner

paidia

Agility in body management   Ability with manipulative objects

tific field. Increasing learner understanding of the vocabulary of movement is its main objective, which it secures through a gradual unfolding of movement experiences. The *what,* the *where,* and the *how* of movement are learned through a thematic spiral progression that results in a readiness to learn. Individual play with movement leads to play with others, with self-testing evolving into games with opponents who have similar interests.

Basic movement lessons that focus on time and direction elements may end with culminating activities in which some children make up a game. In effect, they add the ingredient of competition to their partner relationship, and shift the objective from pure cooperation to competitive play. Some form of tag may result, or one dodging the other and trying to run across a goal line. Given the foundational understandings and the incentive, children will use their imaginations to produce a variety of interesting activities that teachers might never consider. If teachers are not careful, competitively oriented children, even of a very young age, will turn almost any activity into a competition. The option to compete, and to what extent, should be clearly stated so that children may choose not to compete if they feel insecure or handicapped by a physical problem or lack of sufficient skill or understanding. Skilled guidance by teachers is needed to assure a smooth transition from exploration and discovery to competition, even when nothing more than fun is at stake.

The games program

363

Competition—
Keep-Away

Children creating
their own contest

Manipulative lessons in basic movement lend themselves exceptionally well to all kinds of culminating activities, which can be self-testing—activities in which the learner seeks control over an object as he would his body in a gymnastics exercise. Self-testing is an activity that appears to fit Caillois's category of simulative play that he calls *mimicry*.[6] Role playing a sports hero or simply getting lost in make-believe characterizes this category, which is what a youngster might do as he shoots baskets, dives into the water, runs a football around imaginary opponents, or throws "strikes" and "balls" at the target on the wall. Whether self-testing is a fitting exam-

6 Caillois, *Man, Play, and Games*, p. 19.

ple of mimicry or an introductory step to *agon* is of no consequence at the moment. It is important to note, however, that there is a category of activity in physical education that is characterized by a creative spirit.

> *Mimicry:* One is thus confronted with a diverse series of manifestations, the common element of which is that the subject makes believe or makes others believe that he is someone other than himself. He forgets, disguises, or temporarily sheds his personality (sometimes his conventional self) in order to feign another (sometimes his true self).[7]

Huizinga writes of play as being "derived from the two basic aspects under which we meet it: as a contest *for* something or a representation *of* something."[8] A self-testing activity that is designed spontaneously by the child may fit either of these aspects. This might well be the case as the teacher observes an entire class participating in a culminating activity limited to or including self-testing. Some children might be on the verge of *agon* or "contesting," while others are clearly in *mimicry* or the representational aspect of the play function. The point is that children, given the right kind of noncoercive atmosphere, can manage to make decisions that best meet their present needs concerning competition.

Evolution of games from basic movement education

Ideally, games teaching should be an outgrowth of well-conceived and directed basic movement education lessons that have provided the learner with essential body management and manipulative controls needed for the transition from cooperative play to competitive play. (Note: it goes without saying that one must have cooperation to have competition.) The element of competition changes the relationship of the players to one another. This change can result in confusion for certain young or inexperienced players who cannot understand or cope with aggressiveness in attitude or in play on the part of opponents who want to win. Some children find it difficult, if not impossible at the moment, to change their inclination to be passive "nice children who never fight" to aggressive behaviors that seek every possible advantage to win.

Teachers must be alert to the presence of children for whom the shift from cooperative to competitive play may present problems. A sensible solution is to allow children the option of continuing with self-testing or cooperative play if they do not care to compete. Individual counseling may be needed to ascertain the reasons for the dislike of competition with follow-up plans to gradually involve the child competitively.

We believe that games should be outgrowths of a varied program of movement skills instruction for very young children and for inexperienced older children. Gamelike activity should be selected by teachers or children as the culmination of skill learning lessons. This will assure development first of all of a foundation of movement skills. General enough in nature to serve the specific needs of currently relevant games, such a

7 Ibid., p. 19.
8 Huizinga, *Homo Ludens,* p. 13.

Outgrowths of a varied
program of
movement skills

foundation will prevent fragmented or splinter skill learning, which occurs when games are selected first and their limited skills practiced to the exclusion of other, more widely needed skills.

Contests and games

■ The thread connecting the basic movement program with the games program may be the contest called "simple comparisons of ability along special lines" by Mason and Mitchell.[9] Whereas a culminating activity that asks children to test themselves may result in seeing how many times they can jump over a line in ten seconds or how long they can balance a stick on the end of a finger, a contest requires an opponent.

> The object in the various systems of tests is to present standards whereby one may determine his ability, and then attempt to improve his ability and *defeat his own previous record*. In contests he attempts to defeat opponents.[10]

Contests differ from games in three significant ways.

1 In a contest there is no interference with the contestant on the part of his opponents, whereas in a game there is constant and deliberate interference with his plans and plays.

9 Bernard S. Mason and Elmer D. Mitchell, *Active Games and Contests* (New York: A. S. Barnes, 1935), p. 3.
10 Ibid.

Contests

2 Strategy and deception have no place in a contest, while games are full of unexpected situations, strategy, and deception—it is part of a game to outwit one's opponents and confuse them as to what one intends to do.
3 A contest presents few if any situations where the player must exercise choice as to his moves, whereas games are filled with opportunities and emergencies calling for choice.[11]

The culminating activity of a basic movement lesson may result in children making comparisons of their jumps for height or distance. Objective measures are easily compared, either in a self-test or in a contest.

Lessons designed to develop skills make use of the same type of objective measure, with one difference. In basic movement lessons, there is no effort made in the planning stage to have children engage in contests. When a lesson initially planned to help children experience the force of their effort turns into self-testing and contesting, the wise teacher recognizes the need and shifts the focus to the attainment of skills that are important at the moment. Following such a lesson, the teacher should plan for an increased number of lessons aimed at skill development. Self-testing, contesting, and competitive games are planned for in advance, although specific details are often left to the children to work out. More on this subject later.

Classifying contests and games

A classification system for games and contests helps program planners to make decisions concerning appropriate content. Mason and Mitchell have developed a functional system for classifying contests and games. Their classification is shown here in an abbreviated form, with but slight

11 Ibid.

alterations. Space does not permit the extensive elaboration and descriptions of games and contests that this subject deserves. The reader will have to hunt for a copy of this remarkable and useful book to pursue the matter further.

Whereas Mason and Mitchell offer a chapter of variations and descriptions, the categories in the following list are represented by a few of many possible examples. Readers should be able to differentiate other activities and add them to any appropriate category.

Contests

As suggested in chapter 11, a code system for storing and retrieving instructional units permits computerization of physical education program content. The program areas of games, contests, and sports is code numbered (3), the unit area (01) (for contests between individuals), and the subordinate activity in a series of three numbers.

Group I *Between individuals*	*Examples*	*Code ref.* *3-01-000*
Running type	Distance run 40-yd. dash Potato race Sack race	3-01-100
Riding contests	Roller skate races Bicycle obstacle race	3-01-200
Jumping, vaulting, and climbing contests	High jumping Rope jumping Pole vaulting Rope climbing	3-01-300
Throwing and catching	Shot put Beanbag target toss Throw for distance Basketball goal shooting	3-01-400
Striking, batting, and kicking	Soccer kick for distance Fungo hit for accuracy Volleyball serve for accuracy Soccer head butt for distance	3-01-500
Handling mechanical objects	Rope spinning Archery tournament Altitude kite flying	3-01-600
Pushing and pulling, and butting	Tug-of-war Chinning Sit-ups Push-ups	3-01-700

Track meets and sports meets	Track and field meet	3-01-800
	Running events	
	Throwing events	
	Baseball meet	
	Base running	
	Fungo hit for accuracy	
	Home run derby	
	Fielder's throw to home plate	
	Basketball meet	
	Twenty-one	
	Foul shooting	
	Shooting against time	
	Obstacle dribble event	
Contests resembling games	Bowling and variations	3-01-900
		-910
	Skittles	-920
	Hopscotch	-930
	Golf and variations	-940
	Quoits	-950
	Shuffleboard	-960
	Marbles	-970
	Ringer	-971

Group II _Between groups_	_Examples_	_Code ref._ 3-02-000
Mass contests	Tug-of-war	3-02-100
	Touch	
	Centipede race	
	Keep-it-up	
Individual competion with points scored for team	Attention	3-02-200
	Team catch the cane	
	Basketball toss-up	
	Arch goal ball	

Group III _Relays_	_Category_	_Examples_	_Code ref._ 3-03-000
File	Locomotion	Running	3-03-100*
	Passing object	Overhead relay	
	Striking	Goat butting relay	
	Throwing	Corner spry	

* The code number for a file relay using the skill of running should properly be numbered 3-03-101 while the number for file, using locomotion, a more general term, would be 3-03-100. Skipping, hopping, and other locomotor activities should have different numbers, according to their rank on a list of locomotor actions; i.e., 3-03-102 (skipping), 3-03-103 (hopping); and so on.

The games program

Shuttle	Locomotion	Running	3-03-200
	Passing object	Ball hand-off	
	Striking	Hockey dribble	
	Throwing	Chest passing	
Circle	Locomotion	Circle and touch off	3-03-300
	Passing object	Hand-off beanbag	
	Striking	Soccer dribble	
	Throwing	Bounce pass	
Pursuit	Locomotion	Running	3-03-400

Group IV *Goal, tag, and combat games*	*Examples*	*Code ref.* 3-04-000
Goal games*	Run for your supper Beater goes round Forest lookout Squirrels and trees	3-04-100
Tag games, simple	Simple tag Seat tag Cat and rat Fox and geese Cross tag Three deep	3-04-200
Tag games, all players equally liable to be tagged but with an exempt place or position	Old mother witch Duck on a rock Spud	3-04-300
Tag games, dramatic features, and simple cooperation	Run, rabbit, run Midnight Sheep, sheep come home New Orleans Dodgeball Crows and cranes	3-04-400
Tag games, team loyalty	Steal the bacon Prisoner's base Three-team dodgeball	3-04-500
Combative games	Wrestling Jousting (tilting) Pillow fighting	3-04-600

* "Competition centers around getting possession of, or reaching a goal or base." (Mason and Mitchell, *Active Games and Contests*, p. 217.)

Cockfight
Hand wrestle
Leg wrestle
Hat boxing
Balloon busting
King of the mountain

The classification of games involving manipulative skill is taken from Mauldon and Redfern.[12] There are only three categories of games and three types of skills involved, which helps to simplify the progressions.

Category 1			Code ref.
Net		Badminton	3-05-100
Games	3-05-000	Volleyball	-200
		Tennis	-300
Category 2			
Batting		Baseball-softball	3-06-100
Games	3-06-000	Kickball	-200
		Cricket	-300
Category 3			
Running		Basketball	3-07-100
Games	3-07-000	Football	-200
Territorial		Soccer	-300
games that		Hockey	-400
require enter-		Lacrosse	-500
ing the		Rugby	-600
other team's			
area			

The types of skills identified by Mauldon and Redfern[13] closely approximate the categories described in chapter IV.

Type 1
Striking and throwing—propulsion
A The fundamental striking patterns are, and lead to:
  Blocking (as in bunting a baseball or intercepting a volleyball spike)
  Punching (as in serving a volleyball or the goalie's defense against a scoring kick in soccer)
  Kicking (as in punting a football, kicking a soccer ball, passing a soccer ball, kicking a field goal)
  Batting (as in hitting a tennis ball, a golf ball, or any specific type of ball with whatever kind of implement the activity requires)
  Butting (as in heading a soccer ball)

12 Mauldon and Redfern, *Games Teaching*, pp. 29, 30.
13 Ibid., pp. 43-67.

B The fundamental throwing patterns are, and lead to:

Pushing (as in the basketball chest pass)

Underhand (as in the softball pitch)

Overhand (as in baseball pitching, javelin throwing, or football passing)

Heaving (as in throwing a life preserver or a discus)

Type 2

Catching and collecting—reception

A Catching skills include those using either hand or both hands with or without a glove in relation to a variety of balls. Catching also includes the reception of the ball in the game of lacrosse.

B Collecting skills include the variety of ways in which the feet and other body parts receive a ball in soccer and the techniques of receiving in games of hockey that employ the same principle of "giving."

Type 3

Carrying and propelling—manipulating on the move

A Carrying includes ways of holding and carrying a football or rugby ball and of cradling the ball in the crosse or on a hockey stick.

B Propelling involves prehensile dexterity (see chapter IV) and includes dribbling with the foot or hand in such games as soccer, basketball, and speed ball. It involves controlling the ball. In some games, such as hockey, an implement is used to propel the ball or puck.

Analysis of skills

■ Whether performed intuitively or scientifically, analysis of skills precedes selection of a particular game. Children as well as teachers modify games so that they will be both challenging and fun. A game for which children lack skills is no fun, and this lack may turn children away from participation. For this reason, different levels of the same game may have to be used as culminating activities to properly test skill levels of all children rather than just the few. The instructor must know the skill requirements of games and make whatever modifications are necessary to assure success.

Analysis of skills involves the application of the following:

1 *The sequence of the action pattern:* The principle to remember is that skills are movement patterns, in which body parts perform specific movements in a specific order and in conjunction with other body parts to fulfill the purpose of the mover.

2 *The shape of the action pattern:* The principle to remember is that actions of the various body parts and the body as a whole move in various directions in space and follow pathways clearly identifiable as belonging to the skill being analyzed.

3 *The effort-rhythm of the action pattern:* The principle to remember is that all movement has rhythm, either free or metric, which can be described apart from the action itself as having a certain tempo with a

strength factor exhibited by force and accents at various points. Skills are precise demonstrations of Laban's Theme IV, paraphrased as the flow of the strength of an action in space and time.

4 *The relationship of the action pattern*: The principle to remember is that the skill is performed in a specific environment that involves persons and/or things, such as targets, boundaries, landing areas, take-off points, or balls, depending on whether or not the skill is manipulative or nonmanipulative. Where is the foot in relation to the crossbar at the moment of take-off? To which side of the body should the ground ball or fly ball come for greatest efficiency of the return throw? Toward which part of the goal is the kick to be directed?

Differentiation of skills

The skill analyzer must be knowledgeable about the "root" pattern or fundamental motor pattern from which the skill to be analyzed is derived. Sometimes more than one fundamental motor pattern is involved because many skills are combinations of fundamental motor patterns. Figure 12.2 will help to clarify the concept of how a fundamental motor skill becomes differentiated as it is adapted to a variety of purposes.

The process of differentiation of any motor skill or pattern involves change in one or more of the aspects of movement.

The relationship of
the action pattern

Fig. 12.2 A simplified progression of differentiation of the fundamental jumping pattern

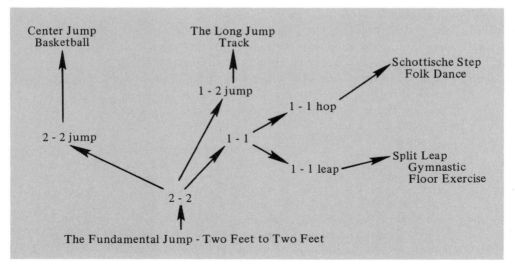

WHAT the body is doing	the ACTION
WHERE the movement is going	the DIRECTION in SPACE
HOW the movement is going	the EFFORT RHYTHM

because of change in the factors of *relationship* directed either by change or greater specificity of purpose on the part of the mover.

The fundamental jumping pattern undergoes many changes even before the child enters school. By the time he has his first formal physical education lesson, he has already learned to push off with two feet either to jump over something, onto something, or just up and down. He can connect a run with a simple long jump, even though he may not always land on his feet. With more opportunity and time to grow stronger, he will acquire a variety of jumping patterns sufficient to permit his participation in a variety of activities. Some of the patterns he develops may not turn out to be very efficient, but unless it is important for him to make specific modifications he will probably just let them alone while he attends to the refinement of skills in some other, more interesting area. However, should he be challenged in some way to modify his jumping patterns to make them more efficient, he will proceed in accordance with what he knows to improve his skills.

Guiding skill differentiation

As the learner shows interest in learning, the teacher guides the process of differentiation in one of two ways: (1) by structuring the environment of things or people so that the learner will be required to make adaptations to the motor pattern or (2) by structuring movement tasks in a manner that evokes change in the aspects of the motor pattern. Learners cannot handle change of several aspects at one time. A change in a single aspect at a time, as illustrated below, will enable learners, when they are ready by virtue of their movement experience, to make step-by-step modifications until either the terminal skill is acquired or the learner's need is directed elsewhere, a signal that he has advanced far enough for now.

Progression in learning to high jump

The situation. The children in this third-grade class have spent many lessons this year and in previous years exploring ways to jump over, on, and off. They demonstrate agility and body control in their jumping behaviors. Now some of them have requested the opportunity to learn how to perform a straddle-roll form of the high jump. The rest of the class is also interested, at least at the moment. All agree to have a lesson on this special way of high jumping that may enable them to go higher than ever before. The field day that is still several weeks away may also have something to do with their interest in improving their high jumping.

The teacher. Recognizing that many of the children are not ready to follow the entire sequence of steps leading from their present knowledge to the specific high-jump style that the class desires to learn, the teacher prepares for this eventual discovery by some children by explaining that any children who wish to stop at some point in the progression are free to do so. They may follow other options.

Organization of the class. Groups of three scattered about with one jump rope for each group. Two students kneel with the jump rope stretched between them at knee level. The third student stands ready for the first task.

The sequence of tasks. Each student takes four turns at each task before replacing one of the rope-holders. If one group finishes a task ahead of others, that group may repeat, with each member taking fewer turns until the others are ready or the teacher signals a halt.

Task No. 1: Find a way to connect a run with a one-footed takeoff into a jump over the rope to a continuation into a run in a figure-eight pattern around the rope-holders (action focus).
Explanation: Start with a task at which everyone will be successful. Third graders not familiar with the figure-eight floor pattern could observe and follow directions or form a circle around one rope-holder and then around the other, the flow connection forming the figure eight.

Task No. 2: Perform the same type of takeoff, but always land on the opposite foot (action focus).
Explanation: A leaping action is the objective, which might also be a scissors jump. It makes no difference at the moment.

Task No. 3: Adjust the figure-eight pattern so that you always approach the jump rope at a forty-five-degree angle (relationship focus).
Explanation: With a single-foot takeoff, this angle of approach will require most if not all students to perform at least one scissors jump,

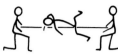

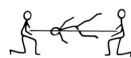

either from the left or from the right, and possibly a very simplified roll if the outside foot is not used for takeoff.

Task No. 4: Approach the rope head-on and experiment with adding a turn in the air before landing (action focus).

Explanation: The change in relationship presents no problem, so it will not be a focus. It will facilitate the execution of a turn either to the left or to the right.

Task No. 5: Decide in which of the two directions you prefer to turn. Then decide from which direction you must approach the rope to make the turn and begin (space focus).

Explanation: The jumpers will discover that it works better to approach the rope from the left if the takeoff foot is the left. The turn also goes to the left.

Task No. 6: Using the basic safety roll, either to the right or to the left, add it to the landing, arrive back on your feet, running to repeat (action focus).

Explanation: This completes the basic elements of the action sequence. Smoothing out the sequence, and perhaps working with the rope at a somewhat higher level, will occupy the remaining time allotted to this portion of the lesson.

Task No. 7: Concentrate on smoothing out the approach to develop a nice rhythm going into the jump that you can remember and either repeat or improve.

Explanation: The most efficient rhythm must be discovered so that children have the opportunity to experience to the best of their ability the joy of accomplishment in motor learning. There's really nothing like it.

Manipulative skill analysis

The analysis of a manipulative skill follows the same pattern as that of a nonmanipulative pattern. More attention to changes in relationship is necessary in these situations because the difficulty in progression can suddenly become too great. Changes must be made gradually, so that learners can make whatever adaptations are necessary to continue their successful ventures into learning skills.

The situation. The sixth-grade girls have taken a sudden interest in learning how to play basketball. Their immediate concern is to learn how to perform the lay-up shot off the dribble in a "fast break." Among their abilities are pushing the ball up for a lay-up shot from a standing position to the right of the hoop.

The sequence of tasks

Task No. 1: Take turns pushing the ball up with your right hand, as you have done before, but make sure that as your right hand pushes, your left foot steps in opposition (action focus).

Explanation: The basic pattern of opposition is fundamental and should be emphasized immediately so that the lower and upper halves of the body will coordinate.

Task No. 2: Accent the push off your left foot and bring your right knee up. Make sure that you continue the same ball-handling action (effort focus with a continuing relationship emphasis).

Explanation: This is the main action of the lay-up shot. Its rhythm must not suffer drastic change because of the addition of the dribble.

Task No. 3: Move away from the basket a distance of four walking steps. Walk into the lay-up shot with three steps, starting with the left foot, L-R-L, and shoot (action focus, but with a change in the relationship to the basket).

Explanation: The angle of approach should be about forty-five degrees. As the three steps are taken, preparations are made to shoot off the accented last step.

Task No. 4: Are you still accenting the push into the lay-up shot? If so, then let's change the rhythm of the first two steps. Instead of walking one, two, and shooting the ball on the third step, let's make one change in that sequence. Change the second step from a walk to a leap. The rhythm now is step, *leap, step* and *shoot* (effort rhythm focus).

Explanation: This is a major change but one that children can usually manage unless they have problems with fundamental locomotor skills like hopping and leaping. It adds an accent to the leap for a total of two accents in the phrase, step, *LEAP*, step, *SHOOT*. This task requires considerable practice and problem solving until smoothness has been well established.

Task No. 5: Now we can introduce the dribble into the sequence we have learned. The trick is not to disturb the rhythm of the action while we change the focus of the relationship to the ball. Take one dribble using your right hand (for a right-handed lay-up shot to the right of the basket) on the first step of the sequence, catch the ball during the leap to your right foot, and immediately follow with a step left and shoot as before.

Explanation: Only the one dribble is used so that proper adjustments can be made. Later, children start from further back and take several dribbles. Speeds will vary but the basic elements of the whole skill are there, ready for further refinement at the discretion of the learner or the instructor.

Many variables constitute a skill. They all fall into one of the categories or aspects of movement mentioned.

> *To teach a new skill, the instructor must start with the simplest form of the motor pattern to reduce the number of variables to which the learner must attend.*

Children must be able to relate successfully to the content of a new skill. Any new skill can be subjected to the following questions to analyze its content.

The games program

1 What is the *root form* of the sequence of actions to which the learner can relate from previous experience?
2 In what ways can the rhythm of the action be simplified without destroying the characteristic effort requirement?
3 What elements of space can be eliminated temporarily without changing the essential shape of the action?
4 Can the variables of environmental relationship be modified so that more attention can be given to the execution of the skill until such time as the pattern has been acquired and can be used at will?

All games
are space games

Space, direction,
awareness

■ A contest brings a change in one major element of relationship. The social factor changes from everyone doing "his own thing" independently of others to rivalry between learners. Suddenly, it is time to see just how good one really is. The winner of a contest is not always the person who was the best in practice or in self-testing. A competitive focus often causes a change in the effort rhythm or in the preciseness of the environmental relationship; for example, loss of timing under pressure or consistently fouling a foot on the takeoff board. Children should be helped to understand that coping with the pressure of competition in a contest can be handled through an attitude that seeks the best accomplishment of which one is capable while acknowledging that the major fun is in participation rather than in winning or losing.

Games analysis is somewhat more complex than contests because of the continuous changes in spatial relationships with other players, with boundaries, and with the ball (if the game requires one, and it will be assumed for purposes of discussion that it does). The same four aspects of movement may be employed both for the analysis of a desired game and for establishing the progression from the simple to the more complex terminal activity.

1 In addition to knowing what actions (skills) the learner must be able to perform, there are certain offensive and defensive maneuvers essential to successful participation. Certain safety skills, such as rolling after taking a fall, may also be required.

2 Spatial awareness is of utmost importance. The player must be able to move within the ever-changing spatial relationships of many games, particularly in running games, where the other team's territory or one's own territory is constantly being invaded. Awareness of direction of movement of others, of the ball, and of one's self is very important. The larger the number of participants, the greater the number of spaces to which one must relate. Pathways through the spaces may also have to be of a certain kind.

3 Control of self and control of the ball within the surrounding space and in relation to boundaries, goals, teammates, and opponents is the essential feature of the good games-player. The faster the play, the greater the difficulty in controlling the ball—or one's self, for that matter. Small spaces in combination with aggressive opponents complicate matters for the less skilled.

4 Relationship variables in games are numerous and often unpredictable. For this reason, games are a great attraction both for players and spectators. Beginners are disadvantaged when they must relate to many players, rules, and physical elements associated with the mature form of the game.

The major variables to reduce for the beginner are those in the aspects of relationship and actions.

The analysis of games

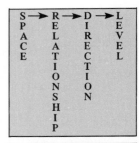

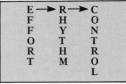

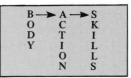

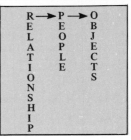

Effort, rhythm,
control

Relationship

Space and relationship constituents of games

In determining the complexity of a game, in analyzing a game, or in simply selecting a game, little thought is often given to the actual difficulties that might be encountered by children deficient in spatial or relationship awareness. Children with visual perception problems have good reason to avoid certain games because they cannot "see." Problems with space and relationship awareness may have as their cause some kind of disability. More often, though, they are the result of inexperience in the right kind of movement learning experience.

For simplicity of analysis, the two aspects of space and relationship are often dealt with at the same time. Therefore, interrelationships are utilized to full advantage in analysis of desirable or required player competencies.

Space, in the context of games, should be considered from three main perspectives: (1) self-space (personal space, already explained); (2) common space (general space, already explained), which may be either the available space for all players or a portion assigned to a group or individual; and (3) position, a specified spot either chosen or given that bears a significant relationship with teammates and opponents. Self-space awareness enables a first baseman to reach out and catch a ball while maintaining contact with the base. The concept can be projected to others, so that a ball is propelled to the appropriate portion of a teammate's self-space. Sudden or impending decrease in self-space is the reason for executing a pass or making some protective movement to avoid loss of the ball. All of this activity goes on while playing one's "position" in relation with others in the assigned area of play (common space).

Relationship variables in games

Spatial relationships in games include three categories of relationship.

Category 1. The player's relationship with others may be cooperative or competitive, depending on whether the others are teammates or opponents. In batting and net games, the offensive player tries to place the ball in a space away from the defending player, while in running games the effort is to run into open spaces. The defensive player in batting and net games tries to play the space in a manner that will put him in an advantageous position to make the play on the ball. Defensive players in running games protect the path to the goal and interfere, in all allowable ways, with the personal space of the offensive player to force release of the ball or a halt in progress, to prevent reception or achieve interception of a passed ball.

  a) *One-on-one* is a competitive relationship between two players. The offensive player continuously attempts to gain spatial advantage to put the ball past or to run past the defensive player, who does his or her best to deny any advantage.

  b) *Two-on-two* offers (1) the opportunity to work cooperatively with a teammate to secure a common goal and (2) a competitive relationship with two other players. For the beginner on offense the difficulty is severe when both defensive players in a running game gang up on him or her. The ability to relate skillfully to a partner has not yet developed sufficiently, perhaps because of a lack of judgments concerning both personal space and the partner's personal space along with the pathway between these spaces. In beginning two-on-two running games defensive players usually have the advantage over offensive players, who must have sufficient skill to force opponents into a one-to-one defensive relationship.

  Batting games with only two members per team allow the defenders to divide the space in the field, cover a base, pitch, or operate in other cooperative ways. Relaying the ball from the outfield is now possible.

Net games, such as volleyball, require cooperation to get the ball across the net and permit sharing defensive responsibilities. Game-like challenges by more skilled players permit introducing setting and spiking, although beginners cannot manage these maneuvers. Tennis doubles require the ability to relate to one's partner without watching that partner because one's concentration must be directed to the opponents' half of the court. Spatial relationships with partners are determined by the tactical situation presented by the offensive players, a condition that changes every time the ball crosses the net, as in other net games. The most vulnerable spaces must receive the greatest attention.

c) *Three-on-three* games offer still greater opportunities for either attacking or defending space. Batting games demand more players as batting skills increase and the mode of play changes from no bases to one base or more. Net games offer more offensive variety with three players than with two and more tactical play on defense, as well. Running games permit faking to one player and passing to another, continuous passing, and using teammates for shields, while leaving the option to pass open. Defensive players have more problems now. The path to the goal is harder to defend against three opponents.

d) Players in larger groups (four-on-four, five-on-five, etc.) often act in two-on-two or three-on-three groups within the larger one. Continuously working with all other teammates but dealing immediately only with one or two is easier on the offensive player than trying to relate to everyone at once. (It must be remembered that the number of players is really doubled by the presence of the defensive team.) A beginner's offensive problem in passing is made easier if he works within a two-on-two or three-on-three setting until such time as he is able to relate to more people simultaneously.

Category 2. Players of games have a number of physical variables within the environment to which they must relate during play. Players must know where they are in relationship to the goal being defended, the goal being attacked, the net, home plate, a certain base, the boundary lines of the field or court. Movements must be in relationship to these variables, as must decisions to change direction or hold a position. Goals are targets, while nets and field or court lines present certain limitations. At any moment during play, decisions to move in certain ways depend upon the situation with reference to positions of the opponents and of the ball.

Physical variables include equipment used in a game. In some cases this includes footwear attire, such as sneakers. However, the equipment usually referred to is that required to play the game—balls, bats, gloves, hockey sticks, rackets or paddles. In beginning baseball-type activities, a batting tee may be used. Regulation balls are usually replaced with such substitutes as the colorful plastic balls found in grocery stores. Junior-sized equipment is easier for children to handle. Because it is both lighter and smaller than regulation equipment, the child finds it easier to position the fingers to achieve the feeling for accurate throwing, passing, and shooting. "Shorty" rackets make learning tennis skills easier for the child under twelve. More accurate timing and ball-on-racket placement is possible. The player gets in front of, moves toward, swings at, gathers in, and performs hundreds of other acts that require manipulation of the space-object-performer variables in relationship to other players and to the playing space and targets. Manipulative and nonmanipulative relationships are interwoven; players manipulate a ball while relating to a base or target, they watch their opponents as well as their teammates, if they are in position to assist.

Category 3. The spatial relationship factor is based upon players knowing where they are and where they are going, so that proper orientation is maintained. Players just beginning to guard or mark opponents in basketball or soccer will often get "lost" when they follow an opponent and leave the path to the goal open. Being aware of how far it is to the sidelines when either running or passing in that direction is important so that play will be contained within bounds and maximum use will be made of available space. When all necessary awarenesses of spatial relationship to people and things are operative, players are in proper position for play and able to function as skilled players. Of course, players must have the requisite skills. However, a participant who cannot relate spatially, no matter how skilled, cannot display those skills in the context of competitive play. The space necessary for a display of skills will be unavailable.

■ The purpose of this and the following two selections on progression is not to provide instructors with a series of ready-made steps to follow in developing a unit of instruction for each grade level in net games. The needs of children vary; therefore, what instructors require is a guide that will enable them to develop their own progressions. That type of guide is what these sections attempt to supply.

Progressions in net games

A Relationship variables
1 Size and weight of the ball, racket, paddle, or other object (*adjust if possible or necessary*)
2 Size of the playing area (*reduce*)
3 Height of the net (*lower*)
4 Number of players (*reduce to three or two*)
5 Intensity of competitive relationship (*play practice games, in which opposition is controlled to improve the caliber of play.*)

B Action variables
1 Skills that are not yet of sufficient quality to stand competition without breaking down (*Eliminate them temporarily; i.e., the spike in volleyball; the power serve in any net game.*)
2 Skills that need to be included for which the opposition does not yet have an adequate defense (*Include them at reduced power.*)

There are several considerations when constructing a sequence of activities to lead to the ability to participate successfully in net games, in ad-

Properly controlled competition can support beginners' efforts.

dition to those that immediately come to mind, such as lack of equipment or court space. It is not too soon to start a progression in the primary grades, if the terminal activity is to be tennis at the junior or senior high school level. The activities do not have to be complicated or need much space.

Suggestions

1 Begin with "keep-it-up" self-testing in which the learner attempts to either keep the ball bouncing on his hand, on the floor, or against the wall. Use balloons, large plastic balls, or tennis balls, and strike with the palm of the hand.
2 Progress from self-testing to contesting to simple learner-designed or teacher-designed games as ball control develops.
3 Progress to defined "courts," where a rope becomes the "net." Ropes secured above learners' heads are for the volleyball progression; ropes lying on the floor or just above the floor are for the tennis progression.
4 Progress in differentiation of skills for volleyball type activities, such as allowing the ball to strike the floor once before returning it.
5 Progress in differentiation of tennis skills by using the back of one hand, adding a paddle or shorty racket, etc.
6 Progress in development of handball from simple tennis beginnings by using available wall space.

Progressions in batting games

■ Batting games provide a rather unique situation, in which a batter competes against the entire opposing team. Each defensive player protects a space against invasion by a batted ball. A ball legally batted into the field of play results in a race between the batter/runner and the fielding team, one running, the other catching and throwing. Victory for batter's team results in a run or a base for safety; victory for the defense results in an out for the batter's team. Because of the quickness with which the fielding team must react to the situation presented by the batter/runner, an adequate level of throwing and catching skill must prevail. The batter, also, must be able to manage the task of handling a bat, if one is used.

A **Relationship variables** *(simplify)*

1 Use of the bat *(eliminate)*
2 Length and weight of the bat *(reduce)*
3 Type of ball, size and weight *(adjust—softer, lighter, or larger)*
4 Size of the area, number of bases, pitching distance *(reduce proportionately)*
5 Number of players per team *(reduce)*
6 Rules of the game *(modify)*

B **Action variables** *(simplify)*

1 Pitching technique *(substitute an appropriate pattern that will not deliver the ball too fast.)*
2 Catching skill *(substitute a rule that permits infielders to throw to the mound instead of to a base.)*
3 Batting skills *(Use a tee to support the ball; increase size of the ball; eliminate the bat and either kick, punch, or throw the ball instead.)*

C Effort-rhythm variables *(simplify)*
1 Lack of pitcher control (*substitute a batting tee or let the pitcher pitch for his own team.*)
2 Control problems that lead to many errors. (*Review the entire purpose of playing the game and consider the possibility of poor progression requiring an easier version of the game or its elimination.*)
D Spatial variables *(clarify)*
1 The pitcher "creeps up" on the batters (*Require the pitcher to pitch from a specific line or "rubber."*)
2 Infielders play the bases instead of the ball, or the other way around (*Alert players to the "rule" that they, the fielders, protect space first and, perceiving no threat, cover the bases* [see the section on spatial progression, p. 380-81].)
3 Players become disoriented and go in the wrong direction (*Insufficient experience with the relationship of players to bases can be corrected only through participation. Reduce the number of players per side and have more teams.*)

Batting games are easily arranged in a progressive sequence. The most important concept to get across to very young children who want to play is that the game is a series of contests between a "runner" and the fielders. Following are a few suggestions for developing a progression in batting games.

Simple progression
1 *Three-player "baseball."* A whiffle-ball game for primary age.
Main objective: For the batter to acquire space-time relationship concepts that enable him to hit the ball away from the fielders; for the fielders, to divide the space so that one covers the smaller infield and the other the larger outfield.
Description: A traffic cone or batting tee is used to support the ball. The batter hits the ball into the field of play and runs to "first base" and back. If the batter returns to the batting position before the infielder has possession of the ball while "on the mound," the batter bats again. If a fly ball is caught or if the ball is "at the mound" before the runner returns "home," the batter is out and rotates to the outfield. The outfielder takes over the infield position and the new batter is the former infielder.
Rationale: The basic concepts of relationship of the players to the playing space and to each other are easily taught through this game. Many opportunities to bat, throw, and field are available.
2 *Even-side progression "baseball."* A whiffle-ball, kickball, or other simplified form of batting game for primary-grade and inexperienced intermediate-grade children.
Main objective: To progressively develop additional space-time concepts; for example:
a) With one or more teammates, it is not necessary to return home from the base or bases before the ball reaches the mound. A teammate can hit the ball and send the runner home from the base.

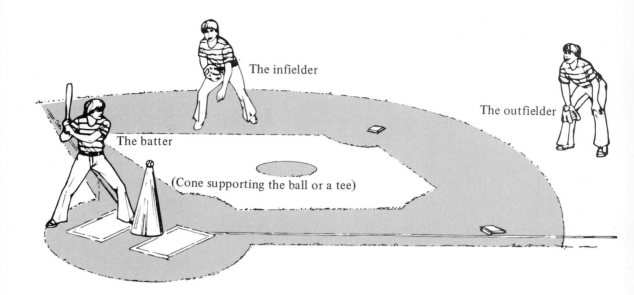

The infielder

The outfielder

The batter

(Cone supporting the ball or a tee)

b) When runners can stop on a base and be safe, it is important to get the ball "to the mound" quickly.

c) As players and bases are added to the game, the new players fill infield positions first because the ball gets to the infield so much faster than it does to the outfield; therefore, that space is attacked first and is the most difficult to defend.

d) Infielders protect spaces when the batter is up and protect bases if the ball is hit to a distant space.

e) Fielders in the "attacked area" play the ball first and then either cover a base or, in the case of a long hit, relay the ball back to the infield.

f) The catcher protects the space in front of and around "home." As soon as the batter becomes a runner, the catcher moves in front of the plate.

Description: After first base is part of the game and the concept is understood, a second base is placed in the vicinity of the normal location of third base. Later, add the last base to give the traditional diamond shape (really a square). In this progression the space-time concepts and skills needed for successful play develop concurrently with the gradual addition of players to each side.

Progression in running games

■ Running games are the most confusing to children, even through the skill requirements are not as high as they are for net games and batting games. These games may frustrate children who lack skill, but at least they know what they are trying to do. This is not the case for running games because the "play space" for each player changes continuously as his relationship to others changes. A partial exception is American football, in which play stops and restarts. This gives the momentarily disoriented player a chance to get straightened out before the next play begins. However, players who lack speed or ball-handling skill will either have to quit or modify the rules with the consent of teammates.

The major problem of change in spatial relationships is best handled by developing a progression along the following lines:

1 The first "game" should be one-on-one in limited space with limited objectives. Example: One-on-one Keep-Away for either soccer or basketball emphasizes ball control. Points are awarded on the basis of time.

2 Two-on-one Keep-Away is a game between an offensive team of two and a single defensive player who attempts to become a member of the offensive partnership by interfering with the play of one member and gaining possession of the ball. Dribbling can be eliminated to focus on the skills of passing the ball.

3 Two-on-two Keep-Away is the first team-versus-team game that can be used as a vehicle for learning rules associated with the long-range terminal objective. Two-on-two Keep-Away can help to develop basic concepts of space relationships to teammates, to opponents, and to the ball. Either a soccer goal of some sort (traffic cones) or a basketball goal (wastebasket if no regulation basket is available) can be used to focus attention on scoring when the offensive team maneuvers close enough to the goal.

4 Three-on-three Keep-Away stresses the development of a number of concepts that, like two-on-two relationships and the primary one-on-one relationship, are carried forward to the final form of the game. Threes (trios) form either lines or triangles. (See Laban's Theme V.) In this relationship of threes alternatives are offered that the partner relationship cannot provide. Players can pass off to one and go between or around. Progressions to secure attainment of new concepts may utilize the following steps, from practice to competition.

   a) Threes practice "giving" and "going," with the "rule" that after passing the ball to either teammate the passer goes to a different space by traveling between the other two.

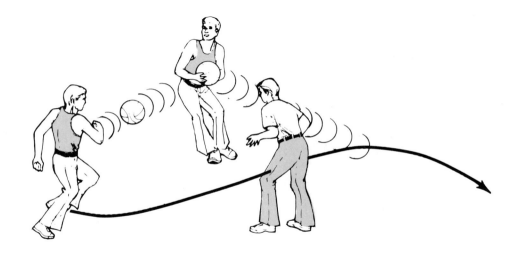

b) Threes practice dribbling the ball between or around teammates before passing ("going" and "giving").

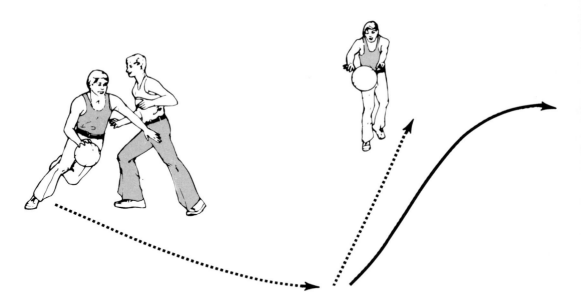

c) Threes compete with threes, emphasizing either or both of the above modes of control in a game of Keep-Away (3-on-3).

d) Threes compete with threes, emphasizing the addition of scoring to the game of Keep-Away (three-on-three basketball or soccer).

5 The addition of more players does not change the focus, which is still a triangular relationship between a ball-handler and two teammates.

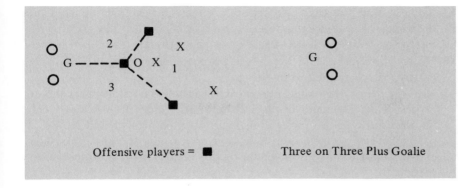

Offensive players = ■   Three on Three Plus Goalie

Note that the player with the ball has three possible triangular relationships, depending on which way he turns.
1 He can relate to both forwards.
2 He can relate to the goalie and left forward.
3 He can relate to the goalie and right forward.
With this many options to learn to exploit, there is no need to hurry children into eleven-on-eleven games.
In three-on-three basketball, as there is no specific player to defend the basketball goal as the goalie does in the game of soccer, little purpose is served by adding a fourth player. However, when the children are ready, usually around fifth grade, the box formation provides important alternatives to an offensive player.

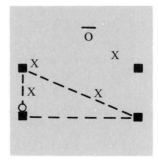

This illustrates four-on-four basketball and shows the three-plus-one concept of offense. Each time the ball changes hands, a different person is "out of the triangle," usually the player furthest from the ball at the moment.

■ Teaching games may utilize procedures that result in the children-designed or instructor-designed games. Before discussing any procedures for teaching games, the fundamental structure of a game should be analyzed. Seven parts are identified on the *activity analysis form*. These seven parts should describe the essential aspects of the game.

Procedures for teaching games to children

1 *Name*: Activities that bear repetition need to be given names. Children may name games that they design, as well as those designed by the instructor. Games selected from books should retain their own names.

2 *Major objectives*: The important purposes of the game should be clearly stated and understood.

3 *Mode of play*: How the game is played to achieve its purposes should be described. The mode of play of traditional games often varies greatly. Modifications are most often made to minimize the difficulties a particular group of children may have in learning the game. As skills and understandings improve, the mode of play can be adjusted accordingly.

4 *Equipment*: Any equipment required should be carefully identified. If a plastic bat is desired, say so. The amount and kind of equipment is important information that serves to limit play in some manner, often by determining the amount of space required and the manipulative skills needed.

5 *Space*: The amount of space required should be described with as much detail as necessary. "A large space" is not as clear as "a 60 × 40 foot area."

6 *Number and organization of players*: The number of players needed and how they are organized in general terms is also important. Are they on teams, on opposite sides of a net, in lines of scrimmage? Are they outdoors or in a gymnasium? Are they in relay formation, scattered about, in a triangular relationship, in two lines of three, or what?

7 *Rules*: The final set of limitations is the formalized rules that amplify the mode of play and include penalties for violations or infractions. Rules written for established games, such as those published by the NCAA or by the authors of game books, should not be repeated. A note to that effect with citation of the resource is sufficient. Another way to simplify descriptions of rules is to refer to the teacher's own file or to the curriculum guide being used. New games require descriptions of essential rules so that the specific restrictions and penalties are spelled out.

How many players should be on a team? A good rule of thumb is to keep the number as small as possible consistent with the purpose of the game. The practice of putting extra players in the outfield or in some other part of the playing area where they will participate only minimally should be discouraged. Only through many opportunities to catch, pass, bat, kick, or whatever will the learner develop and refine the basic game skills needed for successful play.

The following chart will guide teachers in planning play for the various lead-up activities. Small groups are essential to provide opportunity for all children to develop skills. Not included are social games, like Drop-the-Handkerchief or relays, which usually require teams of four, although a few more may be used.

ACTIVITY ANALYSIS FORM

For use in analyzing competitive play forms: i.e., self-tests, contests, games

Name of Activity. _____

Major Objectives. _____

_____

Mode of play. _____

_____

_____

_____

_____

LIMITATIONS

Equipment. _____

_____

Space. _____

_____

Number and organization of players. _____

_____

RULES

Restrictions	Penalties for violation and infraction

Activity	Grade 3:	III	IV	V	VI
Basketball		2	3	3-5	3-5 players*
Touch/Flag Football		2-4	4-6	4-8	4-8 players
Soccer		3-4	3-6	5-8	5-8 players
Volleyball		1-3	1-3	3-6	3-6 players
Softball/Whiffleball/Baseball		3-6	3-6	6-9	6-9 players

* Recommended number of players per team. The lower limits are the most useful for players with limited skill and gamesmanship.

Note: Physical education class time should be devoted to instruction as much as possible. Large games are not particularly good for this purpose. However, children can absorb only a certain amount of instruction at any given time. Just as adults do, children need time to play in a recreational setting. Daily supervised play periods, in addition to regular physical education time, serve to provide both recreational opportunities and a chance to develop further the skills learned in class.

The following pages contain additional information of importance to the skills lesson. Although the format might be applied to any program area wherein specific skills are taught, the application is made to games as the area most likely to be the focus of specific skill learning in the physical education program.

Description of the skills lesson plan

Program area: Identify whether Game, Gymnastics, Dance, or Aquatics Program.

Unit: Identify the specific part of the program to which the lesson belongs.

Lesson focus: Identify the specific skills or activities that will receive attention through specified objectives.

Objectives: Performance objectives to be acquired by the learner are identified in a short form that includes assumption of the following criteria, unless specified otherwise.

1 The skill or activity descriptions noted require the learner to demonstrate the essentials of technique and associated understandings of the mechanics or strategies involved.

2 The competency is demonstrated during the normal events of a physical educational class.

3 The acceptable criterion standard is the minimum level acceptable to the learner and the instructor, rather than a norm. Note: The desired standard of motor behavior is one that permits the learner safe and easy access to the utilization of skill and progression to increasingly more challenging performance levels.

Materials: Equipment needed for the game, scoring sheets, watches, or any other needed items should be identified.

Arrangement of facility: Location of apparatus, boundaries, play stations, and other aspects of the physical environment need description, which may be simplified by inclusion of a supplementary diagram.

SKILLS LESSON PLAN FOR GRADE 6

PROGRAM AREA: Sports   UNIT: Track and Field

LESSON FOCUS: Basic Sprinting, Starts, and Relay Handoff

OBJECTIVES: 1 Arm and leg action with maintenance of forward focus in 50-yd dash
                2 Selection of sprint starting technique out of blocks: **a)** bunch start; **b)** medium start with "set" and "on marks" position
                3 Visual baton pass in exchange zone

MATERIALS NEEDED: 4 sets of starting blocks; 1 baton for every 4 students; 6 jump ropes for temporary zone boundaries

ARRANGEMENT OF FACILITY: As per diagram with lanes and exchange zones marked.

INSTRUCTIONAL SEQUENCE	ORGANIZATION AND PROCEDURE
PREINSTRUCTIONAL ACTIVITY: Agilities warm-up, self-directed, whole body, etc.	O: Freely dispersed or with partners to help
TASKS AND ANTICIPATED DEVELOPMENT	
T^1: Review sprinting with heats of 4 at ¾ speed	O: Group in 4s for later relays. Use as heats; travel 50 yd C: Before repeating, discuss emphasis on opposition and forward focus
T^2: Experiment with and select starting technique D^1: Emphasis on knee lift out of blocks	C: Push off ball of foot; stay erect P: Demo of bunch and medium starts O: Use lanes; rotate turns taking marks, getting set, and starting. Sprint 10 yd
D^1: 25-yd sprints with command start D^2: Increase distance gradually	P: One heat at a time in simulated races. C: Concentration on technique of run and start regardless of competitive focus.
T^3: Group practice visual baton handoff	O: Each team spreads out with 5 yd between each runner P: On "Go," 1st runner carries with left, 2d runner receives with right and immediately changes to left, etc. C: Palm up to receive; place down in hand.
D^1: Each team marks off own zones for 2d, 3d, and 4th runner—practice	P: Give out ropes and have teams spread out farther C: Rule re: passing baton in zones; stress receiving on run late in zone.
CULMINATING ACTIVITY	
Relay races using 200-yd straightaway	O: 4 teams at a time; divide in heats P: Students decide whether boys vs. boys and girls vs. girls or otherwise. C: 1st runner may use blocks for start

Key: T = task sequence and initial task; D = development or additional challenges;
       O = organization, formation, use of space; P = procedure, directions given;
       C = clarification, comments, "hints," points to stress.

SKILLS LESSON PLAN DIAGRAM

PROGRAM AREA: Sports   UNIT: Track and field

LESSON FOCUS: Basic sprinting, starts, and relay handoff

ARRANGEMENT OF FACILITY:

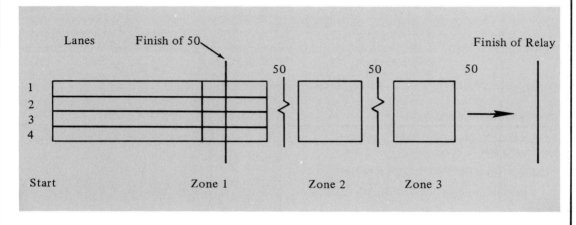

Notes:

Use agricultural lime or limestone to mark lanes. Repeat applications daily for a week.

Mark zone endings with either a traffic cone or a flag to make rule violation easier to observe.

For more permanent marking use kerosene over the lime to kill the grass. Use only where grass is thick and rain washes lime away.

All lines should be straight. Use a mason line and spikes to anchor line to ground while line marker is used.

Use either 30-inch or 36-inch lane width.

Number lanes from left to right.

Arrangement of groups for preliminary instruction in baton passing

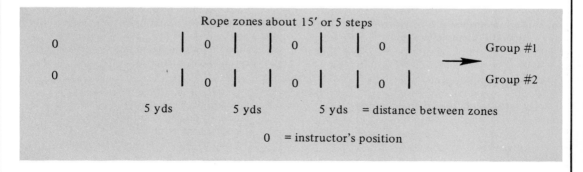

SKILLS LESSON PLAN FOR GRADE _____

PROGRAM AREA: UNIT:

LESSON FOCUS:

OBJECTIVES:

MATERIALS NEEDED:

ARRANGEMENT OF FACILITY:

INSTRUCTIONAL SEQUENCE	ORGANIZATION AND PROCEDURE
PREINSTRUCTIONAL ACTIVITY	
TASKS AND ANTICIPATED DEVELOPMENT	
CULMINATING ACTIVITY	

SKILLS LESSON PLAN DIAGRAM

PROGRAM AREA: UNIT:

LESSON FOCUS:

ARRANGEMENT OF FACILITY:

Organization: A running description of how the class is organized for the beginning activity and all subsequent activities that require changes. Free formation, partners, groups of three, and groups of five are common. Note where the players are to be in relation to activity equipment, boundaries, and other groups; for example, scattered throughout the area, behind the lines, with a ball for every group, and two-on-two.

Procedure: The process used to implement the instructional sequence is identified. This tells what the teacher does, such as demonstrate, explain, tell students to make decisions and what about, direct the progression of events, and officiate. Partners might be directed not to be very aggressive until greater skill is developed.

Clarification: Essential understandings are identified. Certain points may be stressed to assure learner acquisition of certain desired behaviors.

Task: The initial task of a task sequence is clearly stated. The objective of Task Sequence 1 (T^1) is the behavior described by Objective 1. Each task sequence is related to a previously identified objective.

Development: Tasks that follow the initial task of a sequence are called developmental challenges. These tasks further stimulate acquisition of the behaviors identified in the statement of objectives for the lesson.

Culminating activity: The activity used to incorporate the lesson's skills.

■ The approach to games teaching varies with the teacher, the class, the game, and the circumstances under which it is to be played. Some teachers prefer to describe the game first, then teach it in a sequence of steps. Others generalize the activity to get everyone involved in a very simplified form as the first step; if successful, a second step of one or more limitations (i.e., rules) follows. Additional limitations are introduced as rapidly as the necessary adaptations are made.

The role of the teacher

Whichever method of presenting a game is used, it is important to get the activity started as quickly as possible. Long explanations bore children. Get ready to start the game.

1 Have the necessary equipment on hand. (Be sure that balls are inflated properly.)
2 Have the play area's boundaries clearly defined.
3 Have a way of identifying the members of teams playing a running game.

Steps in teaching games (direct method)

Primary age children are grouped in formation before instructions regarding play are given. If the game is to be played in a circle formation, the teacher should first help the children form a circle: "Let's join hands and make a circle." Then the instructions and comments follow to properly orient everyone to the main objective. This is the direct method of teaching a game.

Step 1 Get the children into the proper formation for play.

Step 2 Name the game.

Step 3 Describe the main idea, the major objective, relating it to previous experience (if possible).

Example: One person will be "it" and . . . .
The team with the ball will . . . .

Step 4 Walk through the first description. Simulate the activity.

Step 5 Describe what happens next or what the remaining people do.

Step 6 Walk through the second description. Simulate the activity.

Step 7 Describe the climax, the "punch line," the tag pursuit, the ball hit fair or the kick going into the goal.

Step 8 Walk through the third description. Simulate the activity.

Step 9 Start the game and monitor it until satisfied the children know how to play the game.

Step 10 Divide the class into smaller groups so that more children will get turns.

Note: As a rule, it should take less than three minutes to get the game started. If it takes much longer than that, the game either is too complicated or needs to be presented in a different way. Immediate modification of the rules is called for whenever children have difficulty that cannot be corrected immediately.

The direct method of teaching leaves no room for learner decisions regarding rules, mode of play, and other considerations. A less-direct method is needed if learners are to operate creatively.

Steps in teaching games (indirect method)

When the teacher instructs children to make up a game or contest, they are being asked to make decisions concerning one or more of the five aspects previously discussed. The children may have to make decisions.

A The objective

1 Who can run the fastest?

2 Who is more agile—the quickest?

3 Who is more accurate?

4 Who is the better player?

B The play area

1 How big will it be?

2 Where are the boundaries located?

3 Where are the goals to be placed?

C The rules

1 Who is eligible to play?

2 What must the players do to win?

3 What are the limitations

a) on the start of the activity?

b) on scoring?

c) on the use of the area—unrestricted or restricted movement?

d) on contact with the body or body parts?

e) on the type of personal equipment permitted, such as cleats?

D The game equipment

What kind of bat, ball, glove?

E The players

How many players per side?

The technique for presenting children with options for playing a game, engaging in a contest, or testing themselves is essentially the same for all situations. (The teacher may first wish to give learners the option of using the skills and the equipment, if any, in one of the three forms of competitive activity.)

1 The children decide

on self-testing, a contest, a game; or

between self-testing and a contest with someone; or

between a contest and a game; or

on any game they can devise; or

on any contest they can devise.

Depending on the circumstances, the teacher will offer them one of the options listed.

2 The teacher may decide on the type of competitive activity, and permit the students to make all the other decisions. For example,

a game involving kicking and trapping; or

a contest involving different jumping skills.

The students work out a solution within the limitations given and design the activity, complete with rules and anything else needed.

3 The teacher sets limitations on the type of behavior, perhaps eliminating hazardous play, contact, hitting above the waist, or, because of slippery conditions, running.

The students work out activities within the framework given.

4 The teacher determines the equipment to be used.

The students are free to devise a game using the designated equipment in any legitimate fashion.

5 The teacher determines the number of players per side.

The students devise a competitive activity with the specified limitation on number of players per side.

Of course, teachers may make decisions about any of the components of competitive activity, at the same time making clear to students exactly what their choices are. Students with experience in making decisions will enjoy the opportunity for increased roles in the decision-making process. They will also profit considerably from the experience of creative management of ideas, equipment, time, space, and people. Less-experienced children will want more direction. Children unaccustomed to thinking for themselves will need the most help to get started. However, once they learn the options and have some success they, also, will find creative game development a challenging venture.

The games program

As children progress to sports activities, more highly regulated than games, they will still have decision-making opportunities. While sports are fixed forms, their lead-up activities do not have to obey the same rules, at least not exactly. In a basketball activity, for example, children can be given the option to play their culminating activity, three-on-three basketball, with certain options relevant to rules, such as no dribbling, passing away from the basket after the defensive team rebounds, and lay-up shots only. Naturally, these options would be for highly skilled players, but the less skilled can have similar options.

Summarizing the games program

■ Little has been said in this chapter concerning which games should be played at each grade level. In reality, this cannot or, in our opinion, should not be done. Children's needs vary, but given the opportunity to express themselves in movement and in words, they will quite adequately inform their teachers what they ought to be learning. Taking their cues from the children, teachers structure the culminating activities to lead children into relevant competitive activities. There are only a few options. Children will show by their demonstrated understandings and movement abilities which of these lines of competitive activity they can manage.

Self-testing, contest, or game in		
Running	leads to	chasing and fleeing; racing; running games; relays.
Striking	leads to	batting, punching, and kicking contests; net games; batting games; running games involving kicking.
Throwing and catching	leads to	contests for accuracy or distance; batting games; or running games.

The starting point is determined by the children's understanding of or skill in such prerequisites as techniques, concepts of play, formation, use of space, rules, and game objectives and their predisposition to participation in competitive activities.

Children show what they know by what they do. Teachers find out in a hurry about children simply by observing and analyzing. Through careful observation, teachers can discover the following.

1 How well and varied the movement patterns are executed, regarding control, the use of space, and adaptations to physical and social relationships

2 How easily children accept new challenges that lead them into additional limitations, partner work, and (if ready) small group work.

3 The correct time to introduce the competitive element as the final stage of problem solving in self-testing, contesting with others, or in playing a game

Relay contests

Baton exchange

The games program

401

Although many children enjoy certain activities in standardized forms, being able to create their own games is often the most fun of all. Learning how to make choices and how to live up to rules that one has participated in creating are excellent educational contributions to good citizenship training.

The end of this chapter includes a list of references from which may be drawn a countless variety of games, contests, and ideas for self-testing that may be transformed into either games or contests. You must remember that the games program, like the other programs in physical education, serves both as a way to guide children to become more fully functioning and as an important skill and knowledge area for building competence. For the games program to fulfill this dual purpose, the teacher must know when to "push," when to "guide," and when to let the child alone.

Assignments

■ The following assignments are designed to give experience in relating the games area of instruction to the total program of physical education.

1
Research available physical education books containing descriptions of games and contests for elementary school children. Classify a given number as net, batting, or running games.

2
Select a contest or game from the list of activities compiled in assignment 1 and teach it to two different groups of people, one of which must be elementary school children, to demonstrate your ability to modify appropriate aspects of the activity according to the abilities of the class.

3
Observe a group of children engaged in free or supervised play and list the fundamental manipulative skills observed during a thirty-minute period.

4
Select a fundamental motor pattern (i.e., running, throwing, or jumping) and describe a sequence of changes in the four aspects of movement that show step-by-step progression to a highly differentiated terminal activity skill such as the dance run, pitching a baseball, or the triple jump.

5
Demonstrate ability to teach any of a given group of game skills for net games, batting games, or running games to an intermediate grade level by introducing the skill or skills in the simplest form (the *root skill*) and proceeding from there to present a sequence of limitations relevant to the shape, the effort rhythm, or the relationship of the activity.

6
Prepare a progression of activities in one of the following games that demonstrates changes in the rules of play as the social relationship changes from one-on-one progressively to five-on-five: Football, rugby, soccer.

7
Teach a game to children using the directed teaching method.

8
Teach a lesson that stresses such skills as striking, collecting, kicking, or quick changes of directions. Culminate the lesson by presenting children with options that include the opportunity to self-test, to contest, and to create their own game.

Readings

Caillois, Roger. *Man, Play, and Games*. New York: Free Press, 1961.

Dauer, Victor P., and Pangrazi, Robert P. *Dynamic Physical Education for Elementary School Children*. 5th ed. Minneapolis: Burgess, 1975.

Fabricius, Helen. *Physical Education for the Classroom Teacher*. 2d ed. Dubuque, Iowa: Wm. C. Brown, 1972.

Fait, Hollis F. *Physical Education for the Elementary School Child*. 3d ed. Philadelphia: Saunders, 1976.

Huizinga, Johan. *Homo Ludens: A Study of the Play Element in Culture*. New York: Roy, 1950.

Humphrey, James H. *Child Learning Through Elementary School Physical Education*. 2d ed. Dubuque, Iowa: Wm. C. Brown, 1974.

Hunt, Sarah Ethridge. *Games and Sports the World Around*. 3d ed. New York: Ronald, 1964.

Kirchner, Glenn. *Physical Education for Elementary School Children*. 3d ed. Dubuque, Iowa: Wm. C. Brown, 1974.

La Salle, Dorothy. *Guidance of Children Through Physical Education*. New York: A. S. Barnes, 1946.

Mason, Bernard S., and Mitchell, Elmer D. *Active Games and Contests.* New York: A. S. Barnes, 1935.

Mauldon, E., and Redfern, H. B. *Games Teaching.* London: MacDonald & Evans, 1969.

Miller, Arthur G., Cheffers, John T. F., and Whitcomb, Virginia. *Physical Education, Teaching Human Movement in the Elementary School.* 3d ed. Englewood Cliffs, N. J.: Prentice-Hall, 1974.

Schurr, Evelyn L. *Movement Experiences for Children.* 2d ed. Englewood Cliffs, N.J.: Prentice-Hall, 1975.

Siedentop, Daryl. *Physical Education, Introductory Analysis.* Dubuque, Iowa: Wm. C. Brown, 1970.

Spath, Martha. *Elementary School Physical Education.* Rev. ed. Kirksville, Mo.: Simpson Publishing Company, 1975.

Chapter XIII

Gymnastics

In gymnastics movement is considered
in relation to such matters as the mobility
of joints, and the tone of muscles;
it is concerned with the full physiological
functioning of the body, and is based on
the study of anatomy and physiology.
The underlying purpose is that
of all-round harmonious development.

Moving and Growing, p. 109

■ There is a variety of programs labeled gymnastics, which they most
certainly are, even though they pursue different objectives. The selection
of any one of these subprograms or gymnastics areas depends on the purpose it is intended to serve.

■ The most recent development in gymnastics programs has been the
emergence of educational gymnastics as an alternative to the conventional
forms of gymnastics. Educational gymnastics is most important for children through the primary grades. Stressing problem solving, inventiveness,
and exploration, it is a creative way of teaching gymnastics. Properly
taught, it is an extension of the basic movement program, the purpose of
which is wholly the acquisition of awareness and enrichment of one's
movement vocabulary for the purpose of acquiring skill in the management
of one's body. The basic movement program should operate concurrently
so that its lessons introducing new concepts and awarenesses are immediately linked to gymnastics themes and lessons to which they can apply.

Educational gymnastics

Gymnastics focuses attention on what the body does as its center of
gravity is manipulated and placed in a variety of relationships to its physical environment. Gymnastics does not have to be competitive, although
one could call it a self-testing form of movement in the sense that fundamental game skills are. Educational gymnastics has two aims, according to
Mauldon and Layson:

1 To develop efficiency and a skilled use of the body in practical situations
  when working alone and with others, on the floor and on apparatus

2 To stimulate an understanding and appreciation of objective movement coupled with an ability to invent and select appropriate actions.[1]

"Above all else," states Buckland, "Educational Gymnastics is concerned with assisting the child's natural process of growth, giving him opportunities to exercise and develop his social, creative and physical skills."[2] Bilbrough and Jones list eight aims of the physical education teacher:

1 To contribute to the physical development of each child
2 To increase the physical skill of each child, developing versatility, adaptability and the ability to cope with various tasks and situations
3 To enable each child, through physical activity, to experience a sense of achievement as frequently as possible
4 To help children to experience the enjoyment associated with well-planned, stimulating and purposeful lessons
5 To help children to learn how to co-operate with each other and to work successfully as members of a group
6 To exercise the natural learning processes of enquiry and discovery through creative and imaginative physical activity
7 To develop physical and mental co-ordination, self-control and confidence
8 To provide opportunities for a wide experience in all types of movements and activities, both with and without apparatus, and for using all kinds of apparatus in as many different ways as possible.[3]

The aims of educational gymnastics clearly direct the teacher toward helping each child become more fully functioning by being challenged to learn at his or her own rate and in accordance with his or her own abilities. It has been evident to us for some time that a well-balanced program of physical education in the United States cannot be achieved without the inclusion of educational gymnastics. Present gymnastics programs are either poorly taught or aimed at the abilities of those who intend to specialize. Instructional programs for the undergraduate physical education major and classes in continuing education programs should include this modern concept of educational gymnastics with its aims of meeting the functional needs of all children.

Equipment

Equipment for the modern educational gymnastics program is of three kinds, each serving special needs: hand apparatus, portable apparatus, and fixed apparatus.

Hand apparatus. Hand apparatus is manipulated not for the competitive purposes of contests and games but for the development of agilities. A partial list of such equipment includes the following.

1 Hoops, either plastic or wooden, for rolling, tossing, catching, jumping

1 E. Mauldon and J. Layson, *Teaching Gymnastics* (London: MacDonald & Evans, 1965), p. xii.
2 Don Buckland, *Gymnastics: Activity in the Primary School* (London: Heinemann, 1969), p. 2.
3 A. Bilbrough and P. Jones, *Physical Education in the Primary School,* 3d ed. (London: University of London Press, 1969), pp. 10-11.

Developing efficiency
and skilled use of
the body

Discovery through
creative and imaginative
physical activity

into and out of, and so forth. Rolling, tossing, and catching actions are performed in conjunction with such bodily actions as jumping, turning, rolling, and running to achieve harmony between the actions of both the body and the object.

Opportunities to learn
with apparatus

2 Wands or sticks that are strong enough, while being held by one or more people, to support a child hanging from it. Wands and sticks can also be used for stepping over, around, and under or for supporting and hanging activities in groups of three.

3 Ropes for jumping over, going under; for breaking up the large spaces between more or less fixed apparatus into smaller areas to stimulate inventive movement.

4 Traffic cones for going around and over; for supporting hoops and wands for jumping over and going under.

5 Ribbons and scarves for creative gymnastics, to accent the feeling of movement qualities, and to stimulate the development of appropriate sequences.

6 A parachute for large group activity to stimulate the development of group effort, new ideas for movement, and the creative use of space.

7 Bongo boards, skateboards, roller skates, stilts, pogo sticks, and short vaulting poles offer a variety of challenges in dynamic activities.

Manipulative equipment like ropes, wands, and hoops should be available in sufficient supply so that every child has at least one of the items to use. If such equipment is in short supply, instruction in small groups, while other groups are busily involved with other challenges, assures the most efficient use of time and equipment. In a station method of organization, the instructor places items of a kind at one station so that as the children rotate from one station to another they have the opportunity to work on the special challenges each piece of equipment provides. Long lines should be avoided.

The station method is a good way of rotating the use of equipment like skates and bongo boards. Challenges to improve balance evoke problem solving and the sharing of solutions. In a day or two everyone has rotated

Harmony between
actions of both
body and object

through each of the stations and is ready to start over with either the same or different challenges. Repetition is essential to the acquisition of skill.

Portable apparatus. Portable apparatus consists of equipment like trestles, benches, stools, connecting bars, planks, ladders, and boxes. This type of equipment may be used indoors or outdoors. Children should be taught the correct way of lifting, carrying, and placing the equipment by the time they complete the third grade. Interesting ways of arranging the equipment can be shared between the teacher and the class. Supporting, climbing, hanging, and, if performed carefully, swinging activities of all kinds extend the movements from the floor to another dimension. For variety children may carry and use hand apparatus like hoops, ropes, and wands while traveling across benches or beams.

Fixed apparatus. Fixed apparatus is attached in some fashion to the ground outdoors and to walls, floor, or even the ceiling indoors. It is not readily transportable but is sometimes hinged so that it can be swung against a wall. Apparatus for hanging, climbing, and swinging calls for stability that is best afforded by fixed apparatus, but good quality portable equipment can be very adequate, which means safe. The attachment of portable equipment to fixed apparatus increases the versatility of portable equipment even more. Ropes attached to equipment and strung across the floor to be attached to walls or other equipment make for challenging

Gymnastics

spatial problems to be solved during travels from one piece of apparatus to another.

Actions in educational gymnastics

The actions of the body that constitute the bulk of activity in educational gymnastics are fundamental.

1 Locomotor actions, particularly running, jumping, and rolling
2 Axial movements of all kinds with extensive use of the stretch, bend, and twist
3 Suspended actions, such as hanging and swinging, in all positions
4 Climbing activities using hands, feet, or hands and feet
5 Supporting activities for traveling and balancing, using as many different parts of the body as possible

Hanging and swinging—
feeling the stretch

Exploratory experiences

When these actions are employed in sequences of movement on the floor or in relation to different arrangements of the apparatus, one sees the great variety and individuality that is possible without sacrifice of gracefulness or efficiency. Except for safety requirements, educational gymnastics is free of restrictive limitations and is a continual source for further creation.

In educational gymnastics, exploratory experiences involving the use of the floor and apparatus place emphasis on the development of agility and the full use of the body with control and efficiency. Suitable themes for educational gymnastics lessons will be described later in this chapter.

■ Although the term *artistic* is often used to describe modern competitive gymnastics, the term *Olympic* may be better understood. Olga Korbut has done much through the medium of television to publicize women's gymnastics. Clubs offering instruction in gymnastics have sprung up all over this country. Most of them are staffed with highly competent instructors, but their objectives are those of competitive gymnastics. The public schools are not staffed with personnel capable of providing equivalent instruction, nor is the pupil/teacher ratio favorable to it. Yet the public schools still emphasize the highly restricted forms of Olympic gymnastics that seek to match performance with the ideal. Considering that gymnastics for competition entails very careful training in highly specific events and countless hours of repetition to perfect even the smallest detail, it is questionable whether the best interests of the public school learner are served when the teacher asks for the pursuit of Olympic objectives in skill learning.

Olympic or artistic gymnastics

Olympic gymnastics consists of four events for women: floor exercise, vaulting, and work on balance beam and uneven bars. There are six men's events; floor exercise (without music), vaulting, and work on pommel horse, rings, parallel bars, and horizontal bar. Outside Olympic gymnastics there is competition in tumbling and trampoline.

Unless the physical education teacher is extremely competent, there is little room for Olympic gymnastics in physical education beyond those skills that are natural extensions of the discovery process and the search for efficiency in educational gymnastics. An instructor capable of bridging the outcomes of the two programs is required either to structure a given task in such a manner that the product will be "the forward roll" for example, or some other skill with a standardized form or to teach the skills desired in the most direct manner possible.

Teaching methods

The two methods for teaching Olympic gymnastic skills may be described as the indirect method and the direct method.

Indirect method. The instructor structures a sequence of tasks, making one change at a time while increasing the constraints within which the learner may operate until the final form is achieved. Each step taken is based upon the attainment of a satisfactory standard for the previous task.

Here is an example of a lesson in the forward roll, using the indirect method.

Gymnastics

Find some ways of connecting your rolls with a jump or a turn.
Can you make the first roll a forward roll?
Show me a pencillike stretch jump after your roll.
Can you make the same jump with a turn?
Rather than performing another forward roll, can you put a backward roll into the sequence after the jump and turn?
Eliminate all extra or unnecessary actions so that the sequence consists only of forward rolls alternating with backward rolls connected by the stretch jump with a turn. Let us work out a beginning position, perhaps by following the group leader, and all ending the same way, also.

Direct method. The instructor either demonstrates, has a student demonstrate, uses film, or uses language punctuated by gestures to clarify the form of the gymnastics movement. A step-by-step approach is used, with each step clearly explained. Wrong movements are corrected immediately. If they cannot be corrected, special exercises aimed at isolating the difficulty are identified and performed until the learner is ready to go on with the progression. The outcomes of instruction are meant to be as close to the Olympic standard as possible. Depending on age and experience, lower levels of skill are accepted until sufficient strength, speed, flexibility, or connecting movements have been acquired.

Here is an example of a direct-method lesson in the forward roll.

From a stretched standing position, dive into forward roll. Ready? Go!
Add a stretch jump to the roll, making sure that the direction is straight up and that the body is held in good alignment.
Add a half turn to the jump, being careful to refocus at eye level, and follow it with a backward roll to stretch stand.
Each group—follow the leader and execute the sequence continuously down the mat.

The direct method assumes learner readiness. It should be used only when the instructor knows that the learner has the understandings and movement abilities to follow the specific instructions being given. The instructor must be an analyst of every gymnastics movement and must be able to read knowledgeably the behaviors of the students so as not to risk their safety or embarrass them with instructions they cannot follow properly.

Note how, in the following example of teaching children the forward roll, the instructor must be aware of the components of each of the four aspects of movement.

Assumptions in teaching the forward roll

Instructions	Aspect of movement	Movement Concepts
Stand on the mat with feet together.	Relationship	on, together
Bend down and reach both hands forward.	Body	reach hands, bend

	Space	down, forward
Place them on the mat so that you are now in a bridge on hands and feet.	Body	bridge, place hands, feet
	Relationship	on
Curl your head under and push your hips over while bending your arms and straightening your legs and roll forward.	Body	curl, bending, straightening, roll
	Space	forward
	Relationship	under
Hold the curl of the body and put the feet close to the seat and reach forward beyond your knees so that your weight will roll from the spine to your feet and you can stand up in balance.	Body	curl, seat, knees, roll, spine, feet, balance, stand
	Relationship	beyond
	Effort	weight
	Space	forward, up

The child lacking sufficient body, spatial, or relationship awareness suffers from such instruction. The child is just not ready for directed instruction, nor is it really important at this time. Why is it necessary to learn a forward roll? Because it says so in the curriculum guide? Because the instructor does not know what else to include that is simpler and more appropriate? Either of the two reasons is usually given for a mismatch between learner ability and instructional objectives.

Olympic gymnastics not for everyone

Regardless of the level of gymnastic skills, the Olympic program is not right for everyone. If the instructor has a group of students with a good foundation of basic movement education and educational gymnastics, it is possible to prepare the majority of such students for some kind of directed instruction in specific gymnastics skills. But there will usually be some who have not had adequate background or who simply do not have the ability to engage profitably in Olympic gymnastics.

The instructor who has prepared the children with a background in educational gymnastics sufficient for use as a springboard for Olympic forms is perfectly free to go on to Olympic gymnastics without harming the child who does not wish or who is unable to engage in the activity by making participation voluntary, either after school or in class as additional challenges. Obviously those who do not volunteer should not be pe-

Gymnastics

nalized with poorer grades. Olympic gymnastics is a matter of personal preference. Like tackle football, ski jumping, or springboard diving, its value lies in what it does in helping individuals meet their objectives in life. Olympic gymnastics is not an important educational objective for all children.

<table>
<tr><td>

Rhythmic gymnastics

</td><td>

■ Among the world's most beautiful sports is that of modern rhythmic gymnastics with its artistic blending of body movement and the manipulation of such things as balls, hoops, scarves, ropes, ribbons, and clubs. It is not a common activity in the United States but may grow in popularity as the current movement receives increased television, newspaper, and magazine coverage. Competition includes group exercises for six gymnasts as well as individual routines.

Rhythmic gymnastics appeals to many girls. Creative individual routines as well as group routines are performed to music. Activities include interesting manipulative patterns, nontumbling body movements, and for-

</td></tr>
</table>

Routine with ribbons

Rhythmic gymnastics

mational changes or, in individual routines, versatile use of the body and space. Further information may be received from the United States Gymnastics Federation.[4]

■ Gymnastics activities in the schools are often directed toward some sort of show such as a PTA performance or an exhibition to raise money for additional equipment. Exhibition gymnastics includes individual artistic gymnastic routines, rhythmic gymnastic routines, group exercises using the floor or apparatus, stunts and tumbling, acrobatics, and pyramid building.

Exhibition gymnastics

Stunts are to be found in most books on elementary physical education and in some of the older books on gymnastics. Tumbling involves springing, somersaulting, turning, and rolling in straight pathways with an effort to connect a sequence of skills as smoothly as possible.

4 United States Gymnastics Federation, P.O. Box 4699, Tucson, Ariz. 85717.

Gymnastics

Acrobatics is heavily oriented toward balancing activities. Children do not have the strength to engage in very complex two- or three-person balances, but they do enjoy experimenting with various supports and shapes. Routines are developed in which the participants shift their positions or change their relationships, ending with a climactic balance.

Pyramids are also balances, but they are static shapes that attempt to create interesting designs. Boxes, bars, trestles, and other apparatus are used as supports to raise the levels of the pyramids and to create interesting variety.

Scheduling the gymnastics program

■ The gymnastics program in the elementary school should consist largely of educational gymnastics to assure that all children receive instruction in body management. Any other programs of gymnastics may be added as time, interest, and instructor competence permit. The major objective of gymnastics for all should never be abandoned in favor of programs that meet only a narrow purpose.

Gymnastics as a year-round activity

Gymnastics should be a year-round activity—an outgrowth of the basic movement program by the third grade and a forerunner of both track and field and specialized gymnastics programs. To be a year-round activity and still leave time for important other programs, gymnastics must either be scheduled only on some days of the week or be one module of a multimodular daily lesson. Figure 13.1 illustrates some options. It is essential that basic movement be on a continuing basis. The schedule with a once-a-week program in basic movement is for the upper grades. Lower grades require a minimum of three lessons a week, with K-1 having programs exclusively of basic movement until the children are ready for an exclusively games lesson. This suggests that there is such a time. Some physical education authorities insist on early separation of programs, while the opposite view has equally strong support from others. We agree with the latter group, but we believe in experimentation in program design.

Block programming

Block programming consists of emphasizing single programs through concentrated study. This usually means a "beads-on-a-string" sequence of units throughout the year, with each unit having autonomy. Conventional programs are usually conducted in such a manner. The fall is devoted to outdoor games and sports, winter has units on dance, basketball, gymnastics, and perhaps a little volleyball. Spring ushers in track and field, softball, and perhaps baseball. Rainy days may be devoted to some elementary wrestling. Occasional breaks from such a program include recreational game days, bicycle field days, and other special events. Basic movement education, if included, is relegated to the primary classes either as a block unit or as the prevalent activity with heavy emphasis on exploring different ways of doing things.

Despite the fact that block programming has many shortcomings, it is

Fig. 13.1 Options in program scheduling

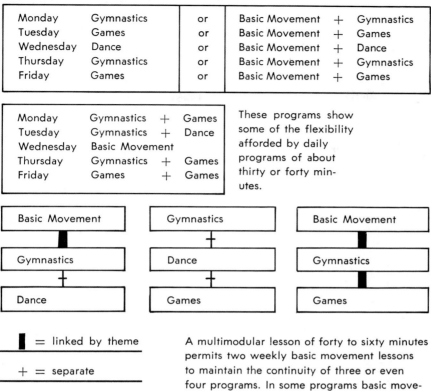

Monday	Gymnastics	or	Basic Movement	+	Gymnastics
Tuesday	Games	or	Basic Movement	+	Games
Wednesday	Dance	or	Basic Movement	+	Dance
Thursday	Gymnastics	or	Basic Movement	+	Gymnastics
Friday	Games	or	Basic Movement	+	Games

Monday	Gymnastics	+	Games
Tuesday	Gymnastics	+	Dance
Wednesday	Basic Movement		
Thursday	Gymnastics	+	Games
Friday	Games	+	Games

These programs show some of the flexibility afforded by daily programs of about thirty or forty minutes.

Basic Movement		Gymnastics		Basic Movement
∎		+		∎
Gymnastics		Dance		Gymnastics
+		+		∎
Dance		Games		Games

∎ = linked by theme

+ = separate

A multimodular lesson of forty to sixty minutes permits two weekly basic movement lessons to maintain the continuity of three or even four programs. In some programs basic movement themes support the following lesson of gymnastics, games, or dance, while some instructors prefer to keep some or all separate so that the modules have no connection with each other.

sometimes unavoidable because gymnastics equipment is not in sufficient quantity for every school to have its own. Under such circumstances, the apparatus portion of the lessons has to be blocked so that maximum use is made of the equipment. However, substitutions for certain kinds of apparatus activity can be made through group work. Children can support each other, pull, push, and hang from wands held by others. Tables, chairs, bleachers, and stage platforms can substitute for apparatus.

> *Large muscle movement must be a continuing experience if the children are to make progress in the development of strength and essential body management skills.*

Modified block programming is an alternative illustrated by figure 13.2. It shows how one program at a time may receive the major emphasis, with periodic rotation assuring all programs equal time. Meanwhile, programs receiving lesser attention maintain some kind of progression, possibly with some attention to follow-up during other times at school or at home.

Fig. 13.2 Variations of blocking that maintain program continuity

		Weeks 1 and 2	Weeks 3 and 4	Weeks 5 and 6
The	Monday	Games	Gymnastics	Gymnastics
Block	Tuesday	Gymnastics	Games	Dance
Program	Wednesday	Gymnastics	Games	Dance
	Thursday	Gymnastics	Games	Dance
	Friday	Dance	Dance	Games
Basic	Monday	Basic movement + Games		
Movement	Tuesday	Gymnastics		
and	Wednesday	Gymnastics		
Gymnastics	Thursday	Basic movement + Games		
Blocked	Friday	Dance		
Maxiblocking	Monday	Basic movement + Games		
of Basic	Tuesday	Basic movement + Dance		
Movement	Wednesday	Basic movement + Gymnastics		
Miniblocking	Thursday	Basic movement + Gymnastics		
of Gymnastics	Friday	Basic movement + Games		
Six-Day	Monday	Basic movement + Dance		
Rotation				
Schedule				

The lesson plan for the gymnastics program

■ The plan of the gymnastics lesson coincides with the thrust of the entire gymnastics program—total body development as demonstrated by the smooth, efficient manner in which the body is managed under a variety of environmental circumstances. The plan consists of three parts, each to be given equal emphasis at least over the course of a week if not during each day's lesson.

Part One: Preinstructional activity

The preinstructional activity, called *limbering* by the British, that takes the form of either free or structured movement starts the lesson and usually lasts from three to five minutes.[5] If particularly good self-directed work is going on, the teacher may choose not to interrupt it for some time, but that situation occurs only with unusually mature, intelligent, and self-disciplined classes.

Free movement allows choice of activity, with the only limitation that the activity be related to previously experienced themes. Structured tasks,

5 Inner London Educational Authority, *Educational Gymnastics* (London: County Hall, 1969), pp. 4, 5.

Preinstructional
limbering

on the other hand, may be used for reviewing or strengthening previous work. Either free or structured movement gets the lesson off to a good start by preparing the children physically and psychologically for the activity to follow.

Learning is a step-by-step process that can only be assessed through observation of behavior. The best time for such assessment, other than when children are involved in set tasks, is when they engage in preinstructional activity. The degree to which new concepts and skills have been assimilated during this activity will be demonstrated quite clearly so that adjustments can be made to the lesson plan before the lesson begins. This most valuable time for observation must never be slighted or treated as though the children are just warming up with the real instruction still five minutes away. During the preinstructional activity, as well as during culminating activities, there is opportunity for children to operate independently, make decisions about what is best for them to do, set tasks for themselves to solve, and in other ways demonstrate their growth toward becoming fully functioning, responsible citizens. There will be many times when the older children will want to discuss some of the directions they would like the lessons to take. Such attitudes should be encouraged, as they in no way infringe on the teacher's prerogative to be the final judge.

Part Two: The floor lesson

The floor lesson that the British call *movement training*[6] introduces and develops the main theme of the lesson, as in basic movement education or in modern educational dance. Three sets of gymnastic tasks to which equal emphasis must be given for all-round development constitute the format of the floor lesson.

1. Tasks for whole body work stress movement in place as well as when traveling.
2. Tasks in which the weight of the body is supported on the hands. The development of strength for these tasks must be emphasized in early lessons until support on the hands is well established, along with controlled landings on the feet. Transfer of weight to the hands for balancing and, eventually, for traveling results in a variety of handstands and traveling actions in which the hands and feet alternate support. Cartwheels and round offs are easiest, but some children will acquire skill in walkovers, tinsicas, and handsprings.
3. Leg work emphasizes three types of landings. They are given here in descending order of difficulty.
   a) Landing so as to continue with traveling without loss of control.
   b) Landing with immediate rebound.
   c) Landing for the purpose of arresting motion entirely, including controlled collapse.

In the following simplified floor lesson plan, *T* refers to task and *D* to development in problem areas as they relate to the lesson theme.

A simplified floor lesson plan

Theme: Making smooth connections with different transitions
Preinstructional activity: Free limbering
Floor lesson

Whole body	T^1	Combining the curl, the stretch, and the twist in different sequences on the spot.
	D^1	Stressing direct transitions
	D^2	Stressing the use of turns in transitions
	T^2	Traveling with different actions, emphasizing different transitions between the main actions
	D^1	Using turns of various kinds
	D^2	Using a sequence on the spot between the main traveling actions
Leg work	T^3	Stressing leaps and jumps in the main traveling actions
	D^1	Arresting the landings to make smooth transitions to the next sequence either on the spot or traveling
Arm work	T^4	Traveling on the hands or alternating hands and feet
	D^1	Adding a sequence to the foregoing patterns in which the hands are used for support
	D^2	Smoothing the connections

6 Ibid., p. 5.

Movement training

Part Three: The apparatus lesson

The apparatus lesson may utilize either large apparatus or hand apparatus, but large apparatus is preferred by children. New dimensions of movement possibility are opened through the extension of the theme from floor to apparatus. Special subthemes are sometimes included to give additional emphasis to actions, space, quality, or relationship ideas appropriate to apparatus experiences. There is an attitudinal difference between the apparatus work of young or inexperienced children and that of older children who have had a year or more of gymnastics work. Young children need to play on the apparatus, to operate as spontaneously as possible until they are well acquainted with the apparatus and have the security of experience to guide them in their further explorations. Older, experienced children maintain continuity among the lesson themes.

To enhance the learning experience, efforts should be made to provide some challenges for arm work, leg work, and whole body actions. Arm work involves gripping, holding on during a swing, providing support, and traveling on the apparatus. Getting on and off the apparatus in different ways usually involves the hands and arms in meaningful and functional ways.

Leg work on landings should always be stressed until the minimal standards are met. Hips, knees, and ankles should be involved in shock absorption after a landing in which the ball of the foot makes the initial contact.

Gymnastics

Whole body actions such as jumping, hanging, swinging, and balancing are as important to apparatus work as to work on the floor. Curling, twisting, and stretching the whole body while hanging promotes development of the musculature and increases awareness of future movement possibilities. Such activity also provides many children with the immediate satisfaction of having hung on long enough to change the shape of the body several times. Other whole-body movements include going under, over, around, and through the apparatus in various ways. The inventiveness of the teacher determines the degree to which exploration of the apparatus environment becomes a challenging adventure.

The difficulty of the challenges is increased in proportion to the development of skilled body management abilities. Tasks are structured in a manner that encourages either inventiveness or refinement. It is important in apparatus work, as in floor lessons, that individual actions be incorporated into sequences as soon as possible. Isolated skills are particularly useful in developing the feelings for transitions and main efforts in the flow of movement.

The apparatus portion of the lesson may culminate in free activity if time permits. Group or partner work may follow, and children who enjoy music might like to add that element to the apparatus or floor work they have chosen.

The division of time between floor and apparatus work is usually about

Springing rearward to
the hands

equal with older children but should be slanted in favor of apparatus work for young children. The seemingly natural inclination of children to work on apparatus, often to the exclusion of everything else, is a familiar one in schools that provide the opportunity for such explorations. Perhaps the children instinctively choose the activity that is best for them. The emphasis on apparatus work has not appeared to hurt the children's progress in psychomotor development according to our experience, but controlled research on the subject is needed.

**Further
considerations
in program
planning**

Changes in activity interests beyond primary grades

As children leave the primary grades, the need for greater program diversification is demonstrated by changes in activity interests. Games for boys are an early need, while girls are content to continue with various kinds of gymnastic experiences. Rhythmic gymnastic work with balls seems to have more appeal than soccer and basketball for some fourth- and fifth-grade girls. However, there is a sharp change in interest in the spring when the same girls, at least partially, abandon gymnastics for track and field and then softball. These activities and a growing interest in the opposite sex appear to usher in the period of interest in competitive team games, contests, and competition in gymnastics if it is available.

The primary child's need for gymnastics

How much gymnastics does the primary school child need? British texts on educational gymnastics and our experience indicate the need for a considerable amount to assure the maximum development of the total body. One of our experiences involved a program with a games emphasis that left a large number of children ill-equipped to participate in many of the physical education program offerings. Too early emphasis on competition that crippled their self-concept appeared to be the crux of the problem. The situation changed dramatically with the installation of movement education in the primary grades. Heavy emphasis on basic movement education and gymnastics appeared to prepare the children better for their changing needs in the upper elementary grades. Controlled research is needed to confirm this experiential evidence.

Suggested time allotments for gymnastics and other activities

Program planners in need of assistance in determining the place of gymnastics and other programs in the physical education curriculum should know that, according to Schurr, there is general agreement among many authors on basic movement as "the core content of the physical education program,"[7] even though there is no agreement on exactly what basic movement education is. However, the content areas listed for basic movement and for gymnastics suggest that a rather large percentage of time in the primary grades should be devoted to these activities. Dauer and Pan-

---

7 Evelyn L. Schurr, *Movement Experiences for Children,* 2d ed. (Englewood Cliffs, N.J.: Prentice-Hall, 1975), p. 44.

grazi suggest percentages for combined movement experiences, body mechanics, apparatus, stunts, and tumbling of 55% for kindergarten to 44% in the third grade and, with the inclusion of combatives, 24% by the sixth grade.[8] Kirchner suggests 60% for these activities for kindergarten and 30% by the sixth grade, with dance held at 20% and games increasing from 20% to 50%.[9] Schurr appears in agreement with Kirchner insofar as gymnastics is concerned.[10]

Multiple unit teaching in program planning

The suggested time allotments for gymnastic activities and our recommendation of a continuing emphasis on basic movement education either as a separate program in the early grades or in alliance with gymnastics, dance, and games poses problems for the program planner that appear to require the multiple unit teaching concept for solution. How else can program continuity be maintained throughout the year? Academic subjects are not taught by the block method until children reach secondary school and college. With block programming, can the agilities, fitness levels, and body management skills of gymnastics be developed during the period of time when the body structures continue to grow and change in proportion to one another? Experience has proved to our satisfaction that in a block program there is rapid deterioration of abilities and functional levels of physical fitness during the long periods of time when the emphasis is on a different part of the program. From research on learning skills, Singer concludes that "gross motor skills can be learned more efficiently with shorter but more numerously spaced sessions over a longer time period. Of the many studies found in experimental literature, the vast majority have demonstrated the immediate superiority of distributed practice over massed practice using a wide range of learning materials and methods."[11] Block programming for the development of the gross motor skills inherent to gymnastics is contraindicated.

Efforts to install multiple unit teaching should not be abandoned because of administrative problems. The problem is almost always a lack of understanding by those in charge. This includes many physical education directors whose background has been team sports in many instances and elementary supervisors who see physical education as generalized motor activity of one kind. Recent developments in our experience bring a degree of hope that the new concepts in physical education expressed in this book and supported by an increasing body of literature will be understood by persons in charge of school administration, by parents and educators in general, and by increasing numbers of physical education teachers in particular.

8 Victor P. Dauer and Robert P. Pangrazi, *Dynamic Physical Education for Elementary School Children,* 5th ed. (Minneapolis: Burgess, 1975), p. 21.
9 Glenn Kirchner, *Physical Education for Elementary School Children,* 3d ed. (Dubuque, Iowa: Wm. C. Brown, 1974), p. 126.
10 Schurr, *Movement Experiences,* p. 45.
11 Robert N. Singer, *Motor Learning and Human Performance* (Toronto: Macmillan, 1968), p. 206.

■ The reader may think that the use of themes in basic movement, educational gymnastics, and educational dance has great potential for confusing the teacher. Actually such confusion does not exist. Children are children, and the scheme of development, whether through basic movement education, gymnastics, or dance, remains essentially the same. The difference lies in the objectives of the lesson.

Basic movement lessons seek to increase the learner's awareness of the possibilities for moving the body in different ways with no concern for skill acquisition. In similar fashion the learner becomes more aware of the influence of the motion factors of time, weight, space, and flow upon actions, and of the quantitative aspect of surrounding space through which the body moves. Awareness of change in environment goes beyond the mere size and shape of it to (1) the arrangement of fixtures within it, (2) the nature of manipulative objects, and (3) the influence of other people upon one's movement behaviors. *To the extent that the learner's movement is movement for its own sake, it is basic movement education.* The reservoir of experiences, feelings, knowledge, and understandings gained is the foundation for their application to practical or expressive situations.

Educational gymnastics is practical. It is concerned with the application of one's ability to move, to orient oneself spatially, to control quality, and to achieve mastery of movement—a high degree of body management skill. *Its themes focus on increasing the learner's mastery of the body in objective movement situations in environments offering a variety of challenges.*

Educational dance is expressive rather than practical. It strives to communicate and to serve as an outlet for moods, attitudes, and feeling. Its themes stress action and movement ideas aimed at enhancing the learner's expressive abilities.

Basic movement and gymnastics

With very young children, preschoolers to as high as first grade (although first grade would be unusual except where there are no kindergartens), entire lessons consist of basic movement education following the modular plan outlined earlier in this book. The second module of each day's lesson rotates the environmental emphasis from apparatus to manipulation to rhythm. Water activities would be included if at all possible, for the aquatic area is rich in opportunities for exploration.

Within the basic movement lessons using apparatus, a gradual shift from movement for its own sake to movement for the purpose of acquiring competence takes place. In other words, the emphasis in some parts of the lesson for some learners shifts to objectives associated with educational gymnastics. The two programs are quite compatible, so it should not seem strange that this happens. There is no need to be tidy and force a separation that exists only in a lesson plan. We often conduct a movement lesson at the beginning of an educational or Olympic gymnastics lesson to focus on certain elements of movement that must be improved or felt if significant progress toward certain objectives is to be made. The next part of the lesson utilizes the felt changes in basic movement awareness to attain such objectives. Therefore, whether a lesson is called basic movement or gymnastics depends upon the extent to which attention and time are devoted to the objectives of the one or the other.

The basis for theme selection

The selection of themes depends upon what the teacher knows about the learner, information that the teacher should get firsthand. Unit themes describe only the general area of attention, not the specific thematic steps that should be taken to attain the objectives. The specific steps must be worked out by the teacher and are governed by the ability to analyze and evaluate the movement status of the learner. The themes of educational gymnastics appear very much like basic movement themes. The main difference is the intention, in educational gymnastics, of arriving at psycho-motor outcomes that demonstrate increased agility, efficiency, and skill in relation to various tasks in certain kinds of environmental settings, as well as skill in relating to others in a physically cooperative manner.

Analyzing the parts of a theme

Williams suggests the following headings as a means for analyzing and categorizing the parts of a theme.[12]

Name of theme: Classification: (action, effort, etc.) (Note: code number may be used)

Group: (introductory, intermediate)

Reasons for selection: (rationale)

Definition: (definition of the limits of the theme and implications)

Aims: (to achieve what should be answered here)

Objectives: (the creation and perfection of sequences from different categories)

Movement material: (Movement tasks derived from the objectives start with exploration and then develop through relationship with a partner and/or relationship to apparatus.)

    I. Exploration
   II. Development
 III. Realization of objectives (the formation of sequences)

The program planner will find these headings useful in the development of a format for unit plans for educational gymnastics. Themes may be selected from a list previously drawn up to assure the inclusion of all the major aspects of work needed to achieve movement competency in body management. Each theme belongs to a classification. The category of body

12 Jean Williams, *Themes for Educational Gymnastics* (London: Lepus Books, 1974), pp. 20 ff.

Spotting the handstand—
cooperative relationship

actions includes all kinds of motor behaviors: space, the pathways, directions, levels, and size of movement; effort, the dynamics affecting the rhythm, control, and flow of the actions of the body; and relationship, the environmental relationship to floor and apparatus or to other people like partners or small groups.

The group (introductory, intermediate) signifies the learner's operational stage. Our book suggests Operational Stage I as an introductory period, Stage II as intermediate, and Stage III as advanced levels of learner behavior. Either set of designations may be used.

A brief statement of rationale explains why a particular theme is selected. Reasons include priority, appropriateness to the sequence in light of previous work, the need to broaden understandings or to improve quality, to provide variety, accent, timing, and flow, and as an introduction to a new line of work.

The definition of the theme sets the precise limits of the work to be done. It identifies the options afforded and clarifies the intention of the theme, as explained in an example from Williams:

This theme is concerned with the ways in which it is possible to change the body weight from one weight-bearing position to another. The focus is on the method of transference which may be stepping, jumping, tipping, twisting, sliding or rolling.[13]

13 Ibid., p. 83.

Gymnastics

Williams defines the aims of the theme as "to bring about certain changes in the understanding and behaviour of the children in the class. These may be concerned with the social aims of creating an atmosphere of discipline or a climate of learning, or of developing co-operative effort between members of a group."[14] She continues by stating that aims may also include new gymnastic concepts like balance, flight, and weight transfer, or improvements in body awareness relevant to shape, or the acquisition of some specific skill.[15]

The final section of this format for a unit plan identifies the objectives of the theme that are transformed into movement tasks by the instructor. A theme is concluded when the objectives have been met. Objectives are in the form of sequences selected from the following list suggested by Williams.[16]

1 Individual floor sequence	A movement pattern without partner or apparatus based on set tasks.
2 Individual sequence using beams, benches, and mats	The inclusion of low apparatus increases the range of possibilities.
3 Partner sequences	A cooperative relationship lends itself to varied possibilities.
4 Sequences on large apparatus	Bars, ropes, ladders, and poles enable the learner to extend further the development of the theme with finished sequences.

Objectives of a unit level theme describe what the learner should be able to do by its conclusion. For example, at the conclusion of the theme, balance and imbalance, the learner should be able to fulfill these objectives.

1 Form a floor sequence with a minimum of five different balances, using different body parts for support.
2 Perform momentary balances on the hands, returning to place, unbalancing into a roll, and twisting to land in a different place.
3 Form a sequence of locomotor actions and balances to connect the floor and either a bench or beam with controlled unbalance onto different body parts.
4 Create a sequence on a large apparatus, showing clear beginnings and endings with a minimum of four balances on different body parts.
5 Form, with a partner, a sequence illustrating a variety of balances, with clear beginnings and endings.

Not all the categories Williams suggests need to be included in the statement of objectives. Young children would not be able to manage partner relationships or create sequences on large apparatus. The program planner in the statement of objectives, however, clearly establishes the desired outcomes, which gives direction to the instructor for planning the lessons.

14 Ibid., p. 21.
15 Ibid., pp. 21-22.
16 Ibid., p. 22.

The remainder of the chapter will be devoted to suggestions for themes and theme progression and to a final commentary on gymnastics in the school based on our experience in the field.

■ Commonly used themes are listed below, with those most suitable for beginners or beginning programs in the first group. Note that most themes are variations of Laban's Themes I and VI. Ideas for additional themes may be found by referring to the appropriate chapter. However, there is enough information here for many years of work. Each theme can be treated as in the following section, and each is subject to variation in the form of subthemes as required by the class. The procedures for developing units may be followed if need exists.

The code numbers opposite the major themes are keyed to the themes in previous chapters, to which the reader should turn for explanation. For example, 01-200 means Laban's Theme I, Symmetry and Asymmetry.

Introductory themes	Reference
Going and Stopping[17]	01-121
Transferring Weight	01-510
Receiving and Bearing Body Weight*	
Shifting Weight on Different Body Parts	
Using Legs and Feet	01-311
Using All the Spaces	03-110

*Themes like these may be added by the instructor and given an appropriate code number.

Intermediate themes	Reference
Rolling, Falling, and Recovery	01-132 and 512
Twisting and Turning	01-112 and 06-250
Use of Hands and Arms	01-321 and 06-110
Using Legs in Different Ways	06-120
Flight	06-240
Levels and Directions	03-200
Balance	01-520 and 06-260
Relationship of Body Parts	01-300
Symmetry and Asymmetry	01-200
Jumping in Different Ways	06-300
Leading Movements *onto, along, off*	01-430
Sequences	01-130 and 06-400
Shapes	03-420 and 09-200
Working with a Partner	05-100
Traveling and Gesturing in Different Directions	11-100
Patterns in Space	09-100

17 Ibid., pp. 17-18. See reference at end of chapter in section of readings on educational gymnastics.

Theme modifications for young or handicapped children

The introductory themes listed may not be appropriate for very young children or for EMRs, for emotionally disturbed, physically handicapped, or exceptional children, or for clumsy children with poor self-concepts. Severe modifications should be made until the children are able to manage the two parts of an educational gymnastics lesson, which may take some time.

Apparatus work. In our experience apparatus work is most beneficial because the children are able to recognize their own accomplishments. Jumping down from a stool, bench, or beam onto a squashy mat for the first time is a thrill that the child will want to repeat over and over again. What is needed is time and encouragement to explore. To that end, the learning environment is set up in advance to stimulate exploration. Interesting arrangements of the apparatus with challenges appropriate to the ability of the class are important. The limited movement abilities of the children would very quickly exhaust the novelty of the environment if it remained the same from one day to the next.

Rules for an apparatus lesson. The following rules are suggested for use in apparatus lessons.

Rule 1 Plan an apparatus lesson only where there are obviously interesting places to do things: places to jump from, swing from, climb up to and over, balance on, slide down, and crawl through, around, and over.

Rule 2 Keep the rules governing exploration simple and very clear. Enforce them kindly but firmly with reminders, elimination from participation for short periods to reinforce the ruling, or removal altogether until the next time.

Rule 3 Expect children to be considerate of each other in demonstrable ways by sharing space, taking turns, and looking out for each other.

Rule 4 Landing mats must be reserved for landings only, to avoid accidents.

Rule 5 Allow children to explore without putting pressure on them, aside from occasionally suggesting some possible action when no ideas for exploration come forth.

Rule 6 Be prepared to change the look of the environment by adding, removing, lowering, raising, or moving equipment during the lesson if the situation warrants.

Rule 7   Respect the individualized nature of the learning experience by permitting children to decide to sit out, participate on the fringe of the group, or participate actively.

Rule 8   Keep the atmosphere friendly, even affectionate, relaxed, and encouraging.

Rule 9   Be prepared in planning lessons to include music; pathways of boards, hand and foot cutouts, and "stepping stones"; a parachute draped over the apparatus to make tunnels and hiding places; mats tipped on their sides to form mazes; and any kind of object to support or broaden the concept or actions stressed by the theme.

Rule 10   Praise achievement both verbally and physically with an affectionate pat or hug.

Suggested themes.   Educational gymnastics lessons for "the little people" and children with learning disabilities must be carefully planned and conducted to assure successful experiences. The most important outcomes result when "I can" feelings replace "I can't."

Themes that use apparatus for both gross motor activity and manipulative experiences are the most useful. Some of them are as follows.

Pathways through different spaces	Arrange beams, ladders, and anything else available to form pathways from one piece of apparatus to another. Make pathways on the floor with tape for balls and hoops to follow.
Big and little	Arrange the apparatus so that there are contrasting big and little spaces and places. Use little balls and big balls, and so on.
Under, over, and around	Arrange the environment so that there are many places in which to explore the lesson theme. Make objects like balls go under, over, and around oneself or the apparatus.
Animal day	Put equipment on its side, if possible, for cages or new places. Add drawings of animals.

■   The teacher new both to gymnastics and to the apparatus to be used presents an interesting situation that is not uncommon today. Many communities have invested in equipment like Whittle, Gym Things, Lind Climbers, and Southampton Caves—either British equipment, Europe-

Hints for the new gymnastics teacher

an equipment, or similarly designed equipment. How to manage this situation is shown in the following instructions.

Step One

The teacher should become familiar with the apparatus by setting it up and hooking it together in several different ways. It is important to learn the operation of any locking braces on the trestles as well as gravity locks or other devices that secure bridges, trestles, and hook-end bars. The teacher should consider how the children might be organized to assist in setting up and taking down the apparatus. Careful attention to this problem makes it easier to use the apparatus as a way of helping children learn to work together in handling basic responsibilities.

Step Two

The teacher must familiarize the children with the apparatus and the behaviors expected in the educational gymnastics program.
A The apparatus should be set up in some simple arrangement to allow the children to explore it freely under the following conditions:
    1. They must stop immediately on a signal by the teacher, for example, "Freeze!"
    2. They must be courteous to each other, sharing the space and not bumping into others.
    3. They must operate within their own abilities with no showing off.
B Challenge the children to go *under* wherever they can, while demonstrating the above behaviors. Then praise them liberally for good conduct and good thinking.
C Challenge the children to find *different* ways of going *under*.
D Apply the conditions of (A) and steps (B) and (C) to the challenges of going *around* and *over*.
E Mentally note the variety of movement behaviors elicited by the challenges and praise ingenuity exhibited to encourage additional efforts to explore creatively. Repeat the challenges with different apparatus arrangements.
F As the children gain confidence, help them to see smoothness and efficiency as exhibited by various children. Especially note the control of landings in descending from apparatus. Stress *soft landings* by bending ankle, knee, and hip joints. Speed must never be stressed. Smooth control enhances safety.

Step Three

Develop simple sequences through an extension of the awareness of basic spatial relationships. Give the children a series of directions such as the following.

A From a spot on the floor, travel to the apparatus and return to place, showing an *over*, an *under*, and an *around*.

1. Vary the sequence, i.e., *under, over, around,* etc.
2. Vary the quantity of relationships within the sequence, i.e., *over, under, under, around, over,* etc.
3. Ask the children to make up their own sequences and perform them using the apparatus. Let children observe others for the purpose of reproducing the sequence of relationships exactly in a different apparatus area.

B Explore ways of going *along* the apparatus, incorporating the additional actions in (A).
C Explore different actions of the body in going *under, around,* and *along.* (Try other combinations, too.)
1. Take the weight on different parts of the body when traveling.
2. Balance in the *on* position.
3. Use different body parts for support.
4. Vary the direction of the movements.
D Develop sequences starting in one place and ending in another.
E Watch your partner's sequence and reproduce it.
F Perform a sequence in unison with your partner.

Step Four

Set up apparatus stations in preparation for a theme emphasis. Decide on an action or a movement idea for a theme, such as *landing and rolling* or *different ways of transferring weight.* Teach the essential concepts and abilities through tasks in a developmental sequence in a floor lesson without apparatus for ten minutes or so. Divide the children into groups of five or six for the apparatus stations where the same concepts are developed further, along with the appropriate efforts to create sequences before moving on to the next station. This may take several days. Review and discuss the basic concepts before beginning each day's lesson. Talk about new ideas and creative thinking. Use floor lessons to clarify the movement ideas further before using the apparatus, but remember that children love apparatus best.

When a theme has been developed into sequences of appropriate movements, it is time to change themes. Some suggestions are:

A Stretching and curling in different ways
B Twisting and turning
C Rocking and rolling
D Wide and narrow shapes
E Working with a partner
F Taking the weight on the hands
G Showing strength and lightness
H Angular and curved pathways
I Emphasizing clear beginnings and endings to movement phrases
J Balances using the hands to assist
K Designs with partners, trios, and small groups.

Gymnastics

Step Five

The teacher increases the challenge and the novelty of apparatus arrangement by the addition of different environmental elements.

A Challenge the children to perform selected movement sequences to different kinds of music.
  1. By themselves all at the same time
  2. Taking turns with a partner
  3. Performing in unison with a partner
  4. Performing in groups of 3 to 5
B Challenge the children to find ways of using an object like a beanbag, ball, hoop, or jump rope while using the apparatus.
  1. Balancing or carrying the object
  2. Manipulating the object in different ways
  3. Sharing the object with a partner, i.e., throwing and catching.
C Attach stretch ropes to connect the apparatus so that children must go over or under the ropes while traveling to different pieces of apparatus.
D Cover the apparatus with a parachute and explore the variety of spaces thus formed.
  1. With little children, make tunnels to go through and explore secret hiding places.
  2. With older children, use a dance theme and develop ideas that incorporate the dramatic use of the design and shapes created.

It would be possible to go on with ideas for using or arranging the apparatus—making it higher, more slanted, selecting more difficult themes, and so forth. It is hoped, however, that by the time the teacher has reached the fifth step the art of programming for educational gymnastics will have been acquired.

Summary

■ The reader may be disappointed in not finding in the gymnastics chapter progressions in Olympic gymnastics or concrete explanations of exactly what children should learn. Such specifics have been avoided for very good reasons. We are of the opinion that a lot of bad gymnastics is being taught and that a lot of gymnastics is being badly taught. Change is needed.

Teachers who still have the idea that performing "coffee grinders," "tip-up," and "seal crawl" is gymnastics can find many books filled with that kind of thing. In our opinion, such activities are not gymnastics but isolated stunts that are not part of sequential development of body management skill. Unfortunately, many of these stunts are even dangerous for some children. The most flagrant example is the dive forward roll over people, which soon becomes a contest to see who can perform the longest dive. These stunts are even included in PTA shows to stimulate excitement. Exhibitionism without a proper foundation leads to injuries, which results in increased insurance costs and the cutting back of programs.

School dollars and the objectives of education dictate the development of educational gymnastics programs first. Anything beyond such programs should be considered extra and added when and if there is instructional competence, student interest, and parent and taxpayer support. The priorities of educational gymnastics are aimed at achieving the highest level of body management skill possible for every child. Optimum development is the goal. No other gymnastics program can attain such objectives because the performance standards are beyond the abilities of the average child.

This does not mean that children should not be taught specific skills like forward rolls, cartwheels, walkovers, somersaults, and handsprings. The gifted movement educator finds it easy to include tasks that lead children into these areas of movement study, but they are optional and involve decision making on the part of the learner. Olympic apparatus may be used to attain similar skills by those gymnastically gifted, but the expectations for the class remain individually oriented.

After-school club programs are the best means for providing the time and the direction for the development of specialized skills. Such programs meet the needs of the few without jeopardizing the overwhelming priority of the many.

Young gymnasts pose a problem for themselves when engaged in educational gymnastics lessons. They are often so specialized already in their movement behaviors that they merely repeat the same sequences over and over again. Many club programs, particularly private clubs, emphasize routines too soon. Children learn them and practice them continuously, thereby losing the opportunity to develop other skills, many of which they will need later. In this country, competition is often entered into at the expense of training in the fundamentals.

A proper blend of educational gymnastics and Olympic gymnastics lends itself well to the all-round development of the boy or girl with gymnastics talent. The specialized coaching and direction in the Olympic program is complemented by the creative thrust of the educational gymnastics program. One program seeks depth in a narrow line of pursuit, while the other looks broadly and gradually selects, arranges, and refines. The programs are not incompatible.

"Let's put on a show" is the cry of those who see the potential of gymnastics for exhibition. How the potential is used will determine its educational soundness. An expression of what is going on in the schools, a way of informing parents and friends, an opportunity to work together to produce something for an audience—all this is the potential of a gymnastics show. But why stop at gymnastics? Why not let children create sequences in other activities as well to show not only what they learn but how they learn? Each program makes a special contribution to the education of the whole child.

Assignments

1
Prepare a sequence of lesson plans for beginners in educational gymnastics with descriptions of the amount and kind of apparatus required.

2
Research the area of educational gymnastics and prepare an annotated bibliography of at least ten books.

3
Observe a selected number of gymnastics classes in local schools and write a summary of what was observed, listing objectives, tasks, and the appropriateness of student responses.

4
Teach educational gymnastics in an after-school program for a period of at least four weeks and report.

5
Prepare a unit plan for educational gymnastics for either kindergarten or first grade, for either third or fourth grade, and for either fifth or sixth grade. Write a rationale for the gymnastics program in the elementary school, including some of the objectives from the instructional units in the statement.

Readings

Educational gymnastics

Bilbrough, A., and Jones, P. *Physical Education in the Primary School.* 3d ed. London: University of London Press, 1969.

A major reference work that includes lesson plans, pictures, methods and learning principles, and a section on the use of manipulative objects. It should be part of every physical education teacher's personal library. Offers a wealth of material for both the experienced and the new teacher.

Buckland, Don. *Gymnastics.* London: Heinemann, 1969.

A useful work for lesson plans, understandings of the role of gymnastics, facilities, apparatus, and ideas for movement material for preschool to junior high school.

Cope, John. *Discovery Methods in Physical Education.* Don Mills, Ontario: Thomas Nelson, 1967.

Contains a description of activity lessons and theme lessons, a useful concept for developing gymnastics lessons.

Inner London Education Authority. *Educational Gymnastics.* Publication R11E. London: County Hall, 1969.

First printed in 1962, this little book was the forerunner of the educational gymnastics books printed thereafter. It is a simple, clear exposition of the principles of lesson planning and the sequence in which they might be conducted. No pictures, just a basic guide.

Mauldon, E., and Layson, J. *Teaching Gymnastics.* London: MacDonald & Evans, 1965.

A masterful work that includes pictures and diagrams, progressions, methods and materials, this book is another for the personal library when only a few selections can be made.

Moving and Growing, Physical Education in the Primary School, Part One. Education Pamphlet No. 24. London: Her Majesty's Stationery Office, 1952.

Williams, Jean. *Themes for Educational Gymnastics.* London: Lepus Books, 1974.

A straightforward description of the themes in gymnastics progression. Examples are presented sequentially. Probably the clearest of all presentations. Particularly useful for the student as a text for courses in educational gymnastics.

Competitive gymnastics

Bengtsson, Nils. *Beginners' Gymnastics.* Palo Alto: National Press Books, 1969.

A useful book for boys' gymnastics with lead-up skills for all events and separate chapters on exercises for developing strength, flexibility, balance, and agility. Line drawings of good technical quality and teaching progression for all skills are particularly helpful.

Bowers, Carolyn Osborn; Fie, Jacquelyn Uphues; Kjeldsen, Kitty; and Schmid, Andrea Bodo. *Judging and Coaching Women's Gymnastics.* Palo Alto: National Press Books, 1972.

A necessary book for the person interested in such features as mechanical analysis, the code of points, and information on the conduct of women's gymnastics. For the club program only.

Carter, Ernestine Russell. *Gymnastics for Girls and Women.* Englewood Cliffs, N.J.: Prentice-Hall, 1969.

An authoritative and well-written book that includes ballet exercises. Although some of the drawings are technically incorrect, the text is explicit and supported by some interesting pictures. Helpful for the beginning club program.

Claus, Marshall. *A Teacher's Guide to Gymnastics.* Palo Alto: National Press Books, 1967.

A book on boys' gymnastics useful for teaching fundamental skills in floor exercise, apparatus events, and rope climbing. Includes spotting techniques, teaching hints, and sequence pictures.

Cooper, Phyllis. *Feminine Gymnastics.* 2d ed. Minneapolis: Burgess, 1973.

Dance and trampoline skills supplement the four competitive events with excellent drawings by Bruce Frederick. Spiral bound, easy to use, but most useful for the club program.

Drury, Blanche, and Schmid, Andrea Bodo. *Gymnastics for Women.* 3d ed. Palo Alto: National Press Books, 1970.

Particularly helpful in describing modern rhythmic gymnastics with techniques and movements for balls, clubs, ropes, hoops, and wands. Includes historical résumé, curricular materials for gymnastics units, and information on class management, judging, weight training, and dance.

Judd, Leslie J.; DeCarlo, Thomas J.; and Kern, René J. *Exhibition Gymnastics.* New York: Association Press, 1969.

The only book written for exhibition gymnastics. The authors bring their considerable knowledge to descriptions of the organization, administration, and production of gymnastics and dance acts. Includes suggestions for climactic performances and comedy.

LaPorte, William R., and Renner, Al G. *The Tumbler's Manual.* Englewood Cliffs, N.J.: Prentice-Hall, 1938.

A classic of its kind that still has much to offer particularly in ideas for two-person acrobatics and floor patterns for demonstrations and exhibitions.

McClow, L. L., and Anderson, D. N. *Tumbling Illustrated.* New York: A. S. Barnes, 1930.

Profusely illustrated with stick drawings, this classic has much of interest for the teacher in search of variations and something different. Includes novelty exercises and work for partners, trios, and groups. Many ideas for demonstrations and exhibitions or just for a change of pace in lessons.

Norman, Randi. *Gymnastics for Girls and Women.* Dubuque, Iowa: Wm. C. Brown, 1965.

The author presents gymnastics from the Norwegian point of view. Beautiful pictures, excellent exercises for technique and rhythmic gymnastics, with nicely presented fundamentals in tumbling, vaulting, and beam. Illustrates how the Scandinavians are able to develop their group gymnastics demonstrations.

Taylor, Bryce; Bajin, Boris; and Zivic, Tom. *Olympic Gymnastics for Men and Women.* Englewood Cliffs, N.J.: Prentice-Hall, 1972.

A general book that covers the fundamental skills of men's and women's gymnastics. Its value lies in its descriptions of skills for the individual events. Helpful for the teacher/coach in need of basic information.

Additional resources

Gymnastics Guide, NAGWS

AAHPER Publication, Sales
1201 16th St. NW
Washington, D.C. 20036

Acrosports, the magazine of the United States Sports Acrobatics Federation

P. O. Box 7
Santa Monica, Calif. 90406

Gymnasts of America, a magazine that reports on gymnastics events, interviews, and technical features

P. O. Box 1310
Durango, Colo. 81301

International Gymnast, the oldest gymnastics magazine in the United States. Pictorial

Sundby Sports Publications
410 Broadway
Santa Monica, Calif. 90401

USGF News, the official publication of the United States Gymnastics Federation

P.O. Box 12713
Tucson, Ariz. 85717

Gymnastics

Chapter XIV

Dance

The sense of satisfaction and achievement
which arises from creating sequences,
dances and dramatic plays is allied to
that experienced in painting a picture
or completing a piece of modelling.
One of the great values of such work
is the power of absorption and
concentration brought into play, for one must
give oneself fully to the dance if one
is to gain from it.

Joan Russell
Modern Dance in Education, p. 88

■ Of all the programs, dance is probably the most neglected. However, it is slated by many authorities for as much as one-third of the total program for primary school children and 20 percent of the program for sixth graders. This situation is akin to not having any of, or having very little of, an essential vitamin, except that there is no way of assessing the damage being wrought by this neglect.

Physical educators are not often drawn from the ranks of those who have studied dance or even movement. Most have been team-sports people engaged in directed play. Few male physical educators have much dance background to draw upon in making determinations about curricular content for dance in the elementary school. Hesitant about their abilities, they avoid dance except for an occasional unit in square dancing with calls on a record and descriptions on the jacket. But it is a step and should not be belittled. If the children find enjoyment in the results, at least one objective has been realized.

This chapter is dedicated to the task of helping the individual who feels uncomfortable about selecting, writing, and ordering dance objectives for inclusion in the physical education program. It is a chapter of beginning steps in each of several types of dance programs with suggestions for future involvement.

Educational dance

■ The forerunner of modern dance is the area of educational dance that has developed mainly through the work of Rudolf Laban, on whose Themes it is based, and his many followers, whose work has enriched the concept of dance for children many times over. Representative examples of their work are to be found in the references at the end of the chapter.

Dance—an innate urge

Young children, even older ones today, participate spontaneously in dancelike movements. Heads move, shoulders and hips wiggle, and feet shuffle as the urge to move expressively is allowed release. The innate urge to move and express through movement is common to children everywhere and suggests an education responsibility to strengthen and give further exercise to them. In the introduction to the little book that enunciated the concept of thematic progression, Rudolf Laban described what he considered the tasks of schools to be.

Expression through
movement

The first task of the school is to foster and to concentrate this urge, and to make the children of the higher age-groups conscious of some of the principles governing movement.

The second and no less important task of education is to preserve the spontaneity of movement and to keep this spontaneity alive up to school-leaving age, and beyond it into adult life.

A third task is the fostering of artistic expression in the medium of the primary art of movement.[1]

The third task is further elaborated as having two aims:

1. . . . to aid the creative expression of children by producing dances appropriate to their gifts and the stage of their development.
2. . . . to foster the capacity for taking part in the higher unit of communal dances produced by the teacher.[1]

An observer of classes in beginning educational dance is apt to mistake the initial challenges for basic movement or gymnastics classes. It is only as the tasks are developed further that one perceives a focus directed toward a different outcome.

Can you find ways of making yourself very small, slowly growing bigger and suddenly exploding to full size?

The exuberance of the action conveys an expression of joy or excitement with anticipatory signs of feigned calmness or growing pressure from within to explode. Is it dance or just the natural reaction of young children to the challenge of this kind of movement problem? It is no matter. Many things are happening at the same time, and attempting to classify every action at this stage is unnecessary.

What really counts is the variety of responses and the fullness of their expression. As a lead-up to dance, the responses should be expressive: for gymnastics, fullness of movement range and control; for basic movement, the awareness of change in size and contrast in the dynamics of the movement. Basic movement for dance is different from basic movement for gymnastics or games only when it is followed by some form of specific application. The momentary isolation of shape or effort in the investigation of various movements is followed by the process of selection.

The basic principles of movement, although grouped in a manner that implies isolation from application, are found, in actual practice, to be presented always in the context of some specific activity, such as children's rhythms or dance; manipulation or rhythmic gymnastics or games; and apparatus and floor patterns or gymnastics. Movement grammar must be given purpose to be a viable, exciting part of the movement experience. The younger the child, the sooner must there be an extension from grammar to application, a few minutes at the very most. Older learners will put off application longer so they can clarify feelings or actions. Isolating the elements of actions to select the appropriate relationship is common practice in the refinement of skills, in making adaptations or modifications, and in the process of creating new patterns. Players returning to action after injury will often play with movement patterns in an effort to recall the exact combination of efforts that made up the skill they once had. Children will spontaneously play with a new action and exhaust its present level of possibilities before selecting a particular pattern or quality to repeat.

1 Rudolf Laban, *Modern Educational Dance*, 3d ed. (London: MacDonald & Evans, 1975), p. 12.

The message of movement

To have an educational dance program, the communicative features of movement must be given the opportunity to be fully expressed. The bonds that prevent children from being themselves—from fully releasing their emotions—must be allowed to slip occasionally. Movement without noise of any kind describes a form of repression, a binding, that cannot be maintained for very long. The naturalness of children's reactions to doing, to being alive, and simply to being where they are should be appreciated for what it signifies and enjoyed for the promise it holds.

The most natural way to introduce young children in basic movement education to educational dance is by asking them to "say something" with their actions, efforts, space, or sounds—with their movement phrases. This requires refining those aspects of an effort action that will give the movement the desired expression. In the same manner, manipulative experiences become contests and games as the ingredient of competition is added to the social setting; apparatus-floor relationships become gymnastics when the body management aspect is stressed to the point of exclusiveness.

Of course, dance can be an outgrowth of experiences without the accompaniment of rhythm or sounds. It is the quality of the movements that signals their purpose. A leap is a leap is a leap. If said in a monotone, it conveys a sameness in the dynamics of the action. But for a game the leap has a functional value: extending to catch a pass, to avoid a fallen opponent, to score a goal. In gymnastics, a leap demonstrates competence, achievement in momentarily conquering the force of gravity or in meeting a performance standard. The leap is product-oriented in all these cases.

This is not so in dance. In dance the leap says something. Perhaps it expresses the quality of flight, of freedom from the restrictive force of gravity or from oppressive rule. Perhaps it just says "Look at me!" Children —and adults also—if caught up in the emotional aspects of a close game or other competition, are likely to jump and leap about to express their joy or elation. No one leaps for sadness, anger, or feelings of futility. These emotions are accompanied by other actions.

The spatial characteristics of movement provide another view of dance and its relation to other program activities. The player of games attacks and defends space while engaged in moving an object through it in the direction of a goal. The gymnast employs the constraints of space as a means for demonstrating competency in body management. This is most vividly demonstrated in balance-beam routines, where the narrowness of the movement sphere presents a severe challenge to the gymnast. Dance abilities are required in floor exercises and balance-beam work to demonstrate movement mastery within the designs of compulsory or optional exercises. In dance, space is the medium to be shaped, surrounded, and exploited.

Lessons in educational dance proceed along the same theme progressions as basic movement and educational gymnastics do. The simple addition of an expressive focus changes the emphasis of a basic movement lesson to dance—very beginning dance, of course, but dance, nevertheless.

Each area of the dance program has an emphasis and/or some specific limitations that distinguish it from all other dance areas. Educational dance is a creative learning experience. Children create dances with their bodies, with or without musical or other accompaniment. At first, these dances are very short, only a phrase or so in length. They may express only a single thought, but as the smallest common denominator of full-blown dance compositions, they contain the main ingredients of dance, children's dance.

Other dance forms are characterized by structure. Most of these structures are imposed by a set of directions for performing the dances. Sometimes these directions come from a book or record; other times they come from the teacher. There is a third possibility, which combines the creative aspect of educational dance with the structure of folk forms. Children can be taught to create their own patterns, that is, to form their own structures, the elements of which are spatial. A teacher who has helped children to discover through exploration of possibilities can also help children to be creative by assembling elements in different ways.

■ Beginning lessons in educational dance look like basic movement lessons, except that they are directed toward clarity of expression and achievement of meaning. Freeing children to be expressive in their movements yet to stay within bounds when necessary is an important first task for the teacher. Some teachers prefer to be very strict at the beginning so that they can relax the rules later on. This may be better than chaos, but fear that the teacher's boundaries may be overstepped will inhibit expression severely in many instances. "The environment created by the teacher for dance learning must be one in which the principles of democratic living are constantly practiced," states Ruth L. Murray.[2] It would be difficult to foster freedom of movement otherwise.

Beginning lessons in educational dance

The teacher, also, must be free—free of false pride, free of the fear of looking ridiculous, free of the fear of making a mistake, free of the fear of being wrong in front of the children. It helps for a teacher to feel and show enthusiasm, to get emotionally involved, to clap hands and shout, "Great! Beautiful! Let's do it some more." It helps when the teacher can laugh and kid or coax with a smile. "One's heart must be in it if what emerges from the act is a genuine dance experience for both dancer and observer."[3] The children have to really want to do it.

It is true that children can be directed through the patterns of a folk or square dance and drilled until the patterns are perfect, but it will end up being something other than dance. The children's movements will say "I don't want to be here. I don't like this stuff. Why do I have to do this?" and so on. Educational dance falls absolutely flat without voluntary involvement.

2 Ruth Lovell Murray, *Dance in Elementary Education*. 2nd ed. (New York: Harper & Row, Publishers, 1963), p. 17.
3 Ibid., p. 18.

Dance

Teachers must know the objectives of the subject they are teaching, or the hoped-for outcomes will never be realized. Ruth L. Murray discussed this concern in the publication *Children's Dance,* the very fine product of the Task Force on Children's Dance sponsored by the American Association for Health, Physical Education and Recreation, as the Alliance was called at that time.

> There is danger that teachers who have had no creative dance in their training and who have been taught only to look and work for efficient, functional movement, will not encourage or even be receptive to a different kind of movement response. They will not see a child's work for what it is, and may even suggest some kind of remedial practice so that the problem is solved more adequately according to their standards rather than the child's.[4]

Dancing is for boys, too

The beginning dance teacher may also not realize the importance of making sure that the needs of boys are met and not just those of girls, who usually like dance from the very start. If dance is taught in ways that suggest that it is effeminate, you will lose the support of the boys in the class. And without their support, the program for the entire class will suffer. However, boys should not be allowed to dominate the dance program. That would not be fair either. A shared relationship gets the best results.

Bruce King shares our opinions about boys and girls in dance.

> If there is a difference in the attitude of boys and girls toward learning, it is that boys seem more eager for results. Boys want to do, rather than to be told how to do. It is easier to teach girls process and techniques. Only the specially motivated boy will submit to the "long working toward" period that is the essence of training a body for professional dance.[5]

By making lessons vigorous and challenging, by avoiding the temptation to refine too soon, and by keeping an atmosphere of fun and liveliness throughout the lesson, the teacher will have met most of the important criteria for having a successful dance program for boys as well as girls.

To be a good teacher of dance, one must have abilities over and above those normally required of good teachers. The good dance teacher is one who (1) loves movement, (2) has a good sense of rhythm, and (3) possesses a creative imagination.[6] Of the three, the love of movement has the greatest value and the highest priority. Next comes the sense of rhythm, the ability to be "on the beat." Imagination can be helped through the development of clearer understandings of subject matter or "from an identification with the insights of childhood and the realization that all of life should be a continuum of new and fresh learnings, of deepening appreciations, of widening horizons."[7]

4 Ruth Lovell Murray, "Competencies of the Teacher of Children's Dance," *Children's Dance* (Washington, D.C.: AAHPER Press, 1973), p. 77.
5 Bruce King, "Who Says Boys Don't Like Dance?" *Children's Dance* (Washington, D.C.: AAHPER Press, 1973), pp. 54-56.
6 Murray, *Dance in Elementary Education,* pp. 26-29.
7 Ibid., p. 29.

A final word from Bruce King on the subject of creative dance for boys before we shift attention to the matter of lessons. King agrees with our belief that if the teacher possesses the basic ingredients of love, rhythm, and imagination, it should not be difficult to understand the concept of creative dance as

> the areas of dance that allows the participant to move impulsively. It uses a problem-solving approach to dance. When the child is challenged to find a new way of moving, he is solving a problem creatively. It may be as simple as working out how to change the direction of a movement; it may be making use of imagery; it may be making use of human actions or feelings. When the participants select and develop the movements for their dance, then that dance must be appropriate for them.[8]

Dance is an art form relevant to the lives of boys and girls; it should be taught in a manner that permits the greatest individual expression. It is a mistake to structure lessons for outcomes that are important to the teacher rather than to the student. This can be avoided by maintaining continual contact with the children by asking questions and by observations. Note how educational dance is handled by different physical educators and teachers of dance in the following series of lesson plan descriptions.

Joan Russell

Stage I: Infants [sic kindergarten]
Infants, first year: material to be covered

How others do it: Sample dance lesson plans

Body Awareness—Laban Theme 1

Activities which involve the "total stir of the whole being" are most appropriate. . . . These include stepping and running, galloping and skipping, spinning and turning, leaping, hopping and jumping and locomotion on all fours. Experience shows that children at this stage of their development find it difficult to stop the flow of movement.

Body parts: in addition to the activities involving the whole body, exploration of possibilities with the extremities can take place. *Feet* will be used in beating on the floor, in travelling on the heels and on the toes, in coming close to each other, in taking big wide steps and in kicking. *Hands* will be used for grasping and releasing, shaking, beating the floor, clapping and tapping. *Knees* will be much in evidence in hopping and jumping.

Effort—Laban Theme 2

Speed can be experienced in variations of quick and slow, especially with the help of sound.

Weight can be experienced in the strength of gripping hands and pushing the feet into the floor. In "pushing" feet the result is not a sustained pressure but this word-suggestion seems to produce more strength than the word "stamping." Contrasts can be achieved through loud and soft stepping and hand-beating, through vigorous leaping and jumping and quiet light-footed stepping and creeping.[9]

8 King, "Who Says Boys Don't Like Dance?" p. 56.
9 Joan Russell, *Creative Dance in the Primary School* (London: MacDonald & Evans, 1965), p. 33.

Freedom to express
through movement

The use of the feet—
exploration of
possibilities

Commentary. These descriptions are really units of work to be covered during the year. Altogether there are four, space and relationship being the other two.

Lesson plans that stress the elements of activities and movement ideas would follow a spiral sequence: an introductory lesson series on Theme I followed by a lesson series on the awareness of speed and weight in connection with the previously explored body actions. As concepts and actions fuse into generalized abilities, additional actions are explored through a review of Theme I.

The same procedure is followed with a sequence of lessons on spatial relationships and directions with various locomotor activities. Attention to factors of weight and time may follow, then some more lessons on actions and the movements of body parts. As soon as the children feel comfortable moving about with each other and with the teacher, the relationship to the teacher can be emphasized by making the teacher the leader or focus for going toward and away from.

Is this dance? Not yet, but the basic movement lessons are given dance-like qualities as the inner life of the child is revealed through the playfulness of his explorations. "We shall expect him to enjoy the explorations and discoveries of what he can do with his body, to enjoy the feeling of repetition when doing an activity over and over again and to enjoy the fun of the unexpected movement happening."[10]

10 Ibid., p. 32.

Various locomotor
activities

Dancelike qualities as
the inner life of the
child is revealed

Mary Joyce

Lesson 4

element: steps
helper: shapes

Go anywhere you want to go in the room. When the drum stops, make a
shape. Head for the open spaces—fill the whole room! Ready, go. And
make a shape.

This time you have to walk, but show me walking in many directions,
with body shapes. Go. Shape.

In order to make good shapes while doing steps, that spine has to move.
Show me how you can move your back. Arch it. Round it. Twist it. Lean
to the side. This time, I want you to run, not only changing directions,
but also trying to make shapes with your back. Go. And shape.

What is leaping? Yes, a high, wide run. Let's take several runs and a leap.
Go. Let's do it again. Can you make a shape when you're in the air? Can
you leap sideward? Backward?

Jumping: remember, jumping is landing with two feet at the same
time. Make shapes as you jump. How many ways can you jump. With
crossed feet? With feet together? Feet apart? Small jumps? Big jumps? Let's
see what can happen with jumping. Go. Shape.

Show me hopping. Can you hop and turn? Can you hop slowly? Can you
hop and make shapes? How many ways can you move your arms as you
hop? Ready, go. Shape.

Dance

Skipping: what can you do with a skip? (Etc.)

Galloping: how many ways can you gallop? (Etc.)

Sliding: slide out that foot as you start. What can you do with a slide? (Etc.)

Everyone line up on the black line ready to come all at once across the room. Combine at least two steps before you reach the far side of the room. What are the steps? Walk, run, leap, jump, hop, skip, gallop, slide. Make your steps interesting by changing your level or your direction or your tempo. Always make shapes. Ready. See what you can do.

Now come two at a time so you can watch each other. Ready, first two.

Today let's do a good-bye dance. Do any steps you like, and come one at a time from your side of the room over to where I am sitting on the floor. Make a shape when you reach me, and then sit next to me. As soon as the person ahead of you finishes, you can start. Ready. (*Play music—something lively, like "Tijuana Taxi."*) Go.[11]

Commentary. The elements referred to are those that have been previously identified in this book under body, space, and effort. "A helper is an image or way of working. It makes an element more interesting and more fun. It can clarify a dance movement or be a vehicle through which an element is used."[12] The two, element and helper, make up the theme of the lesson. This lesson is listed for kindergarten and up. Adjustments in the quantitative aspects of the content as well as the approach are made to conform to age-level needs and expectations.

Note the mixture of directness and problem solving within very limited tasks. As the lesson draws to an end there is a brief analysis, "What are the steps?" followed by the culminating activity, a simple dance. The preceding activity of basic movement is given a final focus.

Sheila Stanley

Sample Lesson Plan Two

Grade: Four, Five, or Six with little experience

Theme: Effort elements—strong and sudden; strong and sustained

Subthemes: 1. Compensating effort element—fine touch
2. Relationships—four individuals meeting and parting

Introduction

Challenge:

1 "Dance to this music (*Baby Elephant Walk* by Henry Mancini) quite freely bringing out the cheerful, cheeky, jaunty spirit of the music," or

2 "Sit and listen to the music. Clap the rhythm." The teacher should discuss briefly the spirit of the music and help the pupils to think of the kinds of movement that would be suitable, and what parts of the body might be stressed. Immediately the pupils should be allowed to try out their ideas moving freely about the room to the music.

Observation: (Optional) One half may watch the other half of the class to see what responses are made to the music noting the stress given to dif-

11 Mary Joyce, *First Steps in Teaching Creative Dance* (Palo Alto, Calif.: National Press Books, 1973), pp. 68-72.

12 Ibid., p. 56.

ferent parts of the body and the general carriage. Note the general expression of the movement.

Challenge: "All work again, trying to keep the movement gay."

Observation: One half observes the other half of the class noting how the dancers pass each other and interweave.

Challenge: "Work again, trying to meet and pass several different people. How do you react to these people?"

Development

Challenge: "Sit and listen to the music, *The Comedians.* ° What is the spirit of the music? Where does it seem to suggest strong, sustained movements?"

Challenge: "This time, work by yourself. Experiment with movements which are as big and strong as the music seems to require. You may find that your body shapes are big and queer also."

This may be a difficult challenge and the teacher may replay the music for further exploration.

Observation: Some pupils may be observed for: i) strong actions or; ii) large shapes; or iii) floor patterns.

Culmination

Discussion—sit in a close group: Exchange a few ideas as to what the music and movement reminded them of. Recall the quality of strength with slowness, also the possibility of large movements and floor patterns.

Challenge: "Make up a dance for four. The requirements are that you must start in a position which allows you to meet at least once in the dance. Try to show the quality of the music in your movements."

Arrange the groups and starting positions. Play the music for experimental work.

The teacher must judge how many replays are necessary for the exploratory stage. He must remind groups of the requirements: 1. meeting at least once; 2. quality of movement. He must regulate the use of the time, indicating when the dancers must select the movements which they want to use. He must control the interval between the replaying of the music, thus influencing the amount of verbal planning which is used.

Observation: Use an observation of a group even while the dance is unfinished and somewhat confused. If this is done, it will be for the purpose of helping the class on a specific point. For example, one group may meet and pass each other dancing as individuals throughout the composition. The teacher should coach the dancers to be aware of the ending. "What meaning does it give to the dance?"

Conclusion

Challenge: "Practice once more before you show your dance to us." Each group should be warned of the last practice.

Observation: If possible, each group should dance for the rest of the class. If a title can be given to the dance, it tends to give satisfaction. Some word of praise should be found for each group's work.[13]

---

13 Sheila Stanley, *Physical Education: A Movement Orientation* (Toronto: McGraw-Hill of Canada, 1969), pp. 284-86.

° R.C.A. Victor LE 1000 *Adventures in Music*, Kabalevsky, "The Comedians": Pantomime.

Commentary. Stanley's lesson plan illustrates how upper-level elementary schoolchildren may become involved in simple dance composition. It is important that something like a finished product come out of the dance experience. "These children are capable of practicing, refining and perfecting their dance sequences, and the form of their dances will tend to become increasingly well defined. This will probably mean that the accents, contrasts, emphases and logical flow from one movement to another will begin to receive some consideration."[14]

There are several points that should be noted about this particular lesson. First, the introduction or preinstructional activity is very closely related to the content of the lesson to follow. It sets the stage with a holistic approach to the subject of the lesson. The "whole idea" is presented in generalized form, followed by a sequence of alternating challenges and observations that gradually clarify the parts within the "whole."

Observation involving first one half of the class and then the other helps to continue the stress on analysis. What are others doing? How is space or effort being manipulated? Is there something new here, something different? In addition, children are quick to note attitudes toward the lesson. Those who may feel a little uncertain about letting themselves go may see behaviors that encourage them to be less inhibited. Of course, while the class is working on a movement task it should be absorbed in exploration, selection, and refinement problems, and not in what others are doing. Children should be doing their own work, and this should be praised until it is accepted practice in every physical education lesson.

Geraldine Dimondstein

Problem III: To explore spatial relationships created by group shapes.

A   Explore a shape where you are touching or connecting with each other.
1. Even when you close the spaces in between, each body will have its own shape.
2. Work with partners or in small groups.
3. Feel the difference between leaning on someone and just touching them. What happens to your balance?
4. Work at different levels and fill in the space around, under, and over.
5. You will be meeting and staying together like "frozen" shapes.

Solutions

a. (Partners.) Sitting on floor facing each other, both with knees flexed and feet on floor. One partner with legs extended in diagonal position encloses other child's legs; heads are downward and touching; arms grasp each other's shoulders.
b. (Partners.) Standing side by side, with weight balanced on one leg, other leg slightly lifted off floor, arms raised and flexed at elbows, inside elbows touching.
c. (Trio.) First and second child sitting on floor, with backs touching, knees flexed, feet on floor, hands on each other's heads; third child sitting, with knees flexed in same position, facing second child, with elbows on his knees

14 Ibid., p. 278.

d. (Trio.) Two children standing in wide lateral stride, side by side, with both inside legs crossed, torsos curved forward, inside shoulders pressed against each other, both holding crossed arms of third child lying on back on floor with hips elevated and legs extended forward through supporting arms of partners.

B Each time you make a shape with another person or with a group, the space around you changes.
1. Divide in small groups and explore movements that take you *over* and *under* each other.
2. Are you touching, or are there spaces between you?
3. Is everyone in your group on the same level in space?
4. Are you moving and staying together, or are you meeting and moving apart?

The lesson continues with each group working out the next part of the problem.[15]

Commentary. The focus of the lessons is conceptual, based on the framework of Laban's work in separate chapters titled "Space," "Time," and "Force," in that order, followed by a chapter on the use of imagery in exploration, a most useful extension of the fundamental concepts. "Explored in innumerable combinations and in varying intensities, these elements give expressive qualities to a child's interpretation of movement, which transforms imagery from storytelling to dance."[16]

Progression in educational dance

■ After the teacher has gained dance teaching experience and feels comfortable with dance lessons, usually after a year or so, attention should be turned to the task of clarifying the objectives of the dance program. It should no longer be characterized as "fun time" for the children and "in-service" for the teacher who is exploring all the possibilities for teaching dance with no progressions in mind. It should continue to be fun but should contain the serious elements of planned development of basic movement and its expression through dance.

Teachers who follow the plan of teaching in accordance with the dual-track approach should find no difficulty at all in shifting from the exploration of movement possibilities to dancelike culminating activities for floor or rhythm lessons that permit such as emphasis. The shift from basic movement education to educational dance could occur while the manipulative modules of the lesson plan continue stressing manipulative exploration and self-testing or even contesting activities.

Remember that the dual track is a convenience for identifying objectives that have two different kinds of purpose in the immediate aspects of the curriculum but that serve the same ultimate goals of the dance, games, gymnastics, or aquatics programs. Consequently, basic movement lessons will gradually take on more and more of the character of games lessons,

---

15 Geraldine Dimondstein, *Children Dance in the Classroom* (New York: Macmillan, 1971), pp. 112-14.

16 Ibid., p. 218.

dance lessons, or any other kind of specific program lesson. This is to be expected, but the timing of the transition should coincide with the readiness of the child to make the transition from exploration to specific application. Day-to-day changes in emphasis will be reflected as lessons return to a deeper exploration of certain elements or principles of movement after a day or two of stressing application.

Educational dance lessons are more easily begun in kindergarten than games lessons. Progressions that follow the suggested basic movement themes are readily shifted to a dance emphasis coordinated with the child's growing awareness of sounds and their relationships to the rhythms of movement. If there are teachers who prefer not to involve themselves immediately in dance progression, the basic movement track with its emphasis on rotating environmental relationships for each new thematic concept will, nevertheless, assure progression in the relationship of movement to sounds as the weight-time elements are explored. If a change of physical education teachers brings in a "dancer" the following year, the children will not be totally lacking in a feeling for the elements of rhythm.

Joan Russell's comments regarding the planning of a syllabus or guide suggests the inclusion of two stages in the learning process similar to the operational stages described earlier in this book. The following paragraphs describe major characteristics of these stages.

Stage I is for infants and for juniors 5 to 8 years old, but this is approximate, as the next stage will overlap, rather than begin at precisely a certain age. It is readiness that determines the end of one stage and the beginning of the next.

"First the young infant is at the stage where he learns directly from personal experience and action. His knowledge of himself must derive from personal experience and experiment with movement." All manner of whole-body and body-part actions are explored and enjoyed. "At this stage then we shall expect the child to produce an immediate response to the stimulus of words, to the tone of voice, to a variety of sounds."

A considerable amount of time is devoted to permitting, in fact encouraging, repetition and the continual emphasis on exploration to discover additional capacities for movement.[17]

Stage 2 is for upper-level infants and for juniors 7 to 11 years of age. This stage grows out of the first stage and signifies readiness to move from exploration for the purpose of gaining comprehension to application, selective analysis, and creative structuring of movement sequences. A gradual increase in ability to operate with others in working relationships is evidenced all the way to group work.

"In this second stage the child begins to be able to use his activities to get data about the world into his mind and there transform them so that they can be used selectively to solve problems." Russell points out further that the child at this stage is only able to " 'structure' immediately present

---

17 Joan Russell, *Creative Dance in the Primary School*, pp. 31-32.

reality and has not reached the stage of conjuring up systematically the full range of alternative possibilities that could exist."[18]

To sum up this all-too-brief section on educational dance, and to clarify the objectives of this important part of a total physical education program in the elementary school:

> We are not concerned with training dancers, with producing a skilled technical performance, nor are we concerned with developing a set style. We are concerned with educating through movement, with fostering the child's love of movement and with giving scope for discovery, imagination and intuition . . . . In the primary school we should aim to increase the child's power of observation and his sensitive awareness to movement, sound, shape, texture and rhythm.[19]

Given this overall description of purpose, the physical educator has sufficient guidelines for developing program objectives at any level for educational dance.

Creative dance

■ The term "creative dance" is tentatively applied to an area of dance that could very well be an extension of educational dance, and therefore, needs no separate designation. However, many teachers have objectives that separate the two dance areas from each other. Educational dance is limited to movement explorations without the benefit of objects to manipulate. Creative dance uses a variety of materials whose properties are explored and then used in the creation of dances.

Props are important

Murray discusses properties of various kinds as aids in exploration and improvisation. After describing a variety of props, such as bandannas, beanbags, scarves, hoops, and hand instruments, she makes the observation that, "Props, of course, should always be seen for what they are, a quick means of helping children to explore a great variety of movements . . . . The next step would be to reproduce these movements freely and accurately in dance improvisation with only imaginary props to control."[20]

Creative dance as described here is a blending of body and object movements for the purpose of developing dance for which the inclusion of props is essential. The following descriptions of lessons will clarify this point further.

Gladys Andrews Fleming has succeeded in developing very effective work using props and costumes. "Props," she writes, "include a variety of objects which help to stimulate or communicate a dance. They not only add to the setting but are also essential to some dances."[21]

---

18 Ibid.
19 Ibid.
20 Murray, *Dance in Elementary Education*, p. 69.
21 Gladys Andrews Fleming, *Creative Rhythmic Movement* (Englewood Cliffs, N.J.: Prentice-Hall, 1976), p. 308.

As props, she lists the following (which are not meant to be all-inclusive):

1. Cartons for building things like planes and ships.
2. Ropes, clotheslines, nylon, string, elastic, nets, packing barrels, transparent plastic, furniture, benches, bleachers, chairs, balloons, hoops, balls, sacks, newspapers, portable screens.
3. Construction materials and art supplies such as brown wrapping paper, newsprint, chalk, magic markers, construction paper.
4. Charts to help children remember sequences of ideas, people in groupings, cues, floor patterns, words of a song, or orientations to spatial relationships.
5. Murals as visual resources for backdrops or the intensification of the work of children's dances.
6. Graphically represented sound compositions to colorfully present enlarged musical scores.
7. People to read poems or words to accompany dance, to help children to orient themselves to new spaces.[22]

Costumes are called "trimming" and are meant to give the dance something extra; however, the dance itself should stand on its own.

> When children feel comfortable in creatively and esthetically communicating the essence of the dance, this is a time to consider costumes, rather than before the dance has been designed. Costume ideas include items like masks and eye patches that help change the personality of the dancer, hats, gloves, scarves, shirts and other wearing apparel, towels, curtains, feathers, burlap and other kinds of bags, and wrist and ankle bells.[23]

Creative dance and language arts

The creative rhythmic dance experiences advocated by Fleming are not a departure at all from the elements of basic movement and educational dance discussed previously. Creative dance is discussed and presented separately because of its very distinct form, which makes it easy to correlate with other subject matter. It can be tied directly to the language arts through stories—particularly those written by the children—poems, and even words alone. The graphics arts and music are equally available for extensive correlation. A great emphasis is put upon chants—talk songs—and Fleming investigates these thoroughly for a variety of uses as accompaniments. "The classification of chants includes work chants, sea chants, religious chants (taking the form of prayer and worship), street chants, and nonsense chants."[24]

Dance songs are used to stimulate creativity. Singing and moving are performed together. "Dance songs are a way of helping children identify and show relationships between movement, sound, and experiences; there is far more to dance songs than just singing with motion."[25]

22 Ibid., pp. 308-9.
23 Ibid., p. 309.
24 Ibid., p. 144.
25 Ibid., p. 163.

This brief description of what may be a separate dance form or just an extension of educational dance, perhaps is characterized best by the title of Dr. Fleming's book, *Creative Rhythmic Movement*. Creative rhythmic dance has great potential for stimulating children to dance and helping to interrelate the art of movement with other subject areas in a school. Creative dance invites inclusion in the curriculum as a planned sequence of dance movement learning experiences.

■ As illustrated in Figure 14.1, dance has two main divisions, creative dance forms, which are unstructured, and structured dance forms, which tend to be noncreative, adult-imposed dance forms. The latter circumstances do not have to prevail. Structure forms can be the foundation of creative dance experiences or an extension of the concepts of spatial relationship and group relationships acquired in educational dance.

Structured dance forms

The most common forms of structured dance are folk dances and square dances. Two others are included in many programs, round dances and novelty dances. The latter form will often complement a folk or square dance program to provide some light-hearted amusement, with movements that entertain both participants and onlookers. The Bunny Hop and the Hokey Pokey have not lost their popularity since their birth in the fifties. Others, such as Alley Cat, have been added to them to continue to stimulate young and old alike to move in very simple rhythmic patterns.

Record companies have produced a tremendous number of dance records for all sorts of patterned dances. Sometimes the calls or directions are on the record. Walk-through and talk-through sides are accompanied by instrumentals so that once the dance is learned the dancer can dance without direction. Square-dance records have calls on one side and music alone on the other, so that the teacher can either reproduce the call exactly or improvise.

The emphasis of this concluding part of the chapter on dance will not be on listing the folk and square dances children should learn. There is some question in our minds about the propriety of suggesting such a progression in elementary schools although there was a time when we vigorously pursued the objectives of such progressions—such objectives as developing appreciations of dance, foreign cultures, and the opposite sex, and developing fitness through dance.

The status of structured dance forms in physical education is not very clear today. Many teachers still believe in a sequential program of children's folk dances from kindergarten to grade three, beginning with such playparty dances as How Do You Do My Partner? and extending to dances with step patterns, such as Cshebogar and Korobushka. Square dancing usually begins at the fourth-grade level but sometimes starts as early as the second grade.

There is no denying that folk and square dance can be fun and tremendously interesting, particularly in the hands of a teacher who can call the dances or prompt them with no notes in hand to distract the learners.

Round dances may be included, particularly if they have interesting names, syncopated rhythms, and novel steps, as do The Salty Dog Rag or The Tennessee Wig Walk.

Fig. 14.1 Dance: A type of "dicotyledonous plant"

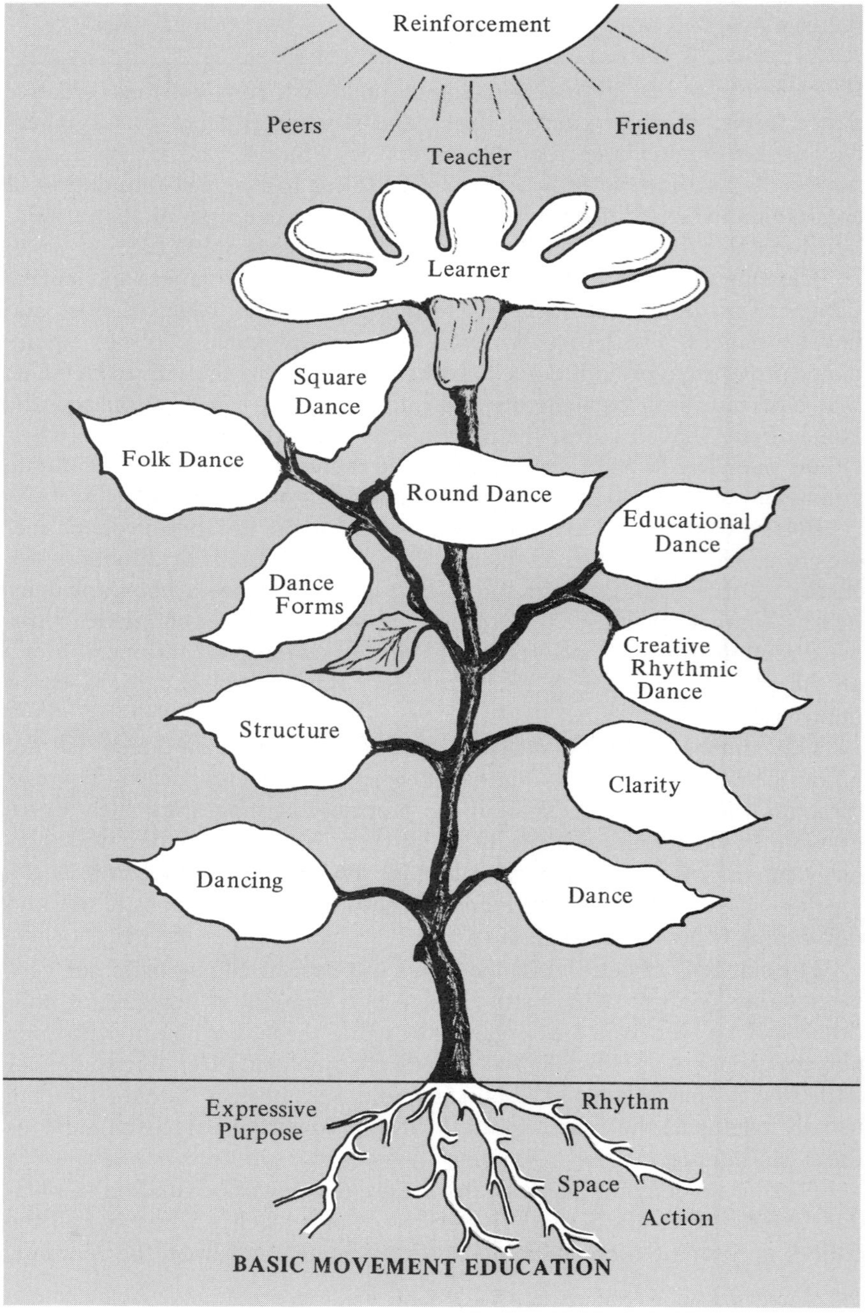

Reinforcement

Peers   Friends

Teacher

Learner

Square Dance

Folk Dance

Round Dance

Educational Dance

Dance Forms

Creative Rhythmic Dance

Structure

Clarity

Dancing

Dance

Expressive Purpose   Rhythm

Space

Action

BASIC MOVEMENT EDUCATION

The danger of using exclusively structured dance forms in the physical education program is that this part of the program may become merely a series of memorized dances and not Dance. Dances are taught as specific patterns to be followed in precise ways using certain steps, also in precise ways. Relationships to others are specified as side by side; back to front; facing; in circle, square, or line formation; and with certain contacts or linkages of hands, elbows, waists, and shoulders. Obviously, the would-be dancer must have either a great deal of knowledge before beginning to participate or the ability to learn rapidly from the directions given. Otherwise the inevitable failures will be all too public and a hindrance to others who cannot proceed until the mistakes are corrected.

If part of the responsibility of teaching includes helping children to understand the structure of the subject they are learning, then it would seem appropriate to search for the means to make square dance, folk dance, and other structured dance forms understandable as structures that can be disassembled and reassembled in the same or in different ways. Murray says that

> In the light of modern educational psychology teacher directed exercises
> per se for children have long been discarded in favor of problem-centered
> movement experiences. Such experiences are stimulating to the learner,
> and the rewards for his efforts are much more immediate and vital to him.
> In all aspects of children's movement education such a method is to be
> preferred.[26]

Is it undesirable to teach children square dancing, folk dancing, and other forms that require learning steps, formations, sequences, and changes in relationships in precise ways? Should all of this type of dance be discarded because it is educationally unsound? In our opinion, the answer is "No." We believe that there is room for all kinds of structured forms, as long as they are not theatrical (tap dancing), erotic (belly dancing), or demanding of expertise beyond the capabilities of the teacher (ballet). The way to make folk, square, round, and circle dances related parts of a conceptually oriented movement education program is to subject them to the same kind of analysis as the other aspects of the program.

Step patterns, from the simple shuffle to the Schottische, the Highland Fling, and the Salty Dog, fall into the category of actions involving certain body parts, movements, and relationships. Formations are spatial structures involving people relationships. Directions belong to the spatial aspect, and the musical rhythms belong to the aspect of effort. Manipulation of the proper variables enables the learner to structure his own forms if he chooses to do so. Creating dances with specific patterns is fun, meaningful, and a direct extension of concepts acquired in basic movement or educational dance.

■ This section will include some ideas for creating dances complete with formations, steps, and patterns. It will not be all-inclusive, but it will be in

Creating dance

26 Murray, *Dance in Elementary Education*, p. 9.

sufficient depth so that the basic concepts may be applied in different ways by readers who see the principles as a way to encourage creativity in the folk forms.

Starting a square dance from scratch

The following steps are suggested for persons who have never danced before from fourth-grade children to adults. Using a single record like *A and E Rag* or similar square-dance instrumental music, the teacher adds the music to a lesson exploring locomotor activity with the feet.

1 Travel following the music.

Adjustments of the actions are made to the tempo of the music.

2 Select an appropriate locomotor pattern and eliminate the others.

The action of walking or skipping may be retained.

3 Clap the accented beat.

The first and fifth beats should be isolated for attention through additional questions and relevant tasks.

4 Select either the first or fifth beat and do something in time to it.

Handclapping or stomping on the beat is usual, but flicking or dabbing actions of the hands or feet might occur. An action has been associated with an accented part of a musical phrase.

5 Find two different movements, one for the first beat and one for the fifth beat.

Further experimentation and questions aimed at firming the position of the two beats in the spatial design of the beats.

6 Let's do something different. Let's change the direction of our movements on the first and fifth beats.

Helping the learner to perceive alternatives, one of which is changing directions. Other alternatives may be added to strengthen the concept, such as stopping on the first and fifth beats, moving the hands about in personal space with change of direction, or changing levels.

7 We can make interesting floor patterns by just using the directions forward, backward, sideways right, and sideways left.

The learners are encouraged to design angular floor patterns. Spatial variables continue to receive the major emphasis.

8 To create some interesting problems, continue what you are doing but with a partner.

Various partner relationships may be explored. Side by side, leader and follower, and facing each other are the most common. All should be explored and the similarities and differences noted, not only of the patterns but also of the changes in spatial relationships leading to meeting and parting, maintaining the space between, or going first with the other following.

9 Work out a pattern with your partner in which you change relationship, i.e., side by side to facing each other, with changes of direction on the first and fifth beats.

Patterns evolve, for example, forward and back (8 beats—side by side), turn to face partner and back up (4) and then move toward each other (4), continue with a do-si-do (8), back up and return, finishing side by side (8), ready to start again. The concept of phrase should be clarified.

1st 8 beats	Forward and back	X O	8 beats
2nd 8 beats	Away from and together	X O	8 beats
3rd 8 beats	Do si do	X O	8 beats
4th 8 beats	Away from and together Finish and turn side by side	X O	8 beats

10 Let's add some kind of partner contact, either just on the first or fifth beat or for as long as eight beats.

Children should be encouraged to experiment with the full range of possibilities. Meeting and touching hands; meeting with elbows or two-hand swinging; parting with a bumps-a-daisy hip or seat bump and returning with a handclap followed by a swing are some of the common possibilities.

11 Patterns can now be made that include traveling together, meeting and parting, and going around.

Optional contact may be made a condition if there is a problem with partner relationships beyond the previous step, but in most cases · the problem solves itself if boys can have each other for partners. Patterns include the promenade, elbow swings, hand swings, and do-si-do.

12 Two people find two more and face each other. Experiment with possibilities for using the old patterns and find any new possibilities.

The results should be meeting and parting with opposites, swinging doing the do-si-do with opposites and diagonally opposite people also. Circling left and right as a group of four is a new pattern that might lead to a duck-for-the-oyster meeting and parting variation. Star figures develop.

13 Create dances in fours that are complete in four phrases of eight.

Dances with specific patterns are created and repeated over and over. The number of figures are doubled and ways are found to put the fours into a circle of progressive fours.

14 Fours join fours to make eight. Experiment with possibilities.

The new formation of the square is exploited with the help of strategic questions by the teacher and sharing experiences. Names are given to the new dances.

15 Working with fixed and changing relationships.	Visiting couple figures and the other variations of simple squares are introduced in traditional ways, but the children add these new figures to what they have to create new dances. Home position and partner changes are added, along with such figures as split the ring, ladies chains, and Texas star.
16 Callers in sets and callers for the floor.	Interested children learn how to prompt dances by calling for their square while they are dancing. Those with special interest and talent are invited to call for the entire class.

Notes and comments. The above sequence is not a single lesson or even two. No effort should be made to arrive at the final step by a specific time. The dance lesson may include other dance problems with this one left for the end as a continuing and evolving problem. The music should be changed frequently after the first lesson so there is opportunity to strenghten recognition of the beat. As the structure of square dance evolves, boys and girls will find great delight in learning new figures and incorporating them in new ways into their own squares. Most of the time, the children will be dancing to their own set callers, but there is certainly nothing wrong with using conventional square dance if that is the experience the children crave most. Having experienced the development of square-dance structure, they can now learn new dances easily and, if they want to, change the figures to suit themselves.

Creating "folk" dances

The problem with many folk dances that are attempted with children is that the children are just not ready to manage so many complicated directions. There are formations, movement with changes in direction, changes in steps, and special relationships with people. In addition, all of this must be done in time to the music. The embarrassment that follows errors or a lapse of memory can make dance an enemy for life, and the teacher who foisted the activity on the unsuspecting learner is not to be trusted again so readily. "I thought you said that was going to be fun."

Many simple folk dances require dancers to do one thing for the first part of the music (A part) and something different for the second part (B part). A simple sequence building up to a folk dance may go like this.

1 Travel about by yourself and stay in time to the music.	The most important first step is familiarization.
2 Let's perform two different actions, one to the first part of the music (A music) and one to the second part (B music).	Solutions may be clapping to the first part and walking to the second; alternating skipping and walking or jumping and turning.
3 Let's find a friend and do it together.	Partner relationships are introduced, with steps that lead to each partner performing the other's sequence alternately.

4 In the middle of the *A* music and in the middle of the *B* music we can change and travel in a different direction.

The simple change of direction eventually leads to changing the direction of a circle which can be developed into circling left and right with a partner in a slow two-hand swing.

5 Variations in partner relationships, foot patterns, or directions of travel may be explored.

Folk dances have many possibilities for variation. Some music will suggest footwork, some clapping patterns. Other music may be more spatially oriented, with meeting and parting or changing directions.

Notes and comments. Folk dancing is fun for those who can manage the variables. Children can be taught to create their own versions from scratch or to adjust existing patterns to suit themselves. Efforts to maintain the so-called integrity of a dance is to lose the opportunity for a great deal of worthwhile learning. Folk dancing will mean much more to children later, when their understandings of the cultures that originated the dances are mixed with their understandings of dance structure. The challenge of adding to their skills is more apt to be met with enthusiasm if their memories of previous involvement are happy ones.

Round dance, anyone?

During the past twenty years or so, coinciding with the growth of the western-style square-dance club, there has been a surge of interest in couple dances called round dances. They were originally included in square-dance programs as a change from squares and as a way of satisfying dancers who liked to waltz, two-step, or polka. The patterns are a cross between ballroom dancing and folk dances.

The teacher interested in teaching round dances must first learn round dancing well enough to understand the additional relationship possibilities; the variations of steps; and the syncopated beat in relation to steps, body movements, and gestures. The same pattern of starting simply and gradually adding variables to the tasks that lead the learner into round dance may be practiced.

Notes and comments. Children become quite sophisticated in their techniques and will utilize concepts learned in one area quite readily in the next area. As a result, there will be much time saved as the sequence of steps is shortened by virtue of children's readiness to accept new and more complicated tasks. The joy of creating is evident no matter what the level of sophistication, as long as one has the knowledge, enjoys the relationships with peers and teacher, and feels comfortable in the physical surroundings. Good music helps and should be secured.

There are many approaches to teaching structured forms. No one way is superior. Adapting dance structures to problem solving within reach of the ability of the learner results in less risk of failure and more chance of success. The outcomes are happier children and better dancers. The problem-solving method scores on three major points: (1) it attains cognitive objectives, (2) it attains psychomotor objectives, and (3) it attains affective objectives.

Dance and dancing	■ This chapter closes with a quotation from Ruth L. Murray: "A dance is movement put into rhythmic and spatial form, a succession of movements which start, proceed, and finish."[27]

To distinguish dancelike movements from dancing, the interpretation given by Murray "is one that emphasizes not only body mastery and discipline in movement but even more the use of such movement for expressive and imaginative purposes."[28]

There is a dire need for physical educators to take up the challenge and include dance as sequentially planned movement learning experiences in physical education from the earliest age on.

Hints to teachers of beginning dance	■ Teachers of dance must be free of inhibitions to movement. They must be able to open up, share, and react empathetically and sympathetically to the behaviors of children. Although basic movement education requires teachers to be free and open, dance requires a greater intensity of free involvement in the emotional overtones of actions. To become a teacher of dance in physical education, the teacher or student should:

1 Get rid of any feelings that dance is for the nonathlete or the sissy. A lot of important sports figures have become dancers, former boxer Sugar Ray Robinson for one. Research the lives of others and find out what made them change or why some have been involved in dance all along.

2 Plan a simple course of self-tuition in dance by reading, listening to dance music, going to the theater, and watching televised dance, particularly on the educational channels. Not all of the dance will be interesting or even good dance. Experience will bring about greater selectivity. Even "Soul Train" has something worthwhile to offer the observer.

3 Gain experience in dance by taking dance classes, joining a dance club at the "Y" or community center, or turning on the record player and practicing privately.

4 Get used to moving without musical accompaniment; utilize free rhythms by experimenting, privately if necessary, with variations of action or idea themes; or join a group that is interested in such activities.

5 Teach a dance lesson to a group of young children. This may be an exploratory lesson that focuses on an action theme with emotional elements as subthemes:

Jumps in surprise
Frightened runs
Careful steps
Timid shapes

It may be a group activity, such as a very simple circle dance in which the children follow the lead of a person in the middle. Playparty

27 Ibid., p. 6.
28 Ibid., p. 7.

dances may be used to gain this kind of experience or emotional elements may be added to explorations of different locomotor patterns or gestures. The latter is a more satisfactory means of getting into dance, but not everyone can take the same beginning steps.

6 Gradually increase the number and variety of dance lessons until a comfortable feeling of competence begins to emerge.

7 Teach a portion of a dance lesson to older children, being careful to select themes familiar to the children; i.e., explore the effects of losing or winning the championship on the movement patterns of spectators, cheerleaders, coaches, and players. The lead into dance may be through exercises that are performed to drumbeats and given an emotional flavor; for example, lively rebounds contrasted with unenergetic work, or very controlled movements contrasted with very sloppy movements. Or it may all begin with running to a drumbeat, changing tempo, directions, and relationships to others with as much exploration and improvisation as possible. Add various kinds of music. Let the children select some of their own music. Be careful not to call the lessons dance if you think the term may have the wrong connotation for the children. Let it be exercise to music, a form of aerobic movement sequences, or some other term.

Assignments

1
Teach one or more lessons in educational dance to elementary schoolchildren. Note the results of each lesson and make comments regarding the readiness of the children either to go on to a different theme or to continue exploring the possibilities of the same themes.
2
Visit an elementary school and discuss the dance program with the physical education teacher. Share the findings with classmates, and summarize the results of all findings with recommendations for change if such is necessary.

3
Select a familiar square dance and teach it to the class with as much problem solving as feasible.
4
Select a dance, such as the Highland Fling, with emphasis on footwork; explore the possibilities for hand-clapping and slapping patterns instead. Add directional actions of the body or body parts. Explore additional possibilities.

5
Prepare one unit on educational dance and another unit on square, folk, or round dancing. Write a rationale for the program objectives selected for each program. Suggest themes or appropriate activities and progressions.
6
Prepare a program in creative rhythmic dance (movement) to enhance the above unit in educational dance. Suggest ways in which props and/or costumes may be used. Incorporate a relationship to some other discipline with at least one of the objectives. Write a rationale for the program.

Readings

AAHPER. *Children's Dance.* Dance Division Task Force, Gladys Andrews Fleming, ed. Washington, D.C.: AAHPER Press, 1973.

Boorman, Joyce. *Dance and Language Experiences with Children.* Don Mills, Ont.: Longman Canada Limited, 1973.

———. *Creative Dance in the First Three Grades.* New York: McKay, 1969.

———. *Creative Dance in Grades Four to Six.* Don Mills, Ont.: Longman Canada, 1971.

Canner, Norma. *. . . and a time to dance.* 2d ed. Boston: Plays, Inc., 1975.

Carroll, Jean, and Lofthouse, Peter. *Creative Dance for Boys.* London: MacDonald & Evans, 1969.

Collins, Claudette. *Practical Modern Educational Dance.* London: MacDonald & Evans, 1969.

Dimondstein, Geraldine. *Children Dance in the Classroom.* New York: Macmillan, 1971.

Exiner, Johanna, and Lloyd, Phyllis. *Teaching Creative Movement.* Boston: Plays, Inc., 1974.

Fleming, Gladys Andrews. *Creative Rhythmic Movement.* Englewood Cliffs, N.J.: Prentice-Hall, 1976.

Goodridge, Janet. *Creative Drama and Improvised Movement for Children.* Boston: Plays, Inc., 1970.

Gray, Vera, and Percival, Rachel. *Music, Movement, and Mime for Children*. London: Oxford University Press, 1962.

Joyce, Mary. *First Steps in Teaching Creative Dance*. Palo Alto, Calif.: National Press Books, 1973.

Kulbitsky, Olga, and Kaltman, Frank L. *Teachers Dance Handbook*. Newark, N.J.: Bluebird Publishing Company, 1959.

Laban, Rudolf. *Modern Educational Dance*. 3d ed. London: MacDonald & Evans, 1975.

Lowndes, Betty. *Movement and Creative Drama for Children*. Boston: Plays, Inc., 1971.

Murray, Ruth Lovell. *Dance in Elementary Education*. 2d ed. New York: Harper & Row, 1963.

Nichols, Bronwen. *Move*. Boston: Plays, Inc., 1975.

Russell, Joan. *Creative Dance in the Primary School*. London: MacDonald & Evans, 1965.

———. *Creative Movement and Dance for Children*. Boston: Plays, Inc., 1975.

———. *Modern Dance in Education*. London: MacDonald & Evans, 1958.

Stanley, Sheila. *Physical Education: A Movement Orientation*. Toronto: McGraw-Hill Company of Canada, 1969.

Taylor, Carla. *Rhythm, A Guide for Creative Movement*. Palo Alto, Calif.: Peek Publications, 1974.

Winters, Shirley J. *Creative Rhythmic Movement*. Dubuque, Iowa: Wm. C. Brown, 1975.

Chapter XV

Goals
and the
curriculum

The stronger the profession is in terms
of the results of its programs,
the less likely it is to be buffeted
by the winds of educational philosophy
or economic change.

Daryl Siedentop
Physical Education Introductory Analysis, p. 230

■ Siedentop is saying in the vernacular, "Physical educators! Let's get on the stick. Let's get the job done that needs doing." You might ask, "What is the job?" One factor Siedentop sees as influencing the future of physical education, "and the one that we can do most about," is to improve "the quality of physical education programs."[1]

A fundamental obstacle to change in the teaching of physical education is the fuzziness with which individual teachers describe the purposes of their programs. Having been graduated themselves from secondary physical education programs based on a "roll-out-the-ball" philosophy, these teachers have difficulty constructing a meaningful framework for their own ideas, the ones that will determine so much of what they will do when it is their turn to teach.

The purpose of this chapter is to clarify the purposes of physical education. At the risk of seeming to give teachers a pat answer to the many unique challenges they will face in their own situations, we offer a curriculum guide for an elementary school physical education program in Appendix A. We have included there the goal statements that we hope will tie the objectives of physical education more clearly to the objectives of the total educational effort and thereby contribute to achievement of its purpose.

---

1 Daryl Siedentop, *Physical Education Introductory Analysis* (Dubuque, Iowa: Wm. C. Brown, 1972), p. 229.

Concerning physical education, Oberteuffer and Ulrich write:

> It seeks to advance and enrich man's culture, foster his best interests, and contribute significantly to his own personal growth through participation in activities which are purposefully selected and carefully taught to provide the desired outcomes.[2]

Desired outcomes are those behaviors children have learned as the result of successful instruction. Undesired outcomes are behaviors that learners sometimes exhibit as a result of some deficiency in the instructor's techniques, teaching strategies, or other factors over which the instructor exercises some control. In any case, the physical education program is evaluated by the quality of its end product, the outcomes it produces in the learners.

Objectives should be selected on the basis of desired end products or behavioral outcomes rather than from a list of teacher objectives that are still confused with learner outcomes. The point is best made by comparing these two objectives.

Objective 1: To teach students how to work cooperatively.

Objective 2: Students will demonstrate cooperative behavior.

Objective 1 describes what the teacher will teach. Goals such as participation in basketball, games of low organization, or relays could be substituted for working cooperatively in Objective 1, and it would still be a teacher objective. There are many such objectives to be found in teachers' lesson plans. Teachers have even been known to argue that there must be something wrong with students who do not learn because, as they put it, the material has been covered. The fault must lie in the student.

Objective 2 indicates, however generally, that the objective is only achieved when students behave in the specified manner. A desirable outcome of instruction is described; the students demonstrate cooperation by behaving in cooperative ways. By describing the circumstances under which students will exhibit such behavior, it is possible to know where or when to look for evidence of learning.

- In relationships with peers and authority figures in the school
- In the classroom
- In physical education classes
- In situations that require team effort to achieve a common goal
- In situations in which individuals must set aside personal ambition for the good of the group.

Assuming that teachers recognize cooperative behavior and make note of its occurrence, the statement of circumstances under which the behavior is to occur amends the original statement and points teachers in the right direction. Now the teacher is left with one decision regarding the evidence of behavior. Is the observed behavior qualitatively or quantitatively good enough to deserve a passing grade; that is, does it meet or go

2 Delbert Oberteuffer and Celeste Ulrich, *Physical Education,* 3d ed. (New York: Harper & Row, 1962), p. 2.

Student-teacher
relationship

Achieving behavioral
outcomes

beyond the minimum standard of acceptability? If the answer is "yes," the learner is credited in some fashion; if it is "no," credit is withheld. Helping the learner achieve the objective is what teaching is all about. The clearer the statement of objectives, the greater the chance that everyone involved, students and teacher, will pull together to achieve the purpose of the activity. Thinking in terms of behavioral outcomes rather than teacher objectives helps teachers know what to teach and how to teach because the proof of the teachers' effectiveness rests on the achievements of the students.

Poor student performance does not automatically disqualify the teacher. Teacher expectations or program objectives may be unrealistic in the first place. Changes will have to be made in the course of instruction before those outcomes are sought again. Instructors must continually revise content, method, and program organization to improve the quality of instruction.

Consider the kindergarten teacher or the physical education teacher of kindergarten children whose objective is securing cooperative student behavior. Among the objectives for the year, the teacher has listed the ability of the children to work and play in a cooperative manner. As evidence that children have learned to cooperate, the teacher then lists the following behaviors and circumstances.

To demonstrate their growth in cooperative behavior, the children will be able to do the following:
1 Perform routine tasks without any fuss.
2 Put materials in their proper places when finished with them.

Goals and the
curriculum

3 Hang outer clothing up before going to assigned places without having to be reminded.
4 Share the use of playthings with others.
5 Willingly change activities when asked to by the teacher.
6 Assist others in cleaning up and putting things away.

If any of these statements needs clarification, such as examples of "routine tasks," details may be added. When the teacher is satisfied with the list, the criteria for determining successful performance must be chosen. The instructor must answer two questions about performance standards.

1 How well must each individual behave, or in what specific manner, before credit for behaving cooperatively will be given?
2 What percentage of the class must learn to behave cooperatively before the class as a whole may be said to have met the standard of acceptability?

In answer to the first question, the teacher may accept "most of the time" or "about 75 percent" as evidence of learning, if 100 percent is unrealistic. The 75 percent figure may be used again in answer to question 2 for the same reason. It may be too much to expect that every child, regardless of personal circumstances, will behave cooperatively 100 percent of the time. Of course, if the performance standard is too low, the teacher will have to raise it, or the school principal may have something to say about the situation. To bring the class up to standard, the teacher will focus instructional tactics on the attainment of the objectives and will praise every child who cooperates as a means of rewarding the child as well as a way of teaching the meaning of cooperation and encouraging others to perform in a like manner.

Stated as a program objective for the first half of the year, the program objective of cooperative behavior may be worded somewhat more broadly.

By the end of the first half of the school year, children should demonstrate a cooperative attitude toward the teacher, their classmates, and the instructional program.

Program objectives identify long-range outcomes of instruction; they are not written for the moment of instruction. Performance or instructional objectives specify more exactly what the students will do to indicate that they have learned. A set of performance objectives is needed for each program objective. Together they describe the behaviors that signify achievement. It takes observable evidence, not all of which is easy to measure.

The rationale for objectives

■ As teachers probe deeper into the purposes for selecting program and performance objectives, they discover the rationale for their selections. Sometimes the rationale is superficial, sometimes obscure, sometimes perfectly clear and acceptable to others, students included.

A rationale should justify the teaching of concepts and skills, that is, justify requiring students to learn them. Put in this context, the rationale for all objectives, from the goals of the school system itself to one of several objectives sought by the class in a single day's work, clarifies why a rationale is valuable. Written statements of rationale are best, of course. Set down on paper, the words stand boldly for examination. Written clearly, they point the way for instructors. A clear statement of rationale helps others, including the learners, understand why the objectives are important.

The choice of rationale for unit level program objectives and specification of instructional outcomes is up to the teacher. Note the variety of expression in the following rationales that may underlie a single program objective.

Program objective: To improve children's awareness of their bodies.
Rationale statements:
Awareness of the body and its parts in motion and at rest is fundamental to learning.
or
Being able to recognize and identify body parts is important to the development of a movement vocabulary.
or
The achievement of mastery over one's body begins with awareness of the most fundamental states, those of motion and stillness.
or
Future skill building lessons will be more satisfying to learners if they have previously acquired the essential body awareness and terminology.
or
The development of the body as an instrument for movement begins with basic awareness of what the body and its parts are doing in a wide range of environmental encounters.
or
Exploration and discovery learning about what the body is doing is made meaningful when the child can verbalize fundamental actions and correctly identify the body parts involved.

Children need to
know the purpose
of the lesson.

Goals and the
curriculum

It is not necessary to write a rationale for every objective. Objectives are easily grouped and covered by one statement. Perhaps the most significant occasion for making a statement of rationale is for the class that is expected to pursue a given set of objectives. Explaining what the lesson is about and *why* covers the matter of rationale for the learners. They now understand the purpose of the lesson. Unfortunately, many teachers fail to inform their students why they are being asked to pursue a particular course of instruction.

Objectives lead to the attainment of goals

■ The physical education curriculum that purports to include movement education consists of two learning tracks, so identified for the convenience of instructional planning, since each seeks the attainment of objectives that differ in purpose. The developmental track contains as many subdivisions as the school system can afford in time, money, personnel, and facilities. For convenience again, this track is divided into four major program areas: games, sports, and contests (competitive activities), gymnastics, dance, and aquatics. Each has its own program objectives.

The basic movement track has its own objectives for activities occurring in a variety of environments, identified generally as floor, rhythmic, apparatus, and manipulative environments. These four environments are singled out as a means of enriching the learning situation rather than as separate programs.

These instructional programs exist for one purpose: as a means for achieving the goals of the physical education curriculum. Goals are major objectives, and goal statements describe long-range outcomes of instruction to which program objectives are responsive. To assure compatibility of purposes, the goals of physical education must in turn reflect the goals of education in general. Before planning objectives for a course of study, it is helpful to have a statement of the goals of the curriculum for guidance.

Assuming that some statement of educational goals exists, the school system is organized to carry out those goals, from the superintendent of schools to the classroom teacher. At least, that is the way the system should work. The managers of the instructional system are arranged in a hierarchy of different operational levels, each with its unique function, performance commitment, and statement of purpose.

Since schools exist to achieve the purposes of society, the goals of society determine what is important and, therefore, what the schools should achieve. Education is supposed to bring about behavioral changes in learners that make it possible for individuals to function as responsible and able citizens in a democratic society. The values of society are expressed as organizational goals by the board of education, which directs what the community will do to attain the goals of society.

The superintendent responds to the board's statements with written administrative regulations that implement the organizational goals. He indicates the kinds of programs needed to achieve them. Curriculum experts develop and administer the programs, and among those experts is a director of physical education.

It is the director of physical education who writes goal statements for the physical education curriculum and all of its subdivisions. He usually requires help from specialists on his own staff or from outside consultants. Program objectives are written first for each of the four major programs—games, gymnastics, dance and aquatics. The objectives for program subdivisions are specified, right down to the instructional level. At this point, the teacher takes over and decides on the instructional units needed to carry out the program objectives. Where there was systemwide uniformity of objectives, there is now individualization of the program school by school, as teachers interpret objectives in light of the unique attributes of the school, the students, and themselves. Instructional objectives are individualized to meet the needs of the learners, so there is even greater divergence at the instructional level. Nevertheless, if properly managed, all individual routes lead to the same desired outcomes.

Although most school systems are organized along lines similar to those shown in figure 15.1 and figure 15.2, it is not often that one finds performance expectations at each level spelled out quite so explicitly. Physical education teachers often are not given lists of well thought-out program objectives. They make up their own program objectives, a fact that is easily confirmed by visiting different schools within a system. The lack of agreement between neighboring schools or different schools that feed the same junior high school about the objectives of elementary school physical education is appalling. Consequently, the children suffer, and they sometimes consider themselves cheated of a proper foundation in physical education. "All we did was play games. No one taught us how to play or how to do anything else," is too often the lament of the educationally deprived student who keenly feels the problem when he competes for a place on the school team. The so-called natural athlete or the go-getter eventually closes the gap and succeeds in spite of his poor physical education. The same cannot be said for other children.

The long-term remedy for inadequate physical education is better administration and adequate statements of goals and objectives. Boards of education must be willing to formulate organizational goals and to accept expert advice and assistance in this task. Their concept of what local society wants should be clearly spelled out and, if necessary, approved by the citizens. With good leadership, those at lower operational levels will understand clearly their responsibilities. In time, good programs will develop out of their collective commitment to implementation of agreed-upon goals of education and physical education.

In the absence of leadership, teachers must make program decisions based on assumed goals. To strengthen their assumptions, they should learn about and keep in mind the chain of objectives and goals running from the instructional to the societal level. Working together, teachers can pool their expertise and design programs that will be accepted by those in middle management—the principals and supervisors. Program acceptance will gradually orient the school system toward the development of a behavioral-outcomes approach to physical education.

Fig. 15.1 The hierarchical commitment of performance by each operational level of an organization*

I Society
  Performance Commitment: Cultural values and educational beliefs
  Unique Function: Makes the ultimate decision concerning the purpose of education.
  Statement of Purpose: Goals of society.

II Board of Education (Board of Directors)
  Performance Commitment: To attain the goals of society.
  Unique Function: Formulates the purpose of the organization.
  Statement of Purpose: Organizational goals.

III Superintendent (President)
  Performance Commitment: To implement the policy organizational goals of the board.
  Unique Function: Formulates the procedures of the organization.
  Statement of Purpose: Superintendent's regulations.

IV Middle Managers (Administrative Council)
  Performance Commitment: To implement the regulations of the superintendent.
  Unique Function: Identify the methods and means of achieving the program objectives.
  Statement of Purpose: Program objectives for courses of study.

V Curriculum Manager (sic Teacher)
  Performance Commitment: To implement the program objectives.
  Unique Function: Identify the methods and means of achieving the program objectives.
  Statement of Purpose: Program objectives for units of study.
  Performance objectives for daily lessons.

---

* John McManama, *Systems Analysis for Effective School Administration* (West Nyack, N.Y.: Parker, 1971), pp. 64-65.

Good elementary school physical education programs eventually force junior high school programs to change. Pressure for change is most effective when it comes from students and their parents who feel cheated by inferior programs. In defense of beleaguered junior and senior high school physical education teachers, we must say that many of them do a superb job under difficult, and often trying, circumstances. After all, they can do only so much with students who come to them with poorly developed skills and negative attitudes. It is almost too late for most students to change attitudes and habits acquired over years of poor teaching or of no physical education at all. However, the handwriting is on the wall; it says that communities are rapidly getting tired of paying high salaries to overpriced recreation leaders when the contracts call for teachers.

There are good teachers everywhere, and a certain number of undergraduates each year are destined to join the fight for better physical education. To them, the following steps in the specification of objectives from societal goals to teacher performance are the first steps in creating a blueprint for change.

Fig. 15.2 The system of links between goals and performance

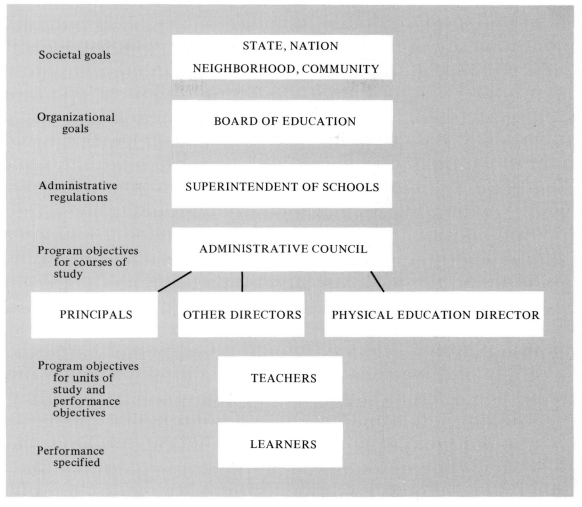

1 Educational goals are dictated by the cultural values of a society. The board of education should write organizational goals based on cultural values they consider relevant.

2 Organizational goals are descriptions of what should be done to achieve the goals of society. They serve as guidelines in decision making at lower organizational levels and as guidelines to evaluation for those who write them.

3 Goals for curriculum may be called *terminal objectives*. They describe the projected behavioral outcomes of complete courses of instruction. Curriculum goals are written for physical education, just as they are for mathematics, history, language arts, and other subject areas.

4 Each goal or set of goals should be accompanied by a rationale that explains why the goals are important. This procedure should be followed even in the writing of instructional objectives. All goal state-

Steps in the specification of physical education, objectives

ments should also be accompanied by organizational statements describing how these goals are to be achieved.

5 Administrative regulations are written to implement organizational goals. These are the policies and procedures that govern the conduct of programs and staff.

6 Program objectives are written for education in basic movement and in the major program areas of developmental movement—games, sports, and contests; gymnastics; dance; and aquatics.

7 Program objectives are written for each of the subdivisions of the major program areas, for example, folk dance, rhythmic gymnastics, and diving. These usually are cast in the form of a course of study so that there is continuity from the introduction of the content to its highest development. Each instructional level contributes program objectives consistent with the developmental needs and interests of the learner and the hierarchical progression from simple to complex. These objectives are usually written by those with expertise in the subject, who could be the director, supervisors, consultants, or teachers. Administrative regulations are written to support these program objectives.

8 The teacher writes objectives for each unit within a course of study or selects unit program objectives prepared by experts. Recognizing that *course objectives may be achieved by different means,* it is often best to leave to the teacher the selection of those alternatives that are most feasible.

9 The teacher writes, or selects from a prepared list the performance objectives that collectively describe the outcomes of instruction called for in the unit level program objectives.

10 The teacher determines the instructional tactics and evaluative criteria to be used in guiding learners in a series of well-defined steps from their present level of competence toward the achievement of program objectives.

Derivation of objectives

■ Objectives are derived from three sources: the learner, society, and the subject.[3] Each of these sources contributes as follows to the formulation of objectives.

The learner

The gap between a learner's present ability and the desired behavioral standard represents the learner's need. As perceived by learners, the gap is between what they think their present abilities are and the level they aspire to achieve. Expressed another way, learners' needs are the difference between where they are and where they want to go educationally. Teachers perceive these gaps differently. Their perception of need is influenced by their knowledge of children and of human growth and development. They are in a position to assess accurately the present condition and the desirable state for a given learner. They know that if certain needs are not

3 Ralph W. Tyler, *Basic Principles of Curriculum and Instruction* (Chicago: University of Chicago Press, 1971), pp. 3-33.

met immediately, the gap between what learners think they can do and what they actually can do will widen, and their problem will be further complicated by their entry into the next developmental stage with its special pressures and challenges.

The successful teacher is one who effects a compromise with students by openly inviting discussion of their needs and helping them reach a more realistic understanding of themselves with the assurance that the teacher will help them achieve any reasonable personal goals they may have. If teachers paid more attention to student needs, they would become more attuned than many teachers are to the selection of alternative instructional objectives that lead students to desired goal states as well or even better than other objectives they might have selected.

Society

A broad concept of society includes the peer group along with the neighborhood and the larger community as a social force that has certain expectations of its membership. Many physical education teachers have ignored peer group pressures, particularly those at variance with the teacher's objectives, and they have paid the price. They found sudden loss of interest in their programs, a turning away from their leadership, and in some places vandalism of physical education equipment and facilities. In pushing too hard for short-range achievement, they lost sight of relevant social goals.

Growing consideration
for the rights of others

Playing as learning

Society at large also has goals that must be considered early in the child's instructional program if the desired attitudes are to be attained. Developing behaviors that show consideration for the rights of others, good humored toleration of individual differences, fair play, justice for all, and acceptance of social obligations imposed on members by a democracy is daily contribution that can be made in physical education to citizenship training long before children reach high school civics classes. Affective behavioral objectives that support long-range societal goals must be included in the cognitive and psychomotor objectives of physical education from the first lesson through all succeeding phases of instruction if students are to make systematic progress in the attainment of these goals.

Sometimes there are formal statements of societal beliefs, such as the one given in the introduction to the curriculum in appendix A. Other beliefs must be deduced by the teacher in interaction with children, parents, and ordinary citizens whose behaviors reflect the value premises of the more immediate community and neighborhood. It is a good idea to stay "tuned in" to people; otherwise one must suffer the indignity of being "tuned out."

The subject

The most common source for objectives is the subject being studied. There is no universally accepted body of knowledge for physical education, but the literature reports that efforts to unify the field in the past ten years and dialogue today are on the increase. Physical education is many subjects, any one of which is rich in content, so there should be no real obstacles to teaching, even while the philosophical debate rages on. Activity courses are not apt to be seriously affected, except in gymnastics, dance, and movement education. Because of their affinity for thematic development, the objectives in these pursuits are still under debate. There are questions also about games and the place of adultlike, varsity-type sports in elementary school physical education. The teacher can only take a stand and choose a direction.

In addition to the many books on sports, dance, and other activities in physical education, many others have been written on principles and laws of movement, physiological factors in exercise, growth, and development, and nutrition. Understanding the "why" of the body and movement is as important as understanding the "what." Laban's vocabulary of basic movement education and description of movement and motion factor principles offer a language that communicates clearly with learners and teachers alike. His work makes analysis of movement immediately available to almost the youngest child, at least as early as the development of descriptive language in early childhood. Teachers of preschoolers can attest to that.

Perhaps the richest source of physical education objectives outside of conventional publishers is the American Alliance for Health, Physical Education, and Recreation. Its monthly journal and publications provide up-to-date information and innovative ideas for all program content areas. The

Alliance also makes available the latest research results relevant to physical education.

A physical education teacher should never be at a loss for resources from which to derive and formulate objectives. However, there are other factors to consider in the process of selecting objectives.

■ Three main factors influence the selection of objectives. They are the philosophical, the psychological, and the environmental considerations of which the curriculum writer is aware, a circumstance that is obviously the result of previous experience and training.[4]

Philosophical considerations determine the value premises upon which selection is based. The teacher who is concerned about affective behaviors will consider the inclusion of objectives that fall in this domain. Attentiveness, commitment to respond, attitudes, and valuing behaviors will serve as sources for objectives. Consciously or unconsciously, however, the teacher or administrator screens out at first glance objectives on any list that are based on conflicting values. This screening process continues right up to the selection of the final list of objectives, and the end product is sometimes a powerful description of the curriculum writer's philosophy of education.

Teachers who undertake to teach children from different socioeconomic and ethnic backgrounds than their own discover that their objectives are at odds with the students' own values. Developing a rationale for these objectives in the face of passive or active opposition will clarify the teachers' points of view, although the teachers' superiors and the parents and children may not accept them. To achieve equilibrium, teachers often need to adopt philosophical positions that are relatively consistent with the values expressed by the goals of the schools in which they are teaching.

Psychological factors are those related to the condition of the learners. Objectives must be appropriate to the readiness level of each learner and consonant with the knowledge of the children's characteristics. Some children are slow learners, some are late in maturing. Some show development in a few areas but not in others. There are those who work well together, pay attention, cooperate, and demonstrate a sense of responsibility. Considering the learners, the teacher must decide which objectives on the list are feasible. The teacher watches and talks with the children to learn about their needs, interests, and abilities. This information may screen out a number of objectives that looked good at first.

The variety of individual characteristics among children should not be considered a serious constraint in an individualized, movement-oriented physical education program. Task-oriented, problem-solving movement experiences do not produce a single right answer anyway. Students' maturity, attentiveness, and task perseverance are much more likely reasons for rejecting objectives than the children's physical abilities. Only when highly specific motor patterns are to be developed do motor ability, strength, and other physical factors make a difference. This is illustrated by the experi-

Factors affecting the selection of objectives

4 Ibid., pp. 33-43.

Goals and the curriculum

ence of one teacher who elected to have the class play softball only to discover that no one could either pitch or catch well enough to play an infield
position.

The importance of
self-initiated tasks

Broadening their
experiences

Making use of
junk equipment

Environmental factors are important in the selection of physical education objectives. Features of the spatial environment, its size, shape, availability of apparatus, and, if outdoors, the texture of the ground and the topography either permit or restrain inclusion of certain objectives. Some schools have no gymnasiums. In others, the floors may be cold, dirty, or warped. The ceilings may be low, the windows unprotected, the fans noisy. Physical educators learn to adjust to all kinds of environmental circumstances and to adapt activities if the objectives cannot be attained any other way. No beginning teacher should reject a position simply because the facilities would severely limit the physical education curriculum. The objectives of physical education can still be met by resourceful and inventive teachers. Being handicapped by poor facilities sometimes offers the best training there is.

■ Writing goal statements for football, basketball, or swimming poses few problems, particularly at the varsity level. The aim is to win, of course, and in the process of winning to succeed as players and as coaches, and as a school. Of course, being easy to identify does not make these goals easy to achieve. Consider, however, a program of a different sort, that of basic movement education. What are its goals? How might those goals be measured?

Goal statements

Goals for basic movement education

Unlike varsity sports and lower level skills programs, basic movement education is not easily analyzed statistically. There are no winning and losing percentages, no measurable times and distances, no value judgments to be exercised by panels of experts applying strict performance criteria. Yet basic movement education has goals, and the criteria for determining goal attainment will surely be found once guidelines for evaluation have been chosen. The following goal statements for basic movement education were derived loosely from ideas expressed by McManama in connection with a hypothetical school math program.[5] Some goals are labeled product goals, while others are labeled process goals. Still others are combinations of the two. Product goals refer to the end product of instruction. Evaluation takes place at the end of the course. Process goals are evaluated while the course is in progress. We have included tentative guidelines for evaluating these goals, but field-testing still is required. The goals also are offered to stimulate discussion and research.

Goal 1 (Product goal)

All students should acquire basic movement competency as the essential ingredient in both the instrumental and expressive functions of the body.

5 John McManama, *Systems Analysis for Effective School Administration* (West Nyack, N.Y.: Parker, 1971), pp. 91-92.

Goals and the curriculum

479

Guidelines for evaluation

1 Determine which operational skills are essential to the movement life of a healthy, fully functioning human being.

2 Identify those movement priorities in both objective and expressive functioning that will further abilities best allocated to the elementary grades in the psychological, physical, social, and intellectual development of the child.

3 Prepare a list of characteristics associated with the identified abilities that can be observed and recorded as not present, or strongly present.

4 Apply these criteria of abilities in a series of planned observations of sixth grade elementary schoolchildren who have had a minimum of five years experience in basic movement education to determine the degree to which the identified abilities are present and to compare them with a sample of scores of children with no basic movement education background.

Goal 2 (Process goal)

The major concepts of basic movement should be learned in a sequence related to the maturational and developmental needs and interests of children.

Guidelines for evaluation

1 Order the major concepts of basic movement and relate them to the activities engaged in by children at play in the early primary, middle, and upper elementary school years.

2 Illustrate the major concepts for teachers and describe what is meant by relating them to developmental skills and activities in physical education.

3 Supervise the teaching to determine if concepts are being taught properly.

Goal 3 (Product and process goal)

A functional and meaningful movement vocabulary should be acquired and applied in the solution of movement problems.

Guidelines for evaluation

1 Identify the sequence of steps and alternatives utilized in movement problem solving and the appropriate vocabulary associated with each step.

2 Observe a random sample of children in each of several grades engaged in movement problem solving to determine if they are applying movement vocabulary in the solution of movement problems.

Goal 4 (Process goal)

The concept of motion factors that make up the movement vocabulary should be interwoven with the acquisition of new skills and extended through involvement with different environmental stimuli.

Guidelines for evaluation

1 Describe and illustrate for teachers what is meant by interweaving skills with concepts that help learners cope with environmental changes affecting the application of skills.

2 Supervise the teaching to determine if concepts are being taught properly.

3 Question a random sample of upper elementary schoolchildren during skill learning and practice to determine their ability to apply concepts to skill refinement and to the correction of errors.

Goal 5 (Process goal)

Creative and independent thinking should be developed through discovery.

Guidelines for evaluation

1 Describe and illustrate for teachers what is meant by instruction in movement education that is conducive to discovery.

2 Supervise the teaching to determine if concepts are being taught properly.

3 Observe children's task behaviors for evidence of creative problem solving and independent thinking.

Goal 6 (Process goal)

The concepts of space, effort, and relationship and the sequence of patterns underlying movement competency should not be abandoned as goals if certain learners are slow to discover them on their own. Directed teaching should assure that these goals are attained.

Guidelines for evaluation

1 Establish a diagnostic measure of movement skills and concept understanding. (This measure should be available as part of the statement of performance objectives.)

2 Establish a time standard for each major learning goal beyond which directed teaching will be undertaken to assure mastery.

3 Supervise the evaluation of progress to assure that this standard is being observed.

Goals for public education

Goals are broad statements of purpose. They stand at some distant point from the present situation but indicate the direction that should be taken. McManama reports on the six educational goals selected by the state of Texas as a clear example of how societal goals expressing the educational values held by society may be stated.[6]

1 Intellectual discipline
2 Economic and vocational competence

3 Citizenship and civic responsibility
4 Competence in human and social relations
5 Moral and ethical values
6 Self-realization and mental and physical health

Although the reader may think that physical health is the only goal to which physical education contributes, the fact is that physical education can contribute significantly to each of these educational goals. Statements of societal goals require proper formulation, according to McManama.[7]

1 The purpose toward which the commitment is made should be clearly stated.
2 The statement should have relevance for performance.
3 The statement should not prescribe methods or means by which the goal is to be attained. (An exception would be process goals.)

Educational institutions are organizations dedicated to the achievement of societal goals. "The essential role of an organization is to provide the management control necessary to attain societal goals."[8] By providing for the expansion of each goal statement, the specifics of accomplishment are described. An accompanying statement of rationale explains why it is desirable to have the goals.

McManama describes two process goals that, when included in a statement of goals, commits the institution to valuing ongoing behavior as well as terminal behavior. These two goals are important to physical education.

1 Each learner is a unique person. Programs should be established which take individual differences into account.
2 Learning how to learn may be as important as the learning itself.[9]

Using the goals for public education in Texas stated earlier and the expanded statements describing what the schools should do to attain those goals, the Farmington, Connecticut, Board of Education adopted a statement of educational goals in June 1970. This statement was accompanied by a description of what the public schools should do to accomplish the goals and was further supported by a complete list of superintendent's regulations.[10]

As an extension of the Farmington goal statement, we have restructured it to illustrate how a statement of goals for physical education might be written in support of goals for an entire educational system.

Goals for physical education in the public schools

Physical education as a phase of the public schools' total educational effort should contribute to the development of each child's maximum capacity to become a fully functioning person with knowledge, skills, and un-

7 Ibid.
8 Ibid.
9 Ibid., p. 67.
10 Ibid., pp. 194-97. This same statement was adapted by the authors in the following section on "Goals for Physical Education in the Public Schools."

derstandings gained through a broad program of movement learning experiences.

1.0 Physical education should foster the development of intellectual discipline.

1.1 Each youngster should acquire knowledge fundamental to basic movement education and its relationship to the development of effective, efficient, and expressive movement. These understandings should be organized and presented in a manner consistent with the developmental needs of children and with respect to their individual needs. To accomplish this, the schools should:

    1.1.1 Determine the concepts basic to the understanding of movement in a developmental curricular program, comprised of basic movement, gymnastics, dance, sports, games, contests, and personal development.

    1.1.2 Describe the major concepts and identify the performance behaviors that will indicate that the learner has learned.

    1.1.3 Develop a system of evaluation that makes it possible to determine where the learner stands before instruction, how each learner is progressing, and how well the end-of-course standards have been met.

    1.1.4 Organize an instructional system that promotes individual progress.

1.2 Each youngster should acquire the ability to solve problems related to general and specific motor learning. To assist children in achieving this goal, the schools should:

    1.2.1 Institute instructional processes that encourage learning through inquiry and problem solving.

    1.2.2 Develop procedures that make it possible for learners to establish personal objectives and evaluate their own progress.

    1.2.3 Develop procedures that make it possible for youngsters to "learn how to learn" so that they can assume responsibility for their own education.

1.3 All youngsters should have an opportunity to investigate many areas of study within the program of physical education that have relevance for them in their personal growth and development. To meet this goal, schools should:

    1.3.1 Make provisions for all youngsters to participate in programs of sports, gymnastics, and dance (and aquatics, when facilities permit) that stimulate progressive development of cognitive, affective, and psychomotor behaviors.

    1.3.2 Provide the resources and opportunities for youngsters to investigate the causal relationship between activity and factors that modify performance.

    1.3.3 Organize the curriculum in a manner that emphasizes the structure of each instructional discipline to provide organizing power for courses of study and units of learning.

2.0 Physical education should foster vocational and avocational competence.

2.1 Each school should help students develop competence in activities that lead to lifetime recreational skills:

    2.1.1 By determining the skills required by each age and sex group for peer acceptance.

    2.1.2 By promoting participation in activities that are both physically and psychologically beneficial.

    2.1.3 By permitting and promoting the use of outdoor and indoor facilities for organized and unorganized play activities before and after regular school hours.

    2.1.4 By organizing field trips to take advantage of recreational opportunities afforded by state and national parks and to engage in activities not feasible at school.

2.2 Each school should help students develop usable vocational and emergency skills:

    2.2.1 By promoting the acquisition of effective and efficient ways of handling small tools and performing tasks such as those that might be required during emergencies.

    2.2.2 By promoting work habits that lead to efficiency in the management of equipment, space, and people.

3.0 Physical education programs should encourage citizenship and civic responsibility.

3.1 Each school should provide experiences that emphasize American heritage and the responsibilities and privileges of citizenship. Physical education should:

    3.1.1 Provide opportunities for students to learn the principles of democratic society and to develop responsible social behaviors through their participation in planning, organizing, and carrying out physical education activities.

    3.1.2 Provide opportunities for youngsters to earn and to assume the responsibilities of leadership through peer group election.

    3.1.3 Function as a vital part of the school's effort to be a democratic society where students can experience both the privileges and the responsibilities of citizenship.

4.0 Physical education programs should develop competence in human and social relations.

4.1 Each school should demonstrate its concern for individuals and their need for acceptance by their peers by:

    4.1.1 Helping them recognize that other children have similar needs that must be reckoned with in planning activities geared to the needs of all.

    4.1.2 Providing opportunities and guidance for children in developing their sensitivity to others who are different, who express themselves differently, or who have aspirations different from their own.

4.2 Each school should develop in students respect for the rights of others and understanding of their responsibility to society. To help students achieve their goals, the physical education program should:

    4.2.1 Provide opportunities for students to make ethical decisions about their rights and responsibilities.

    4.2.2 Help students understand that the school, as a society, sometimes requires individuals to act in the interest of all and with disrespect to none.

5.0 Physical education programs should foster moral and ethical values.

5.1 In keeping with the school's responsibility to foster moral and spiritual values, ethical conduct, and personal integrity, the physical education program should:

    5.1.1 Regularly provide real and simulated experiences in which students make ethical decisions about human conduct. Teachers will be nonjudgmental in discussions of ethical decisions.

    5.1.2 Be conducted by staff members who exhibit ethical conduct and basic integrity themselves.

5.2 To help each student develop life goals, the physical education program should:

    5.2.1 Involve students in discussions and activities related to living and to explorations of existential meaning.

6.0 In support of the school's responsibility the physical education program should promote self-realization and mental and physical health.

6.1 Each school should help students explore their own potential through participation in a broad instructional program beginning in kindergarten.

    6.1.1 The basic instructional program should consist of learning experiences fostering body management and the development of skills in sports and games, dance and gymnastics. Aquatics and outdoor education are recommended.

    6.1.2 The school organization should provide maximum opportunity for instruction geared to individual needs.

        6.1.21 Students whose needs cannot be met through normal instructional channels should be provided with programs adapted to their special needs.

        6.1.22 Students in high school who do not require adaptive physical education should be permitted, insofar as possible, to choose the instruction they feel best meets their special needs and interests.

    6.1.3 The instructional process should encourage students in divergent and creative thinking.

6.2 Each school should guide students in the attainment and maintenance of physical and mental health by:

    6.2.1 Providing them with opportunities for physical activity as well as instruction.

    6.2.2 Supporting health education programs that inform students about physical and mental well-being.

Goals and the
curriculum

485

6.2.3 Providing programs in behavior modification for youngsters whose psychological needs preclude mental health.

6.3 Each school should exhibit concern for development of positive self-concepts by:

6.3.1 Identifying children with poor self-concepts who need special help in physical education.

6.3.2 Establishing a climate that offers maximum opportunity for development of a positive self-concept.

Evaluation in physical education

■ Assuming that the goals of physical education guide the formulation of program and instructional objectives, any directive to pursue process objectives must be honored. Administrative regulation 1.1.4 directs the managers of the system to "organize an instructional system that promotes individual progress." Organizational goal 1.2 states that each youngster will "acquire the ability to solve problems related to general and specific motor learning." An earlier expansion of the intellectual discipline goal determined program content. It was followed by a skills-oriented goal. Together these statements identify both the product and process goals.

It is the process goal commitment to individual progress that led to the development of the pupil progress report form shown in figure 15.3. It has six divisions, each broken down into appropriate factors for assessment of individual achievement.

At regular intervals or when a parent conference is called, the physical education teacher checks the appropriate columns. For those children who are not progressing to the extent of their abilities, the physical education teacher checks the column "needs to improve" alongside the factors or behaviors blocking growth or development. The problem may be lack of courteous behavior toward others, or lack of strength for sport skills, or lack of endurance for repeating activities to refine motor patterns. At no time does the physical educator judge the kind and quality of the skills learned apart from their relationship to the learner's skill objectives.

Administrative regulation 1.2.2 calls for the schools to "develop procedures that make it possible for learners to establish personal objectives and evaluate their own progress." Conferences with the children may reveal that they have not met important individual skill objectives that are necessary to their further progress. Under self-management behaviors, the teacher may note that they need to improve listening skills.

Marked accomplishment deserves special attention because it is not the equivalent of an A performance. This attention is awarded when learners have overcome major impediments to their progress. Expected accomplishment by the highly skilled should not be overrewarded.

Group achievement identifies where a youngster stands in relation to peers. Many parents prefer that these marks be given in the form of letter grades, but support for reporting achievement as "below," "at," or "above" group levels is growing among teachers and parents alike, who agree on the value of individualized learning and are only concerned with general progress of youngsters in relation to others at their grade level.

Fig. 15.3 Elementary school pupil progress report in physical education

	Individual achievement[1]			Group achievement[2]		
	Needs to improve	Satisfactory accomplishment	Marked accomplishment	Below group level	At group level	Above group level
1 Self management behaviors						
Cooperative						
Self-motivated						
Listens and follows directions						
Operates with concern for own safety						
Self-disciplined						
2 Social skill development						
Relates effectively to others						
Respects the rights of others						
Courteous						
3 Body management skills						
Command of fundamental movement skills						
Coordination						
4 Physical fitness						
Strength						
Flexibility						
Endurance						
Speed						
Agility						
5 Activity skills						
Games						
Gymnastics						
Dance and rhythms						
6 Knowledge and understanding						
Recall and comprehend essential information						
Application of rules and principles						
Use of problem-solving approach						

Name ___ School ___ Year ___

Homeroom teacher ___ Physical education teacher ___

1 This evaluation is the teacher's assessment of the child's accomplishment in relation to individual ability.

2 This evaluation is the teacher's assessment of the child's accomplishment in relation to typical age or grade level expectancies.

Movement education

■ We have described a dual-track physical education program, its movement orientation and its relationship to total programming. It may be that two positions need to be reconciled if physical education is to meet the challenges of the next century. On the one hand there are movement teachers who advocate a discovery approach to all physical education instruction, and on the other hand there are conventional teachers who prefer the direct approach to skills teaching. Is there a correct position? Can there be compromise?

Teachers who value attainment of skills above all else and who look down on the movement approach as one that does not go beyond the beginning steps in skills acquisition have been shown, in the chapter on games to be in error. There are as many levels in the movement approach as there are stages in the achievement of the highest level of skill mastery. This is true regardless of the activity. Movement education has succeeded, in part, because skilled individuals have been able to acquire new skills through the application of movement principles or to modify existing skills to coincide with changes in some relationship. Movement-educated persons know how to apply principles to their own learning, how to analyze movement, their own and that of others, and how to make intelligent decisions about alternative approaches to a final solution. The argument that a movement approach does not produce skill acquisition is absolutely false. If skill learning does not take place, the reasons lie elsewhere.

The movement approach does not rule out directed teaching. It only recommends the use of that approach when learner needs and interests, both immediate and future, warrant its application. It is a question of priority. The movement educator continually assumes that learner readiness is the final determinant of method. Having learned to observe and analyze movement, movement-oriented learners are in a good position to take advantage of directed teaching when it is to their advantage to do so. When the teacher is not only expert in the subject matter, such as gymnastics, games, or dance, but is also a movement educator, learners and teacher share a special partnership of understanding and feeling.

Basic movement education is treated as a separate program so that attention can be focused on objectives that are otherwise obscured by the requirements of a specific activity. As their awareness of the body as an instrument for movement through space develops, as their awareness of effort qualities increases their control and fluency in movement, learners draw on reservoirs of concepts and behaviors from moment to moment to cope with the objective and expressive needs in their daily existence. Using new capabilities strengthens them for the next time they will be needed. The satisfaction of achievement is its own reward and a stimulus to repeat the activity and to seek out additional challenges. Knowing that one is ready and equal to the tasks ahead is the state of being toward which basic movement education is directed. It is a preparation for learning whatever movements are important to the learner.

All movement-oriented physical education teachers may not agree with the assignment of basic movement objectives to a separate curricular track. However, our experience has been that students of physical education, both in the field and in undergraduate programs, have less difficulty understanding this "new physical education" when its dual nature is clearly delineated. Educators from other disciplines also are able to make sense out of its organizational structure and to see opportunities for introducing interdisciplinary learning experiences. Elementary supervisors and other administrators, who are concerned about the content-relatedness of subject matter, individualized learning opportunities, and clear statements of objectives are pleased to find that the program has established priorities and that the development of self-discipline is one of them. They are equally pleased to find that the structure is flexible and that its modular lesson format permits teachers to undertake multiple unit instruction in two or more programs concurrently if and when the situation warrants. Most pleasing to us has been the significant improvement in understanding and acceptance of movement education by undergraduate elementary school physical education majors. Appendix A contains a curriculum written by undergraduate students. Their statement of goals and program objectives for the two learning tracks give clear direction for the formulation of instructional objectives. It is not a final statement by any means, as they will discover when they put their curriculum into practice, but it is a significant step in the improvement of physical education.

Readings

Davis, Elwood Craig, and contributing authors. *Philosophies Fashion Physical Education*. Dubuque, Iowa: Wm. C. Brown, 1963.

McManama, John. *Systems Analysis for Effective School Administration*. West Nyack, N.Y.: Parker, 1971.

Mager, Robert F. *Preparing Instructional Objectives*. Belmont, Calif.: Fearon, 1962.

Oberteuffer, Delbert, and Ulrich, Celeste. *Physical Education*. 3d ed. New York: Harper & Row, 1962.

Siedentop, Daryl. *Physical Education Introductory Analysis*. Dubuque, Iowa: Wm. C. Brown, 1972.

Tyler, Ralph W. *Basic Principles of Curriculum and Instruction*. Chicago: University of Chicago Press, 1949.

Goals and the
curriculum

The curriculum guide on the following pages is the culmination of undergraduate student research and course work. It was not an easy project for them to undertake, but their hard work and diligent efforts to organize the new concepts in an effective manner paid off handsomely with clear understandings of goals and objectives in elementary school physical education. The guide has been edited for inclusion in this appendix.

Modern physical education

A curriculum guide for movement in the elementary schools compiled 1974-75

Contents

Authors:
Judith A. Bohl
Virginia M. Burton
Donna A. Gladden
Debra K. Heith
Michael C. Howes
Larry K. Landes
Kathleen T. McIntyre
Linda S. Morrissette
Deborah A. Newman
Catherine E. Nolan
Stacy J. Palczynski
Daniel M. Spallone
Lori S. Tiller
Stephen P. Troxell
Thomas K. Tudor

Preface

■ This curriculum guide is designed to aid administrators and teachers in developing a total physical education program for the elementary school. The focus is on the goals and program objectives for an elementary physical education program with additional guidance through instructional objectives, lesson themes, and example lesson plans. The information was compiled as part of the course requirements of "Movement Education in the Elementary School" and

"Organization and Administration in the Elementary School," offered by the Department of Health and Physical Education at Madison College in Harrisonburg, Virginia.

The authors would like to express special thanks and appreciation to Mrs. Jane Myers Kruger and Mr. Hayes Kruger for their direction and guidance throughout the long year of work on this project.

We would also like to acknowledge the help of Ms. Lynn Loeffler and Dr. Ralph Cohen for their careful examination of the manuscript, and to Mr. Mark Fischman for his help on the aquatics section. Thanks also to Dana S. Warren for typing the final copy of this Curriculum Guide.

Purpose and rationale

■ The purpose of this curriculum is to provide a systematic, progressive approach to teaching physical education in the elementary school. The movement education guidelines established here will allow the instructor to utilize and relate the environment in a way that is naturally stimulating to students and will also enhance the development of those skills necessary for participation in culturally relevant athletic activities.

Through movement education, children will be better able to operate efficiently with a positive self-concept, which, in turn, will allow them to communicate with themselves, with others, and with their environment in a creative and individual manner.

Statement of goals and objectives

I **Intellectual discipline**
  Assist each child in the development of intellectual discipline.
A Adopt an individualized, problem-solving approach in movement-oriented situations.
B Provide an atmosphere where knowledge and understandings of principles of movement can be applied to personal analysis of psychomotor performance.
C Expand the learner's conceptual knowledge of movement through insight into the physiological effects of psychomotor performance.
D Promote esthetic enrichment of the individual's analysis of movement education.
II **Mental health, physical health, and self-realization**
  Assist each child in the development of self-awareness, mental health, and physical health.
A Promote positive self-concepts and an understanding of the student's role in society through participation in the movement program.
B Foster sound mental health and good attitudes toward personal health habits.
C Develop and maintain sound physical health.
D Promote development and maintenance of strength, endurance, flexibility, and agility through learning and executing basic skills and basic movement patterns.
III **Avocational and vocational competencies**
  Assist each child in developing avocational and vocational competencies.
A Provide a foundation for future work skills as preparation for entering a vocationally oriented society.
B Encourage manipulative skills in basic movement efficiency that will promote success in simple task mechanics.
C Foster good attitudes toward sports, dance, gymnastics, and aquatics to promote their use as leisure-time activities to maintain physical fitness.

D Encourage good movement behaviors so that students will feel a confidence in recreational skills that will carry over into avocational areas.

IV **Human and social relations**

Provide for personal development of each child in the area of human and social relations.

A Teach each child that all members of the group have personal needs, and that each member of the group must contribute to the welfare of the group as a whole.

B Promote responsibility for personal behavior that affects the group.

C Foster cooperative attitudes that enable students to reach solutions to common problems through peaceful and orderly methods.

D Develop considerate and friendly children who will recognize and respect the rights and feelings of others.

V **Moral and spiritual values**

Assist each child in developing moral and spiritual values by providing movement experiences aimed toward enhancement of ethical attitudes.

A Willingness to share.

B Sense of fair play.

C Ability to accept the outcome of competition.

D Ability to make value judgments concerning what is right and wrong.

VI **Citizenship and civic responsibility**

Assist each child in the development of citizenship and civic responsibility.

A Develop students' ability to use the most effective and dependable methods of inquiry to discover solutions of proposed problems.

B Foster an abundant social and individual life related to individual capacities and desires.

C Cultivate a deep regard for democracy and an intelligent appreciation of democratic institutions.

D Develop a sense of loyalty and patriotism by showing the relationship among home, school, city, state, and country.

E Provide opportunities for student-oriented leadership that meets the needs of a democratic society.

I **The orientation period**

The basic movement track in the elementary physical education program includes an orientation period during which essential elements of the four basic awarenesses of body, space, effort, and relationship are introduced.

A To attain the program objectives, the learner should:

1 Demonstrate good listening skills and the ability to follow teacher-given directions.

2 Demonstrate a positive self-concept with an "I Can" attitude.

3 Show reasonable self-control.

4 Display cooperation and consideration while working with others.

5 Develop independent work habits with given movement tasks.

6 Demonstrate responsibility for carrying out assigned tasks with a minimum of teacher assistance.

7 Demonstrate basic awareness of safety rules governing the use of apparatus and procedure in the movement laboratory.

B The major program objectives of basic movement education emphasize the aspects of body, effort, space and relationship awareness.

Basic movement program objectives

Modern physical education

493

1 In the development of body awareness, the program should stress:

a) Body actions in the general space, including locomotor, variations, elevations, and turns.

b) Body actions in personal space, including axial movements (curl, stretch, twist) and stillness, with emphasis on symmetry and asymmetry.

c) Identification and recognition of body parts (location and relationship), including body parts used, stressed, and leading an action.

d) The basic functions of curl, stretch, twist, and objective and expressive gestures.

e) Aspects of weightbearing, stressing the specific relationship of body parts involved.

2 In the development of spatial awareness, the program should stress recognition of and adaptation to the environment, including:

a) General space awareness resulting in understanding and awareness of limitations, necessary orientations, and available pathways of movement environments.

b) Awareness of personal space, functioning within its movement limitations, size and orientation of self within that space.

c) Application of personal and general spatial awareness to movements of the learner in both floor and air patterns in different kinds of movement environments.

3 In the development of effort awareness, the program should stress:

a) Awareness of the quality of weight as exhibited by degrees of force or tension in action or stillness.

b) Time awareness as evidenced by change or sustainment of speed of movement.

c) Awareness of the spatial quality of movement characterized by degrees of direct and flexible use of space.

d) Awareness of the flow of movement as evidenced in degrees of bound and free movement quality.

e) Instruction in effort awareness in a progression from emphasis on isolated effort elements to emphasis on combinations and sequential patterns of similar and contrasting effort actions where more than one quality is emphasized.

4 In the development of relationship awareness, the program should stress:

a) Object relationship in which a variety of different forms of manipulation of objects (balls, beanbags, ropes, hoops, etc.) should be experienced by the learner, using different body parts.

b) Nonmanipulative relationships between the learner and such objects as targets and obstacles of many kinds.

c) Relationships with people, especially with other learners, that begin with the learner alone and progress sequentially to partners, threes, and larger groups.

d) Both cooperative and competitive situations that should be experienced in culminating activities and discussed to fully appreciate the difference.

II **K-2 grade level objectives**

The program for grades K-2 should assist the learner to acquire understanding and comprehension of the basic movement vocabulary necessary to improve fundamental psychomotor behaviors and to operate safely within the physical education setting. The program should also assist the learner to understand the necessity for certain courtesies and responsibilities fundamental to cooperative learning within the physical educational setting.

A Period of orientation objectives
1 Listening skills
2 Following directions
3 Positive self-concept
4 Self-control
5 Cooperation
6 Consideration
7 Independent problem solving
8 Responsibility
9 Acceptance of rules and daily procedures
10 Conduct with apparatus and manipulative equipment
B Body awareness objectives
1 Eight basic locomotor skills
2 Takeoff, flight, landing stressing flexion of joints
3 Turns on different body parts
4 Identification of body parts (location, relationship)
5 Body parts used, stressed, leading
6 Basic body functions (curl, stretch, twist)
7 Basic body shapes (pin, ball, screw, wall)
8 Symmetry, asymmetry of shape or action
9 Expressive, objective gestures in dramatic and functional situations
10 Transfer of weight, using a variety of body parts
11 Balanced and unbalanced positions
12 Nonlocomotor movements
C Spatial awareness objectives
1 Difference between general and personal space
2 Understand and work within size, boundaries, and shape as limitations of general space
3 Orientation to "in front," "behind," "to the right," and "to the left," in relation with self, with others, and to objects or aspects of the physical environment
4 Knowledge and application of curved, straight, and twisted pathways to simple movement designs
5 Combine pathways to form floor patterns
6 Variable use of space levels and directions
7 Realize and use the limits of one's personal space
8 Exploration of personal space in relation to extensions and size of movement
D Effort awareness objectives
1 Exhibit the four basic effort qualities (weight, time, space, flow) in single effort expressions
2 Perform combinations of two different effort factors (firm-fine), (free-bound), (flexible-direct), (sudden-sustained), such as (sudden-firm), (sustained-fine), (sustained-free), (direct-firm).
E Relationship objectives
1 Control and manipulation of objects in a variety of ways
2 Relationship to targets or obstacles in a variety of ways
3 Work with one or two partners in a variety of ways
4 Use portable or fixed apparatus in a variety of ways
5 Work with a variety of free and metric rhythms or sounds
III 3-4 grade level objectives
Because of the growing interest in games at the grade 3-4 level, program emphasis should be placed on the further development of spatial awareness,

movement analysis of skills, and analysis of motion factors of play in the physical education setting.

A Body awareness objectives
 1 Further development of awareness of body parts in skill learning
 2 Combining locomotor skills to form more complex patterns
 3 Levels and control of elevation
 4 Incorporating turns into movement skills
 5 Realization of body functions in games, gymnastics, and dance
B Spatial awareness objectives
 1 Further develop orientation to extend understanding of diagonal, planes, 3-D cross in relation to specific points in space
 2 Apply knowledge of general and personal space in the areas of games, gymnastics, and dance
 3 Increased ability to operate within limitations, range, and orientations
 4 Further development of floor patterns and air patterns
 5 Create movement sequences based on spatial elements
C Effort awareness objectives
 1 Identify and execute the eight basic effort actions
 2 Identify opposites of basic effort actions
 3 Relate mood and attitude to effort actions
 4 Be aware of degrees of effort in game skill learning
D Relationship objectives
 1 Increased possibilities for changing the variables of relationships
 2 Relate to different partners in cooperative and competitive situations
 3 Relate to threes and other small groups both cooperatively and competitively

IV **5-6 grade level objectives**
  When learners have mastered basic skills and awarenesses, the program in grades 5-6 should provide an opportunity for them to refine and evaluate these skills through greater movement awareness in skill learning in all areas within the physical education setting.

A Body awareness objectives
 1 Refinement of skills related to more precise awareness of what the body is doing
 2 Flexible and appropriate use of the body related to increasing coordination of different body parts
B Spatial awareness objectives
 1 Refinement of awareness of general and personal space related to the areas of games, gymnastics, and dance
 2 Limitations of range and orientation related to a variety of game, dance, and gymnastics situations
 3 Floor and air patterns related to design
C Effort awareness objectives
 1 Mastery of the eight basic effort actions
 2 Transition from one effort to its opposite and from one effort action to another
 3 Relationship of body parts to effort actions
 4 Apply understandings to refinement of control of the self or object
D Relationship objectives
 1 Leading and adapting to group activity
 2 Understand spatial relationships of game, dance, and gymnastics situations
 3 Variations of formations
 4 Variabilities in the use of targets

5 Increased exploration in utilizing gymnastics apparatus
6 Increased emphasis on the variations of trios
7 Relating to self-imposed limitations, such as rules or constraints forced by environmental arrangements

I Introduction
In the basic movement program, the following themes should be included. These themes suggest tasks and instructional objectives that the learner should attain in the elementary physical education setting. They are based on the themes established by Rudolf Laban.

II K-2 grade level
A Theme I—Body Awareness
1 Utilize the entire body as a unit in motion and stillness
a) Opening and closing
b) Rising and falling
c) Twisting and turning
d) Running, leaping, and other forms of locomotion
e) Maintaining stillness
f) Executing action-stillness sequences
2 Utilize the body both symmetrically and asymmetrically
a) Demonstrate asymmetry by more action on one side of the body than on the other
b) Sense asymmetry by unbalance
c) Feel asymmetry by unbalance in mobility (turning)
d) Emphasize symmetry through equal stress on both sides of the body
e) Link balance and stability through symmetry
3 Recognize body parts
a) Explore the use of the legs in stepping, falling, flying, and leaping
b) Utilize the legs in a supporting role
c) Stress the use of the arms in gathering, twisting, and reaching
d) Create movement sequences
4 Discover movement sequences with different body parts leading
a) Differentiate between movements of the whole body and of specific body parts
b) Demonstrate movement with the arms after movement was started by shoulders, elbow, etc.
c) Lead movement with the legs
d) Create movement sequences
5 Perform gesture and weight-transfer movements
a) Demonstrate weight transfer to different body parts
b) Utilize gesture movements
c) Perform gesture movements with the arms
6 Explore body parts in relation to other body parts
a) Find rhythms with hands and fingers
b) Develop relationships of body parts by
(1) Linking
(2) Intertwining
(3) Avoiding and touching
(4) Surrounding
(5) Meeting, parting, and passing
c) Apply body part relationships to a movement sequence

Themes and activities for the basic movement track

Modern physical education

497

B Theme II—Awareness of Weight and Time
1 Learn the weight qualities of firm and fine touch
   a) Move lightly or strongly
   b) Find light and strong actions
   c) Contrast firm and fine touch
2 Learn the time qualities of sudden and sustained movement
   a) Travel fast or slow
   b) Perform actions fast or slow
   c) Contrast fast and slow movement
   d) Apply time qualities to isolated body parts
3 Combine weight and time qualities
   a) Discover all possibilities when weight and time are combined
   (1) Sustained firmness
   (2) Sudden-fine touch
   (3) Sudden firmness
   (4) Sustained fine touch movements
   b) Sequence phrases involving weight and time qualities
   c) Develop awareness of weight-time qualities by the use of percussion
4 Learn meter
   a) Translate heard meter into movement
   b) Distinguish between duple and triple time
   c) Respond to the time signature of metric movement
5 Show rhythm by the fusion of weight and time
   a) Create a movement phrase by placing strong accents in different parts
   b) Create a movement phrase by placing light accents in different parts
   c) Alternate strong and light accents in the same phrase
C Theme III—Awareness of Space
1 Use of space
   a) Exploring all of the space
   b) Discover what the body can do in relation to space
   (1) Contrast the feelings of penetration of space and of filling space
   (2) Feel the difference between surrounding space and repulsing it
2 Utilize spatial areas around the body
   a) Explore levels of space
   b) Apply space words and phrases such as "in front," "behind," "to the right," and "to the left"
   c) Link awareness of the body and its parts to spatial awareness
   d) Use weight-time qualities in spatial awareness
   e) Create movement sequences based on selected spatial areas
3 Learn the concept of personal space
   a) Explore possibilities for movement in personal space
   b) Vary the size of personal space by changing the base of support
   c) Discover the ranges of personal space
   d) Explore various parts of personal space that surround different body parts
4 Feel extensions in space
   a) Contrast the spatial focus of far and near
   b) Change from inward extensions to outward extensions
   c) Discover the relationship of large and small shapes to various extensions and contractions
   d) Grow and shrink as a whole or with an isolated body part
5 Learn space words and phrases

a) Interpret the meaning of space words and phrases that show relationship, such as under, over, around, through, on, off, toward, away from, up against, next to, close to, far from, above, below

b) Perform specific sequences of space words

c) Apply a given space word to different places

d) Create and execute one's own sequence of space words

6 Discover basic spatial actions

  a) Relate rising and falling to up and down

  b) Use opening and closing in relation to side to side or right to left

  c) Move forward and backward in relation to front and back

7 Link all aspects

  a) Show simultaneous awareness of general and personal space

  b) Display simultaneous awareness of level and direction in both general and personal space

  c) Develop simultaneous awareness of relationship to orientation in the space

  d) Combine far and near with changes in extensions, levels, and directions

D Theme IV—Awareness of the Flow of the Weight of the Body in Space and Time

1 Contrast successive and simultaneous body flow

  a) Experience successive flow with

  (1) Firm and fine touch qualities

  (2) Sudden and sustained qualities

  (3) Large and small positions

  (4) Movement on the spot and while traveling

  b) Experience simultaneous body flow with:

  (1) Firm and fine touch qualities

  (2) Sudden and sustained qualities

  (3) Large and small positions

  (4) Movement on the spot and while traveling

  c) Perform sequences involving particular body parts in successive and/or simultaneous movements

  (1) On a single limb

  (2) Going from limb to limb

  (3) Using different parts

2 Recognize free and bound-flow qualities

  a) Go without stopping and flowing

  b) Move freely flowing while pausing

  c) Move in a bound manner

  d) Stop in a bound manner

  e) Perform phrases of movement involving bound and free

3 Discover flexible and direct space qualities

  a) Contrast straight and round movement

  b) Combine straight and roundabout movements in a sequence or pattern

4 Refine movement with phrasing and punctuation

  a) Emphasize an opening or starting position

  b) Stress ending positions

  c) Emphasize strong and light accents

  d) Perform one or more movement sequences using punctuation

E Theme V—Adaptation to a Partner

1 Adapt to a partner by doing the same movement

  a) Recognize and create the body shape of a partner

b) Sequence levels of a partner in a movement phrase

c) Sequence qualities demonstrated by a partner

d) Feel and do the rhythm of a partner's movement phrase

2 Adapt to a partner by utilizing conversations in movement

    a) React to the final position and shape of a partner

    b) React to the level of a partner's phrase

    c) Speak and answer with movement phrases

    d) Utilize meter as the duration of quality play

    e) Respond with body parts

3 Adapt to a partner through dance

    a) Respond to one another by dancing at the same time

    b) Maintain the space interval

4 Relate to a small group

    a) Utilize trios

  (1) Adapt to a circle and its center

  (2) Respond to relationships by splitting, linking, passing between, and going through

    b) Discover a variety of formations, such as triangles, lines, and circles; discover a variety of couple relationships

    c) Utilize quintets; discover a variety of formations, such as circular, linear, and angular

III 3-4 grade level objectives

A Theme II—Awareness of Weight and Time

1 Use the body to express weight qualities of firm and fine touch through movement

    a) Differentiate between the concepts of firm and fine touch qualities

    b) Utilize whole body parts, as well as isolated body parts, to demonstrate qualities connected with firm and fine touch

    c) Develop an attitude toward the concept of weight, with the ability to differentiate between (1) fine and heavy and (2) firm and heavy

    d) Control the amount of tension associated with firm and fine touch movements

2 Recognition of and application of the body to sudden and sustained movements connected with time qualities

    a) Differentiate between the concepts that deal with sudden and those that deal with sustained movements

    b) Use the whole body along with isolated body parts to stress the qualities in time

    c) Recognize and respond to the dramatic qualities of time that enhance sudden and sustained movements

3 Move the body through sudden and sustained firmness and sudden and sustained fine touch motion

    a) Become familiar with the four attitudes when time and weight are combined

    b) Develop, in sequence, movement phrases associated with different weight and time qualities

    c) Explore the qualities of weight and time through percussive movements

4 Develop the concept of meter, which can be shown as time divided into measurable units of short and/or long duration

    a) Recognize the meter heard and apply it to movement

    b) Create long and short movement phrases to match the meter *c)* Alternate speed and performance on different levels in accordance with the sound heard

d) Explore and create different types of time signatures through meter movement

e) Recognize duple and triple time

5 Exploring the concept of rhythm with creative combinations of weight and time

    a) Stress light and strong accents in different segments of a movement phrase

    b) Stress light and strong accents within the same phrase

    c) Work with stress in weight, perform a metric time with variations

    d) Design and create free rhythmic phrases in correlation with weight and time changes and work them into metrical sequential patterns

B Theme III—Awareness of Space

1 Exploring space

    a) Utilizing all space

    b) Discover the use of the body and its relation to space

(1) Recognize the sensation of penetration of space as opposed to the feeling of filling space

(2) Identify the sensation of surrounding space as opposed to repulsing space

2 Explore the spatial areas surrounding the body

    a) Discover the various levels of space

    b) Learn to orient the body in relation to the directions "in front," "behind," "to the right," "to the left"

    c) Sequence body actions throughout spatial areas

    d) Blend the weight-time qualities of Theme II and spatial areas

    e) Perform movement combinations in designated spatial areas

3 Body regions in personal space

    a) Discover possible movements in personal space as opposed to movements in the general space

(1) Limit personal space by narrowing the base of support

(2) Explore the furthest boundaries of personal space

    b) Discover the regions of personal space surrounding particular body parts: move body parts through their own and adjacent regions

4 Extensions in space

    a) Discover the spatial concepts of far and near

(1) Vary the focus from near (self) to far (outward)

(2) Find extended movement possibilities with an inward focus

    b) Recognize the relationship between large and small shapes as they relate to extensions from and contractions toward the center of the body; contrast growing and shrinking as a whole-body action or an action of individual parts

5 Space words and phrases

    a) Apply various space words and phrases that denote relationship to actions

    b) Link space words

(1) Use the same word in different places and in different ways

(2) Use different words in different places in different ways

    c) Create and apply a linkage of space words

6 Basic spatial actions

    a) Determine the relationship of rising and falling to the concepts of up and down

b) Discover the relationship of opening and crossing to side to side or right to left

c) Demonstrate the relationship of advancing and retreating to forward and backward

7 Unite the concepts of Theme III

    a) Show simultaneous awareness of general and personal space

    b) Show simultaneous awareness of level and direction in both general and personal space

    c) Demonstrate an awareness of space words and phrases in relation to orientation

  (1) Use concepts of toward and away while varying levels or directions

  (2) Use concepts of under, over, and around while varying levels or direction

  (3) Use concepts of on and off while varying body extensions in space

    d) Combine concepts of next to and far from with changes in extension, level, or direction

C Theme IV—Awareness of the Flow of the Weight of the Body in Space and Time

1 Progressive and concurrent body flow

    a) Perform with successive flow related to firm and fine touch qualities; sudden and sustained qualities; large and small positions; stationary movement and movement while traveling

    b) Perform with concurrent flow related to firm and fine touch qualities; sudden and sustained qualities; large and small positions; stationary movement and movement while traveling

    c) Perform consecutive movement phrases involving specific parts of the body

  (1) Shoulder, elbow, wrist, fingers

  (2) Hip, knees, foot

  (3) Foot, knees, hip

  (4) Knee, hip, chest, head

  (5) Finger play

2 Free-flow and bound-flow qualities

    a) Differentiate between free and bound flow

  (1) Freely moving without stopping

  (2) Freely moving while pausing

  (3) Traveling in a bound style

  (4) Sequencing in a bound behavior

    b) Sequence movements, including both free and bound flow

3 Flexible and direct space qualities: differentiate between straight and roundabout movements

4 Flow-space qualities

    a) Differentiate between flexible-free and flexible-bound movement

    b) Differentiate between direct-free and direct-bound movement

    c) Design a development from one space-flow quality to another

5 Flow-time qualities

    a) Differentiate between sudden-bound and sudden-free movements

    b) Differentiate between sustained-bound and sustained-free movements

    c) Design a development from one flow-weight quality to another

6 Flow-weight qualities

    a) Differentiate between firm-touch-bound and fine-touch-bound movements *b)* Differentiate between firm-touch-free and fine-touch-free movements

c) Design a development from one flow-weight quality to another

7 Weight-space qualities

    a) Differentiate between firm-flexible and firm-direct movements

    b) Differentiate between fine-touch-flexible and fine-touch-direct movements

    c) Design a development from one weight-space quality to another

8 Space-time qualities

    a) Differentiate between direct-sudden and direct-sustained movements

    b) Differentiate between flexible-sudden and flexible-sustained movements

    c) Design a development from one space-time quality to another

9 Phrasing and punctuation

    a) Express movements with clearness of quality

  (1) Stress preparatory action to the main action

  (2) Stress ending positions

  (3) Stress beginning positions

  (4) Stress strong and light accents

    b) Accentuate movement phrases

  (1) Link two phrases

  (2) Link three or more movement phrases

D Theme V—Adaptation to a Partner

1 Follow the same movement expressions as the partner

    a) Use a mirror image to express the same movement qualities

    b) Work with a partner to follow the same movement qualities

    c) Use the same body actions to portray a rhythm of the partner's movement

    d) Recognize sequence of body parts and copy movements within the same movement phrase

2 Utilize body parts to respond to a movement phrase in conversation

    a) Acknowledge a partner's final rest position and have body parts respond to that still shape

    b) Recognize a final level position to the partner's movement expression or phrase

    c) Connect body movement to express the feeling of speaking with movement

    d) Use body parts to answer a partner's movement phrase

    e) Control body parts in a response to a partner's movement phrase that expresses agreement

    f) Contrast body parts in a response to a partner's movement phrase that expresses disagreement

    g) Develop a duration of quality play in movement through the use of meter

  (1) Utilize an eight-count phrase for a response

  (2) Utilize eight-count phrases with divisions

    h) Discover different body parts with which to react to, to guide, or to finish movement phrases in accordance with use of specific body parts by a partner

    i) Respond to a partner's movement phrases by stressing specific body parts to lead in the movement conversation

    j) Change roles of a movement phrase from one partner to the other in leading the conversation

3 Move the body parts at the same time as the rest of the group when dancing together

Modern physical education

a) Control the body parts in simultaneous movement

(1) Connect body parts, such as hands, to help move in the same fashion

(2) Change body movements to move in opposite or other directions than the previous movement

(3) Come together and break apart through body movements

b) Travel through the personal or general space maintaining space interval

4 Respond to the properties of small group relationships

   a) Work in trios

(1) Link body movements to a circle or triangle shape and identify the center of that shape

(2) Explore relationships through space-word techniques

(3) Work in a line formation

(4) Discover different formations that may result from two persons working against one

(5) Explore the possibilities of all three working against each other

   b) Work in quartets

(1) Explore possibilities of different arrangements in formations; for example, three versus one

(2) Form paired groups of twos

   c) Work in quintets

(1) Create different formations of circle, line, five-sided setup

(2) Create a wing formation

E Theme VI—The Instrumental Use of the Body

1 Explore possibilities connected with the instrumental use of the body

   a) Create movement gestures that involve a situation

(1) Utilize hands and feet as expressive instruments

(2) Utilize different body parts or the entire body as one instrument

(3) Express actions of leaving, gathering, pulling, gripping, pushing, and scattering

2 Discover the five body activities and stillnesses

   a) Move through space with steps and gesture

(1) Control body action through the transfer of weight back and forth from one support to another

(2) Explore new methods or ways of locomotion through transference of weight

(3) Combine and contrast different forms of locomotion and movement

   b) Explore the five basic jumps through body movement; work on different types of landings from the jumps

   c) Contrast turns with steps and gestures; combine turns with steps and gestures

   d) Utilize body parts to achieve the property of stillness; recognize and control different body parts in the process of stilling certain body parts

   e) Work on balance; develop an awareness of a point of balance and unbalance in different directions and on different levels throughout the body

3 Link the five body activities through movement and the property of stillness

   a) Create gestures through stepping

   b) Utilize locomotor movements through weight transfer

   c) Travel through a space while turning

   d) Work on jumps with an added turn(s)

   e) Utilize body parts to gesture during jumps

   f) Create gestures during locomotion

   g) Discover different types of turns through stepping and added gestures

4 Stress particular body parts in a sequence of body movement activities
   a) Work with one specific action in dealing with a motif and then toward a gradually more complex situation
   b) Develop and create a sequence that enables a particular activity to reach a climactic point, followed by a controlled ending
   c) Stimulate a sequence of activities by use of certain action words, such as skimming, gliding, darting
  (1) Create a collection of action words for activities
  (2) Utilize the action words in a movement phrase or sentence
F Theme VII—The Awareness of Basic Effort Actions
1 Refine thrusting and slashing actions
   a) Differentiate between thrusting and slashing movements
   b) Change from thrusting to slashing actions
   c) Change from slashing to thrusting movements
2 Experience floating and gliding actions
   a) Differentiate between floating and gliding movements
   b) Change from floating to gliding movements
   c) Change from gliding to floating movements
3 Create wringing and pressing actions
   a) Differentiate between wringing and pressing movements
   b) Change from wringing to pressing actions
   c) Change from pressing to wringing actions
4 Show flicking and dabbing actions
   a) Differentiate between flicking and dabbing movements
   b) Change from flicking to dabbing actions
   c) Change from dabbing to flicking actions
   d) Relate jumping to sudden efforts
5 Discover the sensation for countervailing efforts
   a) Thrusting and floating
   b) Slashing and gliding
   c) Wringing and dabbing
   d) Pressing and flicking
6 Create the mood and actions of effort quality
   a) Adjectives
   b) Rhythm instruments
   c) Related body performance with effort actions
7 Associate effort actions to the activities of Theme VI
   a) Relate jumping to sudden efforts
   b) Relate turning to flexible efforts
   c) Relate locomotion to sustained or sudden efforts
   d) Gesture with feeling for all effort actions
   e) Devise activity combinations for each effort quality
   f) Link various effort actions
8 Sense the relationship of specific body parts to specific effort actions
   a) Discover which body part(s) assumes the most important role in specific effort actions
  (1) Emphasize activity of the limbs
  (2) Emphasize activity of the hips, abdomen, shoulders, seat
  (3) Emphasize leading with different body parts
   b) Execute effort actions with specific body parts and the same action with a whole body movement
9 Effort and meter

a) Make significant movements on the strong beat of a measure
b) Effort action accompaniment to accents of the beat
c) Sustain effort actions according to time signature of the meter
d) Nonmetric rhythms and effort actions

G Theme VIII—Occupational Rhythm
1 Refine movement for the timing of working actions
   a) Work with simple actions that are repetitious
   b) Work with movement to time a sequence of events
2 Work in partner relationships or group relationships
   a) Develop a feeling for the industrial actions
   b) Develop a feeling for the commercial actions
   c) Develop a feeling for the farm actions
   d) Recognize the use of body parts through sports, games, and recreational actions
3 Utilize body parts to feel a rhythm action
   a) Apply the body to move in rhythm action sequences consisting of preparation, main action, and recovery
   b) Work with a partner or group on the rhythm action sequence
   c) Respond to the effort rhythm when working with a partner or in a group relationship
(1) Similar actions
(2) Contrasting actions
4 Use body parts to feel different moods and working actions
   a) Create situations that could portray either a hurried or a leisurely attitude toward a working action
   b) Explore all possible moods or attitudes in connection with working actions
   c) Select a particular mood or attitude for a specific working action
5 Move body parts in relation to a work dance
   a) Recognize a working action and apply it to dance
   b) Create a rhythm that could enhance a dance
   c) Create a rhythm that could enlarge a pattern or formation during a dance

IV **5-6 grade level**
A Theme V—Recognizing Partner Relationships
1 Design like movements with a partner
   a) Stress like or similar shapes with another
   b) Utilize sequence of levels in a movement phrase with another
   c) Perform sequence of quality (effort) actions with a partner
   d) Reconstruct the rhythmic phrases of others
2 Communication through movement
   a) Responding, replying to a partner's shape or level
   b) Stressing, emphasizing the expressive quality of movements
(1) Speaking with movement
(2) Answering with movement, as in agreement and disagreement
   c) Emphasize duration of effort qualities in response to a partner
   d) Allow certain body parts to predominate in response to a partner
3 Dancing (that is, moving with others)
   a) With one other person
   b) In groups of threes
   c) With larger groups
   d) Movement with others at the same time

(1) Meeting and parting with others

(2) Maintain designated spatial relationships (intervals)

4 Relationships with more than one partner

  a) Trios

(1) Two against one

(2) Triangles, lines

(3) Linking, weaving, going through

  b) Groups of four

(1) Two-to-two

(2) Three-to-one

  c) Groups of five

(1) Circles

(2) Subgrouping

B Theme VI—The Instrumental Use of the Body

1 Understand the meaning of the instrumental use of the body

  a) Utilize the hands and feet

  b) Use other body parts in movement

  c) Contrast gathering and scattering actions

2 Locomotor movements and stillness

  a) Travel with steps and gestures

  b) Sequential transference of weight from one support to another

  c) Combine different locomotor patterns

  d) Explore basic jumps with variations on landing

  e) Combine turns with steps and gestures; change focus

  f) The body in stillness

(1) Develop awareness of balance

(2) Relationship of body parts to each other during frozen (still) body shapes

3 Combine basic body activities

  a) Gestures while stepping

  b) Travel while turning

  c) Turning jumps

  d) Jumps with gestures

  e) Traveling jumps

  f) Step-jump rhythms

  g) Stepping during turns

  h) Turns with gestures

4 Developing sequential activities

  a) Use of one action motif under increasingly difficult **situations**

  b) Sequence of activities with controlled ending

  c) Create action words to stimulate activity sequences

  d) Build action sentences and translate them into movements

C Theme VII—The Awareness of Basic Effort Actions

1 Thrusting and slashing

  a) Contrast thrusting and slashing

  b) Transitions from thrusting to slashing and from slashing to thrusting

2 Floating and gliding

  a) Contrast floating and gliding

  b) Transitions from floating to gliding and from gliding to floating

3 Wringing and pressing

  a) Contrast wringing and pressing

  b) Transitions from wringing to pressing and from pressing to wringing

Modern physical
education

4 Flicking and dabbing
 a) Contrast flicking and dabbing
 b) Transitions from flicking to dabbing and from dabbing to flicking
5 Create moods with effort actions
 a) Adjectives and adverbs
 b) Rhythm instruments
6 Relate effort actions to the use of the body as an instrument
 a) Jumping with sudden effort actions
 b) Turning and flexible efforts
 c) Locomotion and sustained or sudden efforts
 d) Gesturing with all effort actions
 e) Combine several efforts and activities
 f) Develop sequential patterns using various effort actions and body activities
7 Discover which body parts are best suited for each effort action
 a) Limbs
 b) Trunk, hips, shoulders, seat
 c) Use of one body part, then the whole body
8 Develop awareness of meter in effort
 a) Important movements on strong beat of music
 b) Sustain actions according to given time signatures
 c) Nonmetric rhythms and effort actions
D Theme VIII—Occupational Rhythms
1 Perform working movements
 a) Copy simple working actions
 b) Copy sequences of working actions
2 Perform in groups of two or more
 a) Emphasize industrial actions
 b) Emphasize commercial actions
 c) Emphasize farming actions
 d) Emphasize sport, game, and recreational actions
3 Recognize rhythms of working actions
 a) Stress the three rhythmic parts of action sequences
 (1) Preparation
 (2) Main action
 (3) Recovery
 b) Contrast the effort rhythms of two or more people if performing the same working actions
4 Recognize moods of working actions
 a) Discover different attitudes of people toward working actions
 b) Realize the most appropriate attitude toward working actions
5 Apply working actions to dancing by recognizing rhythms and patterns of working actions as applied to dance
E Theme IX—Awareness of Shape in Movement
1 Utilize basic space patterns
 a) Perform straight and angular shapes
 b) Perform rounded shapes
 c) Perform twisted shapes
 d) Link different space patterns
2 Utilize floor and air patterns

a) Perform patterns on the floor
b) Perform patterns in the air
c) Adapt air patterns from floor patterns
d) Adapt floor patterns from air patterns
3 Stress the size of movements
    a) Recognize the influence of size of movements on shapes and patterns
    b) Contrast growing and shrinking shapes and patterns
    c) Refine spatial patterns by using different body parts to make shapes and varying the size of the shapes
4 Design body shapes
    a) Recognize different body shapes
  (1) Round
  (2) Pinlike
  (3) Wall-like
  (4) Twisted or screwlike
    b) Copy environmental shapes with body shapes
    c) Realize the importance of body carriage to character, mood, and attitude
F Theme —Transitions between the Basic Effort Actions
1 Stress effort actions as transitions from acceleration to deceleration
2 Recognize how the weight factor (increasing-decreasing) affects transitions when using selected effort actions
3 Recognize the importance of flexibility and directness when using effort actions
4 Use gradual or abrupt changes when going from one effort action to its opposite
5 Move from one effort action through the seven other effort actions
G Theme XI—Orientation in Space
1 Discover the dimensional cross
    a) Utilize movements and their variations based on the dimensional cross
    b) Design dimensional step patterns
    c) Stress central and peripheral transitions
    d) Create harmonious transitions as a result of peripheral transitions
    e) Turn, jump, and travel from peripheral transitions
    f) Develop complementary sequences with a partner
  (1) Vary the partner relationship
  (2) Vary the use of different body parts
2 Discover the diagonal cross
    a) Perform sequences of movements along the diagonal scale
    b) Change the movements on the diagonal
    c) Utilize central and peripheral transitions by exploring peripheral movements of the cube
  (1) Recognize variations of movements over plane transitions
  (2) Recognize variations of movements over edge transitions
  (3) Recognize variations of movements over central transitions
3 Discover the three planes
    a) Respond to the door plane
    b) Respond to the wheel plane
    c) Respond to the table plane
    d) Use central and peripheral transitions
H Theme XII—The Combination of Shapes and Efforts

1 Discover the effort

    a) Utilize basic patterns of straight, angular, rounded, and twisted to discover the shape of a sequence of efforts

    b) Investigate the relationship of effort to floor patterns

    c) Investigate the relationship of effort to air patterns

2 Vary the form

    a) Find the natural efforts of straight, angular, rounded, and twisted patterns

    b) Adapt the natural rhythm of a pattern and design one that is different

3 Apply effort and orientation

    a) Combine motion factors with Laban's octahedron of the six basic directions while stressing harmony and discord as related to direction

    b) Understand the effort cube

  (1) Recognize the bridge between basic effort actions and directions based on the diagonal dimensions

  (2) Apply the effort diagonal to direction in contrast to area

  (3) Emphasize feeling actions in the body center

  (4) Link similar actions (efforts) to establish continuity of line

4 Stress movement that contains a free use of effort, shape, and orientation

    a) Practice the effort qualities in all directions

    b) Contrast actions that do not conform to the effort cube with those that do conform to develop differences in expression

I Theme XIII—Elevation

1 Move away from the floor

    a) Rebound in place and while traveling throughout the space

    b) Release tension after the jump to achieve feeling of freedom

2 Lead jumping actions with specific body parts

    a) Lead with the head

    b) Lead with the pelvic girdle

    c) Lead with the chest, front, back, and sides

    d) Lead with parts of the leg

    e) Lead with parts of the arm

3 Combine shapes and elevation

    a) Explore the use of straight, angular, rounded, and twisted shapes in jumps

    b) Create landings with different shapes

    c) Control and emphasize near and far positions of the limbs while jumping

4 Stress effort and elevation

    a) Apply sudden effort actions in elevation

  (1) Stress slashing and flicking while performing turning jumps

  (2) Stress thrusting and dabbing with varying-sized jumps in place

    b) Create floating and gliding sensations in jumping

    c) Stress pressing and wringing qualities prior to elevation

    d) Develop and perform effort-elevation sequences

5 Landing

Discover the three possible methods of coming down

    a) Stress coming down with intention of going up again

    b) Stress coming down and releasing sensation of elevation

    c) Stress coming down and retaining sensation of elevation

6 Elevate the body without jumping

    a) Utilize progressions that move from sensation toward action

    b) Utilize progressions that move from action toward sensation

7 Respond to a partner and to the group in play by transferring the quality of the elevated state from one to another

8 Link music and elevation

    a) Perform dynamic actions in duple time

    b) Practice flowing and swinging actions in triple time

I Introduction

The development track in the elementary Physical Education program should include opportunities for participation in the four program areas of games, gymnastics, dance, and aquatics, if possible.

A In the games program learners should acquire skills and understandings that will enable them to participate in a variety of competitive activities.

1 Basic offensive and defensive movement and manipulative running, batting and net games

2 Knowledge and understanding of the rules of principal sports

3 Principles of cooperative behavior with teammates and/or partners

4 Safety skills and knowledge necessary to minimize or avoid accidents

5 Make ethical decisions based on rules of play

6 Development of a good, sportsmanlike attitude

7 Knowledge of the care and storage of equipment

B In gymnastics learners should acquire understandings of movement principles that will influence the development of body management skills.

1 Ability to transfer weight to different body parts with special emphasis on hands

2 Coordinating the large areas of the body, upper and lower halves, right and left sides

3 Development of good landing techniques

4 Ability to work creatively with apparatus

5 Ability to employ fundamental concepts of spatial patterns

6 Development of agility, flexibility, strength, and muscular endurance

7 Attainment of efficient technique in movement

8 Ability to handle the weight of another in performance of balance, agility, and flight movement skills

9 Understandings of mechanical principles associated with gymnastics

C In aquatic skills learners should be able to perform those activities that will enable them to function and travel efficiently and safely within the aquatic environment.

1 Development of techniques and form in diving.

2 Understanding of techniques and form of principal swimming strokes

3 Basic turning techniques

4 Ability to participate in aquatic games

5 Drownproofing safety practices, and basic rescue and lifesaving techniques

D In dance learners should acquire understandings and skills associated with a variety of activities.

1 Ability to share a dance experience with others

2 Fundamental step-patterns for a variety of rhythmic activities and dances

3 Ability to participate in structured dance formations, either their own creations or set forms created by others

4 Ability to function in partner, individual, and group relationships during dance

5 Understanding techniques and terms involved in folk and social forms of dance.

II Games—program objectives

Learners should be able to participate in games of low and high organization and in team and individual sports. Students should have the opportunity to acquire proficiency of skills that will enable them to participate in the following games:

1 Softball

2 Soccer

3 Basketball

4 Tennis

5 Football—touch or flag

6 Field hockey

7 Volleyball

8 Track and field

9 Wrestling

A 5-6 grade level

The program should include instruction in skills for games and sports in accordance with ability levels of students. There are many appropriate skills and understandings to consider for inclusion in the development of unit and lesson plans for fifth and sixth grades.

1 Softball
   a) Throwing with accuracy
   (1) Underhand
   (2) Overhand
   (3) Sidearm
   b) Pitching
   c) Fielding and infield play
   d) Catching
   e) Hitting
   f) Baserunning

2 Soccer
   a) Strategy of individual play
   (1) Offensive use of space
   (2) Defensive use of space
   b) Goalie play
   c) Tackling
   d) Teamwork in use of space
   e) Rules, from student-designed to standard forms

3 Basketball
   a) Dribbling
   b) Passing
   (1) Bounce
   (2) Chest
   (3) Overhead
   (4) Underhand flip
   (5) Hook
   c) Shooting
   (1) Free throws
   (2) Lay-ups
   (3) Field goal
   d) Jump balls
   e) Rebounding
   f) Strategies of individual play
   (1) Offensive use of space
   (2) Defensive use of space

g) Teamwork in use of space
h) Rules, from student-designed to standard forms
4 Tennis
  a) Strokes
 (1) Forehand
 (2) Backhand
 (3) Overhand
 (4) Net play
  b) Serve modified
  c) Volley
  d) Singles play
  e) Rules
5 Football—two-hand touch, flag; six or eight players
  a) Passing and catching
 (1) Laterals
 (2) Pitchouts
 (3) Forward
  b) Kicking
 (1) Punt
 (2) Kickoff
 (3) Extra point
  c) Strategy
 (1) Offensive use of space
 (2) Defensive use of space
  d) Team play
  e) Rules and scoring
6 Field hockey
  a) Dribbling
  b) Passing
  c) Shooting
  d) Tackling
  e) Scoop and flick
  f) Bully
  g) Dodges
  h) Goalie play
  i) Strategy of individual play
 (1) Offensive use of play
 (2) Defensive use of play
  j) Team play
  k) Rules and scoring
7 Volleyball
  a) Passing
  b) Serve
 (1) Overhand
 (2) Underhand
  c) Positioning
 (1) On the court
 (2) Under the ball
  d) Strategy
 (1) Offensive use of space

(2) Defensive use of space
  e) Team play
  f) Rules and scoring
8 Track and field
  a) Running
  (1) Sprint—50-60 yd
  (2) Distance—600 yd
  (3) Relays—relay or pursuit, 200-220 yd
  (4) Hurdling—60 yd
  b) Field events
  (1) Shot put
  (2) Discus
  (3) Long jump
  (4) Triple jump
  (5) High jump
  (6) Softball throwing for distance
  c) Rules and scoring
9 Wrestling—modified, no takedowns
  a) Kneeling and referee's position
  b) Strategies—offensive and defensive
  (1) Riding
  (2) Pinning
  (3) Reversals
  (4) Escape
  (5) Predicament
B 3-4 grade level
  A basic program of lead-up activities should be offered to promote growth and development of basic skills in the sports and games areas listed below. Included in each activity should be an emphasis on partner and various small-group relationships.
1 Softball-type games
  a) Throwing
  (1) Underhand
  (2) Overhand
  b) Catching
  (1) In the air
  (2) On the ground
  c) Batting
  d) Baserunning
  e) Simplified rules concepts
2 Soccer
  a) Trapping
  b) Passing
  c) Shooting
  d) Throw in
  e) Basic positioning, spatial awareness
  f) Basic rules
3 Basketball-type games
  a) Dribbling
  b) Passing
  c) Shooting

    d) Jump balls

    e) Rules

  4 Tennis

    a) Basic stroking patterns

    (1) Volley

    (2) Forehand

    (3) Backhand

    (4) Serve

    b) Eye-hand coordination lead-ups

    c) Boundaries

    d) Modified games

    (1) Individual

    (2) Team

  5 Football-type games

    a) Passing

    b) Catching

    c) Kicking

    d) Boundaries and rules

    e) Adapted games

  6 Field hockey

    a) Basic stick work

    (1) Dribbling

    (2) Passing

    (3) Ball control

    b) Lead-up drills

    c) Adapted game situations

  7 Volleyball

    Basic ball control skills

    (1) Passing

    (2) Receiving

    (3) Serving

  8 Track and field

    a) 40-yd sprint

    b) 160-yd shuttle relay

    c) High jump

    d) Long jumping

    e) Throw for distance

C K-2 grade level

  In the K-2 grade level, activities should provide opportunities for learner de-signed games to culminate space-related and manipulative activities. The skills to be acquired should include: throwing and catching, kicking, striking, tagging, and simple offensive and defensive maneuvers.

III Gymnastics

By the sixth grade the learner should have acquired adequate body management skills to permit creation and refinement of sequences employing the following gymnastics apparatus:

1 Beam	5 Hoops
2 Bars	6 Ropes
3 Floor	7 Balls
4 Box or horse	8 Wands

A 5-6 grade level

Spotting techniques and group work should lead to the completion of sequences commensurate with ability. Concentrate on refinement of beginnings, endings, and main actions. Rhythmic gymnastic routines for groups should include the use of balls, ropes, hoops, and wands.

B 3-4 grade level

Learners should be able to participate in activities that will lead up to the performance of efficient sequences. Foster exploratory development of skills leading to competency.

1 Supporting and suspension on floor, with partners, and on apparatus.
2 Balancing on various body parts with clarity of stretch, curled and twisted shapes of the body or body parts.
3 Landings from various jumps.
4 Turns on different levels, planes, and axes.
5 Rolling in different directions and in combination with landings and balance.
6 Flight onto, over, and from apparatus.
7 Jumps with various leg gestures, body shapes, and turns.
8 Assisting partners in forward and rearward turns and springs.
9 Fundamental tumbling stressing correct technique of forward and backward rolls, cartwheels, and round off.
10 Transitional and preparatory patterns such as the hurdle.

C K-2 grade level

The K-2 grade level of gymnastics should consist of fundamental themes of educational gymnastics and basic movement education. These activities should explore the range of movement possibilities that lead to agility and safety in body management when using both large and small apparatus. All kinds of ways of transferring the weight of the body, balancing, turning, arresting movement, and combining actions in short movement phrases with clarity of beginnings and endings should be stressed.

IV Dance

Learners should acquire a fundamental understanding of various movements, patterns, formations, and rhythms relevant to the following areas of dance:

1 Square dance
2 Round dance and social dance
3 Folk dance
4 Circle dance
5 Modern dance
6 Creative and novelty dance

A 5-6 grade level

On the 5-6 grade level the student should be able to participate in selected dance activities from the following list, whether alone, with partner, or in a set, line, or group formation.

1 Square dance

a) Do-si-do
b) Partner and corner swings
c) Promenade
d) Allemande right and left
e) Lead couple
f) Grand right and left
g) Indian file
h) Stars—right and left
i) Split the ring
j) Active
k) Ladies chain
l) All around your corner
m) Circle
n) Swings
o) Arch through
p) Pass through
q) Reel
r) See-saw

2 Round dance
- *a)* Polka
- *b)* Schottische
- *c)* Two-step

3 Circle dance
- *a)* King and Queen Highway
- *b)* Promenade
- *c)* Swings
- *d)* London Bridge
- *e)* Changing partners
- *f)* Cinnamon twist
- *g)* Shuffle step

4 Folk dance or creative dance representative of various cultures, i.e., European, Indian, African, Polynesian, Middle-Eastern, and so forth.
- *a)* Grapevine
- *b)* Polka—variations
- *c)* Schottische—variations
- *d)* Two-step—variations
- *e)* Shuffle and stomping patterns

5 Modern dance

Learners should be able to participate in the creation of simple dance compositions that express attitudes, feelings, work and play rhythms, or ideas from school studies in the social sciences, art, drama, and music.

B 3-4 grade level

Learners should be able to demonstrate fundamental step patterns and gestures in line or circle formations with and without partners, both in learner-created dances or in teacher-designed or guided structured forms that utilize square and folk patterns. Major emphasis should be given to learner-designed dances emanating from their explorations of spatial designs; dance songs; chants; everyday experiences in school, neighborhood, and home; rhythmic responses; and movement discoveries.

C K-2 grade level

Students should acquire the ability to express themselves rhythmically through such fundamental movements as walking, skipping, galloping, and running to a variety of simple rhythms. Story ideas, movement experiences, and songs should be the main basis for learner-designed, teacher-guided dances that express clear ideas and actions in simple improvisations and compositions.

V **Aquatics**

Learner should acquire aquatic skills that will enable safe participation in water activities.

A 5-6 grade level

Learners should have the following proficiencies: rhythmic breathing, drownproofing, front crawl, elementary backstroke, sidestroke, backstroke, breast stroke, and simple dives, from the deck or board. Underwater swimming and skills and adaptations of strokes for synchronized swimming, water stunts, or games should be taught, if possible.

B 3-4 grade level

Learners should be able to manage themselves safely in deep water, exhibiting basic stroke techniques, water safety, and drownproofing abilities.

C K-2 grade level

Learners should be able to demonstrate safe ways of managing movements in the water and when entering it. Fundamental skills of drownproofing, such as breath control, should be acquired early.

Suggested culminating activities and skills for the developmental track

I Introduction

In the developmental track of the physical education program, emphasis should be placed on skill development. Children in all grades and at all levels of development should be exposed to the activities within each of the media areas. These areas will be further broken down into instructional objectives, which are enabling objectives that provide lead-up skills.

Included in each activity are skills relevant to the activities and the terminal objectives described in the previous section. The instructor is expected to be able to perform a task analysis on each terminal objective to determine lead-up skills and lead-up activities for the objective. The teacher's instructional objective should include emphasis upon acquisition of motor patterns leading up to eventual attainment of specific skill competencies, such as overhand throw from the outfield in softball, underhand pitch in softball, football pass, trap and shoot sequence in soccer, push pass in field hockey, and chest pass in basketball.

Students will participate in the media areas of games/sports/contests, dance, gymnastics, and aquatics. A list of culminating activities follows.

A Games/Sports/Contests
1 Modified games—soccer, basketball, softball, football, hockey, volleyball
2 Regulation games—basketball, soccer, softball, hockey, tennis, volleyball
3 Meets and matches—tennis, track and field, wrestling (modified), volleyball
B Dance
1 Modern dance—playing dramatic roles, small and large group dance
2 Square dance—simple singing dances, patter calls, program presentation
3 Folk dance—dances from various foreign countries, such as France, Scotland, Israel, and Mexico, and program presentation
C Gymnastics
1 Educational gymnastics—demonstration of group work, displaying overall skills, stunts, and tumbling
2 Olympic gymnastics—intraclass competition, performance of routines, demonstrations
D Aquatics
1 Swimming events in class competition or technique demonstrations
2 Synchronized swimming—class presentation, demonstration of skills
3 Survival skills—drownproofing demonstrations
4 Diving demonstrations or competitions with student judges

II Games/sports/contests

To acquire a degree of proficiency in any area of the games media area, activities need to be provided that will not only enhance the skill development of the students but also provide fun and exciting experiences.

A 5-6 grade level

In the developmental track for grade level 5-6, activities should be sufficiently advanced to provide students with both a challenge and a chance to further develop game skills. Sports to be included are softball, soccer, basketball, tennis, football, field hockey, volleyball, track and field, and wrestling.

1 Softball

Skills to be emphasized	*Activities*
a) Batting	
(1) Batting from tee	(1) Bat to a partner or wall
(2) Tee-ball games	(2) Softball without pitcher; modified baserunning
(3) Tossing up ball and hitting it	(3) Bat to a partner or wall

(4) Hitting fungos

(5) Regulation game
b) Throwing
  (1) Keep away

  (2) Hot Potato
  (3) Double-play throws

c) Catching and fielding
  (1) Hitting fungos
  (2) Keep away
  (3) Pepper

d) Base Running
  (1) Tee-ball
  (2) Regulation game

e) Knowledge
  (1) Softball rules
  (2) Concepts of team play, strategy, positioning

2 Soccer
  a) Trapping
    (1) One-on-one
    (2) Three-on-three
    (3) Milk Carton Soccer
  b) Kicking and passing
    (1) Wallkick

    (2) Three-on-three
    (3) Regulation soccer
  c) Heading
    (1) Head ball

    (2) Keep away
    (3) Four-on-four
  d) Punting
    (1) Speedball
    (2) Five-on-five
  e) Dribbling
    (1) One-on-one
    (2) Two-on-two
    (3) Triangle passing
  f) Goal kicks
    (1) Three-on-three
    (2) Minisoccer
    (3) Wall volley
  g) Knowledge
    (1) Ball control and passing strategy
    (2) Soccer rules
    (3) Team play and positioning

---

(4) Bat ball to other players; score kept on caught balls
(5) Bat pitched balls

(1) Different types of throws, keep ball away from "it"; scattered or circle formation
(2) Throwing and catching—fast release of ball
(3) Fast throws simulating double-plays in regulation game

(1) Same as above
(2) Same as above
(3) One batter; two to three fielders who field and then pitch the ball to the batter

(1) Same as above
(2) Baserunning in variety of situations

(1) Situational play—no goals
(2) Situational play—goalies
(3) Modified soccer with modified balls

(1) Target practice to wall; kick, trap, kick sequence
(2) Situational play

(1) Head ball around group; see how long ball can be kept in the air
(2) Head the ball to keep it away from "it"
(3) Situational play

(1) Modified soccer and basketball
(2) Situational play—goalie; alternation with punts

(1) Situational play
(2) Situational play

(1) Situational play
(2) Seven players
(3) Kick-trap-shoot

3 Basketball
  a) Dribbling
    (1) Through obstacle course   (1) Obstacles set up to encourage proper dribbling with both hands
    (2) One-on-one   (2) Situational play
    (3) Through cones   (3) Same as above
    (4) Simon says   (4) Leader demonstrates ball skills while class follows, i.e., left hand, right hand
    (5) Five-on-five   (5) Situational play with two baskets
  b) Passing
    (1) Two-on-two   (1) Situational play
    (2) Keep away   (2) Same as above
    (3) Passing on fast breaks   (3) Situational play, three to four players
    (4) Three-on-three   (4) Same as above
    (5) Regulation game
  c) Shooting
    (1) Three-on-three   (1) Same as above
    (2) Four-on-four   (2) Same as above
    (3) Five-on-five   (3) Same as above
    (4) Twenty-one
    (5) Regulation game
  d) Rebounding
    (1) Five-on-five   (1) Same as above
    (2) Rebounding repetition   (2) Line rebounding against wall or backboard
  e) Guarding
    (1) One-on-one   (1) Man-to-man
    (2) Five-on-five   (2) Man-to-man or zone
    (3) Half-court basketball   (3) Modified basketball
  f) Knowledge
    (1) Basketball rules
    (2) Officiating
    (3) Team play and strategy
    (4) Positioning

4 Tennis
  a) Volley
    (1) Wall volley   (1) Volley against wall individually or with a partner
      (a) Body position
      (b) Racket placement, relationship, grip
    (2) Forehand volley   (2) Against wall or with a partner
      (a) Same as above
      (b) Same as above
    (3) Backhand volley   (3) Against wall or with a partner
      (a) Same as above
      (b) Same as above
    (4) Play skills   (4) Singles or doubles volleying
      (a) Adjusting to changes in player position
      (b) Adjusting to different speeds and trajectories of the ball

   b) Serve
      (1) Wall serves   (1) Serve to wall
      (2) To opponent   (2) Serve until point, with player alternation
      (3) Added to tennis game
   c) Knowledge
      (1) Tennis rules   (1) Keep score
      (2) Scoring   (2) Intramural play
      (3) Singles and doubles strategy   (3) Ladder tournament
      (4) Positioning

5 Football
   a) Blocking
      (1) Flag football   (1) Modified football without tackling
      (2) Four-on-four   (2) Situational play, man-for-man blocking
   b) Running
      (1) Obstacle course   (1) Change of direction and speed run
      (2) Whistleball   (2) Change direction with each whistle
      (3) One-on-one   (3) Situational play
   c) Kicking
      (1) Catch-kick   (1) Two teams, catch and kick to teammate; goal when kicked past end line

      (2) Field goal and punt   (2) Regulation game
   d) Passing and catching
      (1) Two-on-two   (1) Situational play
      (2) Four-on-four   (2) Same as above
      (3) Six-on-six   (3) Same as above
      (4) Hot Potato   (4) Same as above
      (5) Keep away   (5) Same as above
   e) Knowledge
      (1) Rules
      (2) Plays and formations
      (3) Defensive alignments
      (4) Specialty teams

6 Field hockey
   a) Dribbling
      (1) One-on-one   (1) Situational play
      (2) Obstacle course   (2) Dribbling around obstacles
      (3) Push-pull   (3) Dribble forward, back, to left, to right
   b) Driving
      (1) Two-on-two   (1) Control, drive
      (2) With partner   (2) Control, drive
      (3) Goal shot   (3) Dribble down field and shoot at top of circle
      (4) Circle shot   (4) Players line up around circle and shoot at goalie in rapid succession

   c) Passing
      (1) Triangle play   (1) Two against one defender
      (2) Two-on-two   (2) Situational play with flat and diagonal passing
   d) Dodging
      (1) Obstacle course
      (2) Three-on-three

Modern physical
education

e) Tackling
    (1) One-on-one shuttle
    (2) Regulation game
f) Goalkeeping
    (1) Three-on-three

    (2) Goal shot
g) Knowledge
    (1) Hockey rules
    (2) Positioning and strategy
    (3) Cutting to the open space

(1) Two teams face each other—one dribbles in, is tackled; tackler dribbles; etc.

(1) Two players plus goalie; alternate goalie
(2) Same as above

7 Volleyball (use light ball)
  a) Passing
    (1) Foursquare overhead pass

    (2) Wall volley
      (*a*) Overhead
      (*b*) Bump
    (3) Bump pass
  b) Serving
    (1) To wall
    (2) Regulation game
    (3) Newcomb
    (4) Underhand serve
    (5) Overhand serve
  c) Setting
    (1) Three and over
      (*a*) Bump, set, and volley over
      (*b*) Set, set, volley over
    (2) Circle set

  d) Spike and block
    (1) Toss-spike
    (2) Regulation game
  e) Knowledge
    (1) Volleyball rules
    (2) Rotation procedures
    (3) Positioning and strategy

(1) Four players in square who serve, set, and pass
(2) Pass against wall in overhead or underhand method

(1) Serve retrieve

(3) Modified volleyball with serve

(1) Set twice, then volley over

(2) Set ball within group to achieve height and control

(1) Two teams—one spikes, the other team blocks, sets, and spikes

8 Track and field
  a) Running
    (1) Sprints
    (2) Long runs
    (3) Quick
  b) Jumping
    (1) Obstacle course
    (2) High jump
    (3) Broad jump

(1) Sprint races
(2) Line runs with end runner passing group
(3) Line sprints

(1) Jumping over and across obstacles
(2) Work in threes with stretch rope—rotate
(3) Work in threes, each person jumping further than the one before
(4) Sequence of three standing broad jumps in sets to develop power

c) Hurdling
   - (1) Rope circuit
   - (2) Tire jump
      - (1) Hurdle series of stretch ropes
      - (2) Relay hurdling tires

d) Baton passing
   - (1) Regulation races
   - (2) Jack Rabbit Relay
      - (2) Modified 440 relay

e) Throwing
   - (1) Individual shot put
      - (1) Put shot to open space with retriever putting next
   - (2) Shot put with partner
      - (2) Discus throw from in front of softball back stop
   - (3) Softball throw
      - (3) Circuit from shot put, to softball, throw, to discus
   - (4) Discus throw
      - (4) Throw for distance with run-up
   - (5) Frisbee throw

f) Knowledge
   - (1) Understanding rules
   - (2) Understanding equipment and safety
   - (3) Understanding warm-up and warm-down

9 Wrestling

Due to the combative nature of the wrestling program, many injuries may occur during the growing years of a child. The program should not be introduced until late in grade 4. The child should be taught the safety of proper wrestling maneuvers and should practice with a child of like capabilities. Prerequisite strength, flexibility, and body management should be clearly established prior to activity to avoid injury due to poor condition or inadequate fundamental skills in falling and rolling.

a) Awareness of body parts for leverage
b) Basic holds to pin, reverse, or escape
c) Starting positions—kneeling, not standing, and referee
d) Scoring takedown, near fall, pin, reversal, and escape
e) Three one-minute rounds with student referee

B 3-4 grade level

Activities should provide unique ways of employing fundamental games skills. At this level of development, activities that require strong emphasis on competition should be introduced gradually. List or suggest culminating activities under the 5-6 grade level that would also be appropriate for the 3-4 grade level. With learner or teacher modification, all of the activities would be appropriate once adjusted to fit the maturity and ability level of the students.

C K-2 grade level

Activities for the K-2 level in the development track should be of low organization and should emphasize skills and knowledge that will provide a strong foundation for learning advanced game skills.

III Gymnastics

Learners should engage in those activities commensurate with their abilities and understandings which aid him to develop the skills needed to perform fluent movement sequences of his own design using mats, floor, and a variety of apparatus requiring support and suspension.

Modern physical
education

523

A 5-6 Grade Level

1 Floor exercise and tumbling

Skills to be emphasized	Limitations
a) Rolls	Show proper form while executing rolls, and show
(1) Sequence of forward rolls	good finishing position. Transitional movements
(2) Sequence of backward rolls	are needed to connect main actions.
(3) Forward roll, jump one half turn	Good alignment improves efficiency and appearance
(4) Backward roll, jump one half turn	but requires additional practice to achieve.
(5) Sequence of dive forward rolls	
(6) Backward roll extensions	
(7) Sideward rolls	
(8) Handstand forward roll	

Skills to be emphasized   *Limitations*

a) Rolls
- (1) Sequence of forward rolls
- (2) Sequence of backward rolls
- (3) Forward roll, jump one half turn
- (4) Backward roll, jump one half turn
- (5) Sequence of dive forward rolls
- (6) Backward roll extensions
- (7) Sideward rolls
- (8) Handstand forward roll

Show proper form while executing rolls, and show good finishing position. Transitional movements are needed to connect main actions.
Good alignment improves efficiency and appearance but requires additional practice to achieve.

b) Leaps
- (1) Split leap
- (2) Alternating legs, split leap sequences
- (3) Straddle leap
- (4) Stag leap
- (5) Cissone
- (6) Series of three different leaps

Leaps should stress balanced form and hand positioning and light, strong landings. Combinations of leaps with other locomotion skills or tumbling are required before final refinement can begin.

c) Springs
- (1) Kip action to bridge
- (2) Headsprings
- (3) Handspring turnovers
- (4) Handspring
- (5) Backhand spring turnovers
- (6) Backhand spring
- (7) Cartwheel progressions and cartwheel springs
- (8) Roundoffs

Springs should be done with spotters present when necessary. Proper form and good finishing position should be emphasized. Explosive extension is required for spring off the hands or feet. Combinations with rolls and dance permits the development of sequences.

d) Flexibility moves
- (1) Split progressions with alternate legs leading
- (2) Stride split progression
- (3) Forward walkover progression
- (4) Bridges and valdez
- (5) Wall walk-up for needle scale
- (6) Backward walkover progression
- (7) Straddle splits against a wall
- (8) Splits in standing position with partner
- (9) Straddle-leans to chest down
- (10) Split combinations with turns, rolls, cartwheels, and handstands

Flexibility moves should stress progression and proper warm-up. Again, proper form is important. Walkovers should be accompanied with adequate spotting until the desired level of technique is attained.

e) Balances
- (1) Head stand
- (2) Tip-ups
- (3) Handstands and pirouettes
- (4) Shoulder stands
- (5) Lunges
- (6) Arabesques
- (7) Straddle-bent hip

Balances should emphasize good form and be held. Inverted balance positions should show maximum extension in the back, shoulders, arms, and legs.

(8) Forearm stand
(9) V-sit
f) Spotting techniques
   (1) With partner
   (2) In groups of threes
   (one performer, two spotters)

Proper spotting techniques should accompany learning the above skills to assure safety and development of such factors as strength, flexibility, agility, motivation, and understanding.

g) Routines
   (1) Single pass
   (2) Multiple pass

Single pass routines should contain a minimum of three moves and show good starting and finishing positions and transitions. Multiple pass routines should make efficient use of space and include various combinations of each of the above categories (i.e., flexibility, springs, rolls, leaps). Routines may be accompanied with music, particularly if they are performed by groups or individuals in succession.

h) Judging and scoring
   (1) Self-evaluation
   (2) Partner evaluation
   (3) Evaluation of routines
   (4) Mock meet

Students should have an understanding of judging—using either learner-developed or given criteria to apply to performance—to demonstrate ability to evaluate within the limitations imposed.

2 Apparatus
a) Sequences
   (1) Begin a sequence on the floor, move continuously onto the apparatus and back to the floor. Repeat, improving the links between the movements.
   (2) Find a movement on the apparatus which can be repeated in a rhythmic way. Add a starting and a finishing position.
   (3) Create a sequence in which there is
      (a) change of speed
      (b) change of direction.
   (4) Link one piece of apparatus with another in a sequence using the floor.

There should be a definite starting position. Illustrate continuous action, show varied and original work, and have a clearly controlled finishing position.

b) Levels
   (1) Travel on the apparatus at a
      (a) high level
      (b) low level
   (2) Move from
      (a) high-low
      (b) low-high
   (3) Body is kept close to point of support
   (4) Body stretches away from point of support
      (a) above
      (b) below
   (5) Create sequence that contrasts levels

Work at varied levels may be either near the point of support or stretching away from, above, or below it. Control is important, as the levels may be connected by actions involving some risk to the performer.

Skills to be emphasized	*Limitations*

c) Partners and groups
    (1) Following
    (2) Matching
    (3) Contrasting
    (4) Passing over, under, around
    (5) Supporting

Tasks should be kept simple to avoid injury. Routines with or without music, emphasizing mounts, swinging, balancing, and dismounts.

d) Flight
    (1) Find ways of jumping down safely
    (2) Find ways of getting on apparatus with a jump or leap and immediately jumping off
    (3) Find ways to swing (dismount on backswing)
    (4) Hang from the hands, swing, release, and land with control
    (5) Flight to achieve various body shapes in air
    (6) Jump to balanced landing

Control movements in flight. Flight situations need not be high, but aim for proper landings utilizing the principles either of weight absorption or action/reaction.

e) Pathways, symmetry and asymmetry
    (1) Follow varied pathways
    (2) Repetitive air patterns
    (3) Support of the body
        (*a*) Symmetrically
        (*b*) Asymmetrically
    (4) Combine flight with symmetry and asymmetry
    (5) Sequence of asymmetric movements combined with symmetric balances

Child should demonstrate knowledge of the concepts stated through choice of appropriate move- • ments. Combining asymmetric and symmetric actions should be stressed in the asymmetric run to the symmetric jump or vault.

f) Strength and lightness
    (1) Find places on the apparatus where you can use a great deal of strength
    (2) Find ways to move where only a little energy is needed
    (3) Creating a sequence of light, strong actions that show a definite climax at the end.

Child should be able to distinguish whether a movement requires strength or lightness in order to execute movement efficiently.

g) Suggested apparatus
    (1) Hinged climbing frame
    (2) Rope ladders, hand rings, and trapeze
    (3) Mats
    (4) Benches
    (5) Horizontal ropes
    (6) Trestles
    (7) Poles, ladders, beams, and planks
    (8) Vaulting horse, Swedish box
    (9) Parallel and uneven parallel bars

Safety.
Incorporate new skills in sequence.
Control landings to avoid imbalance or to arrest action momentarily.
Employ proper grip to avoid loss of control
Use lead-up skills as enabling objectives to the final outcome desired.

B 3-4 grade level

1 Floor exercises and tumbling
  a) Rolls
    (1) Forward roll to stand
    (2) Backward roll to stand

Correct form and progression used, show good finishing position.

(3) Sequential rolls (forward and backward)
(4) Shoulder stand roll down and stand
b) Leaps
  (1) Split leap
  (2) Other body shape leaps
  (3) Combination of hops, jumps and leaps

Stress holding shape in flight, full extension—
lifting into split leap position.

c) Transferences on hands
  (1) Cartwheel
  (2) Walkover
  (3) Roundoff
  (4) Tinsica

Stretched body parts emphasize stress of arm-head
relationship throughout actions.

d) Springs
  (1) Kip action
  (2) Cartwheel springs
  (3) Lead-ups to roundoff
e) Flexibility moves
  (1) Lead up to splits, kneeling and hurdler
  (2) Straddle-leans to chest down
  (3) Bridges with straight legs
  (4) Rockinghorse
f) Balances
  (1) Tripods
  (2) Tip-ups
  (3) Handstand
  (4) Shoulder stands
  (5) Lunges
  (6) Knee scales
  (7) Bridgelike balances
  (8) One body part
  (9) Headstand

Stress partner work for assistance, observation,
and critique.

g) Spotting technique
  (1) Group of three working together
  (2) Understand importance of spotting
as safety factor
  (3) Lifting, carrying, controlling

Rhythmic cooperation among two spotters and
performer in rotation showing fluency of transitions and actions.
Getting into and out of handstands through rolls
and turns and assistance in flight are stressed.

h) Routines
  (1) Simple three to four item routines
  (2) Sequence in threes

Show good starting and finishing position. Awareness of audience roles in performing (proper
audience behavior).

2 Apparatus
  a) Mounting and dismounting
    (1) Stressing body parts used
    (2) Controlled landings

Adjust apparatus height.

  b) Use of space
    (1) Over, under, through
    (2) Side, front, back, an angle

Sequence actions and work out transitions
to make fluent combinations.

  c) Transfer of weight
    (1) One body part to same
    (2) One body part to another

Stress control, proper grip.

Skills to be emphasized	Limitations

(3) Leaving apparatus with some body part other than the feet touching first
(4) Arriving at balances

d) Lifting and lowering to change position or initiate swinging

Use the momentum created to produce another movement.

e) Joining movements

Avoid extra swings and awkward positions.

f) Twisting-turning

Rotation around the transverse axis and the long axis of the body.

C K-2 grade level

1 Rolls
  a) Transferring weight by rolling
  b) Rolls in different directions
  c) Landing and rolling

Maintain curved body shape, placing hands where the body weight will be shifted for controlled transfer in forward and backward rolling.

2 Leaving the floor
  a) Hops
  b) Jumps
  c) Receiving and bearing body weight upon landing

Using the entire leg for pushoffs and landings.
Place feet in proper relationship to body weight.
Place hands in proper relationship to body weight.

     (1) From one body part to another
     (2) On different body parts
     (3) From feet to hands
        (a) Rabbit hop
        (b) Mule kick
  d) Curling and stretching
     (1) Back arch
     (2) Curl up and stretch to lie down
     (3) Curl on side

Rocking and rolling on large curved surfaces of the body. Changing shape with the addition of leg, arm, or trunk stretching.

  e) Traveling
     (1) Steplike actions on feet
     (2) Wheeling
     (3) Sliding
     (4) Rolling

3 Apparatus
     (1) Get on and off in different ways
     (2) Perform a main action while in support or suspension

Show control, clarity of positions, ability to join different movements. Repeat sequences to clarify the qualities needed to make a finished product.

     (3) Connect different actions
     (4) Land from jumps
     (5) Simple swinging and turning
     (6) Hang from different body parts
     (7) Get over, under and around with different body parts leading
     (8) Balance in various ways
     (9) Develop original sequences on the apparatus
     (10) Join floor actions with apparatus sequences

IV Dance

In the area of dance the program should provide opportunities for expressive movement (creative movement) and folk forms of dance. The program should develop learners' awarenesses of the potential for rhythmic activities of the body, appreciations for fluent expression, and abilities beyond those in evidence at the beginning of instruction.

A 5-6 grade level

1 Creative dance
   Skills to be emphasized

   a) Action words
      (1) Traveling actions
      (2) Vibratory actions
      (3) Jumping actions
      (4) Turning actions
      (5) Stopping actions
      (6) Percussive actions
      (7) Contracting actions
      (8) Expanding actions
      (9) Sinking actions
   b) Effort awareness
      (1) The sensation of time
      (2) The sensation of energy
      (3) The sensation of space
   c) Space awareness
      (1) Floor pattern and design
      (2) Air pattern and design
      (3) Focus
      (4) Spatial actions
   d) Relationship awareness
      (1) Meeting and parting
      (2) Meeting and staying together
      (3) Leading and following
      (4) Shadowing and mirroring
      (5) Action and response
      (6) Relating to shape, quality, and touch
   e) Miscellaneous ideas
      (1) Identification association
      (2) Dramatization

2 Folk dance
   a) Round Dances
      (1) Heel-toe
      (2) Polka
      (3) Reel
      (4) Schottische
      (5) Swing variations
   b) Folk Dances
      (1) Polka
      (2) Varsovienne position
      (3) American square dance movement

Suggestions

Words can be explored singly or can be developed into sentences of actions.
Movements for variety can be accompanied by music, verses.

Lesson plans should be designed to help the student explore the varying degrees along the continuum of the extremes of effort, space, and relationship. These areas can be explored in both partner and group work and should develop from isolated movements to sequential patterns and finished dances.

Any one of a number of choreographed dances and accompanying music can be used to teach the basic steps and sequence. Stick games, such as Tinikling and Lummi Sticks, are fun and offer variety to the program. Studies of different countries can be enhanced by doing the dances and playing the games with which they are associated. Learn square dance by starting with partners and sequencing phrases of eight-count patterns. Work with four

Skills to be emphasized	Suggestions
(4) Stick game	people and the concept of opposite. Add four more
(5) Big circle and clogging	people and form squares.
(6) Tex-Mex dances	
(7) European country dances	

B 3-4 grade level

1 Creative dance
   a) Body awareness
      (1) Action words
      (2) Body parts leading or emphasizing action
      (3) Body shape
   b) Effort awareness
      (1) Separate motion factors of time, energy and space
      (2) Combining two motion factors
   c) Space awareness
      (1) Direction
      (2) Levels
      (3) Rising and sinking
   d) Relationships
      (1) Alone
      (2) Partner
      (3) Group

See suggestions for 5-6 grade dance section.

2 Folk dance
   a) Round dances
      (1) Directions
      (2) Basic locomotor movements
      (3) Schottische
   b) Line dances
   c) Folk dances
      (1) American
      (2) Tex-Mex
      (3) European
      (4) Stick games

Keep folk forms simple and use student versions. Emphasize elements of structure in composition. Explore step patterns and partner relationships. Select patterns and combine them into learner-designed dances. Share by teaching others how to do them.

C K-2 grade level

1 Creative dance
   a) Emotion expression
      (1) In personal space
      (2) With locomotor movements
   b) Rhythmic actions
      (1) Marching
      (2) Body parts moving in rhythm
   c) Dramatization of familiar stories
   d) Use of various stimuli, such as hats, ribbons, and props

In the K-2 program in dance, teachers should continue to stress elements of basic movement education. Lesson plans should be constructed around these elements and the accompaniments kept simple.

2 Folk dance
  a) Simple formations
    (1) Circle
    (2) Line
  b) Change of direction
  c) Recognizing the primary beat in music
  d) Changing partners
  e) Singing games

Stress concept of dancing to the music with proper beginnings, endings, and step patterns. Divide class into group after dances have been learned.

Paw Paw Patch
A-Hunting We Will Go
Bow Bow Belinda
Rig-a-Jig-Jig

  f) Simple folk

Danish Dance of Greeting
Shoemakers' Dance
Kinder Polka
Carrousel

  g) Novelty dances

Bunny Hop
Hokey Pokey

V Aquatics

In the medium of aquatics, developmental achievement is essential if a child is to overcome fear of the water and become self-sufficient as a swimmer.

A 5-6 grade level

The child should have developed basic strokes and been introduced to diving. Further development of skill should be stressed. Many activities can be incorporated into the learning process. For example, water polo will help to develop the body, build discipline, and build the desire to excel.

Activities

1 Techniques of each stroke, adding butterfly
2 Diving skills
  a) Front dive
  b) Feet-first jump
  c) Optional dives
3 Culminating
4 Water polo
5 Innertube polo
6 Water basketball
7 Synchronized swimming
8 Swim races
9 Novelty relays

B 3-4 grade level

Basic stroke development should be encouraged. Activities should include stroke development of the crawl, backstroke, sidestroke, and breaststroke. Low-level diving can be introduced.

Activities

1 Basic strokes techniques—crawl, backstroke, breaststroke
2 Continued work on endurance
3 Introduction to diving—from side of the pool and from the board

C K-2 grade level

Children at this age should be acquainted with the pool and the safety equipment. Endurance development should be stressed through repetition. Breath-

Modern physical
education

531

ing must be taught and then synchronized with the strokes. Fins can often help with the instruction.

Activities

1 Pull self out of pool without the use of ladders
2 Travel in shallow water using the hands to assist
3 Change from vertical to horizontal position
4 Put face in water, blow bubbles
5 Kick on side of pool
6 Swim with fins to develop awareness of action in relationship to pool surface
7 Swim with kickboard to strengthen awareness of function of legs in leveling off
8 Basic strokes—crawl—elementary form of backstroke
9 Change direction and body position so as to sequence strokes

Laboratory experiences (K-6) program objectives	

I Introduction

The elementary physical education instructional program should be supplemented by daily recreational activity periods that enable students to improve their competencies in physical and social skills through guided supervised play. The laboratory experiences should enable the student to

A Develop good individual recreational attitudes provided by pleasant experiences in supervised play and intramural programs.
B Develop responsible and socially acceptable playground behavior.
C Develop an interest and desire to participate in lifetime sports activities.
D Develop a feeling of belonging, a sense of loyalty to a cause that is larger than the individual self, and a willingness to sacrifice one's own interests for the welfare of the group.
E Develop a spirit of play and sense of sportsmanship or sportsmanlike conduct.
F Develop a means by which the individual can relax and release frustrations, anxieties, and hostilities through some form of socially acceptable physical activity.
G Develop a good self-image through successful participation in play.
H Develop skills that will enable the student to participate in extramural and intramural programs in such sports as

1 Soccer	6 Volleyball	11 Tennis
2 Baseball	7 Gymnastics	12 Bowling
3 Basketball	8 Track and field	13 Swimming
4 Softball	9 Field hockey	
5 Flag football	10 Badminton	

I Develop and enjoy through supervised play the skills previously learned in physical education activity classes.
J Improve physical fitness, strength, endurance, agility, and confident control of body movements.
K Develop good mental, emotional, and physical health habits and attitudes.
L Develop the ability to make social contacts that simulate adult social and competitive life.
M Fulfill and satisfy basic human needs, such as the following, through physical activity.

1 Personal satisfaction	5 Self-reliance
2 Accomplishment	6 Recognition
3 Self-expression	7 Belonging to a group
4 Creativity	

II K-2 grade level

Laboratory experience objectives for grades K-2 should provide students with opportunities to improve their physical and social skills through supervised play.

A The program should provide modified lead-up activities through supervised play in such games and activities as:

1 Tee Ball
2 Dodgeball
3 Seat Tag
4 Kick Ball
5 Jump rope
6 Sky Ball (catch and throw back over net)
7 Triangles (throw/catch or kick/trap in trios)
8 Tug-of-War
9 One-on-one contests (low competition)

B Students should be provided with opportunities to safely explore and use gross motor movements on both indoor and outdoor gymnastics equipment. These movements include:

1 Jumping
2 Turning
3 Rolling
4 Swinging
5 Climbing
6 Hanging
7 Descending
8 Balancing

C The program should provide opportunities to move creatively to rhythms by percussive instruments and music in such activities as:

1 Expressive movements
2 Dramatization
3 Fundamental motor rhythms
4 Play party

D The program should provide the opportunity for aquatic movement through such activities as:

1 Exploratory movement
2 Basic strokes
3 Games
   a) Tag
   b) Water polo simplified
   c) Keepaway
4 Water safety, including basic drownproofing

III 3-4 grade level

In grades 3-4, the program should include both supervised play activities and intramural programs (on a low competitive level).

A The program should provide opportunities to participate in individual and team sport activities with emphasis on skill and sportsmanship in supervised play and intramural programs in the following sports:

1 Soccer
2 Softball/baseball
3 Basketball
4 Volleyball
5 Field hockey
6 Football
7 Lacrosse
8 Tennis
9 Badminton
10 Track and field
11 Bowling

B Gymnastics should be offered in both supervised play and intramural program situations on the following equipment:

1 Mats
2 Uneven parallel bars
3 Parallel bars
4 Balance beam
5 Bars
6 Trampoline
7 Horse

C Supervised play experiences should provide for opportunities for movement in folk, square, and creative dance.

Modern physical education

D Recreational swimming and low competition swimming and diving should be provided.

IV 5-6 grade level

In grades 5-6, the program should continue to provide supervised play activities and intramural programs. Extramural programs should be added.

A The extramural program in the previously mentioned sports should be added to the program for the elements of socializing with and competing against other schools.

B Gymnastics should be continued on the supervised play, intramural, and extramural levels.

C The dance program should include folk, square, and creative dance, with the possible addition of recreational dances and dance clubs.

D The aquatics program should continue as already stated with the addition of extramural swimming and diving.

Bibliography and suggested references

Bancroft, Jessie H. *Games.* New York: Macmillan, 1937.

Blake, O. William, and Volp, Ann M. *Lead Up Games to Team Sports.* Englewood Cliffs, N.J.: Prentice-Hall, 1964.

Boorman, Joyce. *Creative Dance in the First Three Grades.* Don Mills, Ont.: Longman Canada Limited, 1969.

———. *Creative Dance in Grades Four to Six.* Don Mills, Ont.: Longman Canada Limited, 1971.

———. *Dance and Language Experiences with Children.* Don Mills, Ont.: Longman Canada Limited, 1973.

Boyd, Neva L. *Handbook of Games.* Chicago: Fitzsimons, 1945.

Buckland, Don. *Gymnastics, Activity in the Primary School.* London: Heinemann Educational Books, 1969.

Carroll, Jean, and Lofthouse, Peter. *Modern Creative Dance for Boys.* London: MacDonald & Evans, 1969.

Clark, Dara E. *A Program of Activities.* St. Louis: Mosby, 1969.

Cooper, Phyllis. *Feminine Gymnastics.* Minneapolis: Burgess, 1973.

Corbin, Charles B. *Inexpensive Equipment for Games, Play and Physical Activity.* Dubuque, Iowa: Wm. C. Brown, 1972.

Cratty, Bryant J. *Developmental Games for Physically Handicapped Children.* Palo Alto, Calif.: Peek Publications, 1969.

———. *Developmental Sequences of Perceptual Motor Tasks.* Freeport, N.Y.: Educational Activities, 1967.

———. *Intelligence in Action.* Englewood Cliffs, N.J.: Prentice-Hall, 1973.

———. *Trampoline Activities for Atypical Children.* Palo Alto, Calif.: Peek Publications, 1969.

Dimondstein, Geraldine. *Children Dance in the Classroom.* New York: Macmillan, 1971.

Frostig, Marianne and Maslow, Phyllis. *Movement Education Theory and Practice.* Chicago: Follett, 1970.

Gilliom, Bonnie Cherp. *Basic Movement Education for Children: Rationale and Teaching Units.* Reading, Mass.: Addison-Wesley, 1970.

Hunt, Sarah E., and Cain, Ethel. *Games the World Around.* New York: A. S. Barnes, 1950.

Jernigan, Sara S., and Vendier, C. Lynn. *Playtime, a World Recreation Handbook.* New York: McGraw-Hill, 1972.

Joyce, Mary. *First Steps in Teaching Creative Dance.* Palo Alto, Calif.: National Press Books, 1973.

Lofthouse, Peter. *Dance, Activity in the Primary School.* London: Heinemann Educational Books, 1970.

Miller, Peggy L. *Creative Outdoor Play Areas.* Englewood Cliffs, N.J.: Prentice-Hall, 1972.

Morison, Ruth. *A Movement Approach to Educational Gymnastics.* London: Dent, 1969.

Morris, David. *Swimming, Activity for the Primary School.* London: Heinemann Educational Books, 1969.

Mulac, Margaret E. *Games and Stunts for Schools, Camps and Playgrounds.* New York: Harper and Row, 1964.

Murray, Ruth L. *Dance in Elementary Education.* New York: Harper and Row, 1963.

Noble, Neal (consultant). *Learning Through Movement Education.* Chicago: The Athletic Institute, 1975.

Pallett, G. D. *Modern Educational Gymnastics.* New York: Pergamon, 1965.

Russell, Joan. *Creative Dance in the Primary School.* New York: Praeger, 1968.

Schurr, Evelyn L. *Movement Experiences for Children.* New York: Appleton-Century-Crofts, 1967.

Slater, Wendy. *Teaching Modern Educational Dance.* London: Mac-Donald & Evans, 1974.

Stanley, Sheila. *Physical Education, A Movement Orientation.* New York: McGraw-Hill, 1969.

Wackerbarth, Marjorie, and Graham, Lillian S. *Games for All Ages.* Minneapolis: Denison, 1959.

Wallis, Earl L., and Logan, Gene A. *Exercises for Children.* Englewood Cliffs, N.J.: Prentice-Hall, 1966.

Williams, Jean. *Themes for Educational Gymnastics.* London: Lepus Books, 1974.

Wise, W. M. *Games and Sports, Activity in the Primary School.* London: Heinemann Educational Books, 1969.

Curriculum materials

Curriculum outline for a physical education program, K-8

Introduction: The rationale for having a systemwide curriculum.

The two learning tracks
  Basic movement education program
    Awareness of motion factors
    Problem solving as the means for learning
      Environmental discovery
      Directed discovery
    Thematic organization
    Spiral curricular sequence
  Developmental movement education program
    Activities and skills
      Description of the games program
      Description of the gymnastics program
      Description of the dance program
    Rationale for instruction in skills
    Seasonal games, sports, dances, and special events
  Junior high school extracurricular program
    Girls' extracurricular activities
      Intramural
      Extramural
    Boys' extracurricular activities
      Intramural
      Extramural
Schools and facilities: The organizational structure
  Elementary schools
    Indoor and outdoor facilities
    Other resources for space and equipment

Part I

Overview of the program: Rationale and purpose

Part II
Instructional program

Description of activities:
　　Name of activity (game)
　　Statement of rationale and purpose:
　　　The course is designed to . . .
　　　The program objectives are . . .
　　Course objectives for each instructional level (K-2, 3-4, 5-6, 7-8):
　　　Objectives
　　　Skills
　　　Knowledge and understandings
　　　Resources for additional information
Course objectives, gymnastics program
　Alphabetical list of activities
　Description of program activities:
　　Name of activity (program area)
　　Statement of rationale and purpose:
　　　The course is designed to . . .
　　　The program objectives are . . .
　　Course objectives for each instructional level (K-2, 3-4, 5-6, 7-8):
　　　Objectives
　　　Skills
　　　Knowledge and understandings
　　　Resources and additional information
Course objectives, dance program
　Alphabetical list of activities
　Description of program activities
　　Name of activity (program area)
　　Statement of rationale and purpose:
　　　The course is designed to . . .
　　　The program objectives are . . .
　　Course objectives for each instructional level (K-2, 3-4, 5-6, 7-8):
　　　Objectives
　　　Skills
　　　Knowledge and understandings
　　　Resources and additional information

PHYSICAL EDUCATION PROGRAM COURSE OUTLINE

Course of instruction: _____
I
Statement of purpose
   A The rationale for this course of instruction is:

   B The program objectives for this course of instruction are:
     1 Outcomes in the psychomotor domain:

     2 Outcomes in the cognitive domain:

     3 Outcomes in the affective domain:

II

Outline of instructional units for _____

                                       (course of instruction)

Instructional level: Grades   K   1   2   3   4   5   6   7   8

                                         (circle)

Title of unit: _____

Program objectives: By the conclusion of this unit the student should be able to

  1 Perform (skills outcomes)

  2 Know or understand as demonstrated by (cognitive outcomes)

  3 Demonstrate favorable attitudes while engaged in the activity by (affective outcomes)

III

Evaluation

Statement of how outcomes are tested for and graded

IV

Instructional activities and resources (aides, consultants, ideas)

V

Textbooks and bibliographical references

VI

Additional information (equipment, permission forms)

Prepared by: _____

_____

Date: _____

Curriculum materials

ACTIVITY UNIT OBJECTIVES

Games ( )   Gymnastics ( )   Dance ( )

Activity sequence: _____

At the conclusion of the instructional sequence identified by the flow chart below, the student should be able to perform the listed skills with acceptable technique and employ them properly in activity appropriate to individual level of maturity and general movement ability.

Skills	K	1	2	3	4	5	6	7	8

LESSON PLAN

Part I of the lesson
  1 Theme:

  2 Preinstructional activity

  3 Floor task (Initial challenge)

  4 Concepts to clarify

  5 Further development (Additional challenges)

Part II of the lesson
  1 Area to which above concepts and skills will be applied:

  2 Equipment needed—kind and amount

  3 Concepts or skills to be emphasized

  4 Initial task

  5 Further development

  6 Culminating activity (describe briefly—use back for additional information)

Guiding Principles

The organization
of the elementary
school physical
education
program

The K-2 program

■ A minimum of 80 percent of the instructional time is devoted to basic movement education.

Themes serve as the organizing principle for concept and body management development.

Progression in themes is accompanied by the incorporation of new concepts and awarenesses into *all* relevant previous material (spiral development).

New concepts are generally introduced through floor-related activities and then enriched through change in environmental circumstances during each lesson.

Apparatus activity is given the major emphasis to assure the development of appropriate gross motor patterns and body management skills. Structural gymnastic skills (set forms) are not emphasized, but the foundation for their later development is provided. Safety training receives immediate and continuous emphasis to assure the development of adequate motor control.

Manipulative lessons encompass a wide range of activity but gradually focus attention on the development of propulsion, reception, and handling patterns fundamental to participation in games and sports that involve a net and batting and running.

Skill learning is accomplished mainly through guided discovery, but all fundamental motor patterns including manipulative and apparatus skills should be acquired by the end of second grade.

Rhythm lessons involve progression from primary attention to the qualities of different sounds to the organization of sounds into free as well as metric phrases to accompany selected actions. The utilization of floor space and rhythm instruments to accompany movement is augmented by investigation into rhythmic movement patterns in manipulative and apparatus environments.

Correlation with the language arts program is fostered through attention to listening skills, movement vocabulary, beginning, middle, and ending of movement phrases, rhythmic relationships of accent, time, and space, the length and structure of movement phrases, and the imaginative use of movement accompanying or following words, phrases, or stories.

Correlation with the social studies program is fostered through attention to the concepts of number and shape as they relate to the body as a resource for movement and space as the medium shaped by movement.

Correlation with the science program is fostered mainly but not exclusively through an emphasis on inquiry learning, problem-solving, and attention to cause-effect relationships in movement learning.

K-2 instructional plan

Thematic units of instruction with clearly stated objectives are used for a period of three weeks to provide sufficient opportunity for the assimilation of concepts and their enrichment through the relation of rhythmic, manipulative, and apparatus environments in the following patterns.

	Mon.	Tues.	Wed.	Thur.	Fri.
Week 1	Floor ↓ App.	Floor ↓ Rhythm	Floor ↓ Manip.	Floor ↓ App.	Floor ↓ Rhythm
Week 2	Floor ↓ Manip.	Floor ↓ App.	Floor ↓ Rhythm	Floor ↓ Manip.	Floor ↓ App.
Week 3	Floor ↓ Rhythm	Floor ↓ Manip.	Floor ↓ App.	Floor ↓ Rhythm	Floor ↓ Manip.

The use of this plan does not forbid the practice of two or even three successive days of one environmental emphasis. It is meant to ensure the development of all movement in relation to the four environmental circumstances simultaneously—floor, rhythm, apparatus, and manipulation.

The 3-4 program

■ Basic movement education is rapidly reduced from 80 percent at the second grade level to 40 percent at the third grade level and a maximum of 25 percent at the fourth grade level.

Themes continue to serve as the organizing principle for concept and body management development, but activities having cultural and social relevance are given emphasis in the developmental skill learning portion of the program.

Progression in themes continues, but there is often direct application made to games.

Educational gymnastics evolves out of the basic movement track as a separate program emphasis but continues with a theme emphasis rather than an activity emphasis to promote development of general body management skills rather than limited selected skills.

Educational dance evolves out of the basic movement track as a separate program area and continues the emphasis on themes as the principal mode for organizing content.

Activity skills are fostered to assure the acquisition of motor behaviors and associated understandings that will enable the learner to participate in an increasing variety of developmental games, contests, sports, gymnastics, and dance activities. The breadth and depth of this program will depend in large measure on the use of time outside of instructional periods for supervised play or refinement of skills.

The emphasis is still on small group participation, with the maximum number of children per activity rarely exceeding eight.

Skill learning tends to be more directed as children's needs and abilities are clarified in relation to a specific goal. The principles of guided discovery are never abandoned entirely but are used whenever it is to the learner's advantage.

Activity units are the dominant program emphasis, but the basic movement program is either integrated directly with the activity concepts or is used to provide relevant preinstructional emphasis relevant to such topics as spatial relationships, sequence, movement phrasing, and tension control.

Themes place great emphasis on spatial awareness, relationship to partners and small groups, the refinement of movement sequences, and concepts relevant to the analysis of motor skills and the circumstances of the learner. Discussions include concepts like gravity, equilibrium, inertia, momentum, and friction to enlarge the purpose of certain motor behaviors.

Correlation with the academic programs is fostered through the inclusion of interdisciplinary concepts relevant to motor learning, refinement, play, and self-expression. Cooperation with other specialists is important.

3-4 instructional plan

Thematic units of instruction are still important and continue to be developed in a curricular spiral but increasingly are developed in conjunction with the developmental program. Basic movement lessons are gradually interwoven with activity units to assure the continued emphasis on the understandings to be derived from movement studies. In this manner developmental movement lessons are not derived from the underlying basic movement structure but rather from the needs of the learner to understand not only skills and activity concepts but also the relationships of these skills to the mainstream of movement knowledge.

Activity units and basic movement units may be taught within the same lesson, the instructor merely closing one activity and beginning a new one as in the following example.

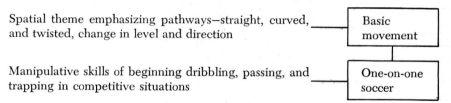

Spatial theme emphasizing pathways—straight, curved, and twisted, change in level and direction — Basic movement

Manipulative skills of beginning dribbling, passing, and trapping in competitive situations — One-on-one soccer

The basic movement lesson may utilize any of the four fundamental environments—floor, apparatus, rhythmic sound, or manipulative objects in a rotation similar to K-2.

Theme: Working with partners emphasizing changes in level, direction, and pathway

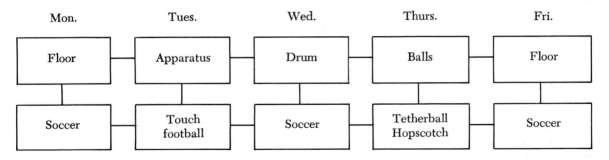

Children with marked deficiencies in arm and shoulder strength would be better off with the following instructional patterns using the same theme.

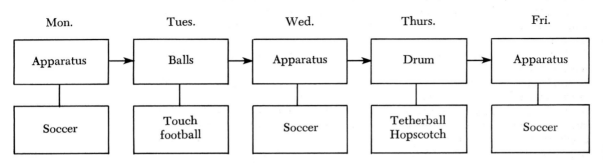

In the above instructional sequence, four units are taught over a three-week period.

Basic movement unit: Working with partners emphasizing changes in level, direction and pathway

Developmental skill unit in soccer: Two-on-two soccer

Developmental skill unit in touch football: Kickoff

Developmental skill unit in playground games: Tetherball and Hopscotch

The three-week plan should take the following form to assure the best use of time.

Week 1	Daily emphasis on space theme	10 minutes
	3 days soccer	15 minutes
	1 day playground	15 minutes
	1 day touch football	15 minutes
Week 2	Daily emphasis on space theme	10 minutes
	2 days touch football	15 minutes
	2 days soccer	15 minutes
	1 day playground game	15 minutes
Week 3	Daily emphasis on space theme	10 minutes
	2 days playground game	15 minutes
	2 days touch football	15 minutes
	1 day soccer	15 minutes

■ Basic movement education is almost always interwoven with specific activities and skills in the games program and is always integrated with the themes of educational gymnastics and dance.

The developmental skills program is organized to achieve the purposes of three distinct program areas: games, contests, and sports; educational gymnastics; and educational dance.

The concepts acquired through the basic movement program during previous learning experiences are elaborated through the acquisition and refinement of many skills.

Skill learning and the application of skills to appropriate problems continues the emphasis on problem solving.

Creativity is fostered through many opportunities to design new or different movement sequences utilizing the floor, the apparatus, and the movements of self and others.

Creativity is encouraged through opportunities to design new dances, to express ideas, or simply to engage others in a socially satisfying experience.

Creativity is fostered by encouraging children to continue the practice of making up their own games and by designing their own offensive and defensive patterns.

Both team and individual sports are taught to provide social outlets in wholesome activity.

Task analysis is taught so it may be practiced by the learners for the purpose of improving their own skills or helping others to improve.

Each of the program areas permits correlation with other aspects of the child's educational program. In class, tasks correlating art, music, movement, or academic subjects may form the basis for an elaboration into PTA presentations that require extensive research and practice of the final form.

Fitness activities focusing on agility and strength may be performed indoors for five minutes and combined with running outdoors to give outdoor activities a stronger fitness emphasis.

5-6 instructional plan

Activity units are organized for a period of three weeks or multiples of three weeks to facilitate coordination with the school calendar and other grade levels. Clear statements of purpose accompany each unit so that the specific objectives may easily be identified. Games, contests, and sports constitute the competitive program area. Gymnastics is concerned with self-testing through the manipulation of body in relation to various kinds of apparatus. Dance is for expressive purposes. Gymnastics and dance continue the use of themes to describe the content emphasis of their programs.

Because basic movement is either integrated in gymnastics or dance movement learning experiences, there is no separation of content into a basic movement lesson. Such lessons occur now to fulfill specific needs for individual classes or groups within classes. Spatial problems in games are clarified on the spot as they occur.

Although block planning utilizes time efficiently for the development of skills, multiple blocks should be considered superior in providing for the broader needs of children. Several examples of activity unit block planning are illustrated.

Outdoor Fall Program

Weeks 1-3	Soccer	M/W/F	9 periods
	Tennis	Tu/Th	6 periods

Weeks 4-6	Soccer	M/W/F	9 periods
	Tennis	Tu/Th	6 periods
Weeks 7-9	Touch football	M/W/F	9 periods
	Recreational games	Tu/Th	6 periods

OR

Weeks 1-3	Touch football	M/W/F	9 periods
	Tennis	Tu/Th	6 periods
Weeks 4-6	Soccer	M/W	6 periods
	Tennis	Tu/Th	6 periods
	Touch football	F	3 periods
Weeks 7-9	Soccer	M/W/F	9 periods
	Touch football	Tu	3 periods
	Recreational games	Th	3 periods

The Indoor Program

Weeks 13-15	Gymnastics	M/W/F	9 periods
	Basketball	Tu/Th	6 periods
Weeks 16-18	Gymnastics	M/W/F	9 periods
	Basketball	Tu/Th	6 periods
Weeks 19-21	Gymnastics	M/W	6 periods
	Dance	Tu/Th	6 periods
	Basketball	F	3 periods
Weeks 22-24	Wrestling, gymnastics	M/W	6 periods
	Volleyball	Tu/Th	6 periods
	Dance	F	3 periods
Weeks 25-27	Gymnastics, dance	M/W	6 periods
	Volleyball	F	3 periods
	Recreational net games	Tu/Th	6 periods

Spring—Outdoor Program

Weeks 28-30	Gymnastics, track and field	M/W/F	9 periods
	Batting games	Tu/Th	6 periods
Weeks 31-33	Track and field	M/W	6 periods
	Batting games	Tu/Th	6 periods
	Recreational games	F	3 periods

Sport Skills

Movement education: its application to teaching sport skills

■ Movement education has brought a methodology to physical education that can be used to help children develop their skills in sports more effectively than the command style of teaching. The skill of teachers in recognizing the levels of readiness for either group or individual activities, their insights into the learning processes, and the effectiveness of their relationships with children must be accompanied by a reasonably good understanding of the skills to be acquired. All of these factors must exist within a learning environment that will encourage all children to develop at their own rate.

Part I of a demonstration of ball handling skills leading to the development of basketball skills concerns itself with the first stage of learning: *self-initiated exploration.*

The Task:
An exploration of how balls of various sizes and weights might be used; self-discovery.
Problem:
For the teacher—To set the environment for discovery
For the pupils—To explore the properties of balls through using them in a variety of ways; to solve those perceived problems involving space; to see how others do it.

Part II involves the teacher more directly in the discovery process.

Who can?
● Problems devised by the teacher to broaden and deepen the awareness of other possibilities than those discovered through self-initiated exploration; leading to pupils to develop new problems for themselves.
How can?

- An extension of the awareness of possibilities to other areas that need increasingly complex movement combinations; space problems require solutions that open the awareness to still more possibilities.
- Working with partners: Cooperative (one-with-one); competitive (one-on-one)
- Emergence of basketball skills as movements are restricted by "rules."
- Games needed to develop skills and create interest:
Keep Away; contests of skill, such as dribbling, passing, and shooting combinations

Part III is concerned with involving pupils in the more structured movement tasks that lead to the development of general game skills that can be successfully employed in peer group activity and that are the foundation for the highly specific skill required for excellence.

- Sequencing movement elements to develop skills
- Accent, time, force, direction modifications that affect skill
- Space, on offense and on defense
- Basketball is a space game from one-on-one to five-on-five.
- The opponent's skill dictates the need for counterskills.
- More rules to restrict movement require skill modifications.

Part IV is concerned with the acquisition of the highly specific skills needed by those willing to devote the time and effort to becoming excellent.

Implementation of basic movement concepts to the development of skills and concepts related to individual and team sports

I Analysis of the basic skills
A Sequence of movements required for efficiency
1 Identification of parts, fundamental movements
2 How action is initiated
3 Part of body leading action
4 Weight transference, from and to
5 Force element
6 Laws of motion
7 Speed (time factor)
II Development of the whole idea
A Focus on the object of the action
B Sequencing the parts, flow
III Developing movement memory
A Repeating the sequence many times
B Awareness of relationship of parts to whole
C Increasing control through understanding of laws of motion to skill
IV Refinement of skill
A Repetition with increasing awareness of the whole until the movement is executed at the unconscious level through overlearning
B Functional application in an increasing number of combinations with other skills

Teaching physical education units

■ The traditional physical education program consists of a series of units that focus on one major activity or a series of related activities. Teachers who have followed this organizational plan find it hard to change to the more fluid organizational format of movement education in which physical education activities are utilized developmentally rather than as objectives in themselves. The distinction I make is only to enable the reader to discern the difference between the traditional orientation of *physical education* and the current meaning of *movement education* with its broader implication for learning through problem solving. The conditions under which the former prevails, regardless of stated objectives aimed at developing a total fitness for living, can best be described as directed learning, while movement education must by the nature of its immediate objectives free the individual to think for himself. It utilizes the innate curiosity of the child to explore, to enjoy challenge, and to delight in discovery—to involve the child more and more deeply in the process of growth and development through movement. To explore, one must have the desire to make the effort. The environment must be enabling. One must live without fear or threat of embarrassment or humiliation. Unit plan teaching has built-in threats—the name of the unit when announced can mean many different things to children depending upon their previous experiences. Be careful how you announce your plans. Remember that not all children are ready to learn what you want to teach.

■ What does volleyball mean to you? It could mean any game in which an inflated object is thrown or batted over a rope or net or skill development to the highest level of competitive sport and strategy. What do you think it means to your students? Try asking them. Begin with general quesions, and if they seem to know some answers, get more specific. You may discover that some know a good deal about the game and others very little. Some might not even be interested. One thing you can count on, they will not be equal in their knowledge, nor will they be equally ready to learn.

Looking ahead to volleyball

Step 1 is finding out where they are in readiness to learn.
Step 2 is helping them improve on present concepts and skills.
Step 3 is giving them a chance to test themselves. Let them play and help them evaluate.

Begin the lesson format (1, 2, or 3) that is easiest for you and the children.

Some things to remember
1 Unless the children have played a lot of volleyball since the last time they had a unit on it, they will need to review. Also, new students may have joined the class.
2 Skills are very specific. Good baseball players may not be good volleyball players.
3 Children must begin from where they are.
4 Drill with no purpose other than skill development is boring for most boys and girls.
5 Children will practice willingly if there's a good reason to practice.
6 Skills, strategies, and rules can evolve or develop through need. To play is the thing. The teacher can use play as a simple way of evaluating readiness for learning.
7 Quality of skill and readiness for learning the next higher order of skill go hand in hand. Work for quality.

■ Before the teacher can begin teaching those skills, strategies, and organizational patterns characteristic of volleyball, the students' readiness level must be assessed. This is best done through activities that the children can handle comfortably, generally some form of the game.

The first volleyball lesson

After an initial warm-up involving large muscle movement, the lesson begins with a task designed to find out where to go from here.

Step 1 Helpful information

1 How skillful are the students at ball handling—throwing, catching, batting with various body parts? Control?
2 What is their ability range?
3 What form of competition will enable children to handle themselves comfortably?
4 Are all of the children socially well adjusted? Can they enjoy group activity?
5 Are they spatially well oriented?
6 Can the children do some thinking for themselves?
7 Is their self-discipline adequate for much individualized programming? Proceed to the lesson—implementation of Step 1.

Preliminary analysis. Children are asked to form groups of three, to take one ball, and to use it in a small space, controlling the ball with the hands and arms.

1 Observation. Can they follow directions?
   a) If not, restate for clarity.
   b) If yes, observe more.
      (1) Whom did they choose?
      (2) Where did they go in gym? To open space? To crowded space?
      (3) Are children showing effort to control ball?
2 Preliminary analysis. Observe as activity goes on.
   a) How well did children handle the assignment?
   b) What were the strong points?
   c) What were the weak points?
   d) What is the range of ability?
3 Stop activity. Have children sit down in front of you. Stress consideration toward you and toward one another.
4 Find out what the students think, what they observed, what they did.
   a) Did they like the activity?
   b) What kinds of problems did they have getting started? Forming groups? Finding space?
   c) What kinds of problems did they have with the activity? Controlling the ball? Determining skills appropriate to the task?
   d) Were any groups able to keep the ball moving (flow)? Any special patterns? Any special way of handling ball? Any specific formation? What shape did the formation assume?

Ask questions. Allow time for "show and tell." Point out similarities and differences. Discuss why some groups had an easier task than others. Did ball control result in everyone having more turns?

Comment. It is not necessary to ask all of these questions the first time. Watch for restlessness and lack of attention. Questions related to items 4*a* and *b* may be enough. Have them go back and try again saying you'll have further questions focusing upon the activity itself. Allow five minutes maximum, then finish asking questions. Be careful. Don't expect too much. Most children will only be aware of the most obvious points until they've had more practice.

Step 2 Learning through problem solving

1 Comment on the strong points you observed, emphasizing them in the following order.
   a) Showed consideration for others
   b) Understood and followed directions with a minimum of time wasted
   c) Individuals and groups showed good control—praise them
   d) Handled the ball skillfully—praise these individuals
2 Comment on weak points noted also in the same order, but make no reference to specific individuals or groups. That can only be done when children can willingly accept objective criticism and recognize its positive aspects both for the individual and the group.
   Note: Mentally rank the weaknesses observed with an analysis of why they occurred.
3 Frame a task that will focus on improving the weak points, again in the order listed. One example for each is listed below.
   a) Can you form groups of four quickly and find a space in which to begin activity?
   b) Listen to and follow these directions in the order in which I give them to you, but wait until you have heard them all.
      (1) Find a partner.
      (2) Choose a ball.
      (3) Find a space.
      (4) Keep the ball moving with control.
   c) Find some *different* ways of controlling the ball without letting it out of your space.
   d) Decide on a ball-handling skill your group needs to work on and practice it for five minutes. Remember that when you help each other you get more turns, as we discovered earlier.

While the students are carrying out your instructions, you should observe, analyze, focus on demonstrations of good quality, praise, and evaluate what happened, how well it happened, and your effectiveness in the process.

Step 3 Competition

Children in groups of two, if possible, or four, if necessary, play a game in which the ball must travel over a net or rope. How to move the ball is left to the group or individual at this point.

The students might be organized in different ways.
1 Creatively; the children find a way.
   a) Stretch rope or wand between two people.
   b) Stretch rope between posts, hooks, apparatus.
   c) Use fixed apparatus like bars and beams.
2 Teacher-directed.
   a) Over nets provided and in spaces provided.
   b) Over ropes stretched about.
   c) Two hold rope, others divide either side, and rotate according to directions given.
   Observe the following points about their play.
1 Ball control
2 How play is started

Sport skills

3 How points are scored
4 What skills do students have? Which ones do they need?
5 Do teammates play cooperatively?
6 Are they ready for pattern play? (Probably not.)

Stop the activity. Find out who won and what were students' major problems as they see them. Note how closely their observations parallel yours. Did they observe anything you didn't?

The second phase in volleyball

■ The following sequence of lessons focuses on the development of skills and play patterns, both offensive and defensive, that meet the felt and observed needs related to volleyball. Students with a movement education background may not need the preparation offered in the foregoing lesson. Even much of the following lesson may be familiar, although the specific skill focus may not have been realized by all.

The term *volleyball* means the child's concept. It may be called Skyball or Newcomb, but designation is only valuable to the teacher. To the children it is volleyball until they know better, and they will know in time.

Problem solving

1 Control thrown ball, catch, bat with various body parts except feet.
2 Use contrasting force to propel ball and to control it, as in catching (absorb force).
3 Change levels of the ball, of the body.
4 Change speed.
5 Change direction, at different levels.
6 Increase and decrease range—near to, far from.
7 Sequence continuous movement of ball in different ways, in gradually selected ways (batting overhand, underhand, with a flat surface, and so on).
8 Do all of the above individually.
9 Do all of the above with a partner.
10 Do all of the above in groups of three.

Task development (with partners or in groups of three)

1 Emphasize control as ball moves from one to another.
2 Restrict ways of moving the ball to batting, with catch only to control.
3 Create a pattern that includes one specific way of handling ball; two ways; three ways.
4 Create a pattern that starts with an underhand serve and keep it going until someone misses. Restart pattern.
5 Work out a way of practicing the serve; the spike; the dig.

Observation and analysis of student performance

1 Who shows good control? Why?
2 What way of controlling the ball was most effective?
3 How can you improve this skill?
4 Is there another way that might work better?
5 What did that group do when they got the ball?
6 How can you use more force and still have accuracy?
7 Did your way of playing provide for rotation of the serve?
8 Considering the amount of time for the game, did your scoring system determine a winner today?

9 As we observe how others play, are we noting the good points of group organization and team play?

10 At this point, who are the best players? Do they all have the best skills? What skills do they have that need improvement? In what way?

Lesson format

1 The entire class works either individually or in small groups on problem solving, task development, and competition.

2 Half of the class works on individual problem solving and on building personal skill; the other half works in small groups. Rotate assignments. All students compete at the end.

3 The class is grouped in threes, and, later, fours, fives, or sixes.

a) Group 1 (one third) engage in competition, using one or more nets.

b) Group 2 (one third) work on offensive or defensive patterns in groups of three.

c) Group 3 (one third) engage in personal skill development. Either alone or with partner students emphasize learning new skill or improving quality.

d) Rotate areas every six to eight minutes.

Suggestions to the teacher

1 You are aiming to achieve format 3 which permits the following.

a) Teacher guidance and specific help where needed

b) Student observation, analysis, and evaluation

c) Opportunity for student-directed learning experiences

d) Opportunity for teacher observation of progress in student behaviors toward student-selected achievement level

2 If you cannot handle format 3, use 2 or 1 and work progressively toward 3. This might take a long time. Don't expect it in one year, although that depends on many factors.

3 Remember, you are not a volleyball coach. The process through which the children go is more important than the end product. They may never play the game again. On the other hand, some may enjoy the challenge so much that they undertake the rigors of training for competition gladly. They must decide for themselves. Look at what is happening to the child. That's what is really important.

Gymnastics

Outline
of gymnastics
for elementary
school

A For the majority of children to handle gymnastic progressions successfully, they should have a rich background in movement from the earliest grade level. Skillful performance requires strength, flexibility, agility, balance, endurance, and movement sense.

1 Exploration and discovery. Individual or group practice in exploring movement, i.e., running, skipping, jumping, dog run, change of direction, turning, combinations, climbing, supporting. Qualities of movement or positions— quick, slow, soft, light, loose, stretched. Explore the use of space.

2 Approach to teaching. As much as possible, direct activities in an atmosphere of freedom. Too many restrictions and overorganization limit learning opportunities and stifle creativity that are so necessary for good gymnastics. Vary from formal to informal; change activities; cover a wide range of activities; do not do too much of any one thing. If possible, let the children go barefoot when working on the floor or on grass. Their movement sense will develop much more rapidly. Guidelines for national certification of gymnastics teachers and coaches are being prepared as of this writing (1977). For information, write Raleigh DeGeer Amyx, USGSA, Dulles International Airport, Box 17241, Washington, D.C. 20041.

3 Working with a partner
   a) Join hands, stand toe to toe, lean away. Change partners.
   b) Join hands, wring the dishrag or swing merry-go-round fashion.
   c) Skip with your partner. Play follow the leader. Play shadow.
   d) Play tug-of-war with partner. Hand wrestle. Push partner like piano.
   e) One child forms a table by kneeling and bending low on hand or elbow support; the other stretches across the first's back and forms a seesaw.

Variations: Jump over; run around partner; crawl under; vault over; seesaw, then reach hands and head under and roll off; do combinations, quick changes.

  f) One supports the other in such activities as jump with elbow-lift assist, handstand on partner's back, thigh stand, one crab bridge on the other, etc.

4 Working in threes—two help one; change or rotate quickly

  a) Three abreast, inside hands joined; center person performs forward roll, neckspring, and flip, spotters move forward.

  b) One forms bridge on hands and knees; performer rolls from bridge and reaches for partner for assisted jump-stand. Rotate positions.

  c) Three abreast; center person handstands, spotters support between knee and thigh; change around quickly.

  d) Two join hands, support third stretched across in front lying position. Set back on feet. Emphasize stretching by performer, spotting high on chest between knee and hip.

  Progression: Stand performer on hands instead of feet and shift to hand-stand spot; from backlying stretch, set performer on hands and push thighs over for snap down.

  e) Two support one in stretched front support on shoulders; spotters support with inside hand under armpit. Later, jump to front support and stretch legs over joined outside hands of spotters.

Special note on teaching: Find out where the children are in their movement education; self-discipline is necessary. Encourage children to find new ways of moving, of getting out of one position into another. Have children demonstrate their discoveries or good techniques. Keep them moving but change the pace frequently. Safety consciousness can be developed only through helping children develop a sense of personal responsibility for themselves and for others. Appreciate the sense of the dictum, "You must learn to walk before you can run." The teacher, not the equipment or the facilities, is the key to success. Much can be done with little equipment. The voice of the teacher sets the tone; the pupil-teacher relationship sets the atmosphere.

B Cross pad movement. Pupils line up along the edge of mat.

1 Command drill

  a) Jumps across, rolls across, turns across, vaults across

  b) Breakfall—forward, backward

  c) Balances—knee-elbow headstand, handstand, headstand, neck balance, scales, bridge, V-sit

  d) Springs—neck, head, to bridge, to feet

  e) Rocking—abdominal, back

2 Creative combinations—movements across, turns, balances, etc.

  a) Created by the teacher

  b) Created by the pupil

  c) Follow the leader

3 Relay teams of three or four. Approach run—do a designated movement across and return; example: run, skip step, roundoff, or cartwheel

C Apparatus

1 Ropes

  a) Climbing—single or double rope

  b) Swinging, single or double—from jump, with running approach *c)* Stunts—heaving, crab run under the rope, skin the cat, inverted hands, bird's nest, chin-ups, angel, skip to bridge, etc.

d) Swing off box—one rope or two ropes. Variation—cross two ropes, swing, turn, swing back. Add mats on box.

2 Box or side horse (no pommels)

  a) Lowest position sideways—add mat for some stunts

    (1) Mount and jump off—stretch, tuck, pike, twist

    (2) Vault over

    (3) Crawl over, crawl away, roll away

    (4) Jump over

    (5) Push off floor to hand support

    (6) Back slide to bridge and kick legs over through handstand

    (7) Forward roll to neckspring.

    (8) Headspring

    (9) From rear sit, fall backward to handstand snap down

  b) Lowest position longways

    (1) Run over and jump

    (2) Squat mount, rabbit hop to the end, and jump off

    (3) Crawl over and reach down to forward roll

    (4) Forward roll and push off

    (5) Backward roll and jump off

    (6) Squat mount and headspring (two spotters)

    (7) Squat mount and handstand turnover (two spotters)

    (8) From stand, roundoff dismount

  c) Lowest position oblique

    (1) Scissor jump mount

    (2) Scissor jump over with hand support (like rear vault)

    (3) Cartwheel over

  d) Two boxes, side by side—one low and one high, or both low

    (1) Up and over first box, second box, and off

    (2) Over high, crawl down, and over low box

    (3) Run and leap from box to box

3 Bar—low position with box in front

  a) Mount box, grab bar, and swing under

  b) Jump to front support and swing under

  c) Jump to front support and turn over

  d) From knee mount, pull to front support

  e) Vault over

  f) Swing leg to stretched split support

4 Bar—low position with box beyond the bar

  a) Swing legs up on box and slide over box

  b) Swing feet up on box and jump off

  c) Swing feet up on box, arch body, half turn and swing back under the bar, or add moves in number 3 above

  d) Mount the bar and crawl over the bar and the box

  e) Rear pull over with kick off from box

  f) Mount the bar and swing under to V-sit on the box

  g) With heel on the box, hands on bar, hang low and muscle up to arch stand on edge of box

Gymnastics

5 Low bar
  a) Front support—turn over forward, under swing, etc.
  b) Knee swing uprise
  c) Backward knee circle
  d) Forward knee or crotch circle
  e) Knee hang, swing dismount
  f) Rear hip pullover
  g) Rear hip circle
  h) Front hip circle
  i) Back knee circle
  j) Kip
6 Rolled mat
  a) Neck roll over, neckspring
  b) Dive roll
  c) Headspring with spotters
  d) Front flip with spotters
7 Balance beam—low, 2-inch width
  a) Walk—forward, backward, sideways
  b) Handstand support
  c) Cartwheel or roundoff over
  d) Dive roll over
  e) With mat over the beam—see the rolled mat exercises
8 Uneven parallel bars—regular bars set uneven
  a) From low, raise legs over high bar
  b) Jump to front support on low bar and swing under
  c) Grasp high bar, raise legs over low and sit, push off
  d) Mount low bar, stand up, roll over high bar
  e) From high bar front support, reach down to low bar with reverse grip, slide down over low bar
  f) Reverse pull over on low bar with push off assist on high bar
  g) From stand on low bar, vault over the high bar
  h) Practice low horizontal bar work
  i) Stem rise
9 Tumbling and practice for floor exercise using elements of tumbling
  a) Approach run with long skip to cartwheel or roundoff
  b) Approach run and dive roll
  c) Roundoff to backward roll
  d) Combinations in one pass for simple tumbling
    (1) Series of forward or backward rolls
    (2) Forward roll, half turn, backward roll
    (3) Cartwheel to forward roll combinations
  e) Headsprings alone, in combination (see number 10 for progression)
  f) Handspring forward (see number 10 for progression)
  g) Back handspring (see number 10 for progression)
  h) Front somersault
  i) Roundoff, flic flac; add back somersault
  j) Walkovers
10 Group work for floor exercise practice. Begin with threes, one performer and two spotters. Rotate positions. Start with simple tricks and progress to variations and increased difficulty.
  a) Turnovers—two support one stretched across joined hands and turn over to handstand and stand.

(1) Front lying position to hands and then feet

(2) Back lying position to hands and then feet

b) Neckspring—inside hands joined, middle performer slow roll to neck and shoulder balance, kip to stand

(1) Spotters assist under shoulder and hips with performer pushing off with hands on kip action

(2) Assist only under the hips

c) Headspring—spotters assist under shoulders and hips, from piked head-stand position of performer

d) Handspring—spotters kneel, facing each other, catch vigorous handstand split legs under hips and assist over if necessary with upper arm spot

e) Back handspring—lead-up following turnover. Performer sits back on spot-ters near joined hands, whips back over the second joined hands with spotters proceeding as in turnover backward to assist in handstand snap down

f Handstand press—spotters assist with press from headstand to handstand, then tripod balance to handstand, then repeats for conditioning

g) Walkovers

(1) Front—split handstand to bridge with spotters assisting under hip with pressure forward for rise to stand

(2) Back—spotters join hands in back of performer and spot against thigh to retard speed and under shoulder to allow hands to position them-selves. Shift weight over hands as performer kicks up and over

h) Front somersault—performer bends over joined hands of spotters, and reaches upward. Spotters grasp wrist, and when performer jumps, they pull upward to assist roll action.

A Tumbling—40 foot minimum length mats

1 A compulsory exercise consisting of at least two passes comprising a degree of difficulty commensurate with the abilities of the majority

2 Optional exercises to motivate and stimulate students of greater ability

B Floor exercise—40 × 40-foot area; music for girls

1 A compulsory exercise containing elements of the dance, balance, tumbling, and strength that will provide practice in the rhythmic blending of move-ments

2 Optional exercises to provide an opportunity for individual interpretation and expression as well as challenge to the creative impulse

3 Group exercises with and without such equipment as ropes, balls, and hands performed rhythmically with or without music

C Swedish box or side horse vaulting—height, 3 feet, 6 inches

1 Compulsory flank, front, or rear vaults to practice controlled approach, vault, and landing

2 Optional vaults as abilities allow

D Horizontal bar—about 5 feet in height or higher

1 Compulsory exercise—mount, circle movements, and dismount in good form

2 Optional exercise—a blending of stunts of greater difficulty

E Trampoline—optional exercises not to exceed twelve bounces with a required extra bounce for safety after full somersault movements*

Gymnastic exercises or routines

---

*Somersaults may be omitted as a matter of safety policy without diminishing the value of trampolining.

F Uneven parallel bars—optional exercises that comprise the basic elements of low horizontal bar work combined now with movements involving the higher bar, turns, supports, suspensions, mounts, and dismounts

Exhibition or competition for elementary boys and girls

A Intergrade—individual competition
B After-school club—exhibitions for primary grades and PTA affairs
C Community teams—community-sponsored gymnastic competition and clinics
1 Townwide competition for individuals
2 District or area developmental meets
3 Junior Olympic Gymnastics*

*Write USGF, P.O. Box 12713, Tucson, Arizona 85711.

Resources

■ This appendix of resources has been divided into sections corresponding with some of the special needs of program planners whether they be students or professionals. It is a severely edited compilation of names, places, books, and things that may be useful either to the planner with limited financial resources or the planner with real or fancied monies with which to purchase whatever is necessary to augment modern educational objectives.

To help the planner of physical education programs, the resources have been grouped to answer some, if not most, of the questions uppermost in the minds of planners as the task of assembling information begins to take shape. The *who, where,* and *what* questions are answered through logical grouping of the suggested resources. In some cases, the answer is provided; in others, the answer may be located in a suggested reference.

Because consultants have a way of moving from one institution to another and because the listing of a few would overburden their already heavy commitment to serving the needs of communities and individuals, this appendix does not list consultants by name. Where to look for consultant help appears a more appropriate form of assistance than to list a few who may no longer be at the address given. The lone exception is the ever helpful and most eagerly sought Dr. Margie Hanson at the offices of the American Alliance for Health, Physical Education and Recreation. It is expected that she will continue to serve the needs of elementary and pre-school educators as she has done so faithfully in the past. *Question*: Who can help answer questions concerning the special problems of my community confronting the physical education program planner?
Answer: Regarding goals, philosophy, and the current trends area, regional, national and international, write:

Dr. Margie Hanson, Elementary Consultant, American Alliance for Health, Physical Education and Recreation, 1201 16th St. NW, Washington, D.C. 20036

Regarding requirements, suggested guidelines, and the possibility of financial grants or a visiting consultant, write your State Director of Physical Education.

(Edited Directory)

Alabama

AKERS, Ghary M., Specialist, Health, Physical Education and Recreation, State Department of Education, State Office Building, Montgomery 36104. Phone: 205-832-6500 (Home) 205-272-5169.

Alaska

WILLIAMS, Vern, State Department of Education, Room 519, Alaska Office Building, Pouch F, Juneau 99801.

Arizona

BEISECKER, Carl E., Consultant, Health and Physical Education, State Department of Public Instruction, 1626 W. Washington, Phoenix 85007.

Arkansas

ALBRIGHT, James G., Director, Specialist in Physical Education, State Department of Education, Little Rock 72201. Phone: 501-371-1962 (Home) 501-753-4659.

California

LANDERS, Barbara, Consultant for Physical Education, 721 Capital Mall, Sacramento 95814. Phone: 916-322-4985.

Canada

CHAISSON, Gilles, Manager, Sports Information Resource Center, 7/8 - 1665 Russell Road, Ottawa, Canada—KIC-ON1. Phone: 613-746-0060, Ext. 288.

DICKSON, Dean, Executive Secretary, Saskatchewan High School Athletic Association, Avord Tower, 2202 Victoria Avenue, Regina, Saskatchewan. Phone: 306-525-1771 (269).

GURNEY, Helen, Chief Educational Officer, Ministry of Education, Mowat Block, Queen's Park, Toronto, Ontario, Canada M7A1L2. Phone: 416-965-6410.

MACMARTIN, Gerry, Assistant Superintendent of Curriculum, Ontario Department of Education, 44 Eglinton Avenue, W. Toronto, Ontario.

MCKENNA, K. E., Supervisor of Physical Education, Province of Alberta, Department of Education, 902-670 7th Avenue, S.W., John J. Bowlen Building, Calgary, Alberta. Phone: 403-268-8306.

NICK, George, Supervisor, Physical Education, Manitoba Department of Education, 404-1181 Portage Avenue, Winnipeg, Manitoba R3N1K4. Phone: 786-0264 (Home) 489-4110.

WARD, C. M., Regional Office, Department of Education, 500 Devonian Building, Edmonton, Alberta. Phone: 403-482-6326.

Canal Zone

ANDERSON, Ross E., Supervisor, Physical Education and Athletics, U.S. Schools, Division of School, Box M, Balboa Heights, Canal Zone. Phone: 52-7873.

Connecticut

HOWELLS, Roberta, Consultant, Physical Education and Girls' Athletics, State Department of Education, State Office Building, Hartford 06115. Phone: 203-566-4424.

Delaware

PARSONS, Howard, Supervisor, Physical Education, Department of Public Instruction, Dover 19901. Phone: 302-678-4886 (Home) 302-764-1967.

District of Columbia

GUIDRY, Mathew, Consultant, President's Council on Physical Fitness and Sports, 400 Sixth Street, Room 303, Washington 20202.

HANSON, Margie (Dr.), Consultant, Elementary Education, American Association for Health, Physical Education and Recreation, 1201 Sixteenth Street NW, Washington 20036. Phone: 202-223-9400 Ext. 581.

STEIN, Julian U. (Dr.), Consultant, Programs for the Handicapped, American Association for Health, Physical Education and Recreation, 1201 Sixteenth Street, N.W., Washington 20036. Phone: 202-833-5547.

Florida

ROUNTREE, Phil, Consultant, Physical Education and Summer Programs, Department of Education, 412 Winchester Building, Tallahassee 32304. Phone: 904-488-3078.

Georgia

SHORT, Jack S., Coordinator, Health, Physical Education and Recreation, Driver Education and Safety, State Department of Education, State Office Building, Atlanta 30334. Phone: 404-656-2581.

Guam

BOTHMER, Richard, Consultant, Health and Physical Education, State Department of Education, Box DE, Agana 96910. Phone: 728-4445.

Hawaii

CURTIS, Delores, Associate Professor, College of Education Department, Curriculum and Instruction, University of Hawaii, Honolulu 96816. Phone: 808-948-7866 (Home) 808-732-1598.

Idaho

KEARNS, Rick, State Department of Education, Len B. Jordan Office Building, 650 West State Street, Boise 83720.

Illinois

KILGORE, Glena, Supervisor, Physical Education, Office of Public Instruction, 316 South Second Street, Springfield 62706. Phone: 217-782-2826.

Indiana

NORDHOLM, Catherine (Mrs.), Consultant, Physical Education, State Board of Health, 1330 West Michigan Street, Indianapolis 46206. Phone: 317-633-4610.

Iowa

COLLISON, Guilford, Consultant, Elementary and Secondary Schools, State Department of Public Instruction, Des Moines 50319.

Kansas

HANEY, Carl J., Educational Specialist, State Department of Education, State Education Building, 120 East Tenth Street, Topeka 66612. Phone: 913-296-3916 (Home) 913-357-7688.

Kentucky

SWAIN, Michael, Consultant, Health and Drug Education, State Department of Education, State Office Building, Frankfort 40601. Phone: 502-564-3572.

Louisiana

MCNABB, Delmon, Supervisor, Health, Physical Education and Recreation, State Department of Education, Box 44064, Baton Rouge 70804.

Maine

LAFOUNTAIN, Wallace, Curriculum Consultant, State Department of Educational and Cultural Services, Augusta 04330. Phone: 207-289-2541.

Maryland

MOLESWORTH, John, Specialist in Physical Education, State Department of Education, Division of Instruction, Box 8717, Baltimore and Washington International Airport, Baltimore 21240. Phone: 301-796-8300 Ext. 399.

Massachusetts

ANDREWS, Paul J., Director, Human Services, State Department of Education, 182 Tremont Street, Boston 02111. Phone: 617-727-5754.

Michigan

QUINN, Lee W. (Dr.), Instructional Specialist, Physical Education, Outdoor Education and Recreation, State Department of Education, Box 420, Lansing 48902. Phone: 517-373-1484 (Home) 517-676-5042.

Minnesota

KNUTSON, Carl, Supervisor, Health, Physical Education and Safety, State Department of Education, 683 Capitol Square Building, St. Paul 55101. Phone: 612-296-4059.

Mississippi

DAVIS, Kermit R., Consultant, Physical Education, State Department of Education, P.O. Box 771, Jackson 39205. Phone: 601-354-6459.

Missouri

TAYLOR, Robert M. (Dr.), Director, Health, Physical Education and Safety, State Department of Education, Box 480, Jefferson City 65101. Phone: 314-751-2664.

Montana

OBERLY, David, Supervisor of Health and Physical Education, Superintendent of Public Instruction, State Capitol, Helena 59601. Phone: 406-449-3861 (Home) 406-442-2569.

Nebraska

GRAY, Roy, Administrative Consultant, Physical Education, Health and Drug Education, State Department of Education, 233 South Tenth Street, Lincoln 68509. Phone: 402-471-2476.

Nevada

COHEN, Paul, Chief, Bureau of Alcohol and Drug Abuse, Department of Human Resources, Capitol Complex, 1803 N. Carson, Carson City 89701. Phone: 702-885-4790 (Home) 702-882-2212.

COOPER, Bert, Director, Curriculum and Instruction, State Department of Education, Heroes Memorial Building, Carson City 89701. Phone: 702-822-7325.

New Jersey

ABITANTA, Sal Edward, School Program Coordinator, New Jersey Department of Education, Somerset County Office, County Administration Annex, 32 Grove Street, Somerville 08876. Phone: 201-725-4700 Ext. 311 (Home) 201-355-3684.

New Mexico

HINGER, Fred J., Supervisor of Student Teachers, Division of Health, Physical Education and Recreation, University of New Mexico, Albuquerque 87110. Phone: 505-277-2048.

New York

GROVER, George H. (Dr.), Director, Division of Health, Physical Education and Recreation, State Department of Education, Albany 12224. Phone: 518-474-5832.

North Carolina

LEAFE, Norman E., Director, Division of Health, Safety and Physical Education, State Department of Public Instruction, Education Building, Raleigh 27611. Phone: 919-829-3906.

Ohio

BRAZELTON, Ambrose E., Chief, Urban Education, Department of Education, State Office Building, 65 South Front Street, Columbus 43215. Phone: 614-466-5077.

Oklahoma

TEDFORD, Harvey, Director, Physical Education Specialist, State Department of Education, State Capitol, Oklahoma City 73127. Phone: 405-521-3361 (Home) 405-789-8681.

Oregon

GODDARD, James D., Educational Program Specialist, Physical Education, State Department of Education, 942 Lancaster Drive NW, Salem 97310. Phone: 503-378-3602.

Pennsylvania

BOELHOUWER, Douglas, Advisor, Health and Physical Education, Department of Education, Box 911, Harrisburg 17126. Phone: 717-787-5423.

Puerto Rico

OTERO, Efrain, Director, Program of Physical Education, Box 1480, Hato Rey 00919. Phone: 764-7615.

Rhode Island

SAVASTANO, Orlando O., Director, Health, Physical Education, Recreation and Athletics, Cranston Public Schools, Cranston 02910. Phone: 401-785-0400.

Samoa

LOLOTAI, Al, Chairman, Health, Physical Education and Recreation, Department of Education, Pago Pago, Tutuila, American Samoa 96799.

South Carolina

SCHREINER, Harold J., Consultant, Physical Education, State Department of Education, Rutledge State Office Building, Columbia 29201. Phone: 803-758-2652 (Home) 803-776-3421.

South Dakota

KING, Larry, Specialist in Health, Physical Education and Recreation, State Department of Education, State Capitol Building, Pierre 57501.

Tennessee

HUNTER, George R., Supervisor, Health, Physical Education, Recreation and Safety, State Department of Education, 132-C Cordell Hull Building, Nashville 37219. Phone: 615-741-2586.

Texas

SESSOM, Ewell, Director, Health and Physical Education, Texas Education Agency, 201 East Eleventh Street, Austin 78701. Phone: 512-475-2608.

Utah

LEAKE, Robert L., Senior Specialist, Health, Physical Education and Recreation, State Department of Education, 250 East 500 South, Salt Lake City 84111. Phone: 801-533-5572 (Home) 801-943-0619.

Vermont

MAGWIRE, Raymond B., Educational Consultant, Health and Physical Education, State Department of Education, State Office Building, Montpelier 05602. Phone: 802-828-3115 (Home) 802-223-3657.

Virginia

MAYS, Frances A. (Miss), Supervisor, Health and Physical Education, State Department of Education, Richmond 23216. Phone: 804-770-2652 (Home) 804-232-9287.

Virgin Islands

SCIPIO, Vernon T., Director, Health, Physical Education, and Recreation, Department of Education, Box 630, St. Thomas 00801.

Washington

SCHAUB, Howard A., Supervisor, Physical Education and Recreation, State Office of Public Instruction, Old Capitol Building, Olympia 98504. Phone: 206-753-6757.

West Virginia

CANONICO, Alan, Supervisor, Health, Physical Education and Recreation, State Department of Education, Charleston 25303. Phone: 304-348-3764 (Home) 304-342-7501.

Wisconsin

JENSEN, Gordon O., Consultant, Physical Education, State Department of Public Instruction, 126 Langdon Street, Madison 53702. Phone: 608-266-3615 (Home) 414-786-2043.

Wyoming
RICKETTS, Walter P., Coordinator, Health, Physical Education and Drug Abuse Education, State Capitol Building, Cheyenne 82002. Phone: 307-777-7411 (Home) 307-634-8421.

Regarding consultant help in curriculum planning, write for suggestions to Dr. Margie Hanson, Elementary Consultant
American Alliance for Health, Physical Education and Recreation
1201 16th Street NW
Washington, D.C. 20036
Expect to pay the usual fee of approximately $100.00 per day plus expenses. If specific kinds of information are needed rather than the consultant's physical presence, describe the situation clearly and ask only for help within the limitations of the problem presented. Do not ask for "everything they have written on movement education" or any other broad topic. A stamped, self-addressed envelope is a courtesy that often brings forth the help requested, but offer to pay a nominal fee also for materials.

No funds available? Write or call your state director of physical education. The help you need may be available.

Question: What professional organizations may I join that will directly benefit my growth and development as a physical educator?
Answer:
American Alliance for Health, Physical Education and Recreation
1201 16th St. NW, Washington, D.C. 20036.
Membership fees range from $25.00 to $45.00 for professionals, $15.00 to $35.00 for graduate students, and $12.50 to $32.50 for undergraduate students depending on the number of periodicals from the following list:
Journal of Physical Education and Recreation
Health Education
Research Quarterly
Update, a news publication, is coupled with any combination of the above.
Your state association for Health, Physical Education and Recreation.
Write AAHPER for the name of the current membership chairperson.
The National Association of Physical Education of College Women.
The National College Physical Education Association for Men.
Publishers of *Quest*. Subscription is $8.00 per year. Write Mrs. Jean K. Marsh, 6140 Sinbad Place, Columbia, Maryland 21045
National Association for the Education of Young Children (NAEYC)
1834 Connecticut Ave. NW
Washington, D.C. 20009
Regular and student membership dues are $15.00 for national level and an additional fee of $8.00 (which may vary) for membership in a local affiliate group. Request information regarding the latter. Bimonthly publication of *Young Children*.
American Dance Guild
1619 Broadway, Suite 603
New York, N.Y. 10019.
Write for information on conferences, literature and membership.

Question: What additional publications may I receive through subscription?

Answer:

The Physical Activities Report, $36.00 per year, monthly. Published by The Institute for Learning, 171 Saybrook Industrial Park, Old Saybrook, Conn. 06475.

The Physical Educator, $8.00 per year, four issues. Subscription office, 9030 Log Run Drive, North Indianapolis, Ind. 46234.

Question: Are there resources available that would help me learn more about homemade or inexpensive equipment?

Answer:

Corbin, Charles B., *Inexpensive Equipment for Games, Play, and Physical Activity*. Dubuque, Iowa: Wm. C. Brown, 1972.

Gallahue, David L., *Developmental Play Equipment*. New York: John Wiley & Sons, Inc., 1975.

Kirchner, Glenn, *Physical Education for Elementary School Children*. Fourth Edition. Dubuque, Iowa, Wm. C. Brown, 1977.

Moran, Joan M. and Kalakian, Leonard H., *Movement Experiences for the Mentally Retarded or Emotionally Disturbed Child*. Second Edition. Minneapolis: Burgess Publishing Co., 1977.

Werner, Peter and Rini, Lisa, *Perceptual-Motor Development Equipment*. New York: John Wiley & Sons, Inc., 1976.

Werner, Peter H. and Simmons, Richard A., *Inexpensive Physical Education Equipment for Children*. Minneapolis: Burgess Publishing Company, 1976.

Question: Which companies are among the recommended that sell good items of small equipment for individual and small group activity.

Answer:

Cossom Corporation 6030 Wayzata Blvd. Minneapolis, Minn. 55416	Floor hockey game, plastic bats and balls, scoops, wands, bowling sets.
Charles H. Demarest Co. 215 Water Street New York, N.Y. 10038	Bamboo poles.
Ed-Nu, Inc. 5115 Route 38 Pennsauken, N.J. 08108	Plastic hoops, "Groove Loops."
J. E. Gregory Co., Inc. West 922 First Avenue Spokane, Washington 99202	Regular and long skip ropes, training hurdles, jump standards, rhythm apparatus, hoops, wands, ribbons, juggle balls, tug of war rope.
Holbrook-Patterson, Inc. Coldwater, Michigan	Basic manipulative equipment, wood blocks, shapes, Indian clubs, dumbbells, bombardment pins, wands.
J. L. Hammett Co. Physical Education Dept. 2393 Vauxhall Road Union, N.J. 07083	Manual dexterity equipment, balls, play tubes, rhythm, hand apparatus, jump ropes, multi-shaped cutouts, push balls, fleece balls, scooters.

Jayfro	Games jump standards, hurdles, water sports
P.O. Box 400	equipment, scooters, parachute, boundary
Waterford, Conn. 06385	cones, tug-of-war ropes.

Physical Education Supply Associates (PESA)
300 Island View Road
Stratford, Conn. 06497

German jump ropes, "magic" ropes, wooden hoops, Wevau balls.

Wolverine Sports Supply
745 State Circle
Ann Arbor, Michigan 48105

Balls, games equipment and games, hoops.

Question: Where can apparatus designed to encourage creative play and the development of agility be purchased?

Answer:

The Delmer F. Harris Co.
P.O. Box 288, Dept. J.
Concordia, Kansas 66901

Outdoor apparatus.

Kidstuff Education Division
WCB Containers Limited
Bayley Street, Stalybridge
Cheshire, England

Equipment for early play, cubes, tubes, construction kits for climbers, slides, bridges, etc. J. L. Hammett Co. is the American distributor.

Lind Climber Company
807 Reba Place
Evanston, Illinois 60202

Beams adjustable to height and position with planks and sawhorse-like supports.

R. W. Whittle, Ltd.
P.V. Works
Monton, Eccles
Manchester, England

Trestles, bars, climbing nets, planks.

Question: What kind of audiovisual information is useful in enhancing the concept of the "new" physical education and where may it be secured?

Answer:

The following are 16mm films available for rental or purchase:

All the Self There is

Thirteen and one-half min. color, sound, 1973. Purchase $90.00, rental (applicable to purchase price) $15.00. Order from AAHPER, c/o NEA Sound Studios, 1201 16th Street NW, Washington, D.C. 20036.

Every Child a Winner

Thirteen and one-half min. color, sound, 1974. Purchase $150.00, 15.00 rental (as above).

Innovation in Elementary Physical Education

Thirty min. sound, color. Order from Pan-Dau Films, Roche Harbor, Washington, D.C. 98250.

Movement Experiences for Primary Children

Seventeen min. sound, color, from Instructional Media Distribution, Altgeld 114, Northern Illinois University, DeKalb, Illinois.

Movement Education in	Twenty min. sound, black and white, 1967.
Physical Education	Purchase $145.00, rental $25.00 from Hayes
	Kruger, James Madison University, Godwin
	Hall, Harrisonburg, Va. 22801.

Additional films that focus more specifically on aspects of movement education are:

Film No. 1: *Introduction*	Universal Education and Visual Arts, 2450
to Movement Education	Victoria Park Avenue, Willowdale 425, Toronto, Canada. (36 min. sound, color.)
Film No. 2: *Developing*	Body awareness focus. (29 min.)
Range and Understanding	
of Movement	
Film No. 3: *Understanding Space and Directional Movements*	General and limited space focus. (26 min.)
Film No. 4: *How to*	Themes for various age levels. (31 min.)
Develop a Theme	
Film No. 5: *Qualities of*	Weight, time, space, and flow. (27 min.)
Movement	

Question: Which record companies provide records for dance, floor exercise, rhythmic gymnastics, fitness and perceptual-motor activities?

Answer:

Bridges, 310 West Jefferson, Dallas, Texas 75208.

Educational Activities, Inc., P.O. Box 392, Freeport, N.Y. 11520.

Hoctor Educational Records, Waldwick, New Jersey 07463.

Kimbo Educational, P.O. Box 477, Long Branch, New Jersey 07740.

Lyons, Dept. P.E., 530 Riverview Ave., Elkhart, Indiana 46514.

Question: Which companies are recommended particularly for square dance records?

Answer:

Blue Star, 323 W. 14th St., Houston, Texas 77008.

Folkraft Records, 1159 Broad Street, Newark, N.J. 10011.

MacGregor, 729 S. Western Ave., Los Angeles, Calif. 90005.

Sets in Order, 462 N. Robertson Blvd., Los Angeles, Calif. 90048.

Windsor, 5530 North Rosemead Blvd., Temple City, Calif. 91780.

Index